OPERATING SYSTEMS: CONCEPTS AND DESIGN

McGRAW-HILL COMPUTER SCIENCE SERIES

OPERATING SYSTEMS: CONCEPTS AND DESIGN

Milan Milenković

McGraw-Hill Publishing Company

New York   St. Louis   San Francisco   Auckland   Bogotá   Caracas
Hamburg   Lisbon   London   Madrid   Mexico   Milan
Montreal   New Delhi   Oklahoma City   Paris   San Juan
São Paulo   Singapore   Sydney   Tokyo   Toronto

This book was set in Times Roman by McGraw-Hill Computer Assisted Publishing, Inc.
The editors were Kaye Pace and Linda A. Mittiga;
the cover was designed by Mersad Berber;
the production supervisor was Phil Galea.
The drawings were done by Volt Information Sciences.
R. R. Donnelley & Sons Company was printer and binder.

OPERATING SYSTEMS

4567890 DOCDOC 943210

ISBN 0-07-041920-5

Library of Congress Cataloging-in-Publication Data
Milenković Milan
    Operating Systems.

    (McGraw-Hill series in computer science)
    Bibliography: p.
    Includes index.
    1. Operating systems (Computers) I. Title.
II. Series: McGraw-Hill computer science series.
QA76.76.063M53 1987   005.4'3   86-20060
ISBN 0-07-041920-5

ABOUT THE AUTHOR

Milan Milenković (M.Sc., Georgia Institute of Technology, Ph.D., University of Massachusetts at Amherst) has extensive teaching and industrial experience in computer systems and operating systems design.

Dr. Milenković has taught operating system design, computer architecture, and systems programming courses at the University of Massachusetts, and to several Route 128 companies. He has authored a monograph on update synchronization in distributed systems, and a number of papers and technical reports.

Dr. Milenković is a principal designer of several commercial products, including an industrial telemetry system and a functionally-partitioned multiprocessor system. He has also consulted for DEC and for ACS International.

To Maria, Alexandros, and to my parents

CONTENTS

3 PROCESSES

6   MEMORY MANAGEMENT: CONTIGUOUS ALLOCATION

7   MEMORY MANAGEMENT: NONCONTIGUOUS ALLOCATION

8   FILE MANAGEMENT

9   DESIGN OF A KERNEL OF A MULTIPROCESS OPERATING SYSTEM (KMOS)

PREFACE

Operating systems are nowadays used by many, understood by some, and designed by relatively few. While a strong interest in mainframes as network hosts and database machines remains, there is a pronounced trend to put a computer on every professional worker's desk. This tremendous growth of the computer-user population is causing an increasing number of people to interact with or to use the services of an operating system at some level or another. It is also forcing operating-system designers to devise innovative and better ways to improve productivity and effectiveness of computer-system users.

With the advent of technology, microprocessors have moved from the realm of embedded and dedicated "intelligent" controllers into powerful desktop computers whose speed and architectural sophistication rival that of some mainframes that are still in active use. Hardware design is increasingly attaining the system-design flavor, with the standard components of the past—such as flip-flops and counters—being replaced by very large scale integrated (VLSI) building blocks such as pipelined CPUs, cache memories, and memory-management units offering a choice of paging or segmentation. Even the entire operating-system kernels on a chip have been made commercially available. With such powerful components available off-the-shelf, operating-system design is no longer the exclusive turf of traditional hardware vendors. Contemporary operating-system designers are in the position to choose the level and functionality of hardware support that best suits their goals and design philosophy. With the operating-system theory having reached a considerable level of maturity and stability, operating-system designers have the foundation, the tools, and the facilities to produce sound and creative systems.

This book is offered as one way of introducing the reader to the principles and practice of operating-system design. It is intended to serve as a textbook for undergraduate and first-year graduate courses in Computer Science and Computer Engineering programs and as a reference for professionals. The reader is assumed to be familiar with the basic principles of computer architecture and data structures, and to be conversant with programming in a high-level language such as Pascal, C, Ada, or PL/I. While not essential, some prior exposure to input/output (I/O) programming in assembly language is advantageous.

Contents of this book

The book's material is organized into eleven chapters. The coverage is modular in the sense that certain chapters or groups of chapters are self-sufficient. As a result, courses may be based on select subsets of chapters, in accordance with the available time, level of the audience, and laboratory facilities. Several possible course organizations are outlined at the end of the overview of the book contents.

Chapter 1 provides an overview of the conceptual evolution of operating systems. Within that framework, the key characteristics of different types of operating systems are identified and classified. The range and nature of operating-system services provided to interactive users (commands) and systems programmers (run-time calls) are then described and used as a basis for a discussion of their implementation considerations.

Chapter 2 provides a detailed introduction to the principles and techniques of the basic input/output (I/O) programming. Special emphasis is placed on analyzing the extent of the CPU's involvement when supporting different I/O strategies, such as program-controlled and interrupt-driven I/O. The management of multiple-level vectored interrupt systems and its application to control of multiple devices is presented in considerable detail as a foundation for the subsequent discussion of concurrency within the I/O section.

Chapter 3 introduces the concept of a process. A detailed timing analysis of a multiprocess example is presented to illustrate the benefits of concurrency and the behavior of processes. After a discussion of the operating system's view and management of processes, a representative set of operating-system calls for process management is outlined. The chapter concludes with a discussion of different types of schedulers and a presentation of scheduling algorithms.

Chapter 4 introduces the synchronization problems related to the concurrent execution of processes. An analysis of the nature of the problem of mutual exclusion is used to motivate the operation of semaphores. After that, a detailed discussion of hardware support and mechanisms for implementation of mutual exclusion and interprocess synchronization in monoprocessor and multiprocessor systems is provided. The chapter concludes with a presentation of some classical problems in concurrent programming.

Chapter 5 introduces additional interprocess synchronization and communication mechanisms, such as critical regions and monitors. Special attention is paid to the functional and implementation aspects of messages, due to their versatility and applicability in both centralized and distributed environments, and to a discussion of interprocess synchronization and communication mechanisms in Ada. The problem of deadlocks arising from concurrent execution of processes is then introduced and common techniques for dealing with it are presented.

Chapter 6 explains the issues involved in the management of main memory and presents several memory-management techniques based on contiguous allocation of memory. Hardware support for static and dynamic partitioning of memory, as well as for segmentation, is discussed in addition to the extent of protection and sharing possible with each of the presented schemes.

Chapter 7 presents techniques based on noncontiguous allocation of physical memory, including paging and virtual memory. As in the previous chapter, a detailed discussion of both functional and implementation considerations is provided for each particular scheme.

Chapter 8 introduces the problems and techniques of secondary-storage management. In addition to presenting typical file-related commands and services, a detailed discussion of disk organization and directory management is provided. Special attention is paid to file and free-space allocation techniques, and to a discussion of address translation. The chapter concludes with a presentation of a generalization of file services that allows uniform treatment of files, I/O devices, and pipes.

Chapter 9 contains requirements and a functional specification of a complete kernel of a multiprocess operating system kernel (KMOS). This kernel embodies many of the ideas presented in earlier chapters. It is provided in order to demonstrate the relationship and interactions between the major components of an operating system, and to illustrate the process and methodology of operating-system design. Within that framework, systems-implementation languages and considerations, as well as methods and techniques of operating-system invocation, are presented and discussed.

Chapter 10 contains a rather detailed description and an implementation of KMOS. Considerations and trade-offs involved in the design of system data structures, process and mailbox lists, and event and timer processing are discussed and analyzed before a specific solution is adopted and implemented for KMOS.

Chapter 11 contains four case studies of commercial systems in order to illustrate current design practices. Three operating systems, PC-DOS, UNIX, and iRMX-86 are presented following a uniform structure of presentation. In particular, command- and system-call user's views are presented before the implementation of each particular system is discussed. Lastly, a detailed case study of software implementation of a remote telemetry unit (RTU) is provided in order to illustrate the formation of processes, the use of operating-system services, and the techniques of real-time programming.

The appendices contain listings of the assembly-language portion of KMOS and of some KMOS utilities.

Method of Presentation

Throughout the book, a uniform method of presentation is followed. It consists of an intuitive motivation of each major topic, followed by a more formal exposition of the underlying principles, and theory, and of some common solutions. After that, the design aspects and considerations are presented and discussed. In order to enable the reader to relate the presented material to his or her experiences, operating-system services are first presented functionally, from a user's point of view. This is followed by a presentation of the system's view of the same services in order to motivate and analyze possible implementations and related considerations. Most major topics are presented as a progression from general, to a sample implementation (KMOS), to a case study.

Alternate Course Organizations

The book is suitable for one-or two-semester courses on operating systems. The core curriculum should consist of Chapters 2 through 5. Chapter 1 may be assigned as introductory reading or covered in a few introductory lectures. The choice of other chapters depends on the orientation of the course and on the emphasis of the instructor.

A standard computer science course at a junior or a senior level will then typically cover the material on memory- and file-management presented in Chapters 6 through 8. If there is sufficient time, a functional specification of KMOS presented in Chapter 9 may be covered to illustrate the relationship between the various system components. Probably the best time to do so is after Chapter 5. A selected case study, such as the one on Unix, may be included to illustrate a concrete application of the presented principles and ideas. In schools where laboratory facilities are used in conjunction with operating-system courses, material on KMOS may be introduced after Chapter 5 so that lab exercises may proceed in parallel with the coverage of Chapters 6 through 8. Alternatively, KMOS may be assigned for reading or independent study to advanced students. In a two-semester course, KMOS and term projects consisting of the modifications to and extensions of KMOS may be covered in the second semester. Many such projects are suggested as exercises following Chapters 9 and 10.

In courses oriented towards microcomputer operating systems, concurrent programming, and/or real-time programming, material in Chapters 6 through 8 is usually omitted and KMOS is taught after Chapter 5. The case studies of most interest in such courses are probably the iRMX-86 and the RTU implementation. The more theoretically and conceptually oriented courses will probably cover Chapters 2 through 5 in their entirety, followed by Chapter 9 and case studies. Practically oriented courses may omit the more advanced mechanisms discussed in Chapter 5, such as monitors and Ada, and concentrate on implementation and design aspects through programming assignments suggested in the exercises and include the more thorough coverage of KMOS provided in Chapter 10.

Since the book's material is modular, professional readers may glance through the text and concentrate on topics that are of special interest or are perhaps less familiar.

In order to assist teaching and experimentation, the complete KMOS software executable on the IBM PC and compatibles is available through McGraw-Hill to instructors who adopt the text for classroom use.

Acknowledgments

Many people have contributed to bringing this book into its present form. I am especially indebted to Harold Stone for his encouragement and insightful comments at virtually all stages of this project. He has not only meticulously reviewed all drafts of the manuscript, but also taught me many things about the technology of publishing. Careful reviews and thoughtful comments on earlier drafts were provided by Steven Bruell of the University of Iowa, Norman Kerth of Portland State University, Donald Thomas of Carnegie-Mellon University, Prasad Vishnubhotla of Ohio State University, Bernard Weinberg of Michigan State University, and by anonymous reviewers. Naturally, all errors and omissions that remain are mine.

The enthusiastic feedback from students at the University of Massachusetts and from some Route 128 companies has been instrumental in improving presentation in several places and in establishing my confidence in the structuring of the material.

Mersad Berber, a renowned artist whose work explores the creative processes of mind in another dimension, has kindly contributed the front cover design.

The University of Massachusetts at Amherst and Energoinvest-IRIS, especially Marko Zirojević, have had unusual understanding and provided support by allowing me to take the time off for writing. Several corporations have kindly donated their time, literature, and evaluation software to this project. Among them are: AT&T, DEC, Digital Research, Hunter & Ready, IBM, Intel, Logitech, Mark of the Unicorn, Microsoft, and Motorola.

Milan Milenković

OPERATING SYSTEMS: CONCEPTS AND DESIGN

ONE

INTRODUCTION

An *operating system* (OS) may be viewed as an organized collection of software extensions of hardware consisting of control routines for operating a computer and for providing an environment for execution of programs. Other programs rely on facilities provided by the operating system to gain access to computer-system resources, such as files and input/output (I/O) devices. Programs usually invoke services of the operating system by means of *operating-system calls*. In addition, users may interact with the operating system directly by means of *operating-system commands*. In either case, the operating system acts as an interface between users and the hardware of a computer system.

The range and extent of services provided by an operating system depend on a number of factors. Among other things, user-visible functions of an operating system are largely determined by the needs and characteristics of the target environment that the OS is intended to support. For example, an operating system intended for program development in an interactive environment may have a quite different set of system calls and commands than an operating system designed for run-time support of a dedicated real-time application, such as control of a car engine.

Internally, an operating system acts as a manager of resources of the computer system, such as processor, memory, and I/O devices. In this role, the operating system keeps track of the status of each resource and decides who gets a resource, for how long, and when. In systems that support concurrent execution of programs, the operating system resolves conflicting requests for resources in a manner that preserves system integrity and in so doing attempts to optimize the resulting performance. In general, the primary objective of operating systems is to increase productivity of a production resource, such as computer hardware or computer-system

1

users. Operating systems designed for million-dollar computers at a time when the minimum wage in the United States was $1 per hour were mostly concerned with producing as much work as possible out of the computer system. User convenience and productivity were secondary considerations. At the other end of the spectrum, an operating system may be designed for a personal computer costing a few thousand dollars and may serve a single user whose annual salary is 10 times as high. In this instance, it is the user whose productivity ought to be increased as much as possible, with hardware utilization being of much less concern.

In this chapter we present the basic characteristics and design objectives of different types of operating systems. We then describe some generic services commonly provided by operating systems regardless of their type. These services are described from two different points of view: those of the command-language users, and those of the system-call users. The chapter closes with a general discussion of the implementation of operating systems, as well as an introduction to the layered structure followed in much of the remainder of this book.

1.1 EVOLUTION OF OPERATING SYSTEMS

An operating system may process its workload serially or concurrently. That is, resources of the computer system may be dedicated to a single program until its completion, or they may be dynamically reassigned among a collection of active programs in different stages of execution. Because of their ability to execute multiple programs in interleaved fashion, such operating systems are often referred to as *multiprogramming systems*. Several variations of both serial and multiprogrammed operating systems exist. In order to motivate the need for the types of services that each of these varieties provide, we briefly and informally sketch the evolutionary path of operating-system development. In particular, we describe serial processing, batch processing, and multiprogramming. No specific dates are attached to some of the events because we are interested in the progression of ideas and not in attempting to chart the history of operating systems. Moreover, much of the historical development of operating systems for mainframes was first retraced by minicomputers and then again by microcomputers and personal computers. Thus many of the concepts and ideas recur and are applicable to different systems at different times.

The mechanics of program execution and a brief sketch of the process of program development, namely, the edit-compile-execute cycle, are described for each type of operating system. While execution of programs is an essential activity in all computer systems, productivity of program preparation is important only in program-development environments, such as university computing centers.

1.1.1 Serial Processing

In theory, every computer system may be programmed in its machine language with no systems-software support. Programming of the "bare machine" was customary for early computer systems. A slightly more advanced version of this mode of operation is common for the simple evaluation boards that are sometimes used in introductory microprocessor courses. Programs for the bare machine can be developed by manually translating sequences of instructions into binary or some other code whose base is usually an integer power of 2. Instructions and data are then entered into the computer by means of console switches or, perhaps, through a hexadecimal keyboard. Programs are started by loading the program counter register with the address of the first instruction. Results of execution are obtained by examining the contents of the relevant registers and memory locations. Input/output devices, if any, must be controlled by the executing program directly, say, by reading and writing the related I/O ports. Evidently, programming of the bare machine results in low productivity of both users and hardware. The long and tedious process of program and data entry practically precludes execution of medium and large programs in such an environment.

The next significant evolutionary step in computer-system usage came about with the advent of input/output devices, such as punched cards and paper tape, and of language translators. Programs, now coded in a programming language, are translated into executable form by a computer program. Another program, called the *loader*, automates the process of loading executable programs into memory. The user places a program and its input data on an input device, and the loader transfers information from that input device into memory. After transferring control to the loaded program by manual or automatic means, execution of the program commences. The executing program reads its input from the designated input device and may produce some output on an output device, such as a printer or display screen. Once in memory, the program may be rerun with a different set of input data.

The mechanics of development and preparation of programs in such environments are quite slow and cumbersome due to serial execution of programs and to numerous manual operations involved in the process. In a typical sequence, the editor program is loaded to prepare the source code of the user program. The next step is to load and execute the language translator and provide it with the source code of the user program. When serial input devices such as card readers are used, multiple-pass language translators may require the source code to be repositioned for reading during each pass. If syntax errors are detected, the whole process must be repeated from the beginning. Eventually, the object code produced from the syntactically correct source code is loaded and executed. If run-time errors are detected, the state of the machine can be examined and modified by means of console switches or with the assistance of a program called a *debugger*.

The described mode of operation was used initially in the late fifties, but it was also common in low-end microcomputers of the early eighties with cassettes as I/O devices.

In addition to language translators, systems software includes the loader and possibly the editor and debugger programs. Most of these programs use input/output devices and thus must contain some code to exercise those devices.

Since many user programs also use input/output devices, the logical refinement is to provide a collection of standard I/O routines for use with all programs. This realization led to a progression of implementations ranging from the placement of card decks with I/O routines into the user code to the eventual collection of precompiled routines and the use of linker and librarian programs to combine them with the user's object code. The details of this process are the subject of systems programming courses, and we do not dwell on them further.

In the described system, I/O routines and the loader program already represent a rudimentary form of operating system. Although quite crude, it still provides an environment for the execution of programs far beyond what is available on the bare machine. Language translators, editors, and debuggers are systems programs that rely on the services of, but are not generally regarded as part of, the operating system. For example, the language translator would normally use the provided I/O routines while obtaining its input (the source code) and producing the output.

While a definite improvement over the bare-machine approach, this mode of operation is obviously not very efficient. Running the computer system may require frequent manual loading of programs and data. This results in low utilization of system resources. User productivity, especially in multiuser environments, is low as users await their turn at the machine. Even with such tools as editors and debuggers, the program development is very slow and is ridden with manual program and data loading.

1.1.2 Batch Processing

The next logical step in the evolution of operating systems was to automate the sequencing of operations involved in program execution and in the mechanical aspects of program development. The intent was to increase system resource utilization and programmer productivity by reducing or eliminating component idle times caused by comparatively lengthy manual operations.

Even when automated, housekeeping operations such as mounting tapes and filling out log forms take a long time relative to processor and memory speeds. Since there is not much that can be done to reduce these operations, system performance may be increased by dividing this "overhead" among a number of programs. More specifically, if several programs are batched together on a single input tape for which housekeeping operations are performed only once, the overhead per program is reduced accordingly. A related concept, sometimes called *phasing*, is to prearrange submitted jobs so that similar ones are placed in the same batch. For example, by batching several Fortran compilation jobs together, the Fortran compiler can be loaded only once to process them all in a row.

In order to realize the resource-utilization potential of batch, a mounted batch of jobs must be processed automatically without slow human intervention. To this end, some means must be provided to instruct the operating system how to process each individual job. These instructions are usually supplied by operating-system commands embedded in the batch stream. Operating-system commands represent statements of the *Job Control Language* (JCL). Typical JCL commands include marking of job beginnings and endings, commands for loading and executing programs, job characteristics such as expected execution time and memory requirements, and the like. These commands are embedded in the job stream, together with user programs and data.

A memory-resident portion of the batch operating system, sometimes called the *batch monitor*, reads, interprets, and executes these commands. In response to them, batch jobs are executed one at a time. A job may consist of several steps, each of which usually involves loading and executing a program. For example, a job may consist of compilation and subsequent execution of a user program. Each particular step to be performed is indicated to the monitor by means of the appropriate command. When a JOB_END command is encountered, the monitor may look for another job which may be identified by a JOB_START command.

As described, the batch monitor augments functions and services of the simple serial monitor discussed earlier. In addition to the loader and common I/O routines, the batch monitor also includes the command-language interpreter capable of recognizing and processing a collection of commands, such as LOAD and RUN.

By reducing or eliminating component idle times due to slow manual operations, batch processing offers a greater potential for increased system resource utilization and throughput than simple serial processing, especially in computer systems serving multiple users. As far as program development is concerned, batch processing is not a great improvement over simple serial processing. The turnaround time, measured from the time a job is submitted until its output is received, may be quite long in batch systems. Phasing may further increase the turnaround time by introducing additional waiting for a complete batch of the given kind to be assembled. Moreover, programmers are forced to debug their programs offline, as opposed to being able to examine the state of the machine immediately upon detection of a failure. While this may enforce use of better programming disciplines, it is difficult to reconstruct the state of the system just on the basis of a post-mortem memory dump.

With sequencing of program-execution mostly automated by batch operating systems, the speed discrepancy between fast processors and comparatively slow I/O devices, such as card readers and printers, emerged as a major performance bottleneck. Further improvements in batch processing were mostly along the lines of increasing the throughput and resource utilization by overlapping input and output operations. These developments have coincided with the introduction of direct memory access (DMA) channels, peripheral controllers, and later, dedicated input/output processors. As a result, satellite computers for offline processing were often substituted for by sophisticated input/output programs executed on the same computer with the batch monitor. These have allowed overlapping of program execution with input/output operations on behalf of other programs. For example, a portion of main memory may be set aside for I/O buffering.

During the execution of a program, the I/O section may concurrently read input cards of the next job into a buffer. When that job is subsequently scheduled for execution, the processor can obtain its input at the fast main-memory rate as opposed to the slow card-reader input rate. Similarly, output of a job may be buffered to memory and subsequently printed concurrently with the execution of the next job. More sophisticated forms of I/O buffering, called *SPOOLing* (for Simultaneous Peripheral Operations OnLine), use disks to temporarily store input and output of jobs. Card-to-disk and disk-to-printer operations for the subsequent and previous programs, respectively, are performed by the SPOOLing monitor concurrently with execution of the current program. Both the input and the output of several jobs may be queued on the disk as necessary to sustain high processor-utilization rates.

Because of their ability to increase the effective I/O transfer rates at program-execution time, versions of SPOOLing are also present in some other types of operating systems. Although significant, performance improvements made possible by SPOOLing and similar enhancements are less dramatic than those of batch relative to simple serial processing.

Many single-user operating systems for personal computers basically provide for serial processing. User programs are commonly loaded into memory and executed in response to user commands typed on the console. The file-management system is often provided for program and data storage. A form of batch processing is made possible by means of files consisting of commands to the operating system that are executed in sequence. Command files are primarily used to automate involved customization and operational sequences of frequent operations.

1.1.3 Multiprogramming

Even with the described enhancements, batch processing essentially dedicates resources of the computer system to a single program at a time. As we shall see shortly, there are more efficient ways to operate a computer. Before presenting some of them, let us briefly review some aspects of program behavior in order to motivate the basic idea of multiprogramming.

In the course of their execution, most programs oscillate between computation-intensive and I/O-intensive phases. This is illustrated in Figure 1.1, where computation-intensive bursts are indicated by shaded boxes and I/O is indicated by dashed boxes. Idealized serial execution of two programs, with no interprogram idle time, is depicted in Figure 1.1a. For comparison purposes, both programs are assumed to have identical behavior with regard to processor and I/O times and their relative distributions.

As Figure 1.1a suggests, serial execution of programs causes either the processor or the I/O devices to be idle at some time or another even when the input job stream is never empty. One way to attack this problem is to assign some other work to the processor and I/O devices when they would otherwise be idling. Ample supplies of pending work to be assigned to underutilized components may be provided by allowing programs to execute concurrently.

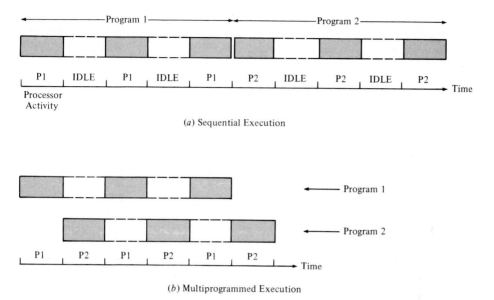

(a) Sequential Execution

(b) Multiprogrammed Execution

Figure 1.1 Multiprogramming.

Figure 1.1b illustrates a possible scenario of concurrent execution of the two programs introduced in Figure 1.1a. It starts with the processor executing the first computational sequence of Program 1. Instead of idling during the subsequent I/O sequence of Program 1, the processor is assigned to the first computational sequence of Program 2, which is assumed to be in memory and awaiting execution. When this work is done, the processor is assigned to Program 1 again, then later to Program 2, and so forth.

As Figure 1.1 suggests, significant performance gains may be achieved by interleaved execution of programs, or *multiprogramming*, as this mode of operation is usually called. With a single processor, parallel execution of programs is not possible, and at most one program can be in control of the processor at any time. The example presented in Figure 1.1b achieves 100% processor utilization with only two active programs. While convenient for the purpose of illustrating the basic idea of multiprogramming, such dramatic results should not be expected very often when real programs are used. In order to increase resource utilization, actual multiprogramming systems usually allow more than two programs to compete for system resources at any time. The number of programs actively competing for resources of a multiprogrammed computer system is often called the *degree of multiprogramming*. In theory, higher degrees of multiprogramming should result in higher resource utilization.

Multiprogramming has traditionally been employed to increase the resource utilization of a computer system and to support multiple, simultaneously active users. A typical example of a multiprogramming system is provided by time-sharing systems found in many university computer centers. Time-sharing systems support multiple interactive users. System and user programs, as well as data, are kept on the secondary storage which is managed by the file system. Programs are developed and executed in the *interactive* mode, as opposed to the noninteractive mode typical of batch systems.

Users normally communicate with an interactive system by means of commands typed at the terminals. The source code of a user program may be entered and edited from a terminal under control of the text editor program. In response to a user's command, a file produced in this manner is processed by a language translator to produce an object file. Syntax errors, if any, are corrected by editing the text file that contains the source code. After a successful compilation, the object-code file is processed by the linker and librarian programs to produce an executable program file. In response to a RUN command, the operating system loads into memory the contents of the designated program file and executes the program. Input data may be supplied to the executing program interactively, by typing them at the terminal, or from a data file. If run-time errors are detected, a program can be debugged interactively under control of a debugging program.

Interactive systems provide a convenient and comparatively productive environment for the development and execution of programs. In contrast to batch systems that impose turnaround delays and force offline debugging, time-sharing systems generally provide relatively quick terminal response-time and allow for rapid cycling between different stages of program development, such as editing and debugging. In essence, time-sharing allows a multitude of users to share the resources of a computer installation as if each user has his or her own machine.

1.2 TYPES OF OPERATING SYSTEMS

In this section we discuss certain characteristics of different types of operating systems. In particular, we discuss general properties, typical applications, and basic requirements of batch and multiprogramming systems. Time-sharing and real-time varieties of multiprogramming systems are also presented in some detail.

In addition to some general comments, each type of operating system is discussed with regard to the following aspects:

- Processor scheduling
- Memory-management
- I/O-management
- File-management

1.2.1 Batch Operating Systems

As discussed earlier, batch processing generally requires that the program, data, and appropriate system commands be submitted together in the form of a job.

Batch operating systems usually allow little or no interaction between users and executing programs. Batch processing has a greater potential for resource utilization than simple serial processing in computer systems serving multiple users. Due to turnaround delays and offline debugging, batch processing is not very convenient for program development.

Programs that do not require interaction and programs with long execution times may be served well by a batch operating system. Some examples of such programs include payroll, forecasting, statistical analysis, and large scientific number-crunching programs. Serial processing combined with batchlike command files is also found on many personal computers.

Scheduling in batch systems is very simple. Jobs are typically processed in the order of submission, that is, in the first come, first served fashion. As discussed in Chapter 3, some other ordering of jobs, such as shortest job next, is sometimes employed to provide a fair distribution of turnaround times.

Memory-management in batch systems is also very simple. Memory is usually divided into two areas. One of them is permanently occupied by the resident portion of the operating system, and the other is used to load transient programs for execution. When a transient program terminates, a new program is loaded into the same area of memory.

Since at most one program may be in execution at any time, batch systems do not require any time-critical device-management. For this reason, many serial and ordinary batch operating systems use the simple program-controlled method of I/O described in Chapter 2. The lack of contention for I/O devices makes their allocation and deallocation trivial.

Batch systems often provide simple forms of file-management. Since access to files is also serial, little protection and no concurrency control of file access are required.

1.2.2 Multiprogramming Operating Systems

As illustrated by Figure 1.1, concurrent execution of programs has a significant potential for improving system throughput and resource utilization relative to batch and serial processing. This potential is realized, or at least exploited, by a class of operating systems that multiplexes computer-system resources among a multitude of active programs. Such operating systems usually have the prefix *multi-* in their names, such as multitasking or multiprogramming. In this section we briefly describe the chief characteristics and functions of such systems.

An instance of a program in execution is called a *process* or a *task*. A *multiprocess* operating system, also called *multitasking* operating systems, is distinguished by its ability to support two or more active processes simultaneously. The term *multiprogramming* denotes an operating system which, in addition to supporting multiple concurrent processes, allows the instructions and data from two or more disjoint processes to reside in primary memory simultaneously. Note that multiprogramming implies multiprocess operation, but multiprocess operation (or multitasking) does not imply multiprogramming. In effect, the multiprocess operation is one of the mechanisms that a multiprogramming operating system employs in managing the totality of computer-system resources, including the central processing unit (CPU), memory, and I/O devices.

Multiaccess, or *multiuser*, operating systems allow simultaneous access to a computer system through two or more terminals. Although frequently associated with multiprogramming, multiuser operation does not imply, nor is it implied by, either multitasking or multiprogramming. An example is provided by some dedicated transaction-processing systems, such as airline ticket reservations, that support hundreds of active terminals under control of a single program. On the other hand, general purpose time-sharing systems incorporate both multiprogramming and multiuser operation. Multiprocess operation without multiuser support can be found in the operating systems of some advanced personal computers and in real-time systems, which are described later in this section.

In general, all multiprogramming systems are characterized by a multitude of simultaneously active programs that are competing for system resources, such as processor, memory, and I/O devices. A multiprogramming operating system monitors the state of all active programs and system resources. When important changes of state occur, or when it is explicitly called to, the operating system is activated to allocate resources and to provide certain services from its repertoire. As we shall see shortly, the requirements of the specific environment being served influence the choice of objectives and policies of the related multiprogrammed operating system.

Time-sharing systems. Time-sharing is a popular representative of multiprogrammed, multiuser systems. In addition to general program-development environments, many large computer-aided design (CAD) and text processing systems also belong to this category. In contrast, dedicated multiaccess systems essentially run a single large application program most of the time. A typical example is provided by a banking application with hundreds of terminals running under the control of a single program and accessing a common database.

One of the primary objectives of multiuser systems in general, and of time-sharing in particular, is good terminal-response time. Giving the illusion to each user of having a machine to himself or herself, time-sharing systems often attempt to provide equitable sharing of common resources. For example, when the system is loaded, users with more demanding processing requirements are made to wait longer.

This philosophy is reflected in the choice of scheduling algorithm. Most time-sharing systems use time-slice (round-robin) scheduling. In this approach, programs are executed with rotating priority that increases during waiting and drops after the service is granted. In order to prevent programs from monopolizing the processor, a program executing longer than the system-defined time slice is interrupted by the operating system and placed at the end of the queue of waiting programs. As discussed in Chapter 3, this mode of operation generally provides quick response time to interactive programs.

Memory-management in time-sharing systems provides for isolation and protection of coresident programs. As described in Chapters 6 and 7, some forms of controlled sharing are sometimes provided to conserve memory and possibly to exchange data between programs. Since they are executed on behalf of different users, programs in time-sharing systems generally do not have much need to communicate with each other.

Input/output-management in time-sharing systems must be sophisticated enough to cope with multiple users and devices. However, due to the relatively slow speeds of terminals and human users, processing of terminal interrupts need not be time-critical. As in most multiuser environments, allocation and deallocation of devices must be done in a manner that preserves system integrity and provides for good performance.

Given the possibility of concurrent and possibly conflicting attempts to access files, file-management in a time-sharing system must provide protection and access control. This task is often compounded by the requirement that files be shared among certain users or classes of users. The issues of file-management, file protection, and concurrency control are discussed in detail in Chapters 5 and 8.

Real-time systems. Real-time operating systems are used in environments where a large number of events, mostly external to the computer system, must be accepted and processed in a short time or within certain deadlines. Examples of such applications include industrial control, telephone switching equipment, flight control, and real-time simulations. Real-time systems are also frequently used in military applications.

A primary objective of real-time systems is to provide quick event-response times and thus meet the scheduling deadlines. User convenience and resource utilization are of secondary concern to real-time system designers. It is not uncommon for a real-time system to be expected to process bursts of thousands of interrupts per second without missing a single event. Such requirements usually cannot be met by multiprogramming alone, and real-time operating systems usually rely on certain specific policies and techniques for doing their job.

Explicit programmer-defined and programmer-controlled processes are commonly encountered in real-time systems. Basically, a separate process is charged with handling a single external event. The process is activated upon occurrence of the related event, often signaled by an interrupt. Multiprocess operation is accomplished by scheduling processes for execution independently of each other. Each process is assigned a certain level of priority that corresponds to the relative importance of the event it services. The processor is normally allocated to the highest-priority process among those which are ready to execute. Higher-priority processes usually preempt execution of lower-priority processes. This form of scheduling, called *priority-based preemptive scheduling*, is used by a majority of real-time systems. The details of its working are described in Chapter 3, and an implementation is presented in Chapter 10.

Memory-management in real-time systems is comparatively less demanding than in other types of multiprogramming systems. The primary reason for this is that many processes permanently reside in memory in order to provide quick response time. Unlike, say, time-sharing, the process population in real-time systems is fairly static and there is comparatively little moving of programs between primary and secondary storage. On the other hand, processes in real-time systems tend to cooperate closely, thus necessitating support for both separation and sharing of memory.

As already suggested, time-critical device-management is one of the main characteristics of real-time systems. In addition to providing sophisticated forms of interrupt-management and I/O buffering, real-time operating systems often provide system calls to allow user processes (programs) to connect themselves to interrupt vectors and to service events directly.

File-management is usually found only in larger installations of real-time systems. In fact, some embedded real-time systems, such as an onboard automotive controller, may not even have any secondary storage. However, where provided, file-management of real-time systems must satisfy much the same requirements as those found in time-sharing and other multiprogramming systems. These include protection and access control. The primary objective of file-management in real-time systems is usually the speed of access, rather than efficient utilization of secondary storage.

1.2.3 Combination Operating Systems

As presented here, different types of operating systems are optimized, or at least largely geared toward serving the needs of certain specific environments. In practice, however, a given environment may not exactly fit any of the described molds. For instance, both interactive program development and lengthy simulations are often encountered in university computing centers. For this reason, some commercial operating systems provide a combination of the described services. For example, a time-sharing system may support interactive users while also incorporating a full-fledged batch monitor. This allows computationally intensive noninteractive programs to be run concurrently with interactive programs. The common practice is to assign low priority to batch jobs and thus to execute batched programs only when the processor would otherwise be idle. In other words, batch processing may be used as a filler to improve processor utilization while accomplishing a useful service of its own. Similarly, some time-critical events, such as receipt and transmission of network data packets, may be handled in real-time fashion on systems that otherwise provide time-sharing services to their terminal users.

1.3 DIFFERENT VIEWS OF THE OPERATING SYSTEM

In this section we present some services of the operating system as perceived by its different classes of users. For the purposes of this discussion, users of operating-system services are divided into two broad classes: command-language users and system-call users. Informally, *command-language users* are those who obtain the services of the operating system by means of commands, say, typed at the terminal or embedded in a batch job. *System-call users*, on the other hand, invoke the services of the operating system by means of run-time system calls. These are usually embedded in and activated during execution of programs.

1.3.1 The Command-Language User's View of the Operating System

Operating-system command languages are usually system-specific. While their syntax differs from one system to another, the range and functionality of system commands are much less varied. Some of the typical functional classes of operating-system commands are given in Table 1.1. Let us briefly elaborate on them.

Log-on and housekeeping operations on multiuser systems include commands for logging into and out of the system, such as LOGIN and BYE, and for password manipulation, such as CHANGE_PASSWORD. After logging in, users may set or change some parameters of their working environment. For example, the characteristics of a user's terminal, such as CRT or hard copy, may be defined at this point. This information is stored by the operating system for further reference and use by other programs. For instance, the text editor may automatically enter the screen mode or the line mode, depending on the type of terminal from which it is invoked. Other commands may allow definition or reassignment of default-device designations for the user, such as the disk drive where user files are to be sought and placed. Commands for volume and media manipulation are discussed later in relation to files.

Commands for program activation and control generally allow programs to be loaded and executed. Explicit commands for program loading are useful for fixing programs in memory, controlling the exact place or partition where the program is to be loaded, and the like. A program can be loaded into main memory with a LOAD command and executed with an EXECUTE command. These two actions are often combined into a single command, such as RUN. Due to the high frequency of usage of this service, many systems allow programs to be executed simply by typing the name of the file that contains an executable program. Running programs can usually be forcefully terminated by means of

Table 1.1 Some operating-system commands

Functional class	Typical operations
Log-on and housekeeping	Login, bye, change password
Program activation and control	Load, run, abort
File-management	Create, delete, rename, copy
Status reporting	List active programs, logged users
System-management	Create account, list error-log

ABORT or a similar command. Some systems provide commands or options to execute programs at the specified time of day or repetitively at specified intervals. Commands to set and modify program attributes, such as the scheduling priority, are sometimes also included in this class.

File-management commands usually provide facilities for creation and maintenance of named files, such as CREATE, DELETE, and RENAME. Catalogs of files, called *directories*, can be listed or printed by means of appropriate commands. Files can also be copied, merged, and printed in response to user commands. Numerous utilities for processing contents of files, such as comparison and sorting, are available on many systems. Some of them are described in Chapter 11. Volumes for file storage can be manipulated by a set of operating-system commands. For example, volumes may be initialized for the needs of the particular operating system and checked for consistency and media defects. While present on most systems, usage of commands for volume maintenance may be restricted to authorized personnel on multiuser systems. Detailed descriptions of file-related commands may be found in Chapter 8.

Commands to report status are quite varied on different systems. In principle, they allow users to obtain information about the state of user-initiated activities and allocated devices or about the state of the entire system. For example, users may inquire about the status of their programs, size and contents of system print queues, and the number or identities of other logged-on users. Some systems provide quite extensive performance reports to users, such as page-fault activity or dynamic display of the summary of system activity. Such facilities are very useful for learning the intricacies of operation and behavior of a particular system. On the other hand, dynamic-performance monitors can consume considerable amounts of system resources. For this reason, their use is often restricted to certain classes of users.

System-management commands are normally reserved for use by system managers and maintenance personnel. These commands provide facilities for the creation and maintenance of user accounts, limit setting on resource usage, and specification of default devices. System managers can often obtain detailed statistical reports on system behavior. This information is invaluable for fine-tuning the system and for identifying potential trouble spots. Special utilities are often provided for analysis of hard and soft errors accumulated and recorded over a period of time. Other commands in this class allow the definition and posting of sign-on messages and system announcements.

Many systems also provide commands that allow terminal users to exchange messages with each other. A popular extension of this service is the mail facility that provides a versatile store-and-forward type of depository for the exchange of messages between members of the user population.

1.3.2 The System-Call User's View of the Operating System

Systems and applications programmers often invoke services of the operating system from their programs by means of system calls. System commands issued by command-language users are normally converted into and executed as a series of system calls. In addition to providing most of the functionality available to command-language users, system calls usually allow finer control over system operations and more direct access to hardware facilities, especially the input/output system.

Except for some of the log-on operations and system-management functions, system calls usually represent a superset of functions available at the command level. Since many of these were described in the previous section, we now discuss some of the functions typically provided primarily by means of system calls.

System calls for the execution and control of programs usually include a full set of services available via the command language, such as RUN, EXECUTE, ABORT, and time-related scheduling. In addition, users of system calls may SUSPEND one or more programs until occurrence of a specific condition, RESUME previously suspended programs, and set or change various execution-time attributes of programs. Some facilities, often extensive in real-time systems, are also provided for interprogram communication and synchronization. For example, programs may exchange data and timing signals to synchronize their execution with certain events. Details of program-related system calls may be found in Chapter 3, and implementation of some of them is discussed in Chapters 9 and 10. Mechanisms for interprogram synchronization and communication are discussed in Chapters 4 and 5.

Resource-management system calls provide services for the allocation, reservation, and reclamation of system resources. For example, system calls exist to extend or reduce the amount of memory owned by the calling program. Other types of system objects may be assigned to or reserved by the calling program and destroyed or returned to the custody of the operating system thereafter.

Although they are treated separately in some systems, system calls for device- and file-management are functionally combined in many contemporary operating systems. Advantages of the latter approach and some examples are presented in Chapters 8 and 11. Basically, this class of system calls provides facilities for communicating with input/output devices. In addition to reading and writing individual items or blocks of data, calls such as OPEN and CLOSE are provided to manage logical connections to devices. While virtually all I/O devices may be accessed serially, special calls are provided for random access to block-structured devices, such as disks. System calls are also provided for device initialization and for selection of specific modes of operation.

1.4 DESIGN AND IMPLEMENTATION OF OPERATING SYSTEMS

In this section we discuss some of the issues and methodology involved in operating-system design and implementation. We begin by outlining the major problems and approaches used in the management of such operating-system objects as processes, memory, and files. We then present a layered view of the internal organization of operating systems.

1.4.1 Functional Requirements

It is the processes, or programs in execution, that do the work of a computer system. Processes are created in response to explicit or implicit user requests. In the course of their progress toward completion, processes issue requests for system services and resources, such as memory and files. In multiprocess systems, several active processes may coexist in main memory and compete for the processor cycles needed for their completion.

The operating system provides various supervisory and control functions for the management of processes. These include services for the creation and removal of processes, for controlling the progress of processes, and for acting on exceptional conditions arising during the execution of a process. The operating system allocates hardware and software resources in response to process requirements and to explicit process requests. In addition, the operating system provides the protection, access control, and security needed to maintain system integrity in multiprogramming environments. Cooperation among processes is facilitated by providing mechanisms for interprocess communication and exchange of information, such as signals and messages.

The concept of a process, the related issues, and system calls are discussed in Chapter 3, together with the scheduling algorithms for allocating the processor among processes. Interrupts and the related concepts of exceptional-condition processing are discussed in Chapter 2. Interprocess synchronization, communication, and cooperation are elaborated in Chapters 4 and 5. Most of these concepts and mechanisms are incorporated into and actually applied in the design and implementation of a complete OS kernel presented in Chapters 9 and 10.

The management of primary memory consists mainly of allocating the physical memory of finite capacity to requesting processes. Demands for memory result from the creation of new processes and from the dynamic expansion of existing processes. Memory is normally freed upon termination of processes. However, the operating system may elect to swap out temporarily inactive processes in order to vacate space needed by the processes otherwise ready to execute. Depending on how objects are placed in memory, memory-allocation schemes can be qualified as contiguous or noncontiguous.

Contiguous allocation of memory implies that each object, such as a program or set of data, is placed into a set of consecutive memory locations. In essence, the main memory is partitioned into a number of areas that are allocated among the requesting processes. This partitioning may be static or dynamic. In either case, contiguous allocation suffers from the problem of memory *fragmentation*, where portions of physical memory are unused but cannot be allocated to requestors.

Noncontiguous allocation of memory implies that a single logical object may be placed in nonconsecutive sets of memory locations. This improves the potential for effective use of main memory by reducing or eliminating fragmentation. However, noncontiguous allocation requires run-time mapping of the contiguous logical addressing space into the actual, scattered physical addresses. This mapping requires both specialized hardware and memory space for storage of the mapping tables. Several different noncontiguous schemes of main-memory allocation, including segmentation, paging, and virtual memory, are presented and compared in Chapter 7.

Memory allocation in multiprogramming systems must satisfy some additional constraints imposed by the coexistence of multiple active processes. For example, unrelated processes must be strictly isolated from each other, that is, placed in nonoverlapping areas of memory and protected from malevolent or erroneous violation of their address spaces by other processes. In this way, adverse effects of programming errors can be localized to offending processes. On the other hand, cooperating processes may want to overlap in some areas of memory in order to exchange data or to conserve space. Although sometimes conflicting, both requirements are legitimate and ought to be supported by the operating system. Mechanisms for enforced separation and controlled sharing of memory among concurrent processes, including the required and desirable hardware support, are discussed and compared for each memory-management scheme presented in Chapters 6 and 7.

Long-term storage of information, including programs and data, is an important function of an operating system. Information is usually stored on secondary storage devices in the form of collections of related entities called *files*. Many contemporary operating systems hide device-specific aspects of file manipulation from users and provide an abstraction of the secondary storage as a simple, uniform space of named files. Individual files often appear to users as linear arrays of characters or records. Some systems extend this view to the entire input/output system by treating I/O devices as files, possibly with some special attributes. Such combined I/O and file systems, where both are accessible to users through a single, unified set of system calls and services, are often referred to as *device-independent I/O systems*. The idea is to relieve users of the burden of having to explicitly move data between the main memory and the secondary storage and of having to handle data differently depending on where it is physically stored. Implementation of these abstractions requires the operating system to map logical access requests to physical file and device addresses, in addition to allocating space and keeping track of the status of secondary storage devices.

A trustworthy long-term storage system must be reliable and capable of preserving file integrity even under adverse conditions, including equipment malfunctions and system crashes. Operating systems employ various techniques for file-system restoration and recovery. Their complexity and effectiveness vary with the demands of the target environment. For example, while simple backup programs may suffice for a microcomputer operating system, an online banking database may require transaction journaling, redundant data storage, and automatic file recovery.

Multiuser and multiprogramming environments impose some additional requirements on file manipulation and storage. Similar to information main memory, information in files must be protected from unauthorized access, while at the same time cooperating users must be allowed to share and even concurrently access common files. The details of file-management, including device-management and access authorization, are presented in Chapter 8.

1.4.2 Implementation

The operating system manages the operation of a computer system and provides a potentially large number of user-accessible services. Acting as a traffic manager, the operating system keeps track of, and provides the working environment for, the execution of programs. The operating system allocates and reclaims resources in response to explicit requests, as well as on the basis of the state of the computer system. Resource-management decisions are governed by policies resulting from the design objectives, such as user convenience and efficiency of operation. Additional complexities are imposed by the requirement to dynamically enforce separation and to facilitate sharing of certain objects in multiuser environments.

One of the major problems facing operating system designers is how to manage this complexity of functions at many levels of detail while providing a product that is reasonably reliable and easy to maintain. The reported experiences with large operating systems designed as monolithic pieces of code have been discouraging in both respects. Contemporary systems are usually designed and implemented in the form of a hierarchy of levels of abstraction. This approach is an outgrowth of the concept of *information hiding*, where the details of data structures and processing algorithms are confined within modules. Externally, a module is known to perform a specific function on objects of a given type. The details of how it does it are neither available nor of concern to users of the module's services.

Modules interact with their environment through well-defined interfaces. *Modularity* basically refers to the partitioning of complex problems into a collection of modules, each of which performs a single function. As a result, modules tend to be small and thus easy to comprehend and implement. Given relatively low degrees of coupling between well-designed modules, modifications tend to be localized to affected modules and to the software that directly interfaces with them. Moreover, changes of the internal structure of a module that do not change its external interface may be done for improved performance or similar reasons without affecting other modules at all. Modules also facilitate encapsulation of data, where objects may be manipulated exclusively by means of a set of meaningful operations provided for the related object-type.

The principle of information hiding has been successfully extended from isolated subsystems to an entire operating system. The basic idea is to create a hierarchy of levels of abstraction so that at each level the details of operation of lower levels may be ignored. Each level of abstraction provides a set of objects and primitive operations that may be used by higher levels. In so doing, each level may rely on the objects and related operations provided by lower levels. In effect, each level of abstraction enriches the set of facilities provided by the hardware and by all intermediate levels.

A hierarchical operating-system model is depicted in Table 1.2. This is not a model of any particular operating system, but a representative structure that is followed in much of the remainder of this book.

Level 1 is the first layer of the operating system that uses only the objects and operations provided by the bare hardware. Depending on the overall functionality of the operating system, the underlying hardware configuration may include interrupt controller, interval timer, and support for memory management. The details of various types of hardware support for the operating system are discussed in several chapters later in this book.

Level 1, often called the *kernel* or *nucleus* of the operating system, basically manages processes. The kernel keeps track of active processes by means of data structures that depict the state of the system. This level contains a scheduler that selects which process to run next when the running process is switched off. Upon allocating the CPU to a new process, the kernel performs a context-switch operation which includes saving the state of the departing process and restoring the state of the oncoming one. Level 1 manages interrupts by masking them as and when required and provides facilities for connecting service routines to hardware interrupts. Basic mechanisms for interprocess synchronization and, possibly, communication, such as semaphores or messages, may also be provided at this level. Material on interrupts and processes is presented in Chapters 2 and 3. Interprocess synchronization and communication are the subject of Chapters 4 and 5. Implementation of these concepts is demonstrated in Chapters 9 and 10, where the design of a complete multiprocess OS kernel is presented.

Level 2 basically provides low-level facilities for management of the secondary storage needed to support the main-memory management on Level 3. Level 2 allows blocks of data to be shuttled between primary and secondary storage. A fairly low-level abstraction of secondary storage as a linear array of data blocks is provided by this level for the purposes of reading and writing. Requests made in this fashion are translated into hardware commands for the movement and positioning of disk heads. Some details of these operations are described in Chapter 8.

Table 1.2 Operating-system layers

Level	Name	Objects	Typical operations
5	Command-language interpreter	Environment data	Statements in command language
4	File system	Files, devices	Create, destroy, open, close, read, write
3	Memory-management	Segments, pages	Read, write, fetch
2	Basic I/O	Data blocks	Read, write, allocate, free
1	Kernel	Processes, semaphores	Create, destroy, suspend, resume, signal, wait

Level 3 manages primary memory. It allocates memory for programs to be loaded and frees it when no longer required. Isolation of distinct address spaces and some controlled forms of sharing of memory are also supported by Level 3. Virtual memory, which gives the programmer an illusion of having a larger memory at his or her disposal than may be physically available, can be implemented at this level. Modules of Level 3 handle hardware interrupts that signal attempts to address data that are not in main memory. In this case, missing blocks of data are brought from secondary storage using facilities of Level 2. If no room is available, the necessary space is freed by temporarily removing some data to the secondary store. Memory-management is discussed in Chapters 6 and 7.

Level 4 provides facilities for long-term storage and manipulation of named files. More sophisticated forms of space allocation and accessing of data on secondary storage than those provided by Level 2 are implemented at Level 4. Files, or portions thereof, may be accessed and updated by means of high-level commands and without the need to specify data-block numbers or addresses, as required by Level 2. At Level 4, information is usually addressed in a file-relative manner.

Level 4 also manages external devices and peripherals, such as printers and terminals. Hardware differences among certain types of devices, such as character-oriented and block-structured, are bridged by software at this level to provide a uniform view of files and devices to higher levels and ultimately to system users. This standard interface may also be extended to an interprogram communication facility, called *pipe*, which is essentially a one-way virtual communication channel. Streams of data may be written at one end of the pipe and read at the other using basically the same set of calls, such as OPEN and READ, that is available for manipulation of files and devices. Details of file-management and some aspects of device-management at Level 4 are presented in Chapter 8. I/O programming at low level for character-oriented devices is discussed in Chapter 2.

Level 5 is the command-language interpreter. It provides the interface between interactive users and the operating system. Modules at Level 5 use facilities provided by the lower levels to accept command lines from terminals. These input lines are then parsed to separate commands from parameters and to identify the type of service required. System calls to other levels are employed to actually render the service. When requested to execute a program, software at this level creates the working environment and invokes the related processes.

1.5 SUMMARY

Following the course of the conceptual evolution of the operating system, we have identified the main characteristics of the program-execution and development environments provided by the bare machine, serial processing (including batch), and multiprogramming.

On the basis of their attributes and design objectives, different types of operating systems were defined and characterized with respect to scheduling and management of memory, devices, and files.

Typical services provided by an operating system to its users were presented from the point of view of command-language users and system-call users.

Functional requirements imposed by the need to provide these services, as well as to monitor computer-system operation and to dynamically allocate its resources to executing programs, were discussed next. In order to cope with these complex requirements, a hierarchical approach to operating-system design was advocated. A result of this process is usually a layered implementation of a progression of levels of abstraction, such as the sample structure described under Implementation in Section 1.4.

OTHER READING

The chronological evolution of operating systems until the late sixties is described by Rosin (1969). More recent historical perspectives can be found in Peterson and Silberschatz (1983) and Deitel (1984).

The various aspects of the different types of operating systems are described by Shaw (1974), Hsiao (1975), Habermann (1976), and Lorin and Deitel (1981).

The services provided by operating-system kernels are discussed in Chapter 3, and some of them are implemented in Chapters 9 and 10. The services provided by commercial operating systems are described in detail in the vendors' manuals. Chapter 11 contains a description of the major commands and system calls for three commercial operating systems (PC/MS-DOS, Unix, and iRMX-86).

The functions and functional requirements of operating systems are described by Lister (1979) and Denning (1971). Other interesting views of operating systems can be found in Madnick and Donovan (1974) and Brinch Hansen (1973). An early layered implementation of a multiprogramming operating system is described by Dijkstra (1968*b*). A 15-level operating-system design hierarchy is presented by Brown et al. (1984).

TWO

INPUT/OUTPUT: PRINCIPLES AND PROGRAMMING

The input/output system is the part of the operating system charged with the management of I/O devices. Acting as the interface between system users and I/O devices, the input/output system provides a means by which files and devices are treated in a uniform manner and are manipulated by means of a set of high-level commands, such as READ_STRING. At the device end, however, the I/O system must supply the device-specific control signals to each particular type of device, possibly many times in the course of execution of a single high-level command. Higher-level functions of the input/output system, placed at Level 4 in the sample hierarchy introduced in Chapter 1, are discussed in Chapter 8. In this chapter we discuss the low-level functions of the input/output system, including the details of device control and I/O programming.

After a brief outline of the structure and role of the input/output section of a computer system, we introduce the notion of an input/output port, stressing the aspects of concern to systems programmers. We then discuss the principles of input/output programming and informally analyze the resulting timing in order to assess performance boundaries of the various I/O schemes. Following the exposition of program-controlled I/O, we present a somewhat more involved discussion of interrupts. The purpose of this discussion is both to explore the kind of hardware support to the operating system normally provided in this area and to indicate the potential for parallel operation that is exploited by multiprogramming operating systems and is discussed in detail in subsequent chapters.

Several characteristics of the input/output subsystem are precursors to many topics that we explore later in this book. For one, significant performance benefits may be attained when input/output devices are operating concurrently. With today's sophisticated I/O controllers, only an occasional, and often brief, inter-action with the CPU may be all that is needed to sustain data traffic through an I/O device. Consequently, it is quite customary to have the CPU initiate a number of independent I/O operations before others in progress are completed. On the other hand, concurrent execution of independent tasks requires careful scheduling of many different code sequences and of time-critical events sensed or caused by input/output devices.

Given its complexity and impact on performance, concurrency is a major topic in operating-system theory. As many of the concurrency-related problems are either originating from or present in the input/output system, our goal in this chapter is to explore the principles of input/output systems, to study the elements of I/O programming, and to introduce the increasing degrees of concurrent execution of I/O operations that the hardware supports. In so doing, we will encounter a number of increasingly difficult scheduling problems that we solve using largely ad hoc and intuitive techniques, mimicking those frequently used by programmers. Toward the end of the chapter we conclude that even higher degrees of concurrency are possible, but that they require a much more rigid and systematic programming discipline, discussed in subsequent chapters.

2.1 THE INPUT/OUTPUT PROBLEM

In this section we focus on the hardware aspects of the input/output subsystem and stress its unique attributes that both necessitate specialized programming and make concurrent operations possible.

There seems to be an endless variety of device types that have been attached to computer systems—each with its own encoding, electrical, and timing require-ments. Many of them operate asynchronously from the CPU, at rates ranging from just a few data transfers per second to millions of data transfers per sec-ond. Input/output hardware and software are charged with the difficult tasks of attending to the individual requirements of I/O devices and providing for their efficient and reliable operation while hiding device-specific details and presenting a uniform abstraction of generic I/O operations to the outer layers of an operating system and, ultimately, to user programs. Before we see how this can be done, let us explore three important characteristics of the input/output problem:

1. Asynchronous operation
2. The speed gap
3. Format conversions

The following sections treat each of these characteristics in detail.

2.1.1 Asynchronous Operation

During program execution, the processor engages in numerous transactions with the main memory and I/O devices in order to fetch instructions for execution and to access data operands. For example, READ operations with both memory and devices are typically initiated by the processor, which, some time later, obtains the required items. However, the timing of memory and I/O transactions is fundamentally different.

Except possibly when errors occur, memory is always ready to furnish a datum whose address is designated by the processor. It does so within a nearly constant time, the *memory-access time*, which generally lasts at most a few cycles of the processor clock. In that sense, memory may be regarded as operating synchronously with the CPU. Another important observation is that the CPU waits until the desired item from memory arrives, as the CPU has nothing to do until an instruction or datum is fetched.

On the other hand, events in the external world and the input/output devices that interface them with the computer system usually bear no relationship to the processor clock. From the point of view of the CPU, I/O data arrival and transfer times are generally unpredictable. Compare an input transaction from a terminal, for example, with a memory fetch. Once the CPU informs the terminal controller that it needs a character, the CPU must be prepared to receive the character whenever the user at the terminal chooses to press a key. That may happen a fraction of a second or minutes later. Memory, however, reports its data to the CPU at a fixed time after the request is issued. In other words, I/O devices, unlike memory, operate *asynchronously* from the CPU. For reasons of device independence and immunity to configuration changes, it is usually beneficial to operate devices asynchronously, including those devices that have predictable data-transfer times and could be operated synchronously.

Given the need to control asynchronous operation, the hardware of the I/O section must include special control signals that enable the CPU and device controllers to indicate to each other their status, intentions, and data availability. These are collectively referred to as *handshaking signals*. Before attempting to obtain a datum from a device, the CPU normally queries the device for status by using the handshaking protocols. If the I/O datum is actually available, the CPU fetches it from the controller; otherwise the CPU has to wait. Since that may be a long wait, the operating system may elect to schedule another program for execution in order to prevent the CPU from idling while awaiting completion of I/O transactions. Note that the currently executing program would first have to be suspended pending arrival of the required I/O datum. At some later time, the handshaking signals may alert the CPU to the fact that the I/O transaction has been completed, and the operating system would then resume the suspended program.

2.1.2 The Speed Gap: CPU versus Peripherals

As pointed out, there is a several orders of magnitude difference in the speeds of I/O devices themselves and of I/O speed in general relative to the CPU-memory bandwidth. When transmitting continuous streams of data, I/O devices may exhibit rates from the order of less than 1 cps (characters per second) to the order of 1,000,000 cps—a full 6 orders of magnitude variation. The low end of the spectrum is represented by slow terminals, switches, and displays, whereas the high end belongs to local-area networks and high-performance disk drives. Very high-speed devices are usually interfaced via specialized I/O channels or dedicated processors. They tend to perform data transfers in blocks using direct memory-access (DMA) techniques. In contrast, programmed I/O, which is controlled directly by the CPU for each individual character, is often limited to the less demanding devices. In this chapter we are mostly concerned with the latter.

In order to appreciate the speed gap, consider a relatively fast CRT terminal with a nominal data-transfer rate of 19,200 Hz (hertz). Many terminals use bit-serial data-transfer techniques, so assuming that one character occupies 10 bits (1 start bit, 8 data bits, and 1 stop bit), the data rate is 1920 cps. In other words, when displaying, say, a long file of text, the computer is able to transmit almost 2000 characters per second to the terminal. In practice, the average data rate is likely to be lower, since alphanumeric terminals can rarely process and display characters that fast. This problem is often solved by incorporating hardware buffers into terminals to smooth the speed differences between the input data rate and the display data rate. As a result, peak data rates can be sustained at least for shorter bursts until the buffer is filled.

In any case, 2000 cps is one character transmission every 500 μs (microseconds). Given a CPU with instruction execution times in the neighborhood of 1 μs, after transferring a datum to the terminal, the CPU has nearly 500 μs to prepare for the next character before the terminal becomes ready to receive it. Assuming that the CPU uses just a few cycles to ready a character, then when servicing a relatively fast (non-DMA) peripheral running at its theoretical speed limit, the CPU may be *idle 99% of the time.*

In the example presented, the *speed gap*, defined as the ratio of the CPU-memory bandwidth to the I/O device maximum data rate, is on the order of 500 : 1. In general, character-oriented I/O devices (as opposed to the block-oriented devices using DMA) operate at rates well below the CPU-memory bandwidth. The speed gap, as defined here, is really the best case, since it assumes that the I/O device is constantly operating at its maximum data rate. In practice, I/O transfers tend to be asynchronous and much less regular. As a result, the CPU can become heavily underutilized when dedicated to servicing a single character-oriented I/O device. One way to improve CPU utilization, that is, the proportion of processor cycles spent doing useful work as opposed to waiting for the I/O device to become ready, is to multiplex the CPU among a number of I/O devices. The idea is to reduce idling by assigning some other work to the CPU while activated I/O operations are in progress. Later in this chapter we present some methods and examples of concurrent I/O operations.

2.1.3 Format Conversions

The third important aspect of the I/O problem is the format conversion necessary to bridge the incompatibilities between computer systems and their many different peripherals. For example, some devices require bit-serial data transfers, and others expect character-parallel data transfers. Both varieties of transfers have numerous data encodings, such as ASCII, EBCDIC, and Hollerith. In addition to encoding and decoding data between binary and whatever code is needed by a specific device, the I/O routines may also have to perform error-checking operations necessary to maintain and verify the integrity of data. Although they are an integral part of I/O programming, format conversions tend to be highly device-specific, and we will not address them in detail in this text.

2.2 INPUT/OUTPUT INTERFACES

Hardware controllers (interfaces) act as intermediaries between the computer system and input/output devices. Their purpose is to bridge the speed and signaling-level incompatibilities between the CPU and peripherals and to translate the generic I/O commands issued by the CPU into device-specific controls. In the previous section we indicated some attributes of the I/O subsystem, such as the need for data buffering. Let us now explore its basic organization more systematically in order to set the stage for the subsequent discussion of I/O programming techniques. To reach our goal, we adopt the I/O programmer's point of view and stress the hardware issues most pertinent in that context.

While treatment of the input/output section as a single functional entity of a computer system is a frequently used and useful metaphor, I/O hardware is often physically distributed over a number of device interfaces or controllers (we use these terms interchangeably). This is demonstrated in Figure 2.1, which depicts a block diagram of a computer system. This logical structure is readily identifiable in the physical structure of a computer system and can be observed by removing the protective cover of one. Usually the hub of the system is the backplane that houses a number of connectors into which various other boards are plugged. The connectors themselves are joined by a number of parallel signal traces, the *system bus*, which serve as a communication medium for interboard exchanges of address, data, and control pulses. The modules above the system bus in Figure 2.1 depict the CPU and memory boards. Our present concern is the input/output controllers (interfaces), three of which are depicted below the system bus in Figure 2.1. The modules, as shown, are divided according to their function. In actual implementations, several different functional units, such as memory, I/O, and even the CPU, may be integrated on a single printed-circuit board.

As their respective labels indicate, the I/O controllers are in charge of the serial, parallel, and DMA devices. Below each of them, a representative device of the type that would normally be connected to the respective I/O controller is shown. Many terminals, as well as short- and long-haul communication links, use bit-serial line protocols and thus require serial interfaces for connection to a computer system. The majority of printers need parallel interfaces, which are also popular for connecting switches, relays, LEDs and other line-oriented displays.

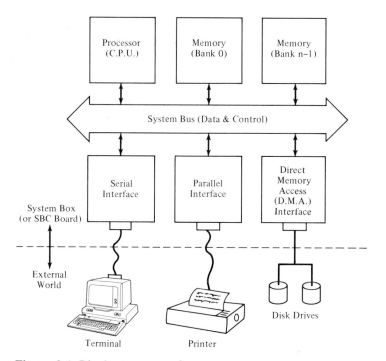

Figure 2.1 Block structure of a computer system.

Finally, DMA-type interfaces are most commonly used by high-performance, block-oriented storage devices, such as disks and tapes, although any other device that exhibits high transfer rates is a candidate for this type of connection. Some examples include local-area networks and sophisticated terminal multiplexers.

An interface board is usually designed to handle one or more devices of the same type or of very similar types. Multiple devices, when supported, are handled either by means of dedicated channels (one per device) or in a daisy-chain fashion (where only one of them may be active at a time). The former method is quite common for terminal controllers, whereas the latter is customary for disk controllers. When the number of similar devices exceeds the capacity of a single controller, more than one controller of the same type may be installed—up to the limit prescribed by the manufacturer. This limit is usually determined by hardware considerations, such as bus loading and the CPU's ability to handle the combined throughput at peak loads.

Figure 2.2 represents a very general block diagram of an I/O controller. The controller is divided into three functional layers: (1) bus interface, (2) generic device controller, and (3) device interface. The rationale for the two interface layers becomes obvious when one refers to Figure 2.1 and observes that an I/O controller is positioned between the computer system bus at one end and the I/O device itself at the other. As we stated earlier, the I/O section is charged with providing a uniform abstraction of I/O devices to the rest of the system.

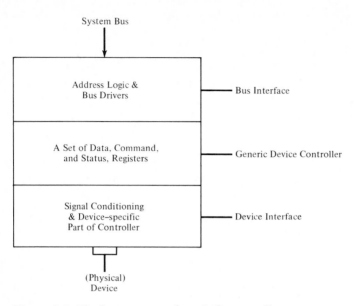

Figure 2.2 Block structure of an I/O controller.

At the hardware level, this means that at the system-bus end each controller must appear as a standard module, capable of participating in all applicable transactions, such as read, write, priority arbitration, interrupt, and DMA cycles. At the device end, the controller must be compatible by providing the specific signals at the required electrical levels. Note that these are device-dependent and typically quite different from the standard computer-logic levels. A variety of binary voltage and current levels, and often some analog signals, are required to drive the electromechanical components found in many computer peripherals. This situation normally restricts each individual I/O controller to interfacing with only a specific collection of functionally similar physical devices.

While the two described layers are of great concern to hardware designers, the middle layer—the generic device controller—is by far the most important to software designers. It provides a uniform abstraction of I/O devices to systems programmers. In particular, it makes every device appear to be a set of dedicated registers. Status queries, issuing of device-specific I/O commands, and data transfers are all accomplished simply by reading from or writing into these registers. A set of such dedicated registers is usually called an *I/O port*. The more common varieties of I/O ports include parallel ports, serial ports, floppy and Winchester controllers, graphic controllers, programmable interval timers, and local-area network controllers. When implemented in LSI or VLSI technology, several I/O ports may be housed in a single integrated circuit.

Figure 2.3 shows the block structure of a typical I/O port. For generality, we are assuming that the port is capable of simultaneous data transmission in both directions. A common convention is to interpret the terms *input* and *output*

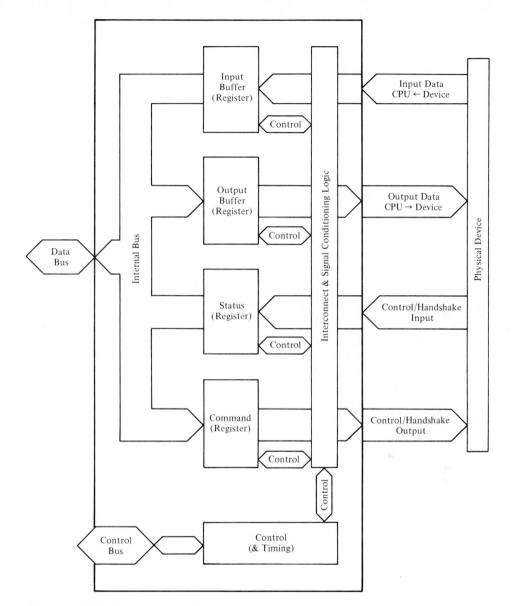

Figure 2.3 Block structure of a typical I/O port.

from the CPU's point of view. With this convention, *input* refers to data transfers from a device to the CPU, and *output* denotes communication in the opposite direction. The port in Figure 2.3 is shown as connecting at its respective ends directly to the computer system bus and to the I/O device. Recall from our earlier discussion that some external drivers and receivers may be needed to connect the bus and device to the port. In any event, the most important part of the I/O port's structure is the set of registers that represents the programmer's view of the attached I/O device. The four register types shown in Figure 2.3 represent the major functional categories commonly found in I/O ports:

1. Input data registers (buffers)
2. Output data registers (buffers)
3. Status registers
4. Command registers

In practice, an I/O port may have several registers in each category or share the functions of a few categories within a single physical register. In general, the number of separate hardware registers in a port tends to be proportional to its functional complexity.

2.2.1 Buffer Registers

The primary function of an input buffer is to hold a datum until the CPU is ready to accept it. This need arises when several I/O activities are executing concurrently, since the CPU may be engaged in one activity when an I/O datum for a second activity becomes available. The I/O device thus may have to wait for the CPU to do the housekeeping necessary to store the state of its current activity for subsequent resumption. Given the transient nature of I/O events, the input datum may no longer be present or valid by the time the CPU is ready to receive the data. To overcome this problem, I/O controllers contain one or more *buffer* registers that hold the data in transit until their target destination is ready to accept the data.

Buffers are frequently implemented as latches strobed by an external signal to guarantee sampling when the data are stable. In multiprogramming systems, I/O from a specific device is overlapped with other activities. As a result, the CPU may not always respond instantly to a signal indicating data availability in a buffer. Because it operates asynchronously, an I/O device may, regardless, produce additional data in the interim. This situation would normally result in lost input characters, as the new data overwrite the current data in the buffer before the CPU manages to retrieve them. Multiple-input buffers in the I/O port can alleviate this problem by providing storage for holding input data until the CPU can process them. In other words, the operating system is given some assistance in handling unanticipated bursty traffic occurring at a bad time. Note that this convenience is limited to a few characters at a time. It is useful for supplying storage for short bursts of input data, but the CPU must be able to process the data at a rate at least as high as the average input rate. If not, buffer overflow will occur with certainty for any size buffer. Thus buffering removes critical timing problems due to peak data rates but does not reduce average rate requirements.

The output buffers primarily serve the purpose of latching the output data written by the CPU so that external devices may be provided with steady signals suitable for their timing requirements. Given that the CPU is essentially the sender of data, there is usually no notion of lost characters on output as far as it is concerned. In many non-DMA uses, output devices do not require data at a sustained rate. Thus, if the system is not very responsive to an output activity, the only harm may be to lower the transfer rate below the potential maximum. For this reason, multiple buffering is much less frequently used on output than on input. Some I/O ports have provisions for output buffering and thus may assist in boosting the output transfer rate if that feature is exploited by the system software. Additional assistance is provided by output devices that contain their own internal buffers in order to boost the peak transfer rate.

Note that our discussion of buffering is limited to what is directly supported by I/O hardware. Software buffering is discussed later in this chapter.

2.2.2 Command Registers

Command registers are in charge of transferring I/O commands between a CPU and an I/O device. Note that regardless of the direction of data transfers, the CPU usually controls an I/O operation by instructing a device when to perform some action. The CPU selects a particular operation from a fixed, device-specific set by writing the corresponding code into the command register. The device usually does not send commands to the CPU; it only indicates its current state, which is accessible to the CPU via port-status registers.

Commands for a specific device tend to fall into one of two general categories:

1. *Mode-designating commands*, which select a particular mode of operation, such as input or output, error-checking algorithm, or type of communication protocol. Mode-designating commands are typically issued only once, during the initialization sequence which is a part of the power-on and reset routines.
2. *Operational I/O commands*, which govern the timing and mechanics of the actual data transfers. Operational commands cause device-specific control actions, such as enable/disable transmission, seek, read, and write. These commands are issued as often as necessary, which typically amounts to once per data transfer.

A command may occupy a full word, but more often it alters the individual control bits within the command register, leaving other bits unchanged. Serving primarily the CPU's need to control devices, command registers are usually write-only registers.

To reduce cost, many interfaces do not dedicate separate port addresses to mode registers, but rather share those of command registers. For such interfaces, the target register of a CPU write is the mode register for the first write after reset or initialization; otherwise, the target is a command register.

2.2.3 Status Registers

As their name suggests, status registers are used to provide information about the status of the I/O device to the CPU. They include such information as device ready or busy, buffer-empty or buffer-full conditions, and error indications. Status registers are usually implemented as a collection of read-only bits in which each bit is associated with some condition, such as READY/NOT_READY. The most common operation on them is testing whether an individual bit is set or not in order to determine the status of the condition it represents.

Both status-register and command-register manipulations are more efficient in systems where input/output ports are memory mapped; i.e., I/O registers are addressed like memory locations, and the full instruction set—especially bit testing and setting—may use them as source or destination operands. Isolated I/O, because of its separate I/O addressing space, requires copying into the CPU registers in order to perform the desired operations, which adds to overhead in I/O processing.

2.3 I/O PORT EXAMPLES

Before illustrating these concepts by giving examples of I/O programming, we briefly describe two types of commonly used I/O ports that will be referred to frequently in this book—the USART and the interval timer. Our exposition again takes the I/O programmer's point of view and concentrates on the control and data registers of each device.

2.3.1 Universal Synchronous/Asynchronous Receiver/Transmitter (USART)

As indicated in our earlier examples, the bit-serial mode is used primarily for computer/terminal communication, with or without modems. It is also encountered in numerous varieties of both short- and long-haul communication links and computer networks.

The universal synchronous/asynchronous receiver/transmitter (USART) is an LSI/VLSI device that is commonly used to implement serial ports. A detailed discussion of serial communication and interfacing is beyond the scope of this chapter. Here we just outline the basic notions in order to aid the understanding of the USART's structure as perceived by an I/O programmer. In addition to explaining the USART itself, this material should serve as an illustration of the extent to which an I/O programmer must understand the hardware and its principles of operation.

There are basically two modes of bit-serial data transfer: *asynchronous*, which is used for lower speeds and requires the receiver to synchronize on a character basis using known line speed and start and stop bits appended to each character by the sender, and *synchronous*, in which synchronization is performed on a block basis by extracting the timing reference provided by the sender in the data stream itself. Typical USARTs can support either transmission mode; selection is usually made by setting the corresponding bits in the mode register. For the sake of hardware simplicity, in this section we focus on the asynchronous mode of data transmission.

Many USARTs support simultaneous bidirectional data transmission, often called *full duplex*, at rates of up to the order of 1 MHz. Depending on the type of connection and the encoding of data, each character consists of 5 to 8 data bits, plus an initial start bit (a zero bit) and one or two stop bits (one bits). The sending USART performs parallel-to-serial conversion and emits data bits on the communication line one at a time. The duration of each bit on the line is determined by the data rate of the link. The USARTs at both ends must be initialized to run at this rate. The sending USART also appends start and stop bits to each character. They are used for synchronization and error detection by the receiving USART, which subsequently strips them off in order to forward only the data bits to its CPU. Naturally, this is done during the serial-to-parallel conversion that brings the character back to its original form.

A USART is also capable of verifying the integrity of the received data by means of the parity bit. When the parity control option is activated by setting the corresponding bits in the mode register, a parity bit is appended to each character by the sending USART. Its value is computed on the basis of the number of ones in the associated data bits and on the basis of the parity mode selected (odd or even). The receiving USART computes its own value of parity on the basis of the received data bits and the parity mode, if any, in effect. The computed parity bit is then compared to the received parity bit and any discrepancy is flagged via the status register to indicate a receive error.

More sophisticated error-control methods may be employed on the blocks of data, but they are rarely supported in the low-end USARTs and are usually implemented in software if desired. As higher levels of integration develop, sophisticated error-control algorithms are moving on chip and are software-selectable as different operating modes of a USART. USARTs without synchronous mode capability are often called UARTs. Several independent, functionally complete UARTs or USARTs may be housed on a single integrated circuit, which is then referred to as a MUART.

These concepts are illustrated in Figure 2.4, which depicts an asynchronous communication link with USARTs at both ends. As shown, system A is transmitting the 7-bit data pattern (1010011 binary) that happens to be the ASCII code for the letter *S*. This value is shown in the output and input buffer registers of the sending and receiving USARTs, respectively, just after the transmission is completed. The corresponding serial bit stream—assuming 7 data bits, even parity, and 1 stop bit—is shown as it would appear on the line. Note how USARTs receive and deliver characters in parallel when interacting with their respective CPUs, whereas the values actually transmitted have quite a different format. Also note that start, stop, and parity bits are stripped off at the receiving end.

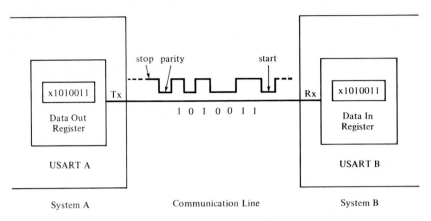

Figure 2.4 An asynchronous communication link.

This is a simple example of an I/O interface handling the idiosyncrasies of a specific device and hiding them from the higher levels of hierarchy, the CPU and the I/O programmer in particular.

From the point of view of the generic I/O controller discussed earlier, a USART consists of input and output buffer registers and command and status registers. Other parts of a USART, which are of lesser importance to a systems programmer, include a fair amount of logic for parallel-to-serial conversions, start-bit and stop-bit mechanization, parity handling, and character synchronization. The number of input buffers typically varies between two and four, whereas one to two buffers are most common on the output. Command and status registers provide the processor with the means of controlling a USART's operation. Their description is a bit more involved, so let us structure it around the sequence of steps typical for programming a USART.

After a power up or a software reset, the USART is brought to a known state. The details of this action are product-specific, but the process commonly readies the USART for a mode command that writes into the mode register. As Figure 2.5a suggests, communication-line parameters—such as asynchronous or synchronous operation, the number of data bits in a character, even/odd or no parity, and line speed—are selected by setting the mode register. Note that this does not result in any actual I/O data transfers, but rather determines the format they will have. Also note that most of these parameters are characteristics of the communication link and must be set identically in the USARTs at both ends. In general, they must not be changed once the link becomes operational, as any disparity would result in garbled data.

The process of programming the mode of operation of a programmable I/O port is usually referred to as *hardware* or *device initialization*. It should always precede normal operation, and no data transfers should take place until all participating interfaces are initialized, e.g., both USARTs in the communication system shown in Figure 2.4.

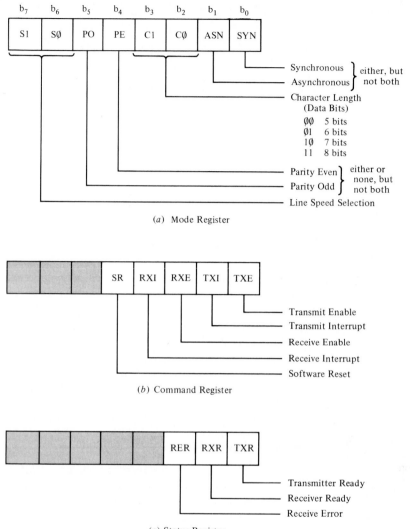

(a) Mode Register

(b) Command Register

(c) Status Register

Figure 2.5 USART registers.

Once initialized, the USART is ready to receive operational commands. As illustrated in Figure 2.5b, these are used to enable or disable reception or transmission of characters or to enable or disable the interrupt-generating logic that signals character arrivals and output-buffer empty conditions. Not shown in the figure are link-handshaking control bits. They may be used to control a modem, when connected, or as a rudimentary line control protocol in computer-to-computer communication via serial links. In addition, some commands, such as local or remote loopback, may be included for testing purposes.

Unlike initialization commands, operational commands may be issued at any time during normal operation.

Finally, a status register dynamically indicates the state of input and output buffers and reception errors. For simplicity, some device-specific features, such as the status of modem-control lines, are not illustrated in Figure 2.5. However, they could be implemented in the unused bits and/or in additional registers.

2.3.2 Programmable Interval Timer (PIT)

Programmable interval timers (PITs) contain one or more programmable counters/interval timers. They are capable of counting external pulses and generating an output signal of the programmable shape and duration. These versatile devices may be used as the system time base, a real-time clock (RTC), baud-rate generator (for USARTs), event counter, motor control, or music generator, as well as in numerous other timing and counting applications. In the discussion that follows, we focus on the PIT as a time base and real-time clock, the functions found in virtually all operating systems.

When used for timing purposes, the PIT generates a periodic interrupt that restores control momentarily to an operating system. The PIT does this by counting external pulses provided by a stable clock of known frequency. The PIT's output is usually set for the pulse mode and connected directly to the CPU's interrupt-request section. The time period between two successive timer interrupts is programmed by writing a pulse-count constant into the PIT's register. The variables that determine the interrupt interval are the clock period or frequency and the count constant according to the formula

$$\text{Interval} = \text{clock period} \times \text{count constant}$$

Most often, the clock frequency and the desired interval are known, leaving the count constant to be calculated. For example, given a 2-MHz clock and desired timing interval of 20 ms (milliseconds), the count constant is determined as

$$\text{Clock period} = \frac{1}{2 \times 10^6} = \frac{1}{2} \times 10^{-6} = 0.5\mu s$$

$$\text{Count constant} = \frac{20 \times 10^{-3}}{0.5 \times 10^{-6}} = 40 \times 10^3$$

In other words, in order to have a PIT fed by a 2-MHz clock generate a pulse every 20 ms, its respective register should be loaded with the counting constant of 40,000. Note that PIT counting registers are often limited to 16 bits or less, which restricts the duration of the maximum interval with a given clock. This limitation may be removed by cascading the output of one pulse-generator register to the clock input of the second pulse-generator register. Many PITs provide this capability through internal paths that are controlled by mode selection. Even longer intervals may be attained by counting PIT interrupts in dedicated-memory locations, often called *software counters*.

From the system programmer's point of view, a PIT is a device that needs initialization and an interrupt service routine. Unlike a USART, no handshaking or extensive status checking is necessary for a PIT. Furthermore, PITs intended for timing applications often include automatic count-register reloading when the register counts down to zero. This reduces the CPU's involvement to initialization and mode selection only and simplifies accurate timekeeping when used for time-of-day applications.

A typical PIT contains mode and command registers to which the CPU may write in order to control the PIT. Mode commands include selection of the output characteristics. Typically, a count register may produce a single event or may be programmed to produce a periodic event by setting the register for automatic reload. The mode may also select a signal source to count, such as a crystal-clock input, an external input, or the output of another counter register. Operational commands are usually limited to START_COUNTING and STOP_COUNTING. The CPU can also query a PIT for status and read the running count of a specified timer. Given the frequent presence of several independent counters on a chip, command registers usually include some provision for addressing them individually.

2.4 PROGRAM-CONTROLLED I/O

In this section we explore the fundamentals of input/output programming. Our emphasis is on the principles, but we also look at the performance and introduce the high-level-language (HLL) notation that will be used throughout this book. In order to concentrate on the basic principles of I/O programming, we first present a simple case of controlling a single I/O device using the program-controlled I/O method. A more realistic situation involving control of multiple devices is discussed in the subsequent section.

2.4.1 Controlling a Single Device

Because of their asynchronous operation, I/O devices rely on handshaking protocols to synchronize their activities with the CPU temporarily in order to exchange data. Signals to assist in this process are usually provided on the system bus and within the status and command registers of device interfaces.

A typical program-controlled input transaction is illustrated in Figure 2.6. Output transactions consist of the same basic steps in a slightly permuted order.

A common practice is to initialize each device before allowing it to participate in input/output operations. Device initialization is normally performed after the system is powered up, although subsequent reinitialization is possible after software-commanded resetting of individual devices. The primary purpose of initialization is to select the desired mode of operation after the device is brought to a known state by a hardware or a software reset. While initialization is

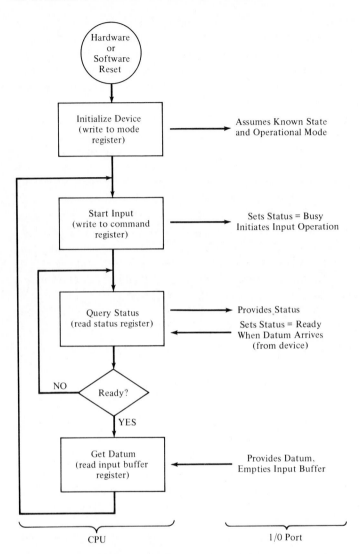

Figure 2.6 A typical program-controlled input transaction.

performed once for each device, other steps depicted in Figure 2.6 are repetitively executed for each individual data transfer.

In general, prior to each I/O transaction, the CPU indicates its desire to transfer or receive data by issuing a START_I/O command. This is accomplished by writing the corresponding bit pattern into the command register of the I/O port in the respective device interface. Upon receipt, the I/O port sets a status bit to *busy*, to indicate that an operation is in progress. When data become available in the input buffer or an output buffer becomes empty, the I/O port signals the event by setting a corresponding bit in its status register to the *ready* state. The CPU may determine the setting of status bits at any time by reading the I/O port's status register. When it discovers that the port is ready, the CPU may read the data from the input buffer or place data in the output buffer—depending on the direction of the transfer in question. At this point, another I/O transaction may be initiated, and the whole cycle is repeated. Note that status flags for input signify the completeness of a data transfer (input buffer full), but for output they indicate the readiness of the device for new data transfer from the CPU (output buffer empty). The I/O command sequences are somewhat automated for many USARTs. In particular, placing a datum in the output buffer and reading a datum from the input buffer also act as implicit START_OUTPUT and START_INPUT commands, respectively.

The assembly language coding of the USART initialization and data input and output sequences for a hypothetical machine are given in Program 2.1. Sample constants follow the format of USART registers given in Figure 2.5, and the initialization is performed for the line characteristics described in Figure 2.4. For simplicity and generality, the only addressing modes used are direct addressing, and immediate addressing which is indicated by a # sign preceding the operand. All instructions have two operands that are assumed to be in the *destination, source* order. For example,

MOVE   USCMD, #RESET

loads literal (immediate operand) RESET into the USART's command register.

Hardware initialization is markedly product-specific. Only a few of its basic operations are shown in the INITUS section of Program 2.1. Note that the RESET command is the first given to the USART in order to bring it to a known state. This usually implies clearing the buffers, status flags, etc. and preparing the USART to receive the mode command. Typically, both hardware and software resets accomplish this purpose. The major difference is that a hardware reset command is a signal broadcast through the whole system as part of the power-up sequence, whereas a software reset command may be issued at any time and selectively to the specific (addressed) device only. Both forms of reset cancel all operations of the I/O port, so they should be used with caution and timed properly.

Initialization in Program 2.1 continues with selecting the mode of operation and, in the example given, enabling transmission. This particular sequence would be used for system A in Figure 2.4 (sender USART), while system B's initialization would differ only in enabling the reception instead. Naturally, for bidirectional links, both should be enabled by writing #RXENAB + #TXENAB into the USART's command register.

The two remaining sections of code in Program 2.1 illustrate the *program-controlled I/O method*, where the CPU is busily testing the status of an I/O device until it becomes ready for the next transfer. The input section consists of testing the status register repetitively until a datum arrives, an event that the USART indicates by setting the RXRDY bit in its status register (this

```
;               USART register addresses

USMODE    EQU       ...              ;mode register
USCMD     EQU       ...              ;command register
USSTAT    EQU       ...              ;status register
USDIN     EQU       ...              ;input data buffer
USDOUT    EQU       ...              ;output data buffer

;               mode definition constant

MODE      EQU       xx011010B        ;mode=async, even
                                     ;   parity, 7bits

;               command definition constants

TXENAB    EQU       00000001B        ;transmit enable
RXENAB    EQU       00000100B        ;receive enable
RESET     EQU       00010000B        ;reset USART

;               status definition constants

TXRDY     EQU       00000001B        ;transmitter ready
RXRDY     EQU       00000010B        ;receiver ready
RXERR     EQU       00000100B        ;receive error

;               USART initialization

INITUS:   MOVE      USCMD,#RESET     ;reset USART
          MOVE      USMODE,#MODE     ;set mode of operation
          ...                        ;other device-specific
                                     ;   commands and housekeeping
          MOVE      USCMD,#TXENAB    ;enable transmission (reception
          ...                        ;   and interrupts off)

;               receive (input) a character

WAITIN:   BITEST    USSTAT,#RXRDY    ;has a character arrived ?
          BNSET     WAITIN           ;   no, try again
          BITEST    USSTAT,#RXERR    ;   arrived, is it OK?
          BSET      RECERR           ;      bad, process error
          MOVE      RA,USDIN         ;      OK char, save it in RA
          ...

RECERR:   MOVE      RB,USSTAT        ;receive-error, save status in RB
          MOVE      RA,USDIN         ;   and clean-up USART inbuffer
          ...

;               transmit (output) a character

WTOUT:    BITEST    USSTAT,#TXRDY    ;ready to send a character?
          BNSET     WTOUT            ;   no, try again
          MOVE      USDOUT,RC        ;   ready, send from RC
```

Program 2.1 Program-controlled input/output

corresponds to READY status in Figure 2.6). The instruction used is BITEST, which is assumed to perform an *and* operation between its two operands and to set the CPU condition-code flags accordingly. BITEST is assumed to affect neither the source nor the destination operand. This type of instruction is often used to test the individual bits of an I/O port's registers. Two types of conditional jumps, BSET and BNSET, are used in Program 2.1 to branch if the bit tested by the BITEST instruction is found to be set or not set, respectively.

Once the character arrives, the program checks for a reception error. If none is detected, the datum is fetched from the input buffer register and placed into the CPU register RA. Alternatively, control is passed to the error-handling section. Its rudimentary form is shown in Program 2.1 beginning with label RECERR. The error-handling code usually determines the cause of the problem by testing the specific error indicators in the status register, e.g., parity, overrun (lost character), or framing error (last bit not a stop bit) for a typical USART. Depending on the findings, a recovery action is taken, and the error is reported or logged. Since USARTs usually do not offer any means for correcting errors, a received character is discarded when an error flag is raised. Note that the character in error is, nonetheless, read by our sample program. This is a common practice with USARTs in order to empty the input buffer and thus reset the RXRDY and RXERR flags. Otherwise, after returning from the error processing, the WAITIN loop would result in rereading of the same character and reprocessing of the same "error" indefinitely.

No error checking is performed in the output section of Program 2.1. In fact, many USARTs do not have error flags for output operations. However, line status is usually provided and an output program ought to verify that a connection exists before each byte is sent. A conscientious I/O programmer would check the line and "liveness" of the receiver by sending test messages at regular intervals or when the normal traffic subsides.

Returning to the output code itself, it, like the input code, consists of a loop that is executed repetitively until the USART becomes ready to receive a new character. This type of loop is used for both input and output and is called the *busy-wait loop.* It is the basis of the program-controlled I/O method. This is the simplest form of I/O programming, which is found only in single-user systems and in some dedicated I/O processors. Its main shortcomings are

1. Low CPU utilization
2. Difficulty in handling multiple I/O devices

A simple timing analysis of the output code, using our earlier assumptions of a 1920-cps transfer rate and 1-μs instruction execution time, indicates that the busy-wait loop is executed approximately 250 times for each character transferred. In other words, even with the relatively fast peripheral driven at its maximum speed, *250 unsuccessful status-register tests are performed for each successful one* (resulting in the actual output), thus yielding an effective CPU utilization of less than 1%. Note that the CPU, by busy-waiting, is devoting the full 100% of its execution cycles to the output device, but only less than 1% of them represent useful work. We should point out that a more accurate analysis would have to take into account the additional instructions necessary to fetch successive characters from memory, update buffer pointers, check for termination, etc. However, those instructions are executed only when the actual character transmission takes place and thus affect neither the busy loop itself nor the order of magnitude of our result.

In any case, the important conclusion is that in our example of program-controlled I/O, the CPU devotes all its cycles to a single device and in so doing may become heavily underutilized. Before we discover ways to remedy these problems, let us introduce a slightly more complicated situation and a new notation.

Program 2.2 is a pseudo-Pascal version of the module COMPUTEPRINT, which alternates between performing some (unspecified) computation and printing its results. The purpose of this example is to introduce the high-level-language (HLL) notation used throughout this book and to look deeper into program-controlled I/O.

Our HLL generally follows the syntax of Pascal, but occasionally we add some notions and constructs of our own. These are necessary when dealing with I/O port addresses and other hardware-specific details that are unavoidable in systems programming. Most of the nonstandard constructs are coded as procedures in order to make them directly implementable in systems that support linking of modules coded in different languages, as many commercial releases of Pascal do. The keyword *program/module* is used to indicate that what follows may be a stand-alone program or a module of a larger system. The issue of separate and independent compilation of modules is discussed in Chapter 9.

Program 2.2, as many others in this book, omits nonessential details in order to focus the reader's attention on the fundamentals of the principles under investigation. Our primary consideration here is the procedure PRINT, which uses the program-controlled I/O method to output OUTCOUNT characters from the array OUTDATA. These are presumed to be produced by COMPUTE.

A statement that warrants some explanation is the second *while* in PRINT. It is intended to represent a busy-wait loop similar to the ones found in Program 2.1. Note that it tests the status of the IOPORT and keeps looping until the OUTRDY (an equivalent of TXRDY in Program 2.1) flag is set, indicating the I/O port's readiness to accept the next character for transmission. The KEEPTESTING comment is included to make the statement more readable by suggesting the repetitive operation in a form that may not be intuitively obvious at first; namely, the value of the IOPORT_STATUS variable is not affected by any statements in the program but is changed only by external events and devices. However, changes of IOPORT_STATUS control the program's execution so that the reader must envision changes to IOPORT_STATUS occurring autonomously and observe how the program behaves in response to them. As suggested by our earlier examples, 99% of a program's execution time may be spent executing this particular statement.

```
program/module computeprint;

  const
    max = ...;            {max length of output}
    outrdy = ...;         {ioport output ready}

  type
    text = array [1..max] of char;

  var
    data : text;
    numberof : integer;

  procedure compute(var comdata : text; var count : integer);
    ...

  procedure print(outdata : text; outcount : integer);

    var
      outindex : integer;

    begin
      outindex := 1;
      while outcount > 0 do
        begin
          while ioport_status <> outrdy do {keeptesting};
          ioport_dataout := outdata[outindex];
          outindex := outindex + 1;
          outcount := outcount - 1
        end {while}
    end; {print}

  begin {computeprint}
    initialize_hardware;
    while true do          {forever}
      begin
        compute(data, numberof);
        print(data, numberof)
      end {while}
  end {computeprint}
```

Program 2.2 Programmed-controlled output

When the flag finally becomes set (IOPORT_STATUS = OUTRDY), control passes to the next statement, which places a new character in the I/O port's output buffer. Figure 2.7 is a timing diagram of the flow of control in Program 2.2. Given that the procedure PRINT uses program-controlled I/O, the CPU utilization while executing PRINT may be as low as 1%. Moreover, all the CPU's cycles are dedicated to this program. The utilization could be improved somewhat by overlapping other computations with the output. Specifically, rather than looping continuously while waiting for the device to become ready, the CPU could be performing the next batch of computations and only occasionally test the status of the device. This approach, while improving CPU utilization, still does not

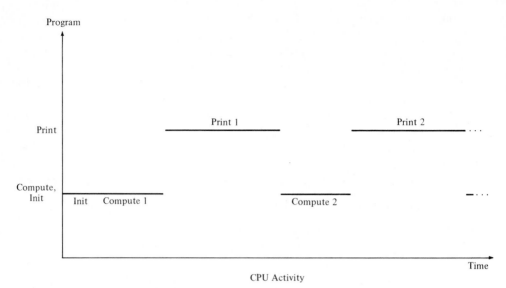

Figure 2.7 Timing diagram of Program 2.2.

solve the problem of handling multiple I/O devices. We discuss a technique for controlling several devices in a more general framework in the section that follows.

2.4.2 Controlling Multiple Devices: Polling

In virtually all computer installations there are several I/O devices. The obvious question is: Can the CPU control more than one device with program-controlled I/O? The answer is yes. The method for accomplishing this capitalizes on the low CPU utilization of the busy-wait loop by expanding the loop to test the status of several I/O devices and to branch to the appropriate I/O service routine of the first device found to be ready. This is called *polling*, and its busy-wait loop has the following format:

Test status of device 1.
If ready, go to its service routine.
Test status of device 2.
If ready, go to its service routine.
.
.
.

Test status of device *n*.
If ready, go to its service routine.
Repeat polling sequence.

The device service routines contain a few instructions for performing the actual I/O and for updating buffer pointers and counters; but they usually do not test the status of the respective I/O device, since the status test is made just prior to entering the service routine. Each service routine terminates with a branch back to a test in the polling sequence. Whether this branch returns to the beginning of the polling sequence (device 1) or to the next status test in line determines the relative device priorities and maximum service rates. To see why this is true, let us explore I/O response times as a function of polling sequence.

When I/O load increases, so does the probability that a device is ready when polled. Its service routine will then be executed, and no other status testing will take place during that time. Upon completion, devices that are both above and below the one just serviced in the polling sequence may be awaiting the CPU's attention. If polling is resumed from the beginning of the sequence after each I/O transaction, devices placed high in the sequence are obviously given preferential service and, in effect, high priority. In such systems, when several devices await service, the one with the highest priority obtains service first. Alternatively, if polling is performed in the round-robin fashion, all devices have essentially equal priority. In fact, device priority rotates depending on the device's distance in the polling list from the status check currently being executed.

I/O response time is closely related to the polling strategy in effect. We consider two related performance measures: *latency*, the time that elapses from the moment a device becomes ready until its service routine is entered, and *I/O bandwidth*, the maximum I/O rate that may be sustained without the loss of data. Let us, without loss of generality, assume that all device service routines are of equal duration T. With fixed polling priorities, the highest-priority device, in the worst case, may experience a latency of T and sustain burst I/O rates of up to $1/T$. Unfortunately, at maximum rate, high-priority I/O may tie up the CPU so that no other device receives service. In practice, because the CPU is much faster than typical I/O devices, rarely does one device utilize the entire capacity of the CPU in a polled system. If this situation occurs, it would best be handled by a dedicated CPU. However, this extreme example shows how fixed-priority systems can be monopolized by a single device. Consequently, I/O performance can be guaranteed only for the highest-priority device. All other devices have to have their expected performance rated relative to the behavior of the higher-priority devices. With a rotating priority, the worst-case latency is $(n-1)T$, and the I/O bandwidth is no less than $1/(nT)$ for *each device* in the system. So, which strategy is better?

Before answering, the reader should realize that our cursory performance analysis is based on extreme assumptions in order to explore the limiting properties of the various schemes. Statistically speaking, we were looking at a very skewed end of the probability distribution, far from the expected system behavior. As we have seen before, typical non-DMA I/O devices operate well below CPU speeds. DMA devices consume higher bus bandwidth but a virtually insignificant fraction of CPU execution cycles. It can be shown that with polling it would take over 100 terminals, all running at full 19.2 KHz, to tie up a 1-MIPS (millions of instructions per second) processor.

The answer obviously depends on the application and on the optimization criteria. Rotating priority gives fair service and predictable performance to all devices. Another viewpoint can be that performance is, in essence, equally bad for all devices. Given that all I/O devices are not created equal, some of them can tolerate latency better than others. If a disk drive's service request is not honored within a fixed time window of data availability, an additional full rotation will be needed before another window is created. On the other hand, being a little lax in providing a buffered printer with a character may result in no measurable loss of performance. Priorities are a convenient way for the system designer to enforce a particular order in servicing concurrent outstanding device requests, as well as to tune the system's I/O performance and response times. These issues are of great importance in operating-system design, and we return to them in the next chapter.

Coming back to polling, we should realize that it is a variation of a busy-wait loop and that continuous polling would most likely result in many unsuccessful tests and low effective CPU utilization. What if we were to reduce polling frequency by allocating the CPU to a more productive, perhaps unrelated, activity and only occasionally execute the polling sequence itself? This is an idea in the right direction, but it suffers from some practical problems. The question is both how often to poll and how to implement that frequency in a general-purpose system. If polling frequency is high, it degenerates to busy-waiting with most of its problems. On the other hand, infrequent polling increases CPU utilization but may also result in higher latency, thereby reducing performance and possibly causing loss of data. The "right" frequency is also system- and configuration-dependent. For example, if some asynchronous lines connected to serial ports are upgraded from servicing "dumb" terminals, with input from humans at rates typically less than 10 cps, to personal computers, with input rates on the order of 1000 cps, the frequency of polling would have to be modified accordingly—a major undertaking requiring the system to be reconfigured. Even when these issues are resolved and the suitable polling frequency is chosen, we must still face the problem of implementation. Whatever the CPU may be doing, it must execute the polling sequence at chosen intervals. In general, this would imply careful analysis of all programs in terms of execution times in order to make sure that branches to polling are inserted at proper places, an unreasonable requirement at best when one wants to consider the changes suggested by the previous example. A more practical approach is to use the programmable interval timer. However, the problem is that when a timed interval expires, the CPU must recognize the fact immediately and initiate polling. Program-controlled I/O does not have the ability to respond to timeouts without latency, so we turn our attention to interrupt-driven I/O, which is ideally suited for such purposes.

2.5 INTERRUPT-DRIVEN I/O

In this section we briefly outline the chief characteristics of interrupt-driven I/O and then explore some advanced features that will lead us to the subsequent investigation of I/O concurrency. Following the structure of the section on program-controlled I/O, we first present the simpler case of a single interrupt-driven device in the system in order to stress the basic principles. The use of interrupts to control multiple devices is then treated in a separate subsection.

2.5.1 Controlling a Single Device

Our previous discussion revealed the basic problem of program-controlled I/O, that is, accurate guessing of the appropriate time to test device readiness in order to maintain satisfactory levels of performance for both I/O and the CPU. On the other hand, we have seen that the I/O interface permanently monitors attached devices and "knows" exactly when an event, such as I/O completion, needs a CPU's attention. The idea behind the interrupt mechanism is to have the interface force the CPU to temporarily relinquish its current activity and to service the significant I/O event. Note that this approach effectively does away with busy-waiting and status testing. In essence, interrupts are a hardware-assisted mechanism for synchronizing a CPU with the (asynchronous) external events. After a device is serviced by executing its associated interrupt-service routine (ISR), the CPU resumes the previous activity at the point of interruption. Some examples of interrupt-generating events are input data ready, ready for next datum on output, and DMA transfer completed. In order to introduce the basic hardware and software aspects of interrupts, we begin with the simple case of a single interrupting device in the system.

With interrupt-driven I/O, the CPU will typically be engaged in some other activity until a significant I/O event occurs and raises an interrupt request. That forces transfer of control to a service routine. Since control will be given back to the interrupted activity after the interrupt request is serviced, the hardware must save at least the current value of the program counter (PC) before reloading it with the address of the interrupt-service routine. Let us, for the time being, defer the discussion of where the address of the interrupt-service routine is found and assume a common simple case that it is found in a fixed memory location dedicated to ISR addresses.

Given that they are triggered in response to external I/O events, interrupt requests themselves are asynchronous with respect to the CPU. This means that the times of their occurrences are unpredictable, and interrupts may suspend other programs at virtually any point in time. When the ISR starts executing, being a sequence of instructions itself, it will inevitably modify the CPU registers, status flags, and possibly, some memory locations. Upon its completion, control is returned to the interrupted activity. The interrupted program can continue its execution correctly only if it finds its view of the machine in the same state as it was just prior to the interrupt. In other words, the *context* of the interrupted program must be preserved while the ISR is executing, and it must be restored before control is subsequently returned to it. If no common variables are shared by the interrupted program and the ISR, the context may be taken to mean the values of all CPU registers and status flags. However, only the part of the context that is actually *modified* by the interrupt-service routine needs to be saved.

The process of changing context from an executing program to an interrupt handler is called the *context switch*, and it requires a combination of hardware and software to control. How can this process be implemented? How much of it should be delegated to hardware?

The first answer should be quite obvious. The interrupted program knows neither when an interrupt will assume control of the processor nor which part of the machine context will be modified by the interrupt routine. Therefore, the interrupt-service routine itself must be charged with context saving and restoring.

There is no definite answer to the question of how much of context saving to delegate to hardware; it is resolved by hardware designers as a compromise among speed, reliability, and user convenience. We have already seen that the program counter is saved as a part of the hardware interrupt-recognition sequence. In some computers, the same hardware also saves the rest of the state, i.e., flags and all other program-accessible registers, thus relieving the ISR of the burden. Another school of thought suggests that saving more than the minimum is too costly and increases the overhead of each interrupt. This reasoning is based on the observation that some interrupt routines modify only a subset of system registers. Consequently, it is more efficient to save only the affected subset of registers during a context switch. Machines based on this philosophy usually save the minimal state automatically and leave the rest to software, since there is no simple way to instruct the hardware as to which particular subset of registers to save (although this has been done in the VAX architecture, for example). Because no single approach is acceptable, many different solutions have been implemented. Some CPUs save only the PC and status flags; others save all registers and flags; and many save selected registers and flags. The recent trend seems to be to provide several options in the instruction set and to let the I/O programmer choose the one best suited for the specific application. In any case, both hardware and software sequences typically use the system stack for temporary storage of program contexts.

The issue here, other than hardware cost and complexity, is the time necessary to perform a context switch—an extremely important factor in real-time and other I/O intensive or time-critical applications. For the same amount of information saved, hardware context save/restore is faster, since no instructions need be fetched from memory. However, the software approach may have an edge where a small subset of the state, which varies from ISR to ISR, is saved. Whatever strategy is chosen, note that the hardware should, just before returning control to the interrupted program, restore the part of context that it saved. This is commonly accomplished by a special instruction, *return from interrupt* (RTI), which is usually the last statement executed in an interrupt-service routine.

Except for context saving and restoring, an ISR is essentially a piece of code that is executed in response to an external event. As such, it usually consists of a few instructions to transfer data, check for errors, and update pointers, which is a structure very similar to the service-routine part of program-controlled I/O.

No testing of device readiness need be performed in the ISR, because an ISR is entered only when an I/O event occurs. Hence readiness may be taken for granted.

An interrupt request that invokes an ISR is an electric signal. That signal must be removed when the corresponding interrupt handler responds to the request. So the ISR code must, at some point, notify the I/O port to remove its interrupt request signal. Otherwise, the same request would interrupt the CPU continuously, even after the I/O processing had been completed. In such a case, the CPU would be prevented from doing any useful work. The process by which a CPU notifies an I/O port or an interrupt controller to remove an interrupt request is called an *interrupt acknowledge*. Many I/O ports combine this function with buffer-register accessing, so that by simply retrieving or supplying a datum, for input and output, respectively, the CPU acknowledges the corresponding interrupt. So, for many USARTs, both start I/O and interrupt acknowledge are side effects of reads and writes to the buffer registers.

A peculiarity of ISR code is that, unlike procedure code, it is not called by other software, although it may share some variables and produce results for other sections of code. Interrupt handlers are invoked indirectly, in response to external events. Except possibly for initialization procedures that set up interrupt vectors, non-ISR code should contain no references to ISR code. Each ISR should terminate with the return-from-interrupt instruction if one exists in the given instruction set. Special provisions to that effect must be provided if an ISR is coded in a high-level language.

Program 2.3 illustrates coding of an interrupt-service routine and demonstrates how computations may be overlapped with I/O in order to improve the system's throughput, even when executing a single program. The program is basically an interrupt version of the COMPUTEPRINT with double buffering added for additional I/O overlap. The two new constructs introduced in this example are the statements for manipulating the interrupt mechanism (enable and disable) and the *process* keyword that designates an interrupt-service routine. Our sample ISR process, PRINT, is embedded in the START_OUTPUT procedure. Syntactically, it follows the structure of a procedure—in terms of declaration and scopes of the variables. Recall that an ISR should never be explicitly invoked by software, so a process should be parameterless. Semantically, a process will, for the time being, represent an ISR, which means that it is invoked by hardware via the interrupt-linkage mechanism and that the last *end* statement of a process should be compiled as an RTI instruction or its equivalent for a given architecture. The example given in Program 2.3 is intended to provide just an intuitive motivation of a process as a separate, asynchronously activated piece of code; the concept of a process is of paramount importance in operating system design, and it is dealt with in detail in Chapter 3.

The main section of the program INTERRUPT_CP begins by initializing hardware. The first statement disables interrupts in order to prevent any I/O processing until the I/O port is initialized for the desired mode of operation. For this reason, one of the effects of the hardware reset in many computers is to disable interrupts. Note that enable interrupts and disable interrupts are simply the HLL representation of the corresponding machine language instructions, such as EI and DI or STI (for set interrupts) and CLI (for clear interrupts). The final step of initialization is to place the address of the interrupt-service routine in the fixed memory location in order to indicate to the hardware interrupt sequence where to transfer control when the I/O port becomes ready. For reasons of compatibility with subsequent programs, this statement uses the term *vector*, which is explained under Controlling Multiple Devices.

Before discussing the overall functioning of Program 2.3, let us explain the logic of the PRINT process. Its purpose is to output OUTCOUNT characters from the OUTDATA array. One character is transferred in response to each interrupt request. Therefore, it takes OUTCOUNT interrupts for PRINT to complete one full cycle. When the IOPORT becomes ready to output a character, it raises

```
program/module interruptCP;

  const
    max = ...;                {max length of output}
  type
    text = array [1..max] of char;
  var
    data1, data2 : text;      {data buffers}
    outdone : boolean;        {flag: done printing output}

  procedure compute(var comdata : text; var count : integer);
    ...

  procedure start_output(outdata : text; outcount : integer);
    var
      outindex : integer;

    process print;
      begin
        while true do
          begin
            {await_printer_interrupt}
            save_context;
            ioport_dataout := outdata[i];
            outindex := outindex + 1;
            outcount := outcount - 1;
            if outcount = 0
              then
                begin
                  disable_interrupts;
                  outdone := true
                end;
            restore_context
          end {while}
      end; {print}
```

(*Continued*)

```
  begin {start_output}
     i := 1;
     outdone := false;
     enable_interrupts
  end; {start_output}

 begin {interruptCP}
   disable_interrupts;
   initialize_hardware;
   connect_interrupt_vector(print);
   compute(data1, num1);                    {compute1}
   start_output(data1, num1);               {start printing1, and}
   compute(data2, num2);                    {compute2 concurrently}
   while not outdone do {keeptesting};      {wait till 1 printed}
   start_output(data2, num2);               {start printing2, and}
   compute(data1, num1);                    {compute3 concurrently}
   while not outdone do {keeptesting};      {wait till 2 printed}
   start_output(data1, num1);               {start printing3, and}
   compute(data2, num1);                    {compute4 concurrently}
     . . .
 end {interruptCP}
```

Program 2.3 Interrupt-driven compute-print

its ready flag, which, in turn, asserts an interrupt request. When interrupts are enabled, an interrupt request invokes the hardware interrupt-recognition sequence. In our example, this sequence transfers control to the PRINT process. PRINT then saves the context of the interrupted activity, outputs the next character, and tests whether all OUTCOUNTs of them have been processed. If not, it restores the saved context and returns from interrupt. Recall that this translates to an RTI instruction that restores whatever part of the context was saved by hardware and resumes the previous activity at the point of interruption. PRINT is coded assuming that the interrupt is implicitly acknowledged by placing the next character in IOPORT's output buffer; otherwise it should include an explicit interrupt-acknowledge statement.

This version of the program relies on software double buffering, global signaling variables, and interrupt enabling/disabling in order to overlap computations with I/O. The main part of the program, after initialization, performs the first batch of computations and instructs procedure COMPUTE to place results in DATA1 and NUM1—the first buffer and its associated character-count variable. It then invokes START_OUTPUT to output the results. START_OUTPUT sets the OUTDONE synchronization flag to false to indicate that output is in progress and enables interrupts. At this point it returns to the main section, since the PRINT process will be servicing the interrupts as they come. While output of DATA1 is taking place at a rate determined by the output device, the second computation is initiated by the main program. This is our first example of interleaved program execution in a computer system.

As the diagram in Figure 2.8 indicates, both the second computation and the first output are concurrently progressing toward their respective completions. The output, being an ISR, preempts computation whenever the device is ready for another transfer. Note that results of the second computation (stored in the DATA2 buffer) may not be printed until the first output (stored in the DATA1 buffer) is completed, because the order of characters in printed output must be identical to the order in which characters are produced. The third batch of computations must also be postponed until DATA1 is printed, since both data buffers are in use until that time.

The main section awaits completion of the printing of DATA1 by testing the OUTDONE flag, which is set to true when a run of PRINT is completed. Note that busy-waiting in the main section while testing the OUTDONE flag does not impede the progress of the interrupt-driven PRINT. When PRINT completes, the DATA1 buffer is freed and becomes available for the next batch of results. The main section then invokes the second output and the third computation. Note that the order of procedure invocation, although arbitrary in principle, must be as indicated in Program 2.3 if overlapped operation is desired.

The final note regards the behavior of the interrupt-service routines illustrated by this program. Note that an ISR may share variables with other sections of code, such as OUTDATA and OUTDONE in Program 2.3. Due to the asynchronous execution of ISRs, the use and updating of shared global variables must, in general, be carefully synchronized in order to avoid timing errors. Program 2.3 is structured in such a way that synchronization is not necessary. However, in

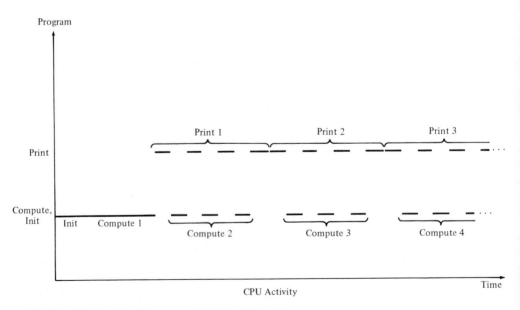

Figure 2.8 Timing diagram of Program 2.3.

many other cases synchronization is absolutely essential. The important issue of interprocess synchronization is dealt with in Chapters 4 and 5.

In terms of behavior, notice how the hardware interrupt-enable/disable mechanism may be used to exchange stop and go timing signals between the ISR and other sections of code. In particular, START_OUTPUT "turns on" PRINT by enabling interrupts, and PRINT shuts itself off, i.e., disables its own continuing operation, by disabling interrupts. A careful reader will notice that PRINT actually disables interrupts even while the transmission of the last character in a string may still be in progress. This, on output, does no harm because it simply means that no interrupt should be accepted when the I/O port's output buffer becomes empty after processing the last character.

How much have we gained in terms of performance by going from the program-controlled to the interrupt-driven version of this program? In the latter case, with sufficient buffering, at best both CPU and I/O utilization of nearly 100% might be achieved. This should be contrasted with the possibly less than 1% CPU utilization in the program-controlled I/O case. Yet the total performance improvement will not be increased by more than a factor of 2! The reason for this is that by overlapping two activities, we cannot do better than reduce the resulting execution time to that of the longer routine. The time for fully sequential execution would equal the sum of the times of the two routines, and that can be at most twice as long as the overlapped time. Another important observation is that program-controlled I/O is, in general, capable of providing higher I/O bandwidth than interrupt-driven I/O. Namely, assuming a single I/O device, the maximum I/O bandwidth for a given computer system is obtained by calculating the time it takes to move data in and out by means of the program-controlled I/O, with all status tests being successful, i.e., with virtually 100% CPU utilization. Under the same assumptions, the data throughput for interrupt-driven I/O would have to be lower, owing to the overhead of context switching (saving and restoring). For this reason, designers of dedicated I/O systems, e.g., a communications front-end processor, should seriously consider program-controlled I/O.

2.5.2 Controlling Multiple Devices

It would appear that we have invested a lot of energy to produce a not so spectacular gain. However, truly significant performance improvement may be obtained by overlapping a *multitude* of interrupt-driven I/O processes with a number of CPU-bound activities. This mode of operation requires support from the operating system in terms of scheduling, synchronization, and protection. Those issues will be our primary concern in this book as we progress toward the design of a complete kernel of a multiprocess operating system. The first stumbling block on our way is dealing with multiple sources of interrupts, which we have tacitly ignored thus far.

When multiple I/O interfaces perform their data transfers in the interrupt-driven mode, the means for recognizing a specific source of interrupt and handling a hierarchy of priority levels must be provided by either the hardware or the system software. Since the number of separate interrupt request lines in a computer system is usually smaller than the number of possible sources of interrupt, the CPU, in general, cannot deduce which particular device needs service just on the basis of having received an interrupt signal on a given line. Obviously, some extensions to the basic interrupt-recognition mechanisms are needed for this purpose. Probably the simplest way is to retain the hardware transfer of control to a fixed memory location, as we have assumed in the single-source case. In other words, every interrupt request in the system, no matter what its cause, forces the CPU to transfer control to the same place. The actual originator of the request may then be determined by a polling routine, such as the one described under Controlling Multiple Devices: Polling in Section 2.4. The essential difference between this method and program-controlled I/O polling is that with interrupts, the polling routine is entered only when at least one device is *known to be ready*; i.e., success is guaranteed and only a limited number of CPU cycles may be lost in testing devices that are not ready but precede the active one in the sequence. Note that this approach raises the issue of relative priorities in exactly the same way as described under Controlling Multiple Devices: Polling in Section 2.4. In particular, when several interrupt requests are pending simultaneously, the one with the highest priority is serviced first. As a part of that process, the interrupt is acknowledged to the specific interface in question, and it removes its request signal from the system bus. The remaining interfaces, however, continue to hold their request lines active, pending acknowledgment. In turn, the CPU will be interrupted again, identify another source, and acknowledge and service it. This process is repeated until all outstanding requests are serviced. Note that its success hinges on interfaces maintaining interrupt requests active until acknowledged, a feature commonly provided by I/O ports.

The described scheme is simple and requires minimal hardware support, but it may result in somewhat inefficient use of CPU cycles. This may lead to potentially longer interrupt latency and lower I/O bandwidth than would be possible if each interrupt request were to branch to its service routine directly. *Interrupt vectoring* is a hardware mechanism that accomplishes this task. Although the implementation details vary, vectoring provides direct linkage between each source of interrupt and its associated service routine. The interrupting-device interface provides, as a part of its interrupt request, either its own unique identifier or the very address of the ISR itself. The hardware-recognition sequence uses this information to transfer control to the designated ISR, either by indexing via the obtained identifier into the table of ISR addresses (interrupt-vector table) or by simply loading the program counter with the supplied address. Given its complexity, vectoring requires additional hardware in each interface or, more often, a specialized I/O port, the *programmable interrupt-controller* (PIC), to assist vectoring of interrupts. The trend in high-end microprocessors, an active brewery of new architectural definitions, seems to be the use of fairly large interrupt-vector tables and reliance on cascaded PICs to provide a complex hierarchy of interrupts with support for a number of uniquely identifiable sources. The number of connected physical devices may be enlarged by multiplexing individual levels with the aid of polling. Note that when polling is combined with vectoring, the cycles wasted on polling are significantly reduced, since polling sequences are shorter when interrupt vectors transfer control to the appropriate subgroups of devices.

Vectoring, by means of extensive hardware support, minimizes interrupt latency and provides for the maximum interrupt-driven I/O bandwidth in the environments with multiple sources of interrupts. Virtually all multiprocess and multiprogramming operating systems rely on vectoring as a hardware foundation for concurrent processing. However, multiple sources of interrupt introduce the possibility of having a number of pending interrupt requests at any point in time. Since vectoring eliminates the polling sequence, it must provide some other means for handling device priorities and, consequently, for choosing which of the several active requests should be serviced first.

One approach is to assign a different level of priority to each unique source that can be vectored or to clusters of devices if the number of distinct levels is more limited. This ordering is normally recognized by hardware priority arbiters (resolvers) that honor requests in the order of their relative priorities. The system integrator, and sometimes the end-user, is thus given the freedom to assign relative importance to each peripheral device and to make this decision known to the hardware by programming the PIC and the related I/O port registers. In this way, peripherals may be provided with service tuned to their requirements and high-performance devices can be enabled to operate at the best possible rates and without interference from the lower-speed devices. In addition, time-critical events may be guaranteed the lowest possible latency, an extremely important requirement in real-time systems. All this suggests the need for a responsive priority structure, but it also motivates the need to explore some related issues. What should be done when a higher-priority interrupt request occurs in the midst of an interrupt-service routine? What if a lower-priority request occurs?

In our previous discussion, and in the Program 2.3, we have made an implicit assumption that an ISR has higher priority than the (background) activity that the CPU engages in when there are no interrupts. Whenever an interrupt occurs, the CPU suspends the background program and enters the ISR. A simple expansion of this logic suggests that a higher-priority request should likewise preempt the service routine for a lower-priority interrupt. Note that because each ISR saves and restores the context of the preempted activity, any depth of interrupt nesting may be supported without problems. Naturally, when an ISR is completed, its return instruction should transfer control to the place of interruption, i.e., to the next-lower-level ISR that was not completed. In other words, like subroutines, nested interrupt returns follow last-in-first-out (LIFO) ordering, which makes a push-down stack the perfect place to store contexts. Going in the opposite direction, a request of lower priority than the one currently being serviced should be made to wait until it becomes the highest-priority active request. As a practical example, we do not want to service a printer interrupt in the midst of receiving a high-priority network broadcast.

The enforcement of this logic imposes considerable demands on the interrupt-recognition mechanism. In particular, it must be able to permanently weigh priorities of the routines being executed against the incoming requests and to decide accordingly whether to invoke context switching and vectoring and updating of the current highest active priority or to let an interrupt remain pending without interfering with the execution in progress. Obviously, this is a job to be done by hardware, but one that is perhaps too costly to support in architectures that may not be intended exclusively for multiprogramming environments. Many microprocessors rely on sophisticated PICs to provide the full range of these services in hardware. Fortunately, by following some relatively simple rules and utilizing interrupt-related features commonly provided by hardware, this task may also be accomplished by software with relatively little overhead. Before outlining the usual approach to this problem, let us first explore the available tools.

We have already mentioned the existence of machine instructions to enable and disable interrupt recognition. This is a rather coarse brute-force method that is found in virtually all computer systems. These instructions may have mnemonics suggestive of their role in a particular system, such as EI for enable interrupts and DI for disable interrupts. Generally, such instructions turn the whole interrupt system on or off—the feature that we have already used in Program 2.3.

The next-finer level is the ability to enable or disable selectively certain interrupt levels or related clusters, which is often called *interrupt masking*. This is usually accomplished by providing an interrupt mask register and some means of altering its contents. Interrupt masking typically consists of a collection of bits that, depending on their settings, enable or disable the corresponding interrupt levels. Thus, by programming ones and zeros into these bits, one may "mask out" specific levels and permanently or temporarily prevent recognition of the requests from so designated sources. Other than priority control, the ability to mask interrupts is useful for dealing with spurious interrupts by disabling all levels unused in a given configuration. As usual, the implementation details vary; interrupt masks may have dedicated registers within the CPU, may be a part of the processor status word, or may require the addition of the PIC to provide them.

The last and finest level of interrupt control is an individual interface. By manipulating the interrupt-enable/disable bits within the command registers of I/O ports, even specific devices within a group sharing a priority level or an interrupt-request line may be selectively allowed or prohibited from interrupting the CPU. Sample interrupt-control bits for a USART are shown in Figure 2.5.

The final touches are provided by turning interrupts off automatically after the hardware reset and during the hardware portion of an interrupt-recognition sequence. The latter gives the programmer the flexibility to manipulate interrupt levels within an interrupt-service routine. As discussed, the common practice is to enable higher-priority levels and to disable the lower-priority ones immediately upon entering an ISR. Note that this may be done even before the software portion of the context save. An interesting question is whether the interrupt level that the ISR is itself running at should be enabled or not. Leaving that level enabled usually results in problems. In systems where several devices may share the same priority level, enabling that level within an ISR could result in preemptions between equals and lock up the entire system, as none of the routines may be able to reach the point of acknowledging its own interrupt request.

A more subtle problem, encountered even when interrupt levels are not shared, is the issue of an interrupt- service routine preempting itself. Namely, if the interrupt is acknowledged early enough within the ISR, the same device—especially if multiple buffered—may be ready for another I/O transaction and may generate a new interrupt. In general, this is both difficult to handle correctly (the ISR would have to be reentrant) and undesirable, since it could irrecoverably disturb the order of transferred data. For these reasons, it is common practice to enable all higher levels and disable all lower levels, including a routine's own level, in an interrupt-service routine. Some computer systems have these rules implemented in hardware, and others have them in software—typically in the operating-system kernel—using the hardware provisions described in this section. A similar scheme is supported by the sample operating system described in Chapters 9 and 10.

Before illustrating the use of multiple interrupts, let us summarize the steps involved in interrupt-driven I/O. The example sequence refers to a typical input operation, assuming that the I/O port in question has already been initialized for interrupt-driven I/O and that the associated priority level is enabled. Output transactions follow the same logic, with slightly permuted initial steps. Naturally, owing to the many different practical implementations, the exact order of individual steps may vary somewhat in different computer systems.

1. The CPU initializes input by issuing a start-input command to the I/O port. The CPU may begin and/or continue executing some unrelated sequence of instructions until the activated input is completed by the I/O port.
2. The I/O port sets its input-status bit to BUSY and initiates the device-specific input action.
3. When the input datum is assembled in the I/O port's input buffer, the port sets its input-status bit to READY and raises its interrupt-request line.
4. When the CPU is in an interruptible mode (the instruction in progress is completed and interrupts are enabled) and the I/O port's request becomes the highest-priority pending interrupt request, the hardware interrupt-recognition sequence is initiated on the device's behalf:
   a. Interrupts are disabled.
   b. The hardware part of the context is saved.
   c. The source of interrupt is identified (through polling or vectoring).
   d. Control is transferred to the ISR.
5. Within the interrupt-service routine, the following actions take place:
   a. Higher-priority levels of interrupt are enabled (lower and equal remain off).
   b. The software part of the context is saved.
   c. A datum is obtained from the I/O port's buffer.
   d. The interrupt is acknowledged and the I/O port responds by removing its interrupt request; possibly, another start-input command is issued.
   e. Other interrupt processing and housekeeping are completed.

    f. The software part of the saved context is restored.

    g. The return-from-interrupt (RTI) instruction is executed.

  6. Whether by means of RTI or some additional instructions, the hardware part of context is restored, and the interrupt-priority levels, up to that of the interrupted program, are enabled.

2.6 CONCURRENT I/O

After completing our exposition of the principles of input/output programming, in this section we illustrate how multiple interrupts may be employed to improve system performance and component utilization through interleaved operation. Our primary aim here is to motivate the potential for concurrent operation normally provided by the I/O hardware. Operating-system modules that support and control concurrent operation and some related theoretical considerations are discussed in subsequent chapters.

Program 2.4 is used as a vehicle for demonstration and illustration of the main points to be made in this section. Many details of the interrupt handling, especially priorities, are hidden or just implied in Program 2.4 because of the HLL coding. This is the level of I/O programming involvement often encountered by application programmers. In a way, this example demonstrates the importance of understanding the interrupt-handling strategy of the underlying system, even if one does not have to manipulate the interrupts directly. Naturally, operating-system designers and system programmers would have to be intimately involved in its details and especially observe the interplay and implied interaction between program components resulting from the particular interrupt priority and management scheme at hand. We highlight some details as we proceed with the explanation of Program 2.4.

The program basically consists of three related, but not too tightly coupled activities:

1. Interrupt-driven input of a line of text from the terminal
2. Some unspecified processing of that data
3. Interrupt-driven output of the data collected by the input routine

This program is a simplification of some of the functions performed by a terminal I/O driver and by an operating-system routine for handling the human interface, often called the *console-monitor routine*. Note that both I/O sections deal with a single physical device—a terminal. However, from the system's point of view, those are two independent logical devices: an input device (keyboard), and an output device (CRT display or hard-copy output). As explained in the description of a USART, each of these devices possesses its own set of data registers, as well as dedicated portions of the command and status registers. This is clearly illustrated by the fact that many terminals, when online, do not echo input characters. More specifically, anything typed on the keyboard is sent directly to the system, which, in turn, typically echoes some characters back to the display via a separate output routine for the users's convenience and verification. The output routine in Program 2.4 has exactly this function; it simply echoes (displays or prints) a line of text to an output device. Finally, the processing is assumed to use the input data for some purpose, but not to modify them in any way before their output is completed. For example, PROCESS_DATA might simply parse the input searching for valid commands to the operating system in order to invoke the appropriate service. Alternatively, if no match is found, it could output an error message and prompt the user to enter corrected text. Neither the OS invocation nor the communication with the user is implemented in Program 2.4. Our emphasis there is simply to study the functioning of multiple interrupts and some aspects of their interleaved operation.

In summary, we have the three functions delegated to three different procedures and a main program that acts as a traffic controller. An important observation is that the two I/O processes KEYBOARD and DISPLAY are permanently active, awaiting the user's input for processing. This is customarily the case with the system I/O routines that must be available whenever a device needs service. Consequently, the main program never terminates. In terms of data structures, the input routine uses the INDATA array to assemble a line of text, and both the output routine and PROCESS_DATA work from the OUTDATA array. Sharing of the OUTDATA array is not a problem in this example, since both procedures use OUTDATA in a read-only fashion. Almost all variables are made global in order to avoid possible distraction of the program's logic through lengthy lists of parameters.

Program 2.4 actually contains three versions of the main section in order to introduce increasing degrees of concurrency. The first version is strictly sequential, and its primary purpose is to illustrate the required order of events and the logic of the three procedures. As before, the main program disables interrupts in order to initialize the hardware and to place addresses of the two interrupt-service routines into the appropriate entries of the vector table. In Program 2.4, interrupt enabling and disabling is done at the port level, thus affecting only the individual device. Note that by choosing the specific vectors, relative priorities are, in effect, assigned to the two ISRs. After that, the main section enters its forever (while true) part. This structure, namely, the initialization part executed only once followed by a nonterminating loop, is typical for permanently active programs and will be frequently encountered in this book.

The repetitive sequence consists of obtaining a line of input, processing it, and echoing via the output routine. Input-line variables in this example are assumed to be of variable length up to MAX characters. This parameter is usually chosen to match a full line of output, typically 80 or 132 characters. All data buffers are, of course, dimensioned to this value. Given that any particular line may be shorter, the KEYBOARD process keeps track of the actual number input. An input sequence is assumed to be terminated by a special character, such as RETURN (carriage return). When the terminator is received, the KEYBOARD process deactivates itself and sets the INDONE flag to announce the availability

```
program/module concurrentIO;
    const
        max = 80;                 {max length of output}
        line_end = return;        {line termination character}
    type
        text = array [1..max] of char;
    var
        indata, outdata, save_data : text;      {data buffers}
        indone, outdone : boolean;              {completion flags}
        inindex, incount, outindex, outcount, save_count : integer;
    procedure start_input;
        process keyboard;
            begin
                while true do
                    begin
                        {await_kbd_interrupt}
                        save_context;
                        kbd_status := ioport_status;
                        kbd_data := ioport_datain;          {interrupt acknowledge}
                        if kbd_status = OK
                            then                            {error-free reception}
                                begin
                                    indata[inindex] := kbd_data;
                                    inindex := inindex + 1;
                                    incount := incount + 1;
                                    if kbd_data = line_end
                                        then                {line of input completed }
                                            begin
                                                ioport_command := kbd_interrupts_disable;
                                                indone := true
                                            end {if}
                                    end {if}
                            else handle_error(kbd_status);   {reception errors}
                        restore_context
                    end {while}
            end; {keyboard}
        begin {start_input}
            indone := false;
            inindex := 1;
            incount := 0;
            ioport_command := kbd_interrupts_enable
        end; {start_input}
    procedure start_output;
        process display;
            begin
                while true do
                    begin
                        {await_dsp_interrupt}
                        save_context;
                        ioport_dataout := outdata[outindex];
                        outindex := outindex + 1;
                        outcount := outcount - 1;
```

(Continued)

```
              if outcount = 0
                  then                            {line printed}
                      begin
                          ioport_command := dsp_interrupts_disable;
                          outdone := true
                      end; {if}
                  restore_context
              end {while}
          end; {display}

    begin {start_output}
        outdone := false;
        outindex := 1;
        outcount := save_count;
        ioport_command := dsp_interrupts_enable
    end; {start_output}

{MAIN - version 1}
begin {concurrentIO}
    ioport_command := kbd_and_dsp_interrupts_disable;
    initialize_hardware;
    connect_interrupt_vectors(kbd, dsp);
    while true do                            {forever}
        begin
            start_input;                         {activate input(x)}
            while not indone do {keeptesting};   {await completion}
            copy(indata, outdata);
            save_count := incount;
            process_data;                        {process input(x)}
            start_output;                        {echo input(x)}
            while not outdone do {keeptesting}
        end {while}
end {concurrentIO}

{MAIN - version 2}
begin {concurrentIO}
    ioport_command := kbd_and_dsp_interrupts_disable;
    initialize_hardware;
    connect_interrupt_vectors(kbd, dsp);
    while true do
        begin
            start_input;                         {activate input(x) }
            while not indone do {keeptesting};   {await completion}
            copy(indata, outdata);
            save_count := incount;
            start_output;                        {echo input(x), and }
            process_data;                        { process it concurrently}
            while not outdone do {keeptesting}
        end {while}
end {concurrentIO}
```

(Continued)

```
{MAIN - version 3}
begin {concurrentIO}
    ioport_command := kbd_and_dsp_interrupts_disable;
    initialize_hardware;
    connect_interrupt_vectors(kbd, dsp);
    outdone := true;
    start_input;                                        {activate input(1)}
    while true do
        begin
            while not indone do {keeptesting};          {await input(x)}
            copy (indata, save_data);                   {save input (x)}
            save_count := incount;
            start_input;                                 {activate input(x+1)}
            while not outdone do {keeptesting};          {await output(x−1)}
            copy(save_data, outdata);                    {input(x) to outdata}
            start_output;                                {echo input(x), and}
            process_data                                 {process it concurrently}
        end {while}
end {concurrentIO}
```

Program 2.4 Concurrent input/output

of a line of input to the rest of the system. The main program awaits this event by busily testing the flag. Note that this assumes that the main program is running at a lower priority than the KEYBOARD process. No explicit priority is assigned to the main program, following the usual convention that each hardware priority level takes precedence over the default priority for non-I/O-related routines. Alternatively, a level of priority lower than that of either ISR should be assigned to the main routine.

With input completed, the main program copies the input buffer to OUTDATA for the echoing that follows processing. Note that the DISPLAY process echoes exactly the number of characters designated by KEYBOARD. In practice, an additional line-feed character might need to be appended, but we ignore it here.

The second version of the main program introduces some interleaving by coactivating the output and processing of a line of data. Since processing is compute-bound and output is interrupt-driven, the two activities may be conveniently interleaved. As indicated by the timing diagram presented in Figure 2.9b, this strategy is very similar to the one used in Program 2.3.

The third version goes a significant step beyond, by allowing all three activities to be progressing toward their completion concurrently. This is accomplished by overlapping output and processing of a batch of input with assembling of the next line of input. This is sometimes referred to as a *type-ahead feature*, where the user may start entering a line of input even before the previous one has been echoed.

In order to make this mode of operation possible, characters collected by a complete cycle of the KEYBOARD process are copied to the SAVE_DATA array for subsequent echoing by the DISPLAY process. This frees the INDATA

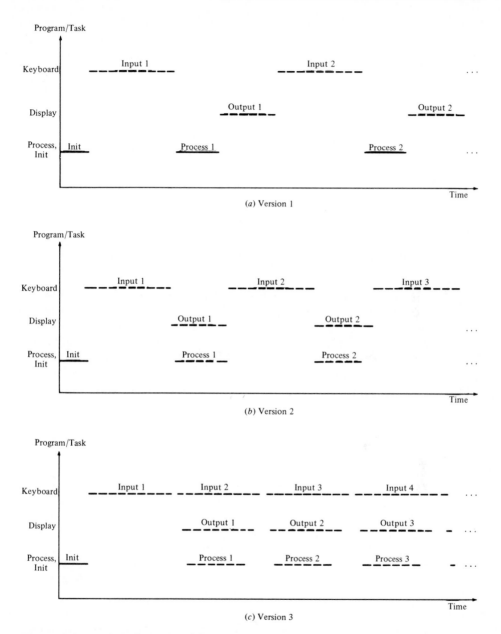

Figure 2.9 Timing diagram of Program 2.4.

buffer for the next line of input, thus allowing immediate activation of the input routine. When output (echoing) of the previous line of text is completed, the line of text saved in SAVE_DATA is copied to the OUTDATA array and the output routine is activated. Being interrupt-driven, both input and output routines operate concurrently. A possible occasional competition between the two when they simultaneously need activation is resolved by the interrupt priority-arbitration logic. The reader should observe that the two ISRs must run at different levels of priority but that it does not really matter which one is higher. Naturally, interleaved execution may result in occasional preemption of the lower-priority level, but that should not be a cause for concern in our example. The common practice is to assign higher priority to the input routine and thus minimize the possibility of losing characters. This, as explained before, is not a problem on output.

Unlike the two I/O routines, PROCESS_DATA is compute-bound. As a result, once invoked, PROCESS_DATA executes to completion before returning control to the next statement of the main routine. As a result of context saving and restoring, occasional preemptions by I/O routines are practically transparent to PROCESS_DATA and main routines.

Following processing of a line of input, the main program awaits completion of the next line of input if it is not already assembled by the KEYBOARD process. Input data are stored in the SAVE_DATA array until their output can be initiated, and the described sequence of events is repeated. This process is illustrated by the timing diagram in Figure 2.9c. Note that owing to limited buffering, input cannot get ahead of output by more than one line at a time. This is enforced in the main program by means of testing the two completion flags.

A final, but important, note is that the expected levels of CPU and I/O utilization depend on the relative execution times of the three functions. Most likely, processing will be the shortest of the three, with output (especially to a CRT) taking less time than the input at typing speed. In other words, with a single-line type-ahead, the CPU and the display may experience low utilization factors. Adding more buffers to increase the degree of interleaving would not help much in the long run because of the inherent disparity in data production and consumption rates in this example, to say nothing of user confusion and the errors likely to be introduced when echoing lags input for several lines at a time.

In general, careful tuning of a program in order to increase the degree of concurrency among its routines may be rendered obsolete by changes in configuration, say, from human input to computer-computer input. For this and other reasons, overlapping within a program should not be carried to extremes. The best way to improve system performance and component utilization is to introduce concurrency at the *system level* and to charge the operating system with multiplexing a system's resources among all active programs. This, obviously, increases the probability of having some useful work assigned to the CPU without indulging in a study of the timing patterns of any single program. We study the benefits and implementation techniques of this approach in Chapter 3 and turn to the more esoteric topic of synchronization among concurrent programs in Chapters 4 and 5.

2.7 SUMMARY

In Chapter 1 we indicated that the multiprogramming and multiprocess modes of operation can significantly increase throughput and component utilization of a computer system. In Chapter 2 we have investigated the nature and timing of input/output operations in order to informally assess the potential for concurrent operation embodied in the input/output system.

Owing to the pronounced speed gap between processor and I/O devices, the CPU may be heavily underutilized if it is dedicated to servicing a single device at a time, as in the program-controlled method of I/O. Having discovered that there is a need (and usually the processing capacity) to handle I/O devices concurrently, we looked at the available hardware support.

Concurrent operation of I/O devices is supported by input/output ports that provide handshaking signals and buffering of data. Handshaking is necessary to synchronize devices with the CPU in order to exchange data. Owing to the asynchronous operation of I/O devices and the CPU, input buffering is desirable to help prevent loss of data until the CPU can switch attention to the I/O transaction in progress.

CPU utilization, interrupt latency, and compound-system I/O bandwidth may all be improved by using vectored interrupts and hardware-assisted enforcement of interrupt priorities. Such elaborate interrupt mechanisms facilitate multiplexing of the CPU among a number of devices. In addition, they allow tuning of individual device-response times in accordance with the relative importance of the related operations.

Interrupt-driven I/O operations may be interleaved to improve throughput even when executing a single program, but this requires careful timing analysis and tuning of individual programs, which are difficult and impractical to do in many cases. Moreover, while the interrupt mechanism facilitates interleaving of I/O operations, it is of little help when concurrent execution of computationally intensive activities is desired.

Thus our major conclusion is that the I/O system provides the potential for concurrency and that the I/O hardware and the interrupt system provide the necessary support. Starting with this foundation, the operating system may exploit parallelism at the system level by taking into consideration all outstanding input/output and computational activities. Such an approach can have a greater potential for global optimization of system performance. It can also relieve programmers by automatically scheduling activities for concurrent execution. In the chapters that follow, we investigate how such a facility can be built.

OTHER READING

Input/output ports and elements of I/O programming are described in the many books on microcomputer interfacing, architecture, and assembly-language programming. Among these are books by Leventhal (1978) and Wakerly (1981), which provide an excellent foundation for the material presented in Chapter 2. More general treatment of I/O systems, including mainframes and I/O channels, can be found in Stone (1980) and in Baer (1980). Examples of interrupt and channel I/O programming are provided by Madnick and Donovan (1974). A discussion of CPU and I/O overlap can be found in Hsiao (1975). Hunt (1980) discusses some architectural and design issues related to interrupts.

The best source for actual device descriptions is the literature provided by the hardware manufacturers, such as Intel (1984a) and Motorola (1984a). A wealth of useful practical information for implementation of communication links may be found in manufacturers' application notes, such as Smith (1976). Readers with access to a personal computer should by all means study the actual examples of low-level input/output programming provided in the BIOS (Basic Input/Output System), whose source code is available for many CP/M and MS-DOS (PC-DOS) machines. One of the best documented examples may be found in *Technical Reference for the IBM Personal Computer* (IBM, 1983).

More advanced material on serial data communication may be found in books by McNamara (1982) and Stone (1982). Many data-communication standards, including the RS-232C, are reprinted in Folts and Karp (1978).

EXERCISES

2.1 Obtain a specification (data sheet) of an actual USART or UART and study the organization and functioning of its mode, command, and buffer registers. Describe how the USART may be initialized to operate in program-controlled and interrupt-driven modes. If a loopback option is available, discuss how it may be used to check the communication link during the power-up operational test and possibly during the normal system operation.

2.2 Preferably using an actual device specification, write USART initialization sequences for both ends of the communication system depicted in Figure 2.4. Make sure to maintain the compatibility and symmetry necessary to make the communication link functional. If an actual device is used, the baud-rate generator should also be initialized for the desired line speed.

2.3 Using the program-controlled I/O method, write an XMIT routine that accepts a string of ASCII characters and transmits it to the communication line via a USART. One possibility is to store the target string in the calling routine's address space and pass the starting address of the string to the XMIT routine. Designate a special character, an ASCII NUL (0), for example, to denote the end of string. When this character is transmitted, the XMIT routine should terminate transmission and return control to the caller. If an actual device is used, link-control signals, such as request to send (RTS), may need to be activated as required by the communications interface at hand.

2.4 Using program-controlled I/O, write a RECEIVE routine that accepts a string of characters up to and including the end-of-string character as defined in Exercise 3. One way to effect exchange of data between the RECEIVE routine and its callers is to pass as the calling parameter the address of the caller's data buffer where the input string is to be placed. RECEIVE should also test the relevant USART status bits after reception of each character to detect possible reception errors. Devise a method to deal with reception errors once they occur. Do you think that the caller of RECEIVE should be alerted when errors are detected? Why or why not? When an error is detected, should RECEIVE terminate immediately or continue reception of characters?

2.5 If a communication link and two computer systems are available, combine the initialization, XMIT, and RECEIVE routines from the previous exercises to form a simple communication facility and try to make it operational. Make sure that the cable used for the purpose is configured for a sender/receiver setup at its opposite ends. For example, in RS-232C systems, the null-modem cable must be used, so that the XMIT pin of a sending USART is connected to the RECEIVE pin of the receiving USART, and vice versa. Books by McNamara (1982) and Stone (1982) may be consulted for details on how to set up a communication link. A test instrument, such as a logic analyzer, an oscilloscope, or a logic probe, might be useful while debugging the hardware connection.

2.6 Identify the maximum actual data-display rate that your CRT terminal can sustain over a period of time, and compare it to the maximum nominal data-reception speed declared by the manufacturer. In the likely case of a discrepancy, discuss the circumstances under which the vendor's specification does and does not hold. *Hint*: Try displaying a sequence of characters whose number exceeds the buffering capacity of the terminal. Set the communication link for the maximum nominal data rate, but experiment with the terminal by causing the CPU to pause between successive character transmissions. Gradually increase the transmission speed by reducing the intercharacter wait until you either reach an error-free maximum data rate or observe reception errors on the terminal. (Some terminals indicate reception errors by displaying special characters, while others simply ignore the problem and display the garbled data without any warning.)

Explain what may be done to circumvent the problem, if one exists, and to allow the operating system to operate the terminal at the maximum nominal data rate without the observed problem. Discuss why the simple synchronous solution of reducing the effective output rate by causing the processor to idle between successive character transmissions is undesirable and inferior to the asynchronous approach.

2.7 Write the polling sequence and the individual device service routines for a computer system that consists of at least three program-controlled I/O devices, such as a keyboard, a CRT display, and a printer. Assume that each individual device service routine, when entered, just accepts or transmits a character from a buffer and updates the pointers for the next data transfer.

(a) Explain the differences between two possible polling strategies, one that assigns rotating priorities and one that assigns fixed priorities to individual devices. For the fixed-priority case, indicate how you would assign priorities to each of the three devices and why. On the basis of the two polling programs, estimate the maximum system I/O bandwidth attainable by each method and the maximum I/O bandwidth for each individual device.

(b) Assess the average CPU idle time when servicing the three devices. To do this, you may need to assume some representative data rates, such as 5 cps for the keyboard, 960 cps for the display, and 160 cps for the printer. One way to make rough performance estimates is to count the number of bytes read and written by the CPU while executing the related program, including all instruction and data references. Assume that all instructions and data references (registers, memory) are 2 bytes wide and that the CPU memory bandwidth is 1 million accesses per second, 2 bytes per access.

2.8 Using the byte-counting method described in the previous exercise, discuss the relative performance of the various ways of fielding interrupts. Assume that you need to perform a "timer" type of operation, where the interrupt program just increments a single memory location using the INCREMENT MEMORY instruction. Also assume that the timer device has the third highest interrupt priority in the system. Consider the following cases:

(a) All interrupts are tied to a single line, and the interrupt handler must use polling to determine the identity of the interrupting device. The state saved by the hardware upon acceptance of an interrupt request consists of the program counter, processor status word, and two accumulators. Count the number of bytes accessed while servicing a single timer interrupt under these assumptions.

(b) What is the performance difference, expressed as a percentage increase or decrease relative to the previous case, if the number of accumulators saved by hardware is 0? is 8?

(c) Assuming that all interrupts are vectored, calculate the number of bytes needed to service a single timer interrupt under the same assumptions as in part a.

(d) How does performance in part c change if the number of accumulators saved by hardware is 0? is 8?

2.9 Consider a time-sharing computer system that services 10 terminals concurrently. Suppose that each terminal interrupts the CPU 10 times a second on the average. Using the results obtained as a solution to the previous exercise, derive upper and lower bounds on the amount of *interrupt overhead* required to service these terminals. Interrupt overhead includes all byte accesses related to getting into and out of an interrupt routine, but it does not include the work done in the body of the interrupt routine. Assume that each terminal interrupt routine modifies a single CPU accumulator. If the memory can support 1 million accesses per second, 2 bytes per access, derive the upper and the lower bounds on the fraction of memory bandwidth used for interrupt overhead.

2.10 Write and test interrupt-driven versions of the XMIT and RECEIVE routines introduced in Exercises 3 and 4. Indicate how parameters and control may be transferred between routines that call on their services and XMIT and RECEIVE routines. Contrast and discuss the relative advantages of program-controlled and interrupt-driven versions of XMIT and RECEIVE routines. If tested on the actual hardware, also compare the program-development and debugging efforts expended to make each version work.

2.11 Following the same basic model and reasoning used to develop Program 2.4, modify Program 2.4 so that echoing on the terminal follows the input as closely as possible rather than taking place only after a full line of input is completed. Without assuming anything about relative speeds of input and output operations, attempt to achieve maximum possible concurrency and avoid copying of data whenever possible. In other words, both input and output processes should operate concurrently and probably use some global shared data as opposed to the private copies used in Program 2.4. Otherwise, input and output processes must be strictly independent from each other; a simple solution of having the input process echo the characters or invoke part of the output process directly is not acceptable. Be very careful to synchronize properly the updating of global data shared by the two processes. Also watch that one or more processes do not "hang up" due to race conditions. Make whatever (reasonable) assumptions about the underlying hardware interrupt system that you deem necessary. *Hint*: You will probably need to establish some synchronization protocol between the input and output processes. The interrupt-enable/disable mechanism may be useful for this purpose.

2.12 Consider the third, concurrent version of Program 2.4. Assuming that output is produced by the PROCESS_DATA routine as opposed to simply being a copy of the input, write a program that allows input, processing, and output to be overlapped to the same extent as in the original Program 2.4. Given that the PROCESS_DATA routine now modifies input and produces the output data, what is the minimal number of buffers needed to support this level of concurrency? Using a timing chart if necessary, describe clearly which buffer is used by whom and when it is acquired and released by the individual routines. Also indicate how the input, process, and output routines synchronize with each other in order to maintain the overall system integrity.

THREE

PROCESSES

As we saw in the preceding chapter, significant performance gains may be achieved when system resources are multiplexed among a number of active programs, thus increasing the probability of having some useful work to allocate to temporarily idle components. However, rather than attempting to accomplish this purpose by identifying and exploiting the parallelism possible within any given program, a common practice is to organize relatively independent activities into separate processes (tasks) and have the operating system execute them concurrently.

The concept of a process is either implicitly or explicitly present in all multiprogrammed operating systems. Its significance has also been recognized by the designers of some high-level languages, such as Ada and Modula, that provide mechanisms specifically for management of concurrent processes. In essence, a *process* or *task* is an instance of a program in execution. It is the smallest piece of work that is individually schedulable by an operating system. Each multiprogramming OS keeps track of all active processes and allocates the system's resources to them according to policies devised to meet design-performance objectives. Just how the operating system knows when to step in and how to allocate resources in a given situation is the subject of this chapter.

We begin by describing the concept of a process and illustrating how it may be employed by systems programmers to improve throughput and response time even within a single program. A subsequent section explores the system's view of processes and how they are managed by the operating system. We then discuss the typical system services provided for that purpose in operating systems and mention the equivalent facilities in Ada. The chapter concludes with an analysis of scheduling—its purpose, goals, commonly used mechanisms, and enforcement policies.

3.1 THE PROCESS CONCEPT

The operating-systems literature seems to be roughly evenly split in its use of two different terms to denote the concept of a sequence of code in execution. Many books and articles use the term *process*. On the other hand, vendors' manuals and systems programmers almost exclusively refer to the same concept as a *task*. Designers of Ada have also opted for the latter. The term *process* may be somewhat confusing when used to describe a multiprogramming environment, because *multiprocessing* is usually understood to mean a system with multiple hardware processors rather than a single processor with multiple processes running concurrently. Where necessary to distinguish it from multiprogramming, we use the term *multiprocess* to denote an operating system that supports concurrent execution of programs on a single processor without necessarily supporting elaborate forms of memory-management and file-management. This form of operation is also known as *multitasking*. *Multiprogramming* is a more general concept that denotes an operating system that provides memory-management and file-management, in addition to supporting concurrent execution of programs. Thus a multiprogramming operating system is also a multiprocess operating system, while the converse is not implied.

In this chapter we introduce the concept of a process and explain it from three different viewpoints—those of the user, the systems programmer, and the operating system.

According to Denning (1983), the operating system may be defined as the computer-system software that assists hardware in performing process-management functions, including

1. Creating and removing (destroying) processes.
2. Controlling the progress of processes, that is, ensuring that each logically enabled process makes progress toward its completion at a positive rate.
3. Acting on exceptional conditions arising during the execution of a process, including interrupts and arithmetic errors.
4. Allocating hardware resources among process.
5. Providing a means of communicating messages or signals among processes.

A process is an instance of a program in execution. An intention to activate an executable program (compiled and linked) is announced to the operating system by means of a specialized command, such as RUN, or a system call provided for that purpose. The operating system responds by creating a process. In general, this activity consists of creation and initialization of operating-system data structures for monitoring and controlling the progress of the related process. In order to focus our attention on concurrent process execution, in this chapter we ignore the related activities of memory allocation and loading of the related program in memory. Discussion of memory-management and its relationship to program execution is presented in Chapters 6 and 7.

Once created, a process becomes active and eligible to compete for system resources such as processor and I/O devices. Given typical program behavior, a process cycles between periods of active execution and of waiting for completion of I/O activities. When a running process becomes suspended, say, by issuing an I/O request and pending I/O completion, the operating system may schedule another process for execution. Each active process is an individually schedulable entity. By means of defining the boundaries of a particular process, systems programmers can inform the operating system which activities may be executed concurrently.

A familiar example that should help in making the distinction between the static concept of a program and the dynamic concept of a process created to execute the program is provided by executing the text editor in multiprogrammed, multiuser systems. The file containing the editor program in its executable form is the template for all editor processes. When a user invokes the editor, the operating system loads the editor program (instructions and data) into memory, creates an editor process, and schedules it for execution. The editor process then begins executing the editing commands issued by the user from the terminal. In so doing, the editor process uses a specific set of user-designated input and output files. When the editing session is complete, the user issues some sort of an EXIT command to the editor process, which in turn does some housekeeping and terminates itself by calling the operating system. At this point, the OS closes the data files and erases the activation record of that specific instance of the editor process, which then ceases to exist. Deletion of the editor process affects neither the results of its work stored in data files nor the editor program that resides in its own file.

If another user invokes the editor before the first user terminates the session, *a separate version of the editor process* is created by the OS. Although the same editor-program file is used for the purpose, each concurrent invocation of the editor causes the creation of a new and unique editor process. Note that this is necessary because each process represents a different thread of control, accepts commands from a different user, and has a different run-time state, including the contents of CPU registers, memory buffers, and data files. The two processes would not only be completely independent from the point of view of the OS, but would in fact compete with each other for allocation of the CPU, memory, and disk I/O.

In multiprocess systems, a number of active processes are typically in various stages of execution at any point in time. A particular process usually cycles through various states, such as running and suspended, a number of times before terminating and departing the system. The operating system dynamically tracks the state of each process and records all the state changes as they occur. This information is used for scheduling and other resource-allocation decisions made in response to demands of the active processes.

Thus, in addition to the static process template—consisting of the related program code and data—each process possesses certain *attributes* that assist the OS in managing it. Process attributes include current state, scheduling priority, access rights, and other information described in more detail in a subsequent section. Depending on the type of operating system and on the target program-execution environment, division of labor into tasks that will be executed as independent processes and initial assignment of process attributes may be performed by the operating system or by the systems programmer. In other words, what will constitute a separate process at run-time can be either *system-defined* or *programmer-defined*. As is usually the case with automatic versus manual control, the tradeoff here is one of convenience and ease of use versus performance and control of system operation.

System-defined processes are commonly encountered in general-purpose multiprogramming systems, such as time-sharing. In this approach, each program submitted for execution is treated by the operating system as an independent process. Thus, in response to the user's RUN command, the system creates a process to execute the program. A single-batch job may give rise to several processes. For instance, a separate process may be created for each of the job activities—including compilation, linking, and execution of the user program. Initial values of process attributes, such as scheduling priority and access rights, are assigned by the operating system at the process-creation time on the basis of the related user's profile and system defaults. Processes created in this manner are usually transient in the sense that they are destroyed and disposed of by the system after each run.

The confines of a process are usually defined by programmers when high performance or explicit control of system activities is desired. Systems programs, such as parts of the operating system, and real-time applications are common examples of programmer-defined processes. After dividing the work of the application at hand into the desired number of independent chunks, a systems programmer defines the confines of each individual process. A parent process is then commonly added to create the environment for and to control execution of individual application processes. During program development, or at run-time by embedding the related system calls, the programmer can assign initial values of process attributes and control various aspects of process execution. This is illustrated in detail in the next section. System processes, such as the console-monitor routine, tend to be permanent in the sense that they exist throughout the lifetime of the system and never terminate.

By virtue of sharing resources of a single system, all concurrent processes *compete* with each other for allocation of system resources needed for their operation. Another fundamental relationship among the concurrent processes is that of *cooperation*. This relation holds in systems in which activity is carried out by a group of related processes, each charged with a specific function. Cooperating processes exchange data and synchronization signals necessary to orchestrate their collective progress. Both competition and cooperation of processes require proper OS support. Competition requires careful resource allocation and protection in terms of isolation of different address-spaces. Cooperation depends on the existence of mechanisms for controlled usage of shared data and the exchange of synchronization signals. These are demanding and often conflicting requirements that must be addressed when designing multiprogramming operating systems, and we devote a lot of attention to them in subsequent chapters.

Cooperating processes typically share some common attributes, in addition to interacting with each other. For those reasons, they are often grouped together into what is called a *family* of processes. Although complex relationships within a family are possible, the notion most frequently supported by operating systems is that of a parent-child. Children processes usually inherit attributes from their parents at the process-creation time. These attributes may be changed at run-time by invoking the operating-system calls. A parent process normally terminates only after all its children have done so.

The Ada language explicitly supports both these notions. An Ada-language construct, called *task*, is used to allow programmers to designate a collection of executable statements and data declarations that will constitute an independent process at run-time. Ada documentation also uses the term *task* to denote the dynamic notion of a process. We follow this convention when referring to Ada. The reader is reminded to think of *tasks in execution* as processes. Ada provides for task types—program templates similar to the data-type templates available in Pascal. Once a task type is declared, a number of instances of it may be created by designating them as being of a given type. Families of tasks are treated in a manner similar to arrays—each member of the family is uniquely identified by its own subscript. This feature is useful for manipulating a number of tasks that have identical programs. For example, a family can be the printer handlers in a system with multiple physical printers, each controlled by a separate task. Nested tasks declared within another (parent) task follow conventional rules of scope; i.e., children must be terminated before the parent. The significance of tasks in Ada may be deduced from the fact that Ada treats each main program as a task, even when the main program is not explicitly declared as such.

3.2 SYSTEMS PROGRAMMER'S VIEW OF PROCESSES

Systems programmers often must explicitly deal with processes. The operating system, or a systems-implementation language in some cases, provides them with the facilities for defining the confines of a process, its attributes, the nature of residence in memory (fixed or swappable), etc. It is by means of this mechanism, called *tasking* in Ada, that the systems programmer informs the operating system which activities may be scheduled for concurrent execution. By defining the values of process attributes, systems programmers can control or influence many important aspects of run-time process behavior and management. Processes and the related system calls can be used for fine-tuning of the time-critical applications and for assisting the operating system in resolving conflicting resource requirements.

3.2.1 A Multiprocess Example

In order to illustrate these ideas and to demonstrate the use of processes as experienced by systems programmers, we present a simplified example of a data-acquisition system (DAC). Our hypothetical data-acquisition system is supposed to monitor some process continuously, to record the process behavior, and to identify and report significant changes to an operator, or perhaps a robot, who may take some further action. These changes may be some statistically significant departures of measured values of the process variables from their expected or desirable ranges.

From the systems programmer's point of view, the related program should collect the input data from an external sensor, say, by means of an analog-to-digital (A/D) converter, log them on disk for archival purposes, perform some statistical operations in order to identify the significant changes from the previous sample, and report those, say, by printing them or by sending a message to the eagerly awaiting robot. This sequence of activities is assumed to be performed repetitively during the lifetime of the system. Although the description is quite simplified, this example typifies the nature of operations encountered in data-acquisition systems.

Given that the listed activities appear to require sequential processing, the simplest approach is to write a single program to carry them out one after another. A possible implementation of the presented problem is given as Program 3.1. For ease of reference, the four identified activities are named as follows: COLLECT (from A/D), LOG (to disk), STAT (statistical processing), and REPORT (print significant changes).

The deceptive simplicity of this example is intentional. It demonstrates how one could logically reason one's way into an inadequate implementation. If performance is no problem, our approach is acceptable, and it may in fact be used by an experienced systems programmer while testing the logic of the four activities. However, if response time is critical and the hardware is fixed, a

```
program sequential_DAC;

    . . .

    begin
        while true do        {forever}
            begin
                collect_ad;      {data from A/D converter}
                log_d;           {to disk}
                stat_p;          {statistical processing}
                report_pr        {print significant changes}
            end {while}
    end {sequential_DAC}
```

**Program 3.1 Sequential implementation of
the Data-Acquisition System (DAC)**

multiprocess approach can produce better performance. How are we to know that? The suggestion is provided by our earlier conclusion that I/O, in general, is quite slow when compared to the CPU-execution rates. If our sample program is strictly sequential, as in Program 3.1, then the CPU idles during the A/D conversions, while waiting for disk seeks, and while printing. However, if the four required activities are split into separate processes, they may be able to run concurrently. This, in turn, can improve performance by having a compute-bound activity run on the CPU while the I/O of another process is in progress.

From the problem definition, it follows that we must first collect the data, and then log them and perform the statistical processing. The relative ordering of the latter two activities is neither specified nor important. One of them (LOG) is mostly I/O-oriented, whereas the other (STAT) is compute-bound. These two are perfect candidates for concurrent execution; there is no precedence relationship between them, and they have practically nonconflicting resource requirements. So, instead of idling while disk seeks are in progress, the CPU can be executing STAT. With LOG and STAT interleaved, we are entitled to expect better performance. As for REPORT, it can run only when STAT is completed, because it prints the data provided by STAT. These precedence relationships are represented by the directed graph in Figure 3.1b. Each circle represents one run of the activity identified by the first letter of its name. Next to it is the number of the particular run. For example, starting with a freshly initialized system, COLLECT runs first (C1). It prepares data for the first run of LOG (L1) and STAT (S1), the two of which are executed concurrently. When they finish, another run of COLLECT (C2) begins, concurrently with the first run of REPORT (R1), which prints the changes furnished by STAT (S1). The arcs in the graph indicate causal and precedence relationships. For example, C2 may begin its execution only after both L1 and S1 have completed their respective runs. For comparison, a precedence graph for sequential execution of the four activities is given in Figure 3.1a. Assuming approximately equal execution times for all four activities, Figure 3.1 suggests that concurrent execution in this example may result in a twofold performance improvement over the sequential case.

On the basis of the previous discussion, we may code the four identified activities as separate processes. Their pseudocode is given in Program 3.2. In order to focus on multiprocess operation, the program omits data specifications altogether. In the first approximation, let us assume the existence of two global buffers (accessible to all processes): IB1, an input buffer where COLLECT stores a batch of input collected on one run; and OB1, an output buffer where STAT places data to be output by REPORT. Both LOG and STAT are assumed to obtain their respective inputs from IB1, but not to modify the contents in any way; i.e., for them, IB1 is strictly read-only. Each process may also have its own private data, but this is unimportant for the purposes of our discussion.

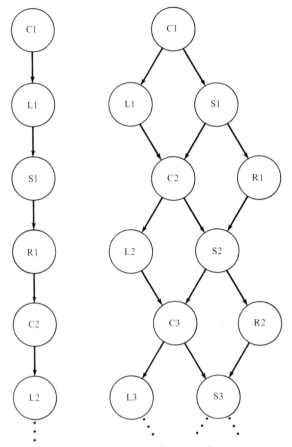

Figure 3.1 Precedence graphs of the multiprocess example.

(a) Sequential Execution   (b) Concurrent Execution

3.2.2 Interprocess Synchronization

The new concept introduced in Program 3.2 is the sending and receiving of signals. The purpose of these signals is to provide the synchronization necessary to enforce the outlined precedence relationships among our assemblage of cooperating processes. Note that we used the enable/disable-interrupt mechanism for a similar purpose in Chapter 2. This should provide some intuitive motivation in understanding their role, but by no means should signals be thought of as interrupts. Signals are one of the interprocess synchronization mechanisms that, as a group, are among the most important services provided by multiprocess operating systems. Their detailed treatment may be found in Chapters 4 and 5. For the time being, let us assume that a process waiting on one or more signals is suspended by the operating system, that is, made ineligible for execution until all required signals arrive. A signal is assumed

program/module *multiprocess_DAC*;

  . . .

  process *collect*;
    begin
      while *true* **do**
        begin
          wait_signal_from(*log, stat*);
          collect_ad;
          send_signal_to(*log, stat*)
        end {*while*}
    end {*collect*};

  process *log*;
    begin
      while *true* **do**
        begin
          wait_signal_from(*collect*);
          log_d;
          send_signal_to(*collect*)
        end {*while*}
    end; {*log*}

  process *stat*;
    begin
      while *true* **do**
        begin
          wait_signal_from(*collect, report*);
          stat_p;
          send_signal_to(*report, collect*)
        end {*while*}
    end; {*stat*}

  process *report*;
    begin
      while *true* **do**
        begin
          wait_signal_from(*stat*);
          report_pr;
          send_signal_to(*stat*)
        end
    end; {*report*}

  {*parent process*}
  begin {*multiprocess_DAC*}
    initialize_environment;
    send_signal_to(*collect, collect, stat*);   {*for the first run*}
    initiate *collect, log, stat, report*
  end {*multiprocess_DAC*}

Program 3.2 Multiprocess implementation of the DAC System

to arrive after it is sent by another process. Sending a signal per se does not suspend the sending process. In order to understand the need for signals as used in Program 3.2 and the interleaved execution of processes in general, the reader must learn to think "parallel" and to interpret various events from both a particular process's viewpoint and the system's viewpoint at the same time.

The first important observation is that with the problem split into four processes, each process executes its own sequential stream of instructions more or less independently. Interleaving is performed by the operating system in a manner largely transparent to the concurrent processes themselves. The processes are dynamically cycling through their active and suspended states, and only the operating system knows their collective state at any point in time. An individual process has no way of knowing the state or the progress of any other process, unless specifically informed about it by a signal. In other words, a process may assess only a subset of the global state that is explicitly made visible to it. The systems programmer controls this aspect of interprocess synchronization by defining the identity and the meaning of signals exchanged among the cooperating processes.

Probably the most understandable use of signals in Program 3.2 is the one depicted in the LOG process. The precedence relationships dictate that LOG must wait for COLLECT to provide the data in IB1 in order to save them on disk. Without awaiting the signal from COLLECT to indicate that event, LOG could behave erratically and store a single sample several times (if it is faster than COLLECT), not at all (say, if COLLECT cycles twice), or only partially when the two processes overlap. Once LOG completes its operation, it sends a signal to COLLECT to indicate that data have been logged. This also implies that the contents of IB1 are no longer needed by LOG. A similar stop/go protocol is employed by STAT and REPORT in negotiating the use of OB1. From the problem statement, it follows that the next run of COLLECT may be initiated only after both LOG and STAT have processed the previous batch of collected data. In other words, COLLECT must receive signals from both LOG and STAT that signify that fact. However, whenever the system is brought up, COLLECT must be the first process to run. In Program 3.2 this is accomplished by having the parent process send the signal necessary for proper initiation of children processes. In a sense, these signals are "fakes," because they must appear to the receiving process as if they were coming from their usual source. The first two signals sent to COLLECT, for example, should act as if they were sent by LOG and STAT, respectively. The parent process, to whom control is transferred by the OS whenever the system is brought up, is also in charge of initializing the environment and activating the four children processes. In other words, the parent process creates the run-time environment for execution of the application. Initializing a process implies creating it and making it known to the operating system. In an Ada environment, the INITIATE statement initiates all listed tasks (processes) concurrently.

3.2.3 Behavior of Sample Processes

In order to demonstrate the run-time behavior and interleaved operation of the four processes, it is necessary to make some further assumptions about them. Figure 3.2a graphically depicts their assumed behavior, which will serve as the basis of a number of diagrams throughout this chapter. Solid blocks indicate the CPU-bound portions of each process, dashed lines represent the I/O, and up-arrows mark occurrences of interrupts. Down-arrows indicate the instants when the STAT process, which is not interrupt-driven, becomes ready to run. For example, one run of COLLECT consists of servicing three consecutive interrupts from the A/D converter. Each run of its interrupt-service routine (ISR) is assumed to take $\frac{1}{4}$ time unit, and two adjacent A/D interrupts are 1 time unit apart. Similarly, LOG is assumed to require two disk writes, each taking $\frac{1}{2}$ time unit for setup and $1\frac{1}{2}$ time units for the disk I/O. STAT is CPU-bound, taking 2 time units per run. Finally, REPORT consists of processing two printer (or robot) interrupts, $1\frac{1}{2}$ time units apart. With these assumptions, COLLECT, LOG, STAT, and REPORT take 3, 4, 2, and 3 time units, respectively, for one cycle of their execution. As Figure 3.2b illustrates, one sequential run of our data-acquisition application takes 12 time units. As we are interested only in the process behavior and relative comparisons, we leave the value of a time unit unspecified. Readers with an insatiable urge for quantification are advised to think in terms of a millisecond as the order of magnitude of 1 time unit.

The last assumption to be made before analyzing the behavior shown in Figure 3.3 is an assignment of priorities to processes. For reasons similar to those described for the interrupt-service routines, each process is assigned a *software priority level*. The primary purpose of software priorities is to indicate to the operating system the relative importance of a specific process and thus assist it in resolving scheduling conflicts. In particular, when two or more processes concurrently request a single resource, it will be assigned to the one with the highest priority.

In the diagram given in Figure 3.3, the priorities—in decreasing order—are assumed to be as follows: LOG, COLLECT, REPORT, STAT. Priority assignment is an important component in tuning the performance of systems with time-critical requirements. This is another area without hard rules, requiring systems programmers to rely on both problem analysis and educated guessing in assigning priorities. Subsequent timing analysis of the running system may be needed to arrive at the "best" assignment for a given situation. In the example at hand, our guess is based on the observation that LOG drives the disk and thus requires a quick response to interrupts in order to avoid losing disk rotations. COLLECT is assigned the next highest priority because it is also interrupt-driven and provides data that all other processes depend on for their execution. REPORT is of higher priority than STAT only because REPORT is interrupt-driven and we want to keep both I/O and CPU busy. Thus, while waiting for printer interrupts, the CPU may execute STAT if STAT has a lower priority than REPORT, and the CPU automatically reverts to REPORT when an interrupt is posted. If the

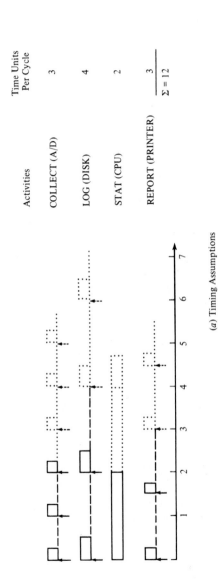

(a) Timing Assumptions

Activities	Time Units Per Cycle
COLLECT (A/D)	3
LOG (DISK)	4
STAT (CPU)	2
REPORT (PRINTER)	$\dfrac{3}{\Sigma = 12}$

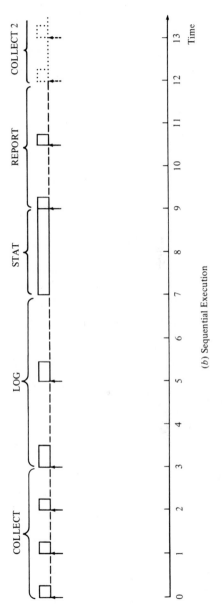

(b) Sequential Execution

Figure 3.2 Data-acquisition system.

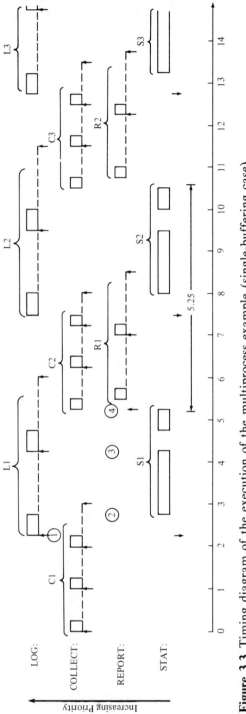

Figure 3.3 Timing diagram of the execution of the multiprocess example (single-buffering case).

priorities were reversed, REPORT would not be able to gain control from STAT. In the previous chapter we indicated that interrupt-driven I/O consists of short CPU bursts to execute the ISR and relatively long periods of device business. Therefore, with REPORT having a higher priority than STAT, both REPORT and STAT have an opportunity to receive the processor's attention and thus make progress toward completion.

The system's view of execution of the four processes, beginning immediately after their initialization, is shown in Figure 3.3. Initially, COLLECT is the first process to run, as it is the only process that does not need signals in order to proceed. LOG, STAT, and REPORT are suspended by the OS pending arrival of the respective signals for which they are awaiting, as indicated by their first executable statements. When the first run of COLLECT completes, COLLECT announces the event by sending signals to LOG and STAT. This, in turn, makes both LOG and STAT eligible for execution, but LOG has higher priority and is therefore allowed to proceed by being allocated the CPU (Figure 3.3, Event 1). When LOG finishes its first CPU-bound burst and waits for disk I/O to complete, the OS allocates the CPU to STAT (Event 2). How does the underlying operating system know that the CPU is idle and may be reassigned? We answer this question in detail later in this chapter; let it suffice for now to point out that I/O routines themselves are part of the OS, so LOG must invoke the operating system to perform the desired I/O on its behalf. As a side effect, the OS is alerted to the fact that LOG (its caller) is awaiting completion of that I/O, so another process may be scheduled for execution. STAT, being CPU-bound, continues to run until the point labeled as Event 3. Here, disk I/O is completed, so LOG is ready to continue its execution (OS is alerted to this event by the disk I/O-completion interrupt). Because of relative priorities, OS chooses to preempt STAT and to run LOG. This is the so-called *priority-based preemptive scheduling* discipline that is frequently encountered in real-time operating systems. Other scheduling disciplines are discussed in Section 3.5.

Now let us assume that writing to disk uses some internal buffers of the I/O system and that the global buffer IB1 need not be used for that purpose. In this case, LOG may send a signal to COLLECT just after setting up the second disk write needed to complete its run and without waiting for the write to be carried out by the disk controller. At the point in Figure 3.3, designated as Event 4, STAT finishes its run and also sends a signal to COLLECT. As a result, COLLECT runs again, accumulating a new batch of input data in IB1, and sends signals to LOG and STAT, thus initiating their second run. Then the process is repeated. Note that STAT sends signals to both COLLECT and REPORT, making them both eligible for execution—but COLLECT wins out due to its higher priority.

So what have we gained by introducing multiple processes in our data-acquisition system? There is better than a *twofold* increase in throughput as a result of interleaved process execution. In other words, the same hardware may be able to monitor the physical process twice as fast as it would when programmed in the strictly sequential manner. This may be deduced from Figure 3.3, which shows that a full cycle of all four processes may now be completed in 5.25 time units, as opposed to 12 time units in the sequential case. Even with concurrent process execution, there is still some room for improvement suggested by the periods of CPU idle time in Figure 3.3. How can the degree of concurrency in our example be increased? In Chapter 2 we accomplished this by using multiple buffering, so let us try it here too.

Figure 3.4 is a precedence graph of a sequence of events with double buffering (B1 and B2). It shows that the degree of concurrency possible in this case is twice that of the single-buffering case shown in Figure 3.1b, as four processes may run concurrently at a time. Figure 3.5 is a timing diagram for the double-buffering

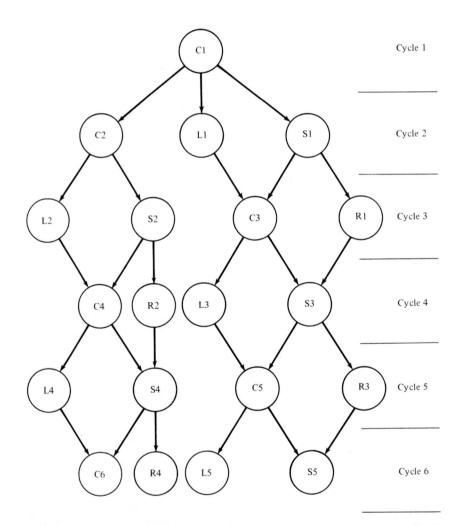

Figure 3.4 Precedence graph of the multiprocess example (double-buffering case).

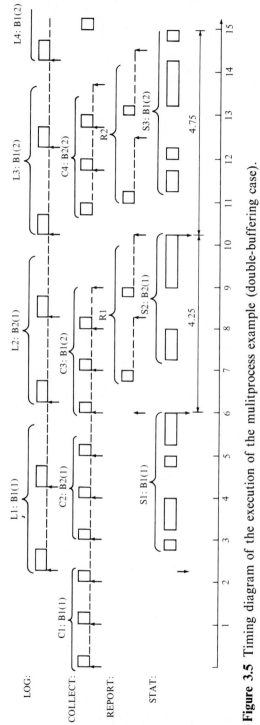

Figure 3.5 Timing diagram of the execution of the multiprocess example (double-buffering case).

case using the same timing assumptions for each individual process. In order to assist tracing of this diagram, each run of a process indicates the buffer used. The number in parentheses denotes the number of the process run that filled it. For example, COLLECT on its first run fills B1(1) for use by LOG and STAT and immediately embarks upon its second run, which fills the second buffer, B2, for the first time, B2(1). When the first run of LOG and STAT completes, B1 is no longer needed and the third run of COLLECT fills B1 a second time, denoted B1(2). Output from STAT (which is input to RECORD) is also assumed to be double-buffered, but those buffer identities are omitted for clarity.

As both Figures 3.4 and 3.5 suggest, this approach results in 100% CPU utilization, rendering further increase in the level of buffering useless. As is usually the case with double buffering, the input process COLLECT is one step ahead of processes LOG and STAT. The reader is strongly encouraged to verify that events depicted in Figure 3.5 conform to our assumptions and that the buffers are used properly. The code in Program 3.2 still describes the spirit of the solution, but some modifications in terms of specifying buffer identities and signaling should be introduced.

The double-buffering version of the program requires 4.5 time units, on average, for completion of one full cycle of all processes. Compared to the previous leap from 12 to 5.5 time units, this change is a very modest improvement. It is understandable, though, given that both solutions rely on concurrent processes and that single buffering alone ensures a rather high CPU utilization factor, leaving a small margin for double buffering. Buffering generally improves throughput up to the point that some bottleneck limits additional improvement. In this example, the bottleneck is CPU time, and it develops when two buffers are used. In other situations, three, four, or more buffers might be useful. The designer usually selects the optimum buffering by analyzing performance and by verifying the design through timing measurement.

3.2.4 Postlude: Systems Programmer's View of Processes

Our example illustrates that the benefits of multiprocess operation do not come for free. In order to split what looked like a simple program into a number of processes, we had to introduce the additional complexity of signals and priority assignments—a process that requires careful coding and may take several iterations to perfect in real-life implementation. Moreover, multiple processes require more debugging than sequential operation owing to synchronization complexities that are absent from the sequential code. This point should be taken with caution, however, because large applications may best be implemented by dividing a large program into a number of simple, straightforward modules with well-defined points of interaction. This approach encourages loose coupling among processes and the design of interprocess interactions well ahead of the actual coding. Such a structure enables incremental program development and debugging of separate modules using stubs (dummy modules) for the ones that remain to be implemented. This technique tends to find problems early, when they are easily discovered and remedied. Not surprisingly, the use of process modules and structures is very much related to structured programming, which many systems programmers were intuitively practicing even before its name was invented.

Coming back to our example, we note that multiprocess operation may dramatically improve the performance of even small, closed systems. Of course, performance improvements from concurrent processing may vary considerably from application to application, thereby making general estimates unjustifiable. The power of concurrent processes lies in being able to specify the sequences of code that can be executed concurrently, thus allowing the operating system to exploit the parallelism possible in a given environment. This is an extremely valuable feature in programming real-time systems or any system in which there is a pronounced need to respond to time-critical events.

However, programmer-defined processes may require intimate knowledge of the scheduling strategies and process-management facilities, such as signaling mechanisms and attribute assignments, of the underlying operating system. In addition, analysis of the timing and behavior of the specific application may also have to be performed. In noncritical applications, systems programmers often informally and intuitively assess the functions likely to benefit from being executed as independent processes. The analysis and design process illustrated by means of our example is usually performed only for production programs that run hundreds of times a day or for some highly specialized applications. Some examples include systems programs and utilities, online reservation and banking systems, and dedicated process-control systems, such as nuclear-reactor monitoring. Casual application programs, as exemplified by student Pascal runs, are usually not subjected to performance analysis for reasons of cost-effectiveness. Multiuser operating systems, instead, treat each user's program as a process by default and exploit concurrency between processes rather than within one application program.

3.3 OPERATING SYSTEM'S VIEW OF PROCESSES

In illustrating the systems programmer's view of processes, several references had to be made to certain aspects of the operating system's management of processes. In this section we expand on those notions and present the process-management system services (OS calls) typically provided by multiprogramming OS kernels.

A *process* was defined as an instance of a program in execution. From the operating system's point of view, a *process* is the smallest individually schedulable entity, consisting of code and data and characterized by attributes and dynamic state. The code is composed of machine instructions and system services calls (OS calls). Attributes associated with a process are assigned by the systems programmer or the operating system itself and include such things as software priority and access rights. The operating system views the execution of a typical process in the course of its activity in the form of a progression through a succession of states.

A general form of the process state-transition diagram is given in Figure 3.6. As we have pointed out earlier, a created process (made known to the OS) is running, ready to run, or suspended awaiting an event. Consequently, four general categories of process states may be introduced: *dormant, ready, running,* and *suspended.*

The *dormant* state is sometimes left out because it denotes processes that are not known to and therefore not tracked by the operating system. All process templates awaiting activation, as well as the programs not yet submitted to the operating system, may be regarded as dormant in this classification.

A *ready* process possesses all resources needed for its execution, except for the CPU. Processes usually assume the ready state immediately upon creation. All ready processes are waiting to have the CPU allocated to them by the operating system in order to run. An operating-system module, called a *scheduler*, selects one ready process for execution whenever the OS has control of the CPU and is about to return the CPU to a new process.

A *running* process possesses all resources needed for its execution, including the CPU. On a single-CPU system, at most one process may be running at any point in time. The running process executes its sequence of machine instructions and may call upon the operating system to perform services such as I/O or synchronization via signal exchange on its behalf. Depending on the particular scheduling policy in effect, the OS may return control to the running process after performing the service, or the OS may schedule another process if one is ready to run.

A *suspended* process lacks some resource other than the CPU, such as a synchronization signal. Such processes are normally left out from competition for execution until the related suspending condition is removed. The running process

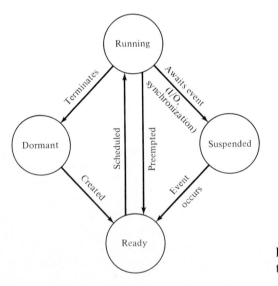

Figure 3.6 Process state-transitions.

may become suspended by invoking an I/O routine whose results it needs in order to proceed or by awaiting a signal that is not yet produced. The operating system then records the reason for suspension, so that it may resume the process at a later time when the suspending condition is removed by the actions of some other process or by the arrival of an external event. If the OS does not return to the process in execution when an interrupt invokes the OS, we say that the running process has been preempted by a higher-priority process. Note that a preempted process remains in the ready state rather than in the suspended state, since the only resource it lacks is the processor.

At any time, a number of active processes occupy different states. The collective states of all processes and resources (busy, free) in the system may be regarded as the *global system state*. In response to both internal and external events, the processes may rapidly change their states and form another global state of the system. A multiprogramming OS continuously tracks changes of the global state that occur as a result of both external and internal events. Using the global system state as an input, the operating system employs its scheduling algorithms to decide how to allocate resources to the requesting processes in such a way that the resulting system performance satisfies design objectives. In this section we explore the mechanisms employed by multiprogramming operating systems in tracking the global state of the system.

The view of the operating system emerging from our discussion thus far is that of a traffic manager. The operating system tracks all processes, suspends and resumes them when appropriate, allocates the CPU and other system resources when called upon to do so, and provides a number of run-time services to executing processes. Let us first investigate how a multiprogramming operating system keeps track of a single process and then construct the picture of its overall operation.

The operating system groups all information that it needs about a particular process into a data structure called a *process descriptor* or a *process control-block* (PCB). Whenever a process is created (initialized, installed), the operating system creates a corresponding process control-block to serve as its run-time description during the lifetime of the process. When the process terminates, its PCB is released to the pool of free cells from which new PCBs are drawn. The dormant state is distinguished from other states because a dormant process has no PCB. A process becomes known to the operating system and thus eligible to compete for system resources only when it has an active PCB associated with it. The process control-block, as a data structure, may be viewed as a record with fields for different static and dynamic process attributes. Our view of the PCB developed so far is summarized as follows:

1. Process name (ID)
2. Priority
3. State (ready, running, suspended)
4. Other fields

Readers accustomed to the Pascal style of data typing, may regard this as a list of fields of the PCB record-type definition. "Other fields" in the list above refer to the additional information about a process that a PCB may contain, such as a process activation record (all registers and status flags), a list of requested and allocated resources, and accounting data. Accounting information is recorded by some systems in order to charge individual users for the CPU time, I/O operations performed, and other resource usage. Embedded and real-time systems generally do not incorporate this feature in order to conserve the precious CPU execution cycles.

Once constructed for a newly created process, the PCB is filled with the programmer-defined attributes found in the process template or specified as the parameters of the CREATE_PROCESS operating-system call. Default values for other fields are usually assigned by the operating system at this time. For example, when a process is created, the activation record entries are set to the values provided by the linker/loader. Whenever that process is suspended, the contents of the CPU registers are saved in its activation record for subsequent restoration when the process is scheduled to run again. The state field is used by the operating system to track each and every state change of the process for as long as its PCB exists.

As explained earlier, a state of a process is just a component of the global system state, which encompasses all processes and resources. In order to keep track of all processes, the operating system maintains lists of process control-blocks classified by the current state of the related processes. In general, there is a *ready list*, which contains PCBs of all ready processes, and a *suspended list*. (Having a list of running processes hardly makes sense in uniprocessor systems in view of the fact that it can contain no more than a single entry at any point in time, so a single pointer to a process in the ready list is sufficient to identify "the list" of running processes.)

By means of these lists, the operating system forms pools of processes in similar states that are likely to be examined by the OS resource-allocation routines. For example, the scheduler should search for the next process to run only in the ready list. Operating-system performance may then be improved by sorting and updating these lists in ways that are most suitable for the routines that are known to operate on them. We will discuss these issues in considerable detail in Chapters 9 and 10, where the design of a complete multiprocess kernel is presented.

Membership of a PCB in a given list is granted on the basis of the current state of its process. Whenever a process changes its state, the operating system reacts by placing the process's PCB in the list that corresponds to its new state. In other words, PCBs are bound to processes but not to lists. A PCB is moved between lists as often as its process changes states. Because of the frequent insertions and deletions of PCBs, OS process lists are almost always implemented as linked-lists, sometimes with multiple pointers, in order to speed up their processing.

Figure 3.7 is a snapshot of system lists for the multiple-process example introduced earlier. This particular configuration of PCBs depicts the global system state, as observed by the scheduler, just after the first run of COLLECT and prior to launching of the LOG process—an instance denoted as Event 1 in Figure 3.3. LOG and STAT processes are ready, whereas REPORT and COLLECT processes are suspended pending arrival of signals, as indicated in the figure below their respective PCBs. In keeping with usual practice, the ready list is assumed to be sorted by process priority in order to facilitate scheduling. The suspended list is managed in FIFO order. One or more link fields are included in each process control-block for formation of lists.

Figure 3.8 illustrates a state transition of a control-block. In Figure 3.8a, system lists are shown at the time when process STAT is running, after LOG has been suspended pending completion of disk I/O. This is a snapshot of the multiple-process example between Events 2 and 3 in Figure 3.3. In Figure 3.8a, dashed arrows indicate the PCB manipulation necessary to reflect a change of the

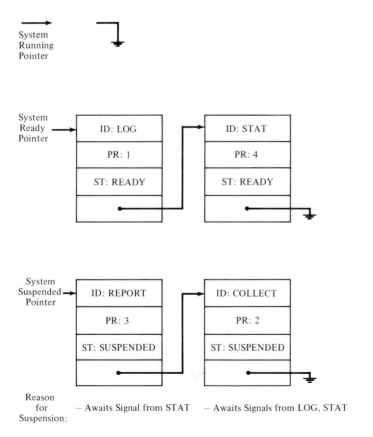

Figure 3.7 System lists: ready and suspended.

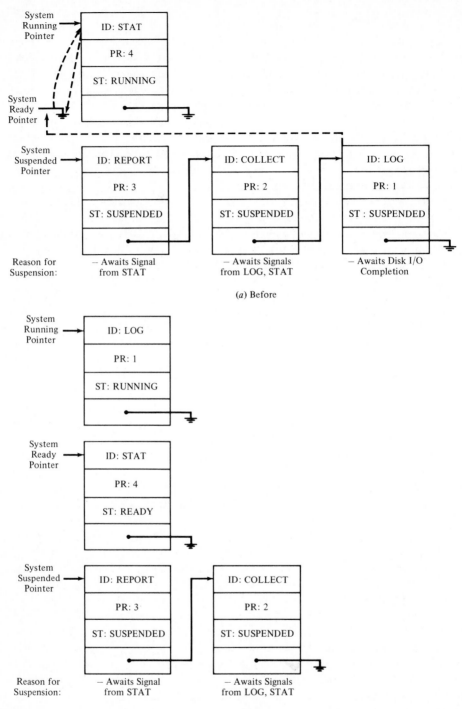

Figure 3.8 Process state-change.

system's global state. In particular, when disk I/O is completed, the corresponding interrupt alerts the operating system to that event. Because LOG's suspending condition has been removed, the operating system makes the LOG process ready by moving its PCB into the ready list (Figure 3.8a, Transition A). The scheduler is then invoked to select the next running process, and LOG is chosen because of its high priority. This effectively preempts STAT, the running process, whose PCB is moved into the ready list (Figure 3.8a, Transition B). LOG then becomes the running process. The resulting state of the system's lists after these changes is depicted in Figure 3.8b.

This example illustrates the essence of the mechanisms used by multiprocess operating systems to detect, record, and manage all changes of the global system state. Whenever a transition from one user process to another has to be made, the OS intervenes and updates the system lists accordingly. The first step is to record the state of the running process that is about to become suspended or preempted. The run-time state of a process typically includes the program counter, stack pointer, processor status word, and all other program-accessible registers. Unlike the interrupt context-save, the full state must be recorded because there is no way for the operating system to know which particular registers the running process may use in its future runs. This information is stored in the activation-record portion of the process's PCB, whose other fields are also updated at this time: state, accounting information, reason for suspension, etc. The PCB is then moved to the ready or suspended list, depending on whether a preemption or a request for a resource that cannot be granted, resulting in suspension, has caused the process switch. In any case, the scheduler is then run to select another process for execution. Any of the number of scheduling policies described in Section 3.6 may be employed for that purpose. The related PCB is then used to create a running environment for the selected process. The activation record is used to set the CPU registers, the interrupt mask register is set to reflect the priority of the new process, and then control is surrendered to the process. This activity is called a *process switch* or a *task switch*.

Process switching is a considerably more complex and overhead-prone operation than context switching, and it can become quite involved in large operating systems with detailed resource accounting and sophisticated scheduling schemes. Given its complexity and relatively high frequency of occurrence, process switching can significantly affect the performance of a multiprocess operating system. For this reason, the speed of process switching must be high in performance-oriented systems, such as real-time applications. A hardware scheme often employed to speed up process switching is to have multiple, structurally identical sets of CPU registers. The minimum is two, one for the operating system and another for user processes. A dedicated bit in the (single copy) processor status word indicates the current mode of operation, supervisor or user, and the corresponding set of active registers. This scheme may be expanded in multiprocessor systems by providing a multitude of CPUs, up to one per process. Such systems may eliminate the problem of process switching, at least the overhead attributable to preemptions, by allocating a dedicated CPU to each active process. The user/supervisor scheme is quite common in contemporary architectures because it also provides the added benefits of system protection and address-space isolation, to be discussed in Chapters 6 and 7.

3.4 OPERATING-SYSTEM SERVICES FOR PROCESS MANAGEMENT

In this section we describe the run-time services (system calls) typically provided by kernels of multiprogramming operating systems for process management. By *run-time services* we mean the predefined system calls that may be invoked by user processes, either directly, via supervisor calls embedded in the user's code, or indirectly, via commands typed at the terminal and translated into OS calls by the console-monitor routine.

Although multiprogramming systems often differ in their design philosophies and objectives, their innermost kernel layers exhibit a striking similarity in the type and range of the process-management primitives they provide. While the details and parameters inevitably vary from one system to another, the functions provided by the total collection of OS calls are very similar. This means that there is a tacit agreement among the operating-system designers as to what constitutes a minimal set of functions and services necessary to support process management in a multiprocess environment. Our aim in this section is to identify and describe the functions belonging to that minimal set. Other services, which are basic functions on some systems, may be implemented from a combination of ones described in this section. In other words, we are interested in OS kernel primitives only. They are described in the format typical for supervisor calls. Readers accustomed to issuing OS commands from terminals rather than programs are more likely to recognize the functions than the syntax. The mechanism for invoking the operating system from a user's program (supervisor calls) is explained in Chapter 9. For the time being, OS calls should be regarded as parametrized procedure calls that are in some way predefined and accessible from all systems-programming languages for a particular installation.

In particular, we describe the following process-management OS calls: CREATE, DELETE, FORK/JOIN, ABORT, SUSPEND, RESUME, DELAY, GET_ATTRIBUTES, and CHANGE_PRIORITY. Each call is introduced in the format of a procedure call, with the names of likely generic invocation parameters enclosed in parentheses. Following a brief description of the OS actions necessary to process a particular request, the possible error conditions for a given call are discussed. Equivalent or similar services provided in the Ada programming language are also described for some calls. Ada is one of the few programming languages that directly supports various forms of process management (called *task-management* in Ada), as opposed to relying on the operating system to provide those services.

CREATE (processID, attributes);

In response to this call, the operating system creates a new process with the specified or default attributes and identifier. As pointed out earlier, a process cannot create itself—because it would have to be running in order to invoke the OS and it cannot run before being created. So a process must be created by another process. In response to the CREATE call, the operating system obtains a new PCB from the pool of free memory, fills the fields with provided and/or default parameters, and inserts the PCB into the ready list—thus making the specified process eligible to run. Some of the parameters definable at the process-creation time include

- Level of privilege, such as system or user
- Priority
- Size and memory requirements
- Maximum data area and/or stack size
- Memory-protection information and access rights
- Other system-dependent data

The typical error returns, implying that the process was not created as a result of this call, include wrongID (illegal, or process already active), no space for PCB (usually transient, the call may be retried later), calling process not authorized to invoke this function, etc. In the case of a temporary lack of PCB space, the user should alert the system manager to increase the size of the memory pool. Ada uses the INITIATE statement to create and activate one or more tasks (processes). When several tasks are created with a single INITIATE statement, they are executed concurrently.

DELETE (processID);

Invocation of this call causes the OS to destroy and remove the designated process from the system. Unlike CREATE, a process may delete itself or another process. The operating system reacts by reclaiming all resources allocated to the specified process (attached I/O devices, memory), closing files opened by or for the process, and performing whatever other housekeeping is necessary. Following this process, the PCB is removed from the list where it presently resides and is returned to the free pool. This makes the designated process dormant. The DELETE service is normally invoked as part of an orderly program termination. The last END statement of a Pascal program, or an EXIT in Fortran, is often compiled into a DELETE call of the underlying operating system.

Almost all multiprogramming operating systems allow processes to terminate themselves, at least provided none of their spawned processes is active. Operating-system designers differ in their attitude toward allowing one process to terminate others. The issue here is one of convenience and efficiency versus system integrity. Allowing uncontrolled use of this function provides a malfunctioning or a malevolent process with the means of wiping out all other processes in the system. On the other hand, terminating a hierarchy of processes in a strictly guarded system, where each process can only delete itself and the parent must wait for children to terminate first, could be a lengthy operation indeed. The usual compromise is to permit deletion of other processes, but to restrict the range to members of the family, to lower-priority processes only, or to some other subclass of processes.

Possible error returns from the DELETE call include a child of this process is active (should terminate first), wrongID (the process does not exist), and calling process not authorized to invoke this function.

FORK/JOIN

Another method of process creation and termination is by means of the FORK/JOIN pair, originally introduced as primitives for multiprocessor systems. The FORK operation is used to split a sequence of instructions into two concurrently executable sequences. After reaching the identifier specified in FORK, a new process (child) is created to execute one branch of the forked code while the creating (parent) process continues to execute the other. FORK usually returns the identity of the child to the parent process, and the parent can use that identifier to designate the identity of the child whose termination it wishes to wait for when invoking a JOIN operation. JOIN is used to merge the two sequences of code divided by the FORK, and it is available to a parent process for synchronization with a child.

The relationship between processes created by FORK is rather symbiotic in the sense that they execute from a single segment of code and a child usually initially obtains a copy of the variables of its parent. This method of process creation is used by the Unix operating system, and it is described in more detail in the Unix case study in Chapter 11. Mesa, a Pascal-like language, uses the FORK/JOIN mechanism to implement asynchronous procedure calls, where both the caller and the called procedure execute concurrently following an invocation. The JOIN primitive is used to synchronize the caller with termination of the named procedure. In most other respects, asynchronous procedure invocation is identical to the synchronous procedure-call mechanism in Mesa, which is very similar to an ordinary procedure call in Pascal or Algol.

ABORT (processID);

This is a forceful termination of a process. While a process could conceivably abort itself, the most frequent use of this call is to remove a malfunctioning process from the system. The operating system performs much the same actions as DELETE, except that it usually furnishes a register and memory dump, together with some information about the identity of the aborting process and the reason for the action. This information may be provided in a file, as a message on a terminal, or as an input to the system crash-dump-analyzer utility. Obviously, the issue of restricting the authority to abort other processes, discussed in relation to the DELETE, is even more pronounced when implementing the ABORT call.

Error returns for ABORT are practically the same as those listed in the DELETE call. The Ada language includes the ABORT statement, which forcefully terminates one or more processes. Other than the usual scope and module-boundary rules, Ada imposes no special restrictions on the capability of a process to abort others.

SUSPEND (processID);

With this call, the designated process is suspended indefinitely and placed in the suspended state. It does, however, remain in the system. A process may suspend itself or another process when it is authorized to do so by virtue of its level of privilege, priority, or family membership. When the running process suspends itself, it—in effect—voluntarily surrenders control to the operating system. The operating system responds by inserting the target process's PCB into the suspended list and by updating the PCB state-field accordingly.

Suspending a suspended process usually has no effect, except in systems that keep track of the depth of suspension. In such systems, a process must be resumed at least as many times as it was suspended in order to become ready. To implement this feature, a suspend-count field has to be maintained in each PCB. Typical error returns include process already suspended, wrongID, and caller not authorized.

RESUME (processID);

This call resumes the target process, which is presumably suspended. Obviously, a suspended process cannot resume itself, because the suspended process would have to be running to have its OS call processed. So a suspended process depends on a partner process to issue the RESUME. The operating system responds by inserting the target process's PCB into the ready list, with the state updated. In systems that keep track of the depth of suspension, the OS first increments the suspend count and moves the PCB only when the count reaches zero.

The SUSPEND/RESUME mechanism is convenient for relatively primitive and unstructured forms of interprocess synchronization. It is often used in systems that do not support exchange of signals. Error returns include process already active, wrongID, and caller not authorized.

DELAY (processID, time);

With this call, the target process is suspended for the duration of the specified time period. The time may be expressed in terms of a number of system clock ticks (system-dependent and not portable) or in standard time units (seconds, minutes). A process may delay itself or, optionally, delay some other process.

The actions of the operating system in handling this call depend on processing interrupts from the programmable interval timer. The actual details are somewhat involved, and we discuss them in the design of our sample OS kernel in Chapters 9 and 10.

The timed delay is a very useful system call for implementing timeouts. In this application, a caller initiates an action and delays for the duration of the timeout. When the delay (timeout) expires, control is given back to the calling process, which tests the outcome of the initiated action. Two other varieties of timed delay are cyclic rescheduling of a process at given intervals (e.g., running it once every 5 minutes) and time-of-day scheduling, where a process is run at the specific time of day. An example of the latter is printing a shift log in a process-control system when a new crew is scheduled to take over or backing up a database at midnight.

The error returns include illegal time interval or unit, wrongID, and caller not authorized. In Ada, a task may delay itself for a number of system clock ticks (system-dependent and not portable) or for a specified time period using the predeclared floating point type TIME. The DELAY statement is used for this purpose.

GET_ATTRIBUTES (processID, attributeset);

This is an inquiry to which the operating system responds by providing the current values of the process attributes or their specified subset from the PCB. This is normally the only way for a process to find out what its current attributes are, because it neither knows where its PCB is nor can it access the protected OS space where the PCBs are usually kept.

This call may be used to monitor the status of a process, its resource usage and accounting information, or other public data stored in a PCB. The error returns include no such attribute, wrongID, and caller not authorized. In Ada, a task may examine the values of certain task attributes by means of reading the predeclared task-attribute variables, such as T'ACTIVE, T'CALLABLE, T'PRIORITY, and T'TERMINATED, where T is the identity of the target task.

CHANGE_PRIORITY (processID);

This is an instance of a more general SET_PROCESS_ATTRIBUTES system call. Obviously, this call is not implemented in systems where process priority is static.

Run-time modifications of a process's priority may be used to increase or decrease a process's ability to compete for system resources. The idea is that priority of a process should rise and fall according to the relative importance of its momentary activity and thus make scheduling more responsive to changes of the global system state. This call may be abused by low-priority processes, and the whole system may be corrupted by processes competing with the operating system itself. For these reasons, the authority to increase priority is usually restricted to changes within a certain range. For example, an explicit maximum may be specified, or the process may not exceed its parent's or group's priority. Although changing priorities of other processes could be useful, most implementations restrict the calling process to manipulating its own priority only.

The error returns include caller not authorized for the requested change and wrongID. In Ada, a task may change its own priority by calling the SET_PRIORITY procedure, which is predeclared in the language.

Our treatment of error returns and exceptional-condition processing in this book is less emphasized than their role in systems programming dictates. The problem is that error returns are heavily system-dependent and therefore difficult to generalize without making scores of additional, and otherwise distracting, assumptions. However, testing of the success/failure indicators returned by the OS after each invocation of a system call is critical to the correct functioning of a program and of the entire system. Probably the easiest way to spot a novice systems programmer is by his or her failure to test these values *after each and every OS call*.

In many instances, the operating system reacts to illegal invocation parameters simply by returning control to the calling process, with an indication of the reason for refusal or inability to take any action. Moreover, when a request for service must be denied due to a temporary crunch for a specific resource, the OS indicates the fact in the same way. Operating-system designers fully expect users to test these indicators and to retry the call or modify the parameters when necessary. It is very important to remember that just calling on the operating system to perform a service is by no means a sufficient guarantee that the desired service will be rendered. It may or may not be, depending on the validity of parameters, the authorization of the calling process, and the operational state of the system at that time. For example, a request to create a process that is otherwise perfectly legitimate may be denied by the operating system because the memory pool for PCBs is temporarily depleted or a quota of active processes is exceeded. The user can become aware of and handle these kinds of problems only by testing the result code returned by the OS. No amount of structured programming, scrutinizing of the source code for validity of invocation parameters, walkthroughs by fellow programmers, or any other program-development technique can substitute for failure to test the result code.

3.5 SCHEDULING

Scheduling refers to a set of policies and mechanisms built into the operating system that governs the order in which the work to be done is completed. A *scheduler* is an OS module that selects the next job to be admitted into the system and the next process to run. The primary objective of scheduling is to optimize system performance in accordance with the criteria deemed most important by the system designers.

In this section we examine the what, when, and how questions about scheduling in approximately that order. We begin by describing the roles of the three different types of schedulers encountered in operating systems. After a discussion of the various performance criteria that schedulers may be designed to attain, we present several popular scheduling disciplines.

3.5.1 Types of Schedulers

In this section we describe three different types of schedulers that may act and coexist in a complex operating system: *long-term, medium-term,* and *short-term schedulers,* as they are usually referred to. After explaining their overall roles and places of activity, each type of scheduler is discussed in terms of its objectives, operating environment, and relationship to other schedulers in the system.

Figure 3.9 shows the possible traversal paths of jobs and programs through the components of a computer system. Rectangles in Figure 3.9 depict queues in which jobs and processes may wait while being processed. The primary places of action of the three types of schedulers are marked with down-arrows. As shown in Figure 3.9, a submitted batch job joins the batch queue while waiting to be processed by the long-term scheduler. Once scheduled for execution, processes spawned by the batch job enter the ready queue to await CPU allocation by the short-term scheduler. After becoming suspended, the running process may be removed from memory and swapped-out to secondary storage. Such processes are subsequently admitted to main memory by the medium-term scheduler in order to be considered for execution by the short-term scheduler.

The long-term scheduler. The long-term scheduler, when present, works with the batch queue and selects the next batch job to be executed. Batch is usually reserved for resource-intensive (CPU time, memory, special I/O devices), low-

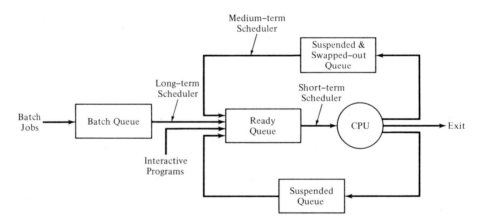

Figure 3.9 Schedulers.

priority programs that may be used as fillers to keep the system resources busy during periods of low activity of interactive jobs. As pointed out earlier, batch jobs contain all the necessary data and commands for their execution. Batch jobs usually also contain programmer-assigned or system-assigned estimates of their resource needs, such as memory size, expected execution time, and device requirements. Knowledge about the anticipated job behavior facilitates the work of the long-term scheduler.

The primary objective of the long-term scheduler is to provide a balanced mix of jobs, such as CPU-bound and I/O-bound, to the short-term scheduler. In a way, the long-term scheduler acts as a first-level throttle in keeping resource utilization at the desired level. For example, when the CPU utilization is low, the scheduler may admit more jobs to increase the number of processes in a ready queue and with it the probability of having some useful work awaiting CPU allocation. Conversely, when the utilization factor becomes high and the response time begins to show it, the long-term scheduler may opt to reduce the rate of batch-job admission accordingly. In addition, the long-term scheduler is usually invoked whenever a completed job departs the system. The frequency of invocation of the long-term scheduler is thus both system- and workload-dependent, but it is generally much lower than that of the other two types of schedulers. As a result of its relatively infrequent execution and the availability of an estimate of its workload's characteristics, the long-term scheduler may incorporate rather complex and computationally intensive algorithms for admitting jobs into the system. In terms of the process state-transition diagram, the long-term scheduler is basically in charge of the dormant-to-ready transitions. Ready processes are placed in the ready queue (ready list in our earlier discussion) for consideration by the short-term scheduler.

The medium-term scheduler. After executing for a while, a running process may become suspended by making an I/O request or by issuing a system call. Given that suspended processes cannot make any progress toward completion until the related suspending condition is removed, it is sometimes beneficial to remove such processes from main memory in order to make room for other processes. In practice, the main-memory capacity may impose a limit on the number of active processes in the system. When a number of those processes become suspended, the remaining supply of ready processes in systems where all suspended processes remain resident in memory may become reduced to a level that impairs functioning of the short-term scheduler by leaving it few or no options for selection. In systems with no support for virtual memory, this problem may be alleviated by removing suspended processes to secondary storage. Saving of the image of a suspended process on secondary storage is called *swapping*, and the process is said to be *swapped out* or *rolled-out*. Details of swapping are described in Chapter 6.

In the system depicted in Figure 3.9, a portion of the suspended processes is assumed to be swapped-out. The remaining processes are assumed to remain in memory while suspended.

The medium-term scheduler is in charge of handling the swapped-out processes. It has little to do while a process remains suspended. However, once the suspending condition is removed, the medium-term scheduler attempts to allocate the required amount of main memory and swap the process in and make it ready. In order to work properly, the medium-term scheduler must be provided with information about the memory requirements of swapped-out processes. This is usually not difficult to implement, because the actual size of the process may be recorded at the time of swapping and stored in the related process control-block.

In terms of the process state-transition diagram, the medium-term scheduler controls suspended-to-ready transitions of swapped processes. This scheduler may be invoked when memory space is vacated by a departing process or when the supply of ready processes falls below a specified limit.

The short-term scheduler. The short-term scheduler allocates the CPU among the pool of ready processes resident in memory. Its main objective is to maximize system performance in accordance with the chosen set of criteria. Being in charge of ready-to-running state transitions, the short-term scheduler must be invoked as often as once for each process switch to select the next process to be run. In practice, the short-term scheduler is invoked whenever an event (internal or external) causes the global state of the system to change. Given that any such change could result in suspension of the running process or in suspension of one or more ready processes, the short-term scheduler should be run to determine whether such significant changes have indeed occurred and, if so, to select the next process to be run. Some of the events introduced thus far that cause rescheduling by virtue of their ability to change the global system state are listed as follows:

- Clock ticks (time-base interrupts)
- Interrupts and I/O completions
- Most operational OS calls (as opposed to queries)
- Sending and receiving of signals
- Activation of interactive programs

In general, whenever one of these events occurs, the operating system invokes the short-term scheduler to determine whether another process should be scheduled for execution.

Most of the process-management OS services discussed in Section 3.3 require invocation of the short-term scheduler as part of their processing. For example, creating a process or resuming a suspended one adds another entry to the ready list (queue), and the scheduler is invoked to determine whether the new entry should also become the running process. Suspending a running process, changing the priority of a running process, exiting or aborting a running process are also events that necessitate selection of a new running process. Some operating systems include an OS call that allows system programmers to explicitly cause invocation of the short-term scheduler, such as the DECLARE_SIGNIFICANT_EVENT call in the RSX-11M operating system. Among other things, this service is useful for invoking the scheduler from user-written event-processing routines, such as I/O drivers.

As indicated in Figure 3.9, interactive programs often enter the ready queue directly after being submitted to the OS, which then creates the corresponding process. Unlike batch jobs, the influx of interactive programs is not throttled, and they may conceivably saturate the system. The necessary control is usually provided indirectly by deteriorating response time, which tempts the users to give up and try again later or at least to reduce the rate of incoming requests.

Figure 3.9 illustrates the roles and interplay between the various types of schedulers in an operating system. It depicts the most general case of all three types being present. For example, a larger operating system might support both batch and interactive programs and rely on swapping to maintain a well-behaved mix of active processes. Smaller or special-purpose operating systems may have only one or two types of schedulers available. A long-term scheduler is normally not found in systems without support for batch, and a medium-term scheduler is needed only when swapping is used by the underlying operating system. When more than one type of scheduler exists in an operating system, proper support for their communication and interaction is very important for attaining satisfactory and balanced performance. For example, workload for the short-term scheduler is prepared by both the long-term and the medium-term schedulers. If they do not provide a balanced mix of compute-bound and I/O-bound processes, the short-term scheduler is not likely to perform well no matter how sophisticated it may be on its own merit.

3.5.2 Scheduling and Performance Criteria

In this section we discuss some of the performance measures and optimization criteria that schedulers may use in attempting to maximize system performance. A list of the frequently encountered ones includes

1. CPU utilization
2. Throughput
3. Turnaround time
4. Waiting time
5. Response time

As discussed earlier, different types of schedulers are concerned with different units of work, such as jobs and processes. For the time being, we use the two terms interchangeably to denote a basic unit of work.

CPU utilization is the average fraction of time during which the CPU is busy. Being busy usually refers to the CPU not being idle, which includes both the time spent executing user programs and the time spent executing the operating system. With this interpretation, CPU utilization may be relatively easily measured, for example by means of a special process introduced in Chapter 9. An alternative is to consider the "useful work" only and thus exclude the time spent executing the operating system. In any case, the idea is that by keeping the CPU busy as much as possible, other component-utilization factors will also be high and thus provide a good return on investment.

Throughput refers to the amount of work completed in a unit of time. One way to express throughput is by means of the number of user jobs executed in a unit of time. The higher the number, the more work apparently being done by the system. Defined this way, throughput is difficult to use for comparisons, because it is dependent on the characteristics and resource requirements of the jobs being considered. The identical workload, e.g., the same job stream, should be presented to different scheduling algorithms in order to compare their performance on this basis.

Turnaround time may be defined as the time that elapses from the moment a program or a job is submitted until it is completed by a system. With the prices of hardware declining and the costs associated with systems programming increasing, improving human productivity by decreasing the turnaround time becomes one of the most important considerations of computer-system design in general and scheduling in particular.

Waiting time is essentially the time that a job spends waiting for resource allocation due to contentions with other jobs in a multiprogramming system. In other words, waiting time is the penalty imposed for sharing resources with others. Waiting time may be expressed as turnaround time less the actual execution time of a job. This measure identifies basically the same source of inefficiency as turnaround time, but waiting time eliminates variability due to the job's execution time. For example, a long job executed without preemptions and a short job executed with several preemptions may experience identical turnaround times. However, the waiting times of the two jobs would differ and clearly indicate the effects and extent of interference experienced by each job.

Response time is most frequently used in time-sharing and real-time operating systems. However, the definitions and the time constants involved in the two systems are quite different. In time-sharing systems, the measure may be defined as the time that elapses from a moment the last character of a command line launching a program or a transaction is entered until the first result appears on the terminal. This is usually called the *terminal response time*. In real-time systems, the response time is essentially latency, and it may be defined as the time from the moment an event (internal or external) is signaled until the first instruction of its respective service routine is executed. This time is often called the *event response time*.

There are many other measures for assessing the performance of an operating system, but they usually can be derived from the ones listed above. In addition to satisfying the chosen design criteria, the scheduler should be concerned with fairness in allocating resources among the users. The scheduler should also strive for predictability and repeatability, so that similar workloads exhibit similar behaviors. Although these considerations may, in a sense, be regarded as scheduling objectives, we will treat them as design constraints.

A typical scheduler-design process consists of selecting one or more of the primary performance criteria and ranking them in a relative order of importance. The next step is to design a scheduling strategy that maximizes performance for the specified set of criteria while obeying the design constraints. We are intentionally avoiding the word *optimization* because most scheduling algorithms actually implemented do not schedule optimally. They are based on heuristic techniques that yield good or near-optimal performance, but they rarely achieve absolutely optimal performance. The primary reason for this lies in the overhead that would be incurred by computing the optimum strategy at run-time and by collecting the performance statistics necessary to perform the optimization. Of course, optimization algorithms remain important, at least as a yardstick in evaluating the heuristics. Schedulers typically attempt to maximize the average performance of a system relative to a given criterion. However, due consideration must be given in controlling the variance and limiting the worst-case behavior. For example, a user experiencing 10-second response times to simple queries has little consolation in knowing that the system's average response time is under 2 seconds.

One of the problems in designing schedulers and selecting a set of performance criteria is that they often conflict with each other. For example, the fastest response time for a given event may result in low CPU utilization. Increased throughput and CPU utilization are usually achieved by increasing the number of active processes, but then response time may suffer.

As is the case with most engineering problems, the design of a scheduler usually requires careful balance of all the different requirements and constraints. Knowing the primary intended use of a given system, operating-system designers tend to maximize the criteria most important in a given environment. For example, throughput and component utilization are the primary design objectives in a batch system; multiuser systems are dominated by concerns about terminal response time; and real-time operating systems are designed for the ability to handle responsively a multitude of external events.

3.6 SCHEDULING ALGORITHMS

The scheduling mechanisms described in this section may, at least in theory, be used by any of the three type of schedulers. As we occasionally point out, some algorithms are better suited to the needs of a particular type of scheduler. Depending on whether a particular scheduling discipline is primarily used by a long-term or a short-term scheduler, we will illustrate its operation by using jobs or processes, respectively.

A major division among the approaches to scheduling may be made depending on whether they rely on preemption or not. Thus, we speak of preemptive and nonpreemptive scheduling disciplines. When applied to short-term scheduling, *no preemption* implies that the running process retains ownership of allocated resources, including the CPU, until the running process voluntarily surrenders control to the operating system. In other words, the running process cannot be forced to relinquish ownership of the CPU when a higher-priority process becomes ready for execution. However, when the running process becomes suspended as a result of its own action, say, by waiting for an I/O completion, another ready process may be scheduled.

With *preemptive scheduling*, on the other hand, a running process may be replaced by a higher-priority process at any time. This is accomplished by activating the scheduler whenever an event that changes the state of the system is detected. Since such events include a number of actions in addition to the voluntary surrender of control by the running process, preemption necessitates more frequent execution of the scheduler.

Regardless of whether preemption is used or not, dispatching of a new running process requires the operating system to save the state of the departing process and to establish the execution environment by loading the context of the oncoming process. Thus each rescheduling necessitates a full process switch. In general, preemptive scheduling may provide for greater responsiveness to events, but at the expense of higher overhead caused by more frequent execution of the scheduler and the associated process switching. As discussed later, the decision whether to schedule preemptively or not, as well as arguments for and against, tends to vary with the environment and the type of application most likely to be supported by a given operating system.

3.6.1 First-Come-First-Served (FCFS) Scheduling

This is by far the simplest scheduling discipline. The workload is simply processed as it comes, with no preemption. For example, jobs are executed in the order of arrival. Implementation of the FCFS scheduler is quite straightforward, and its execution results in little overhead.

As may be expected, by failing to take into consideration the state of the system and the resource requirements of the individual scheduling entities, FCFS scheduling usually results in poor performance. As a consequence of no preemption, component utilization and the system throughput rate may be quite low. Turnaround time is generally bad and unevenly distributed. In particular, short jobs may suffer considerable turnaround delays and waiting times when one or more long jobs are in the system. For example, consider a system with two jobs, J1 and J2, with total execution times of 20 and 2 time units, respectively. If they arrive one shortly after the other in the order J1–J2, the turnaround times are 20 and 22 time units, respectively (J2 must wait for J1 to complete), thus yielding an average of 21 time units. The corresponding waiting times are 0 and 20 time units, yielding an average of 10 time units. However, when the same jobs arrive in the opposite order, J2–J1, the average turnaround time drops to 11 time units and the waiting time is only 1 time unit. This simple example demonstrates how short jobs may be hurt by long jobs in FCFS systems, as well as the potential variability in turnaround and waiting times from one run to another.

Figure 3.10 is a timing diagram of the behavior of FCFS scheduling when it is applied to the double-buffering case of the multiprocess example introduced in Section 3.2. In order to examine the effects of scheduling on concurrent execution of processes, starting with Figure 3.10, all subsequent timing diagrams begin with the state of the system as encountered after the first run of COLLECT. The diagrams do not show the time necessary to execute the OS routines, because the amount of OS overhead is implementation-dependent and generally hard to quantify. While examining the diagrams that follow, the reader should keep in mind that the operating system is invoked to process every state transition and that it consumes processor cycles for scheduling and for process switching.

Returning to Figure 3.10, it demonstrates that FCFS scheduling has relatively low throughput, indicated by taking 5 time units to complete one full cycle of all processes, and poor event response time due to the lack of preemption and process priority. FCFS scheduling effectively eliminates the notion and importance of process priorities; process arrival times (becoming ready) are the sole scheduling criterion. For easier comparison with other scheduling disciplines, the diagram in Figure 3.10 is constructed with the assumption that ties are always broken in favor of what would be a higher-priority process. For example, LOG is always assumed to become ready a fraction of time earlier than STAT, say, due to being the first to receive a signal from COLLECT. It can be shown that if we reverse this assumption, a much worse behavior of FCFS scheduling will be observed.

3.6.2 Shortest Remaining Time Next (SRTN) Scheduling

Shortest remaining time next scheduling is a discipline where the next scheduling entity, a job or a process, is selected on the basis of its having the shortest remaining execution time. SRTN scheduling may be implemented in either the nonpreemptive or preemptive varieties. The nonpreemptive version of SRTN scheduling is often called *shortest job first* (SJF). In either case, whenever the SRTN scheduler is invoked, it searches the corresponding queue (batch or ready) to find the job or the process with the shortest remaining execution time. The difference between the two cases lies in the conditions that lead to invocation of the scheduler and, consequently, the frequency of its execution. Without preemption, the SRTN scheduler is invoked whenever a job is completed or the running process surrenders control to the OS. In the preemptive version, which makes sense for short-term scheduling only, whenever an event occurs that makes a new process ready, the scheduler is invoked to compare the remaining CPU execution time of the running process with the time needed to complete the next CPU burst of the newcomer. Depending on the outcome, the running process may continue or be preempted in order to be replaced by the shortest remaining time process. If it is preempted, the running process joins the ready queue.

SRTN scheduling is a provably optimal scheduling discipline in terms of minimizing the average waiting time of a given workload. It would always schedule the two jobs J1 and J2 introduced in the FCFS scheduling section, when both are available in a queue, in the shorter-longer order and thus

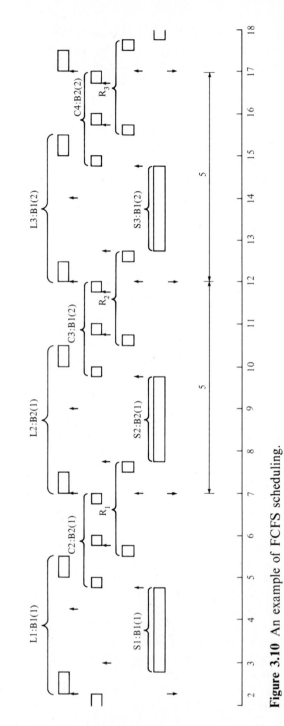

Figure 3.10 An example of FCFS scheduling.

108

achieve the good set of performance figures given earlier. By virtue of taking into consideration the characteristics of the presented workload, SRTN scheduling is done in a consistent and predictable manner, as opposed to FCFS scheduling, whose performance tends to be chancy. In the preemptive version, SRTN scheduling would preempt the executing job whenever a new one arrives in order to examine their respective remaining execution times. Such comparisons take care of the eventuality that a longer job arrives first and starts executing, a situation in which FCFS scheduling performs so poorly. As demonstrated by Figure 3.11, SRTN scheduling with preemption achieves the best throughput (4.25 time units for one cycle of all processes) of all the disciplines considered in this section. SRTN scheduling also provides good event and interrupt response times by giving preference to the related service routines, since their CPU bursts are typically of short duration.

SRTN discipline schedules optimally only when the exact future execution times of jobs or processes are known at the time of scheduling. In the case of short-term scheduling and preemptions, even more detailed knowledge of the duration of *each individual CPU burst* is required. In other words, optimal performance of SRTN scheduling is dependent upon future knowledge of the process/job behavior. This tends to limit effectiveness of SRTN implementations in practice, because future process behavior is difficult to estimate reliably except for some very specialized deterministic (and uninteresting) cases. Moreover, increased accuracy necessitates the use of more complex prediction algorithms, which usually require detailed monitoring and recording of past process behavioral patterns. Implementors of SRTN algorithms must weigh this additional overhead against the benefits of better scheduling performance when based on more accurate predictions.

SRTN scheduling has important theoretical implications, and it can serve as a yardstick for assessing performance of other realizable scheduling disciplines in terms of their deviation from the optimum. Its practical application depends on the accuracy of prediction of the job and process behavior, with the increased accuracy calling for more sophisticated methods and thus resulting in greater overhead. The preemptive variety of SRTN scheduling incurs the additional overhead of frequent process switching and scheduler invocation to examine each and every process transition into the ready state. This work is wasted when the new ready process has a longer remaining execution time than the running process.

This problem can be alleviated in implementations of SRTN scheduling where processes in the ready list are sorted according to the increasing values of their remaining execution times. This approach can also improve the scheduler's performance by avoiding a search to find the process with the shortest remaining time. However, insertions into a sorted list are generally more complex if the list is to remain sorted after inclusion of the new element. An example of a sorted ready list and some related implementation tradeoffs are discussed in the design of an OS kernel in Chapters 9 and 10.

110

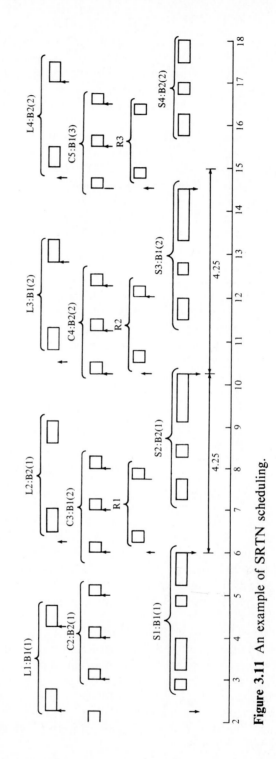

Figure 3.11 An example of SRTN scheduling.

3.6.3 Time-Slice Scheduling (Round Robin, RR)

In interactive environments, such as time-sharing systems, the primary requirement is to provide reasonably good response times and, in general, to share system resources equitably among all users. Obviously, only preemptive disciplines may be considered in such environments, and one of the most popular is *time slicing*, which is also known as *round robin* (RR). Basically, the CPU time is divided into slices, or quanta, that are allocated to requestors. No process can run for more than one time slice when there are others waiting in the ready queue. If a process needs more time to complete after exhausting its time slice, it is enqueued at the end of the ready queue to await the next allocation. Conversely, if the running process surrenders control to the operating system before the end of its allocated time, a significant event is declared and another process is scheduled to run. In this way, CPU time is effectively allocated to processes on a rotating-priority basis (hence the name *round robin*), and every one of them in turn receives $1/N$ of CPU time, where N is the number of ready processes.

Round-robin scheduling achieves equitable sharing of system resources. Short processes may be executed within a single time quantum and thus exhibit good response times. Long processes may require several time quanta and thus be forced to cycle through the ready queue a few times before completion. With RR scheduling, the response times of long processes are directly proportional to their resource requirements. For long processes that consist of a number of interactive sequences with the user, primarily the response time between the two consecutive interactions matters. If the computational requirements between two such sequences may be completed within a single time slice, the user should experience good response time. RR scheduling tends to subject long processes without interactive sequences to relatively long turnaround and waiting times. Such processes, however, may best be run in the batch mode, and it might even be desirable to discourage users from submitting them to the interactive scheduler.

Implementation of round-robin scheduling requires the support of an interval timer, preferably a dedicated one as opposed to sharing the system time base. The timer is usually set to interrupt the operating system whenever a time slice expires and thus force the scheduler to be invoked. The scheduler itself simply stores the context of the running process, moves it to the end of the ready queue, and dispatches the process at the head of the ready queue. The scheduler is also invoked to dispatch a new process whenever the running process surrenders control to the operating system before expiration of its time quantum, say, by requesting I/O. The interval timer is usually reset at that point in order to provide the full time slot to the new running process. Given its frequent setting and resetting, hardware support for a dedicated interval timer is desirable in systems that use time slicing.

Round-robin scheduling is often regarded as a "fair" scheduling discipline. It is also one of the best known scheduling disciplines for achieving good and relatively evenly distributed terminal response time. The performance of round-robin scheduling is very sensitive to the choice of the time slice. For this reason, the duration of the time slice is often made user-tunable by means of the system-generation process. In order to illustrate this important point, round-robin scheduling with three values of time slices is illustrated in Figure 3.12, as applied to our multiprocess example. We use the timing diagrams in Figure 3.12 as a vehicle to discuss the general characteristics of RR scheduling and to point out when some of them are also evident in our example. However, the reader is cautioned against going the opposite way and extrapolating and overgeneralizing the behavior of a single particular example presented here.

The time slice is usually on the order of magnitude of milliseconds—between 1 and 100 ms in many systems—thus allowing on the order of a thousand instructions to the running process. The instructions-per-slice measure is probably more suitable for comparisons of different systems, because the time-duration measure is technology-dependent and may decline with faster CPUs. In general, a shorter time slice should result in better response time. This may be observed in Figure 3.12a, with a time-slice value of .25 time units, where the times elapsed between the occurrence of an event (up-arrows) and its servicing seem to be the shortest for the RR schedulers depicted. Out of necessity, we are restricted to using only qualitative statements, because what is relatively a short time interval in one system may be a long one in another in terms of the number of instructions that may be executed by the CPU within it. By avoiding quantification we are obscuring the fine but important difference between the short and too short.

The relationship between the time slice and the performance of RR scheduling is markedly nonlinear. In other words, reduction of the time slice should not be carried too far in anticipation of better response time. Too short a time slice may result in significant overhead due to the frequent timer interrupts and process switches. For example, during the two execution cycles of all processes marked in Figure 3.12a, RR scheduling with a time slice of .25 time units averages about 16 preemptions and process switches per cycle, including up to four timer interrupts resulting in no rescheduling. Even some of the interrupt-service routines, e.g., LOG, are preempted in the course of their execution. If the overhead of process switching were to be included in the timing diagrams, RR scheduling with a time slice of .25 time units would exhibit much worse behavior than indicated.

By increasing the time slice to .5 time units (Figure 3.12b), the average number of preemptions is reduced to about 11, at the expense of less responsiveness to external events and somewhat lower throughput. When the time slice is set to 1 time unit (Figure 3.12c), the throughput is the best in this example, the average number of preemptions is down to about 8, but the response time becomes worse. Finally, with the time slice set to 2 time units, RR scheduling degenerates to FCFS scheduling (see Figure 3.10), and both throughput and response time deteriorate, with process switches averaging about 8. This example, bearing in mind only qualitative analysis of overhead in terms of counting the number of preemptions and process switches, illustrates the general behavior of round-robin scheduling: too short a time slice results in excessive overhead, whereas too long a time slice degenerates from round-robin to FCFS scheduling as processes surrender control to the OS rather than being preempted by the interval timer.

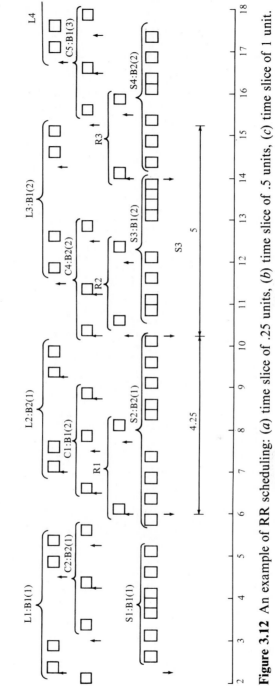

Figure 3.12 An example of **RR** scheduling: (*a*) time slice of .25 units, (*b*) time slice of .5 units, (*c*) time slice of 1 unit.

113

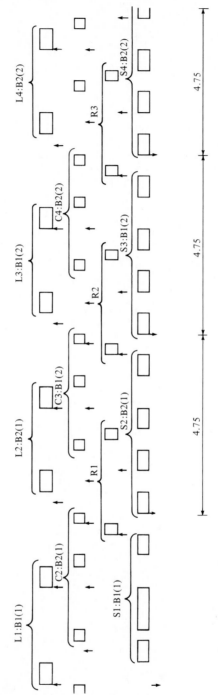
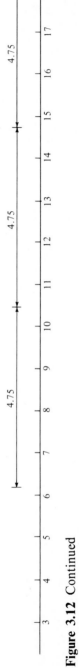

Figure 3.12 Continued

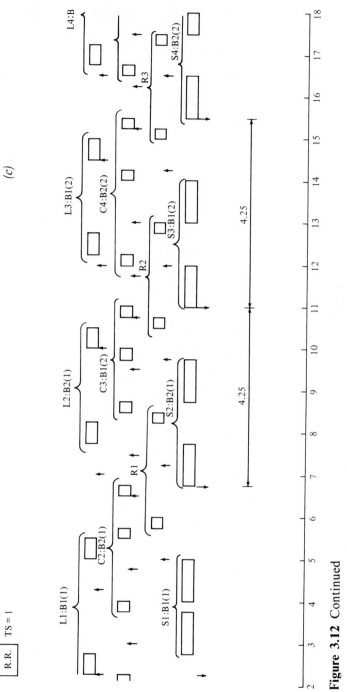

Figure 3.12 Continued

The "optimal" value of the time slice lies somewhere in between, but it is both system-dependent and workload-dependent. For example, the best value of time slice for our example may not turn out to be so good when other processes with different behaviors are introduced in the system, that is, when characteristics of the workload change. This, unfortunately, is often the case with time-sharing systems, where different types of programs may be submitted at different times.

In summary, round-robin scheduling is primarily used in time-sharing and multiuser systems where terminal response time is important. Round-robin scheduling generally discriminates against long noninteractive jobs and depends on the judicious choice of time slice for adequate performance. Duration of a time slice is a tunable system parameter which may be changed during system generation.

3.6.4 Priority-Based Preemptive Scheduling (Event Driven, ED)

Event-driven scheduling is a member of a more general class of priority-based schedulers. In principle, each process in the system is assigned a priority level and the scheduler always chooses the highest-priority ready process. Priorities may be static or dynamic. In either case, their initial values are assigned by the user or the system at the process-creation time. The level of priority may be determined as an aggregate figure on the basis of its initial value, the process's characteristics, resource requirements, and run-time behavior of the process. In this sense, many scheduling disciplines may be regarded as being priority-driven, where the priority of a process represents its likelihood of being scheduled next. Priority-based scheduling may be preemptive or nonpreemptive.

A common problem with priority-based scheduling is a possibility that low-priority processes may be effectively locked out by higher-priority ones. In general, completion of a process within a finite time of its creation cannot be guaranteed with this scheduling policy. In systems where such uncertainty cannot be tolerated, the usual remedy is provided by the so-called *aging priority*. Namely, the priority of each process is gradually increased after the process spends a certain amount of time in the system. Eventually, the older processes attain high priority and are ensured of completion in finite time.

We have already introduced event-driven (ED) scheduling in the earlier sections of this chapter while presenting the multiprocess example. ED scheduling consists of assigning fixed or dynamically varying priorities to all processes and scheduling the highest-priority ready process whenever a significant event occurs. ED scheduling is used in systems where response time, especially to external events, is of utmost importance.

By means of assigning priorities to processes, system programmers can influence the order in which an ED scheduler services coincident external events. As the diagram in Figure 3.5 suggests, ED scheduling is characterized by excellent and predictable response times to high-priority events, low interrupt latency, and high I/O bandwidth. However, low-priority processes may be starved by the high-priority ones. Since it gives little consideration to the resource requirements of processes, event-driven scheduling cannot be expected to excel in general-purpose systems, such as university computing centers, where a large number of user processes are run at the same (default) level of priority.

Another variant of priority-based scheduling is used in the so-called *hard real-time systems*, where each process must be guaranteed execution before expiration of the process's deadline. In such systems, time-critical processes are assumed to be assigned execution-time deadlines. The system workload consists of a combination of periodic processes that are executed cyclically with a known period and aperiodic processes whose arrival times are generally not predictable. An optimal scheduling discipline in such environments is the *earliest-deadline scheduler*, which schedules for execution the ready process with the earliest deadline. Another form of scheduler, called the *least-laxity scheduler* or the *least-slack scheduler*, was also shown to be optimal in single-processor systems. This scheduler selects the ready process with the least difference between its deadline and its computation time. Interestingly, neither of these schedulers is optimal in multiprocessor environments.

3.6.5 Multiple-Level-Queue (MLQ) Scheduling

The scheduling disciplines described so far are more or less suited to particular applications, but with potentially poor performance when applied inappropriately. What is one to use in a mixed system with some time-critical events, a multitude of interactive users, and some very long noninteractive jobs? This description easily fits any university computing center with a variety of devices and terminals (interrupts to be serviced), interactive users (student programs), and simulations (batch jobs). One approach is to combine several scheduling disciplines. A mixed environment may best be serviced by a mix of scheduling disciplines, each charged with what it does best. For example, operating-system processes and device interrupts may be subjected to event-driven scheduling, interactive programs to round-robin scheduling, and batch jobs to FCFS or shortest time next scheduling.

How can this be implemented? The usual practice is to classify the workload according to its characteristics and to maintain separate process queues serviced by different schedulers. This approach is often called *multiple-queues scheduling*. A sample division of the workload might be into system processes, interactive programs, and batch jobs. This would result in the three ready queues depicted in Figure 3.13. A process may be assigned to a specific queue on the basis of its attributes, which may be user- or system-supplied. Each queue may then be serviced by the scheduling discipline best suited to the type of workload it contains. Given a single server (the CPU), some discipline must also be devised for scheduling between queues. Typical approaches are to use absolute-priority or time-slice scheduling with some bias reflecting the relative priority of the processes within specific queues. In the absolute-priority case, the processes from the highest-priority queue, e.g., system processes, are serviced until that queue becomes empty. The scheduling discipline may be event-driven, although FCFS scheduling should not be ruled out given its low overhead and the similar char-

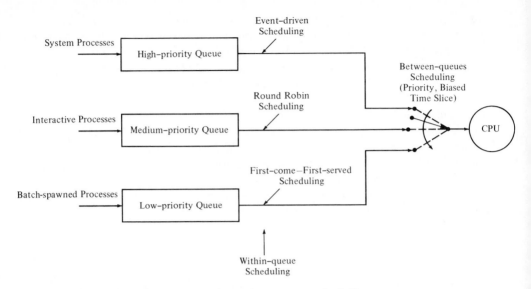

Figure 3.13 An example of multiple-level queue scheduling.

acteristics of processes in that queue. When the highest-priority queue becomes empty, the next queue may be serviced using its own scheduling discipline, e.g., RR scheduling for interactive processes. Finally, when both higher-priority queues become empty, a batch-spawned process may be selected. A lower-priority process may, of course, be preempted by a higher-priority arrival in one of the upper-level queues. This discipline maintains responsiveness to external events and interrupts at the expense of frequent preemptions. An alternative approach is to assign a certain percentage of the CPU time to each queue commensurate with its priority.

Multiple-queues scheduling is a very general discipline that combines the advantages of the "pure" mechanisms discussed earlier. Multiple-level-queue (MLQ) scheduling may also impose the combined overhead of its constituent scheduling disciplines. However, the worst-case behavior of each individual discipline may be offset by assigning classes of processes, those which a particular discipline handles poorly by itself, to a more appropriate queue. Potential advantages of MLQ have been recognized early on by the designers of operating systems that have employed it in the so-called foreground/background (F/B) systems. An F/B system, in its usual form, uses a two-level-queue scheduling discipline. The workload of the system is divided into two queues: a high-priority queue of interactive and time-critical processes (foreground) and a low-priority queue (background) of batch-spawned processes and other processes that do not service external events. The foreground queue is serviced in the event-driven manner, and it can preempt processes executing in the background.

Multiple queues in a system may be used to increase the effectiveness and adaptiveness of scheduling in the form of *multiple-level queues with feedback.*

Rather than having fixed classes of processes allocated to specific queues, the idea is to make traversal of a process through the system dependent upon its run-time behavior. For example, each process may start at the top-level queue. If the process completes within a given time slice, it departs the system after having received the royal treatment. Processes that need more than one time slice to complete may be reassigned by the operating system to a lower-priority queue which gets a lower percentage of the CPU time. If the process is still not finished after having run a few times in that queue, it may be moved to yet another lower-level queue. The idea is to give preferential treatment to short processes and have the resource-consuming ones slowly "sink" into lower-level queues to be used as fillers to keep the CPU utilization high. This philosophy is supported by program-behavior research findings that suggest that the completion rate has a tendency to decrease with attained service. In other words, the more service a process receives, the less likely it is to complete if given a little more service.

On the other hand, if a process surrenders control to the OS before its time slice expires, it may be rewarded by being moved up in the hierarchy of queues. As before, different queues may be serviced using different scheduling disciplines. In contrast to ordinary multiple-level-queue scheduling, the introduction of feedback makes scheduling adaptive and responsive to the actual, measured run-time behavior of processes, as opposed to the fixed classification, which may be defeated by incorrect guessing or abuse of authority. Multiple-level-queue scheduling with feedback is the most general scheduling discipline that may incorporate any or all of the simple scheduling strategies discussed earlier. Its overhead may also combine the elements of each constituent scheduler, in addition to the overhead imposed by the global-queue manipulation and the process-behavior monitoring necessary to implement this scheduling discipline.

3.7 SUMMARY

After exploring the potential for and advantages of concurrent execution of programs and input/output operations in Chapter 2, in Chapter 3 we have shown how multiple processes can be managed at the operating-system level to take advantage of concurrency.

Processes provide a suitable means for informing the operating system about independent activities that may be scheduled for concurrent execution. When user processes are system-defined, as is the case in many time-sharing environments, the operating system exploits the concurrency between programs. Programmer-defined processes can be employed to further improve performance in time-critical applications by exploiting the concurrency possible within a given program or application. This form of operation allows programmers to define process attributes and control and influence the run-time behavior of related processes. For these reasons, portions of operating systems are often implemented as programmer-defined processes. An extensive multiprocess example was presented to illustrate the method of operation, the benefits, and the relative complexity of programmer-defined processes.

A multiprocess operating system monitors and controls the progress of all active processes in the system. The operating system dynamically tracks changes of the global state of the system, which is formed as a collective state of individual processes together with their resource holdings and requirements. This information is used for scheduling and for other resource-allocation and management purposes. Behavior of individual processes is recorded in process control-blocks which are combined into system lists, such as ready and suspended, to monitor the collective state of all active processes.

A multiprogramming OS kernel provides a number of services for process management, such as creation, termination, and periodic execution. These services can be invoked by user processes and by other modules of the operating system. The monitoring of process and system operations and the execution of process-management primitives represent core activities of the OS kernel described as Level 1 in our operating-system hierarchy introduced in Chapter 1. The Ada programming language provides extensive facilities and support for tasks.

An important, although rarely explicit, function of process management is CPU allocation. Three different schedulers may coexist and interact in a complex operating system: a long-term scheduler, a medium-term scheduler, and a short-term scheduler. Of the presented scheduling disciplines, FCFS scheduling is the easiest to implement but a poor performer. SRTN scheduling is optimal but unrealizable. RR scheduling is most popular in time-sharing environments, while ED scheduling is dominant in real-time and other systems with time-critical requirements. MLQ scheduling and its adaptive variant with feedback are the most general scheduling disciplines suitable for complex environments that serve a mixture of processes with different characteristics.

OTHER READING

Ben-Ari (1982) discusses the differences between sequential and concurrent programming and the relationship between concurrency and operating systems. Lorin and Deitel (1981) examine the structure of the operating system by following the flow of a program through the various stages of the development and execution process. Allworth (1981) discusses processes in real-time environments. Denning (1983) provides a concise but thorough introduction to multiprocess operating systems and to some related implementation considerations. The rationale and usage of tasks in Ada are described by Ichbiah et al. (1979). The syntax and semantics of tasks and task-related services in Ada are described in its *Language Reference Manual* (U.S. Department of Defense, 1983).

A discussion of process-management services and their relationship to scheduling is provided by Shaw (1974). Operating-system kernel primitives, including the services for process management, are discussed in Chapter 9, and some of them are implemented in Chapter 10. Other Reading sections of both chapters provide references to literature on both specification and implementation of process-management primitives in various experimental and commercial operating systems. Some experiences with Mesa are discussed by Geschke et al. (1977).

A conceptual introduction to scheduling is provided by Lister (1979) and Peterson and Silberschatz (1983). Analytically oriented textbook treatments are provided by Brinch Hansen (1973) and Habermann (1976). An overview and performance evaluation of several scheduling disciplines are given in Muntz (1975). Deterministic processor scheduling is surveyed by Gonzales (1977). Analytical and theoretical aspects of scheduling are treated by Conway et al. (1967), Coffman and Denning (1973), and Kleinrock (1975). Henry (1984) describes a device scheduler for Unix. Bunt (1976) describes scheduling used in OS/MFT, OS/MVT, Multics, and Unix systems. A practical implementation of a simple scheduler is presented by Comer (1984). The scheduler of the VAX/VMS system is described by Kenah and Bate (1984).

EXERCISES

3.1 Discuss whether there are any advantages to using a multiprocess operating system as opposed to a serial-processing one in a computer system dedicated to serving the needs of a single user. Explain the tradeoffs involved, and describe some representative applications that support your arguments.

3.2 Explain the difference and the relationship between a program and a process. Is this difference important in serial (single-process) operating systems? Why or why not?

3.3 Consider the sequential and multiprocess implementations of the data-acquisition application introduced in Programs 3.1 and 3.2, respectively. Can the I/O-related routines—COLLECT, LOG, and REPORT—use the same method of I/O programming in both implementations? Should they? If interrupt-driven I/O is needed, explain which aspects of interrupt processing should be handled by the underlying operating system and which are best left to user processes. Explain your reasoning.

3.4 Consider the single-buffering, multiprocess implementation of the data-acquisition application whose behavior is depicted by the timing diagram in Figure 3.7. Reassign individual process priorities as follows: (1) COLLECT (highest priority), (2) STAT, (3) REPORT, and (4) LOG (lowest priority). Draw the timing diagram for this situation. Discuss how, if at all, the change in priorities affects the system behavior in terms of throughput, CPU utilization, and interrupt response time.

3.5 Some systems do not allow any form of communication between parent and children processes. Modify Program 3.2 so that this restriction is accommodated while ensuring proper behavior after the system startup.

3.6 In the interprocess signaling mechanism used in Program 3.2, the identities of sender and recipient processes are associated with each specific signal.

Can this explicit naming be avoided at least at the receiving end by allowing a process waiting on one or more signals to proceed whenever the required *number* of signals is received regardless of the identities of their senders? Will such a modified solution be correct?

3.7 Complete the process-state transition diagram given in Figure 3.6 by indicating which system calls, and possibly events, would cause particular state transitions. Add additional transitions if necessary.

3.8 For each process-management system call introduced in Section 3.4, specify whether its processing by the operating system requires invocation of the short-term scheduler. Explain your reasoning.

3.9 Instead of using signals, solve the interprocess synchronization problem posed by the data-acquisition system (the single-buffering version) by using the applicable process-management system calls introduced in Section 3.4. Discuss whether your solution is dependent on certain timing assumptions. If so, state those assumptions and explain which potential timing problems are avoided by their use.

3.10 Which action should the short-term scheduler take when it is invoked but no process is in the ready state? Is this situation possible? If so, suggest a course of action such that further event processing and process-state transitions are not impaired and control over CPU is surrendered to a process as soon as one becomes ready.

3.11 Assume that the three options listed below are being considered to improve performance of a computer system:

(*a*) Divide the workload into n separate queues and have each serviced by a separate CPU whose speed is x MIPS.

(*b*) Keep all workload in a single queue, but have it serviced by n separate CPUs, each of which has a speed of x MIPS, so that the next unit of work is allocated to the first available CPU.

(*c*) Keep all workload in a single queue, but have it serviced by a single, n times faster CPU.

Intuitively argue and rank these options in terms of the average waiting times likely to be experienced by individual programs when FCFS scheduling is used in all cases and no preemption is allowed. It may be helpful to conceptualize these options as a bank where a separate queue of customers is formed in front of each teller, a single queue of customers is formed and serviced on an FCFS basis by all tellers, or a single queue of customers is serviced by a superfast teller.

3.12 An exponential smoothing predictor is proposed to predict CPU execution intervals, so that

$$X_n = aY_{n-1} + (1-a)X_{n-1}$$

where Y_{n-1} is the observed length of the $(n-1)$st execution interval, X_{n-1} is the predictor for the same interval, and a is a number between 0 and 1. Discuss how this predictor changes when different values of parameter a are selected, and argue how effective an SRTN scheduler may be when using such a predictor. Suggest some measures, if any, for coping with situations when the predictor is grossly incorrect.

3.13 A time-sharing operating system uses priority-based scheduling for time-critical processes and round-robin scheduling for interactive user processes. At some point, the hardware is upgraded by replacing the CPU with a functionally equivalent, but twice-faster model. Discuss the changes that different classes of users will experience. Should some parameters of the operating system be changed? If so, which ones and how? Explain the expected system behavior as a result of such changes.

FOUR

INTERPROCESS SYNCHRONIZATION

In previous chapters we discovered that concurrent execution of processes can result in significant performance improvements relative to sequential program execution. System-defined processes are commonly created in general-purpose operating systems to take advantage of the concurrency possible between different programs or applications. When performance is critical, the work may be divided into several programmer-defined cooperating processes to exploit the concurrency possible within a given program or application. However, in order for a group of processes to function properly, their activities must be synchronized in a way that ensures observance of the precedence relationships dictated by the particular problem being solved. Interprocess synchronization is necessary to preserve system integrity and to prevent timing problems resulting from concurrent access to shared resources by multiple processes.

In general, cooperating processes must synchronize with each other whenever they intend to use resources shared by several processes, such as common data structures or physical devices. Examples of interprocess synchronization encountered in previous chapters include implementation of STOP/GO protocols between processes and arbitration of access to shared resources, such as a data buffer. Failure to devise the appropriate synchronization protocols and to enforce their use by each process that uses common resources often results in erratic system behavior and crashes that are notoriously difficult to debug. Concurrency may result in increased productivity when implemented correctly, but it can also degrade reliability when improper interprocess synchronization pollutes the system with elusive timing errors.

This entire chapter is devoted to the study of interprocess synchronization, which is discussed from both the user's and the system designer's point of view. After investigating the nature of the synchronization problem by means of several examples and attempts to solve them, we present an interprocess synchronization mechanism called *semaphores*. In order to assess the feasibility of semaphore implementation, we discuss several hardware mechanisms for mutual exclusion. The chapter concludes with some well-known synchronization problems and their semaphore-based solutions.

4.1 THE INTERPROCESS SYNCHRONIZATION PROBLEM

By definition, all processes executing in a multiprogramming environment compete with other processes for system resources, such as CPU and memory. However, the programmer's awareness and handling of competition among processes in multiprogramming systems depend largely on the nature of the specific process. More specifically, system-defined processes tend to be self-sufficient and separate from other processes, while programmer-defined processes that collectively constitute a single logical application often cooperate and share common resources. Programmers of disjoint processes, as exemplified by student Pascal programs, are rarely explicitly concerned with concurrency. The operating system manages the use of system resources on behalf of such users in a manner that is often transparent to the related processes, and no explicit synchronization statements need to be provided in their source code for that purpose.

In this chapter we are primarily concerned with cooperating processes that typically share some resources that belong to the entire group (family). Given that the operating system does not know, and does not need to know, the precedence relationships within any given collection of processes, the cooperating processes themselves are usually charged with preserving the integrity of the resources belonging to their family. Shared resources may be the family-wide global data or the physical devices that are permanently or temporarily allocated to the application in question. Processes belonging to a family are often loosely coupled, in the sense that they mostly execute on their own, with an occasional need to synchronize with their cooperating peers in order to use the shared resources.

4.1.1 An Example: The Terminal-Handler Problem

Before discussing the synchronization problem and its solutions, let us illustrate by means of an example the nature of the problems that arise when processes are executed concurrently. Program 4.1 (ECHOING) represents a bona fide attempt to solve the character-echoing problem often encountered in terminal drivers. A typical terminal driver accepts data from an input device, usually a keyboard, stores them for subsequent forwarding to the operating system, and outputs (echoes) data to an output device, usually a CRT or a hard copy unit. In practice, terminal drivers can become quite complex when they are

```
program/module echoing;

    . . .

    const
        max = . . .;
    type
        text = array [1..max] of char;
    var
        data : text;
        charstoecho : integer;

    process keyboard;
        var inindex : integer;
            begin
                inindex := 1;
                while true do
                    begin
                        {await_keyboard_interrupt}
                        save_context;
                        data[inindex] := ioport_datain;
                        inindex := inindex + 1;
                        charstoecho := charstoecho + 1;
                        if charstoecho = 1 then enable_out_interrupts;
                        restore_context
                    end {while}
            end; {keyboard}

    process display;
        var outindex : integer;
            begin
                outindex := 1;
                while true do
                    begin
                        {await_display_interrupt}
                        save_context;
                        ioport_dataout_reg := data[outindex];
                        outindex := outindex + 1;
                        charstoecho := charstoecho - 1;
                        if charstoecho = 0 then disable_out_interrupts;
                        restore_context
                    end {while}
            end; {display}

    {parent process}
    begin {echoing}
        disable_interrupts;
        charstoecho := 0;
        initialize_hardware;
        connect_interrupt_vectors(keyboard, out);
        initiate keyboard, display;
        enable_keyboard_interrupts
    end {echoing}
```

Program 4.1 Character echoing

equipped to handle a multitude of different I/O devices and to support a variety of operational modes, such as ASCII or binary data transfers over simplex or duplex communication links. It is a common practice to service a multiterminal environment with a single copy of the terminal driver. The code of such a driver is usually reentrant and capable of concurrently maintaining a number of separate data buffers and communication-line parameters for the individual terminals.

In order to focus on interprocess synchronization, we single out the echoing problem and ignore other complexities of realistic terminal drivers. One important aspect of terminal-driver design is the ability to handle a wide range of input and output data rates produced by or expected by different types of I/O devices that may be attached to a standard terminal interface line. In a particular system-configuration, a standard video terminal may provide the input data from a human user and feed the output to a CRT. In another configuration, the same terminal driver may be required to handle input from a computer-computer communication link, with the output fed to a slower serial printer. Given such potential variations between the relative input and output rates, terminal drivers usually contain an internal buffer to smooth the input-output speed differences while avoiding the loss of data. With buffering, a number of input characters may be accepted and stored before the output device becomes ready to process them. In order to handle both activities at their respective speeds, it is common to provide separate input and output processes that execute concurrently within the terminal driver itself.

Program 4.1 consists of two such cooperating processes, KEYBOARD and DISPLAY, charged with accepting characters typed at the terminal and echoing them on the display. The code and data structures of the two processes are very similar to those presented in Program 2.4. The important difference is that processes in Program 4.1 operate concurrently on the same global buffer, DATA, in order to echo characters as soon as possible following their entry. The KEYBOARD process fills the DATA buffer with input characters, and DISPLAY prints the entries shortly thereafter. For simplicity, the DATA buffer is assumed to be of sufficient capacity to handle the needs of both processes, and error-handling code is omitted.

The nature of the problem implies that the two processes must synchronize with each other. In particular, DISPLAY must never get ahead of KEYBOARD, because it must not attempt to display something that has not yet been entered. Given adequate buffering capacity, KEYBOARD may get ahead as much as necessary at any time and let DISPLAY catch up when it can. In a sense, the KEYBOARD process may be regarded as a producer and the DISPLAY process may be regarded as a consumer of items stored in the DATA buffer. Each process keeps track of its own progress by maintaining a private index to the buffer array, ININDEX and OUTINDEX, respectively. The global variable CHARSTOECHO is used by both processes to keep track of the difference between characters input by KEYBOARD but not yet processed by DISPLAY. Whenever a character is accepted, KEYBOARD increments CHARSTOECHO.

Upon displaying a character, DISPLAY decrements CHARSTOECHO. The contents of this variable is crucial for proper synchronization of the two processes.

The parent process activates input interrupts, and from that point on, the KEYBOARD process remains active and ready to accept input data. Permanent alertness of the input process (KEYBOARD) is necessary to prevent the loss of input characters, which may arrive at any time. DISPLAY, on the other hand, needs to be active only when there is some work for it to do, that is, a positive number of characters is produced but not yet displayed. Program 4.1 relies on the KEYBOARD process to activate the DISPLAY process by means of enabling the output (DISPLAY) interrupts whenever CHARSTOECHO becomes equal to one. Note that output interrupts remain enabled for as long as CHARSTOECHO contains a positive integer, thus keeping DISPLAY active and progressing at the rate of output interrupts. When the last produced character is processed, DISPLAY shuts off the output interrupts. Arrival of one or more input characters causes KEYBOARD to update CHARSTOECHO and to keep the DISPLAY process active until the new batch is processed.

This simple form of STOP/GO protocol implemented by means of interrupts is often used by assembly-language programmers. The problem is that the correctness of this approach tends to be system-dependent in a somewhat indirect manner, which, when overlooked, may cause serious timing errors. To see why this is true, we digress to observe the effects of interleaved execution of concurrent processes in general and of those presented in Program 4.1 in particular at the machine-level.

The KEYBOARD and DISPLAY processes in our example are essentially interrupt-service routines (ISR). One way to code an ISR is to disable interrupt recognition whenever an interrupt request is being processed by the related interrupt-service routine. In such systems, an interrupt-service routine may not be preempted by any other ISR. The reader is invited to verify that the solution proposed in Program 4.1 ensures correct updating of the variable CHARSTOECHO with nonpreemptive execution of the KEYBOARD and DISPLAY processes. However, nonpreemptive ISR execution may lead to loss of data and is thus generally unacceptable for the terminal-driver processes. This may be illustrated by means of Program 4.1 when executing DISPLAY prevents KEYBOARD from responding to an input interrupt in due time.

Because they are aware of this problem, systems programmers typically enable interrupts immediately upon entering a service routine, say, as part of the SAVE_CONTEXT procedure. In order to prevent loss of data, higher priority is normally assigned to the input process. In our example, this would enable KEYBOARD to respond predictably to input interrupts and to preempt the lower-priority DISPLAY if it is active when a character arrives. With the proposed priority assignment, DISPLAY would not be able to preempt KEYBOARD even when an output interrupt occurs. This does not pose a problem, because data to be output are safely stored in the DATA buffer until they are displayed and cannot be lost due to prolonged interrupt latency.

4.1.2 Concurrent Updating of a Shared Variable

While preemptive execution may remedy the character-loss problem, it may also cause timing errors in updating global variables shared by two or more concurrent processes. In order to appreciate fully the effects of preemption, it is useful to think in terms of machine-level operations. For example, a high-level-language (HLL) statement

$$\text{charstoecho} := \text{charstoecho} - 1;$$

may be compiled and executed at run-time as follows:

```
LDA    CHARSTOECHO    ;copy CHARSTOECHO to accumulator,
DEC    ACC            ;decrement accumulator, and
STA    CHARSTOECHO    ;store its value into CHARSTOECHO
```

The coding details are unimportant; the point is that a single HLL statement is often translated into a number of sequential machine operations during the execution of which local working copies of the global variables may be created. These local copies, such as the one stored in the accumulator in the example above, may be temporarily inconsistent with the value of the related global variable. For example, if CHARSTOECHO contains the value 1 prior to execution of the sequence of machine instructions shown, it will (correctly) contain the value 0 when the local working copy is used to update CHARSTOECHO by means of the STA instruction. However, after execution of the DEC instruction, the value of the local copy (accumulator = 0) is different from that of the global copy (CHARSTOECHO = 1) of the variable.

This kind of temporary discrepancy is often encountered during program execution in von Neumann-type architectures, and it is not very important for normal sequential programs whose variables are not shared among concurrent processes. However, temporary inconsistencies of private (local) and public (global) copies of shared variables are one of the primary causes of timing errors in systems where such variables can be accessed concurrently by separate processes. For example, consider the following scenario in the execution of Program 4.1.

Let us assume that the KEYBOARD process is ahead of DISPLAY by one character, so that the contents of the global variable CHARSTOECHO is 1. Suppose that an output interrupt occurs, to which DISPLAY responds by placing the next character in the output port, thus leaving no more to be processed. An input character occurring at that time may cause KEYBOARD to preempt the decrement sequence of DISPLAY, detailed above, between the DEC and STA instructions. This situation is shown in Figure 4.1. KEYBOARD saves the context of the preempted process (DISPLAY), places the new character in the DATA buffer, and updates CHARSTOECHO accordingly, setting it to 2. This is incorrect; the actual difference should now be 1, but KEYBOARD does not know this because KEYBOARD uses the inconsistent global value of CHARSTOECHO. The KEYBOARD process then restores the saved context, and its RTI instruction returns control to DISPLAY exactly at the point of

VARIABLE CHARSTOECHO:

	GLOBAL COPY	LOCAL COPY IN DISPLAY (ACC)
DISPLAY executing	1	0
KEYBOARD preempts DISPLAY, updates CHARSTOECHO	2	0
KEYBOARD completed, DISPLAY resumed	0	0

Figure 4.1 Lost update of a global variable (Program 4.1).

interruption. As a result, the STA instruction is executed and CHARSTOECHO becomes 0, although there is one character (new arrival) to be echoed. DISPLAY then disables output interrupts, awaiting activation by KEYBOARD.

This particular scenario of the execution of two concurrent processes results in a lost update; namely, CHARSTOECHO fails to record the new arrival. A possible consequence is that the last character is placed in the buffer but not echoed. The alarmed user may think that the key was not pressed properly and reenter the character. Our terminal driver may respond by storing the new entry and echoing the previous one. With everything apparently straightened out, the user enters a new character, only to see an extra copy of the previous one displayed. Even assuming no further inconvenient preemptions, the terminal driver would continue to permanently lag with output by one character. The only way to remedy this behavior would be to restart the system, which would also start the ECHOING process with proper initial values, and hope that no nasty preemptions occur thereafter. An even worse behavior may be observed when the KEYBOARD process happens to cycle twice before DISPLAY is resumed in the example above. This would set CHARSTOECHO to 2 before DISPLAY completes its belated update. As a result, Program 4.1 would be lagging with output by two characters behind input. If any of those two characters happens to be the end of line (processing not shown in Program 4.1), the terminal handler might simply hang up and echo nothing until a few characters of a new line are provided. At that point, the previous line of input might be displayed.

It is possible to construct a number of scenarios with perhaps even more unacceptable behavior on the part of the ECHOING process. For our purposes, the "moral" of the presented example is that unrestrained concurrent execution of cooperating processes may result in timing problems detrimental to the system's reliability. The resulting transient and sometimes intermittent errors may account for a sizable amount of the system debugging time. As evidenced by our example, only a specific set of circumstances may expose the incorrect behavior. The sequence of events leading to the problem may occur infrequently, sometimes defying debugging traps for days. For proper analysis, a trace of all machine operations preceding the error may need to be captured in real time and "played back" as needed. In addition, the source listings of all pertinent processes and of the operating system itself may be needed to reconstruct the sequence of events leading to the erroneous system behavior. Common debugging tools, with some exception of the logic analyzers and in-circuit emulators that are rarely available to software developers on larger computer systems, are usually inadequate for collecting these kinds of data. Even with the system trace available, it is often hard just to identify the processes that are directly involved in the mishap. Synchronization errors are often introduced between processes, as opposed to within a single process. For example, neither of our two sample processes, KEYBOARD and DISPLAY, is the sole cause of the described timing problem. In fact, each of them executing sequentially on its own is correct. It is the concurrent execution and the unpredictable interleaving of the two in response to asynchronous events that bring about the problem (sometimes).

4.2 MUTUAL EXCLUSION

All these reasons strongly favor an alternative approach that provides the methodology and tools to deal with interprocess synchronization problems early in the design process rather than attempting to cure the system once it is infested with concurrency-related timing problems.

The character-echoing problem is solvable as approached by manipulating interrupts and by relying on knowledge of the relative priorities and other details of the operation of the two concurrent processes. However, our aim is not to solve a particular problem, but to study the more general synchronization tools that are not dependent on idiosyncrasies and peculiarities of a specific system or a set of processes. In other words, we want a tool that works without modifications regardless of the specific process priorities and that works with an arbitrary number of competing processes. We do not want to be bound to the specific hardware and to its handling of interrupt-enable and interrupt-disable instructions; our tool should be hardware-independent and portable. In fact, we now abandon consideration of interrupts and concentrate on the general synchronization problem among concurrent processes that may not even have anything to do with interrupts.

Let us first analyze why Program 4.1 fails to ensure consistent updating of the shared global variable. The main problem with the ECHOING process is that it allows temporarily inconsistent values of the shared variable to be propagated through the system. The presented approach works when a process is able to complete its update of the shared global variable, thus ensuring that only its consistent values are seen by other processes. Arbitrary process interleaving is possible when consistency of shared variables is ensured. In particular, it does not matter whether KEYBOARD preempts DISPLAY before or after it updates the CHARSTOECHO variable, as long as each process is spared from reading a value invalidated by the update in progress.

In a sense, updating of a shared variable may be regarded as a *critical section* of code, all or none of which must be performed between two points at which other processes can access the shared variable. Only the process executing the critical section should be allowed access to the related shared resource, and all other processes should be prevented from doing so until proper completion of the critical section. This is often referred to as *mutual exclusion*, whereby a single process temporarily prevents all others from using a shared resource during the critical operations that might otherwise adversely affect the system's integrity.

If a shared resource is a variable, mutual exclusion ensures that at most one process at a time has access to it during the critical updates that lead to temporarily inconsistent values. Consequently, other processes see only consistent values of the shared variables. With shared devices, the need for mutual exclusion might be even more obvious when one considers the problems that may be caused by their uncontrolled use: printed output from several programs may be unrecoverably interspersed on a single form or a pipeline valve may be commanded to be both opened and closed at the same time by two concurrent but unsynchronized processes. With these operations performed in a mutually exclusive way, only one program at any point is allowed to control a *serially reusable* device incapable of providing service to more than one user at a time.

Based on our discussion, we may now outline the desirable properties of an acceptable solution to the mutual-exclusion problem. A "good" solution should

- Ensure mutual exclusion between processes accessing the protected shared resource
- Be system-independent and portable, at least at the system-call level
- Allow arbitrary interleaving of contending processes when not accessing the shared resource in order to increase the degree of concurrency in the system
- Make no assumptions about the relative speeds of the contending processes
- Make no assumptions about the relative priorities of the contending processes
- Have no knowledge about the logic and private data structures of the contending processes

Our previous example and discussion should provide the intuitive motivation for the stated requirements. As we learn more about the problem, a few more properties impose themselves, and we note them when appropriate. Let us now attempt to devise a satisfactory mechanism for enforcing mutual exclusion.

4.2.1 The First Algorithm

The simplest way to ensure mutual exclusion is to outlaw concurrency. This approach is too drastic, as it also annihilates all performance improvements possible with concurrent execution of programs. What we really want to do is to grant temporarily to a process that must complete a critical section exclusive access to a shared resource. A process that wishes to enter a critical section would first have to negotiate with all interested parties in order to make sure that no other conflicting activity is in progress and that all concerned processes are aware of the imminent temporary unavailability of the resource. Only upon making sure that the consensus is reached should the winning process begin executing the critical section of code. Once completed, the process should somehow inform other contenders that the resource is available and another round of negotiations may be started.

Let us attempt to put these ideas into practice. Consider a simple system consisting of only two processes that share a common resource accessed within a critical section in order to maintain the system's integrity. Both processes are cyclic, and each of them also executes some code other than the critical section.

Program 4.2 contains the code of the two processes, with a simple provision for mutual exclusion. A global variable TURN is used to control access to an unspecified shared resource, which may be a data structure, a piece of code, or a physical device. TURN can assume only one of the two values, PROC1 or PROC2, to indicate the identity of the process allowed to enter its critical section. Each process dutifully refrains from entering the critical section when

```
program/module mutex1;

    . . .

  type
    who = (proc1, proc2);
  var
    turn : who;

  process p1;
    begin
      while true do
        begin
          while turn = proc2 do {keeptesting};
          critical_section;
          turn := proc2;
          other_p1_processing
        end {while}
    end; {p1}

  process p2;
    begin
      while true do
        begin
          while turn = proc1 do {keeptesting};
          critical_section;
          turn := proc1;
          other_p2_processing
        end {while}
    end; {p2}

  {parent process}
  begin {mutex1}
    turn := ...;
    initiate p1, p2
  end {mutex1}
```

Program 4.2 Mutual exclusion - algorithm 1

the turn belongs to the other. For example, process P1 busily loops until the variable TURN becomes PROC1, and only then does it enter its critical section. This loop represents the negotiation before use of the shared resource. When it completes its critical section, process P1 sets TURN to PROC2 and thus allows process P2 to use the resource next. The code of the process P2 is symmetrical, so process P2 follows the same protocol in acquiring and releasing the resource.

The first important question is whether this solution ensures mutual exclusion between the two processes? The answer is affirmative. Informally, the control variable TURN has only one value at any time (assuming that the potential hardware transient states are not visible to CPU read and write cycles). Consequently, only one process at a time can have its turn indicated. If the other process wishes to access the shared resource at that time, it is kept waiting in the busy loop until the current owner completes its critical section and then updates TURN.

However, this solution is not without problems. From the aesthetic and safety point of view, the criticism is that it relies on contending processes knowing the identity of each other. The techniques of modular and structured programming favor restricting access to information on a "need to know" basis. The basic idea is that a process cannot erroneously or maliciously hurt the others that it does not know about, say, by aborting or suspending them without reason. Another practical consideration giving rise to this approach is the program-development process, especially when a large number of processes encoded as separate modules are involved. If mutual exclusion requires a process to know the names of all its competitors, any restructuring of programs resulting in different divisions of labor into processes would necessitate updating of the turn-assignment code of all constituent modules, including the ones to which no modifications need otherwise be made. This would be extremely inconvenient and error-prone in large programming projects, where such changes may involve a number of programmers and project administrators.

A much more serious problem is that the solution proposed in Program 4.2 is not really free from assumptions about the relative speeds of the two processes. In fact, in Program 4.2, strict turn-taking is imposed between the two processes. For example, starting with TURN set to PROC1, the two processes can only execute in alternating sequence:

$$P1, P2, P1, P2, P1, P2, \ldots$$

Turn-taking actually forces the two processes to work at the collective speed of the slower one. In terms of the terminal handler, this would imply that KEYBOARD can never get ahead of DISPLAY by more than one character, thus defying the fundamental purpose of that program in the first place. The cause of this unfortunate behavior is that each process explicitly assigns the turn to the other. This is yet another undesirable consequence of forcing synchronizing processes to know too much about each other. We may now disqualify this approach to mutual exclusion on the grounds of failing to meet the requirements of a satisfactory solution. But before we do so, let us point out another of its problems that adds a new requirement to our list of desirables.

What happens in Program 4.2 when either process crashes or terminates outside its critical section? Let us assume that process P1 crashes somewhere in its noncritical code, OTHER_P1_PROCESSING. After exiting the critical section, it would have set TURN to PROC2, thus allowing process P2 to enter its critical section when needed. Once out of critical section, process P2 sets TURN back to PROC1, as usual, but process P1 is no longer active, so it can never give the turn back to process P2. This blocks further execution of process P2 as well, because it busily loops in vain, awaiting its turn to access a shared resource that is actually free. It is obviously unacceptable to allow the malfunction or termination of a single process to incapacitate all other processes that share resources with it. We must, therefore, add another requirement to our list in order to provide a satisfactory solution to the mutual-exclusion problem:

- Guarantee that the crashing or terminating of any process outside its critical section does not affect the ability of other contending processes to access the shared resource.

But what about a process crashing within the critical section itself? In terms of the negotiation protocol outlined at the beginning of this section, the crashed process is not able to announce that the shared resource is available, and all contending processes thus remain unable to access it. In general, operating-system mechanisms for mutual exclusion rarely provide for guarding against this possibility. Why? If a process indeed crashes inside a critical section, there is no easy way of knowing whether the guarded shared resource is left in a consistent state or not. In all likelihood it is not, otherwise the enclosing critical section would not be needed in the first place. With the resource probably left in an inconsistent state, allowing other processes to subsequently access it could conceivably pollute the rest of the system. For this reason, we opt to allow the crashing process to take the resource with it as well. This implies that a satisfactory solution to the mutual-exclusion problem may assume that each process completes its critical section in finite time.

Being aware that critical sections are indeed critical, we may require processes to keep them as short as possible. Better yet, we may provide the code to manipulate the shared resource in the form of well-tested and trusted procedures supplied as a part of the system. Application processes would then only have to negotiate the order of invocation of these, but once inside a critical section, it would be quite likely that no crashes occur. For added safety, the operating system might detect failures by means of time-outs on critical sections and then activate whatever remedial procedures may be appropriate.

In large databases this approach may not be satisfactory. Namely, a process crashing during an update could lock out the system's most valuable resource, the database itself. In an online banking or reservation system this could be disastrous. Such systems guard themselves by maintaining so-called *audit trails*, where values of the relevant shared variables are recorded prior to an update. If an update fails, the related process may be aborted or restarted, but its partial and probably inconsistent update is undone by restoring the logged values; that is, the system is restored to the consistent state as of before the update. Audit trails are of considerable interest in the design of database systems, but we will ignore them in our further discussion of synchronization problems and retain the assumption of no failures within critical sections.

4.2.2 The Second Algorithm

Program 4.3 is another attempt to solve the mutual-exclusion problem that builds on the additional insights gained from analyzing the deficiencies of Program 4.2.

program/module *mutex2*;

　. . .

var
　p1using, p2using : boolean;

process *p1*;
　begin
　　while *true* **do**
　　　begin
　　　　while *p2using* **do** {*keeptesting*};
　　　　p1using := true;
　　　　critical_section;
　　　　p1using := false;
　　　　other_p1_processing
　　　end {*while*}
　　end; {*p1*}

process *p2*;
　begin
　　while *true* **do**
　　　begin
　　　　while *p1using* **do** {*keeptesting*};
　　　　p2using := true;
　　　　critical_section;
　　　　p2using := false;
　　　　other_p2_processing
　　　end {*while*}
　　end; {*p2*}

{*parent process*}
begin {*mutex2*}
　p1using := false;
　p2using := false;
　initiate *p1, p2*
end {*mutex2*}

Program 4.3 Mutual exclusion - algorithm 2

In order to avoid strict turn-taking and overdependence on other processes, Program 4.3 introduces two flags, P1USING and P2USING. Each process updates its own flag to indicate its current activity or intentions regarding use of the shared resource and only reads the flag of the other process when necessary for synchronization. Otherwise, the same basic protocol outlined at the beginning of this section is followed. For example, when process P1 wishes to enter its critical section, it first checks whether the resource is being used by another process by means of inspection of the flag P2USING. If the flag is set, indicating that another process is in the critical section (process P2 in our example), process P1 busily tests the flag until the flag is reset to indicate availability of the shared resource. Process P1 then sets its own flag, P1USING, to inform all other contenders that it is entering its critical section. Following its completion, process P1 resets P1USING, thus making the resource available again. Process P2 uses a symmetrical code and follows the same synchronization protocol.

This program is much safer than the previous one because each process updates only its own flag. As a result, crashing of any process outside of critical section, after having updated the related flag accordingly, does not pose a problem. The turn-taking restriction is also removed, and one process may execute its critical section an arbitrary number of times in a row without depending on its partner to reciprocate. The competing processes are much less tightly coupled, a definite improvement in the right direction. Unfortunately, this program removes too many restrictions, including the essential one that at most one process may be in its critical section at any time.

Consider, for example, a scenario where both processes are outside of their critical sections and both flags indicate that the resource is free. Suppose that both processes decide to enter their respective critical sections at about the same time. Process P1 inspects P2USING, finds it false, sets the flag P1USING, and enters the critical section. Now suppose that process P2 briefly preempts P1 after process P1 has inspected P2USING (finding it false) but before P1USING is set to true. Process P2 is misled into concluding that the resource is available, sets P2USING, and proceeds to its critical section. If process P1 is resumed at this point, it is already past the test loop on P2USING, so P1 sets P1USING and also proceeds to its critical section.

With two processes in the critical section at the same time, Program 4.3 fails to satisfy the mutual-exclusion requirement under the assumption of arbitrary interleaving of competing processes. The reason is, once again, that a process inspects a variable (PxUSING) and then makes a decision based on the value read without making certain that no invalidating intervening updates have been applied in the meantime. In particular, without preventing modifications to P2USING after process P1 inspects it but before P1USING is set accordingly, P1 can never be sure that P2USING has not been modified in the meantime, thus rendering its decision inappropriate. In other words, these operations should also be enclosed within a critical section in order to prevent harmful interleaving.

4.2.3 The Third Algorithm

Program 4.4 copes with this problem by preceding the testing of another process's flag by setting of it's own flag first. For example, process P1 first sets P1USING and then tests P2USING to determine what to do next. When it finds P2USING to be false, process P1 may safely proceed to the critical section knowing that no matter how the two processes may be interleaved, process P2 is certain to find P1USING set and to stay away from the resource. This single change ensures mutual exclusion while preserving all other nice properties of Program 4.3. So does this conclude our quest? Unfortunately, it does not.

Consider a scenario where process P1 wishes to enter the critical section and sets P1USING to indicate the fact. If process P2 wishes to enter the critical

program/module *mutex3*;

  . . .

var
  p1using, p2using : *boolean*;

process *p1*;
  begin
    while *true* **do**
      begin
        p1using := *true*;
        while *p2using* **do** {*keeptesting*};
        critical_section;
        p1using := *false*;
        other_p1_processing
      end {*while*}
    end; {*p1*}

process *p2*;
  begin
    while *true* **do**
      begin
        p2using := *true*;
        while *p1using* **do** {*keeptesting*};
        critical_section;
        other_p2_processing
      end {*while*}
    end; {*p2*}

{*parent process*}
begin {*mutex3*}
  p1using := *false*;
  p2using := *false*;
  initiate *p1, p2*
end {*mutex3*}

Program 4.4 Mutual exclusion - algorithm 3

section at the same time and preempts process P1 just before P1 tests P2USING, process P2 may set P2USING and start looping while it waits for P1USING to become false. When control is eventually returned to process P1, it finds P2USING set and starts looping while it waits for P2USING to become false. And so both processes are looping forever, each awaiting the other one to clear the way. Program 4.4 thus carries mutual exclusion too far and ends up with total exclusion and both processes locked out. In order to outlaw this kind of behavior, we must add another requirement to our list:

- When more than one process wishes to enter the critical section, the decision to grant entrance to one of them must be made in finite time.

4.3 SEMAPHORES

Our discussion should indicate that the mutual-exclusion problem is not a trivial one. The Dutch mathematician Dekker is believed to be the first to solve the mutual-exclusion problem. His solution, presented in Program 4.14 as part of Exercise 4.3, incorporates elements of the solutions attempted in the three programs just presented. Although ingenious, Dekker's solution in its original form works for only two processes and cannot be easily extended beyond that number. This restriction does not diminish the theoretical significance of Dekker's solution, but it tends to limit its direct applicability in practice. Dijkstra's proposal of a mechanism for mutual exclusion among an arbitrary number of processes, called *semaphore*, gained wide acceptance and found its way into a number of experimental and commercial operating systems.

4.3.1 Semaphore Definition and Busy-Wait Implementation

A semaphore mechanism basically consists of the two primitive operations *signal* and *wait* (originally defined as P and V by Dijkstra) that operate on a special type of semaphore variable s. The semaphore variable can assume nonnegative integer values and, except possibly for initialization, may be accessed and manipulated only by means of SIGNAL and WAIT operations. The two primitives take one argument each, the semaphore variable, and may be defined as follows:

wait(s); decrements the value of its argument semaphore s as soon as it would become nonnegative. Completion of the WAIT operation, once the decision is made to decrement its argument semaphore, must be indivisible.

signal(s); increments the value of its argument semaphore s as an indivisible operation.

The logic of busy-wait versions of WAIT and SIGNAL operations is given in Program 4.5a and b, respectively.

A semaphore whose variable is allowed to take on only the values of 0 and 1 is called a *binary semaphore*. The variable of a *general semaphore* may take on any nonnegative integer value. When supported, semaphore operations

---

wait(s):   **while** *not* ($s > 0$) **do** {*keeptesting*};
$s := s - 1$;

  a) Wait Operation

signal(s): $s := s + 1$;

  b) Signal Operation

Program 4.5 A busy-wait version of wait and signal

and declarations of semaphore variables are usually provided in the form of operating-system calls or as built-in functions and types in a system implementation language.

Program 4.6 contains the code for three processes that are sharing a common resource accessed from within critical sections. A binary semaphore MUTEX is used to protect the shared resource by enforcing its use in a mutually exclusive manner. Each process ensures the integrity of its critical section by opening it with a WAIT operation and closing with a SIGNAL operation on the related semaphore, MUTEX in our example. An arbitrary number of concurrent processes might join in and share the same resource safely, provided each of them uses the WAIT and SIGNAL operations as indicated.

In order to illustrate the behavior and functioning of semaphores, one possible scenario of the run-time behavior of the three processes introduced in Program 4.6 is shown in Figure 4.2. Different columns in Figure 4.2 show the activities of each individual process, the value of the semaphore variable *after* the actions indicated on the same line are completed, the identity of the process within the critical sections, and the list of processes attempting to enter the critical section.

Before activating the three processes, the parent process in Program 4.6 initializes the semaphore variable MUTEX to 1 to indicate the availability of the shared resource. The corresponding state of the system is depicted as time M1 in Figure 4.2. At time M2, all processes are active and wish to enter their respective critical sections. To that end, each process executes its WAIT statement. In order to emphasize the dynamics, we are pretending that the processes are executing in a fully parallel fashion. This would not be the case in uniprocessor systems, where processes are normally interleaved. However, with the time frame extended slightly around each point depicted in Figure 4.2, and assuming arbitrary order of interleaving, events depicted in Figure 4.2 may become plausible in both uniprocessor and multiprocessor systems.

Looking back at time M2, we can see that the semaphore variable is decremented to 0, indicating that a process has been granted permission to enter its critical section. Line M3 reveals that P1 is the winner. However, a more important thing here is to convince ourselves that the semaphore indeed admits no more than a single process to the critical sections.

As Program 4.6 suggests, all three WAIT operations in Figure 4.2, time M2, start with testing the semaphore variable in an attempt to decrement it and to proceed to their critical sections. One of the processes (the semaphore rules do not specify which) succeeds, and let us assume that it is P1. The WAIT activated on P1's behalf, after having read the value of MUTEX as 1, must immediately seize the semaphore variable and prevent the other concurrent WAIT operations from reading it until decrementing of MUTEX to 0 is completed. This is the motivation for the partial indivisibility required in implementing the WAIT operation. Note that the total indivisibility of a WAIT operation is neither required nor desirable. In particular, a completely indivisible WAIT looping on a busy semaphore would prevent all other primitives, including SIGNAL operations, from accessing the

program/module *smutex*;

    . . .

  var *mutex* : *semaphore*; {*binary*}

  process *p1*;
    begin
      while *true* **do**
        begin
          wait(*mutex*);
          critical_section;
          signal(*mutex*);
          other_p1_processing
        end {*while*}
    end; {*p1*}

  process *p2*;
    begin
      while *true* **do**
        begin
          wait(*mutex*);
          critical_section;
          signal(*mutex*);
          other_p2_processing
        end {*while*}
    end; {*p2*}

  process *p3*;
    begin
      while *true* **do**
        begin
          wait(*mutex*);
          critical_section;
          signal(*mutex*);
          other_p3_processing
        end {*while*}
    end; {*p3*}

  {*parent process*}
  begin {*smutex*}
    mutex := 1; {*free*}
    initiate *p1*, *p2*, *p3*
  end {*smutex*}

Program 4.6 Mutual exclusion with semaphores

TIME	PROCESS STATUS/ACTIVITY			MUTEX: 1 = FREE 0 = BUSY	PROCESSES: IN CRITICAL SECTION; ATTEMPTING TO ENTER
	P1	P2	P3		
M1	—	—	—	1	— ; —
M2	wait (mutex)	wait (mutex)	wait (mutex)	0	— ; P1,P2,P3
M3	critical_section	waiting	waiting	0	P1 ; P2,P3
M4	signal (mutex)	waiting	waiting	1	— ; P2,P3
M5	other_p1_proc.	critical_section	waiting	0	P2 ; P3
M6	wait (mutex)	critical_section	waiting	0	P2 ; P3,P1
M7	waiting	signal (mutex)	waiting	1	— ; P3, P1
M8	critical_section	other_p2_proc.	waiting	0	P1 ; P3

Figure 4.2 A scenario of execution of Program 4.6.

related semaphore variable. As a result, the guarded resource may never be freed and allocated to another requestor.

After regaining control from its completed WAIT, process P1 enters the critical section and uses the shared resource during the subsequent time slot, M3, depicted in Figure 4.2. Process P1 subsequently relinquishes the resource, leaves its critical section, and announces the fact by executing the SIGNAL operation. The two remaining waiting processes, P2 and P3, have an equal chance of obtaining the next permission. In our sample scenario, process P2 becomes the next to enter its critical section and to use the shared resource.

At time M7, process P2 releases the resource and the semaphore variable MUTEX becomes 1. At this time, the two other processes, P1 and P3, are attempting to obtain permission to use the resource, and the proposed definition of semaphore gives them an equal opportunity to succeed. In Figure 4.2, it is assumed that process P1 wins the contest, although P3 never got the chance to use the resource.

4.3.2 Some Properties and Characteristics of Semaphores

A consequence of not imposing any ordering among the waiting processes is the possibility that a process may be locked out due to contention with others. This situation, when some processes are making progress toward their completion but one or more processes are locked out of the resource, is called *indefinite postponement*. This phenomenon is also known as *livelock*, and the affected processes are referred to as being *starved*. In order to prevent livelocks, actual semaphore implementations often enforce some servicing discipline among the waiting processes. Note, however, that system implementors are neither required nor hindered in doing so by the definition of semaphore.

The choice of servicing discipline is very important, because a biased one may enable a group of processes to conspire against others and to permanently usurp the resource. For example, assuming that the process priority is a criterion for choosing a waiting process in Figure 4.2 and that processes P1 and P2 have higher priority than P3, a continuation of the example may easily be constructed such that P3 *never* obtains the resource. If desired, such starvation of processes may be prevented by adding a new requirement to our list:

● A request to enter a critical section must be granted in finite time.

Keeping in mind our assumption that each process spends a finite time executing its critical section, this requirement can easily be met by using the first-in-first-out (FIFO) discipline when choosing among the waiting processes. FIFO servicing of the waiting processes is regarded as the strongest implementation of semaphores.

Our discussion indicates that semaphores are a relatively simple but powerful mechanism for ensuring mutual exclusion among concurrent processes accessing a shared resource. Instead of users attempting to devise their own synchronization protocols—a difficult and treacherous task, as we discovered earlier—semaphores are provided as a tool by the system implementor. Users are just required to help control access to shared resources by following the standard simple protocol. In particular, each participating process is expected to be aware of possible contention over a specific resource and to enclose statements that may be adversely affected by interleaved execution of processes within a WAIT-SIGNAL pair operating on the related semaphore variable.

When semaphores are used, modifications of code or restructurings of processes and modules do not generally necessitate changes in other processes, even if they belong to the same family and share the same resources. The reason for this may be deduced from Program 4.6, which indicates that competing processes do not have to know even the number of other contenders, much less their identities or internal implementation details. In addition, semaphores are very convenient for interprocess synchronization by means of exchange of signals. Signaling among processes is an important feature in a multiprocess environment, and we have already encountered it on several occasions in earlier chapters where interrupt-enable/disable mechanisms and somewhat vaguely defined signals were used for the purpose (e.g., the multiprocess example in Chapter 3).

A semaphore variable is usually created to guard a specific resource from concurrency-related timing errors. This is accomplished by allowing at most one process at a time to access the shared resource. The resulting run-time serialization of contending processes raises the question of the degree of parallelism between concurrent processes that is attainable in systems which rely on semaphores for mutual exclusion.

The impact of serialization can be controlled to a large extent by varying the granularity of individual semaphores. At one extreme, the finest granularity is accomplished by dedicating a separate semaphore to guard each specific shared resource. In this way, the likelihood of conflict over any given resource is minimized and confined only to the subset of active processes that use that specific resource. The price to be paid includes the storage overhead for maintenance of a potentially large number of semaphores and the run-time overhead of processing numerous WAIT and SIGNAL operations.

On the other hand, granularity of semaphores can be made coarse by having each semaphore guard a collection of shared resources. This approach reduces the storage and run-time overhead at the expense of an increased number of conflicts and a potential forced serialization of processes that do not have any resources in common. In other words, coarse granularity of semaphores may result in a reduction of parallelism beyond what is required by the nature of the problem being solved. The tradeoff of coarse versus fine granularity of semaphores must be analyzed and options evaluated in order to arrive at a satisfactory compromise for each particular application.

4.4 HARDWARE SUPPORT FOR MUTUAL EXCLUSION

After discovering the dangers of concurrent programming, the need for and significance of semaphores become quite obvious. Semaphores solve the mutual-exclusion problem in a simple and natural way from the user's point of view and at the same time boast a number of nice properties. However, the definition of semaphores given in the previous section relies on somewhat peculiar indivisibility requirements in order to function properly. Before discussing potential uses of semaphores in more detail, it seems reasonable to first establish the feasibility of their implementation and to make sure that the problem is not just simply delegated to the next-lower implementation layer, with perhaps the same difficulties ultimately reincarnated at the hardware level. Our goal in sections that follow is to investigate whether the implementation of mutual exclusion in general, and of semaphores in particular, is feasible at the hardware level and, if so, if it can be made efficient.

4.4.1 Pessimistic and Optimistic Concurrency Control

Before discussing the specific hardware approaches, let us point out that they may be generally categorized as being essentially pessimistic or optimistic. *Pessimistic* approaches tend to assume the worst possible case and to defend against it by rather austere measures that often end up limiting concurrency. In terms of updating a shared global variable or a semaphore variable, a typical pessimistic solution may act as follows:

1. Block everything that could possibly interfere, so that nothing will interfere (this often results in innocent victims among the disjointed processes).
2. Update the global variable.
3. Unblock the part of the system blocked in Step 1.

In contrast, *optimistic* approaches are based on the assumption that none or few conflicts are likely to be experienced by any particular user of the shared resource, and consequently, they often allow for rather permissive referencing of shared data. When conflicts do occur, optimistic approaches maintain system integrity by discarding updates invalidated by contending concurrent processes. This usually implies partial rolling back of the system state and redoing of some of the affected updates. For example, a typical optimistic solution may be structured as follows:

1. Read the value of the global variable and prepare the tentative local update based on that value (the global variable remains accessible to other users).
2. Compare the current value of the global variable to the value used to prepare the tentative update. If the value of the global variable is unchanged, apply the tentative local update to the global variable. Otherwise (the global variable

has been modified in the interim, thus obsoleting the prepared update), discard the tentative update and repeat from Step 1.

Thus the optimistic approach to concurrency control neither requires nor enforces serialization of processes that access the global variable. There is no notion of a critical section, and mutual exclusion is not required, except for the very brief comparison of the local and global copies of the shared variable. The price to be paid is the overhead of recalculations necessary when tentative updates are invalidated due to interference from other concurrent processes.

The relative merits of these two approaches obviously depend on the actual frequency of conflicts in any given system. When conflicts are relatively infrequent, the pessimistic approach unnecessarily penalizes all users by over-restricting concurrency. With a high rate of conflicts over shared resources, the optimistic approach may incur significant overhead in terms of wasted work to prepare tentative updates that are made obsolete due to interference and must be discarded.

The frequency of conflicts in a given system typically varies in some functional relation to the workload. In general, this is difficult to measure or to predict reliably. Research results seem to suggest that the frequency of conflicts in database systems is relatively low, thus encouraging optimistic approaches to concurrency control. In general-purpose operating systems, the frequency of conflicts may be quite high among the processes using scarce resources, such as certain I/O devices. For more plentiful resources, the frequency of conflicts depends on a number of factors—including the specific requirements of the set of active processes (time-varying), the granularity of the semaphores, and the prevailing approach to concurrency control (pessimistic or optimistic). In general, pessimistic concurrency control tends to reduce parallelism, but its overhead is not very sensitive to dynamic variations in the frequency of conflicts. On the other hand, optimistic concurrency control has a higher potential for parallelism, but its run-time overhead tends to grow with the increasing frequency of conflicts. This behavior can result in thrashing, as more and more tentative updates have to be discarded and recomputed when interference among concurrent processes increases.

In the following sections we discuss the typical machine-level implementations of mutual exclusion in general and of semaphores in particular. We also argue the applicability of each particular system to multiprocessor environments where global variables may reside in shared memory and may be accessed by truly parallel processes executing on different processors.

4.4.2 Disable/Enable Interrupts

Given the availability of interrupt-disable/enable (DI/EI) instructions in virtually all commercial computers, this is probably the most widely applicable way of implementing mutual exclusion. The basic idea is quite simple, and it follows the principle that the shared resource must exclusively be obtained by the process wishing to enter its critical section and subsequently released for the use by the others. This may be accomplished by the following sequence:

```
DI                ;disable interrupts
critical_section  ;use guarded resource
EI                ;enable interrupts
```

The intent of disabling interrupts is to prevent any interference during execution of the critical section. Interrupt disabling generally defers recognition of external events that may cause another process to run and access the same resource and also temporarily disables the scheduler in order to prevent preemptions due to rescheduling. In effect, whenever a process is in its critical section, it forces the whole system into a state of suspended animation. Thus DI/EI is clearly a pessimistic method of concurrency control.

Simplicity and wide applicability are among the few good things to be said about this approach. It is too pessimistic in that it outlaws concurrency altogether whenever a process is using a shared resource. This disables not only competitors that could potentially access the resource, but also all other processes that may have nothing in common with the blocking process.

This approach can also be dangerous and unreliable because interrupt-disable/enable instructions, potentially a lethal weapon in the hands of application programmers, must be made available for synchronization purposes. For example, the sequence

```
DI
HALT
```

swiftly brings down many a multiprogramming operating system.

Even when users are applying the DI/EI mechanism correctly, they may adversely affect the functioning of the operating system by indirectly suspending the scheduler and violating the assumed priority scheme by having a lower-priority process hold back a higher-priority one. Finally, this approach is unsuitable for multiprocessor systems with shared memory because the DI/EI instructions affect only the issuing processor and cannot prevent interference from processes running on other processors.

An alternative to direct use of enable/disable instructions for mutual exclusion is to implement semaphore WAIT and SIGNAL operations at the system level by employing the DI/EI mechanism to enforce the indivisibility requirements of semaphores. In this way, the improper and dangerous use of interrupt-manipulation instructions can be restricted to system routines and taken away from users. Conflicting processes may then rely on the standard semaphore protocols for guarding their critical operations. On the negative side, user processes are required to invoke WAIT and SIGNAL, which are part of the operating system. This imposes the overhead of process switching which is not incurred by the direct DI/EI approach.

4.4.3 Test-and-Set Instruction

The test-and-set (TS) instruction is intended for direct hardware support of mutual exclusion. Test-and-set is designed for resolving conflicts among contending processes by making it possible for only one process to receive a permit to enter its critical section. The basic idea is to set the global control variable to FREE when the guarded shared resource is available. Each process wishing to access the resource is supposed to obtain a permit to do so by executing the TS instruction with the related control variable as the operand. When several concurrent processes are competing, the TS instruction ensures that only one of them proceeds to use the resource. In principle, the TS instruction takes one operand, the address of the control variable or a register that may act as a semaphore, and works as follows:

1. Compare the value of the OPERAND to BUSY, and set the condition codes to reflect the outcome.
2. Set the OPERAND to BUSY.

Both the preceding steps are performed as a single, indivisible operation. The WAIT operation on the semaphore variable S may be implemented as the following procedure when TS is available in the instruction set of the supporting hardware (S is passed by the caller as an argument of WAIT):

```
WAIT_S    TS        S          ;request exclusive access
          BNFREE    WAIT_S     ;repeat until granted
          RETURN               ;proceed to critical section
```

To see how this approach works, assume that several processes are executing WAIT_S in an attempt to access the resource protected by the global variable S. In this description, we follow the common implementation of the TS instruction, where availability of the resource is indicated by S being set to 0 (FREE), whereas S set to 1 denotes the BUSY state. Let us also assume that the resource is initially available and that S accordingly contains the value 0.

When the TS instruction is executed on behalf of the first process, the global variable S is set to 1 (BUSY). However, the condition codes indicate that the value of S was 0 (FREE) prior to the execution of TS, so the resource may be accessed. In terms of the presented sequence of instructions, the branch back to WAIT_S (BNFREE stands for Branch if Not FREE) is not taken. All other processes, upon executing the TS instruction, find S set to 1 and continue looping. As usual, the process using the resource is supposed to reset the control variable S when finished. When S is reset, one of the processes looping on S gains access rights by observing S to have the value 0. The indivisible part of TS makes certain that only one among several concurrent processes, no matter how they may be interleaved, obtains the desired permit. As with the original definition of semaphores, TS imposes no ordering upon the waiting processes.

The essence of the TS instruction is the indivisible testing of the global variable and its subsequent setting to BUSY. Therefore, other instructions that allow the contents of a variable to be tested and subsequently set as an indivisible operation are also candidates for implementation of mutual exclusion. Examples include INCREMENT MEMORY and SWAP MEMORY AND REGISTER, provided that the read-modify-write cycle of these instructions is indivisible.

IBM series 360 computers were the first to include the TS instruction in hardware, allegedly under pressure from operating-system designers. Virtually all commercial computer architectures designed since that time include some explicit hardware provisions for implementing mutual exclusion—in the form of a TS instruction or one of its functional equivalents.

The TS instruction, with proper implementation, may also be used in multiprocessor systems. To understand the need for the specific hardware support for TS, consider a multiprocessor system with a certain amount of memory shared by and accessible to several processors. Let us assume that several concurrent processes, possibly executing on different processors, share a serially reusable resource whose accessing is controlled by a global variable which resides in shared memory.

If updating of the shared variable is performed by means of the TS instruction, as defined earlier, mutual exclusion may be violated by concurrent processes executing at different processors. In particular, our definition of the TS instruction requires at least two memory cycles to execute, in addition to the memory cycles needed to fetch the instruction itself. One memory cycle (READ) is necessary to compare the value of the global control variable to BUSY. The second cycle (WRITE) is required to set the global variable to BUSY. In a uniprocessor system, these two cycles are executed as a single, indivisible read-modify-write memory cycle.

In multiprocessor systems, the arbitration of access to shared memory is commonly performed on a memory-cycle basis. In particular, each processor may be guaranteed an undisturbed READ or WRITE cycle. Given that execution of the TS instruction requires two such cycles, it is conceivable that another processor's TS instruction may intervene between the READ and WRITE cycles of a TS instruction in progress at a given processor. If both TS instructions have the same target operand in shared memory whose value happens to be FREE prior to their execution, two processes may be allowed to use the shared resource, thus violating the mutual-exclusion requirement.

The problem here is essentially the same old issue of allowing temporarily inconsistent values (global variable after being inspected by the first TS instruction but before being set to BUSY) to be perceived by the rest of the system; only this time the problem manifests itself at a much lower implementation level. One way to make the TS instruction function properly in a multiprocessor environment is to implement an indivisible read-modify-write cycle on the system bus leading to the shared memory. This allows both the consecutive memory cycles required for execution of the TS instruction to be completed without interference from other processors. In other words, each processor's TS instruction can only see a consistent global value of the specific operand, as set before or after completed execution of the competing TS instructions. For example, Motorola's M68000 family of microprocessors includes a test-and-set (TAS) instruction suitable for multiprocessor systems by providing an indivisible read-modify-write cycle on the system bus for the TAS instruction.

The exchange (XCHG) instruction may also be used successfully in a multi-processor environment, as evidenced by the implementation of the WAIT operation in Intel's iAPX-86 family of microprocessors given in Program 4.7. The XCHG instruction used in this example is indivisible within a single processor, but a special system-wide bus LOCK prefix is needed to enforce its indivisibility in a multiprocessor environment. In essence, the LOCK prefix activates an indivisible read-modify-write cycle on the bus. This prefix may also be used with other instructions whose indivisible completion may be desired.

In summary, the TS instruction seems to be just what we need to solve the mutual-exclusion problem. TS is simple to use, it does not affect interrupts or the operating system while doing its job, and it may be used in a multiprocessor environment. The use of TS, however, is not without drawbacks.

Consider a situation where process P1 executes the TS instruction, obtains the permit, and enters its critical section. Suppose that a higher-priority process, P2, preempts P1 and attempts to use the same resource. This scenario may result in P2 looping on the control variable awaiting its resetting, but the only process that could reset the variable (P1) is preempted. With strict priority-based scheduling, it is easy to show that the two processes may become deadlocked. This problem perhaps suggests that a process within a critical section should not be preempted, at least not by its contenders. This seemingly simple proposition is rarely implemented because operating systems usually cannot afford the overhead that would be imposed by having to keep track of the nature of instructions being executed by user processes. As a consequence, the possibility of preemption of a process within its critical section is a serious potential problem in systems that rely on the presented form of enforcing mutual exclusion by means of the TS instruction.

4.4.4 Compare-and-Swap Instruction

The compare-and-swap (CS) instruction is a hardware instruction introduced by IBM in their 370 series. The CS instruction follows an optimistic approach to the mutual-exclusion problem. It is not directly intended for implementation of

```
WAIT_S:              MOV     AL,1      ;set local flag to BUSY
LOOP:       LOCK     XCHG    AL,S      ;exchange global and local flags
                     CMP     AL,0      ;was global = FREE?
                     JNZ     LOOP      ;if not, loop until FREE
                     RET               ;return control, resource is FREE
```

Program 4.7 A multiprocessor wait for iAPX-86 family

semaphore operations, but rather for the consistent updating of global variables in the presence of concurrent activity and without any support from the operating system or interrupt mechanism. The CS instruction is very convenient and efficient for simple updates of shared variables.

As explained earlier, the optimistic procedure of updating a shared variable consists of copying the value of the global variable into the local space, say, into a register OLDREG, and of using that value to calculate the tentative update, which is also stored in the local space, say, a register NEWREG. The update is tentative in the sense that it is correct only provided that no other process modifies the global variable while the described sequence of actions is in progress. Otherwise, the tentative update is obsolete and must be discarded. In that case, the whole sequence needs to be repeated.

The CS instruction plays a crucial role in checking whether the tentative update is still valid and, if so, in making it permanent. The CS instruction takes three operands: a register that contains the value of the global variable on which the tentative update is based (OLDREG), a register that contains the tentative update (NEWREG), and the address of the global variable in question (GLOBVAR). The CS instruction consists of the following sequence of steps, which are executed as a single, indivisible operation:

CS   OLDREG,NEWREG,GLOBVAR:

COMPARE   OLDREG,GLOBVAR
SET CONDITION CODES ACCORDINGLY
IF (OLDREG = GLOBVAR)   THEN GLOBVAR := NEWREG
                          ELSE OLDREG := GLOBVAR

In other words, if the value of the global variable is not disturbed by another process during the calculation of the update, the tentative update is applied to the global variable and thus made permanent. Otherwise, the new modified value of GLOBVAR is read into the OLDREG for a rerun. In any case, the condition codes are set to reflect the result of the comparison and, with it, the outcome of execution of the CS instruction.

The use of the CS instruction is illustrated in Program 4.8. The problem being solved is the updating of the shared global variable SUM in a consistent manner in the presence of multiple concurrent processes that update the same variable. The standard semaphore-inspired solution to this problem using the TS instruction is presented as Program 4.8b. It basically consists of requesting exclusive access to the variable SUM by executing a WAIT operation on the semaphore MUTEX that provides mutual exclusion among concurrent processes that update SUM. Once in the critical section, the variable SUM is updated by having the number 3 added to it in our example. The temporary inconsistency between the global (memory) and local (ACC) copies of the variable is hidden from other processes by the enclosing critical section protected by MUTEX. Following completion of the update, manipulation of SUM by other processes is allowed by setting the value of MUTEX to FREE.

```
...
sum := sum + 3;
...
```

a) The problem: update a shared global variable (sum)

```
TESTSET:   TS      MUTEX            ;wait(mutex)
           BNFREE  TESTSET
           MOVE    ACC,SUM          ;sum := sum + 3
           ADD     ACC,#3
           MOVE    SUM,ACC
           MOVE    MUTEX,#0         ;signal(mutex)
```

b) Test and Set solution (pessimistic)

```
COMPSWP:  MOVE    OLDREG,SUM              ;oldreg := sum
AGAIN:    MOVE    NEWREG,OLDREG          ;tentupd := oldreg + 3
          ADD     NEWREG,#3
          CS      OLDREG,NEWREG,SUM  ;if sum=oldreg then sum:=tentupd
          BNEQ    AGAIN                  ;else redo update with new sum
```

c) Compare and Swap solution (optimistic)

Program 4.8 Updating a global variable (sum)

The CS solution presented as Program 4.8c takes a radically different approach. It begins by copying the value of the global variable SUM (let us assume that it is 5) into the local space, i.e., to register OLDREG. This value is then copied into the register NEWREG, to which the additive constant (3 in our case) is added to produce the tentative update (the value of 8 in our example). The CS instruction is then used to assess whether this update is valid and, if so, to make it permanent by replacing the value of the global copy of the variable SUM (which would be 5 in this case) with its updated value (which is 8 in this case). The success of this operation would imply that no other process has modified the value of SUM from the moment it was read at the COMPSWP line in Program 4.8c until execution of the CS instruction. Therefore, the tentative update is valid and it may be safely applied to the global variable.

In order to make sure that this solution preserves integrity of the variable SUM in the presence of concurrent updating activity, assume that the competing process, P2, executes the identical sequence of code concurrently. For easier reference, let us dub the original process as process P1. Now assume that the two processes are interleaved in such a way that both read the same value of the global variable SUM, thus calculating identical tentative updates, and that each process reaches its respective CS instruction at about the same time. Note that this situation is not permitted in the classical approach, such as depicted by Program 4.8b, because all concurrent processes wishing to access the shared variable SUM would be blocked by the one admitted to the critical section past the semaphore MUTEX, the only place where the variable SUM can be read and updated.

Returning to the CS example, assume that process P1 manages to execute its CS instruction first and to apply its local tentative update to SUM. Following the successful equality test, condition codes cause the branch to the label AGAIN not to be taken, and process P1 continues with its other work. Process P2, however, obtains the inequality setting of its condition codes, indicating that the CS instruction did not apply its tentative update. In terms of our example, the value of SUM is found to be equal to 8, which is different than P2's local copy, 5, stored in P2's copy of register OLDREG. Thus the BNEQ (Branch if Not Equal) branch in process P2 is taken, and control is transferred to the label AGAIN to recalculate the value of the tentative update on the basis of the freshly obtained copy of the value of SUM provided in the OLDREG by the CS instruction.

In other words, only one of the two competing processes is allowed to update the global copy of the variable SUM. If the assumption about the order of execution of the two CS instructions is reversed, only process P2 would update SUM, and process P1 would be forced to redo its tentative update. Thus we can conclude that use of the CS instruction as described ensures consistent updating of global variables in the presence of concurrent execution of arbitrarily interleaved processes. It can be easily shown that this solution works with more than two processes.

The CS instruction accomplishes its purpose without blocking any of the contending processes at any time and by allowing their arbitrary and unconstrained interleaving. As a result, the CS solution does not suffer from the preemption-related problem discussed in relation to the TS instruction. With CS, the running process is always capable of making progress toward its completion, regardless of the state and possible preemptions of other processes. Neither DI/EI nor TS instructions can offer this guarantee unconditionally. Other advantages of the CS instruction include independence from the interrupt mechanism and the ability to ensure safe updating of shared variables without any support from the operating system. Moreover, the CS instruction can be used in multiprocessor environments, where the indivisible read-modify-write cycle is supported for shared memory.

The CS instruction is ideally suited for efficient and safe updating of shared variables in the presence of concurrent updating activity, a situation illustrated by Program 4.8c. However, many of the advantages of the CS instructions are lost when it is used in different applications, such as implementation of the semaphore WAIT primitive.

4.5 SEMAPHORES REVISITED

After having convinced ourselves that hardware implementation of semaphores is feasible, we now pay closer attention to semaphore efficiency.

As defined in this chapter, the busy-wait implementation of semaphores has two drawbacks: potential indefinite postponement and low efficiency due to consumption of CPU cycles by blocked processes. Although a blocked process is not making any progress toward its completion, it nonetheless continues to consume system resources by busy-waiting. Both livelock and inefficient busy-waiting may be alleviated when the so-called *queuing implementation of semaphores* is used.

The data structure and the two semaphore operations with queuing implementation are shown in Figure 4.3. As indicated, a queue of process control-blocks (PCB) is associated with each semaphore variable. Instead of busy-waiting when the desired resource is held by somebody else, in a queuing implementation the affected process is suspended and its PCB is enqueued in the queue associated with the semaphore that the process is waiting on. A suspended process does not consume CPU cycles, so this approach is potentially more efficient than busy-waiting.

However, a process suspended at a semaphore due to a conflicting resource request can no longer rely on its own recognizance to proceed to the critical section when the resource eventually becomes available. Obviously, something else must awaken the process from hibernation at the appropriate time. Since a shared resource is released to waiting processes by means of a SIGNAL operation on the related semaphore, SIGNAL is the perfect candidate for resuming a process suspended on a given semaphore.

The resulting logic of the queueing implementation of SIGNAL is depicted in Figure 4.3c. Note that SIGNAL first attempts to awaken a waiting process, and only when there are none is the semaphore variable incremented. This implies that the semaphore variable is kept in the BUSY state for as long as there are processes waiting in its queue. A new process wishing to access the resource and executing the corresponding WAIT is placed in the queue whenever the queue is nonempty. As a result, this implementation gives higher precedence to processes

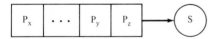

a) Semaphore Structure

---

wait (s):   if not (s > 0) then suspend the caller at s
                     else s := s − 1;

b) Wait Operation

---

signal (s): if queue at s not empty {at least one process waiting}
                     then resume a process from queue at s
                     else s := s + 1;

c) Signal Operation

Figure 4.3 Queuing implementation of semaphores.

already waiting than to new arrivals. One nice consequence of this is that the livelock problem of busy-wait semaphores may be eliminated with a choice of the appropriate queue-service discipline, such as FIFO.

In addition to solving the mutual-exclusion problem, semaphores are very useful and convenient for the exchange of synchronization signals between co-operating processes. In this application, the matching WAIT-SIGNAL pair is formed between two separate processes, as opposed to within a single process, as in the case of mutual exclusion. Our multiprocess example in Chapter 3 demonstrates the need for interprocess synchronization. The use of signals therein was really meant for semaphores, which were hidden under the disguise of signals only because the concept of semaphores had not yet been introduced.

General (counting) semaphores provide additional versatility in some applications. They are especially useful in situations where several resources of the same type are used by a group of processes. Allocation of one type of resource with multiple instances may be governed by a single general semaphore. For example, a system may have a number of functionally equivalent printers or tape drives. When used for allocation of such resources, the general semaphore is initially set to a positive integer value N that corresponds to the number of units of a given type, say, printers. N subsequent WAIT operations on that semaphore succeed in obtaining an instance of the resource, i.e., a printer in our example. Each successful WAIT also decrements the semaphore variable until the semaphore eventually reaches the value 0 (BUSY) when all instances of the resource are allocated to requesting processes. From that point on, further requests are forced to wait until a sufficient number of resources are released by SIGNAL operations. We present some examples of the use of general semaphores in the section that follows.

An important observation is that general semaphores are superfluous in the theoretical sense, because it can be shown that a general semaphore may be implemented by means of binary semaphores. However, the comparative coding efficiency of programs based on the two types of semaphores may differ significantly, and we thus continue to use general semaphores where they result in more compact or intuitively appealing code.

4.6 CLASSICAL PROBLEMS IN CONCURRENT PROGRAMMING

In this section we explore several problems that have a prominent place in the theory and practice of concurrent programming. After analyzing each problem, we present one or more solutions based on semaphores. These problems are also solved using the alternative synchronization methods introduced in Chapter 5. By keeping the overall structure of the solutions based on different mechanisms as similar as possible, our intention is to use the presented problems as a common reference for comparisons.

4.6.1 The Producer/Consumer Problem

In general, the producer/consumer problem may be stated as follows:

- Given a set of cooperating processes, some of which "produce" data items (producers) to be "consumed" by others (consumers), with possible disparity between production and consumption rates,

- Devise a synchronization protocol that allows both producers and consumers to operate concurrently at their respective service rates in such a way that produced items are consumed in the exact order in which they are produced (FIFO).

This problem was actually introduced earlier in this chapter in the form of one of its incarnations—the terminal-handler problem. For instance, the KEYBOARD process may be regarded as an exemplary producer of data items (input characters) for consumption by the DISPLAY process. Processes often tend to behave as a mixture of the two rather than being pure producers or pure consumers. In our earlier multiprocess example, COLLECT is a producer of data, LOG and REPORT are consumers, whereas STAT is both a producer and a consumer of data. Numerous other examples may be found in multiprogramming systems, thus making the producer/consumer problem an important one from both theoretical and practical points of view.

Producers and consumers with an unbounded buffer. In the first attempt to solve the producer/consumer problem, we assume that a buffer of unbounded capacity is set aside to smooth the speed differences between producers and consumers. Obviously, after the system is initialized, a producer must be the first process to run in order to provide the first item. From that point on, a consumer process may run whenever there is more than one item in the buffer produced but not yet consumed. Given the unbounded buffer, producers may run at any time without restrictions. We also assume that all items produced and subsequently consumed have identical, but unspecified structure. The buffer itself may be implemented as an array, a linked list, or any other collection of data items. With these assumptions, the first solution given in Program 4.9 is rather simple.

Before discussing the logic of Program 4.9, let us refine our assumption about the implementation of semaphores, their initialization in particular. In the previous examples we have relied on the assignment statement to initialize semaphore variables, which were accessed only by means of WAIT and SIGNAL operations thereafter. This was done in order to stress the importance and role of semaphore initialization. However, it may be cumbersome and potentially dangerous to implement semaphores in this way. Namely, if assignment to semaphore variables is allowed in a given system, it is difficult to devise and enforce the rules that allow only "good" processes to make such assignments while preventing other processes from doing so. Given their role in interprocess synchronization, a single

program/module *producer-consumer*;

  . . .

  var *produced* : *semaphore*; {*general*}

  process *producer*;
    begin
      while *true* **do**
        begin
          produce;
          place_in_buffer;
          signal(*produced*);
          other_producer_processing
        end {*while*}
    end; {*producer*}

  process *consumer*;
    begin
      while *true* **do**
        begin
          wait(*produced*);
          take_from_buffer;
          consume;
          other_consumer_processing
        end {*while*}
    end; {*consumer*}

  {*parent process*}
  begin {*producer-consumer*}
    {*produced* := 0;}
    initiate *producer*, *consumer*
  end {*producer-consumer*}

Program 4.9 Producer/consumer: unbounded buffer

erroneous or malicious run-time semaphore assignment may create havoc in a multiprocess environment.

In order to encourage safer implementations where semaphore variables are typed in such a way that they cannot participate in assignment operations of any kind, we assume that all semaphores, by being declared, are initialized by the system to 0 (BUSY for binary semaphores). When a different initial value is desired, it must be secured in user code by means of executing the appropriate number of SIGNAL operations before initializing (creating) the processes that use the related semaphore. This assumption is maintained throughout the remainder of this book.

Let us now return to the producer/consumer problem and to Program 4.9. In order to highlight interprocess synchronization, the code of PRODUCER and CONSUMER processes presented in Program 4.9 omits the details of data-item specification and manipulation. A single general semaphore, PRODUCED, keeps track of the number of items produced but not yet consumed. Its initial value is 0, as no items are available in the global buffer at the outset.

With the unbounded-buffer assumption, producers may run at any time. The code of the PRODUCER process reflects this by the absence of WAIT operations. When an item is produced, it is placed in the buffer and the fact is signaled by means of the general semaphore PRODUCED. The nature of the problem implies that the consumer can never get ahead of the producer.

In Program 4.9 this is ensured by having the CONSUMER process wait at the PRODUCED semaphore before consuming an item from the buffer. Since a semaphore is used for interprocess synchronization, as opposed to mutual exclusion, the WAIT and SIGNAL processes are matched between the PRODUCER and CONSUMER processes, rather than within a single process. Given that PRODUCED is initially 0, this solution also satisfies the requirement that the first process to run after the system is initialized must be a producer. After that, indivisibility of semaphore operations ensures that arbitrary interleaving of producer and consumer processes does not introduce timing errors by itself.

Our definition of the producer/consumer problem calls for a number of concurrent producers and consumers, so it behooves us to ascertain whether the offered solution functions properly in such an environment. Absence of critical sections in the code of the two processes in Program 4.9 allows for a high degree of concurrency, but at the expense of generality; namely, by failing to enforce mutual exclusion during execution of the buffer-manipulation procedures PLACE_IN_BUFFER and TAKE_FROM_BUFFER, Program 4.9 cannot, in general, guarantee system integrity when multiple producer and consumer processes are active. For example, even though we have left the details of buffer implementation unspecified, it is obvious that an index or a pointer to the next available buffer slot must be global in order to be accessible to all producers. Its consistency cannot be maintained in the presence of concurrent updates without a synchronization protocol observed by all producers, and Program 4.9 does not provide any.

This situation is remedied by Program 4.10, where buffer-manipulation procedures are placed within critical sections protected by the binary semaphore MUTEX. Consequently, a number of producer and consumer processes may be executed concurrently without adverse effects on the shared global buffer. The code for one producer and one consumer process is shown in Program 4.10, and others are assumed to have the same structure in terms of the ordering of semaphore operations. Note that MUTEX prohibits concurrency whenever a process, be it a producer or a consumer, is placing or removing items from the buffer.

This simple addition must be implemented with caution, because the two semaphores may interact in a rather undesirable manner. Consider, for example, reversing the order of WAIT operations in the CONSUMER process. As a consequence, waiting on the PRODUCED semaphore is moved into the critical section controlled by MUTEX. This, in turn, may deadlock the system from the very start. For instance, assume that while a producer process is busy prepar-

program/module *producers-consumers*;

    ...

   var
     produced : semaphore;   *{general}*
     mutex : semaphore;   *{binary}*

   process *producerX*;
     begin
       while *true* **do**
         begin
           produce;
           wait(mutex);
           place_in_buffer;
           signal(mutex);
           signal(produced);
           other_X_processing
         end *{while}*
     end; *{ producerX }*

   process *consumerY*;
     begin
       while *true* **do**
         begin
           wait(produced);
           wait(mutex);
           take_fm_buffer;
           signal(mutex);
           consume;
           other_Y_processing
         end *{while}*
     end; *{consumerY }*

   { parent process}
   begin *{ producers-consumers}*
     { produced := 0;}
     signal(mutex);
     initiate *producers, consumers*
   end *{ producers-consumers}*

Program 4.10 Producers/consumers : unbounded buffer

ing its first item, a consumer process becomes scheduled. MUTEX is initially FREE, and consumer enters the critical section. It has no items to consume and is thus forced to wait on the PRODUCED semaphore. However, no producer can ever succeed in placing its item in the buffer, because MUTEX dutifully keeps it outside of critical section. Consequently, the consumer remains in the critical section forever and the system is deadlocked. On the other hand, reversing the order of signals in the PRODUCER's code has no such adverse effects. This example demonstrates that although semaphores are a powerful tool, their use by no means automatically solves all timing problems.

Producers and consumers with a bounded buffer. The unbounded-buffer assumption simplifies analysis of the producer/consumer problem by allowing virtually unrestricted execution of the producers. However, this assumption is unrealistic, and proposed solutions based on it may not be directly implementable in real computer systems which have finite memory capacities. In this section we present solutions to the producer/consumer problem assuming a finite capacity of the shared buffer.

The main difference imposed by the bounded buffer is that both consumers *and* producers may be halted under certain circumstances. As before, a consumer may only absorb produced items and must wait when no items are available. Producers, on the other hand, may only produce items when there are empty buffer slots to receive them. Otherwise, new arrivals might overwrite the items produced earlier that are still awaiting consumption and thus violate the requirement that items must be consumed in the same order as they are produced.

At any particular time, the shared global buffer may be empty, partially filled, or full of produced items ready for consumption. A producer process may run in either of the two former cases, but all producers must be kept waiting when the buffer is full. Consumers, when executing, vacate buffer slots, thus enabling producers to run. When the buffer is empty, consumers must wait, for they can never get ahead of producers.

But how do we program these conditions? Let us first formulate our earlier discussion into a few simple expressions. Let *icount* be the number of items produced but not yet consumed, that is

$$icount = produced - consumed$$

where *produced* and *consumed* represent the total number of items produced and consumed, respectively, since the system is started. Given a finite capacity of the buffer, the following must hold

$$0 \leq icount \leq capacity$$

where *capacity* is the capacity of the global buffer. We also know that producers may run only when there are some empty slots in the buffer, yielding

$$mayproduce: \quad icount < capacity$$

Consumers, on the other hand, can execute only when there is at least one item produced but not yet consumed, that is,

$$mayconsume: \quad icount > 0$$

The two conditions, *mayproduce* and *mayconsume*, can now be used to control execution of producer and consumer processes based on the current state of the buffer. In practice, buffers are usually implemented in a circular fashion. This is quite natural for linked-list implementations. Array buffers may be made circular

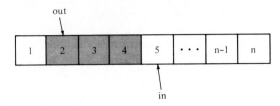

Figure 4.4 Produce/consume buffer.

by "wrapping around" from the last (highest index) to the first (lowest index) position. Figure 4.4 depicts an array buffer with produced but not yet consumed slots shaded in order to distinguish them from the empty (consumed) ones. Two indices, *in* and *out*, point to the next slot available for a produced item and to the place where the next item is to be consumed from, respectively.

Program 4.11 is a solution to the bounded-buffer version of the producer/consumer problem. It contains several details resulting from considerations likely to be followed in an actual implementation. We first explain the overall logic of the solution and then discuss the buffer-manipulation operations. General

```
program/module BB_producers_consumers;
  ...
  const
    capacity = ...;
  type
    item = ...;
  var
    buffer : array [1..capacity] of item;
    mayproduce, mayconsume : semaphore; {general }
    pmutex, cmutex : semaphore; {binary}
    in, out : (1..capacity);
  process producerX;
    var pitem : item;
    begin
      while true do
        begin
          wait(mayproduce);
          pitem := produce;
          wait(pmutex);
          buffer[in] := pitem;
          in := (in mod capacity) + 1;
          signal(pmutex);
          signal(mayconsume);
          other_X_processing
        end {while}
    end; { producerX }
```

(Continued)

```
process consumerZ;
    var citem : item;
    begin
        while true do
            begin
                wait(mayconsume);
                wait(cmutex);
                citem := buffer[out];
                out := (out mod capacity) + 1;
                signal(cmutex);
                signal(mayproduce);
                consume(citem);
                other_Z_processing
            end {while}
    end; {consumerZ}

{parent process}
begin {BB_producers_consumers}
    in := 1;
    out := 1;
    signal(pmutex);
    signal(cmutex);
    for i := 1 to capacity do signal(mayproduce);
    initiate producers, consumers
end {BB_producers_consumers}
```

Program 4.11 Producers/consumers : bounded buffer

semaphores MAYPRODUCE and MAYCONSUME represent the two conditions introduced earlier by the same name which control execution of producer and consumer processes. Two binary semaphores, PMUTEX and CMUTEX, protect buffer and index manipulations of producers and consumers, respectively. As a result, this solution supports multiple concurrent producers and consumers.

Producer processes, as indicated by the code of a sample PRODUCERX, can run only when there are empty slots in the buffer, a condition indicated by the semaphore MAYPRODUCE. This semaphore is initially set to the value corresponding to buffer capacity, thus allowing producers to get up to CAPACITY items ahead of consumers. Whenever a consumer completes its cycle, it empties a slot by removing the consumed item from the buffer and signals the fact via the MAYPRODUCE semaphore to enable a waiting producer, if any. The MAYCONSUME semaphore indicates the availability of produced items, and it functions much the same way as in the unbounded-buffer version of consumer: each run of a producer process increments its value, and consumer processes decrement it by executing a WAIT operation.

Critical sections in producer and consumer processes are introduced to protect buffer manipulation, which is shown in greater detail due to the fact that a more specific implementation of the global buffer, which is an array, is assumed. The *mod* operator is used to wrap an index around when the end of the array is reached, thus making the buffer circular. Producers and consumers use separate buffer indices, IN and OUT, in order to increase the degree of concurrency in the system; namely, the two sets of processes operate at different ends of the buffer and compete with their peers within the group but not between the groups. In the unbounded-buffer solution presented in Program 4.10, this situation is handled by a single semaphore, MUTEX. However, a single semaphore unnecessarily blocks producers whenever a consumer is in its critical section, and vice versa. Given the disjointness of their indices, two semaphores allow for more concurrency, of course, at the expense of additional overhead.

4.6.2 Readers and Writers

Readers and writers is another classical problem in concurrent programming with numerous applications in practice. It basically revolves around a number of processes using a shared global data structure. The processes are categorized, depending on their usage of resource, as either readers or writers. A *reader* never modifies the shared data structure, whereas a *writer* may both read and write into it. A number of readers may use the shared data structure concurrently, because no matter how interleaved, they cannot possibly compromise its consistency. Writers, on the other hand, must be granted exclusive access to data; i.e., they cannot be interleaved safely with either readers or other writers. The problem may be slightly more precisely stated as follows:

- Given a universe of readers that read a common data structure and a universe of writers that modify the same common data structure,

- Devise a synchronization protocol among the readers and writers that ensures consistency of common data while maintaining as high degree of concurrency as possible.

Probably the most obvious example of readers and writers is the file-access control module in multiuser database systems. In fact, any multiuser operating system must provide some sort of concurrency control mechanism to ensure the integrity of files accessible to more than one process. Shared files, such as directories and mail, ought to be available to a number of concurrent users that should not corrupt the public data. In addition to these common examples, the readers and writers problem may be encountered in numerous other manifestations in multiprogramming systems. One such instance may be found in Chapter 3, where the COLLECT process is a writer and the LOG and STAT processes are readers of the incoming-data buffer IB.

One approach to solving the readers and writers problem is to maintain a high degree of concurrency by allowing as many readers as possible to access the shared resource simultaneously. This strategy is implemented in Program 4.12, which contains the code of sample READER and WRITER processes. Writer's

```
program/module readers_writers;

   . . .

   var
     readercount : integer;
     mutex, write : semaphore; {binary}

   process readerX;
     begin
       while true do
         begin
           {obtain permission to enter}
           wait(mutex);
           readercount := readercount + 1;
           if readercount = 1 then wait(write);
           signal(mutex);

                . . .
              {reads}
                . . .
           wait(mutex);
           readercount := readercount - 1;
           if readercount = 0 then signal(write);
           signal(mutex);
           other_X_processing
         end {while}
     end; {readerX}

   process writerZ;
     begin
       while true do
         begin
           wait(write);

                . . .
              {writes}
                . . .
           signal(write);
           other_Z_processing
         end {while}
     end; {writerZ}

   {parent process}
   begin {readers-writers}
     readercount := 0;
     signal(mutex);
     signal(write);
     initiate readers, writers
   end {readers_writers}
```

Program 4.12 Readers and writers

logic is fairly simple, it waits on the binary semaphore WRITE to be granted permission to enter the critical section and to use the shared resource. A reader, on the other hand, goes through two critical sections, one before and one after using the resource. Their purpose is to allow a large number of readers to execute concurrently while making sure that readers are kept away when writers are active.

An integer, READERCOUNT, is used to keep track of the number of readers actively using the resource. What we are really interested in are the first and the last readers of a group; the others do not really matter much as far as synchronization is concerned.

In Program 4.12, the first reader passes through MUTEX, increments the number of readers, and waits on writers, if any. While a reader is reading the shared data, semaphore MUTEX is free and WRITE is busy. This makes it possible for all readers that arrive while at least one is actively reading to quickly pass this critical section and proceed to reading. If there are writers waiting, they are prevented from accessing data by the busy WRITE semaphore. When the last reader of a cluster finishes, it finds READERCOUNT to be 0 and admits waiting writers, if any, by signaling via the WRITE semaphore. When a writer is in the critical section, WRITE is busy and it keeps the first reader to arrive from completing its first critical section. Consequently, any subsequent readers are kept waiting in front of that critical section. When the system is quiescent, both semaphores are free and access to the resource is fair game for both readers and writers.

The solution presented in Program 4.12 maintains a very high degree of concurrency, but it may starve writers by postponing them indefinitely when readers are active. A rather massive instance of the readers and writers problem, the Dow Jones online stock market quotation system, may be used to illustrate the pitfalls of this approach. The quotation system basically consists of a database (stock prices) accessed by a number of reader processes (brokerage houses) and updated by writer processes to reflect changes on the stock exchange. Assuming active trading, there are always readers and writers waiting to be processed. If Program 4.12 were used in that situation, writers would wait for a long time, thus causing the database to lose step with market changes and rendering the whole system useless. Obviously, a fairer scheduling discipline between waiting readers and writers would have to be devised. Giving absolute preference to writers would not help either, because that would keep the database very much up to date, but nobody would be able to read it to find that out. A strategy proposed by Hoare holds promise for both readers and writers to compete in finite time. It suggests that

- A new reader should not start if there is a writer waiting (prevents starvation of writers).
- All readers waiting at the end of a write should have priority over the next writer (prevents starvation of readers).

4.7 SUMMARY

Interprocess synchronization is necessary to prevent and/or to avoid timing errors due to concurrent accessing of shared resources, such as data structures or I/O devices, by multiple contending processes. Interprocess synchronization also allows exchange of timing signals (STOP/GO) between cooperating processes in order to preserve the specific precedence relationships imposed by the problem being solved.

Without adequate interprocess synchronization, updating of shared variables can induce concurrency-related timing errors that are often difficult to debug. One of the primary causes of this problem is the possibility that concurrent processes may observe temporarily inconsistent values of a shared variable while it is being updated. One approach to solving this problem is to perform updates of shared variables in a mutually exclusive manner. This can be accomplished by allowing at most one process at a time to enter the critical section of code within which a particular shared variable or a data structure is updated.

Semaphores are a simple but powerful interprocess synchronization mechanism based on this philosophy. Semaphores satisfy most of the extensive requirements that we have specified for a "good" concurrency-control mechanism, including no assumptions about the relative speeds and priorities of contending processes and no need to know anything about other contenders except that they possibly exist. Of the two presented approaches to semaphore implementation, queuing implementation facilitates elimination of the indefinite-postponement problem and has a greater potential efficiency than busy-waiting.

Hardware support for concurrency control in one form or another is an integral part of virtually all contemporary computer architectures. Some of the available mechanisms, such as interrupt-disable/enable and test-and-set instructions, are suitable for implementation of pessimistic approaches to concurrency control. Others, such as the compare-and-swap instruction, are well suited for optimistic concurrency control. The TS and CS instructions can also function in multiprocessor systems, provided that the indivisible read-modify-write cycle is supported for shared memory.

Some well-known synchronization problems, such as producer/consumer and readers/writers problems, can be solved using semaphores. Because of the large number of their incarnations in practice, both problems are routinely used to test and compare various synchronization mechanisms.

OTHER READING

Discussions of timing problems related to interprocess synchronization are provided by Brinch Hansen (1973) and Wirth (1977).

Dijkstra (1968a) analyzes the mutual-exclusion problem and introduces semaphores. This paper also discusses four attempted solutions to mutual exclusion, three of which are presented in this chapter, and includes an elaboration of Dekker's solution. An *n*-process solution to the mutual-exclusion problem is described by Dijkstra (1965). A different solution to the same problem which is suitable for multicomputer systems without shared memory was devised by Lamport (1974) and later dubbed the "bakery algorithm." An algorithm for mutual exclusion in distributed systems is described by Ricart and Agrawala (1981).

Hardware support for mutual exclusion is discussed by Hwang and Briggs (1984). In addition to TS and CS instructions, the "fetch and add" instruction, which allows a high degree of parallelism in multiprocessor environments, is described. Atwood (1976) presents interprocess synchronization mechanisms in CDC 6000, Cyber, and IBM 360/370 series of computers. Shaw (1974) discusses synchronization primitives in the OS/360, including enqueue/dequeue and wait/post. The wait/notify mechanism of Multics is described by Spier and Organick (1969). The lock/unlock mechanism is proposed by Dennis and van Horn (1966). Bus contention caused by different implementations of mutual exclusion in a multiprocessor system was studied by O'Grady and Lozano (1985).

Habermann (1976) provides a discussion of queuing implementation of semaphores. An efficient hardware-assisted implementation of semaphores in a multiprocessor environment is described by Denning et al. (1981).

The producer/consumer problem is discussed by Dijkstra (1968a and b), and in Dijkstra (1971) another classical synchronization problem known as "dining philosophers" is treated in detail. Concurrent readers and writers were introduced by Courtois et al. (1971). A formal treatment of this problem and a solution that does not require mutual exclusion is described by Lamport (1977). Many of these problems and their solutions are described in Ben-Ari's book (1982), which is dedicated exclusively to the topic of concurrent programming. Other textbook treatments of concurrency are provided by Brinch Hansen (1973), Holt et al. (1978), Peterson and Silberschatz (1983), and Holt (1983).

EXERCISES

4.1 Solve the terminal-handler (character-echoing) problem presented in Program 4.1 using interrupts and possibly the instructions for interrupt control, such as enable/disable. Optionally, implement and test your solution on a computer system. State explicitly all assumptions under which your solution works, and discuss the portability of your solution in terms of dependence on the interrupt-handling mechanism of a particular machine. Does your solution work for more than two processes?

4.2 Does Program 4.13 meet the requirements of a "good" solution to the mutual-exclusion problem stated in Chapter 4? If yes, argue its correctness; if no, provide a counter example and discuss the cause of the failure.

```
program/module mutex4;

   . . .

   var
      p1using, p2using : boolean;

   process p1;
      begin
         while true do
            begin
               p1using := true;
               while p2using do
                  begin
                     p1using := false;
                     {give p2 a chance}
                     p1using := true
                  end; {while}
               critical_section;
               p1using := false;
               other_p1_processing
         end; {p1}

   process p2;
      begin
         while true do
            begin
               p2using := true;
               while p1using do
                  begin
                     p2using := false;
                     {give p1 a chance}
                     p2using := true
                  end; {while}
               critical_section;
               p2using := false;
               other_p1_processing
            end {while}
      end; {p2}

   {parent process}
   begin {mutex4}
      p1using := false;
      p2using := false;
      initiate p1, p2
   end {mutex4}
```

Program 4.13 Mutual exclusion - algorithm 4

```
program/module Dekker;

  . . .

  type
    who = (proc1, proc2)
  var
    turn : who;
    p1using, p2using : boolean;

  process p1
    begin
      while true do
        begin
          p1using := true;
          while p2using do
            if turn = proc2
              then
                begin
                  p1using := false;
                  while turn = proc2 do {keeptesting};
                  p1using := true
                end; {if}
          critical_section;
          turn := proc2;
          p1using := false;
          other_p1_processing
        end {while}
    end; {p1}

  process p2
    begin
      while true do
        begin
          p2using := true;
          while p1using do
            if turn = proc1
              then
                begin
                  p2using := false;
                  while turn = proc1 do {keeptesting};
                  p2using := true
                end; {if}
          critical_section;
          turn := proc1;
          p2using := false;
          other_p2_processing;
        end {while}
    end; {p2}

  {parent process}
```

(Continued)

begin {*Dekker*}
   p1using := *false*;
   p2using := *false*;
   turn := *proc1*;
   initiate *p1*, *p2*
end {*Dekker*}

Program 4.14 Dekker's solution to mutual exclusion

4.3 Program 4.14 represents Dekker's solution to the mutual-exclusion problem slightly modified to suit the notation used in Chapter 4. Explain the logic of this solution, argue its correctness informally, and state explicitly which requirements of a "good" solution are satisfied by Program 4.14. Is the presented value of the initial assignment to variable TURN important for correct functioning of Dekker's solution? Can this solution be implemented in a multiprocessor system with shared memory? If yes, discuss the necessary hardware provisions if any; if no, explain why.

4.4 Program 4.15 is a version of Lamport's bakery algorithm. The relation "less than" on ordered pairs of integers used in this program is defined by $(a,b) < (c,d)$, if $a < c$ or if $a = c$ and $b < d$. Explain the logic of this algorithm, and discuss whether Program 4.15 is suitable for multiprocessor systems. Suggest where (shared or private memory) the individual entries of the arrays CHOOSING and NUMBER should be kept when high efficiency is desired and where they should be kept when resilience to component failures is desired. The algorithm is claimed to be resilient to failures of any single component of the system, e.g., a processor. Discuss the assumptions and the system architecture for which this claim is valid. Can the same claim be made for semaphores? Why or why not?

4.5 Devise a scenario which demonstrates the need for indivisible execution of the semaphore SIGNAL operation.

4.6 In definitions of semaphore WAIT operations presented in Chapter 4, the semaphore variable is decremented only if its value would become nonnegative. In an alternative implementation, the semaphore variable is decremented first and then the test whether to proceed to the critical section or not is made. Give such revised definitions of both busy-waiting and queueing implementations of semaphores, indicate where indivisible operation is required, and discuss the range of values that semaphore variables can attain. What does a negative value of such a semaphore indicate? Does this change affect the SIGNAL operation?

4.7 Implement the busy-wait form of semaphore WAIT and SIGNAL primitives using the various hardware instructions listed below to ensure indivisibility where required. Each solution should meet all the requirements satisfied by Dijkstra's semaphores. Solutions should be coded in a pseudo-assembly language using the standard LOAD, STORE, and COMPARE

program/module *Lamport*;

. . .

  var { *for all processes*}
    choosing : **array** [1..*n*] **of** *integer*;
    number : **array** [1..*n*] **of** *integer*;

{*individual processes*}
process *i*; { *process on processor i*}
    var
      j : *integer*;
    begin
      while *true* **do**
        begin
          choosing[*i*] := 1;
          number[*i*] := 1 + *maximum*(*number*[1],...,*number*[*n*]);
          choosing[*i*] := 0;
          for *j* := 1 **to** *n* **do**
            begin
              while *choosing*[*j*] <> 0 **do** {*keeptesting*};
              while *number*[*j*] <> 0 **and**
                (*number*[*j*],*j* < *number*[*i*],*i*) **do** {*keeptesting*}
            end; { *for*}
          critical_section;
          number[*i*] := 0;
          other_i_processing
        end {*while*}
    end; { *process i*}

  . . .

end {*Lamport*}

Program 4.15 Lamport's bakery algorithm

AND BRANCH instructions in addition to the ones specified below for each particular solution:

(a) DI/EI instructions. When a process enters the critical section guarded by the associated semaphore, interrupts should be on.
(b) XCHG REGISTER,MEMORY instruction.
(c) INCREMENT MEMORY instruction.
(d) COMPARE AND SWAP instruction.

Compare all solutions in terms of the degree of concurrency they permit, and discuss their behavior when a process already in the critical section is preempted. Discuss any other advantages or disadvantages that you consider important, and rank all solutions in the order best/worst according to your findings.

4.8 The FETCH AND ADD (FA) instruction has been proposed for interprocess (interprocessor) synchronization in multiprocessor systems. The instruction takes two arguments: the address of the target global variable, GLOBVAR, and the value of the increment to be added to it, INCR, as a result of execution of the FA instruction. The instruction adds the specified value to the global variable and returns the value of the global variable encountered *prior* to the addition. These operations are indivisible, so that parallel execution of several FA instructions by different processors is equivalent to some (unspecified) serial ordering of those instructions. In other words, assuming positive-integer increments, each processor obtains a different value of GLOBVAR, and GLOBVAR contains the correct sum of all increments plus its value prior to execution of the first parallel FA instruction. Explain how this instruction can be used for interprocessor synchronization, and argue whether it is better suited for pessimistic or optimistic concurrency control.

4.9 A computer system includes three identical printers. Use general semaphore(s) to control access of user processes to the printers. Specify whether any changes to the WAIT and SIGNAL parameter lists are needed when general semaphores are used for device-allocation purposes. Devise the printer acquire and release protocols, and write the code of a typical process that uses a printer. Show the required initialization to be performed by a parent process, and explain how your solution handles the situation when the number of active printer-requesting processes exceeds the number of available printers.

4.10 Show superfluity of a general semaphore by implementing a general semaphore with a binary semaphore or semaphores.

4.11 Use semaphores to implement interprocess synchronization as required by the multiprocess example (DAC) introduced in Chapter 3 and in Program 3.2.

4.12 Devise a queuing implementation of semaphores. Describe the necessary data structures and queue-servicing disciplines. Specify which sections of code are critical, if any. Explain the relationship between a semaphore list and a ready list, and describe traversal of the process control-block of a process executing semaphore WAIT and SIGNAL operations. Discuss whether the queuing implementation of semaphores is susceptible to the preemption-deadlock problem, and explain how your solution behaves when a process is preempted after entering its critical section.

4.13 Given that interrupts essentially signal occurrences of external events, semaphore WAIT and SIGNAL operations can conceivably be used to synchronize interrupt-service routines with external events. For example, an ISR charged with processing keyboard interrupts could execute a WAIT(KEYBOARD) to suspend itself until a keyboard interrupt arrives. The operating system could process an interrupt by simulating a SIGNAL operation on the related semaphore, KEYBOARD in this example. Discuss a possible implementation of such a mechanism, outlining clearly the responsibilities of user processes (ISRs) and of the underlying operating system. Explain how your solution handles the problem of multiple outstanding interrupt requests from the same source (interrupt-request buffering), and discuss the relative advantages or disadvantages of this method of interrupt handling versus the classical approach.

4.14 Modify the solution to the producer/consumer problem given in Program 4.11 so that only binary semaphores are used. Compare your solution to Program 4.10, and discuss the relative advantages or disadvantages of using binary as opposed to general semaphores in this particular instance and in general.

4.15 Write a solution to the concurrent readers and writers problem which implements Hoare's proposal for providing a fair treatment of both readers and writers.

4.16 Discuss the usability of semaphores for synchronization of processes executing at different nodes of a distributed computer system characterized by no shared common memory and by relatively long internode communication delays of variable duration. Suggest where copies of the semaphore variables should be kept, and identify potential performance problems when using semaphores in distributed environments.

chapter FIVE

INTERPROCESS COMMUNICATION AND SYNCHRONIZATION

In the previous chapter we demonstrated that semaphores are a powerful mechanism for interprocess synchronization, mutual exclusion and signaling in particular. Their properties, coupled with the relative simplicity and ease of implementation, have made semaphores a popular tool that is routinely found even in commercial releases of multiprogramming operating systems. Abundant literature on semaphores and the problems they may be used to solve, as well as practical experiences gathered in experimental and commercial systems, not only have increased our understanding of the mechanism itself, but also have contributed greatly to making synchronization one of the central issues in operating-system theory and practice. The intense interest in semaphores has also uncovered some of their drawbacks. Semaphores have been criticized on different grounds, often by proponents of alternative approaches, and various mechanisms have been devised to alleviate some of the identified disadvantages. Most criticisms revolve around the two main themes:

1. Semaphores are unstructured: they make synchronization, and ultimately the system integrity, dependent on strict adherence of all concerned systems programmers to the specific synchronization protocols devised for the problem at hand. Reversing of WAIT and SIGNAL operations, forgetting either of them, or simply jumping around them may easily corrupt or block the entire system.
2. Semaphores do not support data abstraction: even when used properly, semaphores can only protect access to critical sections, but cannot restrict

175

the type of operations on shared resources performed by processes that have been granted access rights. On one hand, semaphores encourage interprocess communication via global variables that are, on the other hand, protected only from dangers of concurrency. Such global variables remain vulnerable to illegal or meaningless manipulation by processes legally allowed to modify them by executing correctly the semaphore operations themselves. A single process that erroneously or malevolently corrupts global data may incapacitate all other users of the data even after the offender itself is removed from the system.

In this chapter we present and discuss certain alternative mechanisms that support or enforce more structured forms of interprocess communication and synchronization. We begin with critical regions and conditional critical regions and then continue with monitors. Subsequent sections are devoted to messages, an extremely versatile and popular mechanism in both centralized and distributed systems, and to facilities for interprocess synchronization and communication provided by Ada. The chapter concludes with a discussion of deadlocks and a presentation of several approaches to handling this problem, which is often encountered in multiprocess and multiprogramming systems.

5.1 CRITICAL REGION AND CONDITIONAL CRITICAL REGION

Many of the programs based on semaphores presented in the previous chapter indicate that once the design considerations are translated into a specific synchronization protocol, each programmer is expected to follow it to the letter when coding processes that use the shared resource. However, semaphores, as defined, cannot actually *enforce* the chosen protocol upon users in a systematic and reliable way, say, by means of compile-time checks. One of the main problems is that semaphores are not syntactically related to the shared resources they guard. In particular, there are no declarations that could alert the compiler that a specific data structure is shared and that its accessing needs to be controlled. Brinch-Hansen has proposed a language construct called *critical region* that alleviates this problem.

A critical region protects a shared data structure by making it known to the compiler, which can then generate a code that maintains mutually exclusive access to the related data. Declaration of a shared variable has the following format:

var *mutex* : **shared** *T*;

where the keyword **shared** informs the compiler that the variable *mutex*, of user-definable type *T*, is shared by several processes. Processes may access a guarded variable by means of the **region** construct as follows:

region *mutex* **do**

where the compound statement following **do** is executed as a critical section. When generating code for a region, the compiler essentially inserts a pair of WAIT and SIGNAL operations, or their equivalents, around the critical section. The necessary declarations enable the compiler to make sure that semaphore operations are not reversed or omitted and to refuse access to shared variables to any statements not belonging to the related region.

Critical regions enforce restricted usage of shared variables and prevent potential errors resulting from improper use of ordinary semaphores. On the negative side, critical regions help structure only one of the two most frequent uses of semaphores—mutual exclusion. The other use, signaling, cannot be performed by a region, because a matching WAIT—SIGNAL pair is formed between two or more processes that may be compiled separately. For this reason, semaphores should be retained even in systems that support critical regions. This results in perhaps a confusing coexistence of two different tools for two instances of what may be considered a single problem—interprocess synchronization.

Semaphore users may sometimes be inconvenienced by the lack of ability to conditionally wait on an event. As defined, waiting on a semaphore is unconditional and irrevocable for a process executing a WAIT operation. A process wishing to execute its critical section only when a particular condition on the components of the shared variable is met may adversely affect the degree of parallelism. Assuming binary semaphores, this can happen when the process enters the critical section and discovers that the desired condition is not met. Such a process may have to idle within the critical section until its condition is satisfied, thus unnecessarily preventing other competing processes from accessing the temporarily unused shared resource. Brinch Hansen has proposed another construct, a *conditional critical region*, to cope with this situation.

A conditional critical region is syntactically similar to the critical region. The shared variable is declared in the same way, the **region** construct is also used to control access, and the only new keyword is **await**. Its use is illustrated in the following sequence of code.

var v : **shared** T;

$\cdots$

region v **do**

begin

$\cdots$

await *condition*;

end;

Implementation of this construct allows a process waiting on a condition within a critical region to be suspended on a special queue pending satisfaction of the related condition. Unlike a semaphore, a conditional critical region can admit another process into the critical section in such a case. Consequently, a process waiting on a condition does not prevent others from using the resource. When the condition is eventually satisfied, the suspended process is awakened.

In general, it is difficult to keep track of the numerous possible conditions, so the common implementation of the conditional critical region assumes that each completed process may have modified the shared variable in such a way that certain of the conditions being waited on are satisfied. In other words, whenever a process leaves the critical section, all conditions that have suspended earlier processes are evaluated and, if warranted, one of the processes is awakened. When that process leaves, the next waiting process whose condition is satisfied is activated. Eventually, no more suspended processes are left, or none of them has the necessary conditions to proceed. In either case, an external process may be admitted to an inactive critical section.

The described strategy gives precedence to the waiting processes, thus ensuring that new entries cannot delay waiting processes indefinitely. The suggested implementation also satisfies the mutual-exclusion requirement by allowing at most one process to access the shared resource at any time. Due to a somewhat involved implementation, conditional critical regions are rarely directly supported in commercial systems.

5.2 MONITORS

As far as mutual exclusion is concerned, all mechanisms discussed so far concern themselves only with making sure that at most one process is allowed to access a shared resource at any time. As pointed out, this is only a part of the problem, because a process allowed to access the resource may erroneously or malevolently corrupt it. Monitors are operating-system structuring mechanisms that address this issue in a rigorous and systematic manner.

The basic idea behind monitors is to provide *data abstraction* in addition to concurrency control, that is, to control not only the timing but also the nature of operations performed on global data so as to prevent meaningless or potentially harmful updates. A way to limit the types of allowable updates is to provide a set of well-tested and trusted data-manipulation procedures. Depending on whether users are just encouraged or actually forced to access data only by means of the supplied procedures, data abstraction may be regarded as weak or strong, respectively. The weak form of data abstraction may be supported in a semaphore environment. However, semaphores do not provide an easy way to enforce the use of supplied procedures for data manipulation, thus making the system vulnerable to the forgetfulness and malevolence of its users.

Monitors go a significant step beyond semaphores by making the critical data accessible indirectly and exclusively via a set of publicly available procedures. In terms of the producer/consumer problem, the shared global buffer may be declared as belonging to a monitor, and neither producers nor consumers would be permitted direct access to it. Instead, producers may be allowed to call a monitor-provided public procedure and to supply the produced item as its argument. A monitor procedure would then actually append the item to the buffer. Likewise, consumers may call on a monitor procedure to obtain a produced item from the buffer. A collection of monitor procedures may thus handle buffer-management and synchronization of concurrent requests internally by means of code and variables hidden from users.

User processes usually have no way of knowing the internal organization of a monitor, such as the number, identities, or structure of monitor variables and internal procedures. Once the public monitor procedures are thoroughly debugged, there is no easy way for users to corrupt the global data. In other words, monitors encapsulate the data used by concurrent processes and allow their manipulation only by means of the meaningful and properly synchronized operations. And this points the way to how interprocess communication and synchronization should be handled.

In terms of structure, a monitor is essentially a collection of data and the procedures to manipulate them. Variables are usually private to the monitor and inaccessible outside of it, whereas procedures may be private or public. A declaration of a monitor typically has the following format:

monitorname : **monitor**;
  begin
    declarations of private data;   {local monitor variables}
    . . .
    procedure *pubname* (formal parameters);   {public procedures}
      begin
        procedure_body;
      end;
    . . .
    procedure *privname*;   {private procedures}
    . . .
    initialization of monitor data;
    . . .
  end *monitorname*;

Unlike processes, monitors are static structures with no life of their own. A monitor becomes active when one of its procedures is invoked by a running process. When its execution is completed, a monitor remains inactive until the next invocation. In a way, monitors may be regarded as external functional extensions of user processes. This may also be claimed for external procedures, but monitors differ from such procedures because monitors provide additional facilities for concurrency control, such as signaling and mutually exclusive execution of monitor procedures.

Much of the logic of structuring and implementation of monitors is conceptually similar to that of monolithic operating systems (sometimes also called monitors). A monolithic OS typically consists of a number of public and private routines. It also has private system data structures, such as lists and tables of processes. Users call on the OS public routines when they wish to perform some system-related work. Concurrency is usually supported at the user-process level, but the monolithic operating system itself typically turns interrupts off whenever entered in order to preserve the integrity of the system data and to avoid synchronization problems.

Monitors fit this description to a large extent, including the execution of monitor procedures in a mutually exclusive fashion. The essential difference between the two approaches is that each monitor oversees a particular resource or a small group of related resources. Consequently, a number of monitors in charge of different resources may coexist in a typical monitor-based operating system. In contrast, monolithic implementation of the whole operating system, essentially amounting to a single, large monitor, results in a complex program with many interactions that may be difficult to conceptualize, to debug, and to maintain. In addition to their unreliability, monolithic operating systems often unnecessarily restrict concurrency by allowing at most one of their routines to be active at a time. With a large number of monitors, mutual exclusion forces serial execution of procedures within each of them, but unrestrained concurrency is possible between processes that use separate monitors.

Finally, monitors borrow from semaphores the idea of internal signaling operations. Processes executing monitor procedures are allowed to wait on a particular condition without affecting other monitor users significantly. A process waiting on a condition remains within the monitor but becomes suspended and is placed in the queue associated with that particular condition. As a result, another process may be allowed to have a monitor procedure executed on its behalf. This particular aspect of monitors is similar to conditional critical regions. Unlike semaphores, monitor conditions are neither true nor false, nor do they assume any integer values. A monitor condition is essentially a header of the related queue of waiting processes. One of the consequences of this is that signaling on an empty condition in the monitor has no effect.

In order to illustrate these ideas, a sample monitor is presented in Program 5.1. It actually implements the WAIT and SIGNAL semaphore operations. The code of user processes that invoke monitor procedures is not shown, but it would simply enclose a critical section between calls to MWAIT and MSIGNAL, as usual. Looking at the monitor itself, let us first observe that it has a body, that is, a sequence of instructions that is executed once when the monitor is activated and before it starts accepting calls. Its purpose is to initialize monitor variables, variable BUSY to false in our example. A "parent" process could not do this, because monitor variables are private and may be accessed only from within the confines of the enclosing monitor.

Since BUSY is initially false, procedure MWAIT invoked by the first caller can be completed without waiting on the condition FREE. After BUSY is set to true, the first caller can leave the monitor and proceed to the critical section controlled by the WAIT_SIGNAL monitor. If another process invokes procedure MWAIT at that time, it would be kept waiting on condition FREE, since BUSY is true. As indicated in Program 5.1, the wait statement within the monitor consists of a concatenation of two names: FREE.WAIT. The second

```
wait_signal : monitor;
  begin
    busy : boolean;
    free : condition;
    procedure mwait;
      begin
        if busy then free.wait;
        busy := true
      end;
    procedure msignal;
      begin
        busy := false;
        free.signal
      end;

    {monitor body - initialization}
    busy := false
  end wait_signal
```

Program 5.1 Wait_signal monitor

name invokes the predeclared monitor primitive WAIT. The first part of the name indicates on which condition WAIT should be executed, because there may be several conditions in a monitor and the desired one must be identified.

After FREE.WAIT is executed on its behalf, the calling process is suspended on the queue associated with FREE. If more callers invoke MWAIT while the first one is still in the critical section, they will also join the queue of suspended processes associated with the condition FREE. When the first caller finally executes MSIGNAL, BUSY is set to false and condition FREE receives a signal. As a result, one of the waiting processes is awakened, and it may complete execution of MWAIT. Each subsequent execution of MSIGNAL awakens another process until there are no more waiting processes. The last process to execute MSIGNAL causes FREE.SIGNAL to be sent, but with no effect because no other processes are waiting. This is not a problem, however, because the next caller of MWAIT will be admitted to its critical section without waiting, since BUSY is false. Although the same variable, BUSY, is used by two monitor procedures, there is no danger of its inconsistent updating due to interleaving of concurrent callers because monitor procedures are executed in a mutually exclusive manner.

This example is used as an introduction to monitors because it is fairly simple and implements a familiar mechanism. The theoretical significance of Program 5.1 is that it demonstrates that semaphores can be implemented with monitors. This implies that anything that can be implemented using semaphores can also be implemented using monitors. In other words, monitors are not a weaker concept than semaphores. Although we do not show it here, the reverse is also true; i.e., monitors can be implemented by semaphores.

Due to its specialized purpose, the example presented does not demonstrate the true power of monitors and their facilities for encapsulation of data. An example that shows a more orthodox usage of monitors is given in Program 5.2, which consists of the BOUNDED_BUFFER monitor, which controls the shared buffer and provides the necessary procedures for handling a standard producer/consumer situation. This particular version supports an arbitrary number of concurrent producer and consumer processes. A sample code of one producer and one consumer process is provided in the separate module presented in Program 5.3. This division is made intentionally in order to stress the fact that monitors are entities separate from their users.

The monitor in Program 5.2 owns the data buffer used to smooth the speed differences between producers and consumers. Other monitor data, needed for proper

```
module m_producers_consumers;

    . . .

    b_b : monitor;
       begin
           buffer : array [1..capacity] of item;
           in, out : (1..capacity);
           count : (0..capacity);
           mayproduce, mayconsume : condition;

           procedure mput(pitem : item);
              begin
                  if count = capacity then mayproduce.wait;
                  buffer[in] := pitem;
                  in := (in mod capacity) + 1;
                  count := count + 1;
                  mayconsume.signal
              end; {mput}

           procedure mtake(var citem : item);
              begin
                  if count = 0 then mayconsume.wait;
                  citem := buffer[out];
                  out := (out mod capacity) + 1;
                  count := count - 1;
                  mayproduce.signal
              end; {mtake}

           {monitor body - initialization}
           in := 1;
           out := 1;
           count := 0
       end b_b;

end {m_producers_consumers}
```

Program 5.2 Producer/consumer: bounded buffer monitor

```
module producers_consumers;

  . . .

  process producerX;
    var pitem : item;
    begin
      while true do
        begin
          pitem := produce;
          b_b.mput(pitem);
          other_X_processing
        end {while}
    end; { producerX }

  . . .

  process consumerZ;
    var citem : item;
    begin
      while true do
        begin
          b_b.mtake(citem);
          consume(citem);
          other_Z_processing
        end {while}
    end; {consumerZ }

  { parent process}
  begin
    initiate producers, consumers
  end {users}
end { producers_consumers}
```

Program 5.3 User processes for program 5.2

operation of its procedures, follow much the same logic and functions of their similarly named counterparts introduced in discussion of the producer/consumer problem in Chapter 4 (Section 4.6 and Program 4.11). The only addition is the variable COUNT, which contains the number of items produced but not yet consumed.

Public monitor procedure MPUT serves producer processes and takes one argument, PITEM, a produced item to be placed in the buffer. Producer processes may invoke MPUT at any time. They are effectively allowed to execute whenever there are some empty buffer slots, indicated by COUNT having a value smaller than the buffer capacity. However, when the buffer becomes full (COUNT = CAPACITY), callers are kept waiting by the condition MAYPRODUCE.WAIT until a consumer frees a slot and sends a MAYPRODUCE.SIGNAL.

Initially COUNT is set to 0, thus allowing up to CAPACITY cycles of producers to be completed regardless of consumer activity. Further execution of producers and consumers is controlled by COUNT according to the momentary state of the buffer. Whenever the buffer is empty (COUNT = 0), consumers are prevented from executing by being suspended on the MAYCONSUME condition. When an item is produced, a consumer is freed and the monitor completes the execution of the MTAKE procedure on the consumer's behalf. This ultimately provides a consumer process with an item from the buffer, after signaling MAYPRODUCE to activate a waiting producer, if any.

Our monitor-based solution to the bounded-buffer version of the producer/consumer problem closely follows the logic of its semaphore counterpart. This is done in order to facilitate comparison of the two mechanisms. The monitor in Program 5.2 and the sample producer and consumer processes presented in Program 5.3 clearly demonstrate the advantages of data abstraction.

The common buffer is protected by the monitor, and it cannot be accessed or manipulated in any way other than those provided by MPUT and MTAKE procedures. MPUT and MTAKE themselves restrict buffer operations to the placing and removing of items, respectively. All synchronization between concurrent user processes, manipulation of buffer indices, and updating of the state variable COUNT is performed by the two procedures. Their internal operational details and variables are concealed from users. All that a user process needs to know is that items may be entrusted to the monitor and obtained from it by following the interface specifications for invoking the MPUT and MTAKE procedures. Conformance of a user's code to the monitor's expectations may be verified at compile-time, and service may be denied if necessary.

Hiding the monitor implementation details from users is advantageous in terms of both providing security and localizing the effects of code modifications. Even a major change of the monitor code, such as switching from an array to a linked-list implementation of the buffer, need not affect the user's code as long as the interfacing rules remain unchanged. This should be contrasted to semaphores, where the synchronization protocol may be a part of each user process and changes in buffer structure and manipulation rules may need to be made in all related user processes.

Monitors tend to bring all parts of a synchronization protocol under one roof, as opposed to semaphores, where the synchronization protocol may be distributed over a number of processes. As a result, monitor code is usually more readable, with complementing synchronizing actions found in the neighboring procedures. This, together with localized changes, may contribute to easier debugging and maintenance of monitor-based programs. For example, conditions that cause producers and consumers to wait are quite readily identifiable from the related monitor statements in Program 5.2. Moreover, the effects of sending of a signal may be deduced by checking the nearby signal-receiving code. When semaphores are used, synchronizing conditions tend to be less intuitively obvious from reading the code itself, partly because pairs of WAIT and SIGNAL operations may be dispersed among different processes and/or modules.

In the examples of monitors presented in this chapter, all signaling is done just before the end of a monitor procedure. Implementation of monitors that mandates this kind of signaling is often referred to as a *restricted version of monitors*. In general, signaling may be followed by some other executable statements, but allowing this to happen in monitors causes some implementation difficulties. For example, a process executing a monitor procedure may, by sending a signal, activate a process waiting within the same monitor on that particular condition. If the signaling process has more statements to execute, the problem is that two processes become ready within a monitor that is, by definition, supposed to enforce mutual exclusion. The option is to allow only one of them to continue, but a difficult question is which of the two processes should it be. The signaled process was waiting, so it is possible that it may have spent more time in the monitor, which should entitle it to claim the right of seniority. On the other hand, it seems unfair to penalize the signaling process for making others eligible for execution. The restricted version of monitors makes sure that this never happens by requiring the signaling process to exit the monitor immediately, thus leaving at most one process active within it.

Paradoxically, some of the major strengths of monitors are directly related to their weaknesses. As stated, having a number of monitors within an operating system may result in increased concurrency and in ease of system design and maintenance. However, the management of system resources entrusted to separate monitors can result in deadlocks. This may happen when a monitor procedure calls another monitor procedure, where it is made to wait, thus blocking the calling monitor as well. If a chain of mutually blocked monitors becomes circular, all participants will become deadlocked, with practically no hope of making progress without outside intervention. On the other hand, the definition of monitors virtually eliminates the possibility of external access to monitor variables, thus leaving little room to system implementers to combat the problem of nested monitor calls.

Another criticism of monitors is that by restricting the nature of global-data manipulations to only those functions provided by the public monitor procedures, users are forced to live with whatever system designers may deem to be appropriate ways to access a given resource. For instance, if a certain file structure is imposed by the file monitor that does all reads and writes, application programmers are effectively denied the freedom to interpret files in any other way. This may be unacceptable to some users, such as systems programmers.

5.3 MESSAGES

In Chapter 3 we demonstrated that splitting a single logical activity into a number of processes that may execute concurrently can result in significantly improved performance. In order to perform their collective functions, cooperating processes must exchange data and synchronize with each other. Since both interprocess synchronization and communication are necessary to support concurrent process execution, it is desirable to integrate the two functions within a single mechanism. Such a versatile tool could provide greater uniformity and ease of use of system services while at the same time being likely to reduce overhead by virtue of having one instead of two separate mechanisms.

Semaphores and critical regions are primarily intended for interprocess synchronization. Monitors additionally provide for data abstraction, but they have some implementation problems and tend to be restrictive in terms of the range of allowable interpretations of data. Moreover, implementations of those mechanisms tend to rely to a large extent on the assumption of a common memory accessible to all synchronizing processes. For example, semaphore variables are global and monitor structures (local data, public procedures) are usually centralized. Accessing such global variables can result in considerable communication delays in distributed systems with no common memory. As a result, the straightforward application of centralized mechanisms for concurrency control to distributed environments is often inefficient and slow.

Messages are a relatively simple mechanism suitable for both interprocess communication *and* synchronization in centralized as well as distributed environments. Many commercial multiprogramming operating systems support some sort of interprocess messages. Sending and receiving of messages is a standard form of intersite communication in computer networks, making it very attractive to augment this facility so as to provide the functions of interprocess communication and synchronization. For this reason, messages are very popular in distributed operating systems. Their importance and usefulness have also been recognized by designers of 32-bit microcomputer system buses, for example, Multibus II and VME bus, which provide specialized hardware facilities for low-overhead, high-bandwidth interprocessor message exchanges.

In essence, a *message* is a collection of information that may be exchanged between a sending and a receiving process. A message may contain data, or execution commands, or even some code to be transmitted between two or more processes. For example, messages are often used in distributed systems to transfer major portions of the operating system and/or application programs to remote nodes.

In general, the message format is flexible and negotiable by each specific sender-receiver pair. A message may be thought of as being characterized by its type, length, sender and receiver IDs, and a data field. A possible format of a message is given in Figure 5.1. It divides the contents of the message into two separate fields: message header and message body. The header usually has a fixed format within a given operating system. A possible arrangement of its fields is depicted in Figure 5.1. The optional message body, when present, typically contains the actual message, and its length may vary from message to message even within a single operating system.

5.3.1 Issues in Message Implementation

The typical message operations that may be provided by the operating system or predeclared in a system-implementation language are *send* message and *receive* message. Implementations of messages may differ in a number of details which,

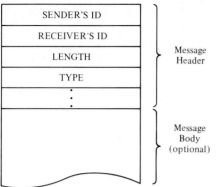

Figure 5.1 Message format.

among other things, affect the functioning and parameters of the SEND and RECEIVE operations. We now describe several important issues in message implementation in order to be able to subsequently give realistic and meaningful examples of their use. In particular, we discuss the following issues:

1. Naming
2. Copying
3. Buffering
4. Length

Naming. One of the major decisions when designing a message facility is whether naming should be direct or indirect. By *direct naming*, we mean that whenever invoking a message operation, each sender must name the specific recipient and, conversely, each receiver must name the source from which it wishes to receive a message. For example, to send a message from process A to process B, the following statements may be necessary when direct naming is used:

> **process** A;
>
> . . .
>
> **send** $(B,\ message)$;
>
> . . .
>
> **process** B;
>
> . . .
>
> **receive** $(A,\ message)$;
>
> . . .

where MESSAGE is the actual message transmitted and B and A are the identities of the receiver and the source of the message, respectively.

This type of message communication is symmetrical in the sense that each sender must know and name its receivers and vice versa. The resulting one-to-one mapping provides a fairly secure message communication as far as mistaken identities are concerned, but it may be inconvenient for implementing service routines. For example, a printer-handler serving the whole system is of little use if it must know the names of all its customers and always specify the particular one from whom the next work-order is to come.

An alternative method is the so-called indirect message communication, where messages are sent to and received from specialized repositories dedicated to that purpose. These repositories are usually called *mailboxes*, due to their way of functioning. For example, if process A wishes to send a message to process B via MAILBOX1, the following statements may be necessary:

> **process** A;
>
>   . . .
>
> **send** ($mailbox1$, $message$);
>
>   . . .
>
> **process** B;
>
>   . . .
>
> **receive** ($mailbox1$, $message$);
>
>   . . .

The first operation places the produced message into the named mailbox, MAILBOX1, and the second removes a message from the named mailbox and provides it to the receiving process via the private variable MESSAGE. When this form of message communication is used, additional system services for maintenance of mailboxes must also be provided, such as CREATE_MAILBOX and DELETE_MAILBOX.

Indirect communication is very versatile in that it can provide one-to-one, one-to-many, many-to-one, and many-to-many mappings between sending and receiving processes. For example, one-to-one mapping is provided simply by creating and dedicating a specific mailbox for the exclusive use of two processes. In a sense, this establishes a private communication channel between them. One-to-many mapping is provided by a mailbox with a single sender and multiple receivers. Many-to-one mapping is important for server processes, and it may be implemented by having a public mailbox with numerous senders (user processes) and a single receiver (server process). If the sender's identity is important for any reason, it may be provided within the message itself.

Copying. Message exchange between two processes, by definition, transfers the contents of the message from the sender's to the receiver's addressing space. This may be accomplished by either copying the whole message into the receiver's addressing space or by simply passing a pointer to the message between the two processes. In other words, message passing can be by value or by reference. In distributed systems with no common memory, copying is obviously unavoidable. In centralized systems, however, the tradeoff is one of safety versus efficiency.

When a message facility is implemented in such a way that the operating system actually copies the entire message from a sender's to a receiver's space, the two processes remain fully decoupled from each other. Essentially, an imprint of the sender's data is made available to the receiver. No matter what the receiver subsequently does with its copy, the sender's original remains unaffected. Likewise, a sender has no direct access to the receiver's data, and any malfunction of either process is localized in the sense that it can corrupt only the local copy of the data. Having multiple private copies of data is an alternative to having a carefully guarded single copy of global data, which is typical in the monitor approach.

On the negative side, copying messages consumes memory and CPU cycles. Asynchronous message communication and/or memory-protection schemes may necessitate that each message first be copied from the sender's space to the operating system's buffer and from there subsequently be copied to the receiver process's space—double copying to deliver a single message. Moreover, a dynamic memory pool usually must be provided and maintained by the operating system to serve as an intermediary in the message-copying process.

This problem tempts some performance-conscious system designers to opt for the less secure but faster solution of simply passing a pointer to the message between the sender and receiver processes. This essentially gives to the receiver a window into the sender's addressing space. One consequence of having a single copy of the message is that while the receiver process is using the message, the sender must not modify any part of it. This is difficult to enforce without some sort of additional mechanism to signal when the message is actually processed by the receiver and may be reclaimed by the sender.

Buffering. The question here is whether the messages sent but not yet received should be buffered or not. The tradeoff is overhead versus flexibility. That is, if outstanding messages are not buffered by the system, both the sender and the receiver must be active and seeking to exchange a message in order for a transfer to take place. In particular, when a sender wishes to send a message for which no outstanding receive is issued, the sender must be suspended until a willing receiver accepts the message. In other words, the sender-receiver communication, when messages are not buffered, is synchronous in the sense that it may take place only between two parties actively seeking the exchange. Consequently, at most one message may be outstanding at any time per a sender-receiver pair.

The avantages of the synchronous message send-receive mechanism are its comparatively low overhead and ease of implementation, as well as the fact that the sender knows that its message has actually been received once the sender is past the SEND-message statement. A disadvantage of this approach is the forceful synchronous operation of senders and receivers, which is undesirable in some cases, as exemplified by the public server processes discussed later in this section.

An alternative, buffering of outstanding messages, allows asynchronous operation of senders and receivers. If no receivers are waiting, a sender delivers its message to the operating system for subsequent forwarding to the recipient. Since the operating system accepts and buffers messages sent but not yet received, a process may continue execution after sending a message and need not be suspended, regardless of the activity of receivers.

This "set and forget" mode of operation tends to increase the degree of concurrency in the system. For example, a process wishing to have something printed may simply place the related data into a message and send it to the printer-server process. Even if the printer-server is busy at the moment, the message is queued by the system and the sender may continue without having to wait. As a matter of fact, the same sender may have several separate print batches outstanding and still not be suspended when creating a new one.

Although asynchronous operation of senders and receivers is a useful feature, it may be dangerous when abused. For example, a runaway process could start producing messages uncontrollably and thereby quickly deplete the system's buffering capacity, thus blocking all further message communication between other processes. One way to alleviate this problem is to impose a system limit on the extent of buffering for each sender-receiver pair or on the mailbox basis.

A related problem, common to both implementations, is that of *indefinite postponement*. This happens when a message is sent but never received, say, due to crashing of the receiver, or when a receiver is waiting for a message that is never produced. Failure to complete a transaction within a finite time is especially undesirable in unbuffered message systems because that automatically blocks the unmatched party. Two common forms of addressing this problem are a nonblocking (waitless) version of the RECEIVE primitive and a timed-wait implementation of RECEIVE.

Nonblocking is a special form of the RECEIVE primitive that is supported in some systems in order to allow receipt of a message if available but without waiting if it is not. The nonblocking RECEIVE primitive returns a message from the designated source if such a message exists. If the message is not available, control is returned to the caller anyway, with an indication of the outcome. Since their functions are sometimes complementary, both nonblocking and blocking versions of RECEIVE are supported in some systems.

A more thorough, but also more complex, approach to the problem of indefinite postponement is to provide a facility for setting a time limit during which a particular message exchange must be completed. Although this limit could be incorporated in both message operations, it is sufficient to implement it in the RECEIVE operation only.

This necessitates a modified calling sequence of message operations, for example:

$$\textbf{receive}(mailbox,\ message,\ time\_limit);$$

where TIME_LIMIT is the maximum time, expressed in clock ticks or standard time units, that the receiver is willing to wait for this message. If none arrives, the operating system returns control to the receiver and informs it, perhaps via a special system message, that a time-out has occurred.

Sender processes can also be protected in this scheme by using an interlock protocol of the form:

> sender :
>
>   . . .
>
> **send** (*mailbox*, *message*);
>
> **receive** (*ackmail*, *ack*, *time_limit*);
>
>   . . .
>
> receiver :
>
>   . . .
>
> **receive** (*mailbox*, *message*, *time_limit*);
>
> **if** message_received_in_time
>
>   **then send** (*ackmail*, *ack*);
>
>   . . .

In this scheme, the sender sends a message and then waits for the related acknowledgment message from the receiver. If the receiver does not receive the original message for any reason, the time limit eventually expires and the sender regains control (from its timed-out RECEIVE operation), at which point it may take some remedial action. The receiver process cannot be held captive by a late message either; it is awakened and informed about the mishap as soon as its own RECEIVE times-out.

Length. The final issue in message design that we discuss in this chapter is whether messages should be of fixed or variable length. The tradeoff here is one of overhead versus flexibility. This problem is not of great importance in systems where message passing is done via pointers, because a different window size for each transmission may be provided by inclusion of a single parameter, window_size, in the message itself. However, when messages are copied and buffered, this tradeoff must be carefully evaluated.

Fixed-size messages usually result in lower overhead by virtue of allowing the related system buffers to be of fixed size as well, which makes their allocation quite simple and efficient. The problem is that messages, when used for communication, naturally come in various sizes, and fitting them into smaller chunks of fixed size often results in additional overhead. For example, short messages waste buffer space, whereas long messages must be split and sent in installments, which may cause sequencing problems at the receiving end. The alternative, variable-size messages, alleviates these problems by dynamically creating buffers to fit the size of each individual message. The problem here is the management of the operating system's dynamic memory pool; allocation of variable-size chunks is costly in terms of CPU time and may also lead to fragmentation of memory, with its related overhead. Details of memory-management, including the problem of fragmentation, are described in Chapters 6 and 7.

5.3.2 Interprocess Communication and Synchronization with Messages

Given a variety of possible message implementations, in the examples that follow we assume a buffered message system with unlimited channel capacity and indirect naming, via mailboxes. This kind of system allows asynchronous operation of senders and receivers. A process may continue executing after sending a message regardless of whether there is a waiting receiver. A process wishing to receive a message is suspended until the message is produced (by a sender), at which point the receiver is resumed. Systems with alternative implementations of messages may differ in certain operational details, but the overall logic and sequence of operations of the programs that follow are generally applicable to most message-based environments.

Although messages are suitable for both interprocess communication and synchronization, we first look at the synchronization aspect of their operation in order to establish a point of reference with the material presented earlier. It is important to realize that exchanging an empty message, with no data field, between two processes is essentially equivalent to signaling. A process, by sending a message, passes a timing signal to another process, the recipient. As far as signaling is concerned, this has the same effect as one process (sender) executing a SIGNAL operation and the other (receiver) executing a WAIT on the same semaphore. In this analogy, the identity of the mailbox corresponds to the name of a unique semaphore variable. As in semaphore systems, the process issuing a WAIT (receiver) remains suspended until the semaphore is signaled (message sent to the mailbox) by some other process. Alternatively, if the semaphore is free (message already in the mailbox), the process issuing the WAIT is allowed to proceed without being suspended.

Given the signaling power of messages, mutual exclusion may be accomplished by following the logic of a similar semaphore solution. This is done in Program 5.4, which contains the code of a representative user process accessing a shared resource protected by the mailbox MUTEX. Following the logic of semaphore implementation, it is assumed that a mailbox is created empty and that it initially contains no messages. This is equivalent to semaphores being initialized by the system to BUSY. In order to make the resource available to the first requester, the parent process sends a message to the mailbox before initiating the users of the resource. Since this message is used solely for signaling purposes, its data content is immaterial, and we assume that it is an empty, NULL, message. Some time later, the first process that wishes to use the resource invokes the RECEIVE operation on the MUTEX mailbox. This results in the initial NULL message being removed from the mailbox and delivered to the process via its MSG parameter. Having received a message, the process is free to continue, and it enters the critical section. If any other process executes a RECEIVE on the MUTEX mailbox during that time, it will be suspended because the mailbox is empty. When its critical section is completed, the owner of the message returns it to the mailbox MUTEX and continues to execute. One of the processes suspended on MUTEX, if any, then receives the message and thus becomes able to proceed.

program/module *msg_mutex*;

  . . .

    type
     message = **record** . . .;
    const
     null = . . .; {*empty message*}

    process *userX*;
     var
      msg : *message*;
     begin
      while *true* **do**
       begin
        receive(*mutex*, *msg*);
        critical_section;
        send(*mutex*, *msg*);
        other_X_processing
       end {*while*}
     end; {*userX*}

    . . .   {*other user processes*}

  {*body of parent process*}
  begin {*msg_mutex*}
   create_mailbox(*mutex*);
   send(*mutex*, *null*);
   initiate *users*
  end {*msg_mutex*}

Program 5.4 Mutual exclusion with messages

The remaining waiting processes, if any, will get their turn, one at a time, as the message is being returned by processes exiting the critical section.

    This scheme is conceptually similar to semaphores. A single message is circulated through the system as a token permit to use the shared resource. Since at most one process may own the message at any point in time, mutual exclusion is ensured. This, of course, depends on the assumption that the RECEIVE operation is indivisible in the sense of delivering the message, if any, to only one caller when invoked concurrently by several. Virtually all implementations of messages provide this kind of SEND and RECEIVE facility, and we assume that this property exists in all further discussion of messages. When used for signaling, the very act of receiving a message accomplishes the desired purpose, and the actual contents of the message are immaterial. As we shall see later, the power and appeal of messages become fully utilized when each message actually transfers data at the same time, thus combining both interprocess communication and synchronization within a single action.

    Program 5.4 informally demonstrates that a message facility may be used to implement binary semaphores. The important implication is that messages, therefore, are not a weaker mechanism than semaphores. General semaphores may be simulated by increasing the number of token messages in the system to match the initial value of an equivalent general semaphore. For example, if three identical printers are to be allocated by means of messages, three tokens should initially be created by sending NULL messages to the appropriate mailbox.

Program 5.5 demonstrates the use of messages in solving the producer/consumer problem. Given that messages may be used to emulate semaphores, a mirror solution of the bounded-buffer version of the semaphore solution may be devised in a fairly straightforward manner. Program 5.5 takes a somewhat different approach in order to utilize fully the ability of messages to transfer data and signals simultaneously. Rather than having a single global buffer accessed by all processes, individual buffer slots are distributed over messages. It is assumed that the data field is present in each message and dimensioned so as to be capable of holding a single produced item.

Two mailboxes, MAYPRODUCE and MAYCONSUME, are used to exchange messages between producers and consumers. Each producer process is supposed to obtain a message from the MAYPRODUCE mailbox—an operation equivalent to reserving an empty buffer slot. After filling the message with the produced item, the producer sends the message to the MAYCONSUME mailbox for consumption. A consumer process removes a message from the MAYCONSUME mailbox, consumes the item contained therein, and returns the empty message to the MAYPRODUCE mailbox.

The buffering capacity is limited by the total number of messages initially made available to producers and consumers. In Program 5.5 this is accomplished by the parent process, which initially sends CAPACITY empty (NULL) messages to the MAYPRODUCE mailbox. This allows up to CAPACITY producer cycles to take place before the first item is consumed. From that point on, producers may run only when there are empty messages available at the MAYPRODUCE mailbox. If none is available, the producers are suspended and kept waiting as a result of executing RECEIVE operations on the MAYPRODUCE mailbox. Likewise, consumers may execute only when there are items produced but not yet consumed, as indicated by messages being queued at the MAYCONSUME mailbox.

The solution presented in Program 5.5 allows a number of producer and consumer processes to run concurrently, and it generally satisfies the requirements imposed by our statement of the producer/consumer problem, provided that messages are queued at mailboxes in FIFO order.

The message approach tackles the problem of global data-manipulation, which is of major concern to the previously discussed solutions, in a rather elegant and decisive fashion—by outright elimination. Other than the names of the two mailboxes, all operational variables in Program 5.5 are local. Elimination of the global buffer in particular makes this solution applicable to both centralized and distributed processing environments.

For all practical purposes, producer and consumer processes may reside and execute at different sites. For example, one site may host producer processes and

```
program/module msg_prods_cons;
    . . .

    type
       message = record . . .;
    const
       capacity = . . .;        {buffering capacity}
       null = . . .;            {empty message}
    var
       i : integer;

    process producerX;
       var pmsg : message;
       begin
          while true do
             begin
                receive(mayproduce, pmsg);
                pmsg := produce;
                send(mayconsume, pmsg);
                other_X_processing
             end {while}
       end; { producerX }

    process consumerZ;
       var cmsg : message;
       begin
          while true do
             begin
                receive(mayconsume, cmsg);
                consume(cmsg);
                send(mayproduce, cmsg);
                other_Z_processing
             end {while}
       end; {consumerZ }

    { parent process}
    begin {msg_prods_cons}
       create_mailbox(mayproduce);
       create_mailbox(mayconsume);
       for i := 1 to capacity do send(mayproduce, null );
       initiate producers, consumers
    end {msg_prods_cons}
```

Program 5.5 Producer/consumer: bounded-buffer version with messages

the MAYPRODUCE mailbox, and another site may handle consumers and the MAYCONSUME mailbox. As long as both mailbox names are globally known or reachable and the operating systems at each end support an intersite-compatible form of the SEND and RECEIVE operations, it is even possible to have the two sites operate under different operating systems. Producer and consumer processes may be independently coded in different programming languages and developed in different program-development environments. Of course, all this would require a number of supporting implementation details and facilities in order to be put into practice. However, our point is that message passing, unlike most mechanisms discussed so far, is a versatile mechanism that may be extended naturally for use in distributed environments. As a result, messages are frequently found in network operating systems.

5.3.3 Interrupt Signaling via Messages

In order to present our final example of the use of messages, let us point out an important possibility for unification of signaling mechanisms and interrupts. As stated in Chapter 2, the interrupt mechanism provides a link between asynchronous external events and the software routines that service them. In other words, interrupts signal the arrival of external events. This is conceptually no different from a process signaling a certain event, such as the completion of resource usage or the emptying of a buffer slot. The question, then, is: Why not provide a uniform signaling mechanism that would encompass both interrupts and ordinary interprocess synchronization? This could result in easier program development and maintenance, since systems programmers would have a single, uniform tool that handles all aspects of synchronization and communication between cooperating processes.

In practice, most commercial systems tend to separate interrupt-service routines from other processes and to provide restricted and exclusive sets of primitives that may be used only by processes belonging to a specific subdivision. This attitude results from the differences in implementation at the system level. In particular, interrupt processes must provide for vectoring, context-switching, and maintenance of interrupt masks and environments commensurate with the priorities of active processes and perhaps do other housekeeping operations that are not required for ordinary, not interrupt-related, processes.

Conceptually, however, synchronization has similar requirements in both cases, and there is little justification in keeping the two sets of processes separate at the user's level. The operating system could simply convert each interrupt into a signal sent by the system to a process or processes waiting for it. For example, a dedicated semaphore may be created for each interrupt. Interrupt-service routines may then connect themselves to external events by executing a WAIT operation on the related semaphore whenever they are ready to service an interrupt. The arrival of an external event, indicated by an interrupt, may be used to activate the server by means of the SIGNAL operation executed by the operating system on the related semaphore.

This approach provides an abstraction that delegates the details of low-level interrupt operations to the operating system while eliminating differences between interrupt and ordinary processes at the user level. The actual servicing of an interrupt still rests with the dedicated server process, thus providing full flexibility and making it unnecessary for the operating system to worry about the device-specific peculiarities of different sources of interrupt. Our sample operating system described in Chapters 9 and 10 handles interrupts in this way and thus demonstrates the feasibility of the proposed approach. The last example in this section, which follows, illustrates the use of such a unified signaling approach.

Program 5.6 contains the sample code of a PRINT_SERVER process that is assumed to act as a printer driver. This process is assumed to be the only one

```
program/module printer;

    . . .

    type
       request = record                    { print-request message}
          length : integer;                { how many to print}
          printdata : array [1..length] of char;   { data to print}
          response : mailbox               { send response here}
       end; {request}

    process print_server;
       var
          newrequest : request;
          synch : message;
       begin
          {initialization}
          disable_printer_interrupts;
          initialize_printer_hardware;
          create_mailbox( printint);
          connect_interrupt_vector( printer-to-printint);
          while true do
            begin
               receive( printmail, newrequest);
               enable_printer_interrupts;
               for i := 1 to newrequest.length do
                 begin
                    receive( printint, synch); {await printer interrupt}
                    print_port := newrequest.printdata[i]
                 end; { for}
               disable_printer_interrupts;
               if newrequest.response <> NIL then send(newrequest.response, done)
            end {while}
       end; { print_server}

    { parent process}
    begin { printer}
       create_mailbox( printmail );
       initiate print_server;
       initiate users
    end { printer}
```

Program 5.6 Message implementation of printer server

directly accessing the printer port and actually transmitting characters to it. In this way, the details of printer operation are hidden from other processes, both in order to relieve them from the idiosyncrasies of the physical device and to protect the printer itself from being used improperly by inexperienced users, which could potentially make it unusable for the entire system.

When a process needs to have something printed, it is simply supposed to forward its request to the PRINT_SERVER. A request is presented as a message of the REQUEST format. All requests are sent to a public mailbox PRINTMAIL. In a buffered message system, a number of print requests may be awaiting processing without the need to suspend the issuing processes unless they desire to wait for some reason. As a matter of fact, a single process may have several outstanding print requests at a time and still continue to execute without waiting for the, usually slower, printer to finish.

The arrival of each printer interrupt in Program 5.6 is assumed to be intercepted by the operating system and converted into a synchronization message that is sent to the PRINTINT mailbox dedicated for that purpose. Prior to sending this message, the operating system is supposed to switch context, to adjust priority masks, and to do whatever else may be required by a specific system when processing a hardware interrupt. At the user level, a printer interrupt is serviced upon receiving the system message (used purely for signaling; its content is immaterial) at the PRINTINT mailbox.

The PRINT_SERVER process begins by initializing the hardware, the printer port and the device itself. As discussed in Chapter 2, the details of this process are markedly system-specific, and we do not discuss them here. The cyclic portion of the PRINT_SERVER consists of accepting a message with a user's request and printing its data portion, one character at a time, in response to printer interrupts. The familiar interrupt-enable/disable mechanism is used to control the printer operation. Probably the best way to manipulate interrupts in this case is at the level of the control bits in the status register of the related device, so as not to interfere with the operation of the entire interrupt system. In any case, when a request is processed, i.e., all the characters contained in it are printed, the PRINT_SERVER process takes a new request, if any, from the PRINTMAIL mailbox. When there are no requests, the PRINT_SERVER is suspended on the PRINTMAIL mailbox. When several requests are outstanding, they are queued at the mailbox, and the server process processes them as fast as it can.

Since messages used to pass print requests also contain data, user processes are decoupled from the server and each is allowed to progress at its own pace. In order to implement the "queue I/O and wait" form of service, the PRINT_SERVER process may send an optional message, when required to do so by the nonnull RESPONSE field, to inform the caller when its service is completed.

Asynchronous operation of sender and receiver processes, made possible by message buffering, is a very desirable feature of the input/output portion of the operating system. If messages are not supported as system primitives, I/O section designers usually emulate a message facility when managing queues of outstanding I/O requests. This is necessary in order to support the two fairly standard options of I/O calls: post an I/O request but allow the caller to continue without waiting (queue I/O call), and post an I/O request and suspend the caller until completed (queue I/O and wait). The callers of such I/O services are thus provided with an option to wait, as is typical of interactive programs when obtaining input, or to proceed after launching an I/O operation. The latter form allows for concurrent operation of user programs and of their I/O operations. Server processes implemented with messages, as evidenced by Program 5.6, naturally support both versions of I/O operations.

5.4 INTERPROCESS SYNCHRONIZATION AND COMMUNICATION IN ADA

Ada is a fairly complex language intended, among other things, for embedded real-time applications. Its specification and development process have been a result of a massive intercontinental cooperation among military, academic, and industrial institutions and individuals. Ada embodies many interesting concepts and facilities useful for multitasking and real-time programming. Some of them include the following:

Modular program development Ada supports separate module compilation in a form that allows compile-time checking of type compatibility (strong typing) across module boundaries. This is accomplished by means of the *package* and *task* constructs that separate module interface specification (publicly visible part) from its body of private data declarations and executable statements (private part). A module that interacts with other modules must be compiled together with their interface specifications, thus enabling the compiler to perform intermodule checks. Ada also provides a rather elaborate scheme for making sure that only up-to-date versions of participating modules (interface specifications and executable code) are combined to form an executable program. This feature is useful for large-scale program development, where a number of programmers may be coding and testing separate modules.

Processes As discussed in Chapter 3, Ada explicitly supports the notion of processes, called *tasks* in Ada, and provides facilities for their creation (initialization) and concurrent execution. Each active process is also characterized by a number of dynamically updated attributes, such as priority and status, which are available for inspection to authorized processes. Ada also provides a DELAY statement, which is useful for timing purposes.

Low-level operations Some facilities for interrupt vectoring and even interfacing with machine-language modules are provided by means of machine-specific libraries that may be combined with other modules. This qualifies Ada as a systems-implementation language, at the expense of possibly restricted portability of the programs that use the low-level facilities.

Exception processing Ada provides a rather thorough set of facilities for dealing with run-time errors. A number of error conditions are defined in the language, and a mechanism is provided for transferring control to user-written code for handling exceptions once they occur. This allows systems programmers to separate the ordinary code from the error-handling routines, as opposed to the usual practice dictated by other languages of having the two intertwined. In principle, errors should account for a relatively small percentage of a program's execution. Their processing usually consists of identifying and attempting to remedy, or at least localize, the resulting negative effects. Since the goals of normal and error processing are quite different, interspersing their code often results in obscuring the logic of both. Given the importance and extensiveness of error processing in systems and real-time programming, Ada's approach facilitates development of more readable and potentially more reliable programs.

All these features, as well as many others not mentioned here, make Ada a fairly complex language that cannot be described in one section of a chapter. In keeping with our present main theme, our primary focus remains on Ada's facilities for interprocess synchronization and communication. Ada is very interesting in this respect, because it is expressly intended for multiprocess systems in both centralized and distributed environments. With practically all presented interprocess synchronization and communication mechanisms already known at the time of its inception, designers of Ada were able to draw on a considerable body of existing research ideas and experiences. As a result, Ada combines a number of familiar concepts in a different and sometimes innovative way.

Rendezvous is the primary interprocess synchronization and communication mechanism in Ada. As is the case with messages, a single set of tools is used for both signaling and data exchange. However, data exchanged between two processes in Ada are structured and typed in a way that may be checked at compile-time, a significant departure from the permissive and potentially obscure formation of messages.

Basically, in order to rendezvous, two processes wishing to exchange timing signals and/or data must both be active and seeking interaction with each other. A rendezvous actually takes place only when both parties are ready and willing to synchronize. Otherwise, the first party to arrive waits. When the second party eventually arrives, the two processes are synchronized briefly to exchange data and possibly to execute some code whose results may be required for their continuation. In any case, after a rendezvous, the parties separate and each continues on its own.

There are actually several different statements in Ada for accomplishing rendezvous. In order to stress the basic ideas, we start by describing what is probably the simplest one, the *entry-accept* mechanism. It allows two or more processes to synchronize with each other and, optionally, to exchange some data during their rendezvous.

5.4.1 The Entry-Accept Mechanism

The syntax and semantics of the entry-accept mechanism are somewhat reminiscent of an external-procedure call. In particular, one of the involved processes contains and owns a sequence of statements to be executed during a rendezvous with another process. Such statements are enclosed within an *accept* construct which may contain no executable statements if only synchronization is required. In order for other processes to rendezvous with it, the owner of the ACCEPT statement gives it a unique name that is made public by placing a corresponding ENTRY statement in the public declaration part of that process.

In order to follow the official syntax of the Ada language, the keyword **task** is used instead of our usual process in all Ada-related examples. To avoid discrepancy between the programs and their textual descriptions, the term *task* is also used instead of process when referring to Ada in the remainder of this section.

As mentioned earlier, statements of a task in Ada are separated into two parts: the public part, where names of the globally accessible variables and procedures are declared for others to reference, and the private implementation part, which is inaccessible to other tasks. Therefore, the identifier of a publicly usable ACCEPT statement must be declared in the public part of its embodying task. An example of this is given in Program 5.7, in which task B contains an ACCEPT statement and provides a corresponding ENTRY in its public part. In this way, task B declares its willingness to accept calls of its ACCEPT statement from other tasks. As Program 5.7 demonstrates, both ACCEPT and its related ENTRY statements have the same identifier (NAME), which may be followed by an optional list of formal parameters to be exchanged during a rendezvous. In our particular example, no data are exchanged, so no parameter list is present.

A sample caller, task A, is also shown in Program 5.7. It declares its intention to rendezvous with B's entry NAME simply by including what looks

```
task A is                     task B is
   {public part of A}            {public part of B}
   .
   .                             entry name;
   .
                                 .
end A;                        end B;

task A body is                task B body is
   {private part of A}           {private part of B}
   .                             .
   B.name; {call entry}          accept name;
   .                             .
end A;                        end B;
```

Program 5.7 Entry - Accept in Ada

like a standard procedure call. The NAME is prefixed by the name of its enclosing task, B, in order to avoid possible ambiguities resulting from identical procedure or entry names in different tasks. Since NAME is an external reference, as far as compilation of task A is concerned, Ada language requires task A to be compiled together with the public part (interface specification) of task B, where NAME is defined. In this way, intermodule checks of proper naming, typing, and matching of parameter lists can be performed at compile-time.

When a call of an entry NAME is encountered during an execution of task A, Ada's run-time system checks whether the matching ACCEPT statement has been executed by task B. Two things may happen: either A arrives first or B is already waiting to have its ACCEPT matched. If task A arrives first, it is suspended and placed in the queue of tasks associated with the ACCEPT NAME statement in task B. Conversely, if task B executes its ACCEPT before A's call, task B is suspended at that point, pending an execution of the B.NAME call by an authorized task. Once both parties arrive, the rendezvous takes place and the two tasks are kept until completion of the ACCEPT sequence of statements, if any.

In Program 5.7, no executable statements are enclosed within the ACCEPT NAME statement, so the rendezvous between tasks A and B is only momentary, after which the two tasks continue on their own. However, even this momentary synchronization is sufficient to serve as an exchange of a timing signal between two tasks, since each task, once past its respective call to the B.NAME and ACCEPT NAME statements, knows that it was in brief synchrony with the other.

As Program 5.7 illustrates, the entry-accept mechanism is asymmetrical. In particular, the calling task must name the owner of the ENTRY, whereas the latter may accept calls from any task that knows the name of the ENTRY and satisfies other compile-time and run-time checks. In Ada, callers must know the name of the service they desire, whereas the service need not name all its users. This is a many-to-one mapping, which is, as we recall, necessary for implementation of server tasks. Of course, the one-to-one mapping may be easily accomplished with this scheme by having a single calling task for a given ENTRY.

The entry-accept mechanism requires two tasks to be in synchrony in order to exchange timing signals and/or data by suspending the first party until the second arrives. While synchronization may reduce concurrency, it generally improves safety in the sense that the caller knows for sure that the rendezvous has been successfully completed once it is past the ENTRY call. Given synchronous intertask signaling and communication in Ada, an interesting question is: What happens if the owner of the ENTRY terminates and a caller attempts to rendezvous with it? This rendezvous, obviously, would never take place, and Ada's run-time system would intervene by raising an ACCEPT exception, which in turn would transfer control to the associated caller's error-processing routine.

Program 5.8 illustrates an implementation of semaphores in Ada, as used for mutual exclusion. Task SEMAPHORE, which actually implements the mecha-

```
task semaphore is
  entry wait;
  entry signal;
end semaphore;

task body semaphore is
  begin
    loop
      accept wait;
      accept signal;
    end loop;
  end semaphore;

... {callers}

task X body is
  begin
    loop
      semaphore.wait;
      critical_section;
      semaphore.signal;
      other_X_processing;
    end loop;
  end X;
```

Program 5.8 Semaphore implementation in Ada

nism, and a sample user task, X, are shown. Task SEMAPHORE has two public entries, WAIT and SIGNAL. As the code of task X indicates, the two entries are used in the same way as the equivalent semaphore operations. The first user task to execute the SEMAPHORE.WAIT call achieves a momentary rendezvous with the matching ACCEPT WAIT statement in the SEMAPHORE task. The two tasks then separate, allowing the caller to enter its critical section.

Other callers of WAIT, if any, are kept waiting in its queue, because task SEMAPHORE is willing to rendezvous only with the callers of SIGNAL after having executed the ACCEPT WAIT statement. Once a user task executes the SEMAPHORE.SIGNAL call, the corresponding momentary synchronization takes place. The two tasks are then free to continue on their own, the user task to do whatever other processing it needs to do, and the SEMAPHORE task to await a rendezvous with the next call to WAIT. If one or more calls are queued in its ACCEPT WAIT queue, task SEMAPHORE performs a rendezvous with the first in the queue.

ACCEPT queues in Ada are, by definition, handled in FIFO order, thus providing for the strongest possible implementation of semaphores. Task SEMAPHORE implements the mutual-exclusion function of binary semaphores by accepting calls only in strict alternation of WAIT and SIGNAL in that order, although not necessarily from the same task. Consequently, task SEMAPHORE is not suitable for signaling.

5.4.2 The SELECT Statement

Ada's *select* statement for concurrent programming builds on the already presented rendezvous mechanism but adds to it the power to choose among alternatives. SELECT is a very versatile and powerful statement with nontrivial semantics. We first present some examples in order to give an intuitive motivation for the functioning of the SELECT statement and then give a more systematic description of its semantics.

Program 5.9 shows how SELECT may be employed to modify somewhat the restrictive behavior of the SEMAPHORE task from Program 5.8. The task SIGNAL presented in Program 5.9 is actually a generic task predeclared in Ada. The SELECT statement, as used in Program 5.9, consists of two alternative code sequences. One of them, beginning with the keyword **when**, is conditional, or the so-called *guarded statement*. In Ada's terminology, depending on whether the associated condition evaluates to true or false, the guard is said to be open or closed, respectively. Note that this is a dynamic property; a guard may oscillate between open and closed states in the course of execution of tasks that affect the constituent variables of its condition.

A snapshot of a guard's state is important when a SELECT statement is evaluated, because on each run, SELECT considers only open guards for execution. The first part of SELECT in Program 5.9 is unconditional, so it is always ready to rendezvous with callers of SEND. An unconditional part of a SELECT statement may be regarded as having its guard always open.

An execution of a SELECT statement begins by the evaluation of all guards. An alternative with an open guard, leading to an immediate rendezvous with some other task, is then selected and executed in a mutually exclusive fashion

```
task signal is
   entry send;
   entry wait;
end signal;

task body signal is
   received : boolean := false;
   begin
     loop
       select
         accept send;
         received := true;
       or when received =>
         accept wait;
         received := false;
       end select;
     end loop;
   end signal;
```

Program 5.9 Ada implementation of a signaling semaphore

with respect to other alternatives. If several open alternatives qualify as leading to immediate rendezvous, say, by having callers waiting in queues associated with their ACCEPT statements, an arbitrary one is chosen. If no alternative leads to an immediate rendezvous, the SELECT statement waits for an alternative to become ready for a rendezvous and then executes it.

In terms of our example, the first alternative is always open, and the second depends on the current state of the variable RECEIVED. This variable is initially set to false right after being declared, since Ada allows compile-time initialization of variables. Therefore, initially only the first alternative is open, and only calls on SEND can rendezvous with the task SIGNAL. Similarly to the queuing implementation of semaphores, the SELECT statement is supposed to be implemented in such a way that no code is executed when there are no outstanding calls to SEND.

The first caller of SIGNAL.SEND has a brief rendezvous with the matching ACCEPT SEND, after which both tasks continue on their own. As far as the task SIGNAL is concerned, this means continuation of the mutually exclusive execution of the selected alternative, setting RECEIVED to false in our particular example. Completion of that assignment statement concludes an execution of the alternative that it belongs to and thus completes the particular execution of the SELECT statement. Being within an endless loop, the next execution of SELECT follows shortly. It begins by evaluating the guards and now finds both to be open. That means that an alternative which has outstanding callers, if any, will be executed. If none does, SELECT waits for the first call to *either* SEND or WAIT. An execution of either call by another task causes SELECT to start executing the related alternative in order to complete a rendezvous.

This example shows that SELECT is an open-minded wait flexible enough to follow the route leading to some useful work if such a route exists, as opposed to ordinary conditional statements that tend to make a choice first and then pursue it irrespective of its fruitfulness. In a way, the SELECT statement is event-driven and dormant in the absence of significant events. In Program 5.9 the use of SELECT allows implementation of a binary semaphore usable for both signaling and mutual-exclusion purposes. This informally demonstrates that Ada's mechanisms are not weaker than semaphores. A more involved example is given in Program 5.10 to illustrate further the use and power of SELECT.

The task BOUNDED_BUFFER in Program 5.10 controls the buffer used by producers and consumers for the exchange of data items and provides two entries for buffer manipulation, PLACE and TAKE. The buffer itself, as well as other operational variables, is private to the BOUNDED_BUFFER task and is thus not directly accessible to producer and consumer tasks. Instead, user tasks can only call on PLACE and TAKE entries in order to furnish data to the buffer or have them removed from there, respectively. This approach is very similar to the monitor version of the same problem.

In keeping with the nature of the problem, produced items may be placed in the buffer only when the buffer has some room. This is ensured by the first condition, which allows calls to PLACE to be accepted only when there is some

```
task bounded_buffer is
  entry place(pitem : in item);
  entry take(titem : out item);
end bounded_buffer;

task body bounded_buffer is
  capacity : constant integer := ...;
  subtype index is integer range 1..capacity;
  buffer : array[index] of item;
  in, out : index;
  count : integer range 0..capacity := 0;
  begin
    loop
      select
        when count < capacity = >
          accept place(pitem : in item) do
            buffer[in] := pitem;
          end;
          in := (in mod capacity) + 1;
          count := count + 1;
      or
        when count > 0 =>
          accept take(titem : out item) do
            titem := buffer[out];
          end;
          out := (out mod capacity) + 1;
          count := count - 1;
      end select;
    end loop;
  end bounded_buffer;
```

Program 5.10 Producers/consumers in Ada

unused buffer capacity. Producers, on the other hand, are allowed to execute only when the buffer is nonempty. This is ensured by the second guard, which remains closed otherwise, thus effectively causing consumers to wait in the associated queue when the buffer is empty. When the buffer is neither full nor empty, both guards are open and producers and consumers may execute concurrently.

The variable COUNT is used by both alternatives to keep track of the number of items produced but not yet consumed. The contents of the variable COUNT are rather critical in that their value affects the states of both guards. Given mutually exclusive execution of the alternatives in SELECT, there is no danger of inconsistent updating of COUNT in the presence of concurrent execution of producers and consumers.

With two examples behind us, we now give a more systematic description of the semantics of Ada's SELECT statement. The full definition includes the additional variations introduced by the possibilities of having DELAY statements in the bodies of different alternatives, but we do not consider those here. Although not illustrated by our examples, the syntax of the SELECT statement allows for an ELSE part which may be executed when no guards are open. Keeping in mind mutually exclusive execution of a selected alternative, execution of a SELECT statement may be described as follows:

1. Evaluate all conditions.
2. Select an arbitrary open alternative if the corresponding rendezvous is possible.
3. If no immediately selectable alternative with an open guard exists, execute the ELSE part. If there is no ELSE part, wait until an alternative with an open guard becomes selectable, as per the rule above.
4. If no guards are open, execute the ELSE part. If there is no ELSE part, raise an exception (SELECT_ERROR).

The SELECT statement is evidently a powerful tool in the hands of systems programmers. Efficient implementation of the SELECT itself is quite demanding, but only compiler writers have to worry about that.

A final example of the use of SELECT in this chapter is provided by Program 5.11, which contains the code of the READER_WRITER task that controls a resource shared by concurrent readers and writers. In order to allow for relative comparisons, this program uses the same scheduling strategy as an earlier one implemented by means of semaphores. That is, as many readers as possible are allowed to access the common resource.

Instead of an entry, readers are provided with a public procedure, READ, that must be used to access the resource protected by the READER_WRITER task. The procedure READ itself contains calls to private entries necessary to achieve the desired synchronization. In this way, all readers are forced to observe the prescribed protocol, as opposed to relying on them to do so voluntarily by exporting the entries START_READ and STOP_READ themselves.

The common resource READ_WRITE_STUFF, of unspecified format, is first initialized by a writer. The cyclic part of the code consists of a SELECT statement with three alternatives. Two unconditional alternatives (guards always open) accept calls to START_READ and STOP_READ performed on behalf of active readers by the READ procedure. A rendezvous with each starting reader is used both to allow the reader to access the resource and to update the variable READERCOUNT which keeps track of the number of readers actively using the resource. Only when there are no active readers (READERCOUNT = 0) does the guard that allows rendezvous with writers open. If there are writers with outstanding calls to WRITE, one of them achieves a rendezvous with the READER_WRITER task.

During the rendezvous, as specified by the ACCEPT statement, the resource is updated using the value provided by the writer, at which point both tasks are freed to proceed on their own. As before, mutual exclusion of the SELECT statement's alternatives guarantees that the updating of READERCOUNT remains consistent in the presence of concurrent execution of readers and writers.

```
task readers_writers is
  procedure read(v : out item);
  entry write(e : in item);
end readers_writers;

task body readers_writers is
  read_write_stuff : item;
  readercount : integer := 0;
  entry start_read;
  entry stop_read;
  procedure read(v : out item) is
    start_read;
    v := read_write_stuff;
    stop_read;
  end;
  begin
    accept write(e : in item) do
      read_write_stuff := e;
    end;
    loop
      select
        accept start_read;
        readers := readers + 1;
      or
        accept stop_read;
        readers := readers − 1;
      or
        when readers = 0 =>
          accept write(e : in item) do
            read_write_stuff := e;
          end;
      end select;
    end loop;
end readers_writers;
```

Program 5.11 Readers/writers in Ada

5.5 DEADLOCKS

Generally, high overall resource utilization and the possibility of parallel operation of many input/output devices driven by concurrent processes contribute
significantly to the high performance potential of multiprocess and multiprogramming systems. At the same time, concurrency and high resource utilization also provide the necessary conditions and the fertile soil for deadlocks
that can be detrimental to system performance. A *deadlock* is a situation
where a group of processes is permanently blocked as a result of each process having acquired a subset of resources needed for its completion and having to wait for release of the remaining resources held by others in the same

group—thus making it impossible for any of the deadlocked processes to proceed.

Deadlocks can occur in concurrent environments as a result of the uncontrolled granting of system resources to requesting processes. As an example, consider a system consisting of a printer and two disk drives. Assume that two concurrent processes make the resource requests indicated in Program 5.12. The presented sequence assumes that resources are requested from and released back to the resource allocator by means of the familiar WAIT and SIGNAL operations on semaphore variables PRINTER (binary) and DISK (general, initialized to 2), respectively. Assume that the two concurrent processes, P1 and P2, are interleaved in such a way that at some point in time process P1 is granted the use of the printer and P2 manages to seize a disk drive. In this case, the two processes are deadlocked, since neither of them can acquire the balance of resources it needs to make further progress. As a result, neither of the processes can complete and release the resources that it owns.

Typifying some general characteristics of deadlocks, this example illustrates that the problem is a result of concurrent execution, since each process could complete correctly when executed serially in an arbitrary order. Moreover, the problem occurs only for certain specific scenarios of interleaving of the two processes. For example, if either process manages to seize all its resources before the other process acquires any, both processes complete in finite time the sequences of actions shown in Program 5.12. Semaphore operations, instead of the common system calls to REQUEST and RELEASE resources, are used to suggest that each process continues to hold ownership of the acquired resources while waiting for the new ones. Semaphores also suggest that the resources are used on a mutually exclusive basis and that the respective "critical sections" can only be completed when all the needed resources are acquired. In the presented example, resources are assumed to be actual physical devices. In general, however, deadlocks can occur as a result of competition over any kind of shared resource, including main memory and information, such as global data, buffer pools, and files. For example, deadlocks can result from execution of nested monitor calls, and the

```
process p1;                          process p2;

    ...                                  ...

  wait(printer);                       wait(disk);
  wait(disk);                          wait(printer);
  wait(disk);                          disk_&_print_processing;
  2_disks_&_print_processing;          signal(printer);
  signal(disk);                        signal(disk);
  signal(disk);
  signal(printer);                       ...

    ...
```

Program 5.12 A sequence of resource requests and releases

processes presented in Program 5.12 can become deadlocked while executing the assumed sequence of operations regardless of the nature of resources protected by the two semaphore variables.

The described conditions actually illustrate the necessary conditions for deadlock, which may be stated more explicitly as follows:

1. *Mutual exclusion.* The shared resources are acquired and used in a mutually exclusive manner, that is, by at most one process at any time.
2. *Hold and wait.* Each process continues to hold resources already allocated to it while waiting to acquire other resources.
3. *No preemption.* Resources granted to a process can be released back to the system only as a result of the voluntary action of that process; the system cannot forcefully revoke them.
4 *Circular waiting.* Deadlocked processes are involved in a circular chain such that each process holds one or more resources that are being requested by the next process in the chain.

The simultaneous existence of these conditions defines the state of deadlock. In other words, all four necessary conditions must be present for a deadlock to occur. Thus, one way to handle deadlocks is to ensure that at every point in time at least one of the four conditions necessary for deadlocks is prevented by design. Another possibility is to have the resource allocator examine the possible consequences of allocating a particular requested resource and to avoid unsafe situations that may lead to deadlocks. Yet another option is to grant resources to requestors freely, but to occasionally examine the system state for deadlocks and to take remedial action when necessary. Most of the practical deadlock-handling techniques fall into one of these three categories, which are customarily called *deadlock prevention*, *deadlock avoidance*, and *deadlock detection and recovery*, respectively. Before describing each of these approaches in detail, we briefly outline some characteristics of the different types of system resources.

5.5.1 Reusable and Consumable Resources

Computer-system resources whose allocation is subject to deadlocks can be broadly categorized into two classes: reusable and consumable resources. *Reusable resources* are characterized by being safely usable by at most one process at a time. Such resources are normally granted to a requesting process when available. When explicitly released by its temporary owner, a reusable resource can be allocated to another requestor, if any. Shared hardware resources and static, long-term global-data structures commonly belong to this category. Some examples include main memory, I/O channels, disk drives, and slots of the system buffer pool. There is usually a fixed number of reusable resources in a system.

In general, there may be several instances of the same reusable resource type, such as memory pages and printers. If individual units of a particular type of resource are indistinguishable in the sense that any of them can satisfy a given request, then such units are not separately labeled for deadlock-detection purposes, but only their total count is kept track of by the system. Thus, the most general case is a system with many different types of resources and multiple instances of each type of resource. Some common special cases include multiple types of resources with a single instance of each resource type and a single type of resource with multiple instances of it.

At any time, each reusable resource is either available or temporarily granted to a process. The common assumption is that the temporary owner of a resource will relinquish the resource in finite time unless deadlocked. In order to concentrate on deadlocks, other potential failures leading to indefinite holding of allocated resources, such as program malfunctions and infinite loops, are ignored and assumed to be taken care of by the operating system, say, by imposing the run-time limits.

Consumable resources, such as messages, are produced and consumed by active processes. As a result, the number of such resources in a system can vary with time. One of the common causes of deadlock involving consumable resources is waiting for an event, such as a message or a signal, that will never arrive. This can happen due to improper synchronization, message addressing, or termination of the producer. Such deadlocks may be regarded as being caused by the programming errors, and their handling can be left to individual affected processes. For example, Ada's task-terminated exception can be useful in this context. From the system's point of view, it is important to ensure that such processes do not hold indefinitely the resources acquired prior to waiting. This can be taken care of by placing and enforcing a limit on how long a process can be allowed to wait. A similar facility can be made available to user processes, say, in the form of the time-limited RECEIVE introduced under Issues in Message Implementation in Section 5.3.

5.5.2 Deadlock Prevention

The basic philosophy of deadlock prevention is to deny at least one of the four necessary condition for deadlocks. Mutual exclusion is usually difficult to dispense with, so it is customary to prevent some of the remaining three conditions.

The hold-and-wait condition can be eliminated by requiring or forcing a process to release all resources held by it whenever the process requests a resource that is not available. In other words, waiting processes are not holding any resources and deadlocks are prevented. There are basically two possible implementations of this strategy: all resources are requested prior to commencement of execution, or resources are requested and, if possible, acquired during the execution.

In order to request all resources at the outset, a job or a process must preclaim all its resource needs. Although sometimes requiring additional effort, it is possible to estimate the resource requirements of processes. This task is somewhat easier for batch jobs, whose resource requirements are often deducible from the job-control statements. In any case, the common problem with preclaiming of resource needs is that such estimates tend to be conservative and to err on the overestimating side. In general, preclaiming necessitates inclusion of all resources that could *potentially* be needed by a process at the run-time as opposed to those *actually* used. This is especially a problem for so-called data-driven programs, whose actual resource requirements are determined dynamically at the run-time. A typical example is provided by ad hoc queries in databases, such as "Update salaries of all programmers," which may need to scan the entire database in order to identify and acquire exclusive use of the subset of qualifying entities, such as "programmers" in the previous example. When such transactions are required to preclaim their resources in advance, they may grossly exaggerate by specifying perhaps the entire database, since "managers" or any other category of employees may be specified by a user interactively on another run. The overestimation problem is present whenever resource requirements must be stated in advance of execution.

When all resources needed by a process are acquired at the outset, they are allocated and unavailable to other processes during the lifetime of the owner process. The problem is that some of those resources may actually be used only during a portion of the execution of the related process, say, at the beginning (card reader) or at the end (printer). Therefore, some resources can be idle for relatively long periods of time, but for the sake of deadlock prevention, they cannot be allocated to other requesting processes. Since the preclaiming of resource needs also has the tendency to overestimate resource requirements, deadlock prevention by means of advanced acquiring of all estimated resources can result in low resource utilization and a corresponding reduction of the level of concurrency possible in the system.

An alternative is to acquire resources incrementally, as needed, and to prevent deadlocks by releasing all resources held by a process when it requests a temporarily unavailable resource. This strategy has the advantages of no preclaiming and of not holding all resources from the inception of a process. However, the drawback is that some resources cannot easily be relinquished and resumed at a later time. For example, some irreversible changes made to memory or to files may corrupt the system if not carried to completion. In effect, resumption of a resource is meaningful only if the integrity of the system is not jeopardized and when the overhead of the state save and restore operations involved in resumption is acceptably small.

The no-preemption condition can obviously be denied by allowing preemption, that is, by authorizing the system to revoke ownership of certain resources from blocked processes. Since preemption is involuntary from the point of view of the affected process, the operating system must be charged with saving the state and restoring it when the process in question is later resumed. This makes preemption of resources even more difficult than the voluntary release and resumption of resources discussed in the previous paragraph. Preemption is possible for certain types of resources, such as the CPU and main memory, since the CPU portion of the process state is routinely saved during the process switch operation and the contents of the preempted memory pages can be swapped out to secondary storage. However, some types of resources, such as partially updated files, cannot be preempted without corrupting the system. Therefore, preemption is possible only for certain types of resources, and it can be applied when the benefits of deadlock prevention outweigh the cost of state save and restore operations. However, since some resources cannot be safely preempted, this approach alone cannot, in general, provide complete deadlock prevention.

One way to prevent the circular-wait condition is by linear ordering of different types of system resources. In this approach, system resources are divided into different classes C_j, where $j = 1, \ldots, n$. Deadlocks are prevented by requiring all processes to request and acquire their resources in a strictly increasing order of the specified system-resource classes. Moreover, acquisition of all resources within a given class must be made with a single request, and not incrementally. In other words, once a process acquires a resource belonging to the class C_j, it can only request resources of class $j+1$ or higher thereafter. Linear ordering of resource classes eliminates the possibility of circular waiting, since a process Pi holding a resource in class C_i cannot possibly wait for any process waiting for a resource in a class C_i or lower.

For example, the resources of the sample system assumed while constructing Program 5.12 can be divided in disk and printer classes in that order. Each process would first have to acquire all disks and then all the printers it needs. With this strategy, it is easy to show that the two processes cannot become deadlocked no matter how they are interleaved. Moreover, adherence of processes to the prescribed ordering of resource requests can be checked at compile-time, thus allowing the system to refuse improper requests without imposing run-time overhead.

A disadvantage of this approach is that resources must be acquired in the prescribed order, as opposed to being requested when actually needed. This may cause the acquiring of some resources well in advance of their actual use, thus lowering the degree of concurrency by making unused resources unavailable for allocation to other processes.

5.5.3 Deadlock Avoidance

The basic idea of deadlock avoidance is to grant only those requests for available resources which cannot possibly result in a state of deadlock. This strategy is usually implemented by having the resource allocator examine the effects of granting a particular request. If the granting of such a resource cannot possibly lead to deadlock, the resource is granted to the requestor. Otherwise, the requesting process is suspended until such time that its pending request can be safely granted. This is usually the case after one or more resources held by other active processes are released.

In order to evaluate safety of the individual system states, deadlock avoidance requires all processes to state (preclaim) their maximum resource requirements prior to execution. Once its execution begins, each process requests its resources as and when needed, up to the maximum preclaimed limit. Naturally, processes whose stated resource requirements exceed the total capacity of the system are not admitted for execution.

The resource allocator keeps track of the number of allocated and available resources of each type, in addition to recording the remaining number of resources preclaimed but not yet requested by each process. A process that requests a resource that is temporarily unavailable is made to wait. If the requested resource is available for allocation, the resource allocator examines whether granting of the request can lead to deadlock by checking whether each of the already active processes could safely complete in case all such processes exercise all their remaining options in acquiring resources they are entitled to by virtue of the remaining claims. If so, the system state after the contemplated allocation is safe and the resource is allocated to the requesting process. Alternatively, granting of the resource could potentially lead to a deadlock state and the resource allocator suspends the requesting process until the desired resource can safely be granted.

In order to describe a deadlock-avoidance algorithm more precisely, we introduce a graph-based model of resource allocation. A graph of $G = (N, E)$ consists of a finite nonempty set of *nodes* (*vertices*) N and edges E. If edges are ordered pairs of nodes (x, y), the graph is said to be *directed*. A *path* in a directed graph is a sequence of edges of the form $(x_1, x_2), (x_2, x_3), \ldots, (x_{n-1}, x_n)$. A *cycle* is a path involving at least two nodes, where the first and the last node are the same. A *bipartite* (bicolored) graph is a graph G whose nodes can be partitioned in two disjoint subsets P and R such that each edge of G connects a node of P and a node of R.

A general resource graph of a possible state of the system described in relation to Program 5.12 is depicted in Figure 5.2a. Each process is depicted by a node drawn as a square, and each type of resource is depicted by a node drawn as a circle. Printer and disk nodes are labeled R1 and R2, respectively. Each unit of a given type of resource is denoted by a small circle inside the node representing the corresponding type of resource. For example, the disk node (R2) in Figure 5.2 contains two circles depicting the two disk drives present in the system. Only one circle in the printer node (R1) indicates the presence of a single printer. Ownership of a resource by a process is represented as an edge from the corresponding resource node to the related process node. Thus, in Figure 5.2a, process P1 is assumed to own the printer. A request for a resource is represented as an edge from the requesting-process node to the target-resource node. For example, the request of process P2 for a disk drive is depicted in Figure 5.2a.

The described representation is called *the general resource graph*. The graph is directed and bipartite, consisting of the two disjoint subsets of the process and resource nodes.

In order to present an algorithm for determining the safety of a system state, let us define the data structures needed by the resource allocator. One way to represent the general resource graph in a computer is by means of a two-dimensional matrix with processes as rows and resource types as columns. In

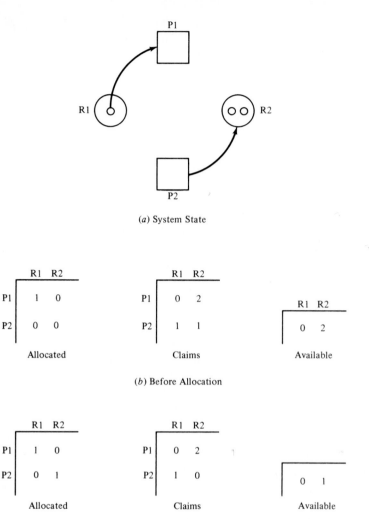

(a) System State

	R1	R2
P1	1	0
P2	0	0

Allocated

	R1	R2
P1	0	2
P2	1	1

Claims

	R1	R2
	0	2

Available

(b) Before Allocation

	R1	R2
P1	1	0
P2	0	1

Allocated

	R1	R2
P1	0	2
P2	1	0

Claims

	R1	R2
	0	1

Available

(c) After Allocation

Figure 5.2 Deadlock avoidance.

this representation, matrix elements correspond to individual edges. Let us call this matrix ALLOCATED, and assume that each of its elements a_{ij} indicates the number of units of the type j held by the process i. An example of the ALLOCATED matrix for the sample system depicted in Figure 5.2a is shown in Figure 5.2b.

The number of resources of each type available for allocation at a given point in time can be represented by an integer row vector AVAILABLE, also shown in Figure 5.2b. Unused resource claims can be represented by means of the CLAIMS matrix, whose structure is identical to that of the ALLOCATED matrix. Elements of the CLAIMS matrix are obtained as the difference between the maximum number of resources of a given type preclaimed by the corresponding process and the number of resources of the same type currently owned by that process. An example of the CLAIMS matrix prior to granting of P2's request for a disk drive is depicted in Figure 5.2b.

The crucial part of deadlock avoidance is the safety test. A state is regarded as *safe* if all processes already granted resources would be able to complete in some order even if each such processes were to use all resources they are entitled to. Thus, a practical safety test must determine whether such an ordering exists.

Let us define a "less than or equal" operation on two vectors C and A of identical size r as $C \leq A$ if and only if $C[i] \leq A[i]$, for every $i = 1, 2, \ldots, r$. In the description that follows, row vectors are denoted by subscripting the name of the enclosing data structure with the identity of the given process (row). For example, $CLAIMS_i$ denotes the ith row of the matrix CLAIMS, that is, the resource claims of the process i.

Resource request

1. For each resource request, verify that the issuing process is authorized to make the request by virtue of having sufficiently many unused claims on the requested type of resource. Refuse to consider unauthorized requests (it is assumed that a static test to verify that the process is preclaiming no more than the maximum number of each type of resource existing in the system is already performed, say, at process-creation time).
2. When a process requests a resource that is not available for allocation, suspend the calling process until its request can be safely granted. When a process requests an available resource, pretend that the resource is granted by updating the ALLOCATED, CLAIMS, and AVAILABLE data structures accordingly. Unmark all processes.
3. Find an unmarked process i such that

$$CLAIMS_i \leq AVAILABLE$$

   If found, mark the process i, update the AVAILABLE vector

$$AVAILABLE := AVAILABLE + ALLOCATED_i,$$

   and repeat this step. If no qualifying process can be found, proceed to the next step.
4. If all processes are marked, the system state is safe, so grant the requested resource, restore the AVAILABLE vector to its value prior to execution of Step 1, and exit to the operating system. Otherwise, the system state is not safe, so suspend the requesting process, restore ALLOCATED, CLAIMS, and AVAILABLE to their values prior to execution of Step 1, and exit to the operating system.

Resource release

When a resource is released, update the AVAILABLE data structure and reconsider pending requests, if any, of that resource type.

The "marking" and "unmarking" of processes required by the stated algorithm can be implemented by modifying some of the existing data structures or by means of a dedicated Boolean column vector MARKED whose entries depict the status (marked or unmarked) of each individual process.

The safety-evaluation portion of this algorithm is known as the *banker's algorithm*, and its time complexity is proportional to $r \times p^2$, where p is the number of active processes, and r is the number of resources. This bound is determined by the repetitive operation in Step 3 of the algorithm, and it is a consequence of the property of the algorithm to determine safety of a state, that is, whether some ordering of resource acquisitions leading to completion of all active processes exists, without backtracking. More efficient algorithms exist for some specialized cases, such as only one instance of each type of resource or only a single type of resource present in the system.

The contents of the data structures after execution of Step 2 of the algorithm are depicted in Figure 5.2c. This is the contemplated state that the system will assume if P2's request is granted. Since Step 3 cannot find a sequence of execution leading to completion of either process, the algorithm determines that the tentative state is unsafe, defers granting of R2 (disk drive) to process P2, and restores the contents of the data structures to the values shown in Figure 5.2b. Although *two* disk drives are in fact available for allocation, the resource allocator does not grant either to process P2. The reason is that there are not enough available resources in the system to complete both P1 and P2 should they choose to exercise all their claims without releasing any of the resources already owned. For the sequence of requests presented in Program 5.12, the resource allocator allows the first process which acquires a single resource to proceed, while the other process is kept waiting after making the very first request. In this particular example, deadlock avoidance imposes strict serialization on the two sample processes.

As indicated, deadlock avoidance does not require acquisition of all resources at once, nor does it necessitate preemption of resources. Resources are requested as and when needed, thus eliminating the problem of resource idling due to premature acquisition which is often encountered with some deadlock-prevention strategies. On the negative side, deadlock avoidance requires preclaiming of resource needs and imposes the run-time storage and execution overhead of detecting the safety of system states. As discussed in the previous section, preclaiming of resources tends to err on the conservative side. This influences the degree of concurrency in systems with deadlock avoidance indirectly but adversely, by causing the resource allocator to perceive a greater number of system states as unsafe. As a result, processes may be kept waiting even when the requested resources are free and allocatable. Even when resource predictions are accurate, the conservative nature of deadlock avoidance tends to reduce the degree of concurrency. This is a consequence of the definition of the safety of a state as a situation only *potentially* leading to a deadlock, as opposed to being a deadlock. In other words, safe states constitute only a subset of nondeadlock states, and unsafety does not imply deadlock. For example, by applying the deadlock-detection algorithm presented in the subsequent section, it can be shown that the unsafe state depicted in Figure 5.2a (data structures in Figure 5.2c) is not a deadlocked state. A deadlock, however, is always an unsafe state.

5.5.4 Deadlock Detection and Recovery

Instead of sacrificing performance by preventing or avoiding deadlocks, some systems grant available resources to requesting processes freely and only occasionally check for deadlocks in order to reclaim resources held by deadlocked processes, if any.

It has been shown that existence of a cycle (or circuit) in a general resource graph is a necessary condition for deadlock. Existence of a *knot*, that is, a cycle with no noncycle outgoing path from any of the involved nodes, is a sufficient condition for deadlocks in a general resource graph. In systems with a single instance of each type of resource, existence of a cycle is a necessary and a sufficient condition for deadlock. Thus, the existence of deadlocks can be determined by using the known algorithms for finding cycles or knots in graphs. It has been shown that a practical approach is to attempt to reduce the general resource graph by removing all holdings and requests of each process whose requests can be granted until all possible reductions are done. If the graph is completely reduced (no edges left) after this process, the system state is not a deadlock. Otherwise, the system is deadlocked and the remaining, irreducible processes are deadlocked. This property of the described procedure is important, because once the deadlock is found, it is necessary to identify the deadlocked processes in order for the system to take some remedial action.

In this section we present a different version of the deadlock-detection algorithm that uses data structures similar to those already introduced in relation to deadlock avoidance. In particular, we use the ALLOCATED matrix and the AVAILABLE integer vector as before. Instead of the CLAIM matrix, we use the REQUESTED matrix of the same format, whose elements identify the number of resources of each type requested but not yet granted to active processes. Naturally, the sum of allocated and requested resources cannot exceed the maximum system capacity. The algorithm operates by accounting for all possibilities of sequencing the processes that remain to be completed. If a completion sequence exists, the system is not in a state of deadlock. Otherwise, the system is deadlocked, since there is no way for all active processes to complete. More specifically, the algorithm can be stated as follows:

1. Update the ALLOCATED, REQUESTED, and AVAILABLE in accordance with the system state. Unmark all active processes.

2. Find an unmarked process i such that

$$\text{REQUESTED}_i \leq \text{AVAILABLE}$$

If found, mark process i, update AVAILABLE

$$\text{AVAILABLE} := \text{AVAILABLE} + \text{ALLOCATED}_i,$$

and repeat this step. If no qualifying process can be found, proceed to the next step.
3. If all processes are marked, the system is not deadlocked. Otherwise, the system is deadlocked and the set of unmarked processes is deadlocked.

The presented algorithm has the same time complexity as the deadlock-avoidance algorithm presented in the previous section, $r \times p^2$. More efficient algorithms exist for specialized cases, such as systems with a single instance of each resource type or with a single type of resource with multiple instances. An algorithm linearly proportional with the number of active processes has been devised for the general case when requests for resources are ordered by size and when a count of the number of resources being requested is associated with each process. This additional bookkeeping overhead is partly offset by facilitating the finding of a blocked process to activate when other processes release resources.

An example of some aspects of the operation of this algorithm is presented in Figure 5.3. A state of the sample system introduced in relation to Program 5.12 is presented in Figure 5.3a. This state can be obtained by granting P2's request for a disk drive (a situation considered unsafe by the deadlock-avoiding resource allocator), then subsequently granting P1's request for a disk drive (still not a deadlock), and then allowing P2 to request the printer and P1 to request a disk drive. Presumably, both processes are blocked due to the unavailability of the requested resources, and the deadlock-detection algorithm is invoked to assess the situation. The contents of the ALLOCATED, REQUESTED, and AVAILABLE data structures for this case are shown in Figure 5.3b. Since no resources are available and both processes have nonzero resource-request vectors, the algorithm cannot find a single qualifying process in Step 2, and it concludes that the two processes are deadlocked.

The frequency of deadlock detection is a system-design parameter. One possibility is to check for deadlocks whenever a resource is requested. An alternative is to activate the deadlock-detection algorithm occasionally, say, at regular intervals or when one or more processes are blocked for a suspiciously long time. Frequent testing for deadlocks has the advantage of early discovery of deadlocks, thus enabling the system to act quickly. Infrequent testing of deadlocks reduces the run-time overhead for deadlock detection at the expense of leaving deadlocks undetected for longer periods of time. This approach can result in lower resource utilization, since deadlocked processes continue to hold resources already granted to them while not making any progress.

Among other things, the frequency of deadlock detection determines the operational details of the resource allocator. For example, if deadlock detection is

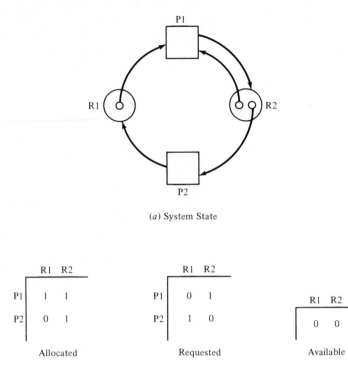

(a) System State

	R1	R2
P1	1	1
P2	0	1

Allocated

	R1	R2
P1	0	1
P2	1	0

Requested

	R1	R2
	0	0

Available

(b) System Data Structures

Figure 5.3 Deadlock detection.

performed upon every resource request, the resource allocator can maintain the deadlock-detection data structures up to date, and they need not be updated in Step 1 of the algorithm. Namely, the ALLOCATED or REQUESTED matrix is updated for each granted or pending resource request, respectively. Moreover, each granting to or releasing of resources by the running process is recorded in the AVAILABLE vector. Since the presented algorithm modifies the AVAILABLE vector while operating, a copy of that vector should be made prior to or during Step 1 and it should be restored for allocation purposes upon completion of the algorithm. With only occasional deadlock detection, there are numerous possibilities for system-resource bookkeeping. In schemes where the AVAILABLE vector is needed for those purposes, performing of the described save and restore operations may be needed. In either case, the minimal resource bookkeeping necessary to allow construction of the data structures described in Step 1 is mandatory in systems where deadlock detection is practiced.

Deadlock detection is only a part of the deadlock-handling task. Detecting of a deadlock only reveals existence of the problem, and the system must then break the deadlock in order to reclaim resources held by blocked processes and to ensure that the affected processes can eventually be completed. The first step in deadlock recovery is to identify the deadlocked processes. This gives an edge to detection algorithms that provide indications of deadlocked processes, such as the one described in this section. The next step is to break the deadlock by rolling back or restarting one or more of the deadlocked processes. Restarting of a process implies the loss of work completed by the process prior to its becoming deadlocked. Since presumably not all processes have progressed equally far, it is desirable to choose the victims among processes whose restarting is less costly. Rolling back of a process requires a facility for recording the run-time states of processes, so that a process can be returned sufficiently deep in the past to break the deadlock. Such facility is provided in some systems where high reliability and/or availability is desired. Common examples include checkpointing in real-time systems and journaling in transaction-processing systems. When present, such mechanisms can be additionally employed for recovery from deadlocks. In general, both rollback and restarting can be difficult, if not impossible, for processes that have done irreversible changes to resources owned prior to deadlock.

In summary, deadlock detection and recovery provides a higher potential degree of concurrency than deadlock prevention or avoidance. Moreover, the run-time overhead of deadlock detection can be made into a tunable system parameter. The price to be paid is the overhead of deadlock recovery once deadlocks are detected and of the usage of system resources wasted by processes that are restarted or rolled back. Deadlock recovery can be attractive in systems with a low probability of deadlocks. In heavily loaded systems, unrestricted granting of resource requests is known to be conducive to overcommitting of resources that can result in frequent deadlocks. The negative effects of allowing deadlocks to occur tend to increase with the system load and with the frequency of deadlocks, thus increasingly wasting system resources when they are needed most.

5.5.5 Combined Approach

It has been argued that none of the presented approaches alone is suitable enough to be used as an exclusive method for handling of deadlocks in a complex system. Instead, deadlock prevention, avoidance, and detection can be combined for maximum effectiveness. This can be accomplished by dividing system resources into a collection of disjoint classes and by applying the most suitable method of handling deadlocks to resources within each particular class. This division can be made along the lines of the design hierarchy of a given operating system or in accordance with the dominant characteristics of certain types of resources, such as tolerating preemption or allowing accurate predictions. Resource ordering, described in relation to deadlock prevention, can be applied to prevent deadlocks between classes. The class-particular deadlock-handling method is then employed to deal with deadlocks within a class of resources.

Consider a system with the following classes of resources:

1. Swapping space, an area of secondary storage designated for backing up blocks of main memory

2. Job resources and assignable devices, such as printers and drives with removable media, e.g., tapes, cartridge disks, floppies
3. Main memory, presumably assignable on a block basis, such as pages or
segments
4. Internal resources, such as I/O channels and slots of the pool of dynamic
memory

The presented enumeration also represents the ordering that must be followed
when requesting resources belonging to different classes. The proposed ordering
is quite logical for the job and process traversal paths described in relation
to scheduling in Chapter 3 (Section 3.5 and Figure 3.9). The order and the
discipline of making requests for resources within a given class is determined by
the applicable local deadlock-handling strategy. The following strategies may be
applied to individual resource classes:

1. *Swapping space.* Prevention of deadlocks by means of advanced acquisition
   of all needed space is a possibility for the swapping-store space. Deadlock
   avoidance is also possible, but deadlock detection is not, since there is no
   backup of the swapping store.
2. *Job resources.* Avoidance of deadlocks is facilitated by the preclaiming of
   resource requirements, which is customarily done for jobs by means of the
   job-control statements. Deadlock prevention by means of resource ordering
   is also a possibility, while detection and recovery are undesirable due to the
   possibility of modification of files that belong to this class of resources.
3. *Main memory.* With swapping, prevention by means of preemption is a reasonable choice. This allows support for run-time growth (and shrinking)
   of memory allocated to resident processes. Avoidance is undesirable because of its run-time overhead and the tendency to underutilize resources.
   Deadlock detection is possible but undesirable due to either the run-time
   overhead for frequent detection or the unused memory held by deadlocked
   processes.
4. *Internal system resources.* Due to frequent requests and releases of resources at
   this level and the resulting frequent changes of state, the run-time overhead of
   deadlock avoidance and even of detection can hardly be tolerated. Prevention
   by means of resource ordering is probably the best choice.

5.6 SUMMARY

In this chapter we have introduced several mechanisms that provide more structured forms of interprocess synchronization and communication than semaphores.
Critical region is a language construct that strictly enforces mutually exclusive
use of a resource declared as shared. In addition, conditional critical region allows
a process to wait on a condition within a critical section without preventing other
eligible processes from accessing the shared resource.

Monitors control not only the synchronization but also the nature of operations that concurrent processes are allowed to perform on shared resources. Shared data can be encapsulated within a monitor body and made accessible only by means of publicly declared monitor procedures. This strong form of data abstraction provides a potential for increased system integrity and tends to localize the effects of program modifications. Mutually exclusive execution of monitor procedures and the signaling facility are available for synchronization among concurrent processes that access the shared resource entrusted to a given monitor. A restricted version of monitors allows a process to signal only immediately prior to leaving the monitor.

Messages allow interprocess communication and synchronization without the need for global variables, which makes them suitable for both centralized and distributed systems. Depending on whether messages are buffered or not, both asynchronous and synchronous operation of sender and receiver processes can be implemented. Mailbox-based exchange of messages can provide very versatile address mapping between sending and receiving processes. Coupled with the ability to be used for signaling interrupts, messages can be used to implement server processes, such as a printer-server, with support for both synchronous and asynchronous forms of I/O calls.

The Ada language relies on various forms of the synchronous rendezvous mechanism for both interprocess synchronization and communication. The entry-accept mechanism allows exchange of data and signals between concurrent processes, while the select statement augments this facility with the ability to choose among alternatives. Strong data abstraction is supported for both mechanisms.

Deadlocks are a common problem in systems where concurrent processes need simultaneous exclusive access to a collection of shared resources. The necessary conditions for deadlock (mutual exclusion, hold and wait, no preemption, and circular waiting) are unfortunately often encountered in multiprogramming systems. Deadlocks can be prevented by designs that deny at least one of these conditions at all times. Deadlocks can be avoided by evaluating the safety of the resulting system state prior to granting each resource request. Another approach is to grant available resources freely and to check for deadlocks occasionally in order to reclaim resources held by deadlocked processes, if any. Each of these schemes has some relative advantages and disadvantages, thus making a combined approach to deadlock handling an interesting alternative.

OTHER READING

Critical regions and conditional critical regions were introduced by Brinch Hansen (1972, 1973).

Hoare (1974) has formalized and expanded the notion of monitors to their present form. Formal treatment and proving of monitors is provided by Howard (1976). The use of monitors in the programming language Concurrent Pascal is described by Brinch Hansen (1977) and in Modula-2 by Wirth (1983). Operating-system applications of monitors are discussed by Keedy (1978). Ravn (1980) explores application of monitors to device drivers. Implementation-related aspects of monitors and processes are discussed by Lampson and Redell (1980).

Messages are described by Brinch Hansen (1970, 1973) and by Peterson and Silberschatz (1983). Comparisons of communication with messages versus procedure calls are provided by Stankovic (1982) and by Staunstrup (1982). A concurrent programming language and notation for interprocess synchronization and communication via messages, Communicating Sequential Processes (CSP), was introduced by Hoare (1978). A programming language based on asynchronous interprocess message exchange in distributed systems, PLITS, was proposed by Feldman (1979). Hardware implementation of a message facility on the i432 processor is described by Organick (1983). A message-based multiprocessor system, called the Cosmic Cube, is described by Seitz (1985). The notion of using messages to signal arrivals of interrupts is described in relation to the Multics system by Spier and Organick (1969).

Interactions between concurrent processes in Ada are described in Ichbiah et al. (1979) and in U.S. Department of Defense (1983). The SELECT statement is based on the idea of guarded commands proposed by Dijkstra (1975). A detailed treatment of Ada's rendezvous mechanism and its applications to standard problems in concurrent programming is provided by Habermann and Perry (1983). An analysis of the efficiency of implementation of Ada rendezvous is discussed by Jones and Ardo (1982).

Dijkstra (1968a) was one of the first to describe the problem of deadlocks. A thorough treatment of deadlocks is provided by Coffman et al. (1971), where the deadlock-detection algorithm presented in this chapter is described. Holt (1972) has formulated the general resource graph model of deadlocks and several algorithms for handling of deadlocks in different situations. Habermann (1969) describes the general resource case of a deadlock-avoidance algorithm. The combined approach to deadlock handling was proposed by Howard (1973). A formal treatment of deadlocks is provided by Shaw (1974). Isloor and Marsland (1980) provide an overview of deadlocks in centralized and distributed systems. Concurrency control and deadlock management in distributed database systems are surveyed by Kohler (1981) and by Bernstein and Goodman (1981).

Textbook treatments of the issues and mechanisms for concurrent programming are provided by Holt et al. (1978), Ben-Ari (1982), and Filman and Friedman (1984). A thorough survey of concepts and notations for concurrent programming is provided by Andrews and Schneider (1983).

EXERCISES

5.1 Identify the system services for interprocess synchronization and communication provided by a multiprogramming operating system accessible to you. Describe what facilities, if any, are available for mutual exclusion, signaling, and data communication. What type of data abstraction is supported by the operating system and/or by the preferred system-implementation language? Write short test programs to explore the functioning of system calls. Describe how processes are developed and executed in the system. Discuss the advantages and disadvantages of the system under evaluation relative to the mechanisms for interprocess communication and synchronization introduced in Chapters 4 and 5. (Small multiprocess operating systems available for many microcomputers and personal computers provide an ideal environment for the experimental part of this exercise. Large time-sharing systems often restrict the range of interprocess services that casual users are allowed to invoke.)

5.2 Show how a monitor can be implemented with semaphores.

5.3 Write a program that solves the readers/writers problem introduced in Chapter 4 by using monitors. Compare and contrast the semaphore, monitor, and Ada solutions to the same problem in terms of the type of data abstraction and of the readability of the code.

5.4 Use monitors to solve the readers/writers problem using Hoare's suggestion for the scheduling of individual readers and writers.

5.5 Can the printer-server introduced in Program 5.6 be implemented using monitors? Assuming that printer interrupts are converted by the operating system into internal monitor signals, provide a monitor-based solution. Discuss whether all properties of the solution in Program 5.6 can be provided with monitors, and compare the two solutions in terms of user-perceived flexibility and the relative degree of concurrency in the system that each of them allows.

5.6 Assuming indirect naming and fixed size of messages, provide a functional specification for the possible implementation of the following varieties of a message facility:

(*a*) Unbuffered messages with no copying
(*b*) Buffered messages with copying

Discuss the relative time and space complexities of the individual implementations of the message facility, and propose an approach that you consider to be the best tradeoff in terms of versatility versus performance.

5.7 Provide some examples where a nonblocking RECEIVE is a better choice than the blocking version of RECEIVE.

5.8 Solve the readers/writers problem using messages. Contrast your solution with solutions to the same problem using other mechanisms (semaphores, monitors, Ada), and discuss the relative advantages and disadvantages of the message approach given the existence of global data. Discuss the possibility and merits of avoiding the global data in a message-based solution.

5.9 What sequence of SEND and (blocking) RECEIVE operations should be executed by a process that wants to receive a message from either the mailbox M1 or the mailbox M2? Provide a solution for each of the following cases:

(*a*) The receiving process must not be blocked at an empty mailbox if there is at least one message in the other mailbox. The solution can only use the two mailboxes and a single receiving process.

(*b*) The receiving process can be suspended (blocked) only when there are no messages in either mailbox and no form of busy waiting is allowed.

5.10 Discuss the implementation issues and tradeoffs (naming, buffering, copying, and length of messages) when designing an interprocess message facility in a distributed computer system with no common memory. Assuming that the internode (intersite) message-exchange facility is already in place, suggest where the message-management data structures, such as mailboxes and the associated process queues, could or should be maintained. Argue the merits of providing separate versus unified calling sequences for intranode and internode message exchanges in relation to user convenience, cost of implementation, and the execution-time efficiency.

5.11 Provide the code for the individual reader and writer tasks that access the shared data structure controlled by the task READERS_WRITERS given in Program 5.11. Discuss whether the READ procedure must be reentrant, and if so why, in order to meet the requirements of the readers/writers problem stated in Chapter 4.

5.12 Show how to implement a general semaphore using the Ada rendezvous mechanism.

5.13 Discuss why the Ada SELECT statement should be implemented without busy waiting, and devise such an implementation. Discuss the potential run-time efficiency of SELECT in relation to the complexity of its implementation.

5.14 Write a program in Ada to solve the readers/writers problem with Hoare's scheduling of individual readers and writers. Contrast and compare your solution with semaphore and monitor-based solutions, if available, to the same problem.

5.15 Can a process be allowed to request multiple resources simultaneously in a system where deadlocks are avoided? Discuss why or why not.

5.16 Write a program that implements the banker's algorithm for systems with a single instance of each type of resource. Can this algorithm be used in the general resource case by being applied individually to each particular type of resource?

5.17 Assume that in the system depicted in Figure 5.3a process P1 does not own a disk drive and that it requests two disk drives simultaneously. Illustrate that situation by means of the general resource graph, and use the deadlock-detection algorithm to evaluate the resulting system state.

5.18 Devise a faster deadlock-detection algorithm than the one presented in Chapter 5 by assuming that only one instance of each type of resource is available in the system.

5.19 Write a simulation to compare the behavior of different deadlock-handling approaches. Provide a suitable representation of the hypothetical system resources, and implement algorithms for deadlock prevention, deadlock avoidance, and deadlock detection. Simulate the acquisition and release of resources by sample user processes, and present the same workload to each of the three deadlock-detection approaches. Record system statistics, including average resource utilization, degree of concurrency, and percentage of unsafe states that are actually deadlocks. Interpret and discuss your findings.

SIX

MEMORY MANAGEMENT: CONTIGUOUS ALLOCATION

In this and the subsequent chapter we discuss the principles of managing the main memory, one of the most precious resources in a multiprogramming system. In our sample hierarchy of operating-system layers, memory-management belongs to Layer 3. The supporting operations of the basic I/O system (Layer 2), which shuttles portions of address spaces between primary and secondary memory in response to requests issued by the memory-manager, are described in Chapter 8 in the more general context of file-management.

Memory-management is primarily concerned with the allocation of the physical memory of finite capacity to requesting processes. No process may be activated before a certain amount of memory can be allocated to it. As indicated in Chapter 3, temporarily inactive processes may be swapped out of memory in order to make room for others. The resulting vacant space can be used to load processes otherwise ready for execution and thus provide the scheduler with a better opportunity to schedule useful work. The overall resource-utilization and other performance criteria of a computer system are thus affected by performance of the memory-management module not only in terms of its effectiveness in allocating memory, but also as a consequence of its influence on, and interaction with, the scheduler.

The coexistence of multiple address spaces belonging to resident processes in main memory poses some additional requirements upon the memory-management layer. For one, active processes must be prevented from erroneously or maliciously accessing and potentially destroying the contents of each other's address spaces. In other words, the memory-manager must ensure isolation between distinct address spaces. At the same time, cooperating processes ought to be provided with some means of sharing common data, such as synchronization variables. Thus a good memory manager in a multiprogramming environment should simultaneously support both protection, by isolating disjoint address spaces, and sharing in order to allow cooperating processes to access common areas of memory. As we shall see, different schemes of memory-management meet these difficult and sometimes conflicting requirements with various degrees of complicity.

In this chapter we present various approaches to memory-management based on contiguous allocation. More specifically, we mean that memory allocation is performed in such a way that each logical object placed in memory occupies a set of locations with strictly consecutive addresses. A common approach with contiguous allocation is to partition the available physical memory and to satisfy requests for memory by allocating suitable free partitions, if any. When a resident object terminates, its partition is freed and made available for allocation to another requestor. Memory partitions may be defined statically, say, during system generation, or dynamically in response to user demands.

When partitioning is static, memory is wasted in each partition where an object of the smaller size than the partition itself is loaded. Wasting of memory within a partition, due to a difference in size of the partition and the object resident within it, is called *internal fragmentation*.

Dynamic partitioning eliminates this problem by making each partition only as large as necessary to fit a given object, such as a program or a shared data area. When an object is removed from memory, the related partition is returned to the pool of free space from which new partitions are created. After some time in operation, dynamic partitioning of memory has a tendency to intersperse the areas of allocated and unused memory. As a result, allocation may fail due to insufficient size of any free block to accommodate a given request even at times when the combined size of free areas exceeds the needs of the request at hand by a wide margin. Wasting of memory between partitions, due to scattering of the free space into a number of discontiguous areas, is called *external fragmentation*.

Regardless of the type of memory partitioning being used, the potential efficiency of a memory-manager is greater in systems where programs are relocatable so that they can be loaded into any area of memory that happens to be available at a given instant. Relocatability usually requires some sort of run-time hardware assistance to map the virtual, program-relative identifiers to the physical addresses where information items are stored at run-time. As we explain later, memory-protection hardware often performs various checks along with the address mapping. The price paid for the added flexibility and security offered by relocation and by the hardware-bound checking is a reduction of the effective memory bandwidth caused by the additional operations involved in accessing memory. Memory-management schemes differ in the relative complexity of address translation and, consequently, in the amount of the related run-time overhead they impose.

In this chapter we present and discuss several approaches to memory-management based on contiguous allocation. Noncontiguous allocation of memory is treated in Chapter 7. In order to provide a common basis for comparison, each scheme is informally analyzed with respect to the following measures:

- Wasted memory
- Time complexity
- Memory-access overhead

Wasted memory is considered to be the fraction of unused physical memory that a given memory-management scheme is unable to allocate when processing a sequence of memory requests. By *unused memory*, we mean memory not allocated to system or user objects. Memory can be wasted by internal fragmentation, by external fragmentation, and by the data structures needed for operation of the memory-manager. The space occupied by the memory-manager, usually dominated by the mapping tables, is sometimes called *table fragmentation*.

Time complexity refers to the computational complexity of allocating and deallocating memory, on a per-request basis, of a particular memory-management algorithm. As indicated, space complexity is included in the previous measure.

Memory-access overhead refers to the duration of the additional operations performed by a given memory-management scheme when accessing memory. It is usually expressed relative to the memory-access time with memory-management turned off.

A broader definition of wasted memory can include the amount of memory wasted by having to maintain multiple memory-resident copies of a single common object due to deficient or restricted sharing. For example, consider a large time-sharing system primarily used for program development. Assume that 20 users on the average are editing programs and that the editor code occupies 50 KB of memory. Without sharing, 1 MB of memory will be occupied by copies of the editor, as opposed to only 50 KB in a system where a single shared copy of the editor may serve the entire user population.

An ideal memory-manager should thus minimize wasted memory and have minimal time complexity and memory-access overhead, while providing good protection and flexible sharing. These requirements are not simultaneously attainable by the memory-management schemes described in this and the subsequent chapter. Therefore, an operating-system designer has to identify and prioritize the goals of a particular design and use or devise the memory-management scheme most suited to the requirements of a given system.

To help in the evaluation process, we describe several standard memory-management schemes along the lines of presented criteria. An added dimension to this design space is provided by some high-end microprocessors, where the designer has the ability to choose the form and the extent of hardware support for memory-management. In the traditional approach to computer-system design, where both hardware and software are typically provided by a single vendor, design teams usually interact in selecting a particular type of memory-management to be employed by the operating system and then provide the necessary hardware support for it. Outside people may study and analyze such designs for educational and informative purposes, but they rarely need to understand the specific details and intricacies of a given architecture. This picture is changing, with the high-end microprocessors offering either onchip or separate memory-management units.

The designer of an operating system for a microprocessor may have to understand the details of hardware support for memory-management well enough to be able to choose the most appropriate hardware for the intended memory-management scheme or, alternatively, to apply the most adequate type of memory-management to a given hardware foundation.

6.1 SINGLE-PROCESS MONITOR

Save for the bare machine, the single-process monitor is one of the simplest ways of managing memory. As suggested by Figure 6.1, the memory is simply divided into two contiguous areas. One of them is usually permanently allocated to the resident portion of the operating system (monitor). The remaining memory is allocated to the so-called transient processes, which are loaded and executed one at a time in response to user commands. When a transient process is completed, the operating system may load another one for execution. Both user processes and nonresident portions of the operating system may be executed in the transient-process area. This form of memory-management is commonly used by single-process microcomputer operating systems, such as CP/M and PC–DOS.

The operating system expends little time and effort when managing memory in this way. Basically, the OS needs to keep track of the first and last locations available for allocation to transient processes. The first location is commonly the one immediately following the resident monitor, and the last one is determined by the capacity of the memory installed in the particular configuration. The latter value may be established by reading the configuration switches or by

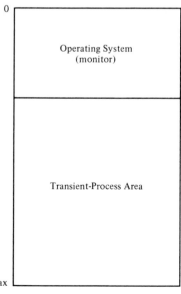

Figure 6.1 Single-process monitor.

having the operating system determine the size of the main memory during the initial system startup. In order to provide a contiguous area of free memory for transient programs, the operating system is usually placed at one extreme end of memory. The choice of a particular end of memory, the top or the bottom, is often influenced by the location of the interrupt-vectoring area (table) for the underlying hardware. In order to protect these vital system data, the interrupt-vector table is usually made a part of the operating system. To that end, the operating system is customarily placed at the same end of memory where the interrupt vectors reside. Portions of the operating system, such as the loader or the command-line interpreter, are sometimes placed at the opposite end of memory, thus leaving a single, large contiguous area of free memory in the middle.

A new transient process may be activated upon termination of the running one. The operating system usually makes sure that the size of the process image to be loaded is within the bounds of available memory. Otherwise, loading cannot be completed and an error message is generated to that effect. Once in memory, the process receives control from the operating system and executes until completion or abortion due to some error condition. The process announces its termination to the operating system by invoking the EXIT service or its equivalent. At this point, another waiting process may be loaded.

Protection between user processes is rarely supported by a single-process monitor, since at most one process is allowed to be resident in memory at any given time. However, it is desirable to protect the operating-system code from being tampered with by the executing transient process. Alternatively, the system may frequently crash and need rebooting when undebugged user programs are run.

A simple way to protect the operating-system code from user programs commonly used in embedded systems is to place the OS in read-only memory. In general purpose applications, such as personal computers, this method is rarely used because of its inflexibility and inability to patch and update the operating-system code. In systems where the operating system is in read-write memory, protection from user processes usually requires some sort of hardware assistance. Two such mechanisms, the fence register and protection bits, are discussed in this section.

Protection may be accomplished by means of a dedicated register, often called the *fence register*, used to draw a boundary between the operating system and the transient-process area. Assuming that the resident portion of the operating system is in low memory, the fence register is set to the highest address occupied by OS code (hence the name *fence*). Each memory address generated by a user process is compared against the fence. Any attempt to access the space below the fence may thus be detected and denied before completion of the related memory reference. Such violations usually trap to the operating system, which in turn may abort the offending program. In order to serve its purpose, modification of the fence register must be a privileged operation not executable by user processes. Consequently, this method of protection requires the hardware ability to distinguish between the execution of operating-system and user processes, such as the one provided by *user* and *supervisor* modes of operation.

Another approach to memory protection is to record the access rights in the memory itself. One possibility is to associate a protection bit with each word in memory. The memory may then easily be divided into two zones of arbitrary size by setting all protection bits in one and resetting them in the other area. For example, initially all protection bits may be reset. During the system startup, protection bits may be set in all locations where the operating system is loaded. User programs may then be loaded and executed in the remaining memory locations. Operating-system protection may be enforced by prohibiting user processes from accessing any memory location whose protection bit is set. At the same time, the OS and system utilities, such as the loader, may be allowed unrestricted access to the memory necessary for their activities. Like most other protection schemes, this approach also requires a hardware-supported distinction between at least two separate levels of privilege when executing machine instructions.

Sharing of code and data in memory does not make much sense in single-process environments, and it is hardly ever supported by single-process monitors. User programs may, of course, pass data to each other in private arrangements, say, by means of memory locations known (or believed) to be safe from being overwritten between executions of participating processes. Such schemes are obviously unreliable, and their use should be avoided.

With straightforward memory allocation and the absence of multiprogramming complexities, single-process monitors are relatively simple to design and comprehend. They are often used in systems with little hardware support for more advanced forms of memory-management or where memory and thus the size of the operating system are at a premium. By relying on overlays, permanently resident portions of some commercial single-process monitors take as little as 4 KB of memory.

The lack of support for multiprogramming results in generally low efficiency of both the CPU and memory. CPU cycles are wasted because there is no pending work that may be executed while the running process is waiting for completion of its I/O sequences. Memory is underutilized because a portion of it between the end of a process's address space and the end of the transient-process area is wasted. On the average, wasted memory in a specific system is related to the difference between the size of the transient-process area and the average-process size weighted by the respective process-execution (and residence) times.

One additional problem is sometimes encountered in systems with simplistic static forms of memory-management. In order to be usable across a wide range of configurations with different capacities of installed memory, system programs in such environments tend to be designed so as to use the least amount of memory possible. Besides the sacrificed speed and functionality, such programs usually take little advantage of additional memory when it is available.

6.2 PARTITIONED MEMORY ALLOCATION—STATIC

One way to support multiprogramming is to divide the available (installed) physical memory into several partitions, each of which may be allocated to a different process. Depending on when and how partitions are created and modified, memory partitioning may be static or dynamic. In this section we discuss static partitioning; the dynamic approach is treated in the next section.

Static partitioning generally implies that the division of memory is made offline and that partitions remain fixed thereafter. The number and sizes of individual partitions are usually determined during the system-generation process, taking into consideration the capacity of the available physical memory, the desired degree of multiprogramming, and the typical sizes of processes most frequently run on a given installation. These statistics may be gathered during the actual system operation. Individual partition sizes are usually adjusted to fit the needs of frequently run processes. Since, in principle, at most one process may execute out of a given partition at any time, the number of distinct partitions represents an upper limit on the number of active processes in a system. This figure is sometimes called the *degree of multiprogramming*. Given the impact of memory partitioning on the overall performance, some systems allow for manual redefinition of partition sizes without having to go through the entire system-generation process.

6.2.1 Principles of Operation

An example of partitioned memory is depicted in Figure 6.2. Of six partitions, one is assumed to be occupied by the resident portion of the operating system and three others by user processes Pi, Pj, and Pk, as indicated. The remaining two partitions, shaded in Figure 6.2, are free and available for allocation.

In order to avoid the details of memory-management, the steps of process creation described in earlier chapters were based on the assumption that the related code and data are already resident in memory. With that assumption removed, it becomes clear that the operating system must first allocate a memory region large enough to hold the process's image. After becoming resident in memory, the newly loaded process can actually make a transition to the Ready state and thus become eligible for execution. Let us now investigate the data structures and software algorithms used by the operating system when managing partitioned memory.

Once partitions are defined, an operating system needs to keep track of their status, such as free or in use, for allocation purposes. Current partition status and attributes of partitions are often collected in a data structure called the *partition-description table* (PDT). A sample PDT format is given in Figure 6.3. As indicated, each partition is described by its starting address (base), size, and status. When static partitioning is used, only the status field of each entry varies in the course of system operation depending on whether the corresponding partition is allocated or not at any given instant. All other fields are static and contain

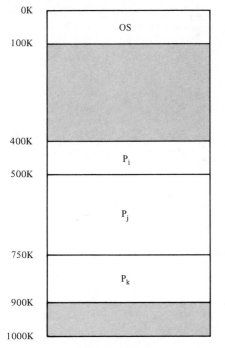

Figure 6.2 Static partitions.

the values defined at partition-definition time. The sample entries in Figure 6.3 correspond to the memory map depicted by Figure 6.2. In particular, Partitions 1 and 5 are assumed to be available for allocation. Partitions 0, 2, 3, and 4 are occupied by some processes, the specific identity of which is usually unimportant for allocation purposes.

When a nonresident process is to be created or activated, the operating system attempts to allocate a free memory partition of sufficient size, if any,

Partition Number	Partition Base	Partition Size	Partition Status
0	0K	100K	ALLOCATED
1	100K	300K	FREE
2	400K	100K	ALLOCATED
3	500K	250K	ALLOCATED
4	750K	150K	ALLOCATED
5	900K	100K	FREE

Figure 6.3 Partition-description table.

by consulting the entries of the PDT. If successful, the status field of the selected entry is marked ALLOCATED and the process image is loaded into the corresponding partition. Since the assumed format of the PDT does not provide any indication as to which process is occupying a given partition, the identity of the assigned partition may be recorded in the process's control-block. When the process terminates or needs to be swapped out, this information may be used to locate and update the related partition's status to FREE. In order to implement these basic ideas, two important facets must be further elaborated and resolved. The first one is the partition-allocation strategy, that is, how to select a specific partition for a given process. The second problem is presented by the situation when no suitable partition is available for allocation.

Assuming that there are some free partitions, allocation of one to the requesting process may be made in several ways, of which the *first-fit* and the *best-fit* are probably the most common. The first-fit approach basically consists of allocating the first free partition large enough to accommodate the process being created. Naturally, the process's size must be made known to the OS, say, by means of the process's image. The best-fit approach, on the other hand, requires that the OS allocate the smallest free partition that meets the requirements of the process under consideration.

When selecting between these two approaches, a tradeoff between execution speed and memory utilization must be made. In particular, both algorithms have to search the partition-description table in order to identify a free partition of adequate size. However, while the first-fit terminates upon finding the first such partition, the best-fit must process all qualifying PDT entries in order to identify the tightest fit. As a result, implementations of the first-fit tend to execute faster. By doing its work more thoroughly, best-fit may achieve higher utilization of memory by creating the smallest possible gap resulting from the difference in size between the process and its allocated (larger) partition.

As an example of the working of the two partition-allocation strategies, consider a system where the 70 KB process Pn is to be created when the memory map happens to have the appearance as presented in Figure 6.2. First-fit allocates Partition 1, thus leaving a 230-KB gap of unusable memory until process Pn terminates or becomes swapped out. Best-fit processes a few more entries and allocates Partition 5, resulting in a more tolerable 30 kB of temporarily unusable memory. In the common case of a relatively small number of fixed partitions in a system, the execution-time differences between the two approaches may not be pronounced enough to outweigh the generally lower degree of memory utilization attributable to first-fit. When the number of partitions is large, as is the case in some systems with dynamic partitioning, neither first-fit nor best-fit is clearly superior.

In general, requests to allocate partitions may come from one of two primary sources: creations of new processes, or reactivations of swapped-out processes. The memory-manager attempts to satisfy these requests from the pool of free partitions. However, certain situations may prevent it from doing so. Some of the more common ones are listed and discussed below:

1. No partition is large enough to accommodate the incoming process.
2. All partitions are allocated.
3. Some partitions are free, but none of them is large enough to accommodate the incoming process.

If the process to be created is too large to fit into any of the system partitions, the operating system cannot do much other than to announce the problem by producing an error message. This situation is basically a design error that may be remedied by redefining the partitions accordingly. Another option is to reduce a program's memory requirements by recoding and possibly by using some sort of overlays.

The case when all partitions are allocated may be handled by deferring the loading of the incoming process until a suitable partition can be allocated to it. An alternative is to force a memory-resident process to vacate a large enough partition. Eviction in order to free the necessary space incurs the additional overhead of selecting the suitable victim and of rolling it out to disk. This technique, called *swapping*, is discussed in the next section.

Both deferring and swapping are also applicable to handling the third case, where free, but unsuitable, partitions are available. If the deferring option is chosen, memory utilization may be kept high if the operating system continues to allocate free partitions to other waiting processes with smaller memory requirements. However, doing so may violate the ordering of process activations intended by the scheduling algorithm and, in turn, affect performance of the system.

The described memory-allocation situations illustrate the close relationship and interaction between memory-management and the scheduling functions of the operating system. Although the division of labor in actual systems may vary, the memory-manager is generally charged with implementing memory-allocation and replacement (eviction) policies. Processor scheduling, on the other hand, determines which process gets the CPU, when, and for how long. The short-term scheduler considers only the set of ready processes, that is, those which have all the needed resources except for the CPU. Ready processes are, by definition, resident in memory. By influencing the membership of the set of resident processes, a memory-manager may affect the scheduler's ability to perform. On the other hand, the effectiveness of the short-term scheduler influences the memory-manager by affecting the average memory-residence times (lifetimes) of processes.

In systems with static partitioning of memory, the number of partitions effectively sets an upper limit on the number of processes resident in memory and, therefore, on the degree of multiprogramming. Within the confines of this limit, CPU utilization may be improved by increasing the ratio of ready-to-resident processes. This may be accomplished by removing suspended processes from memory when otherwise ready ones are available for loading in the related partitions. A removed process is usually kept on secondary storage until all resources needed for its execution, except for memory and the CPU, may be allocated to it. At that point, the process in question becomes eligible for loading into the main memory. The medium-term scheduler and the memory-manager cooperate in further processing of such processes.

6.2.2 Swapping

Removing of suspended or preempted processes from memory and their subsequent return is called *swapping*. Swapping has traditionally been used to implement multiprogramming in systems with restrictive memory capacity or with little hardware support for memory-management. As indicated, swapping may also be helpful for improving CPU utilization in partitioned memory environments by increasing the ratio of ready-to-resident processes.

When the scheduler decides to admit a new process for which no suitable free partition can be found, the swapper may be invoked to vacate such a partition. The swapper usually selects a victim among the suspended processes that occupy partitions large enough to satisfy the needs of the incoming process. Among the qualifying processes, the more likely candidates for swapping are the ones with low priority and those waiting for slow events and thus having a higher probability of being suspended for a comparatively long time. Another important consideration is the time spent in memory by the potential victim. Otherwise, there is a danger of thrashing caused by frequent removals of processes from memory almost immediately following their admissions. Although the mechanics of swapping following the choice of a victim process are simple in principle, implementation of swapping requires some specific provisions and considerations in operating systems that support it. These generally include the file system, specific OS services, and relocation. These issues are elaborated in subsequent paragraphs.

A process is typically prepared for execution and submitted to the operating system in the form of a file that contains a program in executable form and the related data. This file may also contain process attributes, such as priority and memory requirements. Such a file is sometimes called a *process image*. Since it usually modifies its stack and data when executing, a partially executed process generally has a run-time image different from its initial static process image recorded on disk. Therefore, the dynamic run-time state of the process to be swapped out must be recorded for its proper subsequent resumption. In general, the modifiable portion of a process's state consists of the contents of its data and stack locations, as well as of the relevant CPU registers. Code is also subject to run-time modifications in systems that permit the code to modify itself. Therefore, the contents of a sizable portion or the entire address space of a victim process must be copied to disk during the swapping-out operation. Since the static process image is used for initial activation, the (modified) run-time image should not overwrite the static process image on disk. Consequently, a separate swap file must be available for storing the dynamic image of a rolled-out process. There are at least two options regarding placement of a swap file: all swapped processes are kept in a dedicated system-wide swap file or in separate, process-specific files. In either case, swapping space for each swappable process is usually reserved and allocated statically, at process-creation time, in order to avoid the overhead of this potentially lengthy operation at swap time.

A system-wide swap file is usually created in the course of system initialization. The swap file is commonly placed on a fast secondary-storage device so as to reduce the latency of swapping. The usually static address and size of such a swap file may also be beneficial for direct addressing of the swap areas on the disk, thus bypassing the complexities and run-time overhead of disk accessing by means of the general file structure. An important tradeoff when implementing a system-wide swap file is the choice of its size. The primary incentive to keep the swap file small is that space on a fast disk is usually in high demand for system programs and other frequently run or time-critical programs. Obviously, more of this prime space is left for other uses if the swap file is small. On the other hand, the size of the swap file affects the number of active processes in the system, since a new (swappable) process can be activated only when sufficient swap space can be reserved for it. Failure to reserve the swapping space at process-creation time can lead to costly run-time errors and system stoppage due to the inability to swap a designated process.

An alternative is to have a dedicated swap file for each swappable process in the system. These swap files may be created either dynamically at process-creation time or statically at program-preparation time. In either case, the advantages of maintenance of separate swap files include elimination of the system swap-file dimensioning problem and of that file's overflow errors at run-time and no restrictions on the number of active processes imposed by swapping. The disadvantages include usually more disk space expended on swapping, slower access, and more complicated addressing of swapping files scattered on the secondary storage.

Regardless of the type of swapping file being used, the need to access secondary storage makes swapping a lengthy operation relative to the CPU instruction-execution times. For example, swapping out of a 100-kB process using a disk with 30 ms average access time and a transfer rate of 500 kB/s takes, on the average, 30 ms to position the heads and start the transfer and at least another 20 ms to complete it. Loading of another 100-kB process in the vacated partition may take another 50 ms, resulting in 100 ms total idling of at least 100 kB of main memory. This overhead must be taken into consideration when deciding whether to swap a process in order to make room for another one.

Delays of this order of magnitude may be unacceptable for interrupt-service routines or other time-critical processes. For example, swapping out of a momentarily inactive terminal driver in a time-sharing system is certainly a questionable "optimization." Operating systems that support swapping usually cope with this problem by providing some means for system programmers to declare a given process as being swappable or not. In effect, after the initial loading, an unswappable process remains fixed in memory even when it is temporarily suspended. While certainly useful, this service may be abused by declaring an excessive number of processes as fixed, thereby reducing the benefits of swapping. For this reason, the authority to designate a process as being unswappable is usually restricted to a given class of privileged processes and users. All other processes, by default, may be treated as swappable.

An important issue in systems that support swapping is whether processes-to-partition binding is static or dynamic, that is, whether a swapped-out process can subsequently be loaded only into the specific partition from which it was removed or into any partition of adequate size. In general, static binding of processes to partitions may be done in any system with static partitioning of memory, irrespective of whether swapping is supported or not. Static process-to-partition binding eliminates the run-time overhead of partition allocation at the expense of lower utilization of memory due to potentially unbalanced use of partitions. On the other hand, systems where processes are not permanently bound to specific partitions are much more flexible and have a greater potential for efficient use of memory. The obvious price paid for dynamic binding of processes to partitions is the overhead incurred by partition allocation whenever a new process or a swapped process is to be loaded into main memory. The not so obvious aspect of the decision whether to bind processes to partitions statically or dynamically is that some sort of hardware support for dynamic relocation is highly desirable, if not mandatory, for systems with swapping where processes are not statically bound to partitions.

6.2.3 Relocation

The term *program relocatability* usually refers to the ability to load and to execute a given program into an arbitrary place in memory as opposed to a fixed set of locations specified at program-translation time. Since different load addresses may be assigned during different executions of a single relocatable program, a distinction is often made between virtual (programmer-perceived) addresses and the physical addresses where the program and its data are stored in memory during a given execution. More specifically, *virtual addresses* are identifiers used to reference information within a program's address space, while *physical addresses* designate the actual physical memory locations where information items are stored at run-time. Depending on when and how the mapping from the virtual-address space to the physical-address space takes place in a given relocation scheme, program relocation may be regarded as static or dynamic.

Static relocation usually implies that relocation is performed before or during the loading of the program into memory, by a relocating linker or a relocating loader, respectively. Constants, physical I/O port addresses, and offsets relative to the program counter are examples of values that are not location-sensitive and that do not need to be adjusted for relocation. Other forms of addresses of operands may depend on the location of a program in memory, and if so, they must be adjusted accordingly when the program is being loaded or moved to a different area of memory.

A language translator typically prepares the object module by assuming the virtual address 0 to be the starting address of the program, thus making virtual addresses relative to the program loading address. In addition, relocation information, including the designation of all virtual addresses that need adjustment following determination of the physical load address, is customarily provided for subsequent processing by the linker and/or the loader. Either when object modules are combined by the linker or the process image is being loaded, all program locations that need relocation are adjusted in accordance with the actual starting physical address allocated to the program. Once the program is in memory, values that need relocation are indistinguishable from those which do not. (An exception to this rule is provided by the so-called tagged architectures, which set aside a few bits of each memory location to designate the type of datum or instruction contained therein.)

Since relocation information in memory is usually lost following the loading, a partially executed statically relocatable program cannot be simply copied from one area of memory into another and be expected to continue to execute properly. Consequently, in systems with static relocation, a swapped-out process must either be swapped back into the same partition from which it was evicted or software relocation must be repeated whenever the process is to be loaded into a different partition. Given the considerable space and time complexity of software relocation, systems with static relocation are practically restricted to supporting only static binding of processes to partitions.

Dynamic relocation implies that mapping from the virtual-address space to the physical-address space is performed at run-time, usually with some hardware assistance. Process images in systems with dynamic relocation are also prepared assuming the starting location to be a virtual address 0, and they are loaded in memory without any relocation adjustments. When the related process is being executed, all of its memory references are relocated during instruction execution before actually accessing physical memory. This process is often implemented by means of specialized base registers. After allocating a suitable partition and loading a process image in memory, the operating system sets a base register to the starting physical load address. This value is normally obtained from the relevant entry of the partition-description table. Each memory reference generated by the executing process is mapped into the corresponding physical address by having the contents of the base register added to it. Dynamic relocation is illustrated in Figure 6.4.

A sample process image prepared by assuming that the starting address is virtual address 0 is shown unchanged before and after being loaded in memory. In this particular example, it is assumed that address 100000 is allocated as the starting address for loading the process image. This base address is normally available from the corresponding entry of the partition-description table, which is reachable by means of the link to the allocated partition in the PCB. Whenever the process in question is scheduled to run, the base register is loaded with this value in the course of process switching.

Relocation of memory references at run-time is illustrated by means of the instruction MOVE A,1000, which is supposed to load the contents of the virtual address 1000 (relative to program beginning) into the accumulator. As indicated, the target item actually resides at the physical address 101000 in memory. This

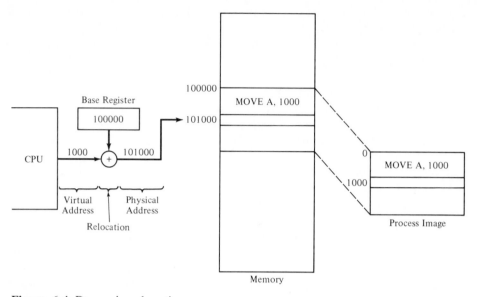

Figure 6.4 Dynamic relocation.

address is produced by adding the contents of the base register to the virtual address emitted by the processor at run-time.

As suggested by Figure 6.4, relocation is performed by hardware and it is transparent to programmers. In effect, all addresses in the process image are prepared by counting on the implicit-based addressing to complete the relocation process at run-time. This approach makes a clear distinction between the virtual-address and the physical-address space. A simple way to conceptualize this distinction is by noting that processor-generated addresses prior to relocation are virtual, whereas physical addresses are produced by the mapping hardware and used to reference memory. This clear separation makes it possible to design optional offchip memory-management units in microprocessor systems and to position them between the CPU chip and the (physical) address-decoding circuitry when advanced forms of memory-management are desired.

Dynamic relocation makes it possible to move a partially executed process from one area of memory into another without any adverse effects on its ability to correctly access instructions and data in the new space. This feature is very useful for support of swapping without binding processes to partitions and for dynamic partitioning, discussed in the next section. In particular, the run-time image of the swapped-out process may subsequently be loaded and executed in a new partition simply by placing its starting address into the base register. The price to be paid is the extra hardware for one or more base registers and some slowing-down of the effective memory-access time due to the relocation process. Contemporary architectures designed for support of implicit-based addressing usually provide a dedicated adder in order to allow address calculations to proceed in parallel with other CPU operations, thus making practically negligible their impact on the effective memory bandwidth.

6.2.4 Protection and Sharing

The integrity of a multiprogramming system depends, among other things, on its ability to enforce the isolation of separate address spaces. Not only must the operating system be protected from unauthorized tampering by user processes, but each user process must also be prevented from inadvertently or maliciously accessing the areas of memory allocated to other processes. Otherwise, a single erroneous or malevolent process may easily corrupt any or all other resident processes. In addition to causing frequent system crashes, uncontrolled access to memory may result in unwanted interactions between processes that are often intermittent and difficult to detect. The consequences may manifest themselves long after the offending process is gone from the system or, worse yet, may result in undetected errors occasionally being injected into other processes. For this reason, multiuser operation should not be provided in systems without adequate hardware support for memory protection. A good illustration is provided by the microprocessor industry, which mostly refrained from offering multiuser operating systems before providing support for memory-management, despite the existence of otherwise powerful and fast CPUs with addressing capabilities in excess of 1 MB.

While closely related to the memory-management scheme, implementation of memory protection in a given system tends to be greatly influenced by the available hardware support. In systems that use base registers for relocation, a common practice is to use limit (bound) registers for protection. The primary function of a limit register is to detect attempts to access an address space beyond the boundary assigned by the operating system to the executing program. The limit register is usually set to the highest virtual address in a program. As illustrated by Figure 6.5, each intended memory reference of an executing program is checked against the contents of the limit register before being forwarded to memory. In this way, any attempt to access a memory location outside the specified area is detected and aborted by the protection hardware before being allowed to reach memory. This violation usually traps to the operating system, which may then take a remedial action, such as to terminate the offending process. The base and limit values for each process are normally kept in its process control-block (PCB). Upon each process switch, the hardware base and limit registers are loaded with the corresponding values for the new running process.

Another approach to protection is to record the access rights in the memory itself. The bit-per-word approach described in Section 6.1 is not suitable for multiprogramming systems, because it can separate only two distinct address spaces. This problem may be solved by adding more bits to designate the identity of each word's owner, but the resulting approach is rather costly. A more economical version of this idea has been implemented by associating a few protection bits with large blocks of physical memory, as opposed to bits used for individual words. For example, some models of the IBM 360 series use four such

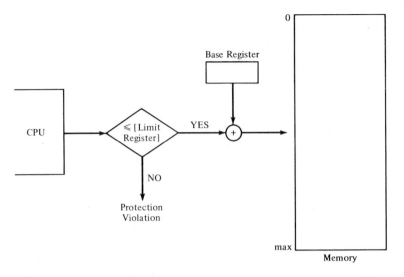

Figure 6.5 Base-limit registers.

bits, called *keys*, per each 2-KB block of memory. When a process is loaded in memory, its identity is recorded in the protection bits of the occupied blocks. The validity of memory references is established at run-time by comparing the running process's identity to the contents of the protection bits of the memory block being accessed. If no match is found, the access is illegal and hardware traps to the operating system for processing of the protection-violation exception. The operating system is usually assigned a unique "master" key, say, 0, that gives it unrestricted access to all blocks of memory. Note that this protection mechanism imposes certain implied restrictions on operating-system designers. For example, with 4-bit keys, the maximum number of static partitions and resident processes is limited to 16. Likewise, associating protection bits with fixed-sized blocks forces partition sizes to be an integral number of such blocks.

In addition to protection, a good memory-management mechanism must also provide for controlled sharing of data and code between cooperating processes. While most memory-management systems offer some sort of memory protection, there are pronounced differences in the extent of sharing that they allow or are capable of supporting. The growing awareness of the importance of interprocess cooperation, many aspects of which are discussed in earlier chapters, has resulted in generally increasing support for this feature in contemporary architectures and operating systems.

Probably the easiest way to implement sharing without significantly compromising protection is to entrust shared objects to the operating system. With the operating system controlling access to shared resources and the guarded mechanism for invoking OS services in place, no additional provisions may be needed to support sharing. Unfortunately, this simple approach is undesirable for several reasons. For one, it encourages growth of the operating system to the point of inclusion of many services normally provided by systems and application programs. All this additional code brought under the OS umbrella usually attains the same level of privilege as the normally well-trusted kernel, thus jeopardizing the overall system integrity and reliability. The resulting large monolithic piece of code also violates practically all rules of structured program development, testing, and maintenance. Another practical, but no less serious, problem with such an approach is the difficulty of protecting dynamically created objects. Namely, the inclusion of new services in many operating systems cannot be performed without disruption of service. In particular, most systems allow incorporation of user-written routines into the operating system only during the system-generation process.

Save for entrusting objects to the operating system, sharing is quite difficult in systems with fixed partitioning of memory. The primary reason is their reliance on rather straightforward protection mechanisms based mostly on the strict isolation of distinct address spaces. Since memory partitions are fixed, disjoint, and usually difficult to access by outside processes not belonging to the operating system, static partitioning of memory is not very conducive to sharing.

A straightforward, but highly taxing, approach is to let a separate physical copy of the shared object reside in the private address spaces of all processes that use it. In effect, a single logical object is represented by means of its multiple "projections"—one per participating process's address space. Since there is no commonly accessible original, each process runs using its local projection of the shared object. Consequently, updates are made only to copies of the shared object. In order for all copies to remain consistent, updates made to any must be propagated to all other copies. The operating system usually accomplishes this chore by copying the shared data from the address space of the running process to all participating partitions upon every process switch. Swapping, when supported, introduces the additional complexity of potentially having one or more of the participating address spaces absent from the main memory. Sharing of code by maintaining multiple physical copies of the shared object does not make much sense in view of the fact that no saving of memory may be expected.

Another traditional simple approach to sharing is to place the data in a dedicated "common" partition. However, any attempt by a participating process to access memory outside of its own partition is normally regarded as a protection violation. In systems with protection keys, this obstacle may be circumvented by changing the keys of all shared blocks upon every process switch in order to grant access rights to the currently running process. Keeping track of which blocks are shared and by whom, as well as the potentially frequent need to modify keys, results in notable OS overhead necessary to support this form of sharing. With base-limit registers, the use of shared partitions outside of—and potentially discontiguous to—the running process's partition requires some special provisions. For instance, separate sets of dedicated base-limit register pairs may be needed for accessing private and shared memory spaces, respectively. This implies the existence of some means, preferably automatic, for designating the appropriate register set to be used for the mapping of each particular memory reference. A way to accomplish this is discussed in relation to segmentation in Section 6.4.

6.2.5 Concluding Remarks

Memory-management based on static partitioning is one of the comparatively simpler ways to support multiprogramming. It may be implemented with modest hardware support which only marginally affects the effective memory bandwidth.

Static partitioning of memory is generally suitable for static environments where the workload is predictable and its characteristics are known. A typical example is provided by a stable production environment running a given application with little or no program development, such as process control or a banking system. Static partitioning is at a disadvantage in environments with varying and generally unpredictable memory requirements of programs prior to their submission, such as a university computing center.

Most of the disadvantages of static partitioning are directly attributable to its inflexibility and inability to adapt to changing system needs. One of its primary problems is the internal fragmentation of memory resulting from the difference between the size of a partition and the actual requirements of the process that resides in it. In general, *fragmentation* refers to the inability of the operating system to allocate portions of unused memory. The extent to which internal fragmentation causes memory to be wasted in a given system varies depending on several factors, such as the number and size of the partitions, the frequency of execution of processes of a given size, the average process size, and its variance. Wasted memory also tends to increase when large, but infrequently run processes must be accommodated, because a large enough partition created for the purpose may be otherwise poorly utilized.

Fixed partitioning imposes more severe restrictions on program sizes than those dictated by the capacity of the installed memory. In particular, no single process or overlay may exceed the size of the largest partition in a given system. Fixed partition sizes are a disadvantage in systems where support for dynamically growing data structures, such as heaps or stacks, is required. Placing such processes in large partitions may result in wasted memory, especially on runs where little expansion of address space actually occurs. Alternatively, an actively expanding process in a small partition may quickly "bump" into its prescribed limit, with no simple operating-system remedy at hand. Fixing the number of partitions has the negative effect of limiting the degree of multiprogramming, which, in turn, may reduce the effectiveness of short-term scheduling. As stated, swapping may be used to increase the proportion of ready processes at the expense of increased I/O overhead.

6.3 PARTITIONED MEMORY ALLOCATION—DYNAMIC

Apparently, internal fragmentation and other problems attributable to static partitioning of memory should be alleviated by defining partitions dynamically, in accordance with the requirements of each particular set of active processes. Starting with the initial state of the system, partitions may be created dynamically to fit the needs of each requesting process. When a process terminates or becomes swapped out, the memory-manager can return the vacated space to the pool of free memory areas from which partition allocations are made.

In principle, neither the size nor the number of dynamically allocated memory partitions need be limited at system generation or at any other time. In practice, the memory-manager may continue to create and to allocate partitions to requesting processes until all physical memory is exhausted or the maximum allowable degree of multiprogramming is reached. The latter limit may be dictated in some systems by design restrictions on PCB queue lengths and on other operating-system data structures.

6.3.1 Principles of Operation

In order to arrive at a specification of data structures necessary to support dynamic definition and allocation of partitions, let us briefly investigate the nature of operations that such memory-managers typically perform.

When instructed to load a process image, the memory-management module of the operating system attempts to create a suitable partition for allocation to the process in question. The first step in this activity is to locate a contiguous free area of memory, if any, which is equal to or larger than the process's size declared with the submitted image. If a suitable free area is found, the operating system "carves out" a partition from it so as to provide an exact fit to the process's needs. The leftover chunk of free memory, if any, is returned to the pool of free memory for further consideration by the allocation module. The partition is created by entering its base, size, and status (ALLOCATED) into the system partition-description table or its equivalent. A copy of, or some link to, this information is normally recorded in the process's control-block. After loading the process image into the created partition, the related process may be turned over to the OS module appropriate for its further processing, such as the short-term scheduler. If no suitable free area may be allocated for some reason, the operating system returns an error indication.

When a resident process terminates or becomes swapped-out, the operating system "terminates" the related partition. This process basically consists of returning the partition's space (defined by PDT) to the pool of free memory and invalidating the corresponding PDT entry. For swapped-out processes, the operating system also invalidates the PCB field where the identity of the allocated partition is normally held.

The operating system obviously needs to keep track of both partitions and free memory. Once created, a partition is defined by its base address and size. Those attributes remain essentially unchanged for as long as the related partition exists. In addition, for the purposes of process switching and swapping, it is important to know which partition belongs to a given process. It turns out that most of these requirements may be satisfied by a slightly modified version of the partition-definition table introduced in the previous section.

Free areas of memory are produced upon termination of partitions and as leftovers in the partition-creation process. For allocation and for partition-creation purposes, the operating system must keep track of the starting address and size of each free area of memory. This information may need to be updated each time a partition is created or terminated. The highly dynamic nature of both the number and attributes of free areas suggests the use of some sort of a linked list to describe them. It is common to conserve space by building the Free list within the free memory itself. For example, the first few words of each free area may be used to indicate the size of the area and to house a link to the successor area.

Figure 6.6a illustrates the basic data structures, the modified PDT, and the Free list used by the operating system when managing dynamically partitioned memory. In order to point out the differences and similarities with static partitioning of memory, the depicted entries describe the memory map identical to that of Figure 6.2. As indicated, PDT entries are used only for the definition of created and allocated partitions, and free areas are described by the Free list. Thus, the second entry of PDT, corresponding to what would be Partition 1, is not used. Unused entries are available for recording of newly created partitions. Note that the size of the PDT is now extended to accommodate a potentially larger number of partitions, up to some system-dependent maximum, which is

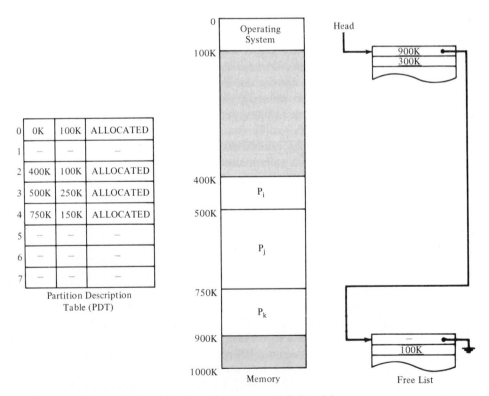

Figure 6.6 Dynamic partitioning of memory. (*a*) Partitions

assumed to be eight for the purposes of our example. The two free areas of memory are recorded in the Free list, whose nodes are shown as sorted by the increasing physical address.

Figure 6.6b illustrates the state of the PDT and of the Free list after creation of a 120-KB partition made out of the larger free area. The new partition is described by the PDT's entry number 1, and the Free list is updated accordingly. Figure 6.6c shows the same data structure after termination of Partition 3, which creates a 250-KB free area.

With data structures outlined, we may give a more specific description of the basic operations of the memory-manager in systems with dynamic partitioning. The system is initialized with all memory available for dynamic allocation declared as free, and all entries in the partition-description table are marked UNUSED ENTRY (no partitions exist). The Free list contains a single entry—all the available memory in a single contiguous block. From that point on, creation of a partition P of size P_SIZE is performed as follows:

1. The Free list is searched for a free area F such that F_SIZE ≥ P_SIZE. If none can be found, the algorithm terminates with an error indication.
2. Calculate DIFF:= F_SIZE − P_SIZE. If DIFF ≤ c, where c is a (small) constant, then allocate the entire free area for creation of the partition P by

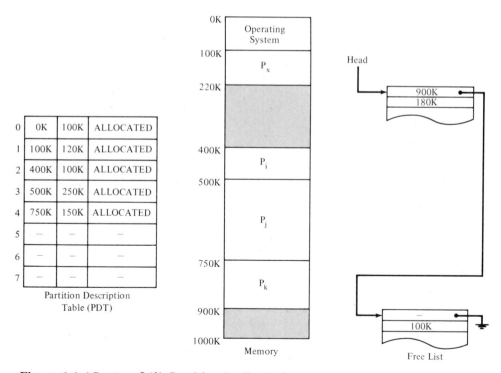

0	0K	100K	ALLOCATED
1	100K	120K	ALLOCATED
2	400K	100K	ALLOCATED
3	500K	250K	ALLOCATED
4	750K	150K	ALLOCATED
5	–	–	–
6	–	–	–
7	–	–	–

Partition Description
Table (PDT)

Figure 6.6 (*Continued*)(*b*) Partition 1 allocated

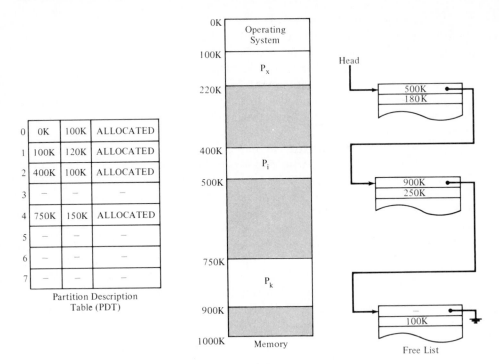

0	0K	100K	ALLOCATED
1	100K	120K	ALLOCATED
2	400K	100K	ALLOCATED
3	–	–	–
4	750K	150K	ALLOCATED
5	–	–	–
6	–	–	–
7	–	–	–

Partition Description
Table (PDT)

Figure 6.6 (*Continued*)(*c*) Partition 3 freed

setting P_SIZE:= F_SIZE, P_BASE:= F_BASE, and adjusting the links of the adjacent blocks in the Free list. If DIFF > *c*, then allocate space for the partition P from the block F, say, by setting P_BASE:= (F_BASE + F_SIZE – P_SIZE) and F_SIZE:= F_SIZE – P_SIZE.

3. Find an unused entry in the PDT and record the base (P_BASE) and size (P_SIZE) in it. Set status to ALLOCATED.
4. Record the PDT's entry number in the control-block of the process T for which the partition P is being created.

Common algorithms for selection of a free area of memory for creation of a partition (Step 1 in the list above) are

- First-fit and its variant next-fit
- Best-fit
- Worst-fit

Next-fit is a modification of first-fit whereby the pointer to the Free list is saved following an allocation and used to begin the search for the subsequent allocation. In effect, the next search continues where the last one left off, as opposed to always starting from the beginning of the Free list, as is the case with first-fit. The idea is reduce the search by avoiding examination of smaller blocks that, in the long run, tend to be created at the beginning of the Free list as a result of previous allocations. Although next-fit is generally faster than first-fit, its effectiveness in reducing the amount of wasted memory was not found to be superior to first-fit.

First-fit and best-fit are among the most popular algorithms for dynamic memory allocation. As indicated earlier, first-fit is generally faster because it terminates as soon as a free block large enough to house a new partition is found. Thus, on the average, first-fit searches half the free list per allocation. Best-fit, on the other hand, searches the entire Free list (unless sorted by size, which is rarely the case for reasons explained later) in order to find the smallest free block large enough to hold a partition being created. In principle, first-fit is faster, but it does not minimize wasted memory for a given allocation. Best-fit is slower, and it tends to produce small leftover free blocks that may be too small for subsequent allocations. However, when processing a series of requests starting with an initially free memory, neither algorithm was shown to be superior to the other in terms of wasted memory.

Worst-fit is an antipode of best-fit, as it allocates the largest free block, provided the block size exceeds the requested partition size. The idea behind worst-fit is to reduce the rate of production of small holes that are quite common when best-fit is used for memory allocation. However, some simulation studies indicate that worst-fit allocation is not very effective in reducing wasted memory when processing a series of requests.

Regardless of the allocation algorithm in use, it is a common practice to avoid creation of too small leftover areas when allocating space for partitions. This consideration is implemented in Step 2 of the presented partition-creation procedure by allocating the entire free block whenever it exceeds the size of the partition only by a small margin determined by the constant c. The minimal value of c in a given system must allow for placement of the links, area attributes, and other information kept in each node of the Free list for allocation purposes. The upper bound of the constant c is a system-dependent design parameter.

Termination of partitions in a system with dynamic allocation of memory may be performed by means of the general procedure given below. Partitions may be terminated following swapping or termination of the inhabiting process R as follows:

1. Use R's control-block to locate the PDT entry, PDT[PCB[R]], describing partition P to be terminated.
2. If process R is to be swapped-out, copy its run-time image from partition P to the designated place in a swap file.
3. Set the PCB[R] pointer to the allocated partition to NONE.
4. Return P to the Free list and coalesce it with the neighboring free areas if possible.
5. Invalidate the PDT entry describing the terminated partition.

As indicated in Step 4 of the presented partition-deallocation procedure, free areas are often recombined when possible in order to reduce fragmentation of memory. When first-fit or best-fit is used, the Free list may be sorted by address to facilitate recombination of free areas when partitions are deallocated. With the Free list sorted, a free area may be returned and recombined with adjacent free areas, if any, by searching half the Free list on the average. At the expense of some extra storage for maintenance of a doubly linked Free list and of some associated information, an algorithm for returning a free area in constant time may be devised.

An allocation-deallocation strategy called the *buddy system* facilitates merging of free space by allocating free areas with an affinity to recombine. Sizes of free blocks in a buddy system are usually an integer power of base 2. In addition to the Free list links, a status field is associated with each area of memory to indicate whether it is in use or not. Free blocks of equal size are often kept in separate Free lists. Requests for free areas are rounded up to the next integer power of base 2. When a free block of size 2^k is requested, the memory allocator attempts to satisfy it by allocating a free block from the list of free blocks of size 2^k. If none is available, the block of the next larger size, 2^{k+1}, is split in two halves (buddies) to satisfy the request. An important property of this allocation scheme is that the base address of the other buddy can be determined given the base address and size of one buddy (for a block of size 2^k, the two addresses differ only in the binary digit whose weight is 2^k). Thus, when a block is freed, a simple test of the status bit can reveal whether its buddy is also free, and if so, the two blocks can be recombined to form the twice-larger original block.

Some effects of the outlined procedures for allocation and deallocation of partitions may be observed in Figure 6.6.

6.3.2 Compaction

Figure 6.6 is also intended to illustrate certain behavioral aspects of systems with dynamic partitioning of memory. For example, the memory map in Figure 6.6c suggests a common situation in such systems—areas of free memory (holes) are interspersed with the actively used partitions throughout memory. This fragmentation of available memory is quite undesirable, as no new partition may exceed the size of the largest hole. For instance, consider the system whose memory is depicted by Figure 6.6c attempting to accommodate a 256 kB incoming process. Although three partitions totaling over twice the needed amount are available, the request cannot be satisfied. As indicated earlier, creation of free areas (holes) between partitions is called *external fragmentation* and is commonly encountered in systems with dynamic allocation of memory.

As indicated, coalescing of adjacent free areas when free blocks are returned is often used to reduce fragmentation and, consequently, the amount of wasted memory. However, such remedies tend to defer the impact of rather than prevent the problem. The primary reason for fragmentation is that due to different lifetimes of resident objects, the pattern of returns of free areas is generally different from the order of allocations. After some time in operation, systems with dynamic allocation of memory tend to reach a state of equilibrium in which the memory wasted by a given allocation scheme can be measured and used for comparisons. It has been shown that when first-fit is used for allocation and free areas are recombined during deallocations whenever possible on a continuous basis so that the system reaches an equilibrium condition where there are N memory blocks in use, on the average, each with a random lifetime, and where DIFF $\geq c$ with probability p, the average number of free blocks tends to be approximately $(1/2)pN$. This rule is sometimes called the *fifty percent rule*. For values of p very close to 1 (this can happen when c is small and there is a pronounced variance of block sizes), the fifty percent rule indicates that we can expect about half as many blocks to be free as there are blocks in use. It can be shown that if a system reaches a state of equilibrium such that the average request size exceeds the average size of a free block, for values of p close to 1, approximately *one-third of memory* is wasted due to fragmentation of memory. Note that this is the case even though adjacent free areas are recombined whenever possible.

When memory becomes seriously fragmented, the only way out may be to relocate some or all partitions into one end of memory and thus combine the holes into one large free area. Since affected processes must be suspended and actually copied from one area of memory into another, it is important to decide when and how this process—called *memory compaction*—is to be performed.

Memory compaction may be performed whenever possible or only when actually needed. Some systems compact memory whenever a free area is created by a departing process, thus collecting most of the free memory into a single large area. An alternative is to compact only upon a failure to allocate a suitable partition, provided that the combined size of free areas exceeds the needs of the request at hand. Otherwise, free memory cannot satisfy the pending requirement anyway, and compaction alone may not be worthwhile.

The potential advantage of incremental and selective compaction may be observed from the memory map depicted in Figure 6.6c. Namely, by moving the process Pi that occupies the 100-KB Partition 2 to the 100-KB free Partition 5, a single 530-KB contiguous hole is created. The resulting memory map is depicted in Figure 6.7a. Unfortunately, this kind of memory compaction is rarely implemented because of the overhead incurred in evaluating the options while selecting the optimal moving strategy. The proposed format of the PDT and of the Free list may also have to be redesigned to facilitate this process. For instance, the contiguity property of free areas may not be immediately obvious from the Free list, and detection of a partition surrounded by free areas may require quite a few CPU cycles. As a result, a more common approach to compacting is to relocate all partitions to one end of memory, as depicted by Figure 6.7b. While no special moving strategy is required, the overhead of copying is usually higher than for more selective moving. In the example presented by Figure 6.7, the number of locations copied from one space to another is 100 KB and 250 KB, respectively. Assuming the best case where a hardware BLOCK_MOVE (move string) instruction is available and may be used for the purpose, at least two

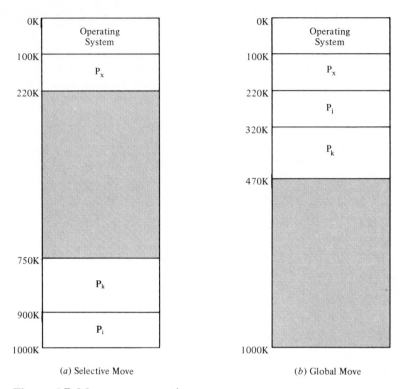

(a) Selective Move   (b) Global Move

Figure 6.7 Memory compaction.

memory references are necessary to move each word—one read and one write. With the .5-μs memory cycle time, the 100-KB move takes approximately

$$100 \times 10^3 \times 2 \times .5 \times 10^{-6}\text{s} = .1\text{s}$$

Thus, the extra 150 KB moved by the second approach results in the additional .15 s of CPU time or thousands of wasted instructions. The presented calculation assumes a common case in which dynamic relocation is supported by hardware. Due to generally excessive compaction overhead, dynamic partitioning of memory is hardly ever supported in systems that lack dynamic relocation hardware.

The compaction process is completed by updating the Free list and the affected PDT entries.

6.3.3 Protection and Sharing

Protection and sharing in systems with dynamic partitioning of memory are not significantly different from their counterparts in static-partitioning environments, since they both rely on virtually identical hardware support. One difference is that dynamic partitioning potentially allows adjacent partitions in physical memory to overlap. Consequently, a single physical copy of a shared object may be accessible from two distinct address spaces. This possibility is illustrated in Figure 6.8, where Partitions A and B overlap to include the shared object placed in the doubly shaded area. The relevant portion of the partition-definition table is also shown in Figure 6.8. As indicated, 500 locations starting from the physical address 5500 are shared and included in both partitions. Although perhaps conceptually appealing, this form of sharing is quite restrictive in practice. Sharing of objects is limited to two processes; when several processes are in play, one of the more involved schemes described under Protection and Sharing in Section 6.2 must be used.

Sharing of code is generally more restrictive than sharing of data. One of the reasons for this is that shared code must either be reentrant or executed in a strictly mutually exclusive fashion with no preemptions. Otherwise, serious problems may result if a process in the middle of execution of the shared code is switched off and another process begins to execute the same section of shared code. Reentrancy generally requires that variables be kept on stack or in registers so that new activations do not affect the state of the preempted incomplete executions. Additional complexities in the sharing of code are imposed by the need that shared code must ensure that references to itself—such as local jumps and access to local data—are mapped properly during executions on behalf of any of the participating processes. When dynamic relocation with base registers is used, this means that all references to itself must reach the same set of physical addresses where the shared code is stored at run-time, no matter which particular base is used for a given relocation. This may be accomplished in different ways, such as by making the shared code position independent or by having the shared code occupy identical virtual offsets in address spaces of all processes that reference it.

Some aspects of the issues involved in self-referencing of shared code are illustrated in Figure 6.9, where a subroutine SUB is assumed to be shared by two

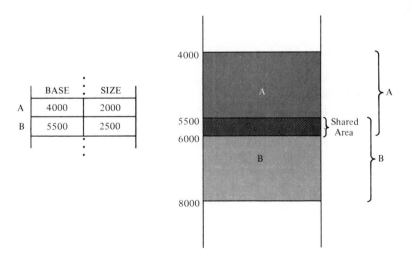

Figure 6.8 Overlapping partitions.

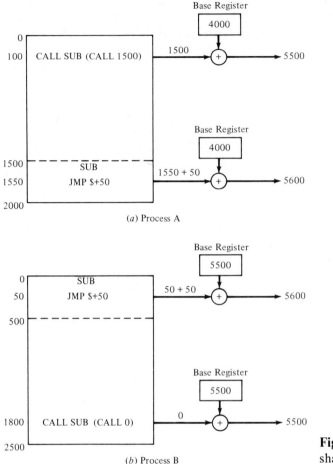

(a) Process A

(b) Process B

Figure 6.9 Accessing shared code.

processes, PA and PB, whose respective partitions overlap in physical memory, as indicated in Figure 6.8. Let us assume that the system in question uses dynamic relocation and dynamic memory allocation, thus allowing the two partitions to overlap. The sizes of the address spaces of the two processes are 2000 and 2500 locations, respectively. The shared subroutine, SUB, occupies 500 locations, and it is placed in locations 5500 to 5999 in physical memory. The subroutine starts at virtual addresses 1500 and 0 in the address spaces of processes PA and PB, respectively. Being shared by the two processes, SUB may be linked with and loaded with either process image.

Figure 6.9 also shows the references to SUB from within the two processes. As indicated in Figure 6.9a, the CALL SUB at virtual address 100 of process PA is mapped to the proper physical address of 5500 at run-time by adding the contents of the PA's base register. Likewise, the CALL SUB at the virtual address 1800 in process PB is mapped to 5500 at run-time by adding PB's value of the base register. This is illustrated in Figure 6.9b. Thus, proper referencing of SUB from the two processes is accomplished even when the two partitions are relocated due to swapping or compaction, provided that they overlap in the same way in the new set of physical addresses. However, making references from within SUB to itself poses a problem unless some special provisions are made. For example, a jump using absolute addressing from location 50 to location 100 within the SUB should read JMP 1600 for proper transfer of control when invoked by PA but JMP 100 if PB's invocation is to work properly. Since the JMP instruction may have only one of these two addresses in its displacement field, there is a problem in executing SUB correctly in both possible contexts.

One way to solve this problem is to use relative references instead of absolute references within shared code. For example, the jump in question may read JMP $ +50, where $ denotes the address of the JMP instruction. Since it is relative to the program counter, JMP is mapped properly when invoked by either process, that is, to virtual address 1600 or 100 in respective cases. At run-time, however, both references map to the same physical address, 5600, as they should. This is illustrated in Figure 6.9.

Code that executes correctly regardless of its load address is often referred to as *position-independent code*. One of its properties is that references to portions of the position-independent code itself are always relative, say, to the program counter or to a base when based addressing is used. Position-independent coding is often used for shared code, such as memory-resident subroutine libraries. In our example, use of position-independent code solves the problem of self-referencing.

Position-independent coding is one of the ways to handle the problem of self-referencing of shared code. The main point of our example, however, is that sharing of code is more restrictive than the sharing of data. In particular, both forms of sharing require the shared object to be accessible from all address spaces of which it is a part. In addition, shared code must also be reentrant or executed on a mutually exclusive basis, and some special provisions—such as position-independent coding—must be made in order to ensure proper references to itself. Since ordinary (nonshared) code does not automatically meet these requirements, some special language provisions must be in place or assembly-language coding may be necessary to prepare shared code for execution in systems with partitioned allocation of memory.

6.3.4 Concluding Remarks

Dynamic partitioning of memory requires basically the same hardware support as does static partitioning. In other words, the main differences between the two memory-management schemes are in software. As a result, protection and sharing in the two approaches are quite similar, except for some additional considerations imposed by compacting of memory when dynamic partitioning is used.

Dynamic partitioning of memory is driven by the specific requirements of the executing processes. As a result of adaptive allocation of memory, internal fragmentation is practically eliminated. Some minimal internal fragmentation may be encountered in systems that manage memory in terms of an incremental number of some basic units, such as those which use the buddy strategy for allocation or keys for protection, where on the average half of one basic allocation unit per partition is lost to internal fragmentation.

In contrast to fixed partitioning, all available memory except for the resident portion of the operating system may be allocated to a single program in systems with dynamic partitioning of memory. Another advantage of variable partition sizes is the ability to accommodate processes whose memory requirements are increasing during their execution. For example, when a process wishes to expand beyond the confines of its current partition, the operating system may create a larger partition and move the process into it. Alternatively, the process's partition may simply be expanded into an adjacent free area if one exists.

Dynamic partitioning of memory is not without disadvantages. It requires more complex bookkeeping and memory-management algorithms, thus consuming more of the operating system's space and time. While internal fragmentation may be negligible, external fragmentation may become a serious problem, imposing a time penalty for compaction. Sharing may also be complicated when shared objects are subjected to compaction of memory.

Real-time and interrupt-servicing processes can rarely tolerate the delays encountered during swapping or compaction of memory. Some operating systems solve this problem by providing a privileged service to fix a designated process in memory. Once loaded in memory, a fixed process remains there until termination. Fixed processes are never swapped or relocated for compaction purposes. While not a problem with static partitioning, fixing of processes in memory may have adverse effects on dynamic partitioning. For example, a process fixed in the middle of memory may effectively half the maximum size of allocatable partitions.

As discussed in the previous section, fixed partitioning of memory may be adequate for stable application environments with known sizes of frequently run processes. Dynamic partitioning is obviously more likely to be used in program-development and other environments where the workload is unpredictable or less well behaved. A compromise used in some systems is to support *both* static and dynamic partitioning of memory at the same time. Namely, a portion of memory may be divided into a certain number of fixed partitions to suit the needs of often-run or time-critical processes. The operating-system kernel and its extensions, such as device drivers and portions of the file system, are good candidates for inhabiting fixed partitions. The remaining portion of memory may then be allocated to other processes by using dynamic partitioning.

6.4 SEGMENTATION

The extent of external fragmentation and its negative impact on wasted memory should be reduced in systems where the average size of a request for allocation is smaller. Since there is not much that the operating system can do to reduce the average process size, a way to reduce the average size of a request for memory is to divide the address space of a single process into blocks that may be placed into noncontiguous areas of memory. This can be accomplished by a memory-management scheme called *segmentation*. Segmentation goes way beyond the simple breaking of address space into several logical entities (segments) by also providing dynamic relocation and sophisticated forms of protection and sharing.

Segments are formed at program-translation time by grouping together logically related items. For example, a typical process may have separate code, data, and stack segments. The data or code shared with other processes may be placed in their own dedicated segments. Being a result of a logical division, individual segments generally have different sizes. While different segments may be placed in separate, noncontiguous areas of physical memory, items belonging to a single segment must be placed in a contiguous area of physical memory. Thus, segmentation shares some properties of both contiguous (with regard to individual segments) and noncontiguous (with regard to the address space of a process) schemes for memory-management. We describe segmentation in this chapter for easier reference to some mechanisms of dynamic memory allocation that are often used in segmented systems.

Segmentation is quite natural for programmers who tend to think of their programs in terms of logically related entities, such as subroutines, and global or local data areas. A segment is essentially a collection of such entities. The segmented address space of a single process is illustrated in Figure 6.10a. In that particular example, four different segments are defined: DATA, STACK, CODE, and SHARED. Except for SHARED, the name of each segment is chosen to indicate the type of information that it contains. The STACK segment is assumed to consist of 500 locations reserved for stack. The SHARED segment consists of two subroutines, SSUB1 and SSUB2, shared with other processes. The definition of the segments follows the typical assembly-language notation, where programmers usually have the freedom to define segments directly in whatever way they feel best suits the needs of the program at hand. As a result, a specific process may have several different segments of the same generic type, such as code or data. For example, both CODE and SHARED segments contain executable instructions and thus belong to the generic type "code."

6.4.1 Principles of Operation

For relocation purposes, each segment is assumed to begin at the virtual address 0. An individual item within a segment is then identifiable by its offset relative to the beginning of the enclosing segment. For example, the subroutine SSUB2 in segment SHARED is assumed to begin at offset 100. However, unique designation of an item in a segmented address space requires specification of *both* its segment and the relative offset therein. While offset 100 may fetch the first instruction of the subroutine SSUB2 within the segment SHARED, the same relative offset may designate an entirely unrelated datum in the DATA segment. Thus, addresses in segmented systems have two components: the segment name and the offset

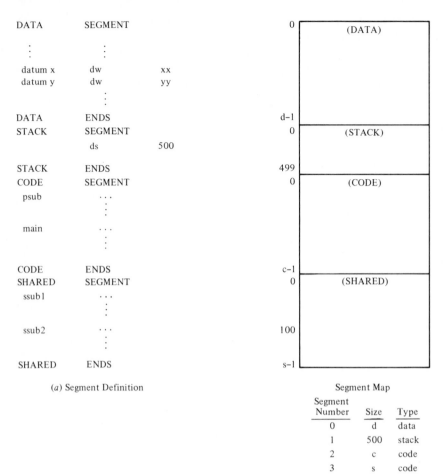

(a) Segment Definition

Segment Map

Segment Number	Size	Type
0	d	data
1	500	stack
2	c	code
3	s	code

(b) Load Module

Figure 6.10 Segments.

within that segment. To simplify processing, segment names are usually mapped to (virtual) segment numbers. This mapping is static, and it may be performed by systems programs in the course of preparation of process images.

A sample linker-produced load module for the segments defined in Figure 6.10a is depicted in Figure 6.10b. Virtual segment numbers are shown as part of the SEGMENT MAP that systems programs prepare in order to facilitate loading of segments in memory by the operating system. When segment numbers and relative offsets within the segments are defined, two-component virtual addresses uniquely identify all items within a process's address space. For example, if the SHARED segment is assigned the number 3, the subroutine SSUB2 may be uniquely identified by its virtual address (3, 100), where 100 is the offset within the enclosing segment number 3 (SHARED).

Since physical memory generally retains its linear-array organization, some address-translation mechanism is needed to convert a two-dimensional virtual-segment address into its physical equivalent. In order to motivate the need for the different components of this mechanism, let us examine the placement of virtual segments in physical memory.

In segmented systems, items belonging to a single segment reside in one contiguous area of physical memory. With each segment compiled as if starting from the virtual address 0, segments are generally individually relocatable. As a result, different segments of the same process need not occupy contiguous areas of physical memory.

When requested to load a segmented process, the operating system attempts to allocate memory for the supplied segments. Using logic similar to dynamic partitioning, a separate partition may be created to suit the needs of each particular segment. The base (obtained while creating the partition) and size (specified in the load module) of a loaded segment are recorded as a tuple called the *segment descriptor*. All segment descriptors of a given process are collected in a table called the *segment-descriptor table* (SDT).

Figure 6.11 illustrates a sample placement of segments defined in Figure 6.10 into physical memory and the resulting segment-descriptor table formed by the operating system. With the physical base address of each segment defined, the process of translation of a virtual, two-component address into its physical equivalent basically follows the mechanics of based addressing. The segment number provided in the virtual address is used to index the segment descriptor table and to obtain the physical base address of the related segment. The physical address is then produced by adding the offset of the desired item to the base of its enclosing segment. This process is illustrated in Figure 6.11 on the example of the virtual address (3, 100). To access Segment 3, the number 3 is used to index the SDT and to obtain the physical base address, 20000, of the segment SHARED. The size field of the same segment descriptor is used to check whether the supplied offset is within the legal bounds of its enclosing segment. If so, the base and offset are added to produce the target physical address. In our example that value is 20100, the first instruction word of the shared subroutine SSUB2.

In general, the size of a segment-descriptor table is related to the size of the virtual-address space of a process. For example, Intel's iAPX 286 processor is capable of supporting up to 16,000 segments of 64 KB each per process, thus requiring 16,000 entries per SDT. Given their potential size, segment-descriptor tables are usually kept in memory. Being a collection of logically related items, the SDTs themselves are often treated as special-type segments. Their accessing is usually facilitated by means of a dedicated hardware register called the *segment-descriptor table base register* (SDTBR), which is set to point to the base of the running process's SDT. Since the size of an SDT may vary from a few entries to several thousands, another dedicated hardware register, called the *segment-descriptor table limit register* (SDTLR), is provided to mark the end of the SDT pointed to by the SDTBR. In this way, an SDT need contain only as many entries as there are segments actually defined in a given process. Attempts to access

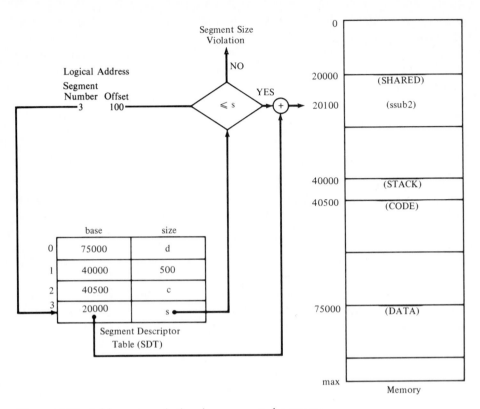

Figure 6.11 Address translation in segmented systems.

nonexistent segments may be detected and dealt with as nonexistent-segment exceptions.

From the operating system's point of view, segmentation is essentially a multiple base-limit version of dynamically partitioned memory. Memory is allocated in the form of variable partitions, the main difference being that one such partition is allocated to each individual segment. Bases and limits of segments belonging to a given process are collected into an SDT which may be assigned a partition of its own. The base and limit of an SDT are normally kept in the PCB of the owner process. Upon each process switch, the SDTBR and SDTLR registers are loaded with the base and size, respectively, of the SDT of the new running process. In addition to the process-loading time, SDT entries may also need to be updated whenever a process is swapped-out or relocated for compaction purposes. Swapping out requires invalidation of all SDT entries describing the affected segments. When the process is swapped back in, the base fields of its segment descriptors must be updated to reflect new load addresses. For this reason, swapping out of the SDT itself is rarely useful. Instead, the SDT of the swapped-out process may be discarded and the static segment map—such as the one depicted in Figure 6.10b—may be used for creation of an up-to-date SDT whenever the related process is loaded in memory. Compaction, when supported, requires updating of the related SDT entry for each segment moved. In such systems, some additional or revised data structures may be needed to facilitate identification of the SDT and its particular entry describing the specific segment scheduled to be moved.

The price paid for segmenting the address space of a process is the overhead of storing and accessing segment-descriptor tables. Mapping of each virtual address requires two memory references: one to the SDT for the virtual-to-physical mapping and the other to access the target location in physical memory. In other words, *segmentation may cut the effective memory bandwidth in half*. With performance of segmented systems so critically dependent upon the duration of the address-translation process, computer-system designers often provide some hardware accelerators to speed the translation up. Memory references expended on mapping may be avoided by keeping segment descriptors in registers. However, the potential size of an SDT and the overhead of process switching make it too costly to keep an entire SDT of the running process in registers. A reasonable compromise is to keep a few of the most frequently used segment descriptors in registers. In this way, most of the memory references may be mapped with the aid of registers. The rest may be mapped using the SDT in memory, as usual. This scheme is dependent upon the operating system's ability to select the proper segment descriptors for storing into registers. In order to provide the intuitive motivation for one possible implementation of systematic descriptor selection, let us investigate the types of segments referenced by the executing process.

Memory references may be functionally categorized as accesses to

1. Instructions
2. Data
3. Stack

Other taxonomies are possible, but this particular one suits our present needs. A typical instruction-execution sequence consists of a mixture of the outlined types of memory references. In fact, a single stack-manipulation instruction, such as a push of a datum from memory onto stack, may require all three types of references in order to be completed. Thus, the working space of a process normally encompasses one each of code, data, and stack segments. Therefore, address translation may be accelerated by keeping the current code, data, and stack segment descriptors in registers. Depending on its type, a particular memory reference may then be mapped using the appropriate register. But can we know the exact type of each memory reference as it is being made by the CPU? The answer is yes, with the proper hardware support. Namely, in most segmented machines the CPU emits a few status bits to indicate the type of each memory reference. The memory-management hardware uses this information to select the appropriate mapping register.

Register-assisted translation of virtual-to-physical addresses is illustrated in Figure 6.12. As indicated, the CPU status lines are used to select the

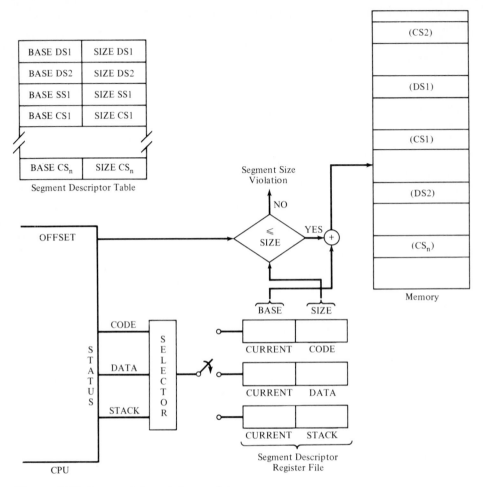

Figure 6.12 Segment-descriptor registers.

appropriate segment-descriptor register (SDR). The size field of the selected segment descriptor is used to check whether the intended reference is within the bounds of the target segment. If so, the base field is added with the offset to produce the physical address. By making the choice of the appropriate segment register implicit in the type of the memory reference being made, segment typing may eliminate the need to keep track of segment numbers during address translations. While segment typing is certainly useful, it may become restrictive at times. For example, copying of an instruction sequence from one segment into another may confuse the selector logic into believing that source and target segments should be of type data rather than code. This problem may be alleviated by using the so-called *segment-override prefixes*, which allow the programmer to explicitly indicate the particular segment-descriptor register to be used for mapping of the memory reference in question.

Segment-descriptor registers are initially loaded from the SDT. Whenever an intersegment reference is made by the running process, the corresponding segment-descriptor is loaded into the appropriate register from the SDT. For example, an intersegment JUMP or CALL causes the segment descriptor of the target (code) segment to be copied from the SDT to the code segment-descriptor register. When segment typing is used as described, segment-descriptor caching becomes deterministic as opposed to probabilistic, which is described in Chapter 7. Segment-descriptors stored in the three segment-descriptor registers define the current working set of the executing process. Since membership in the working set of segments of a process changes with time, segment-descriptor registers are normally included in the process state. Upon each process switch, the contents of the SDRs of the departing process are stored with the rest of its context. Before dispatching the new running process, the operating system loads the segment-descriptor registers with their images recorded in the related PCB.

The benefits of hardware-assisted segment typing are recognized and exploited in many segmented architectures. For example, Multics hardware supports four types of segments: code, data, stack, and linkage segment. Intel's iAPX-86 family maintains four dedicated segment-descriptor registers: code, data, stack, and extra segment. The linkage segment of Multics and the extra segment of iAPX may be used for dynamic linking and loading, sharing, and other purposes described later in this chapter.

6.4.2 Protection and Sharing

The base-limit form of protection is obviously the most natural choice for segmented systems. The legal address space of a process is the collection of segments defined by its SDT. Except for shared segments, separation of distinct address spaces is enforced by placing different segments in disjoint areas of memory. Thus, most of the discussion of protection in systems with dynamic allocation of memory is applicable to segmented environments as well.

An interesting possibility in segmented systems is to provide protection *within* the address space of a single process in addition to the more usual protection between different processes. Given that the type of each segment is defined commensurate with the nature of information stored in its constituent elements, access rights to each segment can be defined accordingly. For instance, while both reading and writing of stack segments may be necessary, accessing of code segments can be permitted in the execute-only or perhaps in the read-only mode. Data segments can be read-only, write-only, or read-write. Thus, segmented systems may be able to prohibit some meaningless operations, such as execution of data or modifications of code. Additional examples include the preventing of stack growth into the adjacent code or data areas and other errors resulting from mismatching of segment types and intended references to them. An important observation is that access rights to different portions of a single address space may vary in accordance with the type of information stored therein. Due to the grouping of logically related items, segmentation is one of the rare memory-management schemes to allow such finely grained delineation of access rights. The mechanism for enforcement of declared access rights in segmented systems is usually coupled with the address-translation hardware. Typically, access-rights bits are included in segment descriptors. In the course of address mapping, the intended type of reference is checked against the access rights for the segment in question. Any mismatch results in abortion of the memory reference in progress and a trap to the operating system.

The flexibility and ease of sharing are among the strongest arguments in favor of segmentation. Shared objects, such as code or data, are usually placed in separate, dedicated segments. A shared segment may be mapped, via the appropriate Segment-Descriptor Tables, to the virtual-address spaces of all processes that are authorized to reference it. The deliberate use of offsets and based addressing facilitates sharing, since the virtual offset of a given item is identical in all processes that share it. The virtual number of a shared segment, on the other hand, need not be identical in all address spaces of which it is a member. These points are illustrated in Figure 6.13, where code segment EMACS is assumed to be shared by three processes. The relevant portions of the segment-descriptor tables of each participating process, SDT1, SDT2, and SDT3, are shown. As indicated, the segment EMACS is assumed to have different virtual numbers in the three address spaces of which it is part. The placement of access-rights bits in segment-descriptor tables is also shown. Figure 6.13 illustrates the fact that different processes can have different access rights to the same shared segment. For example, while processes P1 and P2 can only execute the shared segment EMACS, process P3 is allowed both reading and writing.

Figure 6.13 also illustrates the ability of segmented systems to conserve memory by sharing the code of programs executed by many users. In particular, each participating process can execute the shared code from EMACS using its own *private data segment*. Assuming that EMACS is an editor, this means that a single copy of it may serve the entire user population of a time-sharing system. Naturally, execution of EMACS on behalf of each particular user is treated by the operating system as a separate process. The text buffer of each user is stored in a private data segment of its corresponding process. For example, Users 1, 2, and 3 can have their respective text buffers stored in data segments DATA1, DATA2, and DATA3. Depending on which of the three processes is active at a given time, the hardware data segment-descriptor register points to data segment DATA1, DATA2, or DATA3, while the code segment-descriptor register points to EMACS in all cases. Of course, the current instruction to be executed by the particular process is indicated by the program counter, which is saved and restored as a part of each process's state. In segmented systems, the program-counter register usually contains offsets of instructions within the current code segment. This facilitates sharing by making all code references to itself relative to the beginning of the current code segment. When coupled with segment typing, this feature makes it possible to assign different virtual segment numbers to the

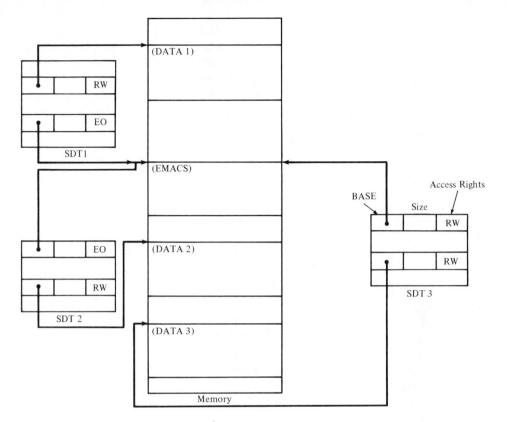

Figure 6.13 Sharing in segmented systems.

same (physical) shared segment in virtual-address spaces of different processes of which it is a part. Alternatively, the problem of making direct references to itself in shared routines described under Protection and Sharing in Section 6.3 restricts the type of code that may safely be shared.

As described, sharing is both encouraged and practiced in segmented systems. This presents some problems in systems that also support swapping, which is normally done to increase processor utilization. For example, a shared segment may need to maintain its memory residence while being actively used by any of the processes authorized to reference it. Swapping in this case opens up a possibility that a participating process may be swapped-out while its shared segment remains resident. When such a process is swapped back in, the construction of its SDT must take into consideration the fact that the shared segment may already be resident. In other words, the operating system must keep track of shared segments and of processes that access them. When a participating process is loaded in memory, the OS is expected to identify the location of the shared segment in memory, if any, and to ensure its proper mapping from all virtual-address spaces of which it is a part.

6.4.3 Concluding Remarks

From the memory-manager's point of view, segmentation is basically a multiple base-limit version of partitioned memory. As such, segmentation allows breakage of the virtual-address space of a process into several pieces, each of which can be assigned a different partition of physical memory. By eliminating the need to assign one contiguous area of memory for the entire address space of a process, the utilization and management of physical memory may be made more efficient. In systems with fixed partitioning, variance of segment sizes may be lower than variances of the sizes of entire processes and thus help reduce the extent of internal fragmentation. In the more common case of variable partitioning, allocation of memory in smaller chunks is likely to slow down the buildup of external fragmentation. As a result, the frequency of compaction may be reduced while retaining the advantage of no internal fragmentation. The logical division of the address space, coupled with typing of segments, provides an excellent foundation for the implementation of versatile protection and sharing mechanisms. With variable partitioning of memory, dynamic growth of segments can be supported more easily.

The potential advantages of segmentation extend beyond the limits and concerns of memory-management. Some of the advantages claimed for segmentation are listed below (those not mentioned thus far are briefly elaborated):

- Elimination of internal fragmentation
- Support for dynamic growth of segments
- Protection
- Sharing
- Modular program development—through segmentation, which naturally leads to the definition of smaller, logically related program entities
- Dynamic linking and loading

With regard to dynamic linking and loading, some segmented systems, such as Multics, provide hardware support for the run-time binding and loading of a procedure only if and when it is referenced during a given program execution. Thus, the address space actually used by a process is determined dynamically to include only what is needed from the full process image. Coupled with the ability to run partially loaded programs, this approach tends to increase memory efficiency.

Memory-management-related disadvantages of segmentation are mostly a result of the variable sizes of segments. When dynamic allocation of partitions is used with segmentation, compaction of memory is usually necessary, although its frequency may be reduced due to the smaller size of segments. Given the possibility of several partitions belonging to a single process, more complex strategies for compaction may need to be employed once it becomes unavoidable. In general, management of segmented memory requires comparatively more complex mechanisms than for either static or dynamic partitioning of memory and thus incurs higher OS overhead. The two-step translation of virtual to physical addresses has to be supported by dedicated hardware to avoid a drastic reduction in the effective memory bandwidth.

Another problem is that no single segment may be larger than the available physical memory. In segmented architectures until the mid-eighties a rather small segment size limit of 64 KB was quite common. Such limits are both inconvenient and taxing when a single logical object, such as a large matrix, must be split into several physical segments. In order to access different parts of a single logical object fragmented into several segments, several different segment base addresses may have to be used for address translations. The resulting run-time overhead may be unacceptable in applications where large data structures must be manipulated as fast as possible, such as in the refreshing of a high-resolution video display.

6.5 SUMMARY

In this chapter we have presented several schemes for management of main memory that are characterized by contiguous allocation of memory. Except for the single-process monitor, which is inefficient in terms of both CPU and memory utilization, all other schemes support multiprogramming by allowing the address spaces of several processes to reside in main memory simultaneously.

One approach is to statically divide the available physical memory into a number of fixed partitions and to satisfy requests for memory by granting suitable free partitions, if any. Fixed partition sizes limit the maximum allowable virtual-address space of any given process to the size of the largest partition (unless overlays are used). The total number of partitions in a given system limits the number of resident processes. Within the confines of this limit, the effectiveness of the short-term scheduler may be improved by employing swapping to increase the ratio of resident to ready processes. Systems with static partitioning suffer from internal fragmentation of memory.

Dynamic (variable) partitioning allows allocation of the entire physical memory, except for the resident part of the operating system, to a single process. Thus, in systems with dynamic partitioning, the virtual-address space of any given process or an overlay is limited only by the capacity of the physical memory in the given system. Dynamic creation of partitions according to the specific needs of requesting processes also eliminates the problem of internal fragmentation. Dynamic allocation of partitions requires the use of more complex algorithms for deallocation of partitions and coalescing of free memory in order to combat external fragmentation. The need for occasional compaction of memory is also a major contributor to the increased time and space complexity of dynamic partitioning.

Both static and dynamic partitioning of memory rely on virtually identical hardware support for relocation and protection. Sharing is quite restrictive in both systems.

Segmentation allows the breaking of the virtual-address space of a single process into separate entities (segments) that may be placed in noncontiguous areas of physical memory. As a result, the virtual-to-physical-address translation at instruction-execution time in such systems is more complex and requires some dedicated hardware support in order to avoid a drastic reduction in effective memory bandwidth. Since average segment sizes are usually smaller than average process sizes, segmentation can reduce the impact of external fragmentation on the performance of systems with dynamically partitioned memory. Other advantages of segmentation include dynamic relocation, finely grained protection both within and between address spaces, ease of sharing, and facilitation of dynamic linking and loading. Unless some additional provisions discussed in Chapter 7 are made, segmentation does not remove the problem of limiting the size of a process's virtual space by the size of the available physical memory.

OTHER READING

Static partitioning and dynamic partitioning of memory in versions of the IBM OS/360, where they are called MFT (multiprogramming with a fixed number of tasks) and MVT (multiprogramming with a variable number of tasks) respectively, are described by Knight (1968) and by Peterson and Silberchatz (1983).

The fifty percent rule is due to Knuth (1973a), who also describes and analyzes first-fit, best-fit, and buddy allocation of memory blocks. Further analysis of dynamic memory allocation, and of first-fit and best-fit in particular, is provided by Shore (1975, 1977), Bays (1977), and Beck (1982). Various forms of the buddy system are described and analyzed by Peterson and Norman (1977). Implementation of a complete memory allocator is discussed by Joseph, Prasad, and Natarajan (1984).

Relocation and position-independent code are described by Wakerly (1981) and by Calingaert (1982). Swapping is discussed by Habermann (1976). Hardware support for protection and sharing, and for some other operating-system functions, is described by Sites (1980).

Segmentation in Multics is described by Organick (1972). The same author (1973) describes the organization of segmented architectures implemented in the Burroughs B5700/B6700 series. Information expressly for operating-system designers using the segmented processor iAPX 286 is provided by Intel (1983b). A thorough treatment of memory-management, including details of segmentation and dynamic binding in Multics, is provided by Madnick and Donovan (1974).

EXERCISES

6.1 Describe how an operating system may determine the capacity of physical memory installed in a given system. Write and test a routine to do this on a specific machine.

6.2 Provide a functional specification for partition allocation in a system with static partitioning (fixed partitions). Design all major data structures, including the PCB, and discuss the advantages and disadvantages of the specific allocation algorithm that you have chosen. Describe the necessary and/or desirable hardware support for protection required by your design.

6.3 Indicate what needs to be changed, and how, in the solution to the previous exercise when swapping is to be supported. Provide a functional specification for the swapper, and discuss when a swapped-out process should be considered for bringing back to main memory. Discuss the type of relocation required by and/or desirable for your design.

6.4 In the base-limit relocation and protection scheme described in the text, each virtual address is first checked against the limit and then mapped to physical address space. Discuss the relative advantages and disadvantages of reversing the order of these operations, that is, checking for a physical as opposed to a virtual bound. Specify the format and manipulation of the relevant PCB fields in both cases. Indicate how and when each of these fields is initialized and/or modified.

6.5 In Step 2 of the dynamic partition-allocation procedure, a partition is "carved" from a larger hole. Assuming that initially all memory is available and represented as a single, contiguous free area (hole), indicate whether the corresponding operation in Step 2 tends to favor one end of physical memory for allocations, and if so, which. Give formulas for allocations that favor the opposite end of memory, and compare the two approaches in terms of time complexity, wasted memory, and the effects on memory coalescing, if any, during deallocations.

6.6 Using the general format of partition allocation and deallocation procedures for dynamic partitioning outlined in the text, provide specifications of the major data structures and write complete routines for the allocation and deallocation of memory. Use the first-fit algorithm for allocation and coalesce adjacent free areas whenever possible during deallocations. Discuss which structure of the Free list is best suited for allocation and which for deallocation of memory, and argue the merits of your particular choice with respect to the combined efficiency of the two operations.

6.7 Repeat the previous exercise, but using best-fit for allocation. Compare the time and space complexities of the two approaches.

6.8 Assume that the head node of the Free list contains a field MAX which indicates the maximum size of a contiguous free area present in the Free list. Explain the use of this field, and indicate which additional operations are necessary to maintain its value up to date during allocations and deallocations of memory. Discuss the advantages and disadvantages of using the MAX field.

6.9 Devise an algorithm for returning an area of memory to the Free list with coalescing of adjacent free areas, if any, in constant time. *Hint*: Use a doubly linked Free list and some extra tags to indicate the status of the adjacent blocks—free or allocated.

6.10 What type of memory fragmentation, if any, may develop when a buddy system is used for the allocation and deallocation of memory? Explain.

6.11 Provide a functional specification and implement routines necessary for buddy allocation and deallocation of memory. Show that the address and size of one buddy provide sufficient information to determine the address of the other buddy.

6.12 Provide a functional specification and write routines to perform compaction "in place," that is, without using the secondary storage. Can all physical memory available for allocation be merged into a single contiguous area using this approach? Why or why not?

6.13 One way to compact memory is to swap all resident processes to the secondary storage, thus creating a single, large contiguous area. The processes swapped for compaction are then brought back into main memory by creating the required number of contiguous partitions. Contrast this approach to the "in-memory" algorithm provided as a solution to the previous exercise in terms of space and time complexity.

6.14 Devise an algorithm for selective compaction of memory, and indicate in which situations it performs better than the brute-force compaction. Discuss the benefits of these savings with regard to the time and space complexities of your algorithm relative to straightforward compaction.

6.15 Provide a general procedure for the allocation of partitions in a segmented system where several partitions may be needed to house different segments of each process. Specify the relevant portion of the PCB structure, show when and how segment descriptors are initialized (allocation must provide for a segment-descriptor table), and discuss how you handle the situation when several partitions are already allocated to a process and then allocation for another segment fails.

6.16 Write software routines for virtual-to-physical-address translation, protection, and other aspects of segmentation so as to emulate segmentation on nonsegmented hardware. Discuss the memory-access overhead of your routines, and identify the critical operations whose implementation in hardware would be most cost-effective.

6.17 Provide a general procedure for preparation, loading, and using of shared code segments in a segmented system without swapping. Discuss whether self-referencing of shared code is a problem in segmented systems, and (if so) indicate how it may be solved. Explain the influence, if any, of segment typing on sharing of code.

CHAPTER SEVEN

MEMORY MANAGEMENT:
NONCONTIGUOUS ALLOCATION

In this chapter we discuss virtual-memory management and memory-management schemes based on noncontiguous allocation of physical memory. By *noncontiguous* we mean that memory is allocated in such a way that parts of a single logical object may be placed in noncontiguous areas of physical memory. Address translation performed during the execution of instructions establishes the necessary correspondence between a contiguous virtual-address space and the possibly discontiguous physical addresses of locations where object items reside in memory. Details of noncontiguous allocation are discussed in relation to paged memory.

The memory-management scheme called *virtual memory* allows execution of processes even when only portions of their address spaces are resident in primary memory. Basically, the actively used portions of an address space are kept in memory, and others are brought in from the secondary storage as and when needed. Depending on whether paging or segmentation is used to manage physical memory, virtual memory-management is referred to as *demand paging* or *demand segmentation*. Thus, in addition to managing the primary memory, virtual memory provides for automatic migration of portions of address spaces of active processes between primary and secondary storage.

Following the approach introduced in Chapter 6, each memory-management scheme is described in terms of its principles of operation and hardware support, followed by a discussion of protection and sharing. Different schemes are characterized and informally compared in terms of wasted memory, time complexity, and memory-access overhead.

7.1 PAGING

Paging is a memory-management scheme that removes the requirement of contiguous allocation of physical memory. Address-mapping is used to maintain the illusion of contiguity of the virtual-address space of a process despite its discontiguous placement in physical memory.

Basically, the physical memory is conceptually divided into a number of fixed-size slots called *page frames*. The virtual-address space of a process is also split into fixed-size blocks called *pages*. Allocation of memory consists of finding a sufficient number of unused page frames for loading of the requesting process's pages. An address-translation mechanism is used to map virtual pages to their physical counterparts. Since each page is mapped separately, different page frames allocated to a single process need not occupy contiguous areas of physical memory.

7.1.1 Principles of Operation

Figure 7.1 demonstrates the basic principle of paging. It illustrates a sample 1-MB system where virtual and physical addresses are assumed to be 20 bits long each. The page is assumed to be 256 bytes. Thus, the physical memory can accommodate 4096 page frames of 256 bytes each.

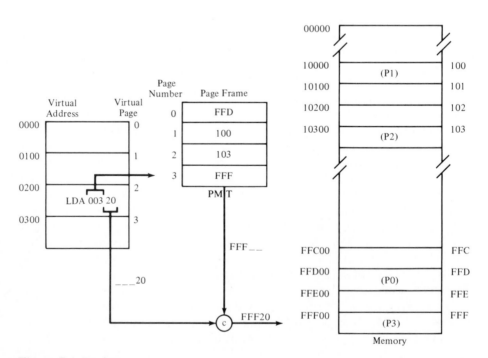

Figure 7.1 Paging.

After setting aside 64 KB of physical memory for the resident portion of the operating system, the remaining 3840 page frames (960 KB) are available for allocation to user processes. For brevity, their addresses are given in hexadecimal notation. Each page is 100H bytes long, and the first user-allocatable page frame starts at the physical address 10000H.

The virtual-address space of a sample user process which is 1008 bytes (3F0H) long is divided into four virtual pages numbered from 0 to 3. A possible placement of those pages into physical memory is depicted in Figure 7.1. The mapping of virtual to physical addresses in paging systems is performed at the page level. In particular, each virtual address is divided into two parts: the (virtual) page number, and the offset within that page. Since pages and page frames have identical sizes, offsets within each are identical and need not be mapped. In our sample system, each 20-bit virtual address may be regarded as a 12-bit page number (high-order bits) and an 8-bit offset within the page. This is adequate for the unique identification of each byte within a page (256 B), and for each page out of the 4096 possible.

In paging systems, address translation is performed with the aid of a mapping table called the *page-map table* (PMT). The PMT is constructed at the process-loading time in order to establish the correspondence between the virtual and physical addresses. A sample format of the PMT, corresponding to the assumed placement of pages in the physical memory, is shown in Figure 7.1. As indicated, there is one PMT entry for each virtual page of a process. The value of each entry is the number of the page frame in the physical memory where the corresponding virtual page is placed. Since offsets are not mapped, only the high-order bits of the physical base-address, that is, the page-frame number, need be stored in a PMT entry. For example, virtual-page 0 is assumed to be placed in the physical page frame whose starting address is FFD00H (1047808 decimal). With each frame being 100H bytes long, the corresponding page-frame number is FFDH, as indicated on the right-hand side of the physical-memory layout in Figure 7.1. This value is stored in the first entry of the PMT. All other PMT entries are filled with page-frame numbers where the corresponding pages are actually loaded.

The logic of the address-translation process in paged systems is illustrated in Figure 7.1 on the example of the virtual-address 0320H (800 decimal). The virtual address is split by hardware into the page number, that is, the high-order 12-bits (003H), and the offset within that page (20H). The page number is used to index the PMT and to obtain the corresponding physical frame number, FFFH in our example. This value is then concatenated with the offset to produce the physical address, FFF20H, which is used to reference the target item in memory.

More formally, in paging systems memory is allocated in fixed-size quanta called pages. Page size is determined by several factors whose influence is discussed later in relation to virtual memory. For convenience of mapping, page sizes are usually an integer power of base 2. In most commercial implementations, page sizes vary between 256 bytes and 4 KB.

The operating system keeps track of the status of each page frame by means of the map of physical memory, which may be structured as a static table. For convenience, we refer to this data structure as a *memory-map table* (MMT). A possible format of an MMT is illustrated in Figure 7.2, assuming that only the process depicted in Figure 7.1 and the operating system are resident in memory. As indicated, each entry of the MMT describes the status, such as FREE or ALLOCATED, of one page frame in physical memory. Therefore, an MMT has a fixed number of entries which is identical to the number of page frames in a given system, that is:

$$f = \frac{m}{p}$$

where f is the number of page frames, m is the capacity of installed physical memory, and p is page size. Both m and p are usually integer powers of base 2, thus resulting in f being an integer.

When requested to load a process of size s, the operating system must allocate n free page frames, so that

$$n = \left\lceil \frac{s}{p} \right\rceil$$

where p is the page size. The notation $\lceil \ \rceil$ denotes the ceiling function which returns an integer result obtained by rounding-up the quotient if the division produces a nonzero remainder. In other words, the operating system allocates

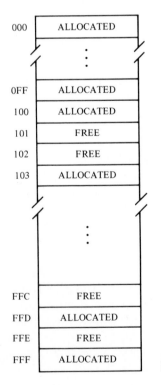

Figure 7.2 Memory-map table.

memory in terms of an integral number of page frames. If the size of a given process is not a multiple of the page size, the last page frame may be partly unused. This phenomenon is known as *page fragmentation* or *page breakage.*

The allocation of memory then simply consists of finding *any n* free page frames. With all page frames having identical sizes, the frame-allocation policy has practically no effect on the memory utilization. There are no first-fit or best-fit considerations; all frames fit all pages, and any fit is as good as any other. After having selected *n* free page frames, the operating system loads process pages into them and constructs the page-map table of the process. Thus, there is one MMT per system and as many PMTs as there are active processes. When a process terminates or becomes swapped-out, memory is deallocated by releasing the frame holdings of the departing process to the pool of free page frames.

This concludes our presentation of the basic principles of operation, and we now turn our attention to some implementation-related aspects of paging. In particular, we discuss frame allocation and the typical hardware support for paging.

Page allocation. Efficiency of the memory-allocation algorithm depends primarily on the speed with which it can locate free page frames. That kind of operation is usually facilitated by having a list of free pages, as opposed to the static-table format of the memory map assumed earlier. Let us briefly evaluate this tradeoff. Assuming that free frames are randomly distributed in memory, the average number of MMT entries, x, that needs to be examined in order to find n free frames may be expressed as:

$$x = \frac{n}{q}$$

where q is the probability that a given frame is empty (free). It is related to the percentage of unused memory u as follows:

$$q = \frac{u}{100} \qquad 0 \le q \le 1$$

In other words, the number of MMT entries searched, x, is directly proportional to kn, where $k = 1/q$ and thus $k \ge 1$. For example, in a system where unused memory percentage is 40% (60% of memory is in use), the probability that any given page frame is free is .4. Thus, to find 10 free frames, 25 MMT entries must be examined on the average. The inverse proportion of x to q implies that the number of MMT entries examined in order to locate x frames increases with the amount of memory in use.

An alternative is to link the free page-frame numbers into a free list. In that case, n free frames may be identified and allocated by unlinking the first n nodes of the free list. Deallocation of memory in systems without the free list consists of marking in the MMT as FREE all frames found in the PMT of the departing process. This operation is also proportional to n when a free list of pages is used. Frames identified in the PMT of the departing process can be linked to the beginning of the free list. Linking at the beginning is usually the fastest way of adding entries to an unordered singly linked list. Since the time complexity of deallocation is not significantly affected by the choice of data structure of free pages, the free list approach has a performance advantage, since its time complexity is not affected by the variation of memory utilization. In a particular implementation, this advantage has to be weighed against other considerations, such as the memory-utilization statistics and the generally higher per-entry space and time complexity of storing and processing linked lists relative to static tables.

Hardware support for paging. Hardware support for paging usually concentrates on conserving the memory necessary for storing of the mapping tables and on speeding-up the mapping of virtual to physical addresses. The multitude of page-map tables in paging systems provides the incentive to minimize the amount of memory necessary for their storage. In principle, each PMT must be large enough to accommodate the maximum size allowed for the address space of a process in a given system. In theory, this may be the entire physical memory. For instance, in a 16-MB system with 256-bytes pages, the size of a PMT should be 64K entries. Individual PMT entries are page numbers that are 16 bits long in the sample system, thus requiring 128 KB of physical memory to store a PMT. With one PMT needed for each active process, the total PMT storage can consume a significant portion of physical memory.

Since the actual address space of a process may be well below its allowable maximum, it is reasonable to construct each PMT with only as many entries as its related process has pages. This may be accomplished by means of a dedicated hardware *page-map table limit register* (PMTLR). A PMTLR is set to the highest virtual page number defined in the PMT of the running process. Accessing of the PMT of the running process may be facilitated by means of the *page-map table base register* (PMTBR), which points to the base address of the PMT of the running process. The respective values of these two registers for each process are defined at process-loading time and stored in the related PCB. Upon each process switch, the PCB of the new running process provides the values to be loaded in the page-map table base and limit registers.

Even with the assistance of these registers, address translations in paging systems still require two memory references: one to access the PMT for mapping, and the other to reference the target item in physical memory. This implies that systems based on paging may suffer a 50% reduction of their memory bandwidth. This problem may be alleviated by providing the specialized hardware to speed up the address-translation process.

One popular approach is to use a high-speed associative memory for storing a subset of often used page-map table entries. This memory is called the *translation-lookaside buffer* (TLAB) or sometimes simply the *mapping cache*. The latter term should not be confused with the associative cache memory used to reduce the effective memory cycle time.

Associative memories can be searched by contents rather than by address. For example, the answer to the question "Is the page number z stored in the TLAB?" can be obtained in a single cycle of the TLAB. If it is in the TLAB, the corresponding page number is furnished within the same TLAB cycle time. Therefore, the main-memory reference for mapping can be substituted by a TLAB reference. Given that the TLAB cycle time is typically an order of magnitude lower than that of the main memory, the memory-access overhead incurred by mapping can be significantly reduced. The role of the cache in the mapping process is depicted in Figure 7.3. The figure also illustrates the roles of the page-map table base and limit registers.

As indicated, the TLAB (mapping-cache) entries contain pairs of virtual page numbers and the corresponding page-frame numbers where the related pages are stored in physical memory. The page number is necessary to define each particular entry, because the TLAB contains only a subset of page-map

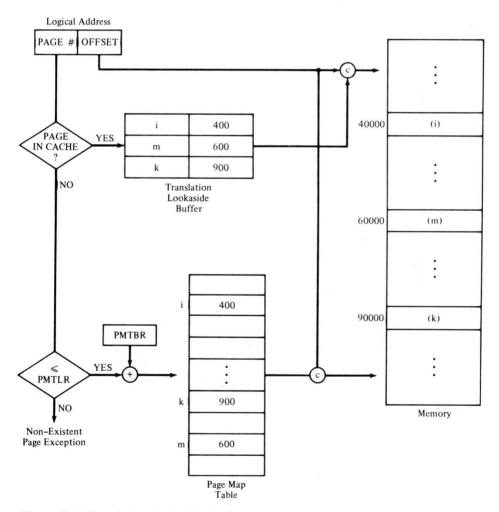

Figure 7.3 Translation-lookaside buffer.

table entries. Address translation begins by presenting the page-number portion of the virtual address to the TLAB. If the desired entry is found in the TLAB, the corresponding page-frame number is combined with the offset to produce the physical address. Alternatively, if the target entry is not in the cache, the PMT in memory must be referenced to complete the mapping. This process begins by consulting the PMTLR to verify that the page number provided in the virtual address is within the bounds of the related process's address space. If so, the page number is added with the contents of the PMTBR to obtain the address of the corresponding PMT entry where the physical page-frame number is stored. This value is then concatenated with the offset portion of the virtual address to produce the physical memory address of the desired item.

Figure 7.3 demonstrates that the overhead of the TLAB search is added to all mappings, irrespective of whether they are eventually completed using the TLAB or the PMT in main memory. In other words, the TLAB actually prolongs the references to the PMT. Thus, in order for the TLAB to be effective, it must satisfy a large portion of all address-mappings. Given the generally small size of a TLAB dictated by the high price of associative memories, only the PMT entries most likely to be needed ought to reside in the TLAB.

The typical strategies for TLAB management in paging systems—such as the fetch, allocation, and replacement policies—are discussed later in relation to virtual memory. For the time being, let us observe that the hardware used to accelerate address translations in paging systems (TLAB) is managed by means of probabilistic algorithms, as opposed to the deterministic mapping-register typing described in relation to segmentation. The reason is that pages are produced by the mechanical splitting of a process's address space into fixed-size chunks. As a result, a page, unlike a segment, in general does not bear any relationship to the logical entities of the underlying program. For example, a single page may contain a mixture of data, stack, and code. This makes typing and other forms of deterministic loading of TLAB entries extremely difficult, in view of the stringent timing restrictions imposed on TLAB manipulation.

7.1.2 Protection and Sharing

Unless specifically declared as shared, distinct address spaces are placed in disjoint areas of physical memory. Memory references of the running process are restricted to its own address space by means of the address-translation mechanism which uses the dedicated page-map table. The PMT limit register is used to detect and to abort attempts to access any memory beyond the legal boundaries of a process. Modifications of PMT base and limit registers are usually possible only by means of privileged instructions which trap to the operating system if attempted in user mode.

By adding the access bits to the PMT entries, as well as the appropriate hardware for testing these bits, access to a given page may be allowed only in certain programmer-defined modes. For example, access bits may allow read only, execute only, or other restricted forms of access. While conceptually similar to the equivalent mechanism described in relation to segmentation, this feature is much less flexible in paging systems. The primary difference is that paging is supposed to be entirely transparent to programmers. Mechanical splitting of an address space into pages is performed without any regard for the possible virtual relationships between the items under consideration. Since there is no notion of typing, code and data, for example, may be mixed within one page. As we shall see, specification of the access rights in paging systems is useful for pages shared by several processes, but it is of much less value inside the boundaries of a given address space.

Protection in paging systems may also be accomplished by means of the protection keys, described earlier. In principle, the page size should correspond to the size of the memory block protected by the single key. This allows pages belonging to a single process to be scattered throughout memory, a perfect match for paged allocation. By associating access-rights bits with protection keys, access to a given page may be restricted when necessary.

Sharing of pages is quite straightforward in systems with paged memory-management. A single physical copy of a shared page can be easily mapped into as many distinct address spaces as desired. Since each such mapping is performed via a dedicated entry in the page-map table of the related process, different processes may have different access rights to the shared page. Given that paging is transparent to users, sharing at the page level must be recognized and supported by systems programs. In particular, systems programs must ensure that virtual offsets of particular items within the shared page are identical in all participating address spaces.

As is the case with data, shared code must occupy the same within-page offsets in all address spaces of which it is a part. As usual, shared code that is not executed in mutually exclusive fashion must be reentrant. In addition, unless the shared code is position-independent, it must occupy the same virtual page numbers in all processes that invoke it. This property must be preserved even in cases when the shared code spans several pages. The reader may recall that these restrictions are necessary for both consistent mapping of self-references and proper invocation of the shared code from different address spaces.

For comparison with segmentation, we use the same example of the reentrant editor code EMACS. Assuming that the program of such functionality is certain to span several pages, we analyze the conditions under which a single physical copy of that code may serve all users of a time-sharing installation. Since writing of position-independent code (PIC) is machine-specific, and thus often restricted to assembly language, we assume the more general case that the EMACS code is not position-independent. As suggested in Chapter 6, the address space of each individual editor process consists of the shared EMACS code coupled with a private data buffer. In the described setup, sharing of the single physical copy of EMACS code is possible in a paged system, provided that EMACS pages have identical virtual page numbers in all participating processes. For example, the shared code might occupy the low portion of each process's address space, with private data mapped above it. If EMACS is not divisible into an even number of pages, the remainder of the last page must be left unused to allow private user data to begin on a page boundary. Restrictions of this kind must be observed by all systems programs involved in preparation of process images if sharing of code is to conserve memory in a given paged system.

7.1.3 Concluding Remarks

Unlike segmentation, paging is managed in its entirety by the operating system and is thus transparent to programmers. Without having to resort to compaction, paging practically eliminates external fragmentation. Allocation and deallocation of memory in paged systems are quite simple, so that management of these functions incurs comparatively little overhead. Utilization of physical memory may be quite high with paging when page size is small and when scheduling is allowed to optimize the usage of memory. In particular, this means that faced with the situation of not having enough free page frames to satisfy the needs of the next process to be loaded, the scheduler may "skip around" the waiting-for-memory queue in order to find a process with smaller memory requirements.

Paging, of course, is not without disadvantages. Its fixed-chunk memory-allocation strategy may result in a partially unused last page of each process. As a consequence, internal fragmentation of one-half page size, on the average, per resident process is inherent in paging systems. Sharing in paged systems is generally more restrictive in comparison with segmentation, and the finely grained protection within the boundaries of a single address space is difficult to realize. The address-translation required by paging imposes the storage overhead of page-map tables, sometimes called *table fragmentation*, which may be quite large in systems with small pages. Moreover, the mapping process either drastically reduces the effective memory bandwidth or requires rather extensive address-translation hardware. Typically, its most expensive component is the TLAB, which is managed using probabilistic algorithms.

7.2 VIRTUAL MEMORY

Virtual memory is a memory-management scheme where only a portion of the virtual-address space of a "resident" process may actually be loaded into physical memory. In other words, virtual memory allows execution of partially loaded processes. As a consequence, the sum of the virtual-address spaces of active processes in a virtual-memory system can exceed the capacity of the available physical memory provided that the physical memory is large enough to hold a minimum amount of the address space of each active process. Thus, while the real-memory schemes strive to approach 100% utilization of physical memory, virtual-memory systems routinely provide apparent utilization factors in excess of 100%! Moreover, the allowable size of the virtual-address space of a single process can exceed the maximum capacity of the physical memory that may be installed in a given system. For example, the virtual-address space of a process of a VAX computer can be up to 4 GB, while some models of VAX support a maximum of only 8 MB of physical memory.

This feat is accomplished by maintaining an image of the entire virtual-address space of a process on the secondary storage and by bringing its sections into main memory when needed. The choices of which sections to bring in, when to bring them in, and where to place them are made by the operating system. These decisions are influenced by the demands of the active processes and by the overall system resource availability. Thus, virtual-memory systems provide for automatic migration of portions of address spaces between secondary and primary storage.

The details of virtual memory-management are generally transparent to programmers. Being provided with the illusion of a much larger memory than may actually be available, programmers are practically relieved from the burden of trying to fit a program into limited memory. Moreover, the same program may run without reprogramming or recompilation on systems with significantly different capacities of installed memory. For example, while a given compiler may run faster in a system with more real memory, its basic functionality need not be affected by memory considerations.

The ability to execute a partially loaded process is also advantageous from the operating system's point of view. For example, a process may be loaded into a space of arbitrary size. This may be used to reduce external fragmentation without the need to change the scheduled order of process executions. Moreover, the amount of space in use by a given process may be varied during its memory residence. As a result, the operating system may speed up the execution of important processes by allocating them more real memory. Alternatively, by reducing the real-memory holdings of resident processes, the degree of multiprogramming can be increased by using the vacated space to activate more processes.

Amidst all these luring benefits, a bit of cautiousness may be in order. The basic idea of virtual memory is to execute partially loaded programs. But does it really make sense? An instruction can be completed only if all code, data, and stack locations that it references reside in physical memory. Can we guarantee that all the proper ingredients will be in main memory at the right time so that each program is making reasonable progress toward its completion? When it references an out-of-memory item, the running process must be suspended for the relatively long time required for fetching the target item from disk. What is the performance penalty incurred by executing a partially loaded process? Are we really gaining anything, or are we just trading programmer's convenience for loss of control over response times and CPU utilization?

Obviously, these questions are too involved to be answered in one paragraph. To that we devote most of the remainder of this chapter. An informal analysis of the program behavior, however, provides an intuitive answer to the basic dilemma of whether it makes sense to execute a partially loaded program. From experience, we may observe that certain portions of a program may not be referenced at all during a specific run. Most programs consist of alternate execution paths, some of which do not span the entire address space. On any given run, external and internal program conditions cause only one specific execution path to be followed. Dynamic linking and loading, described earlier, exploit this aspect of program behavior by loading into memory only those procedures which are actually referenced on a particular run. A typical example of infrequently executed portions of a program are the exception-condition handlers, such as error routines. Moreover, many programs tend to favor specific portions of their address spaces during execution. A typical example is provided by multiple-pass language translators, such as compilers and assemblers. It is quite reasonable to keep in memory only those routines which comprise the code of the pass currently being executed. When another pass over the source code commences, the memory-manager can bring its constituent routines into the main memory and return those of the previous pass back to disk.

7.2.1 Principles of Operation

Virtual memory can be implemented as an extension of paged or of segmented memory-management. Accordingly, address translation is performed by means of page-map tables or via segment-descriptor tables. The important difference, however, is that in virtual-memory systems some portions of the address space of the running process can be absent from main memory. To emphasize the distinction, the term *real memory* is often used to denote the physical memory.

The process of address mapping in virtual-memory systems is more formally defined as follows: Let virtual-address space be $V = \{0, 1, \ldots, v - 1\}$ and the physical (real) memory space $M = \{0, 1, \ldots, m - 1\}$. In many large systems, virtual-address space is larger than physical memory, $v > m$, but the reverse relationship between the two, that is, $v < m$, can be found in some minicomputer and microcomputer systems.

The operating system dynamically allocates real memory to portions of the virtual-address space. The address-translation mechanism must be able to associate virtual names with physical locations. In other words, at any time the mapping hardware must realize the function $f : V \rightarrow M$ such that

$$f(x) = \begin{cases} r \text{ if item } x \text{ is in real memory at location } r \\ \text{missing-item exception if item } x \text{ is not in real memory} \end{cases}$$

Thus, the additional task of address-translation hardware in virtual systems is to detect whether the target item is in real memory or not. The type of missing item depends on the basic underlying memory-management scheme, and it may be a segment or a page. In either case, if the referenced item is in memory, the process of address translation is completed as usual for the related scheme.

For simplicity, we present the operation of virtual memory assuming that paging is the basic underlying memory-management scheme. Where necessary, we indicate the differences between paging and segmentation. A combined segmentation and paging system is discussed under Segmentation and Paging later in this section.

In terms of mechanics, the detection of missing items is rather straightforward. It is usually handled by adding the *presence* indicator, often just a bit, to each entry of the page-map tables. Let us assume that the presence bit, when set, indicates that the corresponding page is in memory. Conversely, when the presence bit is cleared, the corresponding virtual page is not in real memory. Before loading the process, the operating system clears all presence bits in the related page-map table. As and when specific pages are brought into the main memory, the corresponding presence bits are set. When a page is evicted from main memory, its presence bit is reset.

A possible implementation of presence bits is illustrated in Figure 7.4. To simplify the drawing, the presented process's virtual space is assumed to consist of six pages. As indicated, the complete process image is present in the secondary memory. The page-map table contains an entry for each virtual page of the related process. For each page actually present in real memory, the presence bit is set and the PMT points to the physical frame that contains the corresponding page. Alternatively, the presence bit is reset and the PMT entry is invalid.

The address-translation hardware checks the presence bit during the mapping of each memory reference. If the bit is set, the mapping is completed as usual. However, if the corresponding presence bit in the PMT is reset, mapping cannot be completed. In that case, the hardware generates a missing-item exception to announce the fact to the operating system. In paged systems, this exception is often called a *page fault*. When the running process experiences a page fault, it must be suspended until the missing page is brought into main memory. Given that disk accessing is usually several orders of magnitude longer than main-memory cycle time, the operating system usually schedules another ready process in the interim.

The disk address of the faulted page is usually provided in the *file-map table* (FMT). This table is parallel to the page-map table. Thus, when processing a page fault, the operating system uses the virtual page number provided by the mapping hardware to index the FMT and to obtain the related disk address. A possible format and use of the file-map table are depicted in Figure 7.4. For convenience and processing speed, some systems place the disk address of each out-of-memory page into the corresponding PMT entry. This is possible because such entries are otherwise invalid for main-memory mapping purposes.

7.2.2 Instruction Interruptibility

Despite many similarities, the implementation of virtual memory requires certain hardware provisions above and beyond those usually found in systems designed to support real paging or segmentation. Depending on whether these are present or not, a given architecture may or may not be able to support virtual memory. Consider, for example, memory references made by the following instruction:

DECREMENT REG[1] AND BRANCH TO address Y IF the result is ZERO

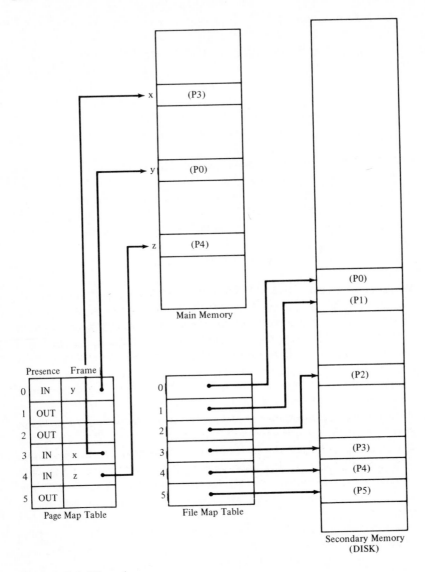

Figure 7.4 Virtual memory.

This instruction is supposed to decrement the contents of the designated register, 1 in our case, and to branch to memory address Y if the register in question equals zero after decrementing. For the purposes of this example, assume that the operation code and address portion of the instruction are encoded in one word each. Since the physical memory is a linear array, we denote the contents of a memory location as $M[I]$, where I is a specific memory address. With the stated assumptions, the instruction under consideration occupies two consecutive words in memory (one contains the operation code and the other the target branch address Y). Assuming that the first word of the instruction is stored at location I in memory, its execution can proceed as indicated below. Memory references made in the process are explicitly indicated for the purposes of further discussion.

1. Fetch the operation code and decode its contents: read $M[I]$
2. Decrement REG[1]
3. Test REG[1], and if ZERO, then set PC = Y: read $M[I+1]$

As outlined, this instruction makes two memory references when the branch is taken. If the first word of the instruction happens to be placed at the last word of a virtual page, the second word will be placed in the adjacent virtual page. In that case, two page faults may occur during its execution. If the first virtual page is not in real memory, a page fault occurs while attempting to fetch the operation-code word. The mapping hardware detects a missing-item exception and traps to the operating system. The page-fault handler then locates the page in question and initiates the process of bringing it into the main memory. An important architectural implication of the described events is that virtual memory may lead to interruption of certain instructions *during* their execution. Most systems not intended to support virtual memory allow recognition of interrupts only between, but not during, execution of instructions. The motivation for this approach is provided both by its simplicity and the significantly smaller amount of state information that must be saved upon acceptance of an interrupt request. Let us briefly discuss the additional hardware provisions necessary to support interrupts during instruction execution, as required by the virtual-memory management.

If the presented instruction experiences a page fault on its first memory reference, it may be simply restarted from the beginning when the related page is eventually brought into the main memory. The address of the interrupted instruction, contained in the program counter, is usually sufficient for restarting. However, when the instruction progresses to the point of deciding to take the branch and faults on fetching the target address Y, subsequent restarting does not work. The problem is that register 1 has already been decremented, and restarting would cause it to be decremented once again when the program is resumed after the page fault is processed. Obviously, the only correct execution of the presented instruction is to decrement the register exactly one time. Consequently, when interrupted after the decrement, the instruction in question must either be resumed from the actual point of interruption or its partial effects must be undone if it is to be restarted. In this particular case, undoing of partial effects implies restoring of the contents of register 1 to its original value prior to the decrement. Having pointed out the problem of instruction interruptibility, let us discuss its common solutions in a more general context.

Depending on the specific instruction set and on the underlying architecture, certain instructions cannot be restarted after experiencing an interrupt in the course of their execution. There are several options in dealing with this problem at the hardware level:

- Partial effects of the interrupted instruction are undone, and the instruction is restarted when the missing-item exception is processed.
- The instruction is resumed from the exact point of interruption when the missing item is brought into memory.
- Memory references are prechecked for page faults before starting execution of the instruction.

All of these approaches have some advantages and disadvantages relative to each other. For example, undoing of partial effects is often instruction-specific and difficult to generalize into a common procedure even for a specific architecture. Moreover, some instructions can make irreversible changes that are extremely difficult or impossible to undo. A typical example is provided by the BLOCK MOVE and TRANSLATE instructions when source and destination strings overlap. However, even when possible, restarting of a string-processing instruction may result in the loss of a significant amount of work. On the other hand, continuation of interrupted instructions from the exact point of interruption requires quite involved storing, and subsequent retrieving, of the internal CPU state, which usually includes considerably more than just the program-accessible registers. Finally, prechecking for page faults may not be possible or justifiable for certain kinds of instructions. In practice, some or all of the presented approaches are often combined for ease of implementation or for improved performance.

The main implication of our discussion is that virtual memory can be implemented only on machines that provide instruction interruptibility for support of virtual memory. An interesting example is provided by Motorola's 68010 CPU, which was essentially a 68000 with the microcode revised to support instruction interruptibility, a feature not provided on the original 68000. Except for some performance differences, the two models are virtually identical in all other respects.

7.2.3 Management of Virtual Memory

Assuming that paging is used as an underlying memory-management scheme, the implementation of virtual memory requires maintenance of one page-map table per active process. Given that the virtual-address space of a process may exceed the capacity of real memory, the size of an individual PMT can be much larger in a virtual than in a real paging system with identical page sizes. The operating system maintains one memory-map table or a free-frame list to keep track of portions of physical memory that are available for allocation. A new component of the memory-manager's data structures is the file-map table (FMT). One such table is maintained for each active process. Its base may be kept in the control-block of the related process. An FMT has a number of entries identical to that of the related PMT. A pair of page-map table base and page-map length registers may be provided in hardware to expedite the address-translation process. As with paging, the existence of a translation-lookaside buffer is highly desirable to reduce the negative effects of mapping on the effective memory bandwidth.

Having described most of these issues in relation to paging, we now concentrate on those aspects which are specific to the management of the virtual memory.

The allocation of only a subset of real page frames to the virtual-address space of a process requires the incorporation of certain policies into the virtual memory-manager. In terms of their relative order of appearance when handling a process, we may classify these policies as follows.

1. Allocation policy—how much real memory to allocate to each active process
2. Fetch policy—which items to bring and when to bring them from secondary storage into the main memory
3. Replacement policy—when a new item is to be brought in and there is no free real memory, which item to evict in order to make room for the new one
4. Placement policy—where to place an incoming item

In most implementations, items are fetched when the running process causes a missing-item exception. In other words, the demands of executing processes dictate the identity and timing of the fetching of items. Accordingly, we speak of *demand paging* or of *demand segmentation.* Although anticipatory or prefetching policies are also conceivable, few implementations of virtual memory rely on these because of the difficulty of making accurate predictions of the future memory requirements of processes.

Depending on the types of items shuttled between the disk and the main memory, the placement policy follows the rules discussed in relation to segmentation and paging. In the case of paging, placement is straightforward, since any free page frame is equally suitable for housing a page.

Replacement and allocation policies are somewhat more involved, and we treat them in separate sections, after a brief overview of program behavior.

7.2.4 Program Behavior

Program behavior, in terms of memory-referencing patterns during program execution, is of extreme importance for the performance of virtual-memory systems. Execution of partially loaded programs generally leads to longer turnaround times due to the processing of missing-item exceptions, which involves relatively long disk-access delays. Both CPU cycles and disk I/O bandwidth are expended for management of virtual memory. Therefore, by minimizing the number of exceptions experienced by a given program, the effective CPU utilization, disk I/O bandwidth, and program turnaround times may be improved. The optimum, of course, is to eliminate the missing-item exceptions altogether by reverting to one of the real memory-management schemes. This, however, eliminates most stated advantages of virtual memory and must be ruled out. We wish to study program behavior and to use our findings to maximize the performance of virtual-memory management under the constraint that the system must be capable of executing programs that are only partially resident in main memory.

In an earlier section, we concluded that some portions of a program may not be referenced and therefore need not be loaded on a particular run. Figure 7.5, which depicts the actual memory-referencing patterns of a program in a paged system, provides a vivid illustration of this point. Unfortunately, in general, we cannot predict the identity of superfluous pages or segments before the program is actually executed. In other words, the fact that some portions of the address space are superfluous on some runs provides mostly the justification for execution of partially loaded programs, but offers little guidance as to which pages to load in order to reduce the number of page faults. Since our interest is in deciding

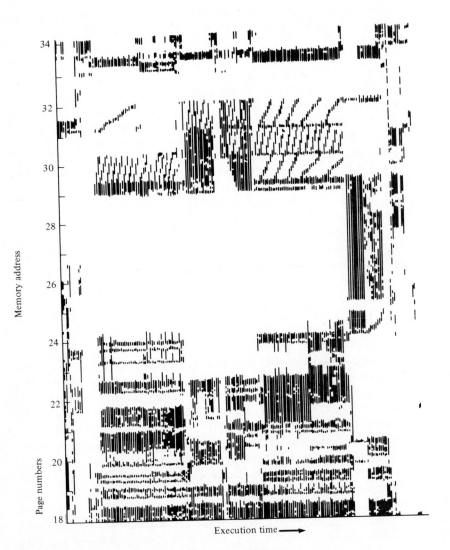

Figure 7.5 Sample memory reference patterns.

how many real page frames to allocate to each process and which pages to load into those frames, we must look for answers elsewhere.

Several studies suggest a strong tendency of programs to favor subsets of their address spaces during execution. This phenomenon is known as the *locality of reference*. Both *temporal* and *spatial* locality of reference have been observed. Intuitively speaking, temporal locality of reference is exhibited by program loops, where a certain set of instructions and data are repetitively referenced for a period of time. Spatial locality suggests that once an item is referenced, there is a high probability that it or its neighboring items are going to be referenced in the near future. This may be illustrated by the straight-line sequences of code, the sequential processing of arrays, and the tendency to reference stack locations in the vicinity of the one pointed to by the stack pointer.

A *locality* is a small cluster of not necessarily adjacent pages to which most memory references are made during a period of time. Both temporal and spatial localities of reference are dynamic properties in the sense that the identity of the particular pages that comprise the actively used set varies with time. As both intuition and research results suggest, the executing program moves from one locality to another in the course of its execution. Statistically speaking, the probability that a particular memory reference is going to be made to the specific page is a time-varying function. It increases when the neighboring pages are being referenced and decreases otherwise. The evidence also suggests that the executing program moves slowly from one locality to another.

From the virtual memory-manager's point of view, locality of reference basically suggests that a significant portion of the memory references of the running process may be made to a subset of its pages. Moreover, there is an increased probability that the recently referenced pages, or their immediate neighbors, are going to be referenced in the near future. These findings may be utilized for implementation of replacement and allocation policies, which are discussed in the sections that follow.

7.2.5 Replacement Policies

A process that experiences a missing-item exception cannot continue to execute until the item is brought into the main memory. Given the tendency of virtual systems to overallocate memory, the memory-manager may have no unused page frames in physical memory for allocation to the incoming item. There are basically two options when handling the described situation: the faulted process may be suspended until some real memory becomes available, or a page may be evicted to make room for the incoming one. The former option is rarely chosen, because missing-item exceptions are really the fault of the virtual memory-manager and not of the process itself. Suspending such processes even further would have adverse effects on their scheduling and turnaround times. Moreover, with all faulted processes holding on to their already allocated real memory, free page frames are not likely to be produced very fast. Thus, eviction is commonly used to free the memory needed to load the missing items.

A replacement policy governs the choice of the victim when eviction is in order. Depending on whether they have been modified or not, items to be removed may have to be written back to disk or simply discarded. We briefly elaborate this possibility on the example of paging.

As indicated, in virtual-memory systems all pages of a process are kept on the secondary storage. As and when needed, some of those pages are copied into the main memory for purposes of process execution. While executing, the running process may modify its data or stack areas, thus making some resident pages different from their disk images. When a page that has not been modified during its residence in memory is to be evicted, it can simply be discarded, since an exact copy of it is available on the disk. However, when a modified page is to be evicted, it must be written back to disk in place of its obsolete copy.

Tracking and recording of page modifications is usually performed in hardware by adding a *written-into* bit to each entry of the page-map table. This "bit" is sometimes also called the *dirty bit*. In any case, it is cleared when the corresponding page is loaded into memory and set by the mapping hardware whenever the page is written into. When a page is selected for eviction, the operating system determines whether or not to write such a page to disk by testing the associated written-into bit. In systems without this hardware provision, performance is adversely affected by having to copy all evicted pages back to disk, irrespective of whether they have actually been modified or not.

When explaining replacement algorithms, which follow, we refer to evicted pages as being removed from memory. Depending on whether the written-into bit is supported by hardware and whether the particular page in question has been modified or not, this may or may not require rewriting of such pages to disk.

Behavior of the various replacement algorithms can be conveniently compared by means of memory-reference strings. Such strings can be synthesized or derived from the actual memory references made by an executing program. We explain the construction of a memory-reference string by means of an example.

A succession of memory references made by an assembler while processing a user program is given below in hexadecimal notation:

$$\ldots, 14489, 1448B, 14494, 14496, A1F8, 14497, 14499, 2638E, 1449A, \ldots$$

When analyzing page-replacement algorithms, we are interested only in the pages being referenced. Assuming a 256-byte page size (100H), the referenced pages are obtained simply by omitting the two least-significant hexadecimal digits (offset within a page), as follows:

$$\ldots, 144, 144, 144, 144, A1, 144, 144, 263, 144, \ldots$$

As far as page replacement is concerned, pages resident in memory may need to be evicted only at times when space in physical memory is needed to accommodate the incoming ones. Once a page is in memory, further references to it cannot possibly result in page faults. This means that when studying page-replacement we should only consider the moments when new pages are being referenced and omit successive references to the same page. Following this logic, the above pattern of page references can be compressed into a reference string for page-replacement analysis as follows:

$$\ldots, 144, \text{A1}, 144, 263, 144, \ldots$$

A reference string obtained in this way is used to illustrate most of the replacement algorithms, whose presentation follows.

First-in, first-out (FIFO). This algorithm replaces the resident page that spent the longest time in memory. Whenever a page is to be evicted, the oldest page is identified and removed from main memory.

In order to implement the FIFO page-replacement algorithm, the memory-manager must keep track of the relative order of the loading of pages into main memory. One way to accomplish this is to maintain an FIFO queue of pages. Both the operation of the FIFO algorithm and its possible implementation by means of a queue of pages are illustrated in Figure 7.6.

Figure 7.6 is constructed by applying the FIFO algorithm to replace pages in a system where the running process is allocated three real page frames. The page-reference string was constructed from a recorded program trace, as explained earlier.

Assuming initially empty memory, the first two page references cause pages 144 and A1 to be brought into the main memory as a result of page faults. The third page reference is made to page 144, which is already in main memory, so

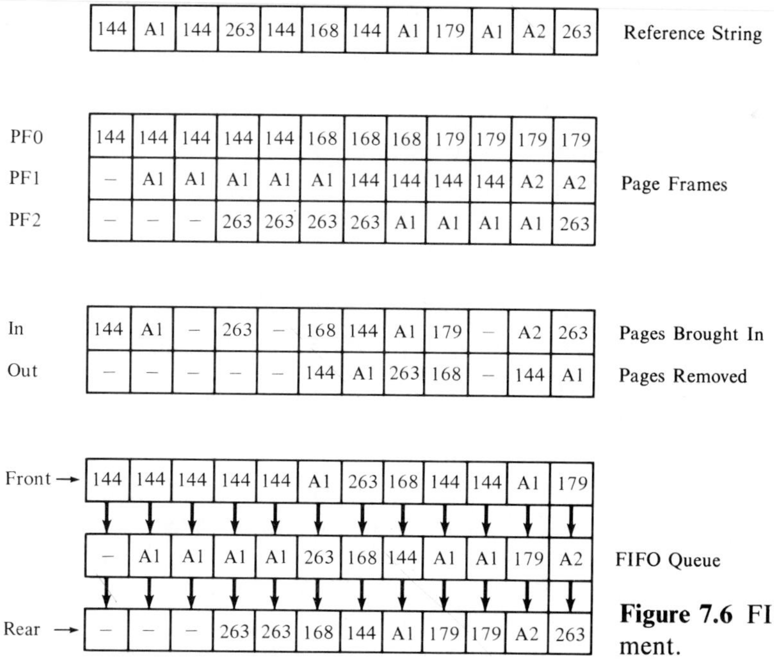

144	A1	144	263	144	168	144	A1	179	A1	A2	263	Reference String

PF0	144	144	144	144	144	168	168	168	179	179	179	179	
PF1	—	A1	A1	A1	A1	A1	144	144	144	144	A2	A2	Page Frames
PF2	—	—	—	263	263	263	263	A1	A1	A1	A1	263	

In	144	A1	—	263	—	168	144	A1	179	—	A2	263	Pages Brought In
Out	—	—	—	—	—	144	A1	263	168	—	144	A1	Pages Removed

Front →	144	144	144	144	144	A1	263	168	144	144	A1	179	
	—	A1	A1	A1	A1	263	168	144	A1	A1	179	A2	FIFO Queue
Rear →	—	—	—	263	263	168	144	A1	179	179	A2	263	

Figure 7.6 FIFO replacement.

that its mapping does not result in a page fault. The fourth memory reference faults again, causing page 263 to be brought in. The first page replacement is made when page 168 is referenced. Using FIFO policy for replacement, the memory-manager consults its FIFO queue in order to choose a victim. As shown in the lower part of Figure 7.6, at that point the oldest page is page 144, which is at the front of the FIFO queue. Thus, page 144 is removed from memory, and page 168 is brought into the vacated page frame. The FIFO queue is updated accordingly. Since the next page reference is made to page 144, it must be brought back in almost immediately after removal. A similar situation is encountered in the next page reference, when page A1—evicted to make room for page 144—must be immediately brought back in.

This kind of behavior contributes to the relatively poor performance of FIFO as a page-replacement policy. By failing to take into account the pattern of usage of a given page, FIFO tends to throw away frequently used pages because they naturally tend to stay longer in memory. Another problem with FIFO is that it may defy intuition by increasing the number of page faults when more real pages are allocated to the program. This behavior is known as *Belady's anomaly*. Although easy to implement, FIFO is not a first choice of operating-system designers for page replacement.

Least-recently-used (LRU). As suggested by its name, this algorithm replaces the least-recently-used resident page. Its operation is shown in Figure 7.7. In general,

	144	A1	144	263	144	168	144	A1	179	A1	A2	263	Reference String

PF0	144	144	144	144	144	144	144	144	144	144	A2	A2	
PF1	—	A1	A1	A1	A1	168	168	168	179	179	179	263	Page Frames
PF2	—	—		263	263	263	263	A1	A1	A1	A1	A1	

In	144	A1	—	263	—	168	—	A1	179	—	A2	263	Pages Brought In
Out	—	—	—	—	—	A1	—	263	168	—	144	179	Pages Removed

	—	—	—	A1	A1	263	263	168	144	144	179	A1
	—	144	A1	144	263	144	168	144	A1	179	A1	A2
TOS →	144	A1	144	263	144	168	144	A1	179	A1	A2	263

Reference Stack

Figure 7.7 LRU replacement.

the LRU algorithm performs better than FIFO. The reason is that LRU takes into account the patterns of program behavior by assuming that the page used in the most distant past is least likely to be referenced in the near future. In the example shown in Figure 7.7, no single page is replaced immediately before being referenced again, which is an improvement over FIFO. Although LRU might behave less ideally in specific instances, on average it does better than FIFO.

The least-recently-used algorithm belongs to a larger class of the so-called *stack* replacement algorithms. A stack algorithm is distinguished by the property of performing better, or at least not worse, when more real memory is made available to the executing program. Stack algorithms, therefore, do not suffer from Belady's anomaly.

Unfortunately, implementation of the LRU algorithm imposes too much overhead to be handled by software alone. One possible implementation is to record the usage of pages by means of a structure similar to the stack. Whenever a resident page is referenced, it is retrieved from the stack and placed at its top. When a page eviction is in order, the page at the bottom of the stack is removed from memory. The appearance of the page-referencing stack is illustrated in the lower portion of Figure 7.7. For example, when a page fault occurs in an attempt to reference page 168, the most-recently-used page before it, 144, is at the top of the stack. The least-recently-used page, A1, is found at the bottom of the stack and is removed from memory.

Maintenance of the page-referencing stack requires its updating for each and every page reference, regardless of whether it results in a page fault or not. In other words, the overhead of searching the stack, moving the referenced page to the top, and updating the rest of the stack accordingly must be added to all memory references. In contrast, the FIFO queue needs to be updated only when page faults occur, an overhead almost negligible in comparison to the time required for processing a page fault. Thus, the implementation of a pure LRU replacement algorithm requires extensive and dedicated hardware support for the described stack operations.

Optimal (OPT). A replacement algorithm due to Belady was proven to be optimal. The algorithm removes the page to be referenced in the most distant future. Since it requires future knowledge, the OPT algorithm is not realizable in practice. Its significance is theoretical, since it can serve as a yardstick for comparison with other algorithms.

Operation of the OPT algorithm is illustrated in Figure 7.8. The number of page faults may be observed from the IN rows, respectively, in Figures 7.6 through 7.8. As indicated, FIFO makes 9, LRU 8, and OPT 7 page faults while processing the sample page-reference string. Given that the presented string was derived from 25 successive memory references, the page-fault frequencies for the three algorithms are .36, .32, and .28, respectively. In practice, page-fault frequencies of typical programs tend to be lower than those suggested by our example.

| 144 | A1 | 144 | 263 | 144 | 168 | 144 | A1 | 179 | A1 | A2 | 263 | Reference String |

PF0	144	144	144	144	144	144	144	144	144	144	144	144	
PF1	–	A1	A1	A1	A1	A1	A1	A1	A1	A1	A1	263	Page Frames
PF2	–	–	–	263	263	168	168	168	179	179	A2	A2	

In	144	A1	–	263	–	168	–	–	179	–	A2	263	Pages Brought In
Out	–	–	–	–	–	263	–	–	168	–	179	A1	Pages Removed

Figure 7.8 OPT replacement.

Approximations. Of the two realizable page-replacement algorithms described above, FIFO has poor performance and potentially anomalous behavior, while LRU is costly to implement. For this reason, several approximations have been developed and used in actual designs. One such popular algorithm combines the relatively low overhead of FIFO with tracking of the resident-page usage which accounts for the better performance of LRU. This algorithm is sometimes called *not-recently-used* (NRU).

The algorithms makes use of the *referenced* bit which is associated with each resident page. The referenced bit is set whenever the related page is referenced (read or written into) and cleared occasionally by software. Its setting indicates whether a given page has been referenced in the recent past. How recent this past is depends on the frequency of the referenced-bit resetting. The page-replacement routine makes use of this information when selecting a victim for removal.

The algorithm is usually implemented by maintaining a circular list of the resident pages and a pointer to the page where it last left off. A sample appearance of such a list just before the replacement routine is invoked to select a page for eviction is illustrated in Figure 7.9a. The assumed referenced-bit settings are shown alongside each page. Starting from the pointer, the algorithm traverses the list until a not-recently-used page, whose referenced bit is cleared, is found. While doing so, the algorithm clears the referenced bit of each examined page. In the example given in Figure 7.9a, the algorithm starts with page A2. Since its referenced bit is set, the page is not selected for removal and its referenced bit is cleared. The next page in line, 144, has not been recently used, and it is removed. The pointer is then advanced to the next item, page A1 in our example, to mark the starting point for the next invocation. This situation is depicted in Figure 7.9b.

Other approximations and variations on this theme are possible. Some of them track page usage more accurately by means of a reference counter or by recording the states of referenced bits by shifting them occasionally into related bit arrays.

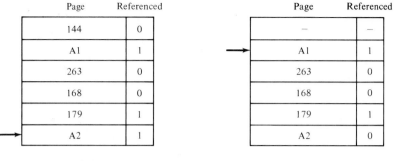

	Page	Referenced
	144	0
→	A1	1
	263	0
	168	0
	179	1
→	A2	1

(*a*) Before

	Page	Referenced
→	—	—
	A1	1
	263	0
	168	0
	179	1
	A2	0

(*b*) After

Figure 7.9 NRU replacement.

When a page is to be evicted, the victim is chosen by comparing counters or bit arrays in order to find the least-frequently-referenced page. In any case, the general idea is to devise an implementable algorithm that bases its decisions on measured page usage and thus takes into account the program-behavior patterns discussed earlier.

As presented here, all replacement policies choose a victim among the resident pages owned by the process that experiences the missing-item exception. This is known as *local* replacement. However, each of the presented algorithms may be made to operate globally. A *global* replacement algorithm processes all resident pages, regardless of the owner's identity, when selecting a victim. In effect, with global replacement, a page fault of one process may be serviced by removing a page held by another. Local replacement tends to localize the effects of the allocation policy to each particular process. Global replacement, on the other hand, increases the degree of coupling between replacement and allocation strategies. In particular, pages allocated to one process by the allocation algorithm may be taken away by a global replacement algorithm. Global replacement is concerned mostly with the overall state of the system and much less with the behavior of each individual process. By varying the number of real pages in use by a given process, global replacement may affect the premises on which the logic and properties of the allocation algorithm in question are based. Not surprisingly, global replacement is known to be suboptimal.

7.2.6 Allocation Policies

The allocation policy in a virtual-memory system governs the operating-system decisions regarding the amount of real memory to be allocated to each active process. In general, the allocation policy must compromise between several conflicting requirements. In terms of paging, giving more real pages to a process should result in reduced page-fault frequency and in improved turnaround time. However, given the limited capacity of physical memory, overly generous allocation of real pages reduces the number of active processes that may coexist in memory at one time. The resulting reduced degree of multiprogramming may lower the CPU utilization factor. On the other hand, if too few pages are allocated to a process, its page-fault frequency and turnaround times may deteriorate to unacceptable levels.

Another problem caused by underallocation of real pages may be encountered in systems that opt for the restarting of faulted instructions. In particular, if fewer pages than necessary for execution of the restartable instruction that causes the largest number of page faults in a given architecture are allocated to a process, it might fault continuously on a single instruction and fail to make any real progress.

For example, consider a two-address instruction, such as ADD @X,@Y, where X and Y are virtual addresses, and @ denotes indirect addressing. Assuming that the operation code and operand addresses are encoded in one word each, this instruction needs three words for storage. With indirect addressing involved, eight memory references are needed to complete execution of this instruction: three to fetch the instruction, two to fetch operand addresses, two to access the operands themselves (indirect addressing), and one to store the result. In the worst case, six different pages may have to coincide in memory in order to complete execution of this instruction: two if the instruction crosses a page boundary, two holding indirect addresses, and two holding the target operands. A likely implementation of this instruction calls for the instruction to be restarted after a page fault. If so, with fewer than six pages allocated to the process that executes it, the instruction may keep faulting forever. In general, the lower limit on the number of pages imposed by the described problem is architecture-dependent. In any particular implementation, the appropriate bound must be evaluated and built into the logic of the allocation routine.

While we seem to have some guidance as to the minimal number of pages, the reasonable maximum number remains elusive. It is also unclear whether a page maximum should be fixed for a given system or determined on an individual basis according to some specific process attributes. Should the maximum be defined statically or dynamically, in response to the system-resource utilization and availability, and perhaps in accordance with the observable behavior of the specific process? Again, we look to program behavior for some answers.

Research results suggest that the relationship between the frequency of page faults and the amount of real memory allocated to a program is nonlinear. While the parameters of this relationship are program-specific, the general shape of the so-called *parachor curve* is similar to the one depicted in Figure 7.10. This specific curve was obtained by measurement of an actual 256-KB program. As indicated, the number of page faults is comparatively very high when the program is constrained to a small amount of real memory. Adding more real memory to a program operating in this area has a significant impact on the page-fault rate. For example, by doubling the amount of allocated real memory from 24 to 48 KB, the number of page faults is reduced by almost four times. However, allocation of the additional 24-KB increment results in a less than three times reduced number of page faults. Still another 24 KB of real memory just about halves the number

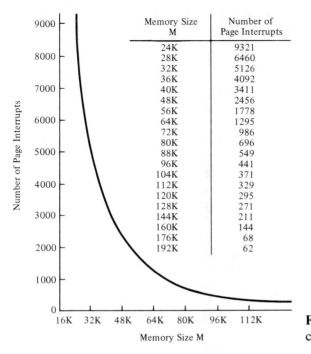

Memory Size M	Number of Page Interrupts
24K	9321
28K	6460
32K	5126
36K	4092
40K	3411
48K	2456
56K	1778
64K	1295
72K	986
80K	696
88K	549
96K	441
104K	371
112K	329
120K	295
128K	271
144K	211
160K	144
176K	68
192K	62

Figure 7.10 Sample parachor curve.

of page faults. The exponential nature of the parachor curve accounts for these observations.

From the allocation module's point of view, the important conclusion is that each program has a certain threshold of the proportion of real to virtual pages below which the number of page faults increases very quickly. At the high end, there seems to be a certain limit on the number of real pages above which an allocation of additional real memory results in little or moderate performance improvement. Thus, we want to allocate memory in such a way that each active program is between these two extremes.

Being program-specific, the upper and lower limits should probably not be fixed, but derived dynamically on the basis of the program-faulting behavior measured during its execution. By defining these guidelines, we are at least qualitatively suggesting how to control the degree of multiprogramming. When resource utilization is low, the degree of multiprogramming may be increased by activating more processes. However, the memory-manager must keep track of the program behavior while doing so. A process that experiences a large number of page faults should be allocated more memory if possible or suspended otherwise. Likewise, a few pages may be taken away without great concern from a process with a low page-fault rate. In addition, the number of pages allocated to a process may be influenced by its priority (higher priority may indicate that a shorter turnaround time is desirable), the amount of free memory, fairness, and the like.

While the complexity and overhead of memory allocation should be within a reasonable bound, the use of oversimplified allocation algorithms is known to have the potential of crippling the system throughput. If real memory is overallocated to the extent that most of the active programs are above their upper page-fault rate thresholds, the system may exhibit a behavior known as *thrashing*. With very frequent page faults, the system spends most of its time shuttling pages between main memory and secondary memory. Although the disk I/O channel may be overloaded by this activity, CPU utilization as low as 1% has been reported for some systems when thrashing.

One way of introducing thrashing behavior is dangerously logical and simple. For example, after observing a low CPU utilization factor, the operating system may attempt to improve it by activating more processes. If no free pages are available, the holdings of the already active processes may be reduced for this purpose. This may drive some of the processes into the high page-fault zone. As a result, CPU utilization may drop while the processes are awaiting their pages to be brought in. In order to improve the still-decreasing CPU utilization, the operating system may decide to increase the degree of multiprogramming even further. Still more pages are taken away from the already depleted holdings of the active processes, and the system is hopelessly on its way to thrashing. From the described scenario, it is obvious that global replacement strategies are susceptible to thrashing.

Thus, a good design must make sure that the allocation algorithm is not inherently unstable and inclined toward thrashing. Knowing the typical patterns of program behavior, we want to ensure that no process is allocated too few pages for its current needs. Too few pages may lead to thrashing, while too many pages may unduly restrict the degree of multiprogramming and CPU utilization. But how can we know how many pages a specific process really needs at a certain point in its execution? This problem is addressed by various allocation policies, two of which are described in subsequent sections.

Page-fault frequency. Keeping a controlled variable within the desired range is a standard problem in control theory. Almost every thermostat in the air conditioner turns the cooler on when the temperature exceeds an upper threshold and turns the cooler off when a lower temperature threshold is reached. This idea may be applied to an allocation module by defining the upper and lower page-fault rates for each process. The actual page-fault rate experienced by a running process may be measured and recorded in the related process control-block. When a process exceeds the upper page-fault threshold, more real pages may be allocated to it. As soon as the process responds by reaching the lower page-fault threshold, allocation of pages to it may be stopped. This relatively simple but effective scheme has been used in actual designs.

Working-set theory. So far, we have discussed page replacement and allocation strategies more or less independently from each other. However, it is obvious that the allocation strategy affects the operating conditions of the replacement strategy by determining the number of pages allocated to each process at a given time. Conversely, the replacement policy may affect the number of pages held by a process and thus indirectly affect the effectiveness of the allocation policy.

The working-set theory takes into consideration the interactive nature of page replacement and allocation by simultaneously addressing how many real page frames to allocate to a given process and which particular pages to keep in those frames.

Much of the program-behavior research described in this chapter either led to or was inspired by the working-set theory. Its three basic premises are

- During any interval of time, a running process favors a subset of its pages.
- The memory-referencing patterns of a process exhibit a high correlation between the immediate past and the immediate future.
- The frequency with which a given page is referenced is a slowly changing function of time.

Ideally, the *working set* of a program is the set of pages that comprises the program's locality at a given time. As the program moves from one locality to another in the course of its execution, the number and identities of the pages in its working set change accordingly. Without knowing the future, the working set of a program is defined to be the set of pages referenced by the program during a recent interval of time. A program's working set at the time of tth memory reference is

$$W(t, \Delta) = \{i \in N | \text{page } i \text{ appears among } r_{t-\Delta+1} \cdots r_t\} \qquad \Delta \geq 1$$

where r_t denotes the memory reference at time t. Thus, $W(t, \Delta)$ is the set of pages referenced during the last Δ memory references. In other words, the working set is the set of pages referenced in a window of size Δ formed by looking backwards in time.

Using this definition, the operating system can determine the working set of each active process in the course of its execution. While unable to predict references to previously unreferenced pages, a realizable form of the working-set replacement and allocation strategy relies on the high correlation of past and future references and on the slowly changing membership of pages in the working set to make a reasonable estimate of the program's current locality.

The *working-set principle* states that a program should be run if and only if its working set is in memory and that a page may not be removed if it is the member of the working set of a running program. Thus, we have guidelines for both the allocation and the replacement of pages. A page should be replaced only if it is not a member of the program's working set. Otherwise, the page-fault rate of the running process is likely to be increased as the pages with a high probability of being referenced in the near future are removed from memory. As for the allocation, the number of real pages allocated to each program should correspond to the size of its working set, that is, to the number of distinct pages contained in the working set. This local replacement and allocation policy helps to prevent thrashing while maintaining a high degree of multiprogramming.

An important parameter for implementation of the working-set principle is the choice of the size of the window Δ. If it is too short, the working set may not encompass the entire current locality. On the other hand, if the window is too long, it may span more than one locality. In practice, accurate tracking of the working set requires the operating system's intervention after each memory reference. For this reason, most implementations are based on some approximation of the realizable definition of the working set. A common practice is to record the page usage at regular intervals during the program's execution by means of the referenced bits. For example, after every few thousand memory references, the referenced bits of the resident pages can be recorded and cleared. The working-set approximations are then constructed by including in them the pages referenced during the few most recent measurements.

7.2.7 Hardware Support and Considerations

In addition to whatever hardware is provided to support the basic underlying memory-management scheme, virtual memory requires some additional provisions. In particular, the presence bit is necessary to aid detection of missing items by the mapping hardware. The written-into bit may help to reduce the overhead incurred by the writing of replaced pages to disk, and the referenced bit is useful for implementation of the replacement policy.

A hardware/software consideration involved in the design of paged systems is choice of page size. Small page size reduces the internal fragmentation and may make better use of memory by containing only a specific locality of reference. For example, research results suggest that procedures in many applications tend to be smaller than 100 words. On the other hand, small pages may result in the excessive size of mapping tables in virtual systems with large virtual addresses. Page-transport efficiency is also adversely affected by small page sizes.

Loading of a page from disk consists of two basic components: the disk-access time necessary to position the heads over the desired track and sector, and the page-transfer time necessary to transfer the page to main memory thereafter. As described in detail in Chapter 8, disk accessing entails rotational latency on the order of milliseconds. A disk seek time of the same order of magnitude must also be added to the average disk-access time. Due to high disk-transfer rates, page-transfer time is practically negligible in comparison to disk-access time. Since page size affects only the transfer time, having larger pages helps to reduce the per-byte overhead of page transportations.

An important consideration in real paging and in virtual-memory systems based on demand paging is the design of a translation-lookaside buffer (TLAB). Although the details of TLAB operation are primarily determined by system architects and hardware designers, management of TLAB is of interest because it deals with problems quite similar to those discussed in relation to virtual memory. In particular, TLAB hardware must incorporate allocation and replacement policies so as to make the best use of the limited number of mapping entries that the TLAB can hold. An issue in TLAB allocation is whether to devote all TLAB entries to the running process or to distribute them somehow among the set of active processes. The TLAB replacement policy governs the choice of an entry to be evicted when a miss occurs and another entry needs to be brought in. These issues are elaborated briefly in the subsequent paragraphs.

Allocation of all TLAB entries to the running process can lead to relatively lengthy initial periods of "loading" the TLAB whenever a process is scheduled. Moreover, this can lead to the undesirable behavior observed in some systems when an interrupt-service routine preempts the running process. Since a typical interrupt routine is only a few hundred instructions long, it may not have enough time to load the TLAB. This can result in slower execution of the ISR due to the need to reference page-map tables in memory while performing address translations. Moreover, when the interrupted process is resumed, its performance also suffers from having to load the TLAB all over again. "Multiprocessing" translation-lookaside buffers combat these problems by containing the PMT entries of several processes. Thus, when a process is scheduled for execution, it may find some of its PMT entries left over in the mapping cache from the preceding period of activity. Management of such TLABs requires the identity of the corresponding process to be associated with each entry in order to make sure that matches are made only with the TLAB entries that belong to the process that produced the addresses to be mapped.

Removal of TLAB entries is usually done after each miss. If the PMT entries of several processes are in the buffer, the victim may be chosen either locally or globally. Understandably, some preferential treatment is usually given to holdings of the running process. In either case, LRU is a popular strategy for the replacement of entries.

The nontrivial problem of maintaining consistency between the PMT entries and their TLAB copies in the presence of frequent page moves must also be tackled by hardware designers. Its solution usually relies on some specialized control instructions for TLAB flushing or for its selective invalidation. While of definite concern to operating-system implementors, these solutions tend to be too machine-specific for a generalized discussion.

Another interesting hardware-related problem is whether I/O devices in virtual-memory systems should use real or virtual addresses. It is addressed by exercises at the end of this chapter.

7.2.8 Protection and Sharing

Protection and sharing in virtual-memory systems essentially retain the characteristics of the basic underlying memory-management scheme, such as paging or segmentation. However, the frequent moves of items between main and secondary memory may actually complicate the management of mapping tables in virtual systems. When an item in real memory is shared by several parties, the mapping tables of all involved processes must point to it. If the shared item, or some portion of it, is selected for removal, all concerned mapping tables must be updated accordingly. All copies of the mapping information must be kept in synchrony and updated to reflect the changes of residence of the shared object. The overhead of known solutions to this problem usually outweighs the potential benefit of removing shared items. Many systems simplify management of mapping tables by fixing the shared objects in memory. A special, privileged OS service is usually provided for that purpose.

An interesting possibility provided by large virtual-address spaces is to treat the operating system itself as a shared object. As such, the operating system is mapped as a part of each user's virtual space. To reduce table fragmentation, dedicated mapping registers are often provided to access a single physical copy of the page-map table reserved for mapping references to the operating system. One or more status bits direct the mapping hardware to use the public or private mapping table, as appropriate for each particular memory reference. In this scheme, different users have different access rights to portions of the operating system. Moreover, the OS calling mechanism may be simplified by avoiding expensive process switches between users and the operating-system code. With the protection mechanism provided by mapping, a much faster CALL instruction, or its variant, may be used to invoke the operating system.

7.2.9 Segmentation and Paging

Although most of our specific examples are based on paging, it is also possible to implement virtual memory in the form of demand segmentation. Such implementations usually inherit the benefits of sharing and protection provided by segmentation. Moreover, their placement policies are aided by explicit awareness of the types of information contained in particular segments. For example, a "working set" of segments should include at least one each of code, data, and stack segments. As with segmentation, intersegment references alert the operating system to changes of locality. However, the variability of segment sizes and the within-segment memory-contiguity requirement complicate the management of both main and secondary memories. Placement strategies, that is, finding of a suitable area of free memory to load an incoming segment, are quite complex in segmented systems. Moreover, as discussed in Chapter 8, the allocation and deallocation of variable-size storage areas to hold individual segments on disk impose considerably more overhead than the handling of pages, that are usually designed to fit in a single disk block.

On the other hand, paging is very convenient for management of main and secondary memory, but is inferior with regard to protection and sharing. The transparency of paging necessitates the use of probabilistic replacement algorithms. Since such algorithms have virtually no guidance from users, they are forced to operate mainly on the basis of their observations of program behavior.

Both segmented and paged implementations of virtual memory have their respective advantages and disadvantages, and neither is superior to the other over all characteristics. Some computer systems combine the two approaches in order to enjoy the benefits of both. One popular approach is to use segmentation from the user's point of view, but to divide each segment into pages of fixed size for purposes of allocation. In this way, the combined system retains most of the advantages of segmentation. At the same time, the problems of complex segment placement and management of secondary memory are eliminated by using paging.

The principle of address translation in combined segmentation and paging systems is illustrated in Figure 7.11. As shown, both segment-descriptor tables and page-map tables are required for mapping. Instead of containing the base and limit of the corresponding segment, each entry of the SDT contains the base address and size of the page-map table to be used for mapping of the related segment's pages. The presence bit in each PMT entry indicates whether the corresponding page is in real memory or not. Access rights are usually recorded as a part of segment descriptors, although they may be placed or refined in the entries of the page-map table. Each virtual address in a combined system basically consists of three fields: the segment number, the page number, and the offset within the page. When a virtual address is presented to the mapping hardware, the segment number is used to locate the corresponding page-map table. Provided that the issuing process is authorized to make the intended type of reference to the target segment, the page number is used to index the PMT as usual. If the

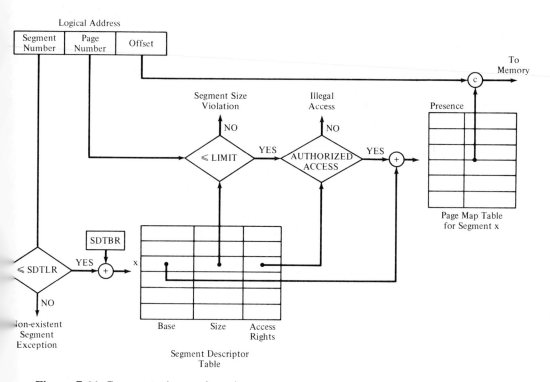

Figure 7.11 Segmentation and paging.

presence bit is set, the mapping is completed by obtaining the real page address from the PMT and combining this with the offset part of the virtual address. If the target page is absent from real memory, the mapping hardware generates a page-fault exception which is processed as usual. At both mapping stages, the length fields are used to verify that the memory references of the running process lie within the confines of its address space.

Naturally, many variations of this powerful scheme are possible. For example, the presence bit may be included with entries of the segment-descriptor table. It may be cleared when no pages of the related segment are in real memory. When such a segment is referenced, the segment fault may be processed by bringing several of its pages into main memory. In general, page prefetching has been more difficult to implement in a way that performs better than demand paging. One of the main reasons for this is the inability to predict the use of previously unreferenced pages. However, referencing of a particular segment increases the probability of its constituent pages being referenced.

While the combination of segmentation and paging is certainly appealing, it requires two memory accesses to complete the mapping of each virtual address. The resulting reduction of the effective memory bandwidth by two-thirds may be too much to bear even in the face of all the added benefits. Obviously, hardware designers of such systems must assist the work of the operating system by providing ample support in terms of mapping registers and lookaside buffers.

7.2.10 Concluding Remarks

From the user's point of view, virtual memory provides the illusion of a large address space that almost eliminates considerations imposed by the limited capacity of physical memory. Thus, both system and user programs can provide the desired functionality without concern for the amount of real memory installed in a particular system. The automatic management of memory sees to it that programs run faster when more real memory is available. These benefits can be made available in both single-user and multiuser virtual systems.

From the operating system's point of view, virtual memory provides the ability to vary the amount of real memory in use by any given program. This enables the operating system to vary the number of active processes in order to increase CPU utilization or to decrease the amount of wasted physical memory. Moreover, effective memory utilization can be higher in virtual-memory systems, because the unused portions of code need not be loaded in main memory. When paging is used, compaction and external fragmentation can be reduced or eliminated.

The main disadvantage of virtual memory is the complex hardware and software needed to support it. Both the space and time complexities of virtual-memory operating systems exceed those of their real-memory counterparts. Large virtual-address space and management of file-map tables contribute to considerably higher table fragmentation. The possibility of thrashing is a serious problem that must be dealt with at the design stage. As a result, more complex replacement and allocation algorithms may have to be devised. Due to processing of the missing-item exceptions, the average turnaround time in the system may increase.

7.3 SUMMARY

The memory-management layer of an operating system allocates and reclaims portions of main memory in response to requests from users and from other operating-system modules and in accordance with the resource-management objectives of a particular system. Processes are created and loaded into memory in response to scheduling decisions that are, among other things, affected by the amount of memory available for allocation at a given instant. Memory is normally freed when resident objects terminate. When it is necessary and cost-effective, the memory-manager may increase the amount of available memory by moving inactive or low-priority objects to lower levels of the memory hierarchy (swapping).

Thus, the memory-manager interacts with the scheduler in selecting the objects to be placed into, or evicted from, the main memory. The mechanics of memory-management consist of allocating and reclaiming of space and of keeping track of the state of memory areas. The objective of memory-management is to provide efficient use of memory by minimizing the amount of wasted memory while imposing little storage, computational, and memory-access overhead. In addition, the memory-manager should provide protection by isolating distinct address spaces and facilitate interprocess cooperation by allowing access to shared data and code.

In the last two chapters we have discussed several schemes for memory-management that satisfy these requirements to various degrees. Partitioned allocation of memory imposes relatively little overhead, but restricts sharing and suffers from internal or external fragmentation. Segmentation reduces the impact of fragmentation and offers superior protection and sharing by dividing each process's address space into logically related entities that may be placed into noncontiguous areas of physical memory. Contiguity of the virtual-address space is maintained by performing address translation at instruction-execution time. Hardware assistance is usually provided for this operation in order to avoid a drastic reduction of the effective memory bandwidth. Paging simplifies allocation and deallocation of memory by dividing address spaces into fixed-sized chunks. Execution-time translation of virtual to physical addresses, usually assisted by hardware, is used to bridge the gap between contiguous virtual addresses and noncontiguous physical addresses where different pages may reside.

Virtual memory removes the restriction on the size of address spaces of individual processes imposed by the capacity of the physical memory installed in a given system. In addition, virtual memory provides for dynamic migration of portions of address spaces between primary and secondary memory in accordance with the relative frequency of usage. As discussed in the next chapter, this feature may be augmented to facilitate uniform addressing of objects regardless of their place of residence in the memory hierarchy.

OTHER READING

Virtual memory, processes, and sharing in Multics are described by Daley and Dennis (1968). Other descriptions of virtual memory in Multics, which was an early and well-described implementation, are provided by Bensoussan and Clingen (1972) and by Organick (1972). Implementations of virtual memory in several commercial and experimental systems are discussed by Doran (1976).

Considerations and issues involved in processor design to support virtual memory in general and instruction interruptibility in particular are discussed by MacGregor and Mothersole (1983). Hardware support for virtual memory in the Maniac II system is described by Morris (1972).

Performance of replacement algorithms in virtual-memory systems was studied by Belady (1966). Results of a study of the performance of page-replacement algorithms as a function of page size are reported by Chu and Opderbeck (1974). Fixed versus dynamic partitioning of real storage in virtual-memory systems is analyzed by Coffman and Ryan (1972). A more recent study by Smith (1980) explores the effects of reduction of the ratio of secondary-storage access time to primary-storage access time that may be expected with faster secondary-storage (paging) devices.

The working-set model and some aspects of program behavior are described by Denning (1968), and by Denning and Schwartz (1972). A more recent paper by Denning (1980) summarizes the issues and research results related to the working-set theory. Smith (1978) describes the techniques and performance of sequential program prefetching in automatically managed memory hierarchies.

A thorough survey of virtual memory and of some aspects of other memory-management schemes is provided by Denning (1970). An indepth treatment of memory-management in general and of virtual memory in particular is provided by Madnick and Donovan (1974). Other textbook presentations of virtual memory are offered by Watson (1970), Shaw (1974), Habermann (1976), and by Peterson and Silberschatz (1983).

EXERCISES

7.1 Describe the function of a translation-lookaside buffer (TLAB) in a paging system, and discuss the issues and operations involved in TLAB management by the operating system. In particular, discuss the options and trade-offs in TLAB entry allocation and replacement policies—such as whether all or some of the TLAB entries should be allocated to the running process, when new entries should be loaded, which entries should be evicted when space is needed, and the like. Indicate which of these operations are time critical and therefore suitable candidates for implementation in hardware.

7.2 Provide a functional specification of operating-system activities involved in management of paged (real) memory in a computer system with no hardware support for paging. Specify major data structures and the format of process control-block (PCB) entries related to management of memory. Discuss the memory-access overhead incurred by your solution, and indicate the operations for which hardware support would be most cost-effective.

7.3 Derive the expression for the effective memory access time in systems with paged memory where virtual to real address translation is assisted by a TLAB. Express the effective memory-access time as a function of the TLAB cycle time, TLAB hit ratio (ratio of address translations satisfied from TLAB versus address translations completed by consulting PMT in memory), and memory-access time in the same system with memory-management turned off. Discuss the range of values of the various parameters for which TLAB is and is not cost-effective.

7.4 Explain why instruction interruptibility is needed in virtual-memory systems. Discuss the issues involved in implementing instruction interruptibility by means of each of the three methods described in the text. Provide examples of actual instructions that are easy to handle and difficult to handle by means of the each individual instruction-interrupt/resume method.

7.5 Discuss whether each of the programming techniques and program actions described below is good or bad with regard to the degree of locality of reference that it is likely to exhibit. Explain your reasoning, and where applicable, state roughly the number of distinct loci of activity (hot spots) that you expect the execution of each of the following to generate:

- Sequential processing of a one-dimensional array
- Sequential processing of a two-dimensional array (state your assumptions)
- Sequential exhaustive search
- Hashing
- Interrupt servicing
- Indirect addressing
- Procedure invocation
- Operating-system invocation

7.6 Explain the role of the written-into (dirty) bit in the management of virtual memory. Provide a functional specification for implementation of this feature in a system without hardware support for the dirty bit, but with hardware support for page-level mode of access control, such as read-only and read-write.

7.7 Describe Belady's anomaly and provide an example that illustrates the anomalous behavior of FIFO.

7.8 Identify and discuss all operations and parameters that influence the effective memory-access time in a virtual-memory system. Indicate the most significant changes that may be expected with future technological improvements, such as introduction of secondary storage devices with access times one or more orders of magnitude faster than those of contemporary devices.

7.9 Indicate the order and relative complexities of operations involved in virtual to real address translation in a virtual-memory system with no hardware support for memory-management. Assess the effective memory-access time of such a system versus the effective memory-access time attainable in the system with complete hardware support for virtual memory described in Chapter 7.

7.10 Provide a rough functional specification of a virtual-memory system based on demand paging. Discuss the tradeoffs involved and the major decisions, including data structures, that must be made when designing such a system. Indicate which information should be kept in PCBs in order to facilitate management of virtual memory in a multiprogrammed system.

7.11 Describe the operation of and provide a functional specification for the memory-management software in a virtual-memory system based on demand segmentation. Contrast demand segmentation with demand paging.

7.12 Provide a functional specification of a virtual memory-manager based on segmentation with paging. Discuss which problems are solved (and created) by this form of memory-management relative to pure demand segmentation and pure demand paging.

7.13 Suppose that three processes concurrently perform compilation of (three different) Pascal programs. Describe the provisions and restrictions necessary to allow the three processes to share a single copy of the code of the Pascal compiler assuming that the underlying memory-management scheme is
(*a*) Real segmentation
(*b*) Real paging
(*c*) Demand paging

7.14 Input/output channels used in high-performance and large computer systems are usually restricted to using physical addresses when accessing their work areas in main memory. Why not virtual addresses? In virtual-memory systems this presents a problem when a page designated by a user process as a source or target of an I/O operation is not in memory at the time when the I/O process effects the transfer in question. For example, this can happen when a user process issues a disk read request by passing the physical address of the page where the data block from the disk is to be placed. In the case of a synchronous I/O request, the issuing process is likely to be suspended until the requested I/O operation is completed. It is conceivable that the physical page designated for the I/O transfer is allocated to another process by the time the disk I/O read is eventually completed. If the I/O channel uses physical addressing, it may not be aware of the change and transfer the data as told, thus causing problems such as destroying the address space of the new owner of the page and not delivering the data to the expecting process. Two common solutions to this problem are

(1) not to do I/O directly to the user space, and (2) to provide the ability to lock certain pages in memory. Discuss the tradeoffs involved in these two approaches, and indicate the changes to routines and data structures of virtual memory-management routines necessary to accommodate these changes.

7.15 Summarize the characteristics of all the forms of memory-management discussed in the last two chapters along the following lines: problem solved, new hardware needed, new software needed, wasted memory, and effective memory-access time.

EIGHT

FILE MANAGEMENT

The file-management portion of the operating system is charged with managing the data that reside on secondary storage. Logically related data items on the secondary storage are usually organized into named collections called *files*. A file, for example, may contain a report, an executable program, or a set of commands to the operating system. In previous chapters we have already encountered some uses of files and secondary storage, such as files containing process images and storage of pages in virtual-memory systems.

The file-management system is supposed to hide all device-specific aspects of file manipulation from users and provide them with an abstraction of a simple, uniform space of named files. A file often appears to users as a linear array of characters or record structures. Some systems augment this view with an abstraction of the input/output system where all I/O devices appear to users as a set of files. Thus, users can rely on a single uniform set of file-manipulation system services for both file-management and I/O device-management. This is sometimes referred to as *device-independent I/O*. For example, a text file may be printed by means of a COPY operation where the destination "file" is the printer device. Another logical but less frequently implemented abstraction is to regard files as an extension of the virtual-address space. The idea is to relieve the users of the burden of explicitly moving data between main memory and secondary storage and of having to handle data differently depending on where it is physically stored. In any case, the common responsibilities of the file-management system include the following:

- Mapping of access requests from logical to physical file-address space
- Transmission of file elements between the main and secondary storage

- Management of the secondary storage, such as keeping track of status and allocation and deallocation of space
- Support for protection and sharing of files, recovery, and possible restoration of files after system crashes

The file-management subsystem can be implemented as one or more layers of the operating system. Its basic services, such as transmission of blocks of data, are necessary to support management of virtual memory and swapping. In the layered implementation of an operating system introduced in Chapter 1, these functions are placed in Layer 2, that is, between the kernel and the memory-manager. Other file-related services, such as directory management and logical to physical mapping of access requests, are provided by Layer 4.

Files of a computer installation can be stored on a number of physical devices, such as disk drives, magnetic tapes, or bubble memory. Depending on whether the specific storage volume that contains a given file is directly accessible by the system or not, the file is said to be online or offline. Volumes may be dismounted for archival purposes or when the combined size of all files in the system exceeds the online capacity of the available storage devices. Our primary emphasis in this chapter is on the management of online files. In order to avoid excessive detail, disks are used exclusively to describe device-related concepts when necessary.

In this chapter we first present the services of the file-management system as perceived by its users. We then discuss the organization and implementation of the file-management functions that provide those services.

8.1 COMMAND-LANGUAGE USER'S VIEW OF THE FILE SYSTEM

According to the type and the method of invocation of file services, users of files may be broadly divided into two categories: *command-language users* and *systems programmers*. The former category includes users who invoke file-management services by means of the operating-system command language. The typical example is provided by interactive users typing commands at their terminals, although similar services may also be invoked in the batch mode, say, by means of command files or job-control cards. In most systems, such users can LIST contents of a file directory (a catalog of file names), COPY files between volumes or devices, CREATE, DELETE, RENAME files, and the like. These services may be invoked directly by means of typing the related command or indirectly by means of an intermediate system program. For example, file creation may be done by invoking the text editor, which, in turn, uses the run-time CREATE_FILE service to pass on the user's request to the file-management system.

Available user and system files are cataloged in *file directories*, which are essentially symbol tables of files. Contents of a directory can be viewed on a terminal or printed by means of a LIST, DIR, CATLIST, LS, or whatever the name of that command is on a given system. File directories in computer systems usually belong to one of two categories: single level or hierarchical.

A *single-level directory*, often called a *flat directory*, contains all files in the system or on a given volume. Their comparative simplicity and ease of implementation make flat directories common in small, single-user systems. However, flat directories are inconvenient and often inadequate for large systems with many files and possibly multiple users. Reviewing of a flat directory can be inconvenient even in a single-user system with a hard disk, because the list of all files may be much too big to display in one screenful of text. More pressing problems with flat directories in larger systems include difficulties in unique naming of files and inadequate support for selective sharing and protection of files in multiuser systems.

These problems can be alleviated by using *hierarchical directories*. In a hierarchical directory system, users can group the related files into subdirectories. All system files are then cataloged in a hierarchy of directories whose structure is similar to that of a rooted tree. By associating different access rights with different subdirectories that need to be referenced when accessing a given file, selective sharing and protection can be easily supported in systems with hierarchical directories. As a side effect, reviewing and displaying of directory contents are much more convenient, as each particular subdirectory usually contains only a small, logically related subset of system files.

Figure 8.1 illustrates a collection of files and directories in a hierarchical system. Directories and subdirectories are denoted by rectangles. Files in Figure 8.1 are denoted by circles. At the top of the hierarchy is the root or the master directory of the system. As indicated, it contains one file, PASLIB, and two subdirectories, named JONES and SMITH. Assuming that these two subdirectories

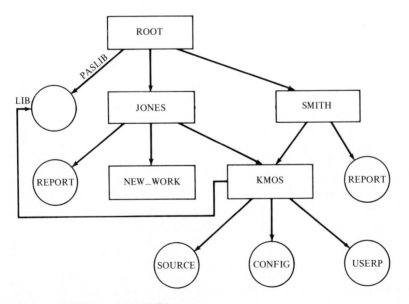

Figure 8.1 Hierarchical file system.

belong to two different users, user Jones has ownership and direct access to the REPORT file and to the subdirectory named NEW_WORK. The subdirectory KMOS is shared by users Jones and Smith, who presumably work together on the project KMOS. By sharing all the KMOS files, the two programmers can have instant access to the up-to-date versions of each other's programs. However, access to private files, such as REPORT, can be easily restricted or denied altogether by means of the access rights associated with the different subdirectories on the path from the root toward the target file.

Access to files in a hierarchical system in principle requires users to indicate all directories that must be searched in order to locate a given entry. Such a specification is often called an *access path* or a *path name*. For example, in order to edit his REPORT file, user Jones can invoke the editor as follows:

EDIT /JONES/REPORT

where the slash (/) indicates a directory, and the first slash refers to the root directory. This form of reference is often called the *complete path specification* or *path name*, because it begins with the root. In systems with complex hierarchies of directories, complete path specifications can be rather lengthy and cumbersome to use. To circumvent this problem, many systems allow users to give only partial path specification beginning with some implicit point of reference, such as the current working directory. For example, assuming that Jones's current working directory is JONES, the command

EDIT REPORT

should have the same effect as the full path specification given earlier. The absence of a slash indicates to the operating system that the name of the target file should be sought in the current working directory. The definition of a user's working directory is usually performed by the system at log-in time, and it may be changed subsequently by means of related system commands.

As perceived by users, the advantages of hierarchical directories include

- facilitated unique naming of files
- support for selective sharing and protection
- convenient directory manipulation

Regardless of the type of directory organization, unique identification of files requires that all file names in a given directory be unique. Enforcing of this requirement may be difficult in large multiuser and network systems with flat file directories. Given that all file names are cataloged in a single directory, the user wishing to name a new file may have to come up with a tentative file name and query the system to make sure that the same name is not used by somebody else. Even so, problems can arise when two or more users are attempting to create different files under the same name at about the same time. This situation might require complex synchronization protocols in network systems when those users reside at different nodes.

Hierarchical directories, on the other hand, alleviate this problem by requiring that only names within a given subdirectory be unique. For example, in Figure 8.1 two different files have the same user-assigned name, REPORT. However, their full access paths are distinct, thus allowing each file to be uniquely specified. By keeping track of each user's working directory, the system can determine exactly which physical file to make available to users Jones and Smith when either of them wishes to edit his REPORT file.

Hierarchical directories also facilitate protection and selective sharing of files. As indicated earlier, protection and sharing are provided by allowing users to access only those files on the path to the root and in the subtree below their own subdirectory. Moreover, hierarchical directories facilitate sharing of files without the need to maintain multiple copies of them. For example, while both users Jones and Smith maintain the KMOS subdirectory in their respective directories, only a single physical copy of KMOS and its member files is actually maintained in the system. This form of file-management also facilitates the use of aliases, that is, referencing of the same file under different names. For example, the same physical file depicted in Figure 8.1 can be accessed under the name PASLIB from the root directory and LIB from the KMOS subdirectory. That is, access paths /PASLIB and /JONES/KMOS/LIB designate the same physical file.

Sharing of files can conserve space on secondary storage in the same way that sharing of common code conserves memory. The creation of a new alias is often called *linking* of the file, because it simply lists in another directory the physical file that already exists. Consequently, an alias is usually handled by means of a system command different from CREATE. In the presented example, the alias LIB can be formed and entered into the subdirectory KMOS by specifying it as a new link to the file /PASLIB. This can be done in order to simplify the specification of the library as the "local" file when preparing for execution of Pascal programs contained in the subdirectory KMOS.

The third user-perceived advantage of hierarchical directories is that reviewing, listing, and general manipulation of shorter topical subdirectories are much more convenient than dealing with a single, large flat directory.

Before discussing details of the specific file-related services, let us point out that specification of file and volume names is markedly system-specific. Some simpler and special-purpose systems require users to specify explicitly the volume where a target file resides. In such systems, volume names become an integral part of each file specification. Default volumes are usually defined in order to omit the volume specification in frequently used commands. For example, the CP/M operating system and its derivatives define a default drive whose identity is indicated as a part of the system prompt. Thus, assuming that Drive A is the current default, command DIR can be used to list the directory of the volume mounted in Drive A. However, to obtain the directory of what is in Drive B, a command of the format DIR B: must be used instead.

More sophisticated forms of binding users to default drives or to volumes are used in more advanced systems. The most advanced form is the automatic binding performed entirely by the operating system. In most large time-sharing installations, users specify directories and file names only without the need to know, or even to be aware of, the actual drive and volume where their files are stored. As with most automated systems, probably the best combination is automatic specification with the possibility of a manual override. For example, when making backup copies of a file, it is rather comforting to be able to force the system to keep them on a different volume.

Other than drive and volume specification, operating systems differ in their approach toward file naming. In some systems a file name may be coupled with the file type and possibly with a version number. Thus a complete file specification may look as follows:

$$\text{drive: /access\_path/filename.type; version\_number}$$

Except for the FILENAME, most of the other fields may be implied, either by means of automatic binding or by the applicable default.

Some systems accept only partial file-name specification, with undefined characters substituted for by the "wild card" character, which is usually denoted by the asterisk (*). For example, the command

$$\text{COPY Z} * \text{LP}$$

may print all files from the current working directory whose names begin with the letter Z. In some systems, the wild card may be used only to substitute for a single character in the designated position, whereas in others it can substitute for a string of characters of arbitrary contents and length. Some systems allow both these interpretations by means of different wild-card characters. In any case, the significance of wild cards is that they may be used to perform a desired operation on several files with a single command.

Some examples of the typical file-related services that users may invoke by means of the command language are given in Table 8.1. A representative list of arguments is also given for each sample command. Although the range of the basic file services is comparative in different operating systems, the variation of command names and specific operational details is quite notable. In the presentation that follows, we summarize the general characteristics of the file-related services in a manner that should enable readers to recognize the equivalent commands in systems familiar to them. In our discussion, we follow the basic order of commands given in Table 8.1.

The general file-manipulation commands usually contain facilities for the creation and deletion of files, such as the CREATE and DELETE commands listed in Table 8.1a. In many systems, creation of a file may be performed indirectly by invoking system programs that subsequently manipulate the newly created file, with the editor probably being the most common example. Deletion of files can be done one-at-a-time or in bulk. In the former approach, full specification of the target file, including the explicit type and version number, may be required for deletion. While perhaps more secure in the sense of being less prone to unintended losses of a collection of files, this approach tends to be tedious when an entire directory or a volume needs to be cleaned up. Another

CREATE	filename
DELETE	filename(s)
RENAME	oldfilename, newfilename
ATTRIBUTES	filename(s), attributes
COPY	source_filename(s), destination_filename(s)

a. General file manipulation

DIR	dirname
MAKE_DIR	dirname
REMOVE_DIR	dirname
CHANGE_DIR	dirname

b. Directory manipulation

INITDISK	drivename
MOUNT	drivename/volumename
DISMOUNT	volumename
VERIFY	volumename
BACKUP	source_file(s)/volume, destination_file(s)/volume
SQUEEZE	volumename

c. Volume/media manipulation

Table 8.1 Command-language file services

extreme is to allow uncontrolled use of wild cards and thus permit the entire file system to be erased with a single command. In order to provide both security and convenience, many systems allow for selective deletion of multiple files in the query mode. In this approach, the user is prompted and expected to give some indication, such as yes/no, for each specific file before it is actually deleted. This form of file deletion may be handled by means of a specialized version of the delete command, such as DELQ—for delete and query—for example.

Renaming and attribute modifications are essentially directory operations. The RENAME command, or its equivalent, allows users to change any or all components of the file name, including the type (sometimes called the file *extension*) and possibly the version number. Although conceivable, it is not common to enable users to transfer files between directories or to establish aliases by means of the RENAME command. The ATTRIBUTE command is available in some systems to change the attributes, such as the allowed type of access, of an already existing file or files.

The COPY command is quite versatile. It is generally used to copy one or more target files to a specified destination. In addition to creating multiple copies of a file, the COPY operation can be used to transfer files between different I/O devices in systems where the device-independent form of I/O is supported. For example, the COPY operation can be used to print files on the laser disk or transfer a file to a remote site. In some systems a single COPY command can be used to back up entire volumes. Another common application of the COPY command is to concatenate several source files into a single destination file. Some systems provide a specialized APPEND command (not shown in Table 8.1) for this purpose. In any case, the COPY command in most systems creates a separate physical copy of the source file, possibly in a different directory or under a new name. Thus, a command

COPY /PASLIB   /JONES/KMOS/LIB

has the effect of creating a copy of the PASLIB file in the directory KMOS under the new name LIB. This is different from creating an alias, the situation depicted in Figure 8.1, in that COPY creates a physical duplicate of the file in question. As a consequence, any subsequent modifications of the file /JONES/KMOS/LIB will generally not be automatically reflected in the file /PASLIB.

The range and effects of the directory-manipulation commands, a representative set of which is listed in Table 8.1b, is usually quite dependent on the type of directories available in a given system. In addition to the DIR command, or its equivalent, used to display the contents of a given directory, typical commands for manipulation of hierarchical directories are given in the remainder of Table 8.1b. The MAKE_DIR command is used to create a new (empty) directory. One of its arguments is usually the name of the new directory, specified in the form of an access path. After creation, the new directory can be populated with files by means of CREATE, COPY, and LINK commands, for example.

The REMOVE_DIR command can be used by authorized users to delete the specified directory. Most systems allow only empty directories to be removed. In other words, all of its constituent files must be deleted or moved to other directories prior to removal of the related subdirectory by means of the REMOVE_DIR command. Finally, the CHANGE_DIR command, or its equivalent, is used to change the current working directory. This command is useful for changing the current default access path when a user intends to work intensively on a set of files in a different directory. Many systems also provide some sort of a query command, such as PWD—for print the (current) working directory—to assist users in navigating through the directory hierarchy.

The last set of commands, listed in Table 8.1c, is used for volume and media manipulation and maintenance. While such commands are usually available in all systems, their use is restricted to system managers and privileged users on larger installations. The INITDISK command is primarily used to initialize new, previously unused volumes before they can be made available to the file system. Like most commands in this group, the functions of INITDISK are highly system- and device-dependent. In general, INITDISK prepares a disk by physically formatting it to conform to the standards of the operating system. This operation usually verifies the physical integrity of the volume, creates a master volume directory, and specifies the volume attributes, such as access authority and the maximum numbers of file and directory entries that may be formed on it. In the case of software-selectable volume sectoring, the INITDISK command writes the address marks and track/sector gaps necessary for subsequent reading and writing of the volume. Some of these device-specific operations are explained in later sections of this chapter.

The MOUNT command is used in conjunction with removable volumes to alert the file system that a new volume is mounted in the designated drive. This information may be used to read and to include the volume directories into the user-visible hierarchy of directories. In a treelike implementation of directories, directories on the mounted volume become a subtree of the designated node of the system directory tree. The DISMOUNT command has exactly the opposite effect. It is required in some systems to break all logical bonds established between the users and the volume about to be removed. The VERIFY command can be used to verify the physical integrity of a suspect volume or for some maintenance purposes. The VERIFY command usually checks the readability of the physical blocks and the consistency of the links used to access files.

The BACKUP command is often used to back up entire volumes for security or archival purposes. While many variations exist, BACKUP is commonly used to make copies of the online volumes onto tape or some other removable, long-term storage medium. A companion command, such as RESTORE, usually exists to restore previously backed up files. Finally, the SQUEEZE command, or its equivalent, is used to restructure the physical layout of files on a volume in such a way that their subsequent accessing is optimized or the available space on a volume is compacted for efficient allocation. The details of its operation are based on the issues discussed in subsequent sections of this chapter.

8.2 SYSTEMS PROGRAMMER'S VIEW OF THE FILE SYSTEM

The second class of users, referred to as *applications* and *systems programmers*, are characterized by invoking services of the file system from their programs by means of run-time calls to the operating system. This division of users is context-dependent in the sense that programmers, in the course of program preparation, can use the full range of services provided by the command language described in the previous section. However, when application and system programs are being executed, they normally use run-time calls to obtain the required file-related services. The run-time calls usually provide most of the file and directory manipulations described earlier. In this section we focus only on those run-time calls which provide additional facilities for file handling. In particular, these include reading and writing of portions of files.

In principle, the file-management subsystem of an operating system provides the means for the creation, manipulation, and accessing of files, with little or no interpretation of information stored within them. The operating system simply views files as arrays of bytes that can be read and modified as required by the programs that manipulate them. It is the responsibility of the manipulating programs to do whatever interpretation of the file contents may be necessary. File-control systems usually allow the file elements to be accessed in sequence or randomly. These two methods of access are often called *sequential* and *random* (direct) file access, respectively. Thus, the operating system can provide services such as READ a byte or a block of bytes from the designated logical position within the file into the designated area of the user virtual-address space. File updating and extensions can be accomplished by means of the WRITE operation, which takes similar arguments but transmits strings of bytes from the user's space into the file.

A possible format of the READ and WRITE run-time commands and their arguments are given in Table 8.2. As specified, only the area in the user's address space, IN_BUFFER and OUT_BUFFER for reading and writing, respectively, are shown. The logical offset within the file where a READ or a WRITE is supposed to take place is not specified. This is assumed to be taken care of by the operating system in the following manner. For sequential access, the operating system directs the first READ or WRITE to the beginning of the file. After transmitting a byte or a block of them, the operating system advances the file pointer, or *marker* as it is often called, to mark the next byte to be processed. Each subsequent READ or WRITE operation begins with the current marker position. Upon completion of the operation, the marker is updated accordingly. For random access, the marker is positioned to the desired logical offset within the file by means of the SEEK command. As described in the table, SEEK is a logical operation that does not result in any data transfer.

In more advanced systems, the binding of programs to files is performed at run-time. This facilitates device independence, which in turns provides for program portability and the added flexibility of changing device and file specifications at run-time. Device independence is discussed in some detail in Section 8.6. Binding of the executing process to a given file at run-time is usually performed by means of an OPEN call. In systems that provide an explicit form of the OPEN service, a program must OPEN each file that it intends to access. The file system responds by establishing a dynamic connection between the calling program and the designated file. In general, the OPEN service allocates buffers, locates the address of the target file by navigating through the hierarchy of file directories, and enforces protection by verifying access rights.

When invoking the OPEN call, the user specifies the name of the file and the intended mode of accessing it, such as read-only (RO) or read-write (RW). On the basis of this information, the operating system can verify the user's authority to access the file in the declared mode. Opening of files can also be used for the purpose of concurrency control. The OPEN command classifies each active user of the related file as a reader or a writer. The operating system can then employ some concurrency-control algorithm, such as the concurrent readers and writers algorithm described in Chapter 5, to allow multiple users to access the same file without compromising its integrity. Each of the concurrent users is supposed to

READ	filename, number_bytes, in_buffer
WRITE	filename, number_bytes, out_buffer
SEEK	filename, logical_position
OPEN	filename, access_mode
CLOSE	filename

Table 8.2 Run-time file services

OPEN the shared file. Thus, a file may be opened by several users, and each user can have several simultaneously opened files.

In addition to file sharing, the OPEN system service allows the operating system to optimize access to actively used files. As we shall see in subsequent sections, faster processing is made possible by keeping some or all access links to the file in main memory. The entire file-accessing information is usually too voluminous to be kept in main memory at all times. One of the useful functions of the OPEN system service is to inform the operating system about the identity of the files in active use. In this way, the file-management subsystem can keep in main memory only those file links which are actually going to be used in the near future. Given that the binding of programs and files performed by means of OPEN commands is of a dynamic nature, it is customary for the operating system to return a unique connection or open ID as a result of each call to OPEN a file. In subsequent operations to such a file, the application program can use the system-supplied ID instead of the name of the file.

The typical order of run-time calls to the file-manager issued by a process when handling a file is depicted in Figure 8.2. As indicated, the new file is first created, or an existing file is opened for access. The desired number of READs and WRITEs can then be performed by the application program. If random access to the file is used, calls to READ and WRITE may be interspersed by calls to SEEK when necessary to reposition the marker. When file processing is completed, the CLOSE service is invoked to break the binding established by the OPEN call. By closing the file, the application program indicates to the operating system that it does not intend to use the related file in the near future. The operating system can respond by releasing the buffers and temporary bonding data structures, such as the connection ID and the file marker, and by allowing other waiting users, if any, to access the file. When the last active bond to a file is detected in the process of closing the file, the operating system can also

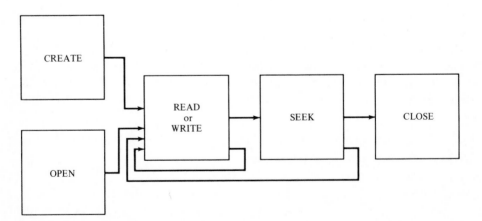

Figure 8.2 Typical file operations.

reclaim the portion of the main memory used to store the accessing links to the file in question.

In addition to our simple model of a file as an array of bytes, some commercial operating systems allow file typing and file structuring to be superimposed upon this basic view. *File typing* refers to the ability of the operating system to distinguish between the different types of files, such as text files and binary files. Different methods can be employed for recognition of the type of each individual file. A simple extreme is to simply encode the file type as a part of its name; the extension field is commonly used for this purpose. Examples of file types encoded as an extension may take on the form of .PAS, .OBJ, .TXT, and .EXE for a Pascal source, object (compiled but not linked), text file, and an executable process image, respectively. Another approach is to encode the file type within the body of the file itself. In any case, the purpose of file typing is to prevent meaningless operation on files, such as execution of a text file or editing of a process image. A disadvantage of typing is that it may restrict the freedom of users to interpret their files in arbitrary ways. For example, with typed files there may be no way to attempt to read volumes created by incompatible operating systems. Another disadvantage may be the additional overhead that typing imposes upon the operating system.

Superimposed forms of file structuring usually include facilities for the definition of fixed- or variable-length records, with user-definable fields, on a file-level basis. For example, a file can be structured as a collection of employee records, and the READ and WRITE services may be able to manipulate individual records and their fields. Thus, a READ may be able to process record *xx*, or a SEEK may be directed to a given employee record defined by some attribute. These services are normally aimed at business data-processing applications as a low-level substitute or a foundation for the database-management system (DBMS). Since there is little uniformity and consensus among operating-system designers as to the form and extent of these services, we will not treat them beyond the level of an occasional reference.

The file-management layers of the operating system are supposed to provide the described user abstraction at the outermost layer and to translate users' requests into device-specific commands at the innermost layer. Before discussing the data structures and the various stages of the mapping process necessary to accomplish this objective, let us briefly explore the physical organization of a typical disk.

8.3 DISK ORGANIZATION

A variety of input/output devices can be used for file storage in a computer system. Their general characteristic is the addressability and transmission of data in blocks, as opposed to the processor main-memory connection, where the unit of data transfer is typically one word. Unlike main memory, file-storage devices usually have a pronounced variance in the average time necessary to access a given block of data. The order of magnitude of this variance depends on the physical implementation of a particular device, and it is quite different for disks, tapes, and bubble memories, to name a few. In this section we discuss magnetic disks as a typical and most pervasive device for online file storage.

A simplified physical organization of a magnetic disk is presented in Figure 8.3. The medium for data storage is the magnetic oxide coated over a disk platter whose appearance is similar to that of a phonographic record. One or more such platters may be available for data storage and retrieval in a single disk drive. Depending of whether the recording platters can be removed from the drive or not, the disks are said to be *removable* or *fixed*. The media for removable disks are often housed in some form of a package, such as a disk cartridge or a floppy disk.

Once a cartridge is in the drive, fixed and removable disks operate in a similar manner. Unlike magnetic tapes, disks platters are constantly rotated by the drive mechanism at a speed of about 3000 rpm; floppy disks rotate at about 300 rpm, and they can be stopped completely between accesses. Data are read and written by means of the read/write heads mounted on a head assembly in such a way that they can be brought in close contact with the portion of disk where the target data reside. Data are stored on the magnetic disk surface in the form of concentric circles called *tracks*. The collection of tracks on all surfaces that are at the same distance from the disk spindle is called a *cylinder*. For example, the disk depicted in Figure 8.3 has two platters and four recording surfaces (two on each platter). Thus, each of its cylinders consists of four tracks. The number of distinct tracks on a single surface determines the total number of cylinders on a given disk. Usually, a number of blocks of data, called *sectors*, are recorded on each track.

Depending on the number of the available read/write heads, disks can be of the fixed-head or the moving-head variety. *Fixed-head disks* usually have a separate read/write head for each track. A given sector is accessed by activating the head on the appropriate track when the target sector passes under it. The time necessary to access the desired sector is called *rotational latency*. On the average, it equals one-half the disk-revolution time, which is on the order of milliseconds for the typical disk-rotational speeds. For example, assuming that the disk is rotated 3000 times per minute, one revolution takes approximately

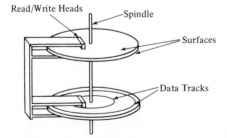

Figure 8.3 Moving-head disk.

20 ms. The average rotational latency of such disks is usually quoted at 10 ms. From the presented description, this means that access to a given sector can take anywhere from 0 to 20 ms, depending on its position relative to the read/write head at the time a READ or WRITE command is issued.

Moving-head disks are characterized by having either one or just a few read/write heads per surface. Removable disks are usually of the moving-head variety in order to allow the head assembly to retract from the cartridge before it is replaced. With moving heads, reading of a sector requires that the head assembly first be moved to the corresponding cylinder. Once this is accomplished, the head on the related track is activated when the target sector passes under it. Thus, the access time of a moving-head disk includes both the head-positioning or *seek time* (circumferential movement) and the rotational latency described above. Disk manufacturers usually quote the average seek time required for the head assembly to traverse one-half of the disk surface. This parameter varies over a larger range than does the rotational latency. Its order of magnitude is in milliseconds, and it may range in actual products from some 20 ms to over 60 ms for lower-performance drives.

These two components of the disk-access time account for its variability of some 2 orders of magnitude, from less than 1 ms to on the order of 100 ms. Once the desired sector is accessed, data are transferred at the rate that is of the order of 1 to 5 Mb/s. Assuming a sector size of 512 bytes, which is quite typical, the sector-transfer time at 5 Mb/s is approximately 781 μs. This is obviously negligible in comparison to the average disk-access time. Given the high data rates of disks, direct memory access (DMA) is almost exclusively utilized to transfer data between disks and main memory.

8.4 DISK CONTROLLER AND DRIVER

Because disks are electromechanical devices, they are capable of carrying out only some rather primitive commands. Typical interface signals between a disk drive and the disk controller of a computer system are depicted in Figure 8.4. Given that a controller is usually capable of handling several drives with similar characteristics, a few control lines are needed to select a drive designated to participate in a given operation. These are indicated as DRIVE SELECT lines in Figure 8.4. Similarly, HEAD SELECT lines are used to activate a specific head on the selected drive. The DIRECTION signal, required for moving-head drives, is used to designate the direction, IN or OUT, in which the heads should be moved starting from the current position. The STEP line is used to provide a timed sequence of step pulses. Usually, one pulse moves the head one cylinder, and a predetermined number of pulses moves the head assembly from its present cylinder to the target cylinder.

The READ and WRITE signals are used to activate the selected read or write head. The DATA IN and DATA OUT lines normally carry the input or the output stream of bits when a READ or a WRITE operation is in progress,

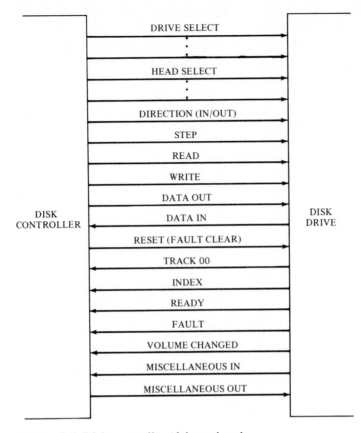

Figure 8.4 Disk controller/driver signals.

respectively. TRACK 00 is a drive-supplied signal that indicates when the head assembly is on cylinder 0, track 0, the outermost or home position. The INDEX signal indicates the time when the drive electronics sense the cylinder or track address mark (index hole on floppy disks). The VOLUME CHANGED signal, usually provided for removable media, alerts the operating system to media changes. Upon detecting this event, the operating system must invalidate in main memory all information regarding the related drive, such as directory entries, free-space tables, and the like.

Other signals include RESET and FAULT indications and a few other device-specific signals collectively labeled as MISCELLANEOUS IN and OUT. Some examples of these include MODE of encoding DOOR OPEN, MOTOR ON, and WRITE PROTECT.

The primary function of a disk controller is to convert higher-level commands, such as SEEK or READ a sector, into a sequence of properly timed drive-specific commands. In addition, the controller provides the serial/parallel conversion and signal conditioning necessary to convert from byte or word format required for DMA communication with main memory into the analog bit-serial streams expected and produced by disk drives. Another important function of disk controllers is error control.

Error control is necessary for detecting transient errors caused by noise and electromagnetic interference and for handling media defects. Whenever a block of data is to be written on disk, the controller calculates the values of and appends the check bits to data. Since disk errors often occur in bursts which produce errors in strings of successive bits, error-detection mechanisms capable of coping with these kinds of errors, such as cyclic redundancy codes (CRCs), are often used in disk controllers. During READ operations, the controller calculates the check bits on the basis of received data. The correctness of the received data is verified by comparing the calculated check bits with the ones received from disk. Any discrepancy indicates an error.

Depending on its cause, a disk error can be transient or permanent. Transient errors are usually dealt with by rereading the sector in question a predetermined number of times. This parameter is often called the *retry count*. If the error persists after a few retries, it is assumed to be permanent. Provided that the drive is fully functional, permanent errors are caused by media defects. Defective sectors are usually called *bad blocks*. Since only premium-priced media are guaranteed to be 100% error free, bad blocks can be present on disks, particularly on high-density, low-cost disks. Instead of throwing away an entire disk because of a single defective sector, the common practice is to exclude bad blocks from further use, say, by marking them as permanently used. Avoidance of the bad blocks is usually delegated to a low-level layer of the file-control system in order to relieve users from the burden. Bad blocks can be initially detected at disk-initialization time. The INITDISK command on many systems returns information about bad blocks.

Except for the basic functions described so far, there is a great variation in the sophistication of disk controllers. The prevailing trend is toward the more "intelligent" disk controllers that take over many functions traditionally delegated to software, such as formatting, buffering, and blocking of data. Sector caching, seek optimizations, and associative disk searches are also provided by some controllers. VLSI implementations of floppy- and hard-disk controllers are commonly employed in new designs, which also frequently feature dedicated microprocessors and large RAM buffers. On the other hand, many classical or "dumb" controllers remain at the rudimentary functional level described earlier. They thus depend heavily on software to provide the other needed functions. In order to avoid generalizations in this nonstandard area, we briefly describe the disk abstraction as provided by the disk driver. The reader should be aware that the described functions in a given system may be carried out predominantly by hardware (disk controller) or by software (disk driver).

A typical disk driver basically allows reading and writing of disk sectors specified by means of the three-component physical disk addresses of the form:

$$< cylinder\ number,\ head\ number,\ sector\ number >\ .$$

Some implementations require READ and WRITE requests to be preceded by head-positioning SEEK commands. For reads and writes, the starting address of a memory area where the data are to be furnished or taken from must also be specified. Typical commands at the driver level are SEEK, READ, and WRITE. Since data transfers between disks and main memory use direct memory access (DMA), the disk driver does not return data to their callers—except for information regarding the outcome of the related operation. When an exception—such as a read error or a drive fault—is detected, the disk driver usually indicates the actual number of bytes that were transferred correctly prior to the error. Other driver commands may include some means for media handling, such as FORMAT a track and MARK a bad block by writing a special deleted-data mark into it.

Some disk drivers and controllers are capable of transferring multiple sectors, or even tracks, in response to a single command. An advantage of this mode of operation is that heads are positioned once, so that the overhead of average access time may be amortized over many sectors. Multisector and multitrack operations usually require all transferred data to occupy consecutive disk addresses. In particular, intervening head movements or sector skipping are usually not allowed.

8.5 OPERATING SYSTEM'S VIEW OF FILE-MANAGEMENT

Figure 8.5 summarizes the various views of the file system described in this chapter so far. Typical commands at each level of abstraction are also given in Figure 8.5. As suggested by the figure, the file system must support the user's abstraction at the outer layer and convert it into the commands understood by the disk driver at the inner layer. From the range of services provided to users and the description of the disk organization, it follows that the basic functions of the file system include

1. Keeping track of all files in the system
2. Controlled sharing and enforcing of file protection
3. Management of disk space and allocation and deallocation
4. Mapping of logical file addresses to physical disk addresses

This list assumes that low-level functions, such as device-management, media-management, and error handling, are provided by the disk driver as described earlier. In other words, the list relies on the disk abstraction provided by the disk driver and includes only the services of the file-system layer depicted in Figure 8.5.

The file system keeps track of files by means of directories. File protection requires enforced separation of distinct files. This means that each user is granted access only to those files which he or she has an explicit permit to use. Moreover,

	Objects Manipulated:	Typical Calls
Interactive Users (Command Language)	FILES	COPY, DELETE, RENAME
Application & System Programs (Run–time Calls)	FILE ELEMENTS (File–relative Logical Addresses)	OPEN, CLOSE, SEEK, READ, WRITE
FILE SYSTEM		
Device Driver	SECTORS (Cylinder, Head, Sector)	SEEK, READ, WRITE

Figure 8.5 File-system layers.

authorized users are allowed access to files only in the specific mode provided by the related authorization, such as read-only or write-only. File sharing, when supported, allows several authorized users to access the same file concurrently. In order to preserve the integrity of shared files, the system may impose some additional temporary restrictions necessary for synchronization purposes. For example, only a set of readers may be allowed concurrent access to a shared file. In any event, file protection should be enforced at all times regardless of the number of concurrent users.

Dynamic changes in both the number and the sizes of files necessitate frequent allocation and deallocation of disk space. The file system usually keeps track of unused disk space by means of a pool of free blocks. Requests for disk blocks necessary for file growth and creation are normally satisfied from this pool. When previously allocated disk blocks are released, say, due to deletions and truncations of files, the file system returns them to the pool of free blocks.

As indicated in the presentation of file-related system calls, users specify portions of files to be read or written in terms of the logical, file-relative addresses. On the other hand, the disk driver handles physical disk addresses, specified in terms of cylinder, head, and sector numbers. In order to bridge this incompatibility, the file system must map user-supplied logical addresses into the physical disk addresses necessary to process read and write requests. Moreover, since the sector is the basic unit of disk transfers, the file system must convert a user's request to access an arbitrary number of bytes into a request to access an integral number of disk sectors.

Having outlined its basic functions, we now proceed to construct the data structures and a functional specification of the file-management system.

8.5.1 Directories

Directories are basically symbol tables of files. A single flat directory can contain a list of all files in a system. When hierarchical directories are used, the collection of all directory and subdirectory entries defines the totality of system files. For generality, we discuss a possible implementation of a hierarchical directory system. Flat directories may be regarded as its degenerate form with no subdirectories and in which the root directory contains all system files.

In principle, an entry in a directory defines a file. A file is usually defined by its name, attributes, and an access pointer. A typical directory entry may contain the following information:

- File name, type, and version number
- File access pointer (starting disk address)
- File attributes:
    Size
    Structure
    Owner
    Access rights
    Date of creation
    Date of last backup
    Date of last reference

The file name, and possibly its type and version number, can be used to uniquely identify a file. The file-access pointer is used to help locate physical blocks for READ and WRITE operations. Numerous file attributes, some of which are given in the list above, may also be stored in directories. One of the more important file attributes is the list of its authorized users and the modes in which each of them is allowed to access the related file. Various dates may be used for archival and management purposes. For example, many time-sharing systems back up the user files at regular intervals. In order to conserve disk space, files not accessed for a long time can be removed to offline storage. Incremental backups of selected files can be made possible by keeping track of the date of the last backup of each file.

Directory entries are added by the creation of files and of aliases to existing files. Entries are removed from directories when files are deleted. Directories are frequently searched to locate and access files for processing and to add or remove entries. With the description of directory contents and the typical operations on a directory outlined, we turn our attention to data structures suitable for implementation of directories.

One of the first decisions to be made concerns the location of file directories. Should directories be kept on disks or in memory? As average disk-access times indicate, much faster access to, and processing of, directories may be accomplished by keeping them in main memory. On the other hand, the space needed for the storage of directories can become quite large, so that directories should be kept on secondary storage. Moreover, having directories on secondary storage allows files on removable volumes to be accessed when volumes are replaced or even mounted on another system. Most systems resolve this dilemma by keeping directories on secondary storage and by copying to main memory the actively used entries. The identities of the actively used entries are made known to the system when files are opened for processing.

Thus, the first simple idea is to organize a file directory as a list of files and to store it on disk. In order to provide uniformity of disk operations, it is customary to regard the directories themselves as files. The somewhat recursive definition of the directory as a file containing a list of all files poses a practical problem of locating the root directory during the system startup. In other words, if the directory lists all files, the question is who then lists the directory? The usual answer is to place the directory, or its root, at a known address of the volume from which the system is booted, so that the operating system can access the root directory directly.

This specification is usually sufficient for implementation of flat directories. Whenever a volume is initialized, an empty directory is created at the known disk address. Upon each file creation, an empty directory entry is located and filled with information about the related file. Thus, each directory entry completely and uniquely identifies one file.

In addition to the unique identification of files, hierarchical directories allow creation of aliases and the use of identical names (in different subdirectories) to designate distinct physical files. This view cannot be easily supported by simple flat directories. Instead, hierarchical directories are usually implemented by separating symbol tables of names from the physical description of files. One such possible organization is depicted in Figure 8.6.

As indicated, file names are kept in symbolic file directories (SFDs). A separate symbolic file directory is maintained for each directory and subdirectory defined in the system. The symbolic directories depicted in Figure 8.6 describe the file system introduced in Figure 8.1. The primary purpose of a symbolic file directory is to establish the correspondence between a user-assigned file name and an internal system-assigned file ID. Each physical file is assigned a unique internal ID that is used by the system to reference the related file. File descriptions, except for the names, are usually kept in a separate directory, called the *basic file directory* (BFD) in Figure 8.6. For reasons of efficiency, a common implementation is to use the internal file ID as an index into the basic file directory. This is shown in Figure 8.6.

The separation of name tables from file descriptions allows for easy handling of aliases and homonyms. For example, note that the physical file whose ID is 4 is known as PASLIB in the root directory and as LIB in the KMOS directory. Consequently, the two names are listed in the symbolic directories ROOT and KMOS. However, both of them designate the same physical file number 4. The

File ID	Type	Address	Size	Usage Count	Access Rights
1	BFD	10	5	1	RW system, No access others
2	DIR	2	1	1	RO everyone
3	–	–	–	–	–
4	OBJ	58	21	2	RW PasMaint, RO others
5	DIR	69	1	1	RO everyone
6	DIR	87	1	1	RO Smith
7	–	–	–	–	–
8	TXT	336	207	1	RW Jones, RO Smith
9	DIR	805	1	1	RO Jones
10	DIR	2318	1	2	RO everyone
11	TXT	1012	118	1	RW Smith
12	–	–	–	–	–
13	OBJ	2586	29	1	RW Jones, RW Smith
14	PAS	2530	55	1	RO everyone
15	TSK	3012	38	1	RW Jones, RW Smith

Basic File Directory (BFD)

ROOT

•	2
PASLIB	4
–	–
JONES	5
SMITH	6
(EOF)	–

JONES

•	5
–	–
REPORT	8
NEW_WORK	9
KMOS	10
(EOF)	–

SMITH

•	6
KMOS	10
REPORT	11
–	–
(EOF)	–

NEW_WORK

•	9
(EOF)	–

KMOS

•	10
SOURCE	14
CONFIG	13
LIB	4
USERP	15
(EOF)	–

Symbolic File Directories

Figure 8.6 File directories.

332

two REPORT files have the same name in JONES and SMITH directories, but different IDs, since they are distinct physical files.

Users' requests for file services are normally processed by searching the symbolic directory specified by the path name in order to determine the related file's ID. This value is then used to locate the file description in the basic file directory. In order to reduce the frequency of directory searches, it is customary to record the file ID and all related directory entries in the connection data structure, often called the *file control-block* (FCB), which is formed when a file is opened for processing. Subsequent references of a process to an open file are made through the file control-block in memory, which contains a copy of or a pointer to the file description contained in the SFD and BFD directories. This approach saves disk accesses normally required for directory searching whenever a given file is to be referenced. Some systems collect names and descriptions of active files into data structures called *active name tables* and *active file tables*, respectively. In any case, a file control-block is deleted when the last active user closes the file in question.

Since directories are stored and accessed as files, the basic file directory in Figure 8.6 contains entries for all system files, including directories, subdirectories, and the BFD itself. Usually the root symbolic directory and the basic file directory are assigned fixed IDs and are placed at known disk addresses. In Figure 8.6, the BFD is assumed to have ID number 1 and to start at block 10 of the system volume. The root directory has ID 2 and starts at disk address 2. It consists of three entries: PASLIB, JONES, and SMITH. Their respective IDs, shown in Figure 8.6, can be used to access those files by means of the basic file directory. For example, directory JONES can be located by means of its ID, which is 5. As the corresponding BFD entry indicates, this file is of type directory (DIR), and it resides at the disk address 69. Since directories may be of variable length, the end of a directory is designated by the end-of-file mark (EOF), as indicated in Figure 8.6. The root directory also illustrates the fact that directories may have unused entries, such as the one following PASLIB. When new files are created, the common practice is to place them at an empty directory entry and to expand the size of the directory only when all of its entries are filled.

A special entry in each symbolic directory, marked by a dot, is used to facilitate references to itself. This feature is useful for supporting the concept of a current working directory and for fast processing of user navigational queries, such as Where am I now?

A new field in the file-description structure is introduced in the basic file directory depicted in Figure 8.6. It is the USAGE COUNT, which indicates the number of references to a given file. The usage count is set to 2 for the files listed in two directories, PASLIB (or LIB) and KMOS, whose IDs are 4 and 10, respectively. The purpose of this field is to facilitate proper deletion of files when aliases and cross-references are possible. For example, if user Smith deletes the KMOS directory, the corresponding entry is supposed to be deleted from his directory. However, the KMOS directory and its files should not be physically deleted, because they are still referenced by JONES. As in our earlier discussion on keeping track of the depth of an interrupt disable, the deletion requests can be handled by keeping track of the file usage count. When a file is created, its usage count is set to 1. Whenever the file is listed in another symbolic directory under the same or a different name, its usage count is increased accordingly. When a file is deleted by a user, the usage count is decremented. The file is physically deleted only when its usage count becomes zero. For example, a DELETE call on the file /JONES/REPORT would be processed by actually removing the file with the ID 8 from the system. This would result in freeing of the BFD entry number 8 and in all 207 blocks owned by REPORT being returned to the free pool. However, the request to delete the file /PASLIB would be processed simply by decrementing its usage count.

The last field of each basic file directory entry depicted in Figure 8.6 contains a list of access rights to the related file. A common restriction, assumed to be implicit in constructing Figure 8.6, is to allow only the system to write directories. In other words, directories are regarded as files that users cannot write. For all other files, only explicitly authorized users should be allowed to access the related file in the specified mode. For example, the directory JONES may be regarded as public in the sense that all users are allowed to read it. However, only users Smith and Jones may read the file /JONES/REPORT, while access to NEW_WORK is restricted to Jones only.

As indicated, access authorizations for a file basically consist of a list of authorized users. However, the actual implementation of access control in this way is cumbersome both in terms of the space needed to record all authorized users of a file and in terms of the time necessary to traverse such lists whenever the related file is accessed. While many variations exist, a common approach is to divide users into a set of categories and to record access rights for categories rather than for individual users. For example, a common division of users of a file is into

owner; group; world

categories. *Owner* is usually the creator of the file. *Group* includes closely related users—such as members of the same team—who are normally given more generous access rights, and *world* includes all other users. Membership of a user in a given category is usually assigned and determined by means of the related password. For example, few dedicated bits of a password may be identical for users belonging to the same *group*. In any case, given a finite number of possible access modes, such as read-only (RO), read-write (RW), write-only (WO), or no-access (NA), complete access rights to a file can be encoded in a few bytes for all types of users.

Returning to our example of Figure 8.6, users Jones and Smith would probably belong to the same group. Thus, access rights to directory JONES, file ID 5, can be recorded as RO;RO;RO for the owner, group, and world, respectively. However, access rights to the /JONES/REPORT file would be RW;RO;NA.

The most frequent operations on directories are searching and addition and removal of entries. Except for the actively used entries, directories are customarily kept on secondary storage. The efficiency of directory operations is therefore primarily affected by the number of disk accesses required to complete a search, to append, or to remove an entry. Although lists are used in our examples for simplicity, a linear-list organization of symbolic directories is not very suitable for searching, since it requires $O(n)$ comparisons to locate a given entry, where n is the number of all entries in a directory. With a good hashing function, hashing can perform a search, append, or a delete operation in constant time. However, the worst-case behavior of hashing is no better than that of a linear list. Moreover, when a directory expands beyond the range that the related hash function can address, all of its entries may have to be rehashed. When such problems are present, they may be circumvented by using tree structures to represent directories. A balanced binary tree may be searched in $O(\log n)$ time. Appending and removing entries can also be performed in this time. An additional advantage of trees is that they facilitate sorted listing of directory entries, which is required by many systems.

8.5.2 Disk-Space Management

An important function of the file system is to manage space on the secondary storage. This includes keeping track of both disk blocks allocated to files and the free blocks available for allocation. File growth consumes free blocks, while deletion and truncation of files produce free blocks for allocation. Thus, in addition to directories that describe existing files, the file system must maintain a pool of free blocks. As shown later, the space-allocation strategy is often closely related to the efficiency of file accessing and of logical-physical mapping of disk addresses. A good space-allocation strategy must take into consideration several related and interactive factors, such as

1. Processing speed of sequential access to files, random access to files, and allocation and deallocation of blocks
2. Ability to make use of multisector and multitrack transfers
3. Disk utilization
4. Main-memory requirements of a given algorithm

Let us briefly review the considerations listed above. Processing speed is usually measured in terms of its dominant factor, that is, as the number of disk accesses required to locate the target block for a read or a write operation. Given their relative frequency of occurrence, the speed of sequential and random access to files is usually more important than the speed of allocation and deallocation of blocks. The ability to make use of multisector and multitrack transfers is advantageous in that it may reduce the effective disk-access time. Disk utilization refers to the percentage of disk space allocatable to users. One of the primary contributors to low disk utilization is external fragmentation, which occurs when free blocks are available but the system is unable to allocate them to requesting users. Main-memory utilization primarily refers to the table fragmentation imposed by a given algorithm.

Management of storage blocks is a familiar problem that we have encountered and discussed in relation to the main memory-management. Secondary storage introduces two additional aspects to the problem: several orders of magnitude slower disk-access time, and possibly an order of magnitude larger number of blocks to deal with. Moreover, the variability and dynamic changes in file sizes make predictions of their resource requirements difficult and unreliable in most cases. Nonetheless, many considerations are similar in both environments. In particular, the basic division of allocation policies into contiguous and noncontiguous is applicable to file systems as well.

The presentation of each space-allocation scheme in subsequent sections follows a similar format. After discussing the principle of its operation, the performance of the related scheme when accessing files sequentially and randomly is assessed. Since a file-management scheme must both provide efficient access to portions of files and manage free space on disks for allocation purposes, we also discuss the behavior of each scheme when managing free space. On the basis of these characteristics, a summary of the advantages and disadvantages of each space-allocation scheme is outlined. In particular, we discuss contiguous allocation of the disk space and two forms of noncontiguous allocation: chaining and indexing.

Contiguous allocation. As is the case with its main-memory counterpart, the basic idea of contiguous allocation is to allocate contiguous areas of disk in response to run-time requests. In systems with contiguous allocation, most files are placed in contiguous blocks on disk. The possible appearance of the BFD file from Figure 8.6, implemented as a contiguous file, is given in Figure 8.7. As indicated, the file occupies five consecutive blocks, starting from block number 10 on disk. As suggested by Figure 8.7, the starting address and the file size, recorded in the directory, are sufficient to access any block of a contiguous file. In particular, sequential access is both simple and fast, because logically adjacent blocks are also physically adjacent on the disk. As a result, multisector transfers can be conveniently used.

Random access to contiguous files is also fast, because the address of the target disk block can be easily calculated on the basis of the file's starting address recorded in the directory. For example, the address of the second logical block (LB2) of the file depicted in Figure 8.7 is obtained by adding its starting address, 10, and the desired offset, 2, to produce the target disk address, 12. The ability to use multisector transfers in the random-access mode depends on the number of consecutive blocks accessed between successive seek operations.

Contiguous allocation of free disk space requires keeping track of clusters of contiguous free blocks and implementation of some policy for satisfying requests for allocation and deallocation of blocks when files are created and deleted, respectively. Addresses and sizes of free disk areas can be kept in a separate list or recorded in unused directory entries. For example, when a file is deleted,

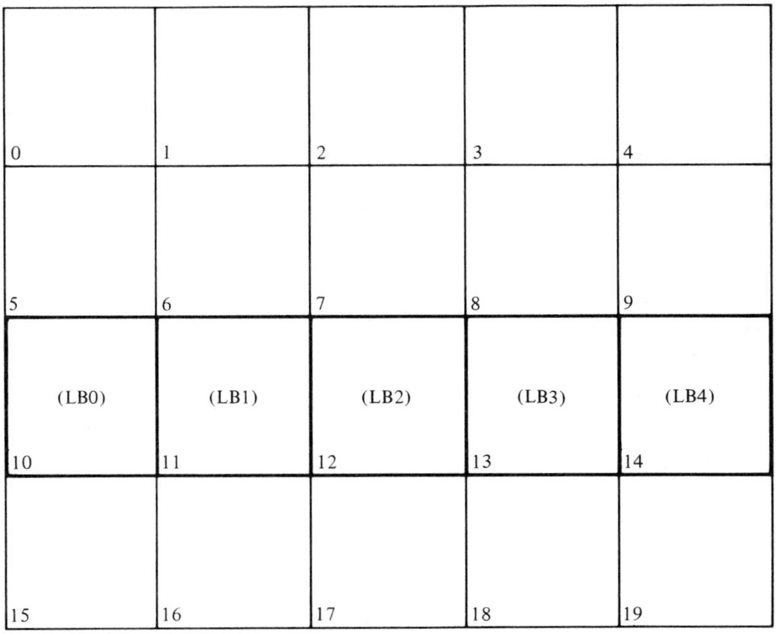

0	1	2	3	4
5	6	7	8	9
(LB0) 10	(LB1) 11	(LB2) 12	(LB3) 13	(LB4) 14
15	16	17	18	19

Figure 8.7 Contiguous allocation of disk space.

its entry in the basic file directory can be marked as unused, but its address and size in terms of blocks can be left intact. When a new file is created, the operating system can search unused directory entries in order to locate a free area of suitable size. Not surprisingly, the first-fit and the best-fit algorithms are often used for this purpose. Depending on the portion of the directory which is kept in main memory, the tradeoff between the first-fit and the best-fit may swing either way. Namely, the first-fit requires fewer directory lookups and it may be preferable when most of the directory is on disk. On the other hand, the best-fit may reduce internal fragmentation by providing a better fit of the requested size to the size of the allocated disk area.

Deallocation of space is almost trivial in systems with contiguous allocation that keep track of at least part of the free space in unused entries of the basic file directory. In such systems, a file can be deleted by simply marking it as absent in the TYPE or PRESENCE field (not shown in Figure 8.6) of the related directory entry.

In summary, contiguous allocation provides for fast file accessing without any intervening disk accesses to locate target blocks. Moreover, very little directory and memory space is needed for keeping track of contiguous files. The main problem with contiguous allocation is the disk fragmentation that it produces. Due to the variability of file sizes, disk space can become heavily fragmented. A combination of internal and external fragmentation may cripple disk utilization.

A form of internal fragmentation is present in all file systems, regardless of the space-allocation policy in use. It is a consequence of the allocation of disk space in terms of blocks, so that one-half of a block on the average is wasted per file. Some systems allocate space in larger units, often called *allocation clusters*, which are an integral number of disk sectors. While clustered allocation of space is generally faster when files grow incrementally, it usually increases internal fragmentation accordingly. Additional internal fragmentation may develop in systems that simplify space-allocation algorithms by allocating a free area of suitable size without returning the remaining blocks to the Free list. As a result, free blocks at the end of each file cannot be allocated until the related file is deleted, and they contribute to internal fragmentation.

External fragmentation refers to scattered groups of free blocks that are too small for allocation but which as a collection may represent a large percentage of the disk size. As in the similar situation found when managing dynamically partitioned main memory, this problem can be dealt with by occasional compaction of the disk. In fact, one of the primary functions of the SQUEEZE utility mentioned in Section 8.1 is to compact the disk space. Disk compaction is usually performed offline on a volume-by-volume basis. As such, it prevents access to related files while being done. Depending on the primary use of a given system, this may or may not be acceptable.

Contiguous allocation of disk space requires the file size to be preclaimed, that is, estimated, at the time of its creation. While this is not a problem when copying files, accurate estimation of file sizes is generally difficult and unreliable. For example, what may be a reasonable basis for estimating the size of a new file being created by the editor? One way to handle this problem is to make some initial estimate and to allocate a suitable free area for the file in question. If the file turns out to be larger than estimated, its extension can be placed in some other disk area. This is often called a *file overflow*. Occasionally, say, as a part of the SQUEEZE operation, overflowed files can be restructured and made contiguous. Accessing of overflowed "contiguous" files is cumbersome, and it loses most of the appeal of contiguous allocation. Finally, contiguous allocation of disk space complicates "mapping around" the bad blocks, which can also contribute to fragmentation by breaking the contiguity of disk areas.

Noncontiguous allocation: chaining. Noncontiguous allocation of disk space, both in terms of files and of free space, is usually some variation of the two basic strategies: chained and indexed allocation.

Chained allocation is essentially a disk-based version of the linked list. Namely, a few bytes of each disk block (or cluster) are set aside to point to the next block in sequence. Both files and free-space lists can be handled in this way. In the case of files, the directory may contain the "head pointer," that is, the address of the first disk block. A possible chained implementation of the BFD file is presented in Figure 8.8. Although the directory entry remains unchanged in the sense that the file starts at disk address 10 and has a size of five blocks, the actual physical blocks occupied by the file are not contiguous. Consequently,

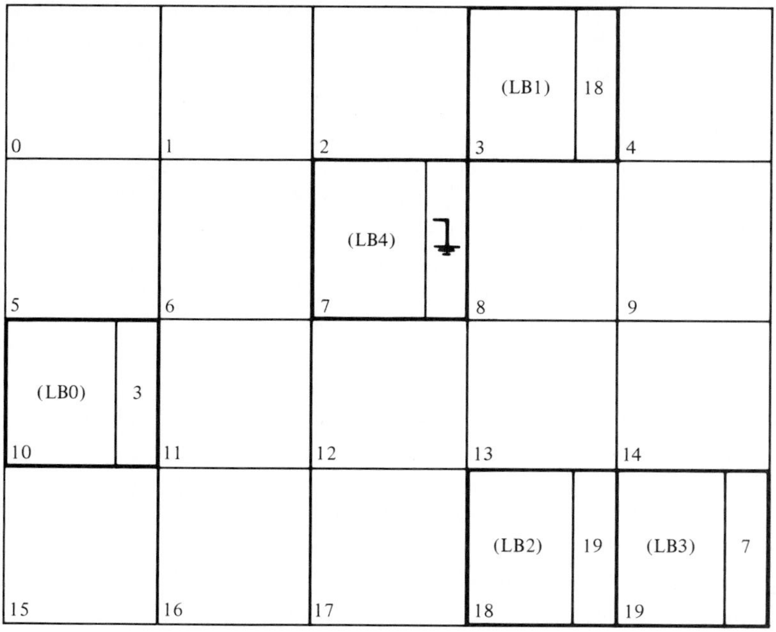

0	1	2	3 (LB1) 18	4
5	6	7 (LB4) ⌐	8	9
10 (LB0) 3	11	12	13	14
15	16	17	18 (LB2) 19	19 (LB3) 7

Figure 8.8 Chained allocation of disk space.

accessing of such files must begin from the first block, whose address is listed in the directory, and proceed by traversing successive physical blocks by means of the next-block pointer fields. For example, logical blocks LB0 through LB4 of the file presented in Figure 8.8 occupy physical block addresses 10, 3, 18, 19, and 7, in that order.

Chained files are well suited for sequential access, because the block currently being processed contains the address of the next block in line. The use of multisector transfers for chained files is, at best, difficult. Namely, even when adjacent logical blocks are physically contiguous, that property cannot generally be known before a given block is accessed. This basically precludes multisector transfers that require prior declaration of the total number of blocks to be transferred. Direct access to chained files is slow, because locating a given block requires accessing of all intervening blocks in the chain.

Chaining of free blocks, on the other hand, is rather simple and convenient. With a single pointer to the free chain kept in memory, allocation of single blocks can be easily performed. Allocation of blocks in groups requires disk accessing to determine the addresses of each subsequent free block. This is rarely a problem in practice, because systems with noncontiguous allocation usually allow incremental growth of files and allocate only single blocks or small groups of them at a time. On the other hand, blocks are commonly deallocated in groups upon deletion of files. By keeping a tail pointer to the free chain in memory, this operation can be performed with a single disk access needed to update the link of the tail block whenever a new free chain is appended to it. Otherwise, one disk access per each block freed may be needed to update the pointers accordingly.

The advantages of chaining include its simplicity and very little storage overhead. Being based on noncontiguous allocation, chaining does not produce external disk fragmentation. As a result, disk compaction may not be needed. Since disk space needed for pointers is usually below 1%, its effects on disk utilization are practically negligible. Moreover, chaining allows easy handling of bad blocks by simply omitting them from both file and free chains. Owing to its linked nature, insertion of a block in the middle of an existing file is quite straightforward, a feature not offered by other space-allocation policies.

The disadvantages of chaining include slow random access to files and the inability to utilize multisector transfers. Some operating-system designers also dislike the sensitivity of chaining to damaged pointers. Indeed, a single damaged pointer can make thousands of blocks inaccessible. Recovering of chained files on damaged disks is an extremely painful experience. Some designs address this problem by keeping pointers in a dedicated file and making redundant copies of it. The idea is to copy the list of chains into the main memory and thus facilitate faster access, especially when accessing files randomly. Redundancy of pointer files is employed for safer recovery. A similar method is used by some versions of the popular MS-DOS and PC-DOS operating systems.

Noncontiguous allocation: indexing. An alternative implementation of noncontiguous allocation of secondary storage space is indexing. While similar to chaining in that it also maintains pointers to allocated blocks, indexing attempts to improve the speed of random access by collecting pointers into the so-called index blocks. The principle of indexing is illustrated in Figure 8.9. As indicated, instead of the address of the first block of the file, the directory contains the address of the index block, which is 10 in our example. The index block, in turn, contains pointers to the data blocks of the related file. Although quite different in their implementation, index blocks basically serve the same purpose as page-map tables do in paged memory systems. At the expense of the overhead of accessing the index block itself, indexing virtually eliminates the time differences between sequential and random access to files. A given block of a file can be accessed by looking up its address at the corresponding offset of the index block. For example, assuming 512-byte blocks and 4-byte pointers, the address of the logical block number 2 of the file BFD can be found in a 4-byte cluster starting at address 8 of the index block. The address of the index block itself can be found in the directory.

With these assumptions, a 512-byte index block can contain up to 128 pointers to file blocks. This means that the largest file in such a system cannot exceed 128 blocks of 512 bytes each. The resulting limit of 64 KB is below the typical file sizes in most systems. This problem may be alleviated by using multilevel indexing, such as the double-level indexing depicted in Figure 8.10. In this scheme, there are two levels of indices that need to be looked up in order to locate a target data block; the first-level index points to second-level index blocks,

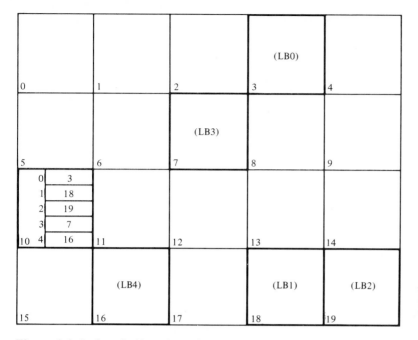

Figure 8.9 Indexed allocation of disk space.

which, in turn, contain pointers to the data blocks. With the same assumptions, this arrangement allows addressing of 128*128 second-level index blocks, capable of supporting file sizes of up to 8 MB of file space. The addressing range grows exponentially with the level of indexing, so that triple-level indexing allows 1-GB files with the same assumptions.

Both sequential and random accessing of indexed files requires one disk access per level of indexing to locate the address of the target block. Successive accesses to file blocks within the addressing range of the current index block need not incur this overhead if recently used index blocks are kept in memory. Naturally, sequential access is more likely to benefit from the buffering of index blocks. In principle, multisector transfers for sequential access are possible by preanalyzing the contiguity of addresses pointed to by successive indices. However, the nature of noncontiguous allocation makes it unlikely to find adjacent logical blocks in consecutive disk sectors. In order to reduce latency, systems with noncontiguous allocation occasionally make their files contiguous by restructuring disks by means of SQUEEZE or a similar utility.

Indexing of free blocks is possible, although perhaps cumbersome, because a freshly initialized volume can have a very large number of free blocks and thus require multiple levels of indexing to account for all of them. Even though the number of free blocks may subsequently be reduced as files are created, allocations and deallocations of blocks may continue to incur the overhead of

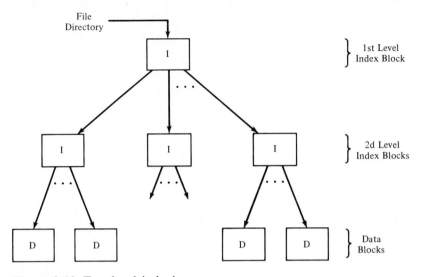

Figure 8.10 Two-level indexing.

multiple-level indexing. As a speedup, keeping of at least one index block of the Free list in memory can result in quick allocation of up to *n* free blocks, where *n* is the number of indices in a block.

A popular variant of indexing the free space on disk is the *bit map*. A bit map is simply a string of bits, each of which indicates the status of one disk sector, such as FREE/ALLOCATED. A possible appearance of the bit map is illustrated in Figure 8.11. That particular example is constructed for the simple 20-block disk illustrated in Figure 8.9. Allocated (and bad) disk blocks are indicated by having a value of 1 in the corresponding bit of the map. In addition to six disk blocks occupied by the BFD file, blocks 0, 1, and 2 are assumed to be occupied by the boot block and the system root directory.

The bit map of a particular volume can be kept in a separate file on that volume and brought into main memory whenever the volume is mounted. An alternative is to construct the bit map on the fly by consulting the directory to determine which blocks are allocated and which are free. In either case, subsequent allocation and deallocation of blocks can be performed quickly by setting and resetting the corresponding bits of the map kept in main memory. To gain some appreciation of the saving of space that it provides, consider an 8-MB disk with 512-byte sectors. The disk has 16 KB of sectors which can be

0	1	2	3	4	5	6	7	8	9	10	11	12	13	14	15	16	17	18	19
1	1	1	1	0	0	0	1	0	0	1	0	0	0	0	0	1	0	1	1

Figure 8.11 Bit map.

indexed by a two-level structure described earlier by using 129 pointer blocks or approximately 64.5 KB for the purpose. With the bit map, the individual states of all 16 kB of available sectors can be described by a 2-KB bit map. Incidentally, note that the storage overhead imposed by double-level indexing of 129 index blocks per volume remains below 1%.

The advantages of indexed file allocation include the absence of external fragmentation and the efficiency of random accessing. Moreover, indexing can easily map around the bad disk blocks. Indexing of free space can be accomplished by means of the bit map.

The primary disadvantage of indexing is the disk accessing necessary to retrieve the address of the target block on disk. As indicated, this overhead can be amortized over several successive disk operations by keeping some index blocks in memory. Another disadvantage of indexing is the space needed to store the addressing information, that is, the index blocks themselves. As shown, this overhead is small for large files, but it can become significant for small files, since at least 1 index block is normally dedicated to each file. For example, 1 index block is needed to describe 5 data blocks of the BFD file in Figure 8.9, which amounts to some 20% overhead.

An interesting variant, used by the Unix system, is to combine direct and indexed addressing in order to save space and to provide faster access to smaller files. In particular, a Unix file-access descriptor, accessible through the directory, contains 13 pointers. The first 10 pointers contain direct addresses of the 10 data blocks on the disk. The eleventh pointer, when needed, points to a first-level index block containing 138 pointers to data blocks. The twelfth pointer points to the first block of the two-level indexing structure, and the thirteenth pointer contains the address of the first block of a three-level indexing structure. With this strategy, files of up to 10 sectors can be addressed directly, one-level indexing is sufficient for files of up to 137 sectors, two-level indexing is sufficient for up to 16,521 sectors, and three-level indexing is sufficient for files on the order of 1 GB.

Unix is just one of the many systems which use some combination of the presented schemes in their space-allocation and file-accessing algorithms. For example, contiguous and chained allocation are convenient for sequentially accessed files, while contiguous and indexed allocation are generally better for random access. Files of predictable sizes may best be handled by contiguous allocation, which seems to make the most use of multisector transfers. By combining both contiguous and noncontiguous forms of space allocation within a single system, disk fragmentation may be kept at acceptable levels. When fragmentation exceeds a certain limit, disk compaction can be used to make all files contiguous and to combine the free space into a single large area.

8.5.3 Address Translation

As described earlier, users perceive information stored on secondary storage as a collection of named files. Users make references to the contents of a given file in terms of file-relative logical addresses. In the common case where files are regarded as linear arrays of bytes, users may make requests to read or to write individual bytes or groups of them. For example, after opening the /JONES/REPORT file, a program can make a request to read 1200 bytes from it, starting from byte number 1600. Assuming that the connection ID given to the program for this file is 3, the following sequence of calls can be used to accomplish the task.

$$\text{SEEK } (3, 1600)$$
$$\text{READ } (3, 1200, \text{ BUFFER})$$

Assuming that no other accesses to the file were made prior to these calls, this is a random-access request. Therefore, the seek command is issued to position the file marker to location 1600. The subsequent READ call instructs the file system to read 1200 B from the file whose connection ID is 3, that is, /JONES/REPORT, into the caller's area named BUFFER. The file system must accept user requests of this form and translate them into disk-driver-understandable three-component physical addresses composed of the cylinder, head, and sector numbers on a given drive.

Although direct logical-physical mapping of disk addresses is possible, most systems perform it in stages. One of the primary reasons for this is a large variability of structure and of other physical characteristics of different secondary storage devices. Even similar devices, such as disk drives, may vary in the number and capacity of platters, sizes of their sectors, number of read/write heads, and the like. Supporting such variety by direct logical-physical mapping of addresses would require knowledge of each specific storage device to be incorporated in almost every layer of the file-management system. Given that the file-management system is usually one of the largest modules of an operating system, this approach would result in a cumbersome and unstructured design. Perhaps an even more pressing problem is the lack of flexibility, which would make it extremely difficult to incorporate new types of drives into such a system after completion of its file-management layer.

In order to avoid these problems, operating-system designers usually follow a more structured approach. In particular, the file system is commonly implemented in the form of several layers, each of which provides its own abstraction of secondary storage devices. Only the lowest layers of this structure, such as device drivers, are explicitly aware of the physical device characteristics. Higher layers operate with abstract virtual devices that embody the common characteristics of the real storage devices, such as block-oriented addressability and transfer of data. The low-level layers, such as device drivers, translate this view into the actual device-specific set of operations. This approach results in a much more manageable and structured design. Moreover, new types of devices may be fairly easily added to the system by writing only a relatively short device driver and leaving the upper layers of the file system intact.

While the details may vary, three levels of device abstraction are commonly identifiable in implementations of the file-management system. The first one is the user view of named files, consisting of a collection of bytes or records. Users address information in files in terms of file-relative logical addresses.

The second, lower, abstraction regards each storage volume as a linear array of logical blocks. Addresses at this level are usually called *volume-relative logical addresses*. This level of disk abstraction is assumed in constructing Figures 8.7 through 8.9, which illustrate various forms of disk-space allocation. The size of the logical block is usually fixed at the system level. Volumes with software-selectable sector sizes are commonly initialized by the system to have sector sizes equal to the logical block size. Devices with fixed but different sector or block sizes are handled by performing the logical-physical block mapping at the driver level. This is usually a simple operation, since most physical block and sector sizes are integer powers of the base 2.

The third abstraction of storage devices is the one provided by device drivers. At this level, disks are addressed by means of three-component physical addresses. As described earlier, the device driver translates these into the actual drive-control signals, such as those depicted in Figure 8.4.

In addition to address translations between different levels of disk abstraction, the file-management system must deal with the possible discrepancy resulting from the fixed-block organization of some storage devices and from the removal of this consideration from the user's view. In particular, a user's request may translate into a fractional number of blocks, while most storage devices are capable of transferring only integral numbers of blocks. Moreover, users may address individual bytes in a file, while disks can address items only on the block level. What happens when a user wishes to access a single byte located in the middle of a disk block? File systems usually handle this problem by maintaining internal buffers from which data are exchanged with secondary storage devices on a block basis. The specific items requested by users are then extracted from such buffers and transferred into the user's space. This process is called *blocking* and *deblocking*, depending on whether data are packed into blocks for output or are unpacked after input from a secondary storage device.

The remainder of this section is rather detailed in its description of the translation process between file-relative to volume-relative and, ultimately, to the physical three-component disk addresses. Readers with little interest in these issues may omit the following material and proceed to the Section 8.5.4 without loss of continuity.

Let us illustrate some aspects of the file-relative to volume-relative mapping of addresses by means of the /JONES/REPORT file example introduced earlier. For generality, let us assume that the file in question is structured as a sequence of logical records of the fixed length of 80 bytes. This might be the case if the file is formatted for an 80-column printer with all trailing blanks included. Let us also assume that we are tracing a request by a program to read 15 logical records, starting from the twentieth, into the caller's BUFFER. Assuming our usual set of file services, the resulting sequence of calls might look as follows:

$$\text{SEEK } (3, \ 20)$$
$$\text{READ } (3, \ 15, \ \text{BUFFER})$$

The first step in mapping is to convert the logical record specification into the file-relative logical byte addresses. After looking up the directory, the file system finds out that the file' in question has fixed-size logical records of 80 bytes. The request may then be translated into byte-relative logical addresses as follows:

$$s = t \times r = 20 \times 80 = 1600$$
$$g = n \times r = 15 \times 80 = 1200$$

where s is the file relative starting address in bytes, t is the target address expressed as a record number, r is record size, g is the number of bytes to be read (get), and n is the number of records to read. Thus, the user's request is translated into file-relative logical addresses expressed in terms of bytes.

The second step of the process is to translate these values into file-relative logical blocks and offsets within those blocks. Assuming that the size of the logical block in the system is 512 B, this may be performed as follows:

$$m = s \text{ div } b = 1600 \text{ div } 512 = 3, \text{ remainder } 64$$

where m is the file-relative marker position, s is the starting address in bytes, and b is the size of the logical block. This translates the starting address for the read into the third file-relative block, at the byte-offset 64. Translation of the number of bytes to transfer into blocks may be done in the following manner. The number of bytes to transfer from the starting block is

$$b - o = 512 - 64 = 448$$

where o is the starting offset (initial marker position). After transferring 448 bytes from the first block that is read, the remaining number of bytes to transfer is

$$1200 - 448 = 752$$

In terms of blocks, this is

$$752 \text{ div } 512 = 1, \text{ remainder } 240$$

or one more complete block and 240 bytes of the third. In summary, the read should encompass file-relative logical blocks number 3, 4, and 5. After bringing these blocks into internal system buffers, the last 448 bytes of the block 3, all of block 4, and the first 240 bytes of the block 5, totaling 1200 bytes, should be copied to the user's address space beginning from the location BUFFER.

Translation of the file-relative block addresses into volume-relative block addresses requires knowledge of the space-allocation scheme. As discussed earlier, space allocation can be contiguous and noncontiguous. Assuming that the file /JONES/REPORT is placed in contiguous disk blocks, the translation of file-relative to volume-relative logical addresses is performed simply by adding the volume-relative starting block address to the file-relative logical block addresses calculated above. In particular, assuming that the first block of the file is at the disk address 336, as indicated in Figure 8.6, the volume-relative block addresses of our read are 339, 340, and 341. If the file in question were chained or indexed, the related pointers to the target logical blocks would have to be obtained at this point by accessing the disk.

In order to translate a volume-relative block address into the corresponding three-component physical disk address, we must assume some particular numbering scheme of logical sectors. Although by no means universal, the following numbering technique is quite common:

1. Start numbering from the outermost cylinder (physical cylinder 0), top surface (head 0). Set volume-relative sector number to 0.
2. Beginning with the track mark (index), number sectors on the current track until the maximum number determined by the sectors-per-track capacity of the device in question.
3. Move to the next surface (head) on the same cylinder and continue numbering sectors on that track in the same way as in Step 2 above.
4. When all tracks (heads) on a cylinder are exhausted in this way, move to the next inner cylinder, start with its head 0, and repeat Steps 2 and 3 above.
5. Continue to perform Steps 2, 3, and 4 until all cylinders on the device, determined by its cylinders-per-device capacity, are exhausted.

The effects of this method of disk numbering are illustrated in Figure 8.12a. Assuming a hypothetical 10-MB disk with 512-B sectors, four heads per cylinder, and 512 cylinders, Figure 8.12a illustrates numbering of sectors on the top surface (head 0) of two consecutive cylinders. Physical sector 0 on head 0 and cylinder 0 is treated as having a logical address of 0. Subsequent sectors on the same head receive consecutive logical numbers up to 9 inclusively, given that there are 10 sectors per track. Numbering continues with other tracks of the same cylinder. Since there are four of them, the last sector (physical number 9) on the last head (3) of the same cylinder (0) is assigned logical address 39. Therefore, the first sector (0) on the top surface (head 0) of the next inner cylinder (1), shown in Figure 8.12a, is assigned logical address 40.

The sector-numbering scheme illustrated in Figure 8.12a does not allow for any processing time between consecutive logical sectors. For example, in a database application a block may be read and searched for some key value. If the value sought is not found, the next logical sector is read and the process repeated. Assuming that this processing takes a little time relative to disk accessing, the idle waiting of almost a full disk-revolution time may be necessary until the next logical block is read. An alternative sector-numbering scheme, called *interleaving*, can be used to offset this problem. As illustrated in Figure 8.12b, interleaving consists of placing consecutive logical blocks into noncontiguous physical sectors on a disk. As a result, some processing time is allowed between passage of two consecutive logical sectors under a read/write head. The duration of such gaps depends on the rotational speed of the disk and on the size and number of intervening physical disk sectors between two consecutive logical blocks. The last component, called the *interleave factor*, is usually programmable to suit the

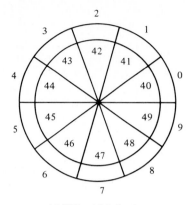

(a) Without Interleaving

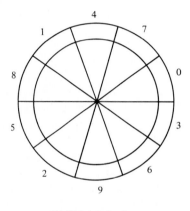

(b) With Interleaving   **Figure 8.12** Sector numbering.

intended use of a given system. In the example presented in Figure 8.12b, the interleave factor is 3. As a result, four logical blocks can be read and processed within a single disk revolution with interleaving as shown in Figure 8.12b. In order to hide the differences between devices that use it and those which do not, interleaving is one of the functions commonly dedicated to disk drivers or other low-level layers of the file system.

The presented order of numbering, without interleaving, is generalized in Table 8.3, where the expressions for the relationships between the logical and physical disk addresses are also given. As indicated for the track 0, sectors on a track are numbered from 0 to $S\text{-}1$, where S is the device's sectors-per-track capacity. The order of tracks and sectors in numbering is shown for the track $T\text{-}1$ on the cylinder 0. The general expression for calculating the volume-relative logical block address in terms of cylinders, tracks, and sectors is shown for the cylinder i, track j, sector k. Its form is

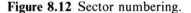

Table 8.3 Physical and logical disk addresses

Physical address			Logical address	
Cylinder $0 \le c \le C-1$	Track $0 \le t \le T-1$	Sector $0 \le s \le S-1$	(Volume-relative) $0 \le l \le CTS-1$	
0	0	0	0	Track 0
0	0	S - 1	S - 1	Cylinder 0
0	T - 1	0	$(T-1)S$	Track T - 1
0	T - 1	S - 1	$(T-1)S + S - 1$	
i	0	0	iTS	Track 0 Cylinder i
i	0	S - 1	$iTS + S - 1$	
i	j	k	$iTS + jS + k$	Track j Cylinder C - 1
C - 1	T - 1	S - 1	CTS - 1	Track T - 1

$$l = iTS + jS + k$$

where S is the number of sectors per track, and T is the number of tracks (and read/write heads) per cylinder. Both of these values are constant for a given device. Lastly, the maximum volume-relative logical block address is

$$CTS - 1$$

where C is the cylinders per volume constant of the device in question, and CTS is its capacity expressed in terms of sectors.

The expression given for the volume-relative logical address, l, above can be used to calculate the three-component physical addresses. Namely, given l, and knowing the device constants T and S, the address triple $< i, j, k >$, where i is the cylinder number, j the head number, and k is the sector number, can be determined as follows. First, l is divided by TS in order to obtain i. That is,

$$\frac{l}{TS} = i + \frac{(jS + k)}{TS}$$

Note that i is the quotient and that the expression in parentheses is the remainder of integer division of l by TS. Since both the head and sector numbers are bundled in the remainder, it is first divided by the constant S in order to obtain the head number j. That is,

$$\frac{(jS + k)}{S} = j + \frac{k}{S}$$

So, as a result of integer division of the previously obtained remainder by the device constant S, we obtain the head number j as a quotient and the sector number k as the remainder. In order to see how this process works, let us apply it to our running example of a READ operation.

Let us assume that we are dealing with a hypothetical 10-MB disk formatted with the sector-size of 512 blocks. There are 10 sectors per track, 4 tracks per cylinder (two platters with four surfaces and one read/write head on each), and 512 cylinders. Thus, the device constants are

$$C = 512$$
$$T = 4$$
$$S = 10$$

Having determined earlier that our starting volume-relative logical block address l is 339, we convert it to the corresponding physical address as follows. First, the logical address is divided by TS, which is 40 in our example.

$$339 \text{ div } 40 = 8, \text{ remainder } 19$$

This gives us the cylinder number 8 and the remainder of 19 for figuring out the head and sector numbers. Dividing this by S, which is 10, we obtain

$$19 \text{ div } 10 = 1, \text{ remainder } 9$$

Therefore, the head number is 1, and the sector number is 9. By repeating this process for the other two block numbers, or by simply incrementing the physical address using the knowledge of the disk-counting scheme, we can obtain the remaining two physical disk addresses, which are <8, 2, 0> and <8, 2, 1>, respectively.

8.5.4 File-Related System Services

In this section we recapitulate and expand the description of the run-time file services to include some of the issues introduced in previous sections.

The basic range of operations of the CREATE call is outlined in the form of a rather abstract functional specification given in Program 8.1. As indicated, the first step is to search the symbolic directory, specified by means of the path name, in order to find out whether the supplied file name already exists in it. Handling of attempts to create a new file under the name which is already in use differs depending on the system in question and on its approach to the naming of files. In general, when file extensions are supported, files with the same names but different extensions are regarded as distinct files. In systems that support version numbers, creation of a new file when the name-extension tuple is already in use results in creation of the file with the same name and extension but with a different version number. If all different components of a file name specified in a CREATE command are in use, some systems simply allow the new file to routine CREATE (filename, attributes);

  begin
    search directory for filename;
      if found report duplicate, or create new version, or overwrite;

    locate a free directory entry;
      if none allocate a new one;

    allocate space for the file; {all, some, or none}
      record allocated blocks in directory;

    record file attributes in directory
  end;

Program 8.1 Functional specification of Create

overwrite the old one, while others treat this situation as an error and refuse to take any further action.

    In any case, the file name is recorded in the related symbolic file directory, and an internal system_ID is obtained for it. The usual practice is to record new entries in the directory in some unused position and to expand the directory only in cases when no room can be found. Some systems limit the size of directories at the volume-initialization time. If this is the case, creation of a new file may result in a directory-full error being returned by the file system. Following recording of the file name, the file system may allocate space for the file being created. Allocation of space at this point is customary in systems with contiguous allocation and not too common for noncontiguous allocation policies. In cases when some space is allocated, this information is recorded in the basic file directory. After recording other file attributes on the basis of user-supplied values and applicable system defaults, most of the CREATE-related work is completed. In some systems, CREATE is regarded as an implicit opening of the same file. In that case, a call to OPEN is made from the CREATE routine.

    The primary purpose of the OPEN file service, whose functional specification is given in Program 8.2, is to establish a run-time bond between the calling program and the specified file. After verifying that the target file exists and that the caller is authorized to access it in the desired mode, the file system usually responds by creating a file control-block (FCB). An active FCB usually contains a copy of the related directory entry, the file marker, the identity of the owner, and whatever other information is maintained by the system for actively used files. The address of the file control-block, or a pointer to it, is usually returned to the calling process in the form of a connection_ID. Since the calling process uses the connection_ID in all future references to the file, the operating system can provide fast directory and file access by using the related information recorded in the file control-block specified by the connection_ID. Finally, by informing the system about the identities of files in active use, maintenance of file control-blocks facilitates concurrency control of shared files. When several distinct users open the same file for concurrent access, each of them is normally assigned a distinct routine OPEN (filename, access_ mode) : connection_ID;

{call: connection_ID := OPEN (filename, access_mode);}

```
begin
    search directory for filename;
        if not found indicate error and return;

    verify authority to access the file in desired mode;
        if not authorized indicate error and return;

    create file-control block FCB;

    create connection_ID for the FCB;

    initialize file marker;

    return connection_ID
end;
```

Program 8.2 Functional specification of Open

file control-block. As a result, each user has its own marker and is thus allowed to address elements of the shared file independently of other concurrent users. Some systems even allow two or more tightly coupled users, such as coroutines, for example, to even share the same file control-block and with it the file marker. This mode of operation is usually announced by means of a separate version of the OPEN call, which returns a copy of an existing connection_ID to the calling process.

As its brief specification given in Program 8.3 indicates, the SEEK command is processed by updating the file marker to point to the byte or to the record whose logical address is supplied by the caller. Naturally, the legitimacy of the user-supplied connection_ID is first checked in order to make sure that an authorized user is making the request. The SEEK command usually has no effect when applied to a sequentially structured file. Some systems simply ignore such calls, while others treat them as errors.

Program 8.4 is a functional specification of operations typically performed by the file system when processing a READ request. Given the possibility of various errors when reading data, the service is assumed to be structured as a function that indicates the outcome of its operation by means of the STATUS

routine SEEK (connection_ID, logical_position);

```
begin
    verify legitimate connection_ID;
    calculate desired position;
    update file marker
end;
```

Program 8.3 Functional specification of Seek

routine READ (connection_ID, num_bytes, in_buffer) : status;

{call: status := READ (connection_ID, num_bytes, in_buffer);}

    begin

        verify legitimate connection_ID;

        verify file open for read; {access authorization}

        synchronize with other active users if necessary; {sharing}

        calculate number and addresses of sectors to read; {mapping}

        verify target addresses are within the file boundary; {protection}

        issue read command(s) to device driver, multisector if possible;

        verify outcome;

        copy num_bytes of data from internal buffers to in_buffer; {deblocking}

        update file marker;

        return status

    end;

Program 8.4 Functional specification of Read

return. After satisfying itself that the user-supplied connection_ID is valid and that the user is authorized to read the related file (file open for read or for read/write), the system checks whether the file is to be accessed concurrently with other users. This check may be performed by traversing the list of file control-blocks. If necessary, the appropriate synchronization mechanism can be invoked at this point. In any case, the user-specified logical address and range are translated into the corresponding number of disk blocks designated by their physical addresses. At this point, the file system may check whether the requested blocks are within the confines of the target file by inspecting the SIZE field of the related directory entry. If applicable, the system may attempt to initialize a multisector disk READ. Otherwise, one or more sector READ commands are issued to the disk driver.

For deblocking purposes, the common practice is to direct such reads into internal buffers of the file system rather than into the user's area designated by means of the IN_BUFFER parameter of READ. The necessary bytes are then extracted from the buffer and copied into the user-designated area starting from the IN_BUFFER location. As discussed in Chapter 3, the use of multiple buffers can significantly improve the effective I/O rate of certain operations. Given relatively long disk-access times and very fast transfer rates, disk I/O is usually extensively buffered. Some systems allow specification of the extent of the file buffering to be made at system-generation time. A more flexible approach is to substitute or to augment this facility by specifying the degree of buffering at the file-open time, subject to available memory. Rather than allocating buffers to each open file connection, some systems attempt to optimize the use of available file buffers by pooling them together. For example, a typical Unix installation may have in excess of 50 buffers. Thus, more than 50 disk sectors may be available in memory at any given time. Potential advantages of disk buffering include

- Overlapped disk I/O operations on different drives and controllers
- Fast file access when index blocks are held in memory
- Fast allocation of space by keeping portions of the Free list in memory
- Prefetching of data
- Ability to reduce the number of disk I/O operations by retrieving blocks from buffers in main memory

The first point follows from our discussion of I/O concurrency in Chapter 3. The remaining points are based on the assumption that the system keeps track of the identity of the specific sectors available in system buffers and attempts to satisfy user request from memory whenever possible. Thus, if a needed index block or a set of pointers to the Free list is found in memory, the disk overhead of indexing may be significantly reduced. Similarly, the potential slowdown of sequentially accessed indexed files can be virtually eliminated by prefetching the next blocks in sequence into system buffers. For example, many implementations of Unix prefetch disk blocks upon detecting a sequential pattern of successive requests made by a given process.

Lastly, the number of disk I/O operations can be reduced with buffering by using a version of the *delayed-write* policy. This policy refers to performing writes on buffers rather than directly to disk. Each buffer that is written into, but not copied to disk, is marked accordingly. When a request for allocation of a new buffer is made and no free buffers exist, some buffer-replacement strategy, such as least-recently-used, is employed to select a victim among the buffers in use. If the buffer selected for replacement is marked as "dirty," it is copied to disk prior to being released for allocation. Otherwise, "clean" buffers are simply overwritten by the new contents. Note that this is very similar to the page-replacement techniques discussed in relation to virtual memory.

The described pool of buffers is usually internal to the operating system. After completion of the requested transfers between disks and internal buffers, the file system performs the necessary blocking or deblocking of data and copies them to the user address-space indicated in respective READ and WRITE calls. In order to avoid the overhead of two buffer-copy operations for reads and writes, some systems allow certain classes of users to access system buffers directly. For example, the RSX-11M operating system allows two modes of data transfer, called the *Move mode* and the *Locate mode*. The Move mode is a classical scheme with full buffer copying. The Locate mode does not copy data to the user's space, but returns pointers to system buffers where the data can be found.

Program 8.5 outlines the basic structure of a WRITE routine. Except for the direction of transfer, the only important difference from the READ service is that WRITES can be used to extend the file. When this is the case, the file system calls the space-allocation module to provide the required number of free routine WRITE (connection_ID, num_bytes, out_buffer) : status;

{call: status := WRITE (connection_ID, num_bytes, out_buffer);}

   begin

      verify legitimate connection_ID;

      verify file open for write; {access authorization}

      synchronize with other active users if necessary; {sharing}

      if file is extended allocate required blocks; {allocation of space}

      update directory if new blocks added;

      calculate number and addresses of sectors to write;

      copy num_bytes of data from out_buffer to internal buffers; {blocking}

      issue write command(s) to device driver, multisector if possible;

      verify outcome;

      update file marker;

      return status

   end;

Program 8.5 Functional specification of Write

blocks, if any. Depending on the particular space-management policy in use, the directory and file-index blocks may have to be updated in order to reflect the new acquisitions. In any case, the file marker is updated accordingly after each disk write.

The last file-related system service described in this section, CLOSE, breaks the connection between the caller and the file whose connection_ID is passed as a parameter. CLOSE, whose functional specification is left to the reader, basically undoes the work of OPEN by closing the references to the file. If the copy of the directory entry held in the file control-block has been updated during its memory residence, it is written back to disk. After performing whatever additional housekeeping may be necessary, CLOSE releases the related file control-block to the free pool from which the FCBs are allocated. In many systems, processing of forceful and voluntary terminations of processes includes the closing of all open files. This can be accomplished by making one call to CLOSE from EXIT or ABORT routines for each file opened by the related process.

8.5.5 Asynchronous Input/Output

Since processing of READ and WRITE calls usually entails one or more disk accesses, their execution times may be relatively long compared to the CPU-bound routines of similar complexity. In order to maintain high levels of performance, many systems allow these operations to execute concurrently with calling processes. Asynchronous execution of file-related services is usually a special case of the general I/O strategy of a given system. Without getting into details, let us briefly outline the skeletal structure of an advanced I/O system.

An input/output system usually includes an I/O scheduler, an I/O traffic controller, and a number of device drivers, such as the disk driver discussed earlier. Like its CPU counterpart, the I/O scheduler decides which process gets a device, when, and for how long. The I/O scheduler is also charged with allocating dedicated I/O processors and channels in systems where they exist. The I/O traffic controller keeps track of the status of devices, such as free or in use. The primary function of device drivers is to convert generic I/O commands, such as READ and WRITE, into device-specific control signals and protocols.

The I/O system usually queues I/O requests issued by user processes until they are actually scheduled for processing. As indicated in Chapter 3, issuing of an I/O request normally suspends the calling process until the related I/O operation is completed. This mode of operation is often called *synchronous I/O*. In terms of flow of control, a synchronous I/O request appears to the issuing process as a subroutine. This is because the called routine retains control until the I/O is fully completed and the caller can make no other progress in the meantime. An alternative implementation, called *asynchronous I/O*, allows both the calling process and the called I/O routine to proceed in parallel after an I/O request is issued. The I/O system usually accomplishes the asynchronous mode of operation by creating a dedicated process to handle each user's request or by means of server processes, such as the printer-server described in Chapter 5.

In any case, the caller is free to continue after issuing an asynchronous I/O request. The two processes must eventually synchronize in order for the I/O system to report the outcome of the related I/O operation to the calling process and to furnish the obtained data in case of READ operations. Depending on the facilities and on the philosophy of the underlying operating system, this synchronization can be accomplished in a number of ways, such as by means of event flags, asynchronous system traps, or signaling messages. In any case, the typical sequence of events may be summarized as follows.

When a user process issues an asynchronous I/O request, it specifies the necessary parameters for subsequent synchronization with the I/O process. The I/O system creates or activates an I/O process to handle the user's request, and both processes continue to execute on their own. When the user process needs the data obtained from the related device, it issues a corresponding synchronization system call, such as wait on the event flag or wait for the synchronization message. Upon completion of the I/O operation, the I/O process signals the fact by setting a specified event flag or by sending a synchronization message. As is the case with most forms of asynchronous operation, when both processes indicate their willingness to communicate, the related exchange of data takes place.

Returning to the file system, better system performance is expected when READ and WRITE operations are asynchronous to the calling process. In such cases, some sort of a WAIT call should be included in the system to allow user processes to synchronize with the I/O system upon completion of a related READ or WRITE request. Some advanced and high-performance systems support both synchronous and asynchronous versions of I/O services and allow the user to choose whichever they deem to be more appropriate for the application at hand.

8.6 A GENERALIZATION OF FILE SERVICES

As suggested on several occasions in this chapter, device-independent I/O provides both an ease of use and flexibility not attainable by most other approaches. Device independence is essentially a form of delayed binding of user programs to I/O devices. User programs are coded and prepared using an abstraction of devices, such as logical I/O ports or logical unit numbers. These abstract devices are bound to actual devices at run-time by means of system calls or the command language. The latter option allows users to ASSIGN logical I/O ports to the actual system devices prior to running their programs.

In order to provide a common abstraction of many different types of I/O devices, it is customary to regard all devices as files in the sense of having a name and allowing bytes to be read from or written into them. A major division between *byte-serial* and *block-structured* devices is usually made. Some systems refer to these as unstructured and structured I/O, respectively. In any case, the former class includes devices capable only of byte-serial transfer, such as printers and terminals. The second class includes block-structured storage devices on which traditional files may be kept. Devices belonging to either class may be accessed by means of the same set of system services, such as OPEN, CLOSE, READ, and WRITE. The SEEK operation may be meaningfully applied only to block-structured devices. While creations and deletions are customary for files, devices are usually regarded as permanent objects created at the system-startup time. Specific device attributes, such as write-only for printers and read-only for keyboards, are also defined at that time. User processes can gain access to a specific device by means of the OPEN call. Depending on the type of device, exclusive or shared type of access may be granted to requestors. After performing a series of READs or WRITEs with the device, the user process can break the connection by means of the CLOSE call.

This uniformity of treatment allows users to handle both files and devices by means of a single set of system calls. Another advantage of device independence is that it facilitates the portability of object code between systems with different hardware configurations. This is made possible by the run-time binding of programs to real devices. As a result, device specifications can be changed without reprogramming.

The basic ideas of uniformity of I/O commands and device independence are powerful concepts that can be applied to other parts of the operating system as well. For example, some systems use an interprocess communication mechanism called a *pipe*, which is similar to messages but can be programmed using the standard set of file and I/O services. A pipe is a virtual communication channel that can be used to connect two processes wishing to exchange a stream of data. The two processes communicating via a pipe can reside on a single machine or on different machines in a network environment. A pipe can be written into at one end and read from the other. The operating system usually provides automatic buffering for the data within a pipe and implicit synchronization between the processes communicating via a pipe. For example, the pipe writer may be delayed while the pipe is full, and the process wishing to read from an empty pipe may be suspended until some data arrive. As indicated, this form of interprocess communication is conceptually similar to the message facility. The difference is that the pipe facility does not require explicit synchronization between communicating processes, does not require explicit management and formation of messages, and is handled at the system-call level in exactly the same way as files and device-independent I/O. At the command-language level, pipes are often used to connect output from one program as the input to another program without any reprogramming and without the use of temporary files. This use of pipes is discussed in Chapter 11 in relation to the Unix operating system.

A pipe can be created, or accessed if it already exists, by means of an OPEN call. A writer process normally produces streams of data that it WRITEs into the pipe. A reader process consumes data from the pipe by means of READ calls. When all data are transferred, the pipe can be closed or destroyed, depending on whether its further use is anticipated or not. Like messages, pipes allow the asynchronous operation of senders and receivers of data, as well as many-many mapping between senders and receivers.

Thus, the same basic set of system calls are used for handling devices, files, and pipes. The generality of this approach allows an additional form of interprogram communication that is established by means of the command language and without any special programming. Namely, since files and devices are treated uniformly, output from and input to a program may easily come from either. Therefore, a program can read a line of input from a terminal, a file, or another program, and these may be varied from one run to another without reprogramming. Similarly, output of a program can be sent to a device or fed directly into another program. For example, a text checked for spelling by the spelling checker can be saved in a file, displayed on a terminal, or passed on directly to the text formatter. By allowing this form of I/O redirection, programs that are not specifically programmed to work together, such as a spelling checker and a text formatter, can be combined to perform a new complex function without any reprogramming. By cascading several utilities in this way, users can construct powerful functions out of simple basic utilities that can go beyond what their original designers may have envisioned.

8.7 SUMMARY

The file-management portion of an operating system manages the information that resides on secondary storage. This information is usually stored on the long-term basis in the form of named files. Lists of file names are cataloged in special files called directories. One-level, or flat, directories contain a list of all files in a system or on a given volume. Hierarchical directories allow grouping of logically related files into subdirectories. Subdirectories are usually managed in the form of a rooted tree. In general, hierarchical directories facilitate the unique naming of files, support more flexible forms of controlled sharing and selective protection of files, and can be more convenient for browsing than large flat files. Hierarchical directories are more complex to manage than flat files, but their advantages are considered to outweigh their drawbacks by many system designers.

Users can manipulate files and directories of a computer system by means of the command language and by means of the run-time system calls. At the command-language level, users can LIST directories, RENAME or DELETE files, CREATE files or directories, and perform other volume and media manipulations. Most of these services are also available to users by means of run-time calls to the file system that can be invoked by executing programs. Moreover, run-time calls can be used to retrieve and modify portions of files by means of the OPEN, READ, WRITE, and CLOSE services.

In addition to providing these services, the file system must also perform other duties, such as enforcement of file protection and access control, managing of storage space, and mapping of user-specified logical addresses to the physical addresses understood by device controllers. File-protection and access-control information is stored as a part of the file description which is available or accessible through the related directory entry. User authorization to perform the requested operation is verified as a part of each file-related operation.

Management of the secondary-storage space consists of keeping track of both the space allocated to existing files and the free space available for allocation. The space-allocation strategy affects the speed of access to files, the complexity of logical to physical address mapping, and disk utilization. Contiguous allocation is generally simple to implement, and it provides efficient sequential and random access to files. On the negative side, contiguous allocation of secondary-storage space suffers from external and internal fragmentation, which can cripple disk utilization unless costly compaction is performed to reclaim the fragmented space.

Chained allocation is a noncontiguous space-allocation scheme conceptually similar to a linked list. Chaining eliminates external fragmentation, facilitates handling of bad blocks, and is relatively simple to implement. The disadvantages of chaining include slow random access to files and sensitivity to damaged pointers. Indexing is a form of noncontiguous allocation that provides faster random access while retaining most of the advantages of chaining. The main drawback of indexing is the disk-access overhead imposed by the need to look up index blocks in order to locate the data blocks of a file. This problem can be alleviated by keeping frequently used indices in main memory.

The mapping of logical file addresses into device-specific physical addresses is usually performed in stages in order to confine device-specific knowledge into the lowest-possible layer of the file-control system. At the user-level, files are perceived and addressed as linear, named arrays of bytes. Requests made at this level are then translated into an intermediate internal view of a secondary storage device as a linear array of logical blocks. This view is mapped by device drivers into physical device addresses — such as cylinder, head, and sector addresses in the case of disk drives. Finally, device controllers produce the device-specific signals, such as SELECT_DRIVE and STEP_TO_CYLINDER, required by the physical drives.

Many advanced operating systems provide device-independent I/O, where files and logical I/O devices are treated by a single, unified set of system services at both the command-language and system-call levels. In such systems, user processes can be interchangeably connected to pipes, files, or I/O devices. This facility is often coupled with the run-time binding of processes to devices, which makes compiled programs insensitive to configuration changes and provides considerable flexibility in managing resources of a computer system.

OTHER READING

A thorough treatment of secondary storage devices and of the file system is provided by Wiederhold (1983). Data structures for the file system are discussed by Dodd (1969), Knuth (1973a and b), and in many books on computer data structures, such as Horowitz and Sahni (1982).

Operating-system texts dealing with the file system include Shaw (1974), Calingeart (1982), and Peterson and Silberschatz (1983). An especially detailed treatment is provided by Madnick and Donovan (1974).

Some aspects of file systems in the IBM OS/360 and in the Burroughs Master Control Program (MCP 1700) are described by Dependahl and Presser (1976). An excellent overview of the requirements and characteristics of database operating systems is provided by Gray (1979). Stonebreaker (1981) examines typical file-related OS services in terms of their suitability for providing a foundation for a database-management system.

Implementations of file systems and of disk drivers are presented by Comer (1984) and by Joseph, Prasad, and Natarajan (1984). Implementation of and improvements to the stream-level I/O in Unix are discussed by Ritchie (1984). A fast file system for Unix is described by McKuscik et al. (1984).

EXERCISES

8.1 Identify the file-related commands and system calls provided by an operating system accessible to you, and discuss their similarities to and differences from the comparable commands and services described in the text. As an exercise, write a program that copies its own source-code file to another file. Run the program, compile the file that it produces, and run the resulting program in order to determine whether it executes correctly.

8.2 What are the tradeoffs involved in choosing one of the three levels of abstraction of disk representation for the storage and addressing of memory pages in a virtual-memory system? Indicate which level of disk abstraction you consider to be the most suitable for that purpose and explain why.

8.3 A disk drive has 305 cylinders, 4 heads, and 17 sectors of 512 B each per track. The disk is rotated at 3000 rpm, and it has a moving-head assembly with an average head-positioning time of 30 ms. The peak data-transfer rate that the drive can sustain is 4 Mb/s. Calculate the best-case and the worst-case times needed to transfer 20 consecutive and 20 randomly distributed blocks (sectors) from such a disk. Indicate the dominant factors in determining the transfer times and the variability between the best-case and the worst-case figures. Specify clearly the best-case and the worst-case assumptions.

8.4 Some operating systems routinely delete files created during an interactive session when the related user logs off, except for those which the user explicitly requests to be retained. Discuss the relative advantages and disadvantages of such systems in comparison with systems that permanently maintain all files until explicitly deleted. For the latter type of systems, discuss how the operating system might guard against excessive consumption of secondary storage space by users who do not clean up the intermediate and temporary files that they no longer need.

8.5 Some commercial operating systems support a restricted form of the hierarchical file system in which each user is assigned a separate subdirectory and no subdirectories can be formed below that level. All user-file directories (UFD) are cataloged in the master-file directory (MFD). In effect, such systems provide a two-level tree directory. Discuss the relative advantages and disadvantages of such systems in comparison to single-level directory systems and to general treelike directory systems, especially with regard to file protection and sharing. Indicate under which conditions a user of such a system might access another user's file, and suggest how system utilities—such as editors, libraries, and compilers—might be accessed without having to maintain multiple copies of them on the secondary storage.

8.6 The concept of the working directory in hierarchical file systems provides the convenience of allowing users to specify only partially qualified file names when manipulating files contained in the current working directory. Devise a method to extend this facility so as to allow users to reference frequently used system utilities stored in other subdirectories by providing only their partial qualification and without leaving the current working directory. Your solution must not require creation and maintenance of multiple physical copies of files. Provide a specification of the additional system commands and services needed to support your solution, if any.

8.7 Provide a functional specification of the data structures and routines necessary to implement a tree-structured hierarchical directory system. Indicate specifically which routines are callable by users and which are internal to the operating system. Your solution should allow the system and possibly the user programs to LOOKUP a directory for a given entry, to ADD a new entry to a directory, and to REMOVE an entry from a directory. Explain how your proposal handles file protection. For simplicity, your solution may be restricted to a single volume, and you may assume that concurrent access to files is not permitted.

8.8 Calculate the number of disk accesses needed to read 20 consecutive logical blocks of a file in a system with:

(*a*) Contiguous allocation

(*b*) Chained allocation

(*c*) Indexed allocation of space

Discuss your findings using the figures from Exercise 3 for illustrative purposes if necessary, and explain the timing differences between the logical block accessing and the physical block accessing.

8.9 Explain what clustered allocation of space is and how it works. Discuss the advantages and disadvantages of clustered allocation when used in conjunction with each of the three disk-space allocation schemes presented in the text relative to their counterparts without clustered allocation of space.

8.10 Indicate at which points and how the address-calculation example presented under Address Translation in Section 8.5 is affected when the underlying file system uses

(*a*) Chaining

(*b*) Indexing methods of disk-space allocation instead of contiguous allocation, as assumed in text.

8.11 Explain what interleaving is, how it works, and how—if at all—it affects the logical-physical translation of disk addresses. In particular, discuss whether interleaving affects the disk-numbering scheme presented in the text, and if so, suggest an alternative scheme suitable for interleaving. In your opinion, can and should knowledge of interleaving be confined only to the related disk driver? Explain your reasoning.

8.12 Consider a system that uses the bit map for free-space allocation. Rather than maintain the bit map on the disk, the system constructs it on the fly on the basis of directory information. Provide a functional specification for the routine and data structures necessary to construct and manage the bit map in such a system. Indicate how your solution handles bad blocks, and specify what information—if any—must be kept on disk for that purpose. Contrast your solution to the alternative implementation in which the entire bit map is kept on the disk and is loaded into main memory when the related volume is brought online (mounted).

8.13 A modified version of chained allocation of disk space is proposed. All linking pointers of a volume are collected in a file called the file-allocation table (FAT). At run-time, actively used portions of FATs belonging to mounted volumes are kept in main memory in order to speed up file access. Provide a functional specification of data structures and routines necessary to support the proposed method of file access. Indicate precisely which data structures are kept on disk, which are kept in main memory, and when each of them is updated. Explain how your solution affects the space-allocation algorithm, and compare its efficiency and speed of file access to the ordinary chained allocation of space.

8.14 Explain what the purpose of the OPEN and CLOSE services is, and suggest a way to eliminate them by making their functionality implicit in other system calls. Discuss the relative advantages and disadvantages of the resulting system in comparison to a system with explicit OPEN and CLOSE services.

8.15 Explain what the purpose of the file control-block is, and provide a functional specification of its structure. Discuss the relationship and linkage, if any, between a process control-block and the file control-blocks of the files opened by a given process. Provide an expanded functional specification of the run-time file services affected by the specification of the file control-block. When a file is concurrently open by several processes, should each process construct a separate file control-block for its connection to the shared file, or should the involved processes share a single file-control block? Discuss the relative merits of each approach, and propose a strategy that you consider to be the most appropriate for managing sharing of files.

8.16 Discuss the tradeoff between a system-wide pool of buffers that are dynamically allocated to handle I/O with actively used files and a static system in which one or more buffers are assigned and dedicated to each opened file. Compare the two approaches in terms of computational complexity and the speed of file access as a function of disk-space allocation schemes and user file-referencing patterns.

NINE

DESIGN OF A KERNEL OF A MULTIPROCESS OPERATING SYSTEM (KMOS)

In this chapter we investigate some aspects of the operating-system design process by means of designing a kernel of a multiprocess OS. Most ingredients of a typical operating-system kernel are described in the preceding chapters. Following the common approach to analysis, specific topics therein are treated with a certain degree of isolation from the rest of the system, thus highlighting the particular and attenuating the effects of interaction with other components. Our goal now is to explore how the individual building blocks presented so far may be combined to form a working system. While integrating the system, our primary concern will be the interactions among its constituents.

The term *kernel* usually denotes the lowest layer of an operating system which is directly above the hardware. In our hierarchy of operating-system layers introduced in Chapter 1, a kernel represents Layer 1. A typical kernel may, among other things, provide the services listed below to other software layers of an operating system and to system users:

1. *Interprocess communication and synchronization.* A set of mechanisms and related primitives necessary to support both functions
2. *Interrupt management.* Typically, vectoring of interrupts, saving and restoring of state, and management of priority levels, including selective level enabling and disabling
3. *Process management.* ·Functions described in Chapter 3, such as creation and deletion of processes, delaying of processes, and the like
4. *Booting and startup of the initial system configuration.*

In addition, a kernel usually handles some supporting activities necessary to provide the services visible to other OS layers. Examples of such internal kernel operations include system time-base management and CPU allocation by means of basic process scheduling. The kernel design discussed in this and the following chapter assumes that all user processes are resident in memory when the kernel receives control of the CPU. This assumption is valid in many embedded computer systems where the application programs are placed in unalterable read-only memory (ROM). In larger, general-purpose systems, the kernel usually relies on other layers to bring the user processes into main memory. Bringing of the kernel itself into main memory is discussed under System Startup in Section 9.4.

In an embedded application a run-time subset of a kernel may be all the system software that is provided on the target machine, whereas in a complex multiprogramming system the kernel is typically enclosed by additional layers of an operating system. Our decision to design a kernel is partly motivated by the fact that it is present in virtually every multiprogramming operating system, from the simplest real-time monitor to the large multiuser system with batch, time-sharing, and possibly real-time and network services provided in parallel. In a sense, a multiprocess kernel may be regarded as a common denominator of multiprogramming operating systems. As discussed in Chapter 3, kernel activities and even the functions of its basic primitives are quite similar across a wide range of operating systems. At least functionally, a kernel is one of the most stable parts of an operating system. Otherwise, any change in the interface specification of a kernel primitive may necessitate changes in all upper layers that call on it. Being closest to hardware, a kernel may be thought of as the first-level functional extension of the bare machine.

As a consequence of all these properties, most attempts to put the operating system in microcode or silicon begin with kernel primitives. Several actual products provide operating-system kernels in read-only memory. These "silicon operating systems," which can be used with a given microprocessor, are largely invariant to the rest of the system hardware configuration. One microprocessor vendor offers an operating-system-firmware (OSF) component consisting of a real-time multitasking (multiprocess) kernel in ROM, programmable interval timers, and a programmable interrupt controller, all housed in a single chip. An interesting aspect of this kernel on a chip is that it has survived, without modifications, several major revisions of the enclosing operating system, which is quite complex. In terms of the layered approach carved in silicon, the same chip is touted as providing some 30 additional operating-system instructions to the instruction set of the basic microprocessor with which it is used. Indeed, with interrupts off while executing a kernel primitive, there is hardly any conceptual difference for the users between "proper" hardware instructions and those handled by the operating-system chip. This chip is described in greater detail in Chapter 11 (Section 11.3).

While designing a sample multiprocess operating-system kernel (KMOS, pronounced "keymos"), we attempt to mimic the actual design process as much as possible, including the motivation for and evaluation of the various design options and tradeoffs as they are encountered. The chapter begins with an informal definition of the range of services to be provided by KMOS. This paves the way for the subsequent discussion of major design decisions and for the functional specification of KMOS services. In the preparation for implementation, some issues regarding the selection of a systems-implementation language and the choice of a method for invoking system services are discussed in the last section of this chapter.

Readers interested in the functional organization of a kernel but not in details of KMOS may read portions of this chapter and omit the entirety of Chapter 10 without loss of continuity. Readers with no interest in kernels may omit most of Chapter 9 and all of Chapter 10 without loss of continuity. Section 9.5 contains a discussion of some implementation considerations, such as characteristics of the systems-implementation languages and hardware instructions for invoking the operating system, which may be of general interest.

9.1 DEFINING KMOS SERVICES

In this section we outline the range of KMOS services, both the services provided to users, that is, directly callable by other software layers, and the internal supporting activities that may not be invoked by routines external to the kernel.

The multiprocess aspect implies the need to support concurrent execution of processes and to provide services for interprocess communication and synchronization. Perhaps less visible but equally important kernel functions include management of interrupts and basic process scheduling.

An early decision to be made when designing an OS kernel involves selection of the interprocess synchronization and communication mechanisms. One of the primary considerations here is to make sure that the chosen set of services (and thus system primitives) is functionally complete in the sense of supporting adequately both forms of interprocess exchange. Messages, which may serve both interprocess synchronization and communication in centralized as well as distributed systems, obviously warrant consideration. Their adoption in KMOS is motivated by the desire to keep the design simple, by virtue of having a single mechanism which, as discussed in Chapter 5, can additionally be used to field interrupts from hardware sources to user's interrupt-service routines.

For the sake of simplicity, and without sacrificing generality, we may opt for event-driven, that is, priority-based, preemptive scheduling of processes. In general, a well-designed kernel should provide flexible mechanisms to be used as building blocks by higher software layers. In particular, a kernel should provide mechanisms and defer implementation of policies such as those governing resource allocation. By choosing event-driven scheduling, it may appear that our KMOS violates this principle. However, this is not the case, because some basic scheduling must be done by the kernel in order to control the execution of processes. In real-time systems, the priority-based scheduling offered by KMOS may be adequate for application to all processes. In systems with more varied requirements, OS processes and interrupt-service routines are often scheduled on the basis of their priority, whereas user processes and utilities may be handled by another scheduling algorithm implemented by an upper-level layer of the operating system. The tools for implementing additional scheduling mechanisms, such as time-slicing, can be provided in KMOS by building on the existing support for interval-timer and system time-base management. Since our list of kernel activities does not include management of input/output devices, we also leave their implementation to the enclosing software layers, which may make the resulting operating system into either a single-user or a multiuser system.

Before deciding on the complete list of services to be provided by KMOS, let us point out that our aim is to illustrate the kernel-design process in a realistic way, but also to keep the outcome simple and comprehensible by, among other things, avoiding unnecessary and distracting details. In this spirit, we strive to provide a small but functionally complete system which combines aspects of all the important issues discussed in previous chapters, such as interrupts, process-management, scheduling, and interprocess interactions. To make things realistic, KMOS is very similar and functionally comparable to several multiprocess kernels. In addition, the version of KMOS presented here is used to control operation of a remote telemetry unit (RTU) in a commercial data-acquisition and control system, which is described in Chapter 11 (Section 11.4).

Having made some major design choices, let us briefly discuss KMOS services in terms of the list of typical OS kernel functions given earlier.

Interprocess communication and synchronization Since messages are to be used for both purposes, we need to implement some sort of SEND and RECEIVE operations. In order to provide the most general many-to-many mapping between senders and receivers, KMOS should manage mailboxes and support at least their creation, say, by means of the CREATEMBOX system call.

Interrupt-management Given that messages are also used to synchronize interrupt-service routines with hardware interrupts, it is sufficient to provide some services for manipulation of the interrupt levels, such as enabling of a level, say, by means of the ENABLEV system call.

Process-management Obviously, the first necessary function is to create a process, so we need a CREATEPROC primitive. Suspending and resuming of processes may be indirectly accomplished at the user level by means of message primitives, so a minimal kernel need not provide specialized system calls for that purpose. In order to support clock-driven forms of scheduling as well as the requirements of real-time applications, we should provide a system call to delay execution of a process for a specified period of time; let us name this KMOS service DELAY.

Booting and startup of the initial system configuration Although they all provide some form of this service, operating systems differ greatly in the details of how system initialization is actually performed. We defer specification of this part of

KMOS until System Startup in Section 9.4, pending elaboration of some related implementation details.

In summary, we need to implement at least the following system calls in KMOS: SEND, RECEIVE, CREATEMBOX, ENABLEV, CREATEPROC, and DELAY. Before discussing the internals of KMOS necessary to provide these services, let us first point out what KMOS does not do. As specified, KMOS provides only the means for creation of objects, such as mailboxes and processes, but not for their termination. For example, services such as DELETE_PROCESS, DELETE_MAILBOX, and DISABLE_LEVEL are missing. These functions, as well as other system services such as the remaining process-management calls discussed in Chapter 3, should be part of a kernel which is to serve as a foundation for a complex operating system. On the other hand, in some embedded applications where the size or the overhead of the executive may be critical (such as the system in which KMOS is actually used), the proposed KMOS kernel may be adequate as is. Namely, system processes and real-time processes tend to be permanent, as opposed to the transient processes common in program-development systems. In order to make KMOS useful in such different environments while keeping it as simple as possible, we opt to implement the kernel as specified with the added provision of designing system-data structures for easy addition of the omitted system calls. As we progress with the implementation, such expansion hooks are pointed out where appropriate. Several problems at the end of chapter involve the design of additional KMOS facilities.

9.2 MAJOR DESIGN DECISIONS

Before specifying the functions and formats of KMOS service calls provided to users, we must decide some issues regarding internal KMOS organization, including messages, interrupt processing, and data structures.

In Chapter 5 we discovered that a message facility may be implemented in several different ways depending on the particular forms of naming, copying, and buffering used in a given system. In the previous section we already adopted the indirect form of message exchange via mailboxes. In order to provide for the asynchronous communication of senders and receivers necessary to support the most general forms of signaling and fielding of interrupts, let us opt for message buffering at the kernel level. For generality, variable-length messages should be supported. Finally, in order to avoid the issue of protection and the details of dynamic memory-management, message-passing in KMOS may be implemented by passing a pointer rather than by copying the contents of a message from the sender's to the receiver's space.

As demonstrated in Program 5.6, the message facility can also be used to signal the arrival of hardware interrupts to the user-provided interrupt-service routines. The appeal of providing a single unified mechanism to handle both interprocess interactions and interrupt fielding is a compelling reason to adopt this approach in KMOS. This feature may be provided by dedicating a mailbox to each potential hardware source of interrupt, such as terminals, disks, and A/D converters. Whenever an interrupt of sufficient priority (higher than that of the running process) is asserted by an I/O port, KMOS should do the preliminary low-level processing and send a system-signaling message to the related mailbox. A process wishing to service interrupts from a given source may do so by receiving the corresponding system messages via RECEIVE calls on the specific mailbox. Obviously, KMOS must also perform the necessary housekeeping operations, such as interrupt-level management by means of masking interrupts according to the priority of the running program, context-switching, and some sort of interrupt acknowledgment. We defer a detailed discussion of these issues until Interrupt-Management in Section 9.4.

In order to support the DELAY function, KMOS must keep track of the elapsed time. This is usually accomplished by means of a dedicated interval timer that is initialized and serviced by the OS. Once started, the timer generates interrupts in approximately regular intervals. If vectored to the operating system, these interrupts may serve as the system time base.

Whenever a computer system is brought up, the operating system must initialize itself and the hardware and create the environment for the initial configuration of processes. When all this is done, control may be passed to the first user process. From that point on, the system becomes event-driven in the sense that the behavioral patterns of executing processes, together with the occurrences of events that cause rescheduling, dictate its further state transitions. In general, an operating system acts both as a watchdog by intervening to do the housekeeping necessary to record and complete the required state transitions and as a controller charged with maintaining a certain level of performance. Allocation of resources and more sophisticated scheduling policies are usually delegated to higher-level layers of an operating system, leaving mostly housekeeping and basic mechanisms to kernels. Save for its simple priority-based scheduler, KMOS is not an exception in that regard.

As discussed in Chapter 3, KMOS can keep track of processes and their individual state changes by maintaining a process control-block (PCB) for each active process. The initial form of a PCB can be established at the process-creation time, which is indicated by invocation of the CREATEPROC primitive. Static process attributes, such as initial priority and starting address, are commonly entered into its PCB at this time.

A newly created process is usually made ready and its PCB is enqueued in the Ready list to await selection by the scheduler. Following a burst of CPU activity, the running process may surrender control to the operating system or be preempted as a result of the occurrence of an interrupt. In either case, the context of the running process must be saved, say, in the related PCB, for subsequent restoration when the process is scheduled to run again. In a multiprocess system, such as KMOS, a number of processes may be active and in different stages of execution at any time. Their collective state can be tracked by the operating system by means of system lists of PCBs. For this reason, KMOS data structures ought to include some form of Ready and Suspended lists. As we proceed with the functional specification of KMOS, we may uncover a need for some additional lists.

9.3 PROCESS-STATE TRANSITIONS IN KMOS

On the basis of the general specification of the range of services to be provided by KMOS, as well as on the basis of the assumptions made in this section, we can construct the KMOS-specific state transition diagram given in Figure 9.1. As discussed earlier, processes are created by means of the CREATEPROC call. A newly created process is assigned a PCB and made ready, as indicated by an arrow between the Dormant and Ready states in Figure 9.1. Whenever an event that causes rescheduling is processed, KMOS schedules the highest-priority ready process to run. A running process has its stream of instructions executed until it is preempted, say, by a higher-priority interrupt, or until it voluntarily surrenders control to KMOS by executing a system call. Depending on the state of the system and on the nature of the invoked service, KMOS may or may not subsequently return control to the calling process.

As indicated in Figure 9.1, the running process regains control immediately after creating a mailbox (CREATEMBOX) or creating a process (CREATEPROC). However, the running process may preempt itself by sending a message to a higher-priority process that is already waiting. Namely, after the

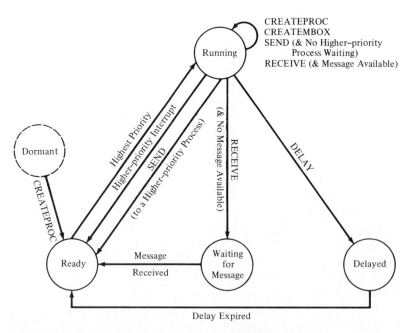

Figure 9.1 Process state-transitions in KMOS.

message in question is delivered by KMOS as a result of execution of the SEND primitive, both the sending and receiving processes are ready, but the receiver is scheduled due to its higher priority. Given asynchronous exchange of messages, sending a message in any other case—such as when there are no waiting recipients or there are one or more but of lower priority than that of the sender—does not cause the running process to lose control of the CPU after execution of SEND.

Situations leading to possible suspension of the running process are somewhat more involved. The simplest one results from invocation of the DELAY function, which simply suspends the running process for the specified period of time. The *Delayed* state is introduced in Figure 9.1 to handle the described situation. The Delayed state is effectively an instance of the more general class of suspended states. As indicated in Chapter 3, it is sometimes desirable to introduce several different instances of the suspended state according to the specific reason for suspension. Another variation of the suspended state suitable for KMOS is the *Waiting-for-message* state also shown in Figure 9.1. Processes enter this state after invoking the RECEIVE call when no messages are available at the specified mailbox. Conversely, invocation of the same KMOS service results in both a message and control being returned to the running process when one or more messages happen to be available at the designated mailbox.

The final note regarding process-state transitions in KMOS depicted by Figure 9.1 concerns the influence of device interrupts and external events in general. Given the use of messages to signal occurrences of interrupts to their service routines in KMOS, interrupt servers spend their time between activities in the Waiting-for-message state. The arrow marked Interrupt, leading from Running to Ready state, refers to the situation when the running process is preempted by a higher-priority interrupt, which causes an interrupt-service routine (ISR) of higher priority than that of the running process to become scheduled for execution. Presumably, such an ISR is hibernating in the Waiting-for-message state until an interrupt from its related source arrives. The (lower-priority) process, which happens to be running when the interrupt occurs, is preempted, but it remains ready and is thus eligible for subsequent consideration by the scheduler.

9.4 FUNCTIONAL SPECIFICATION OF KMOS

Following the usual design procedure, we now proceed with the functional specification of KMOS on the basis of the decisions and assumptions made thus far. This material will serve as a foundation for the subsequent implementation of KMOS described in Chapter 10. Our primary goal in this section is to organize KMOS activities into a set of routines and to specify their activities, interactions, and interfaces. At this stage of the design process, our main interest is in *what* each routine must do rather than *how* it does it. In this way we can focus on designing the overall structure of the system without overcommitment to particular data structures or specific algorithms. Once such a skeleton of the system is built and major interactions are defined, a detailed specification of data structures can be made with much greater confidence that some later "insights" are not likely to necessitate major revisions.

For example, the functional specification should reveal not only the types of operations on the Ready list, but also the specific routines that perform them. As a result, a rough estimate of the frequency and relative importance of a specific operation, such as insert or delete, can be made at this point. Consequently, an adequate data structure and an efficient algorithm for most often or time-critical operations on the Ready list may then be devised and implemented.

It is admittedly very tempting to focus on a specific part of the system, perhaps well known or intriguing to the designer, early on in the design process and to write some code either to establish the feasibility of a conceived approach or to make some "tangible progress" on the project. Failure to resist this temptation almost invariably leads to premature freezing of certain design choices, with the designer's intuition substituting for a more systematic and thorough analysis of their role in the overall structure of the system. In any system of nontrivial complexity, such an approach is likely to result in numerous revisions of already completed modules in order to accommodate the needs of others whose requirements were not anticipated properly. The resulting patched routines and refurbished data structures can hardly be combined to produce a reliable and efficient code.

Even with the disciplined approach to system design, several iterations both within and between different design phases are often necessary to complete the system. However, with the goals and purposes of each iteration clearly defined at its outset, the design process and its final result are much less likely to be frustrating or to get out of control.

9.4.1 Process Dispatching

Let us now return to the functional specification of KMOS. As our earlier discussion and Figure 9.1 suggest, traffic-management is an important function of an operating-system kernel. Whenever a running process is preempted or suspended, the kernel must save the process's context for proper subsequent resumption. In general, the context of a process encompasses that part of the run-time environment which must be recreated by the operating system to ensure proper operation of the process when it is resumed after a period of inactivity. In particular, each system routine in KMOS whose execution results in a rescheduling of processes must save the context of the process which was running when KMOS was entered. As Figure 9.1 reveals, that may be the case with a number of KMOS calls. When a new running process is selected by the scheduler, KMOS must restore the context of that process before actually surrendering control of the CPU to it. This function of an operating system is often called *process dispatching*, so let us entrust it to a DISPATCH routine in KMOS.

DISPATCH is an internal KMOS routine which transfers control to the new running process after restoring its context. In a sense, DISPATCH is an exit routine from KMOS which should be invoked after each rescheduling in order to enforce the scheduling decision. The identity of a new running process must be made known to DISPATCH, so that the related PCB can be found and used to restore the target context. Therefore, functional specification of the DISPATCH routine may be made in the form presented in Program 9.1.

DISPATCH and the subsequent functional specifications of KMOS services are presented in a pseudo-high-level language. The word *routine* indicates a tentative structure which later in the design process may evolve into a subroutine, a process, or perhaps a part or combination thereof. As indicated earlier in this section, the "statements" of a functional specification are meant to serve as a reminder of what the related routine should do rather than how it does it. As a result, rules of syntax are not followed closely, and many details are vague or omitted.

9.4.2 Interprocess Communication and Synchronization

As a consequence of the decision to implement a buffered-message facility for the purposes of interprocess communication and synchronization, KMOS must support management of mailbox and message objects. In addition, SEND and RECEIVE primitives need to be provided to system and user processes that wish to interact with other processes or system devices.

Mailboxes and messages. Operating systems that support a mailbox-based exchange of messages often combine all information necessary for management of a given mailbox into a data structure called a *mailbox descriptor* (MBD). A separate mailbox descriptor is usually dedicated to each active mailbox. An MBD may be formed and initialized at the message-creation time, indicated by execution of the CREATEMBOX call. Not unlike the relationship between processes and PCBs, the user's concept of a mailbox as a repository of messages is supported at the OS level by creation and management of a related mailbox object. Let us briefly review the role of a mailbox descriptor and its possible format in KMOS.

As discussed in regard to process-state transitions in KMOS, when a running process sends a message to a specific mailbox by means of the SEND call, the message can be immediately delivered to a waiting process, if any. However, if there are no processes suspended at that mailbox by an unmatched RECEIVE, the message is left in the mailbox and the running process continues to execute. In this way, several messages can be accumulated in a given mailbox awaiting

```
routine DISPATCH (process); {internal, KMOS use only}
{dispatches a new running process}

   begin
      do {other} housekeeping;
      establish run-time environment for the process;
      restore context of the process;
      surrender control to the process
   end;
```

Program 9.1 Functional specification of Dispatch

delivery to the receiver process. Since KMOS is to buffer outstanding messages, a portion of each mailbox descriptor may be used as a header of the queue of messages awaiting delivery at its related mailbox.

On the other hand, when a running process invokes a RECEIVE system call on a mailbox where no messages are awaiting delivery at that time, the calling process enters the Waiting-for-message state and remains suspended until arrival of a message at the designated mailbox. Due to the nature of message exchanges in KMOS, it is possible that several processes may be awaiting delivery of messages at a given mailbox. Since each such process may be resumed only when a message is delivered to it, mailboxes look like a good place for the matching of processes to messages and vice versa. The idea to queue outstanding messages at a mailbox may thus be extended to include the queuing of processes when receivers temporarily outpace senders of messages to a given mailbox.

The Waiting-for-message state of processes in KMOS can be handled by a fragmented version of the Suspended list, one fragment per mailbox, whereby PCBs of waiting processes are enqueued at the particular mailbox descriptor where the message is to be received. In this way, the reason for suspension of a given process may be deduced from the identity of the mailbox where it is waiting. This approach is likely to be more efficient in KMOS than a straightforward implementation of a single monolithic Suspended list. The reason is that waiting processes can now be directly matched to arriving messages, as opposed to searching about one-half of a potentially large Suspended list in order to find a matching recipient, if any, whenever a process sends a message.

In summary, a mailbox serves as a meeting place of processes and messages. KMOS keeps track of mailboxes by means of mailbox descriptors. A mailbox descriptor in KMOS must be structured in such a way that either messages (resulting from the execution of unmatched SENDs) or control-blocks of suspended processes (resulting from the execution of unmatched RECEIVEs) can be queued at it. Due to the nature of interprocess communication in KMOS, messages or processes, but not both, may be queued at a given mailbox descriptor at any time.

Among the numerous possible service disciplines for waiting processes and messages, FIFO and priority queues are quite popular. FIFO is a likely candidate for KMOS because it is simple to implement and it ensures that, with the proper supply of messages, waiting processes cannot be subjected to indefinite postponement. In addition, the strongest implementation of semaphores and some classical problems in concurrency control may best be served by FIFO delivery of waiting messages. Finally, the use of messages to signal interrupt arrivals in KMOS precludes the use of any queueing discipline other than FIFO.

Some multiprocess operating systems use priority ordering of waiting processes, thus providing for potentially superior response time to high-priority processes than FIFO, but at the expense of the possibility of indefinite postponement and inconveniences when emulating semaphores. An approach adopted in some more complex systems is to support both forms of queuing and to enable system programmers to select the option most appropriate for servicing a particular mailbox.

In order to serve interprocess message communication, a mailbox must first be created by means of the CREATEMBOX call in KMOS. Typically, a sender or the system-initialization module (discussed under System Startup in Section 9.4) may be charged with this task. Creating a mailbox in KMOS is a fairly straightforward operation. It normally results in formation of the related mailbox descriptor capable of queueing messages or processes. When a mailbox descriptor is created, both queues are empty and their headers must be initialized to reflect that fact. As far as message communication in KMOS is concerned, no further operations on a mailbox descriptor need be performed by the CREATEMBOX routine.

In general, however, requests to send messages to or to receive messages from a nonexisting mailbox (deleted or not created) should be denied by the operating system. Although the presented version of KMOS omits this run-time check for reasons of simplicity and performance, we design the mailbox descriptor in KMOS in a way that facilitates the subsequent implementation of this feature. Deletion of an existing mailbox is another service not offered by KMOS but which may be desirable in a larger operating system. Both these extensions call for a list of all mailbox descriptors in the system. Entries to this list can be added whenever a new mailbox is created, and removal of entries can be made when the operating system is required to delete a mailbox. When only a validity check is desired, this list may be searched to find whether the target mailbox descriptor is in active use, say, by virtue of being created but not deleted. Requests to use active mailboxes can then be granted, and others can be denied, with a corresponding error code being returned to the calling process. With the Mailboxes list added to KMOS, the functional specification of CREATEMBOX may be devised as presented in Program 9.2.

Mailbox descriptors and the Mailboxes list can be of further use in operating systems that require processes to declare their affiliation with active mailboxes, for example, by means of an ATTACH(MAILBOX) call. In such systems, a process may DETACH itself from a mailbox that it no longer uses. Similarly, a

```
routine CREATEMBOX (mailbox); {user callable}
{creates a mailbox}
   begin
      save caller's context;
      allocate storage for the mailbox descriptor;
      with mailbox descriptor do
         begin
            initialize queue of messages to empty;
            initialize queue of processes to empty
         end;
      enter mailbox descriptor in Mailboxes list;
      restore caller's context;
      return control to caller
   end;
```

Program 9.2 Functional specification of Creatembox

departing process may be detached from all its mailbox holdings by the operating system as part of the EXIT-call processing.

With ATTACH/DETACH supported, the operating system is enabled to detect unused mailboxes by keeping track of the number of processes actively attached to them. Superfluous mailboxes can then be deleted by the operating system immediately upon detachment of the last related process, reflected by the attached-count in the corresponding mailbox descriptor becoming zero. In this way, the operating system essentially performs event-driven garbage collection of mailboxes. This feature is particularly important in distributed operating systems, where the cost of maintaining an open intersite communication channel may be quite high. KMOS data structures for message exchange allow for the addition of the ATTACH/DETACH mechanism when desired.

SEND and RECEIVE operations. The functional specification of the KMOS facility for sending messages, SEND, is given in Program 9.3. As indicated, SEND needs two parameters: the identity of the MAILBOX (descriptor) where the MESSAGE is to be delivered and the MESSAGE itself. When SEND is invoked by the running process, either processes or messages may be found waiting at the designated MAILBOX descriptor. When no processes are waiting, the MESSAGE cannot be delivered immediately, and SEND enqueues it at the MAILBOX descriptor before returning control to the caller, the running process in this case. Alternatively, if one or more processes are waiting, SEND delivers the MESSAGE to the first in line.

```
routine SEND (mailbox, message); user callable
{sends message to the mailbox}
    begin
      save caller's context;
      if no processes waiting
        then
          begin
            queue up the message at the mailbox descriptor; {FIFO}
            restore caller's context;
            return control to caller {running process}
          end
        else {processes waiting}
          begin
            remove message_recipient from the mailbox process queue;
            deliver the message to the message recipient;
            make message_recipient ready;
            running := schedule the next process to run;
            dispatch (running)
          end
    end;
```

Program 9.3 Functional specification of Send

Since delivery of a message results in both the running process and the message recipient becoming ready, the scheduler should be invoked to determine which process should receive control after the completion of SEND. Prior to that, the context of the running process must be saved in case it is preempted by the message recipient. In any case, the message recipient is made ready and its PCB is moved from the mailbox queue to the Ready list.

Given the priority-based scheduling in KMOS, the next process to run is the highest-priority ready process. The scheduler in KMOS is thus reduced to finding the highest-priority process in the Ready list. Since structure of the Ready list in KMOS still remains to be specified, no particular searching algorithm can be suggested as yet. After scheduling, SEND invokes the DISPATCH routine to establish the run-time environment for, and to transfer control to, the new running process.

Two subtle but relatively important points can be made about the suggested functional specification of the SEND primitive in KMOS. First, like all system routines callable by users, SEND begins by saving the context of the calling process. The saved context is restored when control is eventually returned to the process that has invoked the system service. In the case of SEND, if the message cannot be delivered immediately and control is returned to the sender, the sender's (caller of SEND) context is restored. Alternatively, if the message is successfully delivered, its sender may or may not be the next process to be dispatched. Thus, SEND cannot blindly restore its caller's context, and the restoring of the proper context is left to the DISPATCH routine, which learns the identity of the next running process from the scheduler. The details of the context save-restore operations are system-specific, and they depend on such things as the format of the system data structures, the type of instruction used to invoke the operating system, the amount of context switch (process switch) done by the underlying hardware, the memory-management and protection policies in effect, and the like.

The second point regards potential selection of the next running process within the body of SEND. Namely, when the message is delivered to a waiting process, there are only two viable candidates from which to select the next running process: the caller of SEND (previously running process) and the message recipient. Given the priority-based scheduling in KMOS, probably a more efficient version of SEND may be constructed so that the priorities of the two processes are compared and the scheduling decision is made within SEND. In this way the scheduler need not be invoked, whereas saving the context of the running process and restoring the context of the message recipient are performed only when the priority of the running process is comparatively lower, so that invocation of SEND results in its preemption.

The problem with this approach is that it would build a policy rather than a mechanism into the logic of SEND. Any subsequent change of the scheduling policy would then necessitate corresponding modifications in all routines, such as SEND, which are dependent on it. On the other hand, the functional specification of SEND, as given, is based on the philosophy that each particular OS function should be entrusted to a separate routine that should have the sole authority to perform the given function. Consequently, SEND is not allowed to make any scheduling decisions, even when the algorithm is simple and only two processes are involved. By localizing the focus of each activity into a dedicated OS routine, the system is likely to be easier to comprehend, to develop, and to maintain, thus increasing programming productivity and yielding a potentially more reliable product.

The insights gained by the functional specification of SEND make the process of devising the logic of RECEIVE, whose functional specification is given in Program 9.4, quite straightforward. RECEIVE takes one parameter, identity of the mailbox where the message is to be received, and returns a message to the calling process. For this reason, RECEIVE is specified and intended to be called as a function. When invoked by the running process, RECEIVE may find one, more, or no messages and perhaps some processes waiting at the designated mailbox. Upon finding at least one message, RECEIVE removes the message from the MAILBOX and delivers it to the calling process—in this case the running process, which is not preempted. Alternatively, if no message can be delivered, the running process is suspended at the MAILBOX (descriptor) and a new running process is scheduled and dispatched.

9.4.3 Interrupt-Management

Interrupt servicing in KMOS relies heavily on the message-exchange mechanism. Basically, each hardware interrupt is intercepted by KMOS and converted into a corresponding system message, which is then sent to the mailbox dedicated to

```
routine RECEIVE (mailbox) : message; {user callable}
{delivers a message from the specified mailbox}
   begin
      save caller's context;
      if messages waiting
         then
            begin
               dequeue the first message from the mailbox descriptor;
               give message to the calling process; {running process}
               restore caller's context;
               return control to caller
            end
         else {no message available}
            begin
               suspend the calling process at the mailbox descriptor;
               running := schedule new running process;
               dispatch (running)
            end
   end;
```

Program 9.4 Functional specification of Receive

the interrupt level in question. As discussed in Chapter 2, the operating system should take responsibility for the dynamic disabling of lower interrupt levels and the enabling of higher ones, commensurate with the priority level of the running process. Depending on the available hardware support, the hardware/software division of labor for this activity may vary considerably. In order to avoid machine-dependent details, we assume that KMOS is to be implemented on system configurations that include an interrupt controller or equivalent hardware support for all three levels of interrupt masking discussed in Chapter 2: the system-wide level (interrupts on/off), the individual priority level (selective masking), and the individual device level (I/O port control register). This assumption is satisfied even by microcomputers when they are fitted with a programmable interrupt controller.

In order to support priority-based scheduling, KMOS must keep track of the priority of each process. As discussed in Chapter 3, a common practice is for a system programmer to assign priority to each process and to communicate this parameter to the operating system, so that the priority can be entered into the process's control-block at process-creation time. In order to keep the number of system services low and to reduce the overall system complexity, we opt for static priorities in KMOS.

In principle, an operating system should differentiate between *hardware priority levels*, which may be assumed by the related interrupt-service routines (ISR), and *software priority levels*, which are assigned to all other processes. Hardware priorities are commonly used to drive the interrupt-enable/disable logic and they are placed above software priorities to achieve low latency in response to interrupts. In this scheme, processes are scheduled according to their software priorities when no interrupt-related activities are ready to use the CPU. Due to its uniform handling of interprocess communication and of interrupt signaling via messages, strict differentiation between ISRs and other processes and consequently between hardware and software priority levels is not mandatory in KMOS. However, some means are required for instructing KMOS which particular interrupt levels should be enabled and which disabled when an ISR is running. A simple scheme for accomplishing this may be to partition KMOS priority levels into interrupt-related and other (software) levels. One such sample partitioning is discussed in Chapter 10.

An internal KMOS routine for handling interrupts, ITSERV, is specified in Program 9.5. All hardware interrupts in a KMOS environment are supposed to be vectored to entry of the ITSERV routine. After saving the context of the preempted running process, ITSERV identifies the hardware priority level of the asserted interrupt request. This information is used to send the system-interrupt message to the related interrupt mailbox, designated as MAILBOX[LEVEL]. For reasons of portability and hardware independence, KMOS should not be involved in any device-specific interrupt processing and should not communicate directly with any I/O port other than the programmable interrupt controller (PIC).

A PIC, or its functional equivalent, is a highly desirable form of hardware support for multiprocess operating systems, especially those intended for real

routine ITSERV; {not software callable}
{processing of hardware interrupts}

  begin
    {entered upon a hardware interrupt}
    save context of the running process;
    mark its state preempted;
    identify the source level of interrupt;
    acknowledge interrupt to interrupt controller; {PIC}
    send interrupt_message to mailbox[level];
    if no process waiting at mailbox[level]
      then
        begin
          running := schedule new running process;
          dispatch (running)
        end
  end;

Program 9.5 Functional specification of Itserv

time. Assuming that a PIC is available to KMOS, ITSERV prevents repetitive processing of the same interrupt by acknowledging the request to PIC. Finally, ITSERV sends the interrupt message to signal arrival of the interrupt to the service routine. Naturally, ITSERV should rely on the SEND routine to relay this message and to activate a waiting-service process, if any. If no process is waiting for the interrupt message at the related mailbox, SEND returns control to its caller, ITSERV. Since its work is finished, ITSERV surrenders control to the new running process selected by the scheduler.

Although the proposed specification of ITSERV assumes that individual interrupt levels can be enabled and disabled selectively, we have not specified where and how these operations are done in KMOS. Given the possibility of direct mapping of a KMOS priority level into a corresponding hardware priority level, the DISPATCH routine is probably the best candidate to set the PIC or other interrupt-masking registers so that all higher interrupt levels are enabled and the lower or equal levels are disabled when the running process receives control of the CPU. This operation can be performed as a part of "other housekeeping" in the DISPATCH routine.

In addition to this form of interrupt control, it is customary to allow users to explicitly enable and disable individual levels of interrupt. At system-initialization time, user-serviced interrupt levels are typically disabled and mapped to the operating-system routine for detection and handling of false interrupt requests which could otherwise hang up the system. Some process, most commonly a user-written interrupt-service routine, must then first explicitly enable the interrupt level of the device that it services. One way to implement user-level interrupt enabling is to maintain an internal system-interrupt mask which is initially set to all interrupt levels off. The system service to enable a specific level may then simply turn on the corresponding bit or bits in the system mask. Finally, the operating system, when surrendering control to a process, may enable only those interrupt levels which are both higher than that of the running process and enabled by an earlier system call.

The previous discussion provides the basis for the functional specification of a KMOS routine for enabling an interrupt level, ENABLEV, whose functional specification is given in Program 9.6. Routine ENABLEV takes one parameter, the interrupt level to be enabled. The number of interrupt levels in a given system is generally hardware-dependent, and it may vary between KMOS implementations for different processors. A sample interrupt system is described in Chapter 10. As discussed, ENABLEV simply manipulates the corresponding bit in the system-interrupt mask SYSMASK. This implementation implies that SYSMASK is set to all levels off at the system-initialization time. In principle, ENABLEV can also be charged with creating the interrupt mailbox for the enabled level. To keep things simple, the proposed specification assumes that this is done at KMOS-initialization time for all interrupt levels in a given hardware configuration.

9.4.4 Process-Management

The process-management functions in KMOS are reduced to process creation and to delaying a process for a specified period of time.

Process creation. As discussed in Chapter 3, creation of a process entails initial formation of the process control-block, typically followed by the process's transition to the Ready state. When a process departs the system, its PCB is normally returned to the pool of free PCBs.

For reasons similar to those discussed in relation to the Mailboxes list, a run-time validity check of process names passed as parameters to system calls is a useful feature in an operating system. For example, a request for an indefinite suspension or forceful abortion of a process normally returns an error indication if the specified process is nonexistent, perhaps because it terminated or was never created. Authentication of process names can be conveniently performed when a list of all nondormant processes in the system is maintained by the

```
routine ENABLEV (interrupt_level); {user callable}
{enables a hardware interrupt-level}
   begin
      save caller's context;
      if interrupt_level is valid
         then turn on the sysmsk[interrupt_level] bit;
      restore caller's context;
      return control to caller
   end;
```

Program 9.6 Functional specification of Enablev

OS. Although the validity of process names is not checked by KMOS, such a functional extension is made possible by maintaining the All-processes list. The elements of this list are the process control-blocks, which can be added at the process-creation time and removed when the related process departs the system. With this addition, specification of the CREATEPROC routine in KMOS may be given as presented in Program 9.7.

Routine CREATEPROC associates a process control-block with the newly created process, enters the initial values of the process attributes, such as process priority, and enters the PCB into All-processes and Ready lists. Note that no rescheduling is done following process creation in KMOS, and control is always returned to the calling process. As a result, the newly created process may become the running process only upon occurrence of an event that causes the scheduler to be invoked, such as a timer interrupt.

Delaying of a process for a specified time. Delaying of a process for a specified amount of time is the second process-management function of KMOS. In principle, a process wishing to delay itself invokes the DELAY routine and specifies the duration of the desired delay. The operating system normally services such requests by means of two separate but cooperating activities. The calling process is first suspended and placed in the list of delayed processes, and the number of system clock-ticks corresponding to the duration of the delay is recorded in the related PCB. Secondly, whenever an interrupt from the interval timer is processed, the operating system decrements the number of remaining intervals in the PCBs of all the processes in the Delayed list. Each process whose delay is found to be expired, by virtue of the related count becoming zero, is resumed by being placed into the Ready list.

In keeping with the localization of functions within separate routines in KMOS, we may implement the two described activities as two separate routines. The first of them, DELAY, is specified in Program 9.8. After suspending the caller and recording the number of time intervals (clock-ticks) to delay the caller, DELAY causes dispatching of a new running process in a standard

```
routine CREATEPROC (process_ID, process_attributes); {user callable}
{creates a process and makes it ready}

   begin
      save caller's context;
      allocate space for a PCB[process_ID];
      enter process_attributes into PCB[process_ID];
      initialize other PCB[process_ID] fields;
      enter PCB[process_ID] into All-processes list;
      enter PCB[process_ID] into Ready list;
      restore caller's context;
      return control to caller
   end;
```

Program 9.7 Functional specification of Createproc

```
routine DELAY (time); {user callable}
{places the calling process into Delayed list}

   begin
      save caller's context;
      place caller's PCB into Delayed list; {suspend}
      set caller's status to delayed;
      record time as number of clock ticks to wait;
      running := schedule new running process;
      dispatch (running)
   end;
```

Program 9.8 Functional specification of Delay

way. The functional specification of the routine for processing timer interrupts, KMOSCLOCK, is given in Program 9.9.

The proposed specification of KMOSCLOCK reflects our enhanced understanding of the operation of KMOS. In a typical design process, the definition of each new mechanism may require the redefinition of other functions to incorporate the new mechanisms into previously specified routines. For example, this was the case with our subsequent augmentation of the functions of the DISPATCH routine. In this chapter we take the approach of specifying a routine on the basis of the accumulated knowledge about the KMOS system as discussed up to that point and leave redefinitions to the reader. This should, hopefully, provide a realistic illustration of the various stages of the specification process.

In the particular case of KMOSCLOCK, we rely on the interrupt signaling mechanism of KMOS to do context manipulation and to send a message for each timer interrupt. Consequently, KMOSCLOCK can be conceptualized as a process, as all interrupt-service routines under KMOS should be viewed. In its initialization section, KMOSCLOCK initializes the programmable interval-timer for the desired duration of a system time unit, i.e., clock-tick. Following this, the corresponding interrupt level is enabled in order to allow recognition of timer interrupts. In its repetitive section, KMOSCLOCK is activated upon each timer interrupt (expiration of a clock-tick) to decrement the TICKS_TO_WAIT count of each process in the Delayed list. Processes whose delay has expired are then effectively resumed by being placed into the Ready list.

This concludes our functional specification of KMOS calls. Each major KMOS service is specified for a system in normal operation, that is, the calling processes are in memory and all necessary data structures are properly initialized. We now discuss how a KMOS-based system can be initialized to its operational state.

9.4.5 System Startup

Whenever a computer system is "cold-started," say, after being powered or following a system crash, at least a portion of the operating system must be brought into main memory and given control of the CPU. This activity is often

```
process KMOSCLOCK; {ISR, running under KMOS}
{timer interrupt processing}
  begin
    initialize hardware interval_timer;
    enablev (hardware_timer);
    forever do
      begin
        {enter upon timer interrupt}
        receive interrupt message at timer mailbox;
        decrement ticks_to_wait of each process in Delayed list;
        for all processes where ticks_to_wait = 0 do
          begin
            remove process from Delayed list;
            insert process into Ready list
          end
      end {forever do}
  end;
```

Program 9.9 Functional specification of Kmosclock

called *system booting* or *bootstrapping* of an operating system. Typically, the hardware initially transfers control to a known address where a starting routine in ROM is placed. This routine, called the *bootstrap loader*, can be used to bring the rest of the system gradually to main memory, for instance, from the secondary storage or from another node in a distributed system. In disk-based systems, the core portion of the operating system is often placed at a known address, called the *boot block* or *boot area*, of a known system-disk drive. Thus, the bootstrap-loader routine can include a rudimentary form of a disk driver whose primary function is to load and activate the initialization section of the operating system. This section can, in turn, load into main memory the rest of the operating system and complete the initialization process. In memory-based systems, such as KMOS, the starting routine can simply transfer control to the operating system, which itself may be residing in ROM.

In any case, once in memory, the operating system typically initializes hardware and system data structures, creates the initial configuration of system and user processes, and transfers control to one of them. From that point on, control of the CPU oscillates between active processes and the operating system in response to and in accordance with the changes of system state and the resource-allocation policies in effect.

Initialization of user processes poses a chicken and egg problem: if a process must be created in order to start executing and a process must be executing in order to invoke OS services—including creation of processes—the question is: Who or what creates the first user process in a freshly initialized system? In many interactive multiuser systems this problem is solved by having the operating system create the command-language interpreter process for at least one terminal. This process can then create other processes in response to user commands.

Incidentally, the command-language interpreter is treated as a system process in some operating systems and as a user process in others. Some advantages of the latter approach are discussed in Chapter 11 in relation to the Unix operating system (Section 11.2).

In embedded systems and in many specialized applications, however, there may not be a single-user process—such as the command-line interpreter—which should be present and therefore activated automatically by the operating system in every installation. Thus, a more general solution is for the operating system to create a known process, user-definable but system-initiated, whenever the system is started. At least a portion of the program for this process, let us call it INITPROCESS, can be defined by the system manager or a programmer to include create calls for the initial configuration of user objects, such as processes and mailboxes. By convention, the INITPROCESS is always the first user process to receive control from the operating system.

It is also customary to facilitate creation of a large number of objects by structuring the INITPROCESS so that it can process a set of user-provided object-definition tables. In disk-based systems, this function is often accomplished by having the INITPROCESS routinely execute commands provided in a known file consisting of object-activation commands. The system manager can edit this file or define its entire contents and thus have the desired processes created whenever the system is started.

In any case, a working system is needed to define the initial configuration of a target system. For example, a working system is needed to edit the startup command file or develop the user-specified portion of the INITPROCESS. In large disk-based systems, this problem is often solved by having a version of the operating system that works on the target configuration delivered and installed by the vendor. The system manager can then fine-tune the system and define the desired post-startup configuration of processes by means of *system generation*, a set of programs and procedures for tailoring the operating system for a target configuration. In embedded and other memory-based applications, the target configuration rarely supports program development and the operating system is usually defined on a different host machine. The configured operating system and application programs are then transferred to the target machine by means of some nonvolatile medium, such as ROM or bubble memory, or downloaded from the host through a communication link or an in-circuit emulator. In the downloading case, a resident program (say, in ROM) is required on the target machine to carry out the necessary communication and loading procedures.

Since KMOS is specified as a memory-based system, we assume that all the KMOS code, as well as the code of processes to be run under it, is in memory when control of the CPU is initially transferred to KMOS. In the next chapter we explain how this is accomplished in a sample ROM/RAM-based system. The starting routine of KMOS should thus initialize the hardware needed for the proper operation of KMOS. Based on our previous discussion, this may include initialization of the programmable interrupt controller. In order to be as hardware- and configuration-independent as possible, KMOS should not initialize any other

I/O ports that may be available in a specific system configuration. This task may best be accomplished by the individual interrupt-service routines themselves when they eventually receive control of the CPU for the first time, as illustrated by the KMOSCLOCK process presented earlier. As indicated in Chapter 2 and in our discussion of ITSERV, hardware initialization is customarily done with interrupts off, so that no I/O may take place until the system is ready to handle I/O properly.

Likewise, KMOS must initialize its own data structures before surrendering control to the first user process. These include all system lists and pointers, such as Ready and Delayed lists, and global-system data, such as SYSMASK. At this point, the initial configuration of user processes and their related mailboxes can be created.

A small problem with implementing the INITPROCESS in KMOS is that we do not provide any services for destruction of processes, so that INITPROCESS would unnecessarily have to exist in the system forever. In order to avoid this problem, we can opt for the object-definition table approach with a modification that the KMOS startup module, after initializing hardware and system data structures, creates all processes and mailboxes defined in user-supplied tables. For example, users can provide a list of processes and mailboxes to be created by KMOS by means of two global tables: the initial process table (IPT) and the initial mailbox table (IMT), respectively. With these assumptions, the START routine in KMOS may be specified as given in Program 9.10.

9.5 IMPLEMENTATION CONSIDERATIONS

In this section we discuss two issues that must be resolved in any implementation of an operating system: selection of a programming language or languages, and choice of a method for invoking the operating system.

```
routine START; {internal, KMOS use only}
{initializes the system}

  begin
    {control passed by hardware}
    disable interrupts;
    initialize hardware
      .PIC;
    initialize KMOS data structures
      .list pointers to nil
      .queue headers to empty
      .global variables to initial values;
    create processes supplied in Initial Process Table;
    create mailboxes supplied in Initial Mailbox Table;
    running := schedule new running process;
    dispatch (running)
  end;
```

Program 9.10 Functional specification of Start

9.5.1 Systems-Implementation Languages

Before commencement of coding, a systems-implementation language (or languages) to be used for implementation should be selected. By a *systems-implementation language*, we mean a high-level programming language with provisions for systems programming. Although there has not been official standardization of language support for systems programming, there seems to be some agreement among practitioners as to which features in a language are necessary for systems implementation. Some of those are listed below:

1. Facilities for modular program development
2. Access to hardware and to physical memory addresses

We briefly review each of these in the subsequent sections.

Facilities for modular program development. Facilities for modular program development generally refer to facilities for the individual compilation of modules and for the maintenance of module libraries. These facilities are very useful in large programming projects, both for an individual programmer and for programming teams. Depending on whether type checking is preserved or not across module boundaries when different modules belonging to a single program are compiled at different times, module compilation is said to be separate or independent, respectively. *Independent compilation* refers to the ability to compile individual modules of a single program independently. Independent compilation does not provide type checking across module boundaries; in its basic form only definition of public symbols (defined in one module but used by several) and external symbols (used in a given module but defined elsewhere) is supported. Independent compilation is a familiar tool provided, for example, by Fortran and PL/I compilers and by many commercial assemblers. In systems where standard calling and parameter-passing conventions are observed, independent compilation facilitates the combination of object modules coded in different programming languages.

For example, combining high-level language (HLL) modules with those written in assembly language is a common practice in systems programming. In general, HLLs offer the potential for increased programmer productivity, higher product reliability, and comparative ease of maintenance. Assembly language, on the other hand, offers high performance and allows virtually unrestricted access to hardware. In the absence of appropriate systems-implementation language with facilities discussed later in this section, a reasonable approach to systems programming is to code everything initially in a high-level language. After some operational testing to establish the feasibility and correctness of the logic of the particular solution, certain time-critical operations may be identified and coded in the assembly language. Some hardware and software measuring aids and tools, such as logic analyzers and HLL profilers, are available for pinpointing the areas most likely to benefit from the increased speed of execution. In principle, only operations requiring direct access to hardware and those on which performance of the entire system critically depends should be considered for coding in assembly language. When used, assembler code should be made as structured as possible. An interesting approach that has been used in some commercial systems is to hand-optimize the code generated by the compiler, as opposed to writing the assembly-language portion from scratch. If local per-statement optimization is done, the HLL code can serve for program documentation and testing purposes.

The inability of independent compilation to enforce typing across module boundaries, that is, to ensure that an external identifier is used in a given module in accordance with its type as declared in the identifier's home module, can be a serious problem. For example, referring to nonexistent fields of an external record structure can create havoc at run-time without even an indication at compile-time. This difficulty is directly attributable to independent compilation, since it is not otherwise encountered in strongly typed languages, such as Pascal, when the entire program is compiled as a single unit. Standard Pascal does not allow independent compilation, mainly to enforce the strict compile-time checking of types. As a result, complex Pascal programs can be difficult to develop by a team of programmers, because all of them have to work on a single large program.

Separate compilation, as opposed to independent compilation, provides for separate compilation of modules constituting a single program, with the significant addition of performing compile-time type checking across the module boundaries. Programming languages Ada and Modula-2, for example, include provisions for separate compilation. Basically, both languages require programmers to separate the statements of a module (package or task in Ada) into a module definition part (public part in Ada) and a module implementation part (private part in Ada). The definition portion of a module, which is an externally visible part, includes the declaration of foreign objects referenced within the given module but defined in some other module and the declaration of objects defined in the related module but available to external users. The implementation part contains declarations of the variables private to the module as well as the executable program statements.

Type checking is performed by requiring each implementation part of a module to be compiled with the definition parts of all modules that contain declarations of objects manipulated within the given module. Separate compilation thus combines the advantages of modular program development with the safety of compile-time type checking. Modular program development is generally believed to have a number of advantages, such as data encapsulation, hiding of implementation details and protecting them from outside access, and localization of the effects of changes. In general, all these lead to the decoupling of modules, which is essential for large programming projects where each programmer in a team may be assigned to work on a separate module.

Modular program development usually results in a relatively large number of modules that participate in the mechanics of program development, such as editing, compiling, and linking. For this reason, support for separate or independent compilation is often combined with facilities for the creation and maintenance of program and module libraries. A module library can be a file that consists of a number of object modules produced by separate or independent compilation. For convenience in linking, a library usually contains a list of the names of all the public symbols declared or referenced in its constituent modules. A related utility, often called *librarian*, is commonly provided for the maintenance of program libraries. A typical librarian may provide services for creation and deletion of libraries, for queries about the individual modules or symbols, and for additions or deletions of the individual modules.

Separate compilation coupled with library functions is believed to offer some additional advantages, such as reduction of compilation costs and simplified development and management of program corrections. For example, modifications of the source code can be simplified by being localized only to one or very few affected modules. This results in easier editing and selective backup, since individual source files are comparatively small. Likewise, compilation costs may be reduced by being limited to fewer lines of code per iteration of the edit, compile, and link cycles. Linking of a large number of modules, which is quite common with modular programming, can become cumbersome in terms of unwieldy command lines where each individual module needs to be specified. Libraries are of great help here, because they can be used to group a number of modules together. Linking commands are then reduced to a few module names and to a single specification of a library where other modules are to be found.

Access to hardware and to physical memory addresses. Access to hardware is often made possible by means of a special mechanism rather than by providing specific hardware-manipulation statements in the language. The term generally implies some means for the vectoring of interrupts to user-written service routines and the ability to manipulate certain machine registers, such as the processor status word, interrupt masks, and the stack pointer. Access to hardware is often provided by the use of specialized libraries whose functionality is not defined in the language but is usually informally suggested and often becomes a de facto standard. Independent compilation provides this feature indirectly by allowing object modules produced by compilers to be combined with those produced by the assembler.

Access to physical memory addresses usually refers to the ability to obtain the address of, or to form a pointer to, a static object in memory. For example, this type of operation may include initialization of a pointer to an actual memory address of a named variable. Another common variety is assignment of an address to a variable. For example, a variable of the declared type can be located at a programmer-specified physical address. This feature is useful for accessing I/O ports from a high-level language.

Access to memory words and physical addresses is often coupled with some sort of pointer arithmetic with relaxed type checking, such as comparisons or increments. Pascal, for example, does not aid systems programmers in this respect, because it severely restricts the range of operations allowable on pointer types and permits creation of pointers only to dynamically created objects in memory. Its descendant, Modula-2, provides a range of operations for access to memory words, in addition to a mechanism for controlled type-conversions.

Controlled type-conversions essentially refer to the ability to occasionally escape, with the compiler's consent, the strong type checking if it is otherwise enforced by the programming language in question. Programming languages that support this feature, such as Modula-2 and Edison, differ in the mechanics of this mechanism. In some languages, a given type can be retyped to another type of equivalent length by invoking a system-provided function or procedure. In other languages, a generic type—such as an unsigned integer or a word—is provided and made compatible with other types of the same length. Note that controlled type-conversion may substitute for the pointer arithmetic mentioned earlier.

An uncontrolled type-conversion is often made possible by systems which support independent compilation. Although not allowed in standard Pascal, many commercial versions of Pascal compilers provide independent compilation. In such systems, one may simply call a procedure coded in another language, say, assembler, to equate two Pascal variables of different types. We call this approach *uncontrolled* because the compiler is not alerted to potentially dangerous and often nonportable conversion of types.

The portability of programs that access hardware and physical memory addresses is often restricted to a given type of CPU or even to a specific hardware configuration. Although sometimes indispensable for systems programming, machine-dependent operations should therefore be used only when absolutely necessary. Some systems and compilers flag the use of potentially nonportable or nonstandard features of a language. One such example is the *lint* utility for C code available under the Unix operating system. Lint verifies the potential portability of a program coded in C and advises on constructs and usages that might be portability problems, bugs, or dead code.

9.5.2 Invoking the Operating System

In this section we briefly discuss the common approaches to invoking the operating system. In general, system architects must provide a way to invoke OS services from user programs and to pass some parameters when needed by a specific OS routine. In computer systems that provide some hardware support for protection between the operating system and user processes, an additional requirement is to change the level of privilege whenever crossing the OS-user boundary. Three popular methods for invoking the OS are listed below:

1. Procedure call
2. Supervisor call
3. Software interrupt

Each of them is elaborated briefly in subsequent sections.

Procedure call. A procedure call, in its ordinary form, assumes that the operating-system routines are coded as procedures. Users may invoke them and pass parameters to the OS by means of the standard procedure call. This method is simple and usable on virtually any computer system, since all that it needs is hardware support for the procedure call/return mechanism.

However, procedure calls are generally unsuitable for changing the level of privilege when transferring between a caller and a callee. An exception to this rule may be claimed by some virtual-memory systems, where the operating system is mapped into each user's virtual space. Such systems may use the procedure-call mechanism for its efficiency, since they provide protection to common OS routines through address-space isolation, but privileged access to system facilities may still be difficult to implement.

Another, no less serious problem with invoking the operating system via procedure calls is that of binding. Namely, in most program-development systems the operating system is already in place when user programs are being developed and run. When invoking the OS, the question is when and how to bind user-specified names of OS services to the actual addresses of the corresponding OS routines long since loaded in memory. A straightforward solution, employed in some primitive monitors and early microcomputer systems, is to use direct instead of symbolic addressing and to specify the actual address of the desired operating-system routine. A more convenient approach, used in some larger systems, is to allow symbolic referencing of OS services by their prescribed names. Translation of those names into the entry points of the corresponding modules is performed with the aid of a system-supplied library with public declarations of the names of user-callable operating-system services. The address of each service can be determined and furnished into the OS library by the linker or the linking-loader at the time when the executable version of the operating-system code is prepared. User programs that call on operating-system services directly must specify the OS library as one of the input modules during the linking process in order to have the symbolic references to OS resolved.

Both these schemes are sensitive to changes of operating-system service entry points, which are quite customary in different releases of operating systems, and even in different hardware configurations running under the same release and version (revision level) of a given operating system. As a result, object-code portability is severely restricted, and programs may have to be relinked even in order to work on a given hardware installation when the operating system is upgraded to a new release. Such a mode of operation is obviously undesirable in distributed and network environments, since it may preclude migration of executable programs even among the homogeneous nodes running the same kind of operating system on the same type of the CPU.

Supervisor call. A supervisor call (SVC) is usually a specialized hardware instruction dedicated to invoking the operating system. Common implementations of SVC provide at least one operand, the identity of the desired OS service. Namely, SVC typically provides a common entry point to the operating system. The indicated service may then be invoked on the basis of the supplied parameter by means of a jump or index table. Since it always transfers control to the OS, the SVC instruction may be allowed to switch to Supervisor or some other privileged OS mode. A context switch, if necessary, can also be performed at this point and perhaps be included in the microcode of the SVC instruction. When returning control to a user process, the operating system can do so by means of some sort of (privileged) switch-mode instruction.

Another advantage of the SVC instruction is that it alleviates the problem of knowing the addresses of the OS routines at compile-time or link-time. Users can simply specify a number of the desired OS service as a parameter to the SVC instruction. The key is in the indirect transfer of control by means of the jump table, whereby SVC performs the required run-time binding. Namely, when the OS code is loaded in memory, the SVC jump table is normally filled with the actual address of each numbered OS routine. As long as the service numbers are kept identical between releases, object-code portability of user programs may be accomplished when the SVC instruction is used.

Software interrupt. A software interrupt (SWI) is a versatile instruction that is finding its way into an increasing number of computer systems, especially microprocessors. Basically, a software interrupt instruction triggers the hardware interrupt-processing sequence described in Chapter 2. In other words, an SWI has the same effect as if an external interrupt request were asserted. Depending on the supporting architecture, this may include the context-save and transfer of control to the related interrupt-service routine. The SWI instruction is useful for invocation of operating-system services and the debugging of interrupt-related code.

When used to invoke the operating system, the SWI instruction may provide both context switch and vectoring directly to the related OS routine. In addition, switching to a privileged mode of operation can also be performed at this time. Similar to the SVC instruction, the operating system or some other program can load the address of the corresponding service into each interrupt vector dedicated to an OS service. The users are thus relieved from knowing anything but the number or the "interrupt level" of the corresponding OS service. Due to the resulting run-time binding, the portability of object code can easily be accomplished when the SWI instruction is used to invoke the operating system. By designating a single interrupt vector as an entry point to the operating system, the SWI instruction can be used to emulate the supervisor call described earlier. However, the bottleneck of a single entry point can be alleviated by the software interrupt instruction by dedicating a separate vector to each individual operating-system service.

An additional attractiveness for system architects and programmers is that the SWI instruction can be used to aid in the debugging of interrupt-related code, an area where standard debuggers are of little or no use and where generation and simulation of realistic test cases are difficult. Namely, the SWI instruction can be used to simulate an interrupt coming from a physical device and to trigger the entire event-recognition sequence by being issued from a test program. However, permissive use of this facility can be dangerous in a system in normal operation, and some safeguards must be in place to prevent potentially hazardous uses of the SWI instruction, such as triggering false interrupts at the level assigned to an active device.

9.6 SUMMARY

In this chapter we have provided a functional specification of a small kernel for a multiprocess operating system (KMOS) in order to stress the interactions between the various parts of the operating system discussed in earlier chapters and to illustrate certain aspects of the system-design process. A kernel is a first-level functional extension of the computer hardware corresponding to Layer 1 in our sample hierarchy of operating-system layers introduced in Chapter 1. Kernels are among the most stable layers of operating systems, and their functionality is similar across a wide range of systems.

KMOS provides a message facility for interprocess communication and synchronization, as well as for the signaling of hardware interrupts. Basic process scheduling in KMOS is event-driven and based on the static process priorities. KMOS also supports the delaying of processes for a specified period of time and manages the system time base.

Messages in KMOS are exchanged via mailboxes, where they are buffered if necessary. A mailbox is created in KMOS by invoking the CREATEMBOX system call. The SEND operation is nonblocking, thus resulting in an asynchronous exchange of messages. The RECEIVE operation is used to receive a message.

The system part of interrupt processing in KMOS is performed by the ITSERV routine. Users can selectively enable designated levels of interrupt by means of the ENABLEV system call.

The CREATEPROC service is available for process creation in KMOS. Timed-delaying of processes is performed by cooperation between the DELAY system service and the KMOSCLOCK process which services timer interrupts.

The initial configuration of user processes and mailboxes to be activated upon each system startup is user-definable by means of the initial process table and the initial mailbox table.

Support for modular programming is one of the desirable facilities of programming languages for systems implementation. Separate compilation of modules facilitates a structured form of modular programming by providing compile-time type checking across the module boundaries. Module libraries and related utilities are also useful for modular program development. Access to hardware and to physical memory addresses is often needed in systems programs. Some systems-implementation languages provide these facilities by means of specialized libraries, pointer arithmetic, and controlled-type conversions.

Although widely available, the procedure call/return mechanism is not very suitable for invoking the operating system for reasons of difficulty in managing the protection hardware and the often inflexible binding of operating-system service names to the corresponding addresses. Invocation of operating-system services by means of the specialized instructions, such as a Supervisor call and software interrupt, can alleviate both these problems.

OTHER READING

Issues in kernel design are discussed by Popek and Kline (1979). The duality of operating-system designs based on message exchange and other interprocess synchronization and communication mechanisms is discussed by Lauer and Needham (1978). A conceptual description of operating-system kernel design is provided by Lister (1979) and Denning (1983).

Numerous descriptions of the functions or entire designs of operating-system kernels are available in the literature. Some of them include Brinch Hansen (1970, 1977, 1982), Cheriton et al. (1979), Comer (1984), Hardy (1985), Holt (1983), Hoppe (1980), Joseph et al. (1984), Kepecs and Solomon (1985), Madnick and Donovan (1974), Pohjanpalo (1981), Wicklund (1982), Wulf et al. (1981), and others.

Some aspects of the Unix kernel are described by Ritchie and Thompson (1974), Thompson (1978), Holt (1983), and also in Chapter 11 of this book. Some real-time and interprocess communication extensions to the Unix kernel are described by Lycklama and Bayer (1978).

Vendor's manuals may be consulted for descriptions of the functions provided by the kernels of commercial operating systems. Small systems and embedded real-time kernels are preferable for this purpose in order to avoid sifting through the piles of documentation often provided with large systems. Some good descriptions may be found in Hunter and Ready (1982), Intel (1981), which describes the iRMX 88 system, which has influenced the design of KMOS, and Motorola (1980). The 80130 operating-system kernel on a chip is described in Intel (1983a) and in Chapter 11 of this book.

EXERCISES

9.1 Provide a functional specification for priority queuing, as opposed to FIFO, of processes at mailboxes in KMOS. Discuss the relative advantages and disadvantages of FIFO versus priority queuing with regard to ease of implementation, run-time efficiency, indefinite postponement, and use of the message facility for solving standard problems in concurrent programming, such as producer/consumer. Can priority queuing also be applied to messages?

9.2 Provide a functional specification for a KMOS service to delete a mailbox, DELETEMBOX. Indicate which major system data structures are used by and/or created for your design.

9.3 Provide a functional specification for a KMOS service to delete a mailbox provided it is in the system and to return an error indication otherwise.

Indicate which major system data structures are used by and/or created for your design.

9.4 Discuss the relative merits of requiring processes to ATTACH themselves to an existing mailbox before being allowed to use it for the sending or receiving of messages. Should addition of this feature to KMOS affect the functioning of CREATEMBOX and DELETEMBOX services, and if so, how? Devise functional specifications for ATTACH and DETACH system calls. Indicate all the modifications of the KMOS data structures and routines that may be affected. Discuss what kind of error indications need to be provided by ATTACH and DETACH system calls.

9.5 Discuss the effects on interprocess interactions that would result from disallowing the buffering of messages in KMOS. Devise a functional specification for a blocking version of SEND for this case, and indicate the changes to major system data structures made by your design. Does this change affect the use of messages to signal interrupts, and if so, how?

9.6 Devise a functional specification for a modified version of the RECEIVE operation so that the calling process can specify the time limit on how long it is willing to wait for a message. Explain the method used by your solution to indicate the outcome of the RECEIVE operation to the calling process, and indicate all changes to the original KMOS specification made by your design.

9.7 Devise a functional specification for a KMOS routine to delete a process from the system, DELETEPROC. Discuss the considerations involved in deciding whether a process should be allowed to delete only itself or to delete other processes as well. In the latter case, indicate whether and how deletion is affected by the process state.

9.8 Devise a functional specification for the implementation of the process SUSPEND/RESUME mechanism, discussed in Chapter 3, in KMOS. Indicate whether name checking is used for this purpose and how, specify error returns if any, and describe any changes or additions to the major KMOS data structures made by your design.

9.9 Discuss the possible changes to KMOS behavior and specification resulting from allowing a running process to change its level of priority. Indicate how scheduling may be affected, and devise a functional specification for the CHANGE_PRIORITY system call.

9.10 Devise a functional specification for the queuing implementation of semaphores in KMOS (do not use messages to simulate semaphores). Indicate how semaphores are created and/or initialized in your design, and describe the syntax and operation of the WAIT and SIGNAL calls from the user's point of view.

9.11 Discuss whether the scheduler should be invoked in the KMOSCLOCK process, whose functional specification is provided in Program 9.9, when one or more processes are made ready following expiration of their timed delays.

Describe when and how a process made ready by the KMOSCLOCK is eventually scheduled for execution in the original KMOS specification.

9.12 Devise a functional specification for a KMOS routine, or for modification of an existing one, that would limit the maximum duration of time that a given process is allowed to execute. Should this time limit be system-wide or process-specific? Discuss what other KMOS routines and data structures need to be modified to accommodate this change.

9.13 Discuss the nature and extent of the changes that need to be made to the original specification of KMOS in order to accommodate time-slice scheduling of a group of processes while retaining event-driven scheduling of others. Devise a functional specification for the time-slice scheduler, and describe how a programmer can specify to which scheduler a given process should be subjected.

9.14 When I/O ports are memory mapped, they can be read or written as a memory location. Such ports can be accessed from a high-level language by allowing programmers to specify the physical address of a variable. In that case, a programmer-specified "variable" can be forced to the given I/O port's physical memory address and the port can then be manipulated like any other variable. However, when ports are I/O mapped (also called *isolated I/O*), specialized I/O instructions, such as IN and OUT, must be used by the CPU to access I/O ports. Can the method described for accessing memory-mapped ports from an HLL be used to access I/O-mapped ports? If not, specify an alternative method for accessing I/O-mapped ports from a high-level programming language.

9.15 Find and study a compiler that allows separate or independent compilation, and discuss whether it is usable for systems implementation. Write a simple program consisting of at least two procedures that pass parameters to each other, such as multiplication of two numbers and printing of the result. Code each procedure as a separate module, and go through the complete program-development and testing cycle in order to familiarize yourself with the mechanical aspects of modular programming. If possible, code at least one procedure in a different programming language or in an assembler, and study the parameter-passing conventions for procedure calls in your system.

9.16 Check the instruction set of a computer available to you and indicate which instruction or instructions can be used to invoke the operating system. Discuss the relative advantages and disadvantages of each particular instruction when used for that purpose.

TEN

IMPLEMENTATION OF KMOS

In this chapter we complete the design of KMOS on the basis of the functional specification provided in the previous chapter. The resulting KMOS code, provided at the end of this chapter, can be used on microcomputer and minicomputer systems for operating-system laboratory exercises or as a stand-alone system for real-time applications, such as the control and monitoring of laboratory instruments and automated experiments. Readers not interested in details of the KMOS implementation may omit this chapter without loss of continuity.

Our intent in completing the KMOS design is to provide an illustration of the remaining aspects and intricacies of the system-design process and to provide a realistic example of the application of many concepts discussed in this book. Functional specification, because of the lack of standards and notation for its formal definition, can be presented in many ways that may or may not convey all the important aspects of the system under consideration. For example, our emphasis in Chapter 9 was on what KMOS routines should do, as opposed to how they might do it. Consequently, many details, such as the specification of data structures, remain to be worked out before the coding phase of the design process may be safely begun. In addition, the usual iterations prompted by an increased understanding of the system being designed were left to the reader, thus resulting in a certain lack of uniformity in terms of the level of detail in the specification of different routines.

On the other hand, a reasonably debugged and documented working implementation is definitely a more objective landmark in the system-design process. In proceeding with our design of KMOS, we begin by specifying the KMOS data structures and then present a detailed implementation of its routines. Continuing to mimic the actual design process, we arrive at certain particular solutions by discussing the considerations involved therein and by analyzing implementation tradeoffs as they are encountered.

The KMOS code given at the end of this chapter is written in Pascal, which is chosen mostly because it should be familiar to most readers due to its wide use in educational environments and industry. The programming languages Modula-2 and Ada are in many respects descendants of Pascal, and KMOS code can be translated to either of those languages in a fairly straightforward way. Standard Pascal does not provide many of the facilities described as necessary for systems implementation. This problem is tackled in the design of KMOS in two ways commonly resorted to by practicing systems programmers.

First, an extended Pascal compiler with some systems-implementation facilities is used to implement the HLL portion of KMOS. The extensions for systems implementation provided in this particular compiler follow closely the syntax and semantics of the similar facilities found in popular systems-implementation languages. To make the presented implementation as realistic as possible, and to allow readers to make their own extensions, the code given in this chapter was developed and tested on a personal computer.

Second, a small portion of the machine-dependent part of KMOS is coded in assembly language. In order to facilitate understanding of the functioning of the whole system and to avoid details of the specific machine, a Pascal-like pseudocode is given for routines written in the assembler. For reference, the entire listing of the assembly-language portion of KMOS is provided in Appendix A.

In the presented implementation of KMOS, we use the procedure-call mechanism to invoke the OS because of its applicability to a wide range of hardware. The problem of referencing OS routines is solved by requiring user processes to be linked together with the KMOS modules. This approach is reasonable for embedded real-time systems, such as KMOS in its stand-alone versions. In larger operating systems, the SVC or the SWI approach is preferable.

10.1 KMOS SYSTEM LISTS

The general appearance and functions of the various system lists in KMOS were introduced in Chapter 9. The presented functional specification of KMOS routines also defines most of the operations on the related system lists. As discussed in Chapter 9, the following lists are to be provided in implementations of KMOS (types of their respective entries are indicated in parentheses):

1. All-processes (PCBs)
2. Ready (PCBs)
3. Delayed (PCBs)
4. Waiting-for-message (PCBs, one list per mailbox)
5. Waiting messages (messages, one list per mailbox)
6. Mailboxes (mailbox descriptors)

KMOS data structures include one each of the following lists: All-processes, Ready, and Delayed. In addition, there is potentially one list of messages and one list of processes per each active mailbox in the system. There is no Running list, because in uniprocessor systems the list of running processes can contain at most one entry at any time. Instead of maintaining a degenerate Running list, a pointer in KMOS can be dedicated to always marking the PCB of a running process, which otherwise remains in the Ready list. Each KMOS list is populated by one type of KMOS object: process control-blocks, messages, or mailbox descriptors.

The process control-block of a newly created process in KMOS is placed into the All-processes list and the Ready list. As indicated by the KMOS process-state transition diagram (Figure 9.1), the process may subsequently oscillate between Ready, Running, Delayed, and Waiting-for-message states. Whenever a process changes its state, KMOS routines record the resulting state of the system by moving the related PCB between the corresponding system lists. Processing of an event that results in a change of the system state thus typically causes a system object, such as a PCB, to be removed from one list and placed into another. Due to the generally high frequency of such events in multiprocess systems, the operating system's performance is largely affected by its efficiency in handling the list-processing operations. Careful selection of the data structures suitable for representation and manipulation of system lists is therefore an important part of the operating-system design.

Given the frequent insertions into and deletions of their entries, the OS system lists are commonly implemented using a linked-list representation. Ignoring messages for a moment, a PCB of a KMOS process must provide link fields for the links required by various system lists. For example, a link field can be dedicated for the All-processes list. Since Ready and Suspended states of a process are mutually exclusive, at any time a given PCB may participate only in either the Ready list or one of the two forms of the Suspended list (Delayed or Waiting-for-message). For this reason, a single multipurpose link field in a PCB can suffice for having it placed in any of those three lists.

By having multiple link fields—up to one per each type of list—in a PCB, it is possible to weave KMOS system lists through a set of PCBs statically placed into their allocated memory space and never actually moved. When a PCB needs to be "moved" from one list to another, it is sufficient to update the pointers of adjacent nodes accordingly without ever having to copy the contents of a PCB from one place in memory into another. This point is illustrated by Figure 10.1.

A sample configuration of PCBs and a snapshot of system lists are depicted in Figure 10.1. Also shown are KMOS internal pointers to the various lists. For example, the pointer to the All-processes list is designated as HEADALLP (head of All-processes list). Similarly, HEADREADY and HEADDELAY pointers allow access to Ready and Delayed lists, respectively. In order to facilitate the reading of code, the same acronyms are used to name the corresponding KMOS pointer variables.

Five processes are assumed to be active in the system depicted in Figure 10.1. Their corresponding process control-blocks, PCB1 through PCB5, are connected

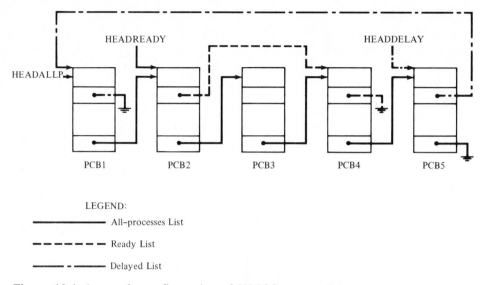

Figure 10.1 A sample configuration of KMOS system lists.

in the All-processes list using the link field dedicated to that purpose in each PCB. As indicated, the Ready list is assumed to contain processes P2 and P4, in that order. The corresponding KMOS list pointer, HEADREADY, is therefore set to PCB2. The Delayed list contains PCB5 and PCB1, thus indicating that processes P5 and P1 are suspended awaiting expiration of their respective timed delays. Process P3 is assumed to be suspended awaiting a message at some unspecified mailbox. The multipurpose link field of its process control-block, PCB3, is left blank pending further elaboration of the structure of the Waiting-for-message lists of processes in KMOS.

10.2 READY LIST AND ITS MANIPULATION

While a process's membership in other lists varies with its state transitions, a process remains in the All-processes list from its creation until it terminates. As suggested earlier, this list may be used to satisfy queries about processes. In general, typical operations on this list are searching for a given process, for example, in order to check the validity of a parameter supplied to a system call, and reading of a process's attributes, such as priority. Since our functional specification of KMOS does not provide any services that require such use of the All-processes list, which is maintained solely for the purpose of KMOS extensions, we have no basis for structuring this list in any particular way. The Ready list, however, is used by several KMOS routines, and the efficiency of certain operations on it may have a significant impact on the overall performance of KMOS-based systems.

10.2.1 Implementation of the Ready List in KMOS

Given that the All-processes list contains PCBs of all active processes, we should consider the possibility of embedding other system lists, such as Ready, within it. For instance, an implied version of the Ready list may be formed within the All-processes list simply by regarding each PCB whose status field is set to READY as also belonging to the Ready list. An alternative is to implement a separate Ready list that contains only the PCBs of processes in the Ready state. In order to choose the most appropriate implementation for KMOS, let us informally analyze the effects that each alternative has on system performance. We may do this by studying the types and frequency of operations performed by KMOS routines on the Ready list and by comparing their relative computational complexities as a function of a particular data structure.

From the functional specification of KMOS routines, we may conclude that the Ready list is updated whenever a process is suspended (removal of the related PCB) and made ready (addition of the related PCB). The Ready list is searched for the highest-priority node whenever a new process needs to be scheduled. Thus, various KMOS routines perform three types of operations on the Ready list: insertion of a node, deletion of a node, and searching to find a node with specific attributes. A cursory examination of the KMOS routines specified in Chapter 9 reveals that scheduling, and thus searching of the Ready list for the highest-priority PCB, is the most frequent operation of the three.

If the Ready list is embedded within the All-processes list, changes of state from Ready-Suspended and Suspended-Ready can be recorded in place without the need to move the related PCB. Assuming that an operating-system pointer points to the target PCB when a state change needs to be performed, all that is needed is to update the PCB's status field accordingly. With this implementation, a new process can be scheduled by searching all PCBs and selecting the one with the highest priority among those whose STATUS field is set to READY. In terms of complexity, state changes may be recorded in constant time, whereas the time complexity of scheduling is on the order of n_t, where n_t is the total number of active processes in a given system at the time of scheduling. By *active*, we mean processes created but not deleted, whose PCBs are recorded in the All-processes list.

A separate Ready list requires updating of the pointers necessary to remove a PCB or to insert a PCB when the corresponding process makes a Ready-Suspended or Suspended-Ready transition, respectively. As illustrated later, these operations may also be performed in constant time independent of the number of nodes in the Ready list. Although both approaches exhibit identical asymptotic behavior (constant time), list manipulations are somewhat more time-consuming than the simple updating of a field required in the embedded implementation of the Ready list. Scheduling of a process with a separate Ready list requires searching of n_r nodes, where n_r is the number of ready processes in a given system at the time of scheduling.

As pointed out, our primary concern is to minimize the time spent searching the Ready list. In order to compare the two alternatives in this respect, let us observe that in multiprogramming operating systems the following relation between the number of ready and the total number of processes holds at all times:

$$n_r \leq n_t$$

On the average, the number of active processes is likely to be strictly smaller than the total number of processes in a given system, with the possibility of being considerably smaller when a relatively large number of processes is suspended for some reason or another. As a result, implementation of a separate Ready list in KMOS is likely to be more efficient than its embedded alternative.

The time complexity of searching can be reduced further, to constant time, when a separate version of the Ready list is sorted by the decreasing priority of participating processes. With this provision, the first PCB in the Ready list always belongs to the highest-priority ready process, and scheduling is reduced to setting a system pointer (running process) to it. However, insertion of a PCB into a sorted Ready list cannot be performed in constant time. On the average, this operation requires searching of $\frac{1}{2}n_r$ nodes in order to find a proper place to insert a PCB. With deletions and scheduling taking constant time and scheduling being the most frequent and time-critical operation that directly affects the interrupt-response time, the implementation of a separate, priority-ordered Ready list in KMOS is likely to yield the best performance of all considered alternatives.

10.2.2 Process Control-Block

The specification of the overall structure of system lists already defines some aspects, links in particular, of the format of a process control-block in KMOS. As discussed in Chapter 3, a PCB usually contains a process's attributes and other information that the operating system needs about a particular process. Some examples of PCB entries include current status, priority, and allocated resources. In addition, a PCB contains the pointer fields necessary to link it into system lists corresponding to the current status of its related process. A PCB commonly provides some means for storing the context of its process when it is suspended or preempted. This function, as well as the problem of the initial entering of a process's attributes into its PCB, must be specified before we can outline the format of a PCB in KMOS.

Hardware interrupt-processing sequences and environment-changing instructions often use the stack for storing and retrieving the parts of context they control. This makes the stack a good place for the operating system to store the remaining part of a process's context that must be saved by software. For reasons of security, it is customary to separate the system stack used by the operating system from the stack accessible to user processes. One way to accomplish this is to save and restore the respective stack pointer whenever a transition from a user's process to the operating system, or vice versa, takes place. Some computer systems facilitate this process by providing multiple stack pointer registers in hardware, sometimes augmented with automatic switching between them when executing instructions that make transitions between User and Supervisor modes. In this way the integrity of the operating system's stack may be preserved in the presence of erroneous handling of the stack by a user process or processes.

However, maintenance of two separate stacks in a system does not solve the problem of a user process disturbing the stack that it shares with other user processes. In particular, if a stack is shared by several user processes, each process making a transition from the Running state must leave the stack exactly as it found it when dispatched. Given that a running process may involuntarily be preempted by an external event, this requirement is both difficult to enforce and restrictive in the sense that it effectively precludes the possibility of processes using the stack for storing temporary variables. A much safer approach is to dedicate a separate stack to each user's process. In this way, whenever a user process is running, the stack pointer (SP) register is set to that process's private stack area. Whenever a process switch takes place, the departing process's value of the SP may be stored in its PCB. Likewise, the hardware SP may then be set for the newly inaugurated running process by restoring the saved SP value from the related PCB.

By allocating private stacks to user processes, the negative effects of improper stack manipulation can be localized to affect only the offending process. In addition, each user process need not worry about matching the number of stack pushes and pops before surrendering control of the CPU to the operating system and, ultimately, to another user process. Other advantages of the private-stack approach regarding context saving and restoring are discussed later in relation to implementation of the ITSERV routine. For obvious reasons, we adopt this form of stack implementation in KMOS.

As discussed in Chapter 3, a systems programmer usually assigns the initial values of certain attributes when submitting a program to the operating system for execution. In general, the program-development tools for systems programming are supposed to assist the programmers in this process. Designing a small memory-based kernel and striving for machine-independence, we may opt for a simple solution to this problem. Let us assume that all initial information about a process to be created is submitted to KMOS in the form of a static record, which we may name a *static process descriptor* (SPD). An SPD in KMOS should contain such information as the process's name, the initial starting address, and the priority. Other details about SPDs are explained in the context of process creation.

With this clarification, we can outline the structure of a process control-block in KMOS. Its precise format is given in Figure 10.2, which is a graphic representation of the PCB record declared in the KMOS code. The first two fields of a PCB in KMOS are links to the Delayed list, which is actually implemented as a doubly linked list for reasons explained later. The THREAD field is the multipurpose link field used to place a PCB into the Ready list or a Waiting-for-message list. The DELAY field is used to record the number of remaining clock-ticks when the process is in the Delayed state. The FRAME field is used to store the stack-frame pointer to the private stack when the process is not running. The STACK field points to the process's stack area whenever the process is not

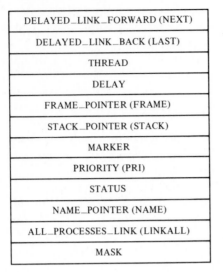

DELAYED_LINK_FORWARD (NEXT)
DELAYED_LINK_BACK (LAST)
THREAD
DELAY
FRAME_POINTER (FRAME)
STACK_POINTER (STACK)
MARKER
PRIORITY (PRI)
STATUS
NAME_POINTER (NAME)
ALL_PROCESSES_LINK (LINKALL)
MASK

Figure 10.2 Structure of a process control-block.

running. For the running process, the hardware stack pointer register and frame pointer register are set to access the process's stack. The MARKER field can be used to indicate the stack limit for a given process. This field is useful for detecting stack overflows and underflows during the system-debugging process. Except for the data structure, run-time testing of stack boundaries is not otherwise supported by the presented version of KMOS.

The PRI field contains the programmer-assigned priority of the process. The STATUS field indicates the current status of the given process, such as Ready or Delayed. The NAME field points to the process's name, which is represented as a string of alphanumeric characters. The LINKALL field is dedicated for linking the PCB into the All-processes list. Lastly, the MASK field is used to store the hardware interrupt mask to be applied when the process is dispatched. As discussed later, this mask is machine-dependent, and it may be computed on the basis of the process's priority.

10.2.3 Insertions into the Ready List

Having specified some major data structures, we are now ready to proceed to discuss the details of the KMOS implementation whose source code is given at the end of this chapter.

KMOS code begins with global constants, type, and data declarations. We explain most of the data declarations in the context of routines that actually use them. At this point, a familiar structure is the PCB record and head pointers to the various system lists. Some initial type declarations make use of the unsigned-integer type, UNSINT or WORD, which is discussed in relation to systems-implementation languages. Other pointer types defined for KMOS data structures include PTRPCB, which points to a process control-block record, and pointers to messages and mailbox descriptors. The last two data types, ADRPCB and ADRLAD, are addresses of the respective variables, a PCB record, and a long address (LADDR) record to be discussed later.

The first KMOS routine to be discussed, INSERTREADY, inserts a process into the Ready list. This internal KMOS procedure is called by other KMOS services whenever a process needs to be "made ready." As indicated by the functional specification, this operation is quite frequently needed by other parts of KMOS. Incidentally, the INSERTREADY itself is not present in the functional specification. The reason is that this procedure implements our decision to maintain a separate, priority-ordered Ready list in KMOS. This decision was made subsequent to completion of the functional specification.

Procedure INSERTREADY inserts a PCB, passed as a parameter, into the Ready list in a manner that preserves its priority ordering. In particular, the new PCB is inserted after all those of higher or equal priority and ahead of all those of lower priority than its own. By *priority* of a PCB, we mean the value in its PRI field. In KMOS, a smaller number indicates higher priority, thus making 0 the highest and 255 the lowest priority in the system. Note that processes of equal priority are placed in the Ready list in a first-come, first-served (FCFS) order.

As indicated, the parameter passed to the INSERTREADY procedure is actually a pointer to the PCB to be processed, denoted as PROCESS in the declaration of the INSERTREADY procedure. In order to find a proper place in the Ready list where the submitted PCB is to be inserted, INSERTREADY searches the Ready list for the first PCB of lower priority. If one is found, the new PCB is inserted *before* that node in order to preserve the priority ordering of the Ready list.

Procedure INSERTREADY uses a standard method of inserting before a given node of a linked list. Two local pointers, CURRENT and PREVIOUS, are used to point to the node currently being visited and to its predecessor, respectively. Both are initially set to the beginning of the Ready list. A search for a lower-priority PCB is then conducted. The search terminates at the first such PCB found or at the end of list if none exists. In either case, the new PCB is inserted after the node pointed to by the PREVIOUS pointer.

As discussed earlier, the THREAD field is used to link PCBs to the Ready list. Once the node after which the new PCB is to be inserted (designated by the PREVIOUS pointer upon exit from the search-loop), the THREAD link of the new PCB is set to point to the node before which it is being inserted. The THREAD field of the previous node is set to the new entry, thus completing the insert. The STATUS field of the new entry is set to READY, and the global variable RUNNING is set to the first entry in the Ready list in case that inserts before the first node takes place. Pointer RUNNING normally points to the running user process, which is the highest-priority ready process in KMOS. When KMOS itself is being executed, RUNNING may take on some transitional states while switching from one running process to another. The pointer to the active user process, RUNNING, essentially marks the only entry, if any, on the Running list.

Two points about the code of INSERTREADY may warrant some explanation. First, the head node of the Ready list is itself declared as a PCB that is initialized as having priority 0 (highest). Therefore, its THREAD field, that is, HEADREADY.THREAD, actually points to the first ready process and the READYLIST points to the head-node PCB. By designing the head node to have a structure identical to other entries, no special code is needed for insertions into the empty list and for insertions before the first (real) node of the list.

The second point is that INSERTREADY, as implemented, never inserts an entry after the last node. This is because the search loop terminates upon reaching the last node regardless of the relative priorities involved, since then the CURRENT^.THREAD pointer becomes NIL. This does not seem to be correct, because the new PCB should be inserted *after* the last node whenever the newcomer's priority is lower than that of the last node in the Ready list. However, this kind of insertion never occurs in KMOS because the last node of the Ready list is *always* reserved for one special process. We now make a digression in order to explain the role of this rather important special process.

A problem that must be resolved by every multiprocess system is what the operating system should do when there is nothing to do. For example, this situation occurs when the running process suspends itself—say, by attempting to receive a message from an empty mailbox—and no other process in the system is ready. As a result of the change of system state necessitating rescheduling (becoming blocked while executing RECEIVE in our example), the scheduler is invoked to select the next running process, but it finds the Ready list empty. In principle, the system has to wait until a process becomes ready and then surrender control to that process. A straightforward implementation of this philosophy is for the scheduler to busily test the state of the Ready list until it becomes nonempty as a result of the occurrence of an event that causes a process to become ready. This approach is ineffective in many systems where the scheduler executes at a higher priority than user processes in order to be protected from potentially harmful preemptions. While in a high-priority wait loop, the operating system may never be able to detect the (lower-priority) event needed to get the user processes back in motion.

This problem is handled in many operating systems with the aid of a special NULL process that is created by the system as a part of the startup sequence. The NULL process is designed to never terminate and to always be ready. As a result, the Ready list is never empty and the problem is solved. Moreover, execution of the scheduler, a time-critical part of the system, can be made faster by eliminating the need to test for emptiness of the Ready list.

The simplest way to implement the NULL process is as a tight busy-wait loop. As described, NULL monopolizes the CPU and therefore must be *the lowest-priority process* in the system. This is exactly what is needed to make sure that all other events have higher priority and will thus preempt NULL and be recognized and processed by the system. Being executed only when the CPU would otherwise be idle makes the NULL process an excellent vehicle for gathering performance statistics. Namely, by keeping track of the time spent executing it, CPU utilization by user processes and by the operating system can be measured. Another useful activity that can be delegated to the NULL process is to execute various diagnostic programs and thus assist in monitoring the system integrity.

The KMOSNUL process is the KMOS version of the do-nothing NULL process. The KMOSNUL process is the lowest-priority process (level 255 in KMOS) which is entirely CPU-bound and thus always ready to execute. The body of KMOSNUL, coded in the assembly language, consists of an unconditional tight loop of the form

$$\textbf{while } true \textbf{ do } \{nothing\};$$

As indicated, the purpose of KMOSNUL is to ensure that the Ready list is never empty. Since priority ordering of the Ready list and event-driven scheduling result in the scheduler being reduced to a single assignment in the course of process dispatching, the DISPATCH routine selects the next process to run in a KMOS system. Thus, existence of the KMOSNUL process makes the execution of DISPATCH faster, since DISPATCH does not have to test for emptiness of the Ready list. In addition, the presence of at least one PCB in the Ready list, ensured by the KMOSNUL, simplifies the work of the INSERTREADY procedure, as described earlier. This can be important in high-performance applications, since DISPATCH and INSERTREADY are probably the most frequently executed portions of a KMOS system.

10.3 INTERPROCESS COMMUNICATION AND SYNCHRONIZATION

As specified, KMOS provides a buffered, indirect message-exchange mechanism via mailboxes. Messages are of variable length, and they are not copied from a sender's to a receiver's space. Each mailbox is visible to KMOS by means of a dedicated message descriptor. A message descriptor must be capable of heading a queue of processes awaiting messages and a queue of messages awaiting delivery to processes. Both queues are serviced in FIFO order. Entries are enqueued at the rear of the queue and removed from its front. Depending on the relative productivity of senders and receivers on a given mailbox, either the process or the message queue may contain entries, but not both. All mailbox descriptors in the system are contained in the Mailboxes list.

10.3.1 Mailboxes and Messages

The format of a mailbox descriptor (MBD) in KMOS is given in Figure 10.3a. It is a graphic representation of the MBD record in KMOS code. As indicated, a mailbox descriptor consists of head and tail pointers to the queue of messages (HEADMES, TAILMES) and head and tail pointers to the Waiting-for-message queue of processes (HEADPROC, TAILPROC). Both sets of head and tail

MESSAGE_HEAD_POINTER	(HEADMES)
MESSAGE_TAIL_POINTER	(TAILMES)
PROCESS_HEAD_POINTER	(HEADPROC)
PROCESS_TAIL_POINTER	(TAILPROC)
MAILBOXES_LINK	(MBOXLINK)

(*a*) Structure of a Mailbox Descriptor

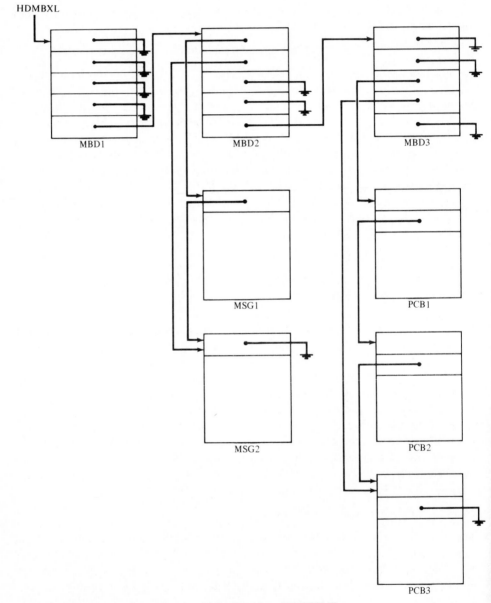

(*b*) A Sample Configuration of KMOS Mailboxes

Figure 10.3 Mailboxes.

pointers are maintained in order to provide for efficient appending and removal of entries at opposite ends of the queues. The MBOXLINK field is used to link the descriptor to the Mailboxes list. When a mailbox is created, all queues are assumed to be empty and their respective pointers are set to NIL. Since memory allocation is not performed by KMOS, a process wishing to create a mailbox must provide a record of the MBD type and invoke the CREATEMBOX routine to initialize the mailbox descriptor.

Procedure CREATEMBOX takes one parameter, the address of the mailbox descriptor. The procedure CREATEMBOX initializes all four pointers of the mailbox descriptor (MBD) to NIL and enqueues the MBD on the Mailboxes list. No particular ordering of this list is required in KMOS, so the simplest and the most efficient method of adding entries to the front is followed. While the created mailbox descriptor is in the process of being inserted into the Mailboxes list, interrupts are turned off to ensure indivisibility of the operation and, consequently, to provide a consistent update of the global variable HEADMAIL.

A sample configuration of the Mailboxes list with three mailbox descriptors is shown in Figure 10.3b. As shown, descriptor MBD1 contains neither processes nor messages. The mailbox descriptor denoted as MBD2 contains two messages, and its message head and tail pointers are set accordingly. The mailbox whose descriptor is denoted as MBD3 contains three processes in the Waiting-for-message state. As discussed earlier, such processes are linked using their respective THREAD fields.

Support for variable-length messages in KMOS requires some sort of message headers where the length of a given message may be recorded by the sender and referenced by the receiving process. Since KMOS is to provide buffering of messages awaiting delivery (sent but not yet received), we must provide some means for linking them at a mailbox descriptor, as depicted by MBD2 in Figure 10.3b. The message header is probably the most convenient place for this link field when unlimited message buffering per mailbox is required, as is the case in KMOS.

The resulting format of a message in KMOS is given in Figure 10.4. As indicated, each message consists of a fixed header and an optional data field of variable length. For example, empty messages used for synchronization purposes normally consist of the header field only. The header contains the LINK and LENGTH fields described earlier. The purpose of its last field, MTYPE, is to allow for differentiation between classes of messages, such as system-sent or user-sent. An example of its use is described in relation to the ITSERV routine. The message header is declared as the MSG record in KMOS code.

In KMOS, a message must be built in the sender's address space before it may be forwarded to a receiving process. Building of a message consists of placing data in the data field, if any, and setting the LENGTH field in the header accordingly. After setting the MTYPE field, if necessary, the message is built, and then it may be sent by invoking the SEND routine. The LINK field of a message header should not be manipulated by the sending process. This field is used by KMOS for queueing messages at mailbox descriptors.

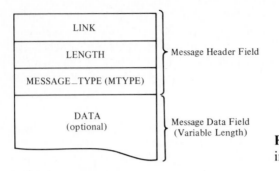

Figure 10.4 Structure of a message in KMOS.

10.3.2 The SEND-Message Operation

As indicated by its code, the SEND procedure takes two parameters: the address of the mailbox descriptor where the message is to be delivered, MAILBOX, and the address of the message itself, MESSAGE. The SEND procedure opens by turning interrupts off in order to ensure mutually exclusive access to the global pointers it manipulates. This is accomplished by the assembly-language procedure INTOFF, which clears the master interrupts-on hardware flag to disable interrupts and leaves all other interrupt masks and control registers intact. Operating-system kernels commonly resort to the disabling of interrupts for providing mutual exclusion and indivisibility of certain sensitive operations, such as message delivery. The relative disadvantages of this method, discussed in Chapter 4, are less pronounced when used in the kernel, which is typically the most trusted layer of an operating system.

The SEND procedure then examines the head of the process queue at the designated mailbox descriptor in order to determine whether some processes are waiting for a message. If the process queue is empty, the message must be enqueued to await delivery. To ensure FIFO delivery of waiting messages, the new message must be enqueued at the tail of the related queue. If the message queue is found empty, the head pointer is set to the new message. Otherwise, the new message is appended in a standard way by setting the LINK field of the last message, designated by the tail pointer as MAILBOX^.TAILMES^.LINK, to point to the new entry. In either case, the new entry is the last message in the updated queue, so its LINK field is set to NIL and the queue-tail pointer is set to the appended message. After turning interrupts back on, SEND returns control to its caller. Note that interrupts are not reactivated if what would be the running process is not active (its STATUS field is not set to READY). This happens when SEND is invoked by ITSERV and not by a user process. In the former case, SEND leaves all interrupt handling to ITSERV, as explained in Section 10.4.

When one or more processes are found waiting at the designated mailbox, the corresponding branch of SEND delivers the message to the first of them. This process, designated as the message recipient and labeled RECIPIENT, is first removed from the front of the queue of waiting processes. After updating the head pointer and the tail pointer in case only the removed process was found in the queue, SEND places the address of the message to be delivered, MESSAGE, into the DELAY field of the RECIPIENT process. The MESSAGE remains there until RECIPIENT eventually becomes the running process and the message is actually delivered to it. Message delivery is completed by the DISPATCH routine described later.

If invoked by a user process, SEND saves its context using the SSTACK procedure. Being very machine- and compiler-specific, the save-stack (SSTACK) procedure is coded in assembly language. Its purpose is to save the stack and frame pointers of the procedure that called the caller of SSTACK, the caller of SEND in this particular case. In other words, procedure SSTACK sets the stage for a return two levels up in a hierarchy of nested calls. This is necessary whenever a user process invokes a KMOS service that causes its caller to be suspended. The KMOS procedure in question, such as SEND, then calls SSTACK to save part of the suspended process's state in such a way that DISPATCH can return control to the user process when it is scheduled to run again.

As illustrated by the SEND procedure, the presented implementation of KMOS takes a somewhat relaxed attitude toward saving the context of processes that remain running following invocation of the operating system. This is illustrated by not saving or restoring the caller's context when the message cannot be delivered and control of the CPU is returned to the caller of SEND. This approach is a result of the choice of the procedure call/return mechanism for invoking KMOS services and of the lack of support for a privileged mode of processor operation while executing the operating system. Thus, KMOS almost appears like a subroutine to its callers, who regain control immediately after the desired service is rendered. Alternatively, if the calling process is suspended, its stack pointers are preserved and later restored, thus emulating a return procedure to the caller when it is eventually scheduled to execute again. A consequence of this approach is that KMOS processes written in a block-structured language that places local variables on stack (the usual practice) perceive KMOS as fully preserving the process's context. However, assembly-language routines that keep some variables in registers cannot expect to have their contents undisturbed upon regaining control from an invoked KMOS service. As indicated by the ITSERV and DISPATCH routines described later, KMOS preserves the full context of involuntarily preempted processes in all cases.

Following invocation of SSTACK, procedure SEND makes the message recipient ready by inserting it into the Ready list. The next active process is then scheduled and dispatched. Given priority ordering, scheduling in KMOS is reduced to a trivial operation of "selecting" the process at the front of the Ready list. The global variable RUNNING points to this process, thus making it possible to combine scheduling and dispatching into an invocation of DISPATCH to prepare the environment for and to surrender control to the running process.

10.3.3 The RECEIVE-Message Operation

Receiving of messages in KMOS-based systems is done by means of the RECEIVE system call. Since it returns a pointer to a message to the calling process, RECEIVE is coded as a function of a PTRMSG type. RECEIVE takes two parameters: pointer to the mailbox where the message is to be received, MAILBOX, and a time limit, TIMLIM. The latter parameter is ignored by KMOS, but it is included for possible expansion in conformance with the discussion of timed receives in Chapter 5.

When the running process wishing to receive a message invokes the RECEIVE function, either messages or waiting processes may be found at the designated mailbox. In the former case, the calling process receives the first message from the queue. Removal of a message in RECEIVE is a standard deletion from the front of a queue. The address of the removed message is placed in the MESSAGE variable. The LINK field of the removed message is set to itself. This is done in order to allow for differentiation between messages that are in a queue and those which are not simply by examination of their LINK field. This is used by the ITSERV routine described in the next section.

After reenabling interrupts, the pointer to the message is returned to the calling process, which resumes its execution. Similar to SEND, RECEIVE runs with all interrupts off and, upon exit, reenables only the interrupt levels that were enabled prior to its invocation. This is accomplished by the assembly-language procedure INTON, which sets the master interrupts-on hardware flag and leaves all other interrupt masks and control registers intact.

When RECEIVE finds no messages, the calling process designated by the global variable RUNNING is labeled as PROCESS and is suspended by virtue of being removed from the Ready list. The removed PROCESS is then placed at the end of the queue of processes waiting for messages at the designated MAILBOX. Context of the PROCESS is saved on its stack using the SSTACK procedure, and the new running process is scheduled and dispatched. Note that interrupts need not be turned back on in this case, because the DISPATCH procedure will establish the environment of the new running process, including enabling of qualified interrupt levels.

10.4 INTERRUPT-MANAGEMENT

As discussed earlier, preliminary processing of all interrupts in KMOS-based systems is performed within the kernel. Consequently, all interrupts are vectored to the operating system, to the ITSERV routine. When an interrupt request is asserted and accepted, control is transferred to ITSERV. This routine identifies the particular source of interrupt, saves the software portion of the preempted process's state, and sends a signaling message to the dedicated mailbox.

10.4.1 Interrupt Mailboxes and Priorities

In KMOS, a separate mailbox must be dedicated to each hardware level of interrupt for the exchange of interrupt-signaling messages between the KMOS and the interrupt-service routines. A process wishing to service interrupts from a given source can do so by invoking the RECEIVE function on the corresponding interrupt mailbox. For this reason, interrupt mailboxes in KMOS systems are publicly declared global variables with names of the format IMBLVx (interrupt mailbox level x), where x is the number of the corresponding hardware level of the interrupt. As a result, KMOS software is capable only of distinguishing between different hardware levels of interrupt. In systems where interrupt-request lines of several devices are connected to a single level, a software routine must be employed to "demultiplex" requests for service by identifying the specific originating device. The logic of such a routine can be structured along the lines of a polling sequence, which was discussed in Chapter 2.

Since a special system message is needed for signaling interrupts occurring at a particular hardware level, for convenience of KMOS software one such message is created and appended to each descriptor of an interrupt mailbox. The resulting data structure of a mailbox IMBLVx is depicted in Figure 10.5. Being used for signaling purposes only, the message contains only the header field and no data. Its MTYPE field is set to a reserved value, 1, to designate the normal, system-sent interrupt message to the receiving process. Interrupt mailboxes and the related messages, of the format depicted in Figure 10.5, are created at the system startup time as described in Section 10.6.

In the particular computer system on which the version of KMOS presented in this chapter is implemented, there are eight distinct hardware levels of interrupt, with level 0 having the highest and level 7 the lowest priority. Due to the lack of difference at the user level between ISRs and ordinary processes in KMOS, discussed in Chapter 9, some means must be provided to the OS for establishing correspondence between the software priority and the hardware priority of a given process. This is essential, for instance, to the DISPATCH routine, which

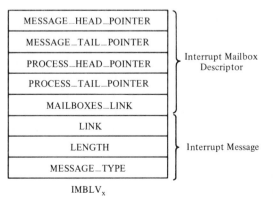

Figure 10.5 Interrupt mailbox in KMOS.

must enable selected priority levels for hardware interrupts when creating an environment for a user process. For this reason, software priority levels of this particular implementation are divided in two groups of 128 levels each. The first group, levels 0 through 127 inclusive, is dedicated to interrupt-related processes. With 8 distinct hardware levels of priority, a straightforward allocation of 16 software levels to a hardware level is made using the following expression:

$$software\_level \ \textbf{div} \ 16 = hardware\_level$$

where *div* stands for the ordinary integer division and the *software_level* must be in the range from 0 to 127. For example, processes running at software levels 0 through 15 inclusive correspond to the hardware level 0, and software levels 112 through 127 correspond to the hardware level 7. Software priorities in the range 128 to 255 are not associated with hardware priorities.

Processes wishing to service interrupts occurring at a given hardware level of priority must be assigned a software priority level in the corresponding range. In this way, a dispatched process is assured that while it is running, all lower and equal hardware levels of priority are disabled by the operating system. For example, the KMOSCLOCK process, described later, which services timer interrupts occurring at level 0, must be assigned a software priority in the range 0 through 15. When KMOSCLOCK is running in response to a timer interrupt, it cannot be preempted by any other source of interrupt in the described system.

The remaining group of software levels, 128 through 255, is treated as being purely software and below all hardware levels of priority. This means that when a process belonging to that range of software priorities is running, all hardware levels of interrupt are enabled and an interrupt from any source may preempt the running process.

10.4.2 Interrupt Servicing in KMOS

Because it involves several machine-specific manipulations of hardware, ITSERV is coded in assembly language. Its pseudocode equivalent in notation resembling Pascal is given as Program 10.1 and the assembler source is provided in Appendix A. As indicated, ITSERV is entered whenever a qualified interrupt request, that is, one explicitly enabled by means of ENABLEV and of higher priority than that of the running process, is recognized by the hardware. In order to distinguish between hardware sources connected to different levels of interrupt, each level is vectored to its own entry point. After recording the identity of the particular hardware interrupt level, a branch to common processing of all interrupt requests, labeled ALLINT, is made. After saving on the stack the software portion of the state of the process preempted by the current interrupt, the updated value of the hardware stack pointer (SP) is stored in the PCB of that process.

In KMOS, the hardware SP register points to the private stack area of the running process whose PCB is identified by the global variable RUNNING. Since the hardware interrupt-processing sequence and ITSERV both use the stack to routine ITSERV; {entered upon hardware interrupt}

  label allint;

  lev0: level := 0;
      goto allint;

  lev1: level := 1;
      goto allint;

  {one vector for each hardware level of priority}

  levx: level := x;
      goto allint;

      begin
allint: save_state_on_stack;
      running^.stack := hardware_SP;
      running^.status := preempted;
      acknowledge_interrupt_to_PIC;
      if intmsg[level].link = self
        then
          begin
            intmsg[level].mtype := 1;
            send (mailbox[level], intmsg[level])
          end
        else intmsg[level].type := 2;
      dispatch (running)
      end; {itserv}

Program 10.1 Pseudo-code equivalent of Itserv

save their respective portions of the preempted process's state, the net effect of these two operations at the beginning of interrupt processing is to save the complete state of the affected processes on its own stack. Subsequent storing of the updated value of the PC into the PCB of the preempted process completes the state-save operation. When the process in question is eventually resumed and its SP restored, the state-restore sequence may be reduced to simply popping-off the saved registers in the reverse order of storing.

After saving the context of the preempted process, ITSERV sets its status to PREEMPTED in order to inform DISPATCH that a full context restore will be needed when the process in question is to be resumed. Routine ITSERV then acknowledges the interrupt being processed to the programmable interrupt controller (PIC) or to its hardware equivalent. This action normally results in deasserting of the corresponding interrupt-request line to the CPU. Note that this does not acknowledge the interrupt to the originating I/O port, whose processing is left to the related interrupt-service routine (ISR). With this division of labor, KMOS handles the CPU part of interrupt logic and ISRs handle the device-specific portions of interrupt processing. This approach relieves the users from handling the CPU and PIC interrupt flags and, in so doing, has the potential of increasing the system reliability by virtue of protecting the common interrupt logic of the system from users. At the same time, KMOS does not become involved in the semantics of the specific sources of interrupt, which otherwise could severely restrict its portability.

As discussed in Chapters 5 and 9, KMOS uses messages to signal arrivals of interrupts to the related ISRs. With KMOS as an intermediary, asynchronous communication between interrupt occurrences and the related servicing processes is possible. In particular, a service process may conceivably be in some state other than Waiting-for-message when an interrupt message is sent to it. Due to buffering of messages in KMOS, the interrupt message in that case is deposited into the corresponding mailbox pending execution of the matching RECEIVE call by the interrupt-servicing process. When consecutive interrupts from the same source are closely spaced in time, a timing error may cause the servicing process to miss one or more interrupts. Being divorced from the device-specific aspects of interrupt processing, there is little that KMOS can do to remedy this situation. However, it should at least alert the user process when interrupts are lost. This poses the problem of detecting missed interrupts in KMOS without getting involved in the details of their processing.

In order to solve this problem, recall that the LINK field of each message is set to point to itself before the message is delivered to a requesting process. The primary reason for doing so is to assist in the detection of missed interrupts. If the LINK field of a given message is set to itself, it may be safely concluded that the message in question is not enqueued at any mailbox. When applied to interrupt messages in KMOS, by examining the LINK field of one, we can determine whether it is enqueued at an interrupt mailbox awaiting delivery or not. Since the same message is sent by the system for each arrival of an interrupt at a given hardware level, the only way for an interrupt message to have its LINK field set to itself is as a result of having been delivered to a requesting process. Conversely, if its LINK field has any other value, the interrupt message is awaiting delivery. Due to the symbiotic relationship between interrupt mailbox descriptors and interrupt messages in KMOS, locating an interrupt message for inspection is not a problem.

Following this line of reasoning, ITSERV checks whether the interrupt message appended to the interrupt mailbox of the level being processed is awaiting delivery or not. If not (LINK = self), the interrupt message is sent to the corresponding mailbox by means of the SEND procedure. Otherwise, the message is still awaiting delivery to signal some previous unprocessed interrupt, and a missed interrupt (KMOS cannot tell how many) is detected. To announce that fact, ITSERV sets the TYPE field of the message to the reserved value, 2, which indicates a missed interrupt. User processes servicing interrupts are assumed to test the TYPE field of the received message in order to be alerted to missed interrupts. Note that the interrupt message is not sent when missed interrupts are detected, because doing so does not serve any useful purpose and it might corrupt system queues.

In normal processing, a service process is waiting at the interrupt mailbox, and it becomes the running process after receiving the message from SEND. However, if service is lagging behind and no interrupt-service process is suspended at the mailbox, SEND enqueues the message and returns control to its caller, ITSERV. In that case, ITSERV schedules and dispatches the new running process. It is for this reason that SEND does not turn the interrupts back on when returning to the caller whose STATUS field differs from READY.

10.4.3 Enabling Hardware Interrupt Levels

The other interrupt-related service of KMOS, enabling of a hardware interrupt level, is quite straightforward. The ENABLEV procedure, coded in assembly language and listed in Appendix A, modifies the system interrupt mask, SYSMASK, to allow recognition of a hardware interrupt level passed as a parameter. Enabling an enabled level has no effect.

Variable SYSMASK is typically a collection of dedicated bits, each of which indicates whether the corresponding hardware level of interrupt has been enabled by means of the ENABLEV call or not. The actual bit settings in SYSMASK are machine-specific. They depend on both the number of distinct levels of interrupt in a given system and the ordering and setting of interrupt-enable/disable bits in control registers of the related hardware interrupt controller. The variable SYSMASK is used by the DISPATCH routine, described next, while creating the interrupt-related part of the environment for the process being dispatched.

10.5 PROCESS-MANAGEMENT

In this section we discuss the dispatching, creation, and timed delaying of processes in KMOS.

10.5.1 Process Dispatching

The DISPATCH procedure in KMOS is coded in assembly language because it directly manipulates certain machine-specific registers and uses special machine instructions, such as interrupt return. The detailed pseudocode equivalent of DISPATCH is given in Program 10.2.

The DISPATCH procedure takes one parameter (PROCESS), a pointer to the PCB of the process to be dispatched. The first action of DISPATCH is to set the hardware stack and frame pointers to the values recorded in the PCB and thus restore the process's stack area. The next activity is to enable the interrupt levels that should be on when the process being dispatched is running. Recall that an interrupt level is recognizable in KMOS only when two conditions are satisfied simultaneously: the hardware priority of the request is higher than that of the running process, and the level at which the request is made has been explicitly enabled by means of the ENABLEV call.

In order to enable the appropriate hardware levels of interrupt, DISPATCH uses the interrupt mask stored in the process's control-block. The value of this

```
procedure DISPATCH (process : ptrpcb);

  begin
      hardware_SP := process^.stack;                    {restore process's stack}
      hardware_FP := process^.frame;
      interrupt_mask := and(sysmask, process^.mask);    {enable higher int-levels}
      if process^.status = preempted                    {if was preempted }
        then                                            {   then}
          begin
            restore_regs                                {    unsave_context}
          IRET {end}                                    {    surrender control}
        else                                            {  else}
          begin
            if process^.delay <> nil                    {    if message to deliver}
              then
                begin
                  message := process^.delay;
                  message^.link := message;             {       then msg.link:=self}
                  receive := message;
                  process^.delay := nil
                end
          EI;                                           {    enable interrupts}
          RET {end}                                     {    exit KMOS}
  end; {dispatch}
```

Program 10.2 Pseudocode equivalent of Dispatch

mask is computed by the CREATEPROC procedure, described next, on the basis of the software priority of the related process. Its format is machine-specific, because the mask is supposed to be directly copyable to the appropriate register of the hardware interrupt controller.

As discussed earlier, the interrupt mask is derived in such a way that only interrupt levels higher than that of the running process may be enabled. In order to enable only a subset of those levels which is defined by preceding invocations of ENABLEV, procedure DISPATCH combines the process-specific mask with SYSMASK. Although variations are possible, depending on the bit polarity of the individual masks, in general the two masks are AND-ed together. The corresponding function call in Program 10.2 is meant to suggest the bitwise AND operation on the two masks, which is not available in standard Pascal. As indicated, the value obtained in this way is applied directly to the appropriate PIC register. This compound mask, however, takes effect only when control is surrendered to the user's process, as interrupts remain off throughout DISPATCH.

If the process being dispatched was preempted by an interrupt during its most recent run, DISPATCH restores its context by popping-off the contents of registers from the stack in the reverse order from their storing by ITSERV. Although not different from other processes at the user level, interrupt-service routines are unique in the sense of being invoked by the hardware interrupt-processing sequence. As discussed in Chapter 2, the effects of this sequence must be undone by the specialized interrupt-return instruction IRET. With the user process's program counter on stack, DISPATCH surrenders control to a preempted process by means of the IRET instruction. In machines where IRET does not restore the value of the hardware interrupt flag, an enable-interrupt (EI) instruction should precede IRET.

When handling a process not preempted on its last run, DISPATCH checks whether a message needs to be delivered. This is normally the case when the process being dispatched is exiting the Waiting-for-message state. If so, DISPATCH must retrieve the address of the message from the DELAY field of the related PCB, where it is placed by the SEND procedure. After setting the LINK field of the message to point to itself, DISPATCH surrenders control to the user process as if it were returned by the RECEIVE routine. In general, this requires emulation of the return function in order to deliver the message destined for the process being dispatched. Many compilers perform a single-value return function such as RECEIVE, by placing a copy of the variable in question into a specific CPU register, so this is all that DISPATCH usually has to do.

With the process's program counter on stack, a convenient way for DISPATCH to finally surrender control is by means of the regular subroutine-return instruction (RET). Since DISPATCH is always invoked with interrupts off, the last instruction prior to RET is customarily enabling of interrupts (EI), subject to masks in effect. The last two instructions are given in the assembly-language form in Program 10.2 in order to indicate the actual point where transfer of control from KMOS to user takes place.

10.5.2 Static Process-Descriptor

The creation of a process basically consists of initialization of its process control-block. In KMOS, systems programmers provide the initial values of process attributes by means of a special data structure, the static process descriptor (SPD). As indicated by the definition of its record in KMOS code, an SPD contains a process's attributes, such as name, priority, and indication of some special hardware requirements, if any, by means of the FLAGS field. In its present form, KMOS makes no use of the latter information, but it is included for future expansion, such as support for a specialized arithmetic coprocessor.

Since memory allocation in the presented implementation of KMOS is static, a process that wishes to create another process must provide sufficient memory space for the PCB and the stack of the new process. Addresses of these memory areas and the programmer-assigned process attributes, such as name and priority, are combined into a data structure called the *static process descriptor* (SPD), whose type is defined as the SPD in the type-definition part of the KMOS code. The INITIALPC field of an SPD record is used to store the starting address of the related process identified by the NAME field. The STACKLOW and STACKLEN fields define the lowest address of the reserved stack area and its maximum size, respectively. The RAMPCB field houses a pointer to the memory area reserved for the process control-block. The RAM prefix indicates that this structure must be maintained in the read/write memory as opposed to read-only memory.

When used in small embedded systems, KMOS can easily make the often useful distinction between static and dynamic data so that they may be placed in ROM or RAM, respectively. The resulting code is often called ROM-able, and it is of great interest in embedded systems with no secondary storage. For example, an SPD record for a process belonging to an initial system configuration—such as KMOSNUL—is static in the sense that it is defined at system-development time and never modified at run-time. Thus, SPDs can safely be placed in ROM. In fact, placing the static data, constants, and the code of KMOS and user processes in ROM greatly simplifies booting and restarting of the system, say, after a malfunction or a program failure. In addition, code and data in ROM are more secure in the sense that they cannot be erroneously or malevolently erased by a running process.

In order to simplify allocation of memory and the entire process of forming a static process descriptor, the present implementation of KMOS provides a set of macros for that purpose. A complete listing of configuration macros is provided in Appendix B. The user only needs to specify the initial process attributes (name and priority) and the desired size of the process's stack area. Macros create an SPD on the basis of this information, including even the starting address of the process, provided its process name corresponds to its public entry label. A more detailed description of SPD-preparation macros is given in Section 10.6.

In any case, with its code in memory and the SPD formed, a process can be created by means of the CREATEPROC call.

10.5.3 Process Creation

The CREATEPROC procedure takes one parameter, the address of the SPD of a process to be created. The CREATEPROC procedure starts by forming a process control-block in the area pointed to by the RAMPCB field of the SPD. While being created, a PCB does not belong to any system list, so all its link fields are set to NIL.

Handling of the stack is somewhat more involved. First, the top of the stack must be calculated and placed into the STACK field of the PCB. This operation can be machine-dependent in the sense that the direction of stack growth, from higher to lower memory addresses, or vice versa, may vary from one computer system to another. Assuming the common case of downward growth, the initial value of STACK can be obtained by adding the stack length to the lowest stack address, which are provided in the STACKLEN and STACKLOW fields of the SPD.

An indirect but important concern of the CREATEPROC is the preparation of the newly formed PCB so that control of the CPU can be surrendered to a new process in a manner that is consistent with the way in which control is transferred to regular processes. As discussed earlier, a process that is not running always has the address of its next instruction (the value of the PC) on its private stack. When such a process is resumed, DISPATCH eventually surrenders control to it by emulating a subroutine return with the process's PC on top of the stack. For reasons of uniformity and efficiency, it is desirable to make both regular and new processes look the same to DISPATCH in this regard. This can be accomplished by having CREATEPROC place the starting address of the new process onto the process's stack.

In particular, if the starting address of the process is pushed onto the process's stack, the subroutine return used by DISPATCH works for all processes. For this reason, procedure CREATEPROC actually places the process's initial starting address, supplied in the INITIALPC field of the SPD, onto its private stack. In addition, the STACK field of the PCB is set to point to the "pushed address" as the current top of stack, thus making it both unnecessary and even impossible for DISPATCH to differentiate between newly created and recurring processes. Naturally, this process is machine-dependent, and it may require some assembly-language code.

The specific machine on which the presented version of KMOS is implemented uses a segmented approach to memory addressing. As a result, addresses of routines are 4 bytes long and consist of two fields: offset and segment, of 2 bytes each. The related, implementation-specific, code of the KMOS procedure CREATEPROC initially sets the STACK to the sum of the STACKLOW and STACKLEN values, reduced by the process-address size, PADSIZE (4 in this implementation), to accommodate the initial address which is to be placed on the stack. Once formed, the STACK is RETYPE-ed to a special long address type and used as a pointer to place the segmented initial address on top of the process's stack in memory.

The next activity of CREATEPROC is to calculate the process's interrupt mask, MASK, on the basis of its software priority indicated in the SPD. The MASK should have the proper format to be directly writable into the hardware interrupt-mask registers in order to enable only the hardware levels of priority higher than that of the process in question. Obviously, this interrupt mask is machine-specific. As discussed in the previous section, MASK is used by the DISPATCH routine while creating the environment for the new running process. Rather then being provided in a separate PCB field, the MASK may be calculated by DISPATCH at run-time. However, the lookup method used in KMOS eliminates this run-time calculation and thus results in comparatively better performance.

Although machine-specific and not portable, we explain briefly the logic of the related KMOS calculation in order to give some flavor of this type of operation. As described earlier, the particular hardware on which the presented version of KMOS is implemented provides eight distinct priority levels of interrupt. The top 128 software priority levels of KMOS are mapped into the 8 hardware levels using a simple 16 : 1 allocation. The corresponding hardware interrupt mask has 8 bits, 1 per level, arranged so that the least significant mask-bit corresponds to level 0. Other bits are dedicated to decreasing levels of interrupts, with bit 7 corresponding to hardware level 7.

When a process at a given level of priority is running, only the interrupt levels of higher priority than its own should be enabled. For example, a process running at software level 1 corresponds to hardware priority 0, and all hardware levels must be disabled when it is running. Assuming that a mask-bit set to 1 indicates that the corresponding level should be disabled, the MASK for such a process should have a value 0FFH or 255 decimal. A process having software priority 125 corresponds to a hardware level of 7. When this process runs, all hardware levels except for 7 should be enabled. Consequently, the MASK of this process should have the value 80H or 128 decimal.

The CREATEPROC code for calculation of masks uses the following equation for processes in the software range of priorities between 0 and 127:

$$MASK = 256 - 2^{p \ div \ 16}$$

where p is process's the software priority. Integer division of software priority by 16 yields the corresponding hardware level of priority. The desired mask may then be obtained by raising base 2 to that power and subtracting the obtained value from 256. The reader is encouraged to verify this for a few test cases, including the two discussed in the preceding example.

The final responsibility of CREATEPROC is to place the newly formed PCB into the All-processes list. Since it is not sorted, insertions into this list are made at its front. The PCB is then inserted into the Ready list using the INSERTREADY procedure described earlier. Both list manipulations are performed with interrupts off in order to protect the global system pointers involved in the process. Note that no scheduling is performed at the process-creation time. Consequently, the newly created process will be considered for execution following the next event that causes the rescheduling.

10.5.4 Delaying of a Process for a Specified Time

An important process-management function of KMOS is delaying of a process for a specified period of time. As indicated by its functional specification, delaying of a process is performed by two separate but related routines. The first routine, DELAY, is called by a user process wishing to be delayed. The calling process is suspended and placed on the list of delayed processes. The second routine, KMOSCLOCK, is actually an interrupt-service routine which decrements the remaining delay of the processes in the Delayed list and makes eligible for execution those processes whose delay is found to be expired.

The Delayed list. Before discussing the details of their implementation, we must specify the common data structure used by both routines—the Delayed list. The DELAY procedure basically inserts entries into this list, whereas KMOSCLOCK searches the list and removes qualified entries. Our task is to choose a data structure that provides for efficient processing of both operations. In most systems, the frequency of timer interrupts is higher than that of processes becoming delayed. Consequently, we should be primarily concerned with the efficiency of clock-tick processing.

The first option to be considered is whether the Delayed list should be sorted or not. Inserts into an unsorted list can be performed in constant time by simply appending new entries. The clock-tick processing with such a list, however, has a time complexity proportional to the total number of delayed processes n_d. On the other hand, insertions into a sorted Delayed list, on the average, take $\frac{1}{2}n_d$ operations. Clock-tick processing with this kind of list apparently has the same time complexity as in the previous case, because the remaining delays of all processes must be decremented upon each timer interrupt. Unfortunately, neither of the two approaches does much for reducing the overhead of the most frequent and time-critical operation. The problem lies with decrementing of remaining delays of all processes in timed wait. One way to alleviate this problem is to make delays relative to each other, rather than absolute in terms of remaining time units. Let us explain this idea by means of an example.

Consider a system in which four processes, P1 through P4, are in the Delayed state. Assume that their remaining delays are 5, 20, 20, and 30 time units, respectively. In a classical scheme, KMOSCLOCK decrements all these values upon each timer interrupt and makes ready those processes whose delay becomes 0. In this example, 30 timer interrupts are needed to empty the Delayed list, assuming that no new entries arrive. In the course of processing these interrupts, 75 decrements of the remaining delay have to be made (5 times 4 entries, 15 times 3 entries, and 10 times 1 entry).

Alternatively, consider the same system where delays are recorded and processed relative to each other. Assume that the Delayed list is sorted by increasing absolute delays, a requirement satisfied by our example. Let us now express an individual process's relative delay as the number of clock-ticks to wait *after* the delay of that process's predecessor expires. The predecessor's relative delay is, in turn, expressed in terms of its predecessor's delay, thus yielding the following expression:

$$\text{reld}_i = \text{absd}_i - \sum_{j=1}^{i-1} \text{reld}_j; \ i = 2, \cdots, n$$

where $\text{reld}(_i)$ is the relative delay of the process i, and $\text{absd}(_i)$ is the absolute delay of the process i. In other words, relative delay of a process is the increment expressed in terms of clock-ticks that must elapse after expiration of all preceding relative delays in order for the process in question to leave the Delayed state. Since the first process in the Delayed list has no predecessor, its relative delay is numerically identical to its absolute delay. In our example, the relative delays of the four sample processes are 5, 15, 0, and 10, respectively.

So what is to be gained by the introduction of relative delays? The primary advantage is that *only the remaining delay of the first process in the list needs to be decremented upon each timer interrupt*. Since all other delays are relative and additive to it, no PCBs of processes beyond the one at the head of the Delayed list need be processed. This results in a significant reduction of overhead of timer-interrupt processing. In particular, only one node is visited and processed per timer interrupt, which brings the time complexity of that operation down to constant time.

In terms of our running example, the first 5 timer interrupts are serviced by decrementing the delay of the first process. When it becomes 0, the process is removed from the Delayed list. The subsequent 15 timer interrupts result in the second process's delay becoming 0. Since its successor has a relative delay of 0, both processes are removed from the Delayed list at that time. Finally, 10 timer interrupts later, delay of the last process expires and it makes the transition to the Ready state. Due to the suggested modification, 30 as opposed to 75 decrements are made in processing the same set of processes. In addition, the node to be processed is accessed in constant time, thus eliminating the node-traversal overhead imposed by the classical approach.

In summary, the proposed form of the Delayed list is sorted by the relative delay recorded in the DELAY field of each participating process. With this structure, inserts into the Delayed list require, on the average, examination of $\frac{1}{2}n_d$ nodes. Given that a much more frequent companion operation, clock-tick processing, is reduced to constant time, this price is well worth paying for the improved performance.

As indicated earlier, the Delayed list is a doubly linked list. Although not essential for the presented implementation of KMOS, double linking is maintained for possible extension leading to the addition of a time-limited version of the RECEIVE call. In order to illustrate management of this type of list and of relative delays, the appearance of the Delayed list with the four processes introduced in this section is given in Figure 10.6. Let us briefly outline the steps involved in adding a new process, Pn, whose absolute delay is 25 time units. Presumably, the process in question invokes KMOS to suspend it for the indicated period of time. As a result, KMOS has to search the Delayed list depicted in Figure 10.6 in order to find where to insert Pn, that is, behind all processes with shorter remaining delays and ahead of processes with longer remaining delays than that of Pn. In so doing, the relative delay of process Pn has to be calculated.

Starting with the first PCB in the Delayed list, Pn's delay is compared to P1's (relative) delay, which is 5. Since Pn's running relative delay is larger, the search proceeds to the next node. Before the new comparison, however, the relative delay of Pn starts being formed by subtracting from it the delay of the examined node, P1. As a result, the running relative delay of Pn, 20, is compared to that of the current node, P2, which is 15. Since Pn's delay is still larger, the process is repeated with P3. When node P4 is reached, Pn's delay equals 5. Since it is smaller than the relative delay of P4, process Pn is to be inserted after the predecessor of P4, which is pointed to by the back-link stored in the field LAST of P4's control-block. The state after insertion of Pn is shown in Figure 10.7.

Note that in addition to updating of the link fields of P3 and P4, the relative delay of P4 is changed. This is because of the cumulative nature of the relative

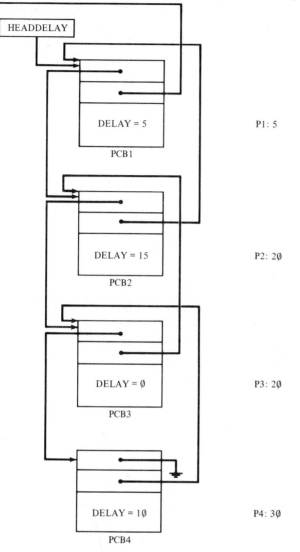

Absolute Delays

P1: 5

P2: 2Ø

P3: 2Ø

P4: 3Ø

Figure 10.6 Sample configuration of delayed list.

delays: the absolute delay of each node is a function of the relative delays recorded
for all nodes ahead of it in the Delayed list. In particular, the relative delay of
Pn is subtracted from the relative delay of P4, thus yielding the value of 5.
The validity of this operation may be verified by establishing that the absolute
remaining delay of P4 remains intact, as it should. In general, whenever a new
node is inserted into the Delayed list, the relative delay of its immediate successor
must be reduced by the value of the new entry's relative delay.

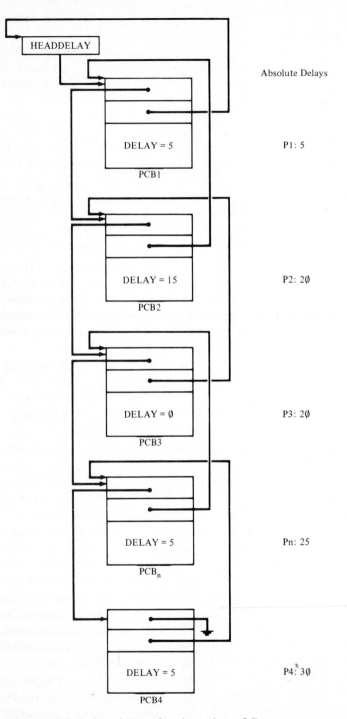

Figure 10.7 Delayed list after insertion of P*n*.

The DELAY operation. These ideas are embodied in the procedure DELAY which is provided in KMOS code. For reasons of potential future compatibility with the RECEIVE call, procedure DELAY takes two parameters: the address of a mailbox, and the delay expressed in terms of system time units. The first parameter is ignored by DELAY. As discussed earlier, specifying the duration of the desired delay in terms of the number of clock-ticks (system time units) is system-specific and generally not portable even within the same family of operating systems. The reason is that the time unit is often a system-generation parameter that may vary from installation to installation. Since conversion of standard time units, such as seconds or minutes, into the corresponding number of system-specific clock-ticks is straightforward, we opt for the simpler and faster approach of using system clock-ticks in KMOS.

The DELAY procedure acts only on those user calls whose desired delay is greater than 1 time unit. When called with an illegal argument, such as negative or zero time to wait, DELAY simply returns to caller with no error indication. For legal invocations, DELAY turns interrupts off in order to preserve the integrity of the Delayed list in the presence of concurrent updates.

Following the logic of relative delays outlined earlier, DELAY scans the list to find a place where the new entry is to be inserted. As with the Ready list described earlier, special processing for inserts at the beginning of the list and into the empty list are avoided by structuring the head pointer of the Delayed list as a PCB whose delay is 0. After visiting each node, the corresponding relative delay of the new entry is formed by updating the variable TICKS. The related WHILE loop terminates either when a place to insert is found or the last node is reached. In the latter case, depending on their relative delays, the new entry may have to be inserted before or after the last node.

If the relative delay of the new entry is smaller than that of the examined node, an insert before the examined node is performed. Accordingly, the relative delay of the examined node is updated and the roving pointer, ROVER, is backed-up to the node after which the insert is to be performed. Alternatively, the insert is to be made after the last visited node, and TICKS is updated. The latter situation includes inserts after the very last node, as well as behind nodes with the same relative delay as that of the new entry. In this way, nodes with identical remaining delays are treated in FCFS order.

Once its place is found, the new entry is marked as PROCESS (delayed process) and inserted into the Delayed list by modifying the forward link of its predecessor and the back link of its successor, if any. Of course, the corresponding links of the PROCESS itself are set to its predecessor and successor, respectively. After updating its status and recording its calculated relative delay, TICKS, the stack pointer of the delayed process is saved in its PCB and the process is suspended by being deleted from the Ready list. Note that the resulting transient state cannot corrupt KMOS because it is made invisible to other routines by virtue of having the interrupts off. With processing of the significant event completed, the new running process is scheduled and dispatched.

Timer-interrupt processing. The companion routine of DELAY, KMOSCLOCK, is effectively a process running under KMOS. It services interrupts from the interval timer by decrementing the remaining delay of the first process, if any, in the Delayed list. If the updated delay becomes 0, the top process and its potential successors with identical delay are removed from the Delayed list and placed into the Ready list. Since standard Pascal does not support the notion of processes, KMOSCLOCK is coded as a procedure. However, being a process, KMOSCLOCK must never be explicitly invoked by any routine or the associated timing it produces will be in error and the system may crash.

In general, when accurate timing is desired, the KMOSCLOCK process or its equivalent must have higher priority than any process which delays itself. In the hardware configuration on which the presented version of KMOS is implemented, the interval timer generates its interrupts at a hardware level of 0. The KMOSCLOCK process is assigned software priority 0, which is commensurate with the hardware level of priority it services. Consequently, no process can preempt the KMOSCLOCK in KMOS-based systems, and the high priority of KMOSCLOCK provides for accurate timekeeping, subject to the accuracy and stability of the hardware clock.

Like most system and real-time processes, KMOSCLOCK consists of the initialization part, which is executed only once, and the forever-do part, which performs the normal processing. The first part of KMOSCLOCK contains a call to enable recognition of hardware interrupts at the level 0 and then forms the address of the corresponding interrupt mailbox, IMBLV0 in this particular implementation, where KMOSCLOCK receives interrupt-signaling messages from KMOS. An implementation of KMOSCLOCK should normally begin with the initialization of the hardware interval timer so as to specify duration of a clock-tick for the particular system configuration. In the presented implementation this is not done because the underlying hardware system on which KMOS runs initializes the hardware interval timer to generate interrupts approximately every 55 ms.

The forever-do part begins by waiting for synchronization with timer interrupts. Given that the address of the interrupt mailbox, TIMERINT, has the proper value but a different type than the parameter required by RECEIVE, this value is RETYPE-ed. Since the very act of receiving a message signals the arrival of the awaited interrupt, KMOSCLOCK practically ignores the contents of the interrupt message (SIGNALMSG) after its receipt. Checking of its MTYPE field is not performed for reasons of efficiency and simplicity. However, this check should definitely be included during program development and system debugging.

Once an interrupt occurs, KMOSCLOCK tests whether there are any delayed processes. If so, the remaining delay of the first one is decremented. Following this, a WHILE loop is entered to remove all processes whose remaining delay is 0, if any. Each qualifying process is made ready and removed from the front position of the Delayed list. If more processes are left, the back pointer of the new first process is set to the list head. Alternatively, if the list is emptied, the roving pointer—DPROCESS—is set to the head node, whose DELAY field is 0, to ensure proper evaluation of the loop condition even when the end of the list is reached. Otherwise, a run-time error may occur, since DPROCESS^.DELAY is undefined for a nonexistent node.

In general, when KMOSCLOCK adds one or more entries to the Ready list, the scheduler should be invoked to select the next process to run. In the proposed implementation this is both undesirable and difficult, since a process, such as KMOSCLOCK, should not and cannot invoke an internal system routine, such as DISPATCH. However, scheduling is implicitly accomplished because KMOSCLOCK continues by invoking RECEIVE to await another timer interrupt. In normal processing, the interrupt is not asserted until the full tick elapses, and KMOSCLOCK is suspended at the TIMERINT mailbox. The ensuing processing of the change of system state (process KMOSCLOCK moving from the Running to the Waiting-for-message state) results in the rescheduling needed to take newly readied processes into consideration.

10.6 STARTUP AND INITIAL SYSTEM CONFIGURATION

The main body of the KMOS program is actually the initialization section, specified as the START routine in Chapter 9. In KMOS-based systems control must be passed to this section of code whenever the system is started (booted). This section turns interrupts off in order to initialize hardware, the programmable interrupt controller in particular. As discussed earlier, other hardware and I/O ports are normally initialized by their related servicing drivers, such as KMOSCLOCK.

With hardware prepared for normal operation, KMOS initializes its global variables. Recalling that head pointers to the Ready and Delayed lists are structured as PCB nodes for efficient processing, pointers to these structures are initialized by means of the ADR operator. Although the static pointer to a data structure is essentially its base address, the address and pointer types are incompatible in the Pascal compiler used to implement KMOS, and RETYPE-ing is necessary to equate the two values. Since the Ready list is initially empty, its pointer, HEADREADY.THREAD, is set to NIL. The priority of the HEADREADY node is set to 0 in order to ensure proper operation of the INSERTREADY procedure. The All-processes and Delayed lists are initialized in a similar manner. The delay of the pointer node HEADDELAY.DELAY is set to 0 to ensure proper operation of the routines that manipulate the Delayed list, such as DELAY and KMOSCLOCK. The described operations conclude the initialization of KMOS data structures.

Before surrendering control to a user process for the first time, KMOS creates the user-specified initial configuration of processes and mailboxes. As discussed in Chapter 9, this initial configuration is defined by means of a table consisting of static process descriptors and mailbox descriptors. The general appearance of the configuration table is depicted in Figure 10.8. As indicated, the table INITAB contains pointers to the table of SPDs of initial processes (IPT) and contains a pointer to the table of addresses of initial mailboxes (IMT). The number of

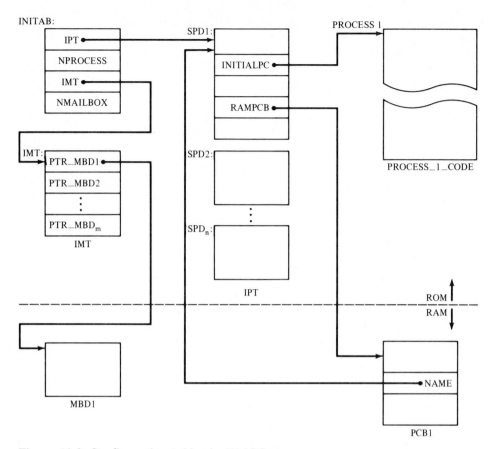

Figure 10.8 Configuration tables in KMOS.

entries in each of those tables, **NPROCESS** and **NMAILBOX**, is also given in the **INITAB** table, whose type is specified as **CRTAB** in KMOS.

A set of macros is provided in KMOS (and listed in Appendix B) for the creation of descriptors for the processes and mailboxes belonging to the initial system configuration. For example, an SPD macro takes three parameters: process name, priority, and desired stack size. The macro then reserves the space in memory necessary for the SPD and PCB records and initializes all fields of the SPD record. Similarly, the MSG macro reserves the space in memory for a mailbox descriptor. Other macros form the **INITAB** table on the basis of the SPDs and mailbox descriptors specified for the initial system configuration. The KMOSNUL and KMOSCLOCK processes are routinely included in the initial configuration of KMOS systems. Naturally, users are free to construct the initial system configuration by other means when desired, such as by constructing their own INITAB, by supplying a program that creates initial processes and mailboxes, and the like. Aside from the initial configuration, processes and mailboxes can be created at any time during system operation by invoking the CREATEPROC and CREATEMBOX services of KMOS.

As indicated, the initialization code invokes CREATEPROC to create each process specified by means of the INITAB table. With the SPDs of initial processes occupying adjacent positions in IPT, the successor to the just processed SPD can be reached by incrementing the pointer by the length of an SPD, indicated by the constant SPDSIZE in KMOS. Since a pointer cannot be incremented in standard Pascal, some machine- and compiler-specific conversion of types is needed to accomplish this process. A similar approach is used to create the initial set of mailboxes. Finally, DISPATCH is invoked to schedule one of the created processes and to surrender control of the CPU to it. As a part of this process, the interrupt system is enabled for the level of priority of the scheduled process.

10.7 SUMMARY

In this chapter we have presented an implementation of the KMOS kernel whose functional specification was given in Chapter 9.

In order to facilitate the frequent insertions and deletions of nodes resulting from changes of system states, KMOS lists are implemented as linked lists. The Ready list is sorted by decreasing priorities of the participating process control-blocks in order to minimize the time complexity of its most frequent and time-critical operation: searching in the course of scheduling the next process to run. Manipulations of the Ready list, as well as scheduling and dispatching operations, are simplified and their performance is improved as a result of the existence of the KMOSNUL process whose function is to provide at least one ready process in the system at all times.

Separate user stack areas are maintained in KMOS in order to localize the effects of improper stack manipulation by user processes and to allow use of the stack for local variables and temporary data storage. This is important for processes coded in block-structured languages.

The message-exchange facility of KMOS is, in addition to support for interprocess communication and synchronization, used to signal the arrival of hardware interrupts. As a side effect of message buffering, asynchronous servicing of hardware interrupt requests is made possible in KMOS. Missed interrupts are detected by the system and indicated to service processes. Selective enabling of interrupt levels commensurate with the priority of the running process, as well as explicitly by means of the ENABLEV service, is also supported in KMOS.

Programmer-specified process attributes are communicated to the system by means of static process descriptors. The presented KMOS implementation facilitates placing of the static portion of the system into read-only memory when desired.

The time complexity of timer-interrupt processing is reduced by ordering the processes in the Delayed list according to increasing relative delays. The initial system configuration is user-definable by means of the initialization table.

OTHER READING

Since our preoccupation in Chapter 10 was the detailed implementation of an operating system, in this section we list several books that provide detailed descriptions of concepts and designs of kernels and, in some cases, of other parts of operating systems.

The design of the operating system Solo and a report on the programming language Concurrent Pascal that Solo is written in are provided by Brinch Hansen (1977). A more recent book by the same author (1982) describes a systems-implementation language, Edison, and the design of a kernel written in that language.

Holt (1983) describes the programming language Concurrent Euclid and Tunis, a Unix-like multiprocess kernel written in Concurrent Euclid. The design of Xinu, another Unix-inspired operating system, is described by Comer (1984). Xinu is written in C and it supports network configurations of Xinu machines.

Wulf, Levin, and Harbison (1981) describe the ideas, concepts, and implementation aspects of the Hydra operating system running on the C.mmp multiprocessor. In addition, a performance evaluation of some of the Hydra mechanisms is provided and discussed. Joseph, Prasad, and Natarajan (1984) report on the design of another multiprocessor operating system written in the programming language CCNPascal, a derivative of Concurrent Pascal.

Implementation details, data structures, and several mechanisms of the VAX/VMS, a commercial virtual-memory operating system, are described by Kenah and Bate (1984).

EXERCISES

The first seven exercises in this section are devised to test and to sharpen the reader's understanding of the implementation of KMOS discussed in this chapter. Consequently, their completion is not dependent on having access to a KMOS system. Although the remaining exercises can more or less be solved on paper, they represent various functional extensions to the KMOS system and the most beneficial approach is to implement and test some of them on a working KMOS system. An additional set of exercises is provided by implementing other KMOS extensions whose functional specification was called for in Exercises 1 through 10, inclusive, of the previous chapter.

10.1 Modify the Ready list so that its head node is not a (fake) process control-block, as is the case in the presented implementation of KMOS. Instead, use an ordinary list head pointer that points to the first (real) PCB of the Ready list. Modify the code of the INSERTREADY and of all other KMOS routines affected by this change, and compare the resulting solution to the original KMOS code. Discuss the relative advantages and disadvantages of the two approaches with regard to the nature and frequency of the various operations performed on the Ready list in KMOS.

10.2 As presented, KMOS manages a separate stack area for each active process. However, no mention of the system stack is made in the text. Explain which stack area, if any, is used by the KMOS system itself. Discuss whether this approach should be changed in systems that support differentiation between the user's and the system's stack in hardware, and if so, how.

10.3 Assume that KMOSNUL or a similar process is not used in KMOS. Identify all KMOS routines affected by this change, modify their code accordingly, and discuss the ramifications of this change for the overall system's operation.

10.4 An alternative way of handling the KMOSNUL process in KMOS is proposed. The proposal consists of simply reserving the lowest priority in the system (255 in the presented implementation) for KMOSNUL and forbidding any other process to use that priority. Discuss whether this change requires modification of the KMOS code as presented, provide the necessary modifications, if any, and modify certain KMOS routines so that denial of the lowest priority to any process other than KMOSNUL is actually enforced.

10.5 Can a user process send a message to an interrupt mailbox? Analyze the resulting behavior of KMOS, and discuss whether this operation should be allowed or not. What would be the use, if any, of sending messages to interrupt mailboxes?

10.6 Discuss the changes needed to be made to KMOS in order to handle absolute delays instead of the relative delays of processes waiting in the Delayed list. Provide the necessary modifications to DELAY, to KMOSCLOCK, and to any other routine of KMOS affected by this change. Discuss the relative advantages and disadvantages of the two approaches.

10.7 Discuss the ramifications of not assigning the highest level of priority to the KMOSCLOCK process.

10.8 Implement and test a printer and/or a display driver for a KMOS by following the logic of an interrupt-driven service routine for the message-based systems presented in Program 5.6. For testing and demonstration purposes, implement at least one test program that invokes the printer-server.

10.9 Assume that the only user activity in a KMOS system consists of execution of three processes: P1, P2, and P3. Each process consists of a forever-do loop, in which the process delays itself by invoking the DELAY service, prints its identity (just the number 1, 2, or 3 will suffice) when the delay expires, and repeats the sequence. Delays of the individual processes are 60, 95, and 110 time units, respectively. Assuming that process P2 has the highest priority and P1 the lowest priority of the three processes, predict the appearance of the first 25 items of output produced as a result of execution of the three processes. Implement the three processes and test your prediction in practice. Explain how ties, when two or more processes exit the Delayed state at the same time, are broken and why.

10.10 In the presented implementation of KMOS, the system saves complete state only when the running process is involuntarily preempted and saves only partial state of the process in all other changes of state. Modify KMOS so that the entire state of the process is also saved when it voluntarily transfers control to KMOS and restored when that process is scheduled to run again.

10.11 Design and implement dynamic memory for the purposes of creation of system objects, such as PCBs, MBDs, and messages. Provide the GET memory and PUT memory services to processes for acquiring and releasing of memory blocks, respectively. Since messages in KMOS are of variable length, indicate how the problem of memory fragmentation is tackled by your design. Provide sample calling procedures that user processes should follow when creating processes or mailboxes with this form of memory allocation.

10.12 Relying on the facilities for dynamic memory-management provided for the previous exercise, modify KMOS so that messages are copied from a sender's to a user's space (with some intermediate system buffering if necessary), as opposed to the current implementation of effectively exchanging a pointer to the message. Discuss the tradeoff of safety versus performance on the basis of the two implementations of the message facility.

10.13 Modify KMOS so that objects, such as processes and mailboxes, can be created and referenced by name as opposed to address of the user-provided record, as is the case in the presented implementation. Assuming that the user specifies only the name and the user-specified attributes (such as priority and the starting address), modify the calling sequences of object-creation services so that the system does the rest of the work in acquiring memory and creating the objects therein. Indicate how users' names are cataloged by the system and when and how name-address mapping is performed. Specify how errors, such as duplicate name during object creation or nonexistent name during object referencing, are handled and indicated to users by your design. Discuss the tradeoff of user convenience versus system complexity of the naming facility on the basis of your experience.

10.14 Modify the RECEIVE and all affected routines of KMOS so that the caller may specify the time limit on how long it is willing to wait for a message to arrive. Use the TIMLIM parameter of RECEIVE for that purpose. If the calling process manages to receive a message before expiration of the specified limit, the normal execution of RECEIVE should be followed. However, if the time limit expires while the process is still waiting for the message, the waiting should be terminated and the process in question readied for execution. In either case, some indication of the outcome of the RECEIVE should be provided to the user. Specify how this is done in your design, and provide some examples of user processes calling the timed RECEIVE and analyzing its response upon regaining control. Is the DELAY routine needed in systems where the described version of time-limited RECEIVE is provided? Why or why not?

10.15 Modify the DELAY routine in KMOS so that it allows users to specify the delay interval in terms of standard time units, such as seconds, as opposed to system-dependent clock-ticks.

10.16 Design and implement a file-management system for the KMOS kernel. Unless a facility for interaction with users and a command language are provided, implement only the file services accessible via system calls.

KMOS KERNEL

```
JG IC  Line#   Source Line        IBM Personal Computer Pascal Compiler
   00    1     {$pagesize:54, $linesize:95}
         2     {$title: 'KMOS KERNEL'}
         3     {$subtitle:'DEFINITION OF DATA STRUCTURES'}
         4     {$nilck-, $debug-, $symtab-}
         5
   00    6     PROGRAM kmos;
         7
   10    8       CONST
   10    9         ready    = 0;              {process states: ready,}
   10   10         delayed  = 1;                      {delayed, and}
   10   11         waitmsg  = 2;                       {waiting-for-message}
   10   12         spdsize  = 24;            {size of SPD; all sizes in bytes}
   10   13         imtesize = 2;             {size of an IMT entry}
   10   14         padsize  = 4;             {size of process address}
        15
   10   16       TYPE
   10   17         unsint  = WORD;           {word allows controlled type-conversions}
   10   18         ptrspd  = ^spd;           {pointer to a static process descriptor, }
   10   19         ptrmbd  = ^mbd;           {pointer to a mailbox decriptor, MBD}
   10   20         ptrpcb  = ^pcb;           {pointerr to a process control block, PCB}
   10   21         ptombd  = ^indirect;      {pointer to an indirect record}
   10   22         ptrmsg  = ^msg;           {pointer to a message}
   10   23         adrpcb  = ADR OF pcb;     {address od a process control block}
   10   24         adrlad  = ADR OF laddr;   {address of a long address record}
        25
   10   26         laddr = RECORD    {long address, for iAPX86 segmentation}
   20   27           offset  : unsint;       {offset within a segment}
   20   28           segment : unsint        {base address of a segment}
   10   29         END;
        30
   10   31         spd = RECORD      {static process descriptor, can be in ROM}
   20   32           name      : ARRAY [1..10] OF char;  {process name - ASCII}
   20   33           initialpc : laddr;      {starting address of the process}
   20   34           stacklow  : unsint;     {lowest address of process's stack}
   20   35           stacklen  : unsint;     {length of process's stack}
   20   36           pri       : integer;    {process priority [0,255]}
   20   37           rampcb    : ptrpcb;     {address of process PCB}
   20   38           flags     : integer     {miscellaneous, e.g. special hardware}
   10   39         END;
        40
```

KMOS

KMOS KERNEL
DEFINITION OF DATA STRUCTURES

```
JG IC  Line#   Source Line        IBM Personal Computer Pascal Compiler
        41     {$page+}
  10    42       pcb = RECORD     {process control block}
  20    43         next    : ptrpcb;     {forward link for delayed list}
  20    44         last    : ptrpcb;     {link-back for delayed list}
  20    45         thread  : ptrpcb;     {multipurpose link}
  20    46         delay   : integer;    {remaining delay for timed waits}
  20    47         frame   : unsint;     {stack frame pointer}
  20    48         stack   : unsint;     {stack pointer to private stack area}
  20    49         marker  : unsint;     {low stack limit - offset}
  20    50         pri     : integer;    {process priority}
  20    51         status  : integer;    {process status}
  20    52         name    : ptrspd;     {pointer to process name in SPD}
  20    53         linkall : ptrpcb;     {link for all processes list}
  20    54         mask    : integer     {process interrupt mask}
  10    55       END;
        56
  10    57       mbd = RECORD     {mailbox descriptor}
  20    58         headmes  : ptrmsg;    {pointer to head of the message queue}
  20    59         tailmes  : ptrmsg;    {pointer to tail of the message queue}
  20    60         headproc : ptrpcb;    {pointer to head of the process queue}
  20    61         tailproc : ptrpcb;    {pointer to tail of the process queue}
  20    62         mboxlink : ptrmbd     {link to Mailboxes list}
  10    63       END;
        64
  10    65       msg = RECORD     {message}
  20    66         link   : ptrmsg;      {link for messages at a mailbox}
  20    67         length : integer;     {message length}
  20    68         mtype  : integer      {message type}
  10    69       END;
        70
  10    71       crtab = RECORD    {create table, initial system configuration, ROM}
  20    72         ipt      : ptrspd;    {pointer to initial process table, IPT}
  20    73         nprocess : integer;   {number of processes in IPT}
  20    74         imt      : ptombd;    {pointer to initial mailbox table, IMT}
  20    75         nmailbox : integer    {number of mailboxes in IMT}
  10    76       END;
        77
  10    78       indirect = RECORD  {indirect, for double indirection}
  20    79         tombx : ptrmbd    {ptr to ptr to a mailbox descriptor}
  10    80       END;
        81
```

KMOS

```
KMOS KERNEL
DEFINITION OF DATA STRUCTURES

JG IC  Line#    Source Line        IBM Personal Computer Pascal Compiler
        82     {$page+}
        83     {external variables: defined elsewhere, used in this module}
   10   84     VAR [EXTERNAL] initab: crtab; {create table, in CONFIG.MAC}
   10   85     VAR [EXTERNAL] imblv0: mbd;   {level_0 interrupt mbx. descriptor}
        86
        87      {public variables: defined here, referenced elsewhere}
   10   88     VAR
   10   89      running [PUBLIC] : ptrpcb;  {pointer to the running process}
        90
        91      {global variables: headers and pointers to system lists}
   10   92      headready  : pcb;        {head of ready list: node}
   10   93      headdelay  : pcb;        {head of delay list: node}
   10   94      headmail   : ptrmbd;     {head mailboxes list: pointer}
   10   95      headallp   : ptrpcb;     {head all processes list: pointer}
   10   96      readylist  : ptrpcb;     {pointer to head ready list}
   10   97      delaydlist : ptrpcb;     {pointer to head delayed list}
        98
        99      {miscellaneous global pointers and variables}
   10  100      staticpd   : ptrspd;     {pointer to a static process descriptor
   10  101      ustaticpd  : unsint;     {unsigned staticpd}
   10  102      inibox     : ptrmbd;     {pointer to a mailbox descriptor}
   10  103      fstep      : ptombd;     {ptr to a ptr to a mailbox descriptor}
   10  104      ufstep     : unsint;     {unsigned fstep}
   10  105      i          : integer;    {loop counter}
       106
       107     {external procedures; in assembly-language module KMOSA.ASM}
   10  108     PROCEDURE inihdw;EXTERNAL;   {initializes hardware}
   10  109     PROCEDURE enablev (level : integer);EXTERNAL; {enable interrupt lev
   10  110     PROCEDURE inton; EXTERNAL;   {turn interrupts on}
   10  111     PROCEDURE intoff; EXTERNAL;  {turn interrupts off}
   10  112     PROCEDURE dispatch (process : ptrpcb); EXTERNAL; {dispatch a proces
   10  113     PROCEDURE sstack (process : ptrpcb); EXTERNAL;   {save process stac
       114

SSTACK
```

KMOS KERNEL
INSERTREADY

```
JG IC  Line#    Source Line      IBM Personal Computer Pascal Compiler
         115    {$subtitle:'INSERTREADY', $page+}
         116    {** INSERTREADY ** is an internal, not user-callable, procedure
         117     that inserts a process identified by PCB whose address is passed
         118     as a parameter, into the list of ready processes. Insertions are
         119     done in a manner that preserves priority ordering of the Ready list.}
         120
   20    121    PROCEDURE insertready (process : ptrpcb);
         122
   20    123      VAR
   20    124        current,                {pointers to the current, and}
   20    125        previous : ptrpcb;       {previous ready-list nodes visited}
         126
   20    127      BEGIN
   21    128        current := readylist;
   21    129        previous := readylist;
         130        {search for a lower priority process, stop if last node}
   21    131        WHILE (process^.pri >= current^.pri) AND (current^.thread <> nil) DO
   21    132          BEGIN
   22    133            previous := current;
   32    134            current := current^.thread
   21    135          END; {while}
         136        {insert after the last higher or equal priority process: previous}
   21    137        process^.thread := previous^.thread;
   21    138        previous^.thread := process;
   21    139        process^.status := ready;
 = 31    140        running := headready.thread
   10    141      END; {insertready}
```

INSERTREADY

KMOS KERNEL
CREATEMBOX

```
JG IC  Line#    Source Line       IBM Personal Computer Pascal Compiler
          142   {$subtitle:'CREATEMBOX', $page+}
          143     {** CREATEMBOX ** is a user-callable procedure that
          144      creates a mailbox by initializing the mailbox descriptor
          145      whose address is passed as a parameter.}
          146
    20    147   PROCEDURE creatembox (mailbox : ptrmbd) [PUBLIC];
          148
    20    149     BEGIN
    21    150       mailbox^.headmes := nil;
    21    151       mailbox^.tailmes := nil;
    21    152       mailbox^.headproc := nil;
    21    153       mailbox^.tailproc := nil;
          154       {insert into mailboxes list}
    21    155       intoff;
    21    156       mailbox^.mboxlink := headmail;
  = 21    157       headmail := mailbox;
    21    158       inton
    10    159     END; {creatembox}
```


CREATEMBOX

KMOS KERNEL
SEND

```
JG IC  Line#    Source Line        IBM Personal Computer Pascal Compiler
       160      {$subtitle:'SEND', $page+}
       161      {** SEND ** is a user-callable procedure that sends a message
       162       whose address is passed as a second parameter to the mailbox
       163       whose address is passed as the first parameter. SEND is
       164       nonblocking and waiting messages are queued in FIFO order.}
       165
   20  166      PROCEDURE send (mailbox : ptrmbd; message : ptrmsg) [PUBLIC];
       167
   20  168        VAR
   20  169          recipient : ptrpcb;    {message recepient process}
       170
   20  171        BEGIN
   21  172          intoff;
   21  173          IF (mailbox^.headproc = nil)
   21  174            THEN    {if no processes waiting, queue up the message}
   21  175              BEGIN
   22  176                IF (mailbox^.headmes = nil)
   22  177                  THEN mailbox^.headmes := message
   22  178                  ELSE mailbox^.tailmes^.link := message;
   22  179                message^.link := nil;
   22  180                mailbox^.tailmes := message;
   22  181                IF running^.status = ready THEN inton
   22  182              END
   21  183            ELSE    {if processes waiting, deliver the message}
   21  184              BEGIN
   22  185                recipient := mailbox^.headproc;
   22  186                mailbox^.headproc := recipient^.thread;
   22  187                IF mailbox^.headproc = nil THEN mailbox^.tailproc := nil;
   22  188                recipient^.delay := RETYPE (integer, message);
       189                {if not called by KMOS, save process's stack pointer}
   22  190                IF running^.status = ready THEN sstack (running);
   22  191                insertready (recipient);
   22  192                dispatch (running)
   22  193              END {if}
   10  194        END; {send}
```

SEND

KMOS KERNEL
DELETEREADY

```
JG IC  Line#    Source Line       IBM Personal Computer Pascal Compiler
        195     {$subtitle:'DELETEREADY', $page+}
        196       {** DELETEREADY ** is an internal procedure that
        197         removes the running process from the Ready list.}
        198
   10   199     PROCEDURE deleteready;
        200
   20   201       BEGIN
 = 21   202         headready.thread := running^.thread;
 = 21   203         running^.thread := nil;
 = 31   204         running := headready.thread
   10   205       END; {deleteready}
```

DELETEREADY

KMOS KERNEL
RECEIVE

```
JG IC  Line#    Source Line        IBM Personal Computer Pascal Compiler
        206     {$subtitle:'RECEIVE', $page+}
        207
        208     {** RECEIVE ** is a user-callable function that delivers
        209       a message, when available, to the caller. RECEIVE is
        210       blocking, and messages queue is handled in FIFO order.}
        211
   20   212     FUNCTION receive (mailbox : ptrmbd; timlim : integer) : ptrmsg [PUBLIC];
        213
   20   214     VAR
   20   215       message : ptrmsg;        {message to return}
   20   216       process : ptrpcb;        {process to suspend}
        217
   20   218     BEGIN
   21   219       intoff;
   21   220       IF mailbox^.headmes <> nil
   21   221         THEN     {if messages available, caller gets the first}
   21   222           BEGIN
   22   223             message := mailbox^.headmes;
   22   224             mailbox^.headmes := message^.link;
   22   225             IF mailbox^.headmes = nil THEN mailbox^.tailmes := nil;
   22   226             message^.link := message;
 = 22   227             receive := message;
   22   228             inton
   22   229           END
   21   230         ELSE     {if no messages, the caller is suspended}
   21   231           BEGIN
   22   232             process := running;
   22   233             process^.status := waitmsg;
   22   234             deleteready;
   22   235             IF mailbox^.tailproc = nil
   22   236               THEN mailbox^.headproc := process
   22   237               ELSE mailbox^.tailproc^.thread := process;
   22   238             mailbox^.tailproc := process;
   22   239             sstack (process);
   22   240             dispatch (running)
   22   241           END {if}
   10   242     END; {receive}
```

RECEIVE

KMOS KERNEL
CREATEPROC

```
JG IC  Line#    Source Line       IBM Personal Computer Pascal Compiler
       243      {$subtitle:'CREATEPROC', $page+}
       244      {** CREATEPROC ** is a user-callable procedure that initializes
       245      a Process Control Block of the process identified by the
       246      Static Process Descriptor whose address is passed as a
       247      parameter. The target process is then placed in Ready list.}
       248
   20  249      PROCEDURE createproc (descriptor : ptrspd) [PUBLIC];
       250
   20  251        VAR
   20  252          memstack : adrlad;         {process stack in memory}
   20  253          process : ptrpcb;          {target PCB}
       254
       255        {Integer function TWOTO raises base 2 to an integer
       256         power passed as a parameter.}
   30  257        FUNCTION twoto (power : integer) : integer;
   30  258          BEGIN
 = 31  259            twoto := TRUNC(EXP(POWER*ln(2)))
   20  260          END; {twoto}

       261
   20  262        BEGIN {createproc}
       263          {initialize PCB fields}
   21  264          process := descriptor^.rampcb;
   21  265          process^.next := nil;
   21  266          process^.last := nil;
   21  267          process^.thread := nil;
   21  268          process^.delay := 0;
   21  269          process^.name := descriptor;
   21  270          process^.pri := descriptor^.pri;
       271
       272          {establish process stack}
   21  273          process^.stack := descriptor^.stacklow + descriptor^.stacklen - padsiz
   21  274          process^.marker := descriptor^.stacklow;
       275
       276          {push process starting address onto its stack -machine dependent}
   21  277          memstack := RETYPE (adrlad,process^.stack);
   21  278          memstack^.offset := descriptor^.initialpc.offset;
   21  279          memstack^.segment := descriptor^.initialpc.segment;
       280
       281          {calculate process's interrupt mask = f(priority)}
   21  282          IF (process^.pri < 128)
   21  283            THEN process^.mask := 256 - twoto (process^.pri DIV 16)
   21  284            ELSE process^.mask :=0;
       285
```

CREATEPROC

KMOS KERNEL
CREATEPROC

```
 JG IC  Line#    Source Line        IBM Personal Computer Pascal Compiler
          286    {$page+}
          287        {insert into all processes and ready lists}
    21    288        intoff;
    21    289        process^.linkall := headallp;
=   21    290        headallp := process;
    21    291        insertready (process);
    21    292        inton
    10    293    END; {createproc}
```


CREATEPROC

```
KMOS KERNEL
DELAY
```

```
JG IC  Line#    Source Line       IBM Personal Computer Pascal Compiler
        294     {$subtitle:'DELAY', $page+}
        295      {** DELAY ** is a user-callable procedure that places the calling
        296          process in the Delayed list for subsequent resumption by KMOSCLOCK.}
        297
   20   298      PROCEDURE delay (fake : ptrmsg; ticks : integer) [PUBLIC];
        299
   20   300        VAR
   20   301          rover   : ptrpcb;      {roving pointer}
   20   302          process : ptrpcb;      {process to sleep}
        303
   20   304        BEGIN
   21   305          IF ticks >= 1         {if called with a legal parameter}
   21   306            THEN
   21   307              BEGIN
   22   308                intoff;
   22   309                rover := delaydlist;
        310                {scan the list until lower delay or end of list reached}
   22   311                WHILE (ticks >= rover^.delay) AND (rover^.next <> nil) DO
   22   312                  BEGIN
   23   313                    ticks := ticks - rover^.delay;
   33   314                    rover := rover^.next
   22   315                  END; {while}
   32   316                IF ticks < rover^.delay
   22   317                  THEN
   22   318                    BEGIN
   23   319                      rover^.delay := rover^.delay - ticks;
   33   320                      rover := rover^.last
   23   321                    END
   22   322                  ELSE ticks := ticks - rover^.delay;
   22   323                process := running;
   22   324                process^.next := rover^.next;
   22   325                process^.last := rover;
   22   326                rover^.next := process;
   22   327                IF process^.next <> nil
   22   328                  THEN
   22   329                    BEGIN
   23   330                      rover := process^.next;
   23   331                      rover^.last := process
   22   332                    END;
   22   333                process^.status := delayed;
   22   334                process^.delay := ticks;
   22   335                sstack (process);
   22   336                deleteready;
   22   337                dispatch (running)
   22   338              END {if}
   10   339          END; {delay}
```

```
DELAY
```

KMOS KERNEL
KMOSCLOCK

```
JG IC   Line#    Source Line       IBM Personal Computer Pascal Compiler
        340      {$subtitle:'KMOSCLOCK', $page+}
        341      {** KMOSCLOCK ** is a process (created during system
        342       initialization) that services interrupts from the hardware
        343       timer, and awakens processes whose timed delay has expired.}
        344
  20    345      PROCEDURE kmosclock [PUBLIC];
        346
  20    347        CONST
  20    348          timerlevel = 0;            {hardware-specific constant}
        349
  20    350        VAR
  20    351          signalmsg : ptrmsg;        {for interrupt-signaling message}
  20    352          dprocess  : ptrpcb;        {delayed process manipulation}
  20    353          timerint  : ADR OF mbd;    {hardware-timer interrupt mailbox}
        354
  20    355        BEGIN
        356
        357          {initialization section, executed only once}
  21    358          enablev (timerlevel);      {enable timer interrupts}
  21    359          timerint := ADR imblv0;
        360
        361          {repetitive, forever do section}
  21    362          WHILE true DO
  21    363            BEGIN
  22    364              signalmsg := receive (RETYPE (ptrmbd, timerint), 0);
  22    365              IF headdelay.next <> nil
  22    366                THEN    {if some processes in timed wait}
  22    367                  BEGIN
  23    368                    dprocess := headdelay.next;
  23    369                    dprocess^.delay := dprocess^.delay - 1;
  23    370                    WHILE (dprocess^.delay = 0) AND (headdelay.next <> NIL) DO
  23    371                      BEGIN
  24    372                        insertready (dprocess);
  24    373                        dprocess := dprocess^.next;
= 24    374                        headdelay.next := dprocess;
  24    375                        IF dprocess <> nil
  24    376                          THEN dprocess^.last := delaydlist
  24    377                          ELSE dprocess := delaydlist
  24    378                      END {while}
  23    379                  END {if}
  22    380            END {while}
  10    381      END; {kmosclock}
```

KMOSCLOCK

KMOS KERNEL
KMOS MAIN SECTION

```
 JG IC  Line#    Source Line       IBM Personal Computer Pascal Compiler
        382    {$subtitle:'KMOS MAIN SECTION', $page+}
        383
  10    384      BEGIN {kmos}
        385        {initialize hardware: PIC etc.}
  11    386        intoff;
  11    387        inihdw;
        388
        389        {initialize head nodes and pointers to system lists}
  11    390        readylist := RETYPE (ptrpcb, ADR headready);
  11    391        headready.thread := nil;
  11    392        headready.pri := 0;
  11    393        headallp := nil;
  11    394        delaydlist := RETYPE (ptrpcb, ADR headdelay);
  11    395        headdelay.next := nil;
  11    396        headdelay.last := RETYPE (ptrpcb, ADR headdelay);
  11    397        headdelay.delay := 0;
        398
        399        {create all processes defined in IPT by module CONFIG}
  11    400        IF initab.nprocess <> 0 THEN
  11    401          BEGIN
  12    402            staticpd := initab.ipt;
  12    403            FOR i := 1 TO initab.nprocess DO
  12    404              BEGIN
  13    405                createproc (staticpd);
  13    406                ustaticpd := RETYPE (unsint, staticpd);
  13    407                ustaticpd := ustaticpd + spdsize;
  13    408                staticpd := RETYPE (ptrspd, ustaticpd)
  13    409              END {for}
  11    410          END; {if}
        411
        412        {create all mailboxes defined in IMT}
  11    413        IF initab.nmailbox <> 0 THEN
  11    414          BEGIN
  12    415            fstep := initab.IMT;
  12    416            FOR i := 1 TO initab.nmailbox DO
  12    417              BEGIN
  13    418                inibox := fstep^.tombx;
  13    419                creatembox (inibox);
  13    420                ufstep := RETYPE (unsint, fstep);
  13    421                ufstep := ufstep + imtesize;
  13    422                fstep := RETYPE (ptombd, ufstep)
  13    423              END {for}
  11    424          END; {if}
        425        {surrender control to a user process}
  11    426        dispatch (running)
  00    427      END. {kmos}
```

KMOS

ELEVEN

CASE STUDIES

In this chapter we present three commercial operating systems, PC-DOS (MS-DOS), Unix, and iRMX 86, and one representative real-time application built on top of the KMOS kernel described in Chapters 9 and 10. The PC-DOS operating system is representative of a class of single-process monitors widely used on personal computers. The Unix operating system is chosen for its availability on a wide range of different hardware, for a variety of interesting facilities, and as an example of a rich set of tools and tool-building utilities. The case study of the iRMX 86 illustrates a contemporary real-time operating system that incorporates several of the interprocess synchronization and communication mechanisms discussed in Chapters 4 and 5. Each operating system is described from two different points of view, in particular those of the command-language users and of the system-call users, followed by a discussion of some implementation aspects of the system. Finally, a description of the design of a remote-telemetry unit (RTU) illustrates the basic principles of real-time system design. That case study emphasizes the general considerations of real-time system design and some of the RTU solutions that are applicable to other environments, such as computer networks and distributed systems.

11.1 PC-DOS (MS-DOS) OPERATING SYSTEM

The PC-DOS operating system is used on a variety of IBM PC models. Its close cousin, the MS-DOS, is available on numerous other computers based on Intel's iAPX 86 family of microprocessors. Although many differences now exist between them, MS-DOS started out as a CP/M-80-compatible operating system. In 1980 Seattle Computer developed the QDOS, an operating system for their 8086 microprocessor-based board. One of its design requirements was to allow applications developed for Intel's 8080 microprocessor under the CP/M-80 operating system to run unchanged when converted to the 8086 code as per Intel's published rules. (The 8080 microprocessor is upward-compatible with the 8086, and the manufacturer provided some predominantly automatic means for converting existing 8080 code to the 8086 machine language when the 8086 was made available.) Other design requirements of the QDOS operating system were to provide speed and efficiency of disk-related operations. Microsoft later acquired rights to this product, which was subsequently marketed as the MS-DOS operating system. After its initial adoption for the IBM personal computer family, the MS-DOS (called PC-DOS in the IBM version) operating system has undergone several major revisions. In this process, PC-DOS has been constantly evolving toward the Unix operating system, both at the command-language and the system-call levels. In this chapter we describe certain characteristics of single-process versions of the PC-DOS operating system.

11.1.1 Command-Language User's View of the PC-DOS

The PC-DOS is a single-user, single-process operating system. It shares many characteristics of similar operating systems for personal computers, the most notable example of which is the CP/M operating system manufactured by Digital Research. The enormous popularity of these operating systems, measured in terms of the number of copies sold, is largely due to the vast array of relatively low-cost software available for them. In addition to hundreds of packages ranging from spreadsheets and word processors to computer-aided design and expert systems, serious program development under the PC-DOS operating system is made possible by the availability of programming languages, such as Pascal, C, Modula-2, PL/I, Fortran, Cobol, Lisp, Prolog, and others.

As a result of its evolution from a CP/M-like operating system toward a Unix-like operating system, later versions of PC-DOS offer a hierarchical file system and some aspects of device independence. The latter facilitates the use of filters and pipes, which are described in the next section in relation to the Unix operating system. We now discuss the facilities of PC-DOS for program development and execution, file manipulation, and volume maintenance.

Programs can be executed under PC-DOS by simply typing the name of the file that contains the image (the linked object code) of the related program. Fully or partially qualified path names, that is, those beginning with the root or with the current working directory, can be used to specify the file that contains the target program image. For example, the program SPSHEET, whose image is stored in the file SPSHEET.COM in the subdirectory SP, can be executed by typing its fully qualified path name beginning with the root directory on the volume C as follows:

$$C : \backslash SP \backslash SPSHEET$$

Note that the PC-DOS uses a backslash character (\) instead of the more common slash (/) as a delimiter in path-name specification. If the default user volume is C and the working directory is SP, the same program can be invoked by typing its name

SPSHEET

in response to the PC-DOS prompt. In addition to user-written and application programs, nonresident commands of the PC-DOS itself are also invoked in this manner. This approach allows easy extension of the basic set of system services by inclusion of additional utilities that appear to users as "standard" system commands.

The PC-DOS also supports the construction and execution of parametrized command files, called *batch files* in PC-DOS terminology. A comparatively primitive but useful command language is available for the construction and execution of batch files. These are especially useful for customizing the system after it is brought up and for automating the process of installing and running software that requires a sequence of more or less standard commands for its operation. A special command file, called AUTOEXEC.BAT, is executed automatically whenever the system is booted. By defining or modifying the contents of this file, users can specify a sequence of operations for the PC-DOS to execute whenever the system is turned on. For example, a given application can be activated automatically when the system is started. This may be useful for the so-called naive users, who may only want to use a given application without having to learn about the operating system in order to operate the machine.

In terms of file manipulation, the PC-DOS provides a more or less standard set of file- , directory- , and volume-related commands. Some of them are listed in Table 11.1 following the order of introduction of the equivalent generic commands discussed in Chapter 8. The basic function of each command in Table 11.1 is specified in the comment field beginning with a semicolon. As discussed earlier, the position of each file within the directory hierarchy can be specified by means of the related path name. Since most of the presented commands follow the names and syntax of the related generic commands presented in Chapter 8, we briefly explain some of them that have different names or no counterpart among the generic file-related commands discussed in Chapter 8.

As indicated in Table 11.1, files can be deleted, renamed, copied, and have some of their attributes modified. Directories, or specific files therein, are listed by means of the DIR command. Since a hierarchical file structure is supported, commands are provided for the creation and removal of directories, as well as for changing the current working directory, CHDIR. The command TREE displays the tree structure of directories present on the specified volume. The set of commands for volume manipulation and maintenance includes commands for formatting, verification, and backing up of selected files or of entire volumes. The command JOIN is used to add the directory tree of a volume to the system hierarchy of directories. This command corresponds to the generic MOUNT command discussed in Chapter 8.

DEL   ; delete files
RENAME   ; rename files
ATTRIB   ; read or modify file attributes
COPY   ; copy files

a. General file manipulation

DIR   ; list filenames
MKDIR   ; create a sub-directory
RMDIR   ; remove a sub-directory
CHDIR   ; change working directory
TREE   ; display all directory paths

b. Directory manipulation

FORMAT   ; format/ initialize a volume
JOIN   ; add volume to directory hierarchy
CHKDSK   ; check disk and reports status
DISKCOPY   ; copy entire volumes
BACKUP   ; back up fixed disk files
RESTORE   ; restore files to fixed disk
RECOVER   ; recover damaged files

c. Volume/media manipulation

Table 11.1 Some file-related commands of the PC-DOS

11.1.2 System-Call User's View of the PC-DOS

System calls of the PC-DOS clearly reflect its evolution from the CP/M-like operating system toward a Unix-like one. Namely, older calls reflecting a flat file system and device-specific I/O are retained in order to allow applications written under earlier versions to execute under subsequent versions of PC-DOS without modifications. While providing user convenience and a stable evolutionary path without obsoleting available software, the compatibility among most versions of the PC-DOS at the system-call level results in a somewhat confusing situation where several different system calls are available for accomplishing a single task.

PC-DOS calls are invoked from a user program by means of software interrupts. When needed, calling parameters are supplied in processor registers or, much less frequently, by means of parameter areas built in the user's address space. In this section we outline the general characteristics of some PC-DOS system calls for program execution and file-management.

Program images are invoked for execution in response to a system call that is patterned after the EXEC call described later in relation to Unix. Programs can also terminate themselves in an orderly fashion by calling the PC-DOS, which releases some of their holdings and writes the related I/O buffers to disk if necessary. Since multiprocess operation is not supported, the PC-DOS does not provide calls for interprogram communication and synchronization. A possibility exists for having two programs simultaneously loaded in nonconflicting areas of memory. This can be accomplished by means of a call that terminates the caller but leaves it resident and adjusts the memory boundary so that subsequent program loading does not overwrite the already resident program. The intended purpose of this arrangement is to allow a user-written interrupt routine to coexist in memory with an application program. By means of a related system call, interrupts from a given source can be vectored to the resident user routine while the coresident application is executing. Although quite limited in scope, this facility has been exploited for a variety of applications, ranging from dynamic key reassignment to quite sophisticated utilities that may temporarily preempt and subsequently return to the application program in response to a few keystrokes. For example, this facility has been employed to allow a calculator program to be invoked at any point in time when running an unrelated application. After performing the desired calculation, the preempted application is resumed at the exact point of interruption, possibly to make use of the preceding calculation.

PC-DOS calls for performing input and output operations include reading of individual characters or of complete and edited input lines from keyboards and outputting of single characters and character strings to displays and printers. Early versions of the PC-DOS were device-dependent in the sense of providing a separate call, or set of calls, for each particular type of supported device. Later versions gravitate toward device independence and treat I/O devices as files, offering a uniform set of system calls for manipulation of both files and devices.

File-related operations include most of the services available to command-language users, such as renaming and deletion of files. Naturally, system calls also allow creation, reading, and writing of files. The PC-DOS provides OPEN and CLOSE services and requires files to be explicitly open prior to being read or written by a given program. In early versions of the PC-DOS, file-related operations were performed by creating a parameter area, called a *file control-block* (FCB), in user space. The address of the FCB is passed to the operating system as a parameter of the software interrupt. Later versions of PC-DOS have adopted the connection_ID approach described in Chapter 8. That is, opening of a file returns a unique ID, called the *file handle* in PC-DOS terminology, that is used to identify the related file in subsequent read and write operations. Early versions of the PC-DOS supported user-definable logical records organized into logical blocks. Files could have been manipulated at the block, record, or byte level. Later versions have shifted toward the Unix approach of treating files as featureless arrays of bytes. In addition to providing operations at the file level, the PC-DOS supports direct reading and writing of volume-relative logical blocks. Multiblock transfers are available for sequential files. An equivalent of the SEEK operation is available for randomly accessed files.

Being essentially a single-user, single-process system, the PC-DOS does not go to great lengths to provide file protection and sharing. With the introduction of support for networks, controlled access to concurrently open files was provided on a first-come, first-served basis without much regard for file ownership.

11.1.3 PC-DOS Implementation

In this section we present some aspects of PC-DOS implementation following the order of introduction of the corresponding topics in earlier chapters of this book.

After a few introductory remarks, we discuss execution of user programs under PC-DOS. The remainder of this section contains an overview of the memory-management and file-management modules of the PC-DOS operating system.

Originally following the philosophy of the CP/M operating system, most of PC-DOS code is independent of the hardware configuration that it runs on. This is accomplished by a layered implementation of device-related code so that only the lowest layer, called BIOS (for basic input output system), is aware of the actual device and port addresses. BIOS provides low-level input/output functions, such as input of a single character from a keyboard or writing of a logical block to the disk. In effect, BIOS provides an abstraction of the underlying hardware for the rest of the PC-DOS operating system. Since DOS code is device-independent, the MS-DOS operating system can be ported to foreign hardware based on iAPX 86 processor by rewriting only the BIOS.

As a single-process monitor, the PC-DOS only needs to provide some means for execution of programs in response to user commands. This can be accomplished in cooperation between the loader and the command interpreter without the need for scheduling, process bookkeeping, or interprocess synchronization and communication. Most devices are handled via programmed I/O in order to eliminate the complexities of interrupt-management.

Management of memory in the PC-DOS is also simple, as all physical memory left over after loading of the resident portion of the PC-DOS is made available for user programs. The memory layout of a typical PC-DOS system is presented in Figure 11.1. As indicated, the lowest memory is reserved for interrupt vectors. These are used for the system-clock interrupt and to direct user software interrupts to the appropriate entry points of the PC-DOS. The next area

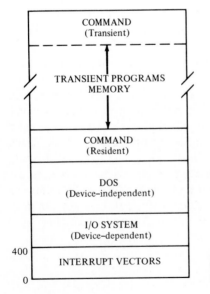

Figure 11.1 A PC-DOS (MS-DOS) memory map.

in memory is occupied by the BIOS code. In IBM terminology, BIOS refers to the low-level I/O code that resides in the read-only memory (ROM) of system boards. The RAM-resident part of BIOS is loaded from the IBMBIO file that augments or replaces some of the ROM BIOS routines. The next area of memory contains the resident portion of the operating system (DOS). The command interpreter, called COMMAND, is the last resident portion of the PC-DOS.

In order to reduce memory requirements, COMMAND is split in two parts. One of them is permanently resident above the DOS area, while the other is placed in high memory, as indicated in Figure 11.1. An interesting solution is provided for restoring this portion of the COMMAND code after being overwritten by a large user program. Namely, after each program termination, the integrity of the transient portion of COMMAND is verified by calculating a checksum of the contents of its memory locations and comparing it against the known expected value. If the two do not match, COMMAND is considered to have been overwritten and DOS reloads it from the disk. Otherwise, COMMAND is assumed to be OK and no further action is taken.

Files in the PC-DOS are cataloged in a hierarchical system of directories. Each volume contains a root directory placed at the known physical address. The size of the root directory is usually restricted on a per-volume basis so that the directory can be placed in a fixed number of sectors. As usual, entries of the root directory can point to ordinary files or to subdirectories. Subdirectories are managed in the same way as ordinary files. As a result, their size is not restricted by the PC-DOS. Each entry of a symbolic directory (root or a subdirectory) contains the following information:

- File name
- File extension
- File attributes (e.g., read-only, system, hidden)
- Date and time of creation or last modification
- Starting cluster address
- File size

Files are identified by means of two components: file name and file extension. Version numbers are not supported. Special characters are used to mark empty and never-before-used directory entries. A number of user-visible and internal system-assigned file attributes are maintained as an array of dedicated bits. Users can specify whether a file may be read and written or just read (RO). Since the PC-DOS is a single-user system, no notion of file ownership exists. In network configurations where concurrent access to a file from remote nodes as well as the local one is possible, a rudimentary form of file sharing is provided on a first-come, first-served basis. System-visible file attributes include indication of the file type, such as subdirectory or an ordinary file, and an archive bit used for backup purposes.

Before explaining the linkage between symbolic file directories and the basic file directory, let us briefly discuss the physical organization of PC-DOS files. Disks are normally divided into 512-byte physical sectors. Space is allocated in terms of clusters, with each cluster containing from 1 to 8 adjacent sectors, depending on the size of the volume that it resides on. A cluster is the basic unit of allocation. Disk space is allocated in noncontiguous fashion using a variant of the chaining technique. Instead of being located in data blocks, chains of file and free-space pointers are collected in a table called the *file-allocation table* (FAT). This table has one entry for each cluster on its enclosing volume. Two identical copies of the file-allocation table are kept on each volume for security. Like the root directory, FATs are located at a known place on each volume. In early versions of the PC-DOS, a complete copy of the file-allocation table was kept in memory in order to speed up disk retrievals. With the introduction of larger Winchester disks, only actively used portions of FATs are brought into memory as needed.

Each entry of a symbolic directory that contains a valid file description points to the starting-cluster address where the first few sectors of the file can be found. Sectors in other clusters can be located by consulting the file-allocation table. Each entry of the FAT contains a pointer to the next cluster of a file, if any. Since the file-allocation table has one entry for each cluster on the volume, there is a one-to-one correspondence between an FAT offset and the related physical cluster addresses. Thus, the starting-cluster address contained in the symbolic description of each file can be used as an index to FAT in order to obtain the volume-relative address of the next cluster. Addresses of other clusters of a file can be obtained by repeating this process and following the chain of pointers contained in the file-allocation table. When the FAT is kept in memory, files can be accessed randomly without incurring the overhead of disk accessing necessary to locate the address of the target sector when pure chaining is used. Special reserved characters are used in FAT entries to mark the end of file, free (unused) clusters, and bad blocks.

Later versions of the PC-DOS use buffering, as described in Chapter 8, in order to improve the efficiency of disk operations. The number of buffers is user-definable by means of the configuration file. All modified buffers are flushed to the disk as a part of the orderly program termination invoked by the PC-DOS equivalent of the EXIT call described in the previous section.

11.1.4 PC-DOS Summary

The PC-DOS (MS-DOS) is a single-user, single-process operating system available for iAPX 86-based computers. Due to confinement of device-dependent code into one layer, porting of the PC-DOS is reduced to writing of the BIOS code for the new hardware. While early versions of the PC-DOS resemble the CP/M operating system, later releases of the PC-DOS have Unix-like features. At the command level, the PC-DOS provides a hierarchical file system, I/O redirection, pipes, and filters. User-written commands can be invoked in the same way as standard system commands, thus giving the appearance of extending the basic system functionality.

The PC-DOS provides both device-dependent and device-independent versions of system calls for input/output and file manipulation. Being a single-user system, the PC-DOS provides only rudimentary file protection and access control. Disk space is allocated in terms of clusters of consecutive sectors. A variant of chaining that allows for relatively fast random access to files is used for keeping track of both file blocks and free space.

11.2 Unix OPERATING SYSTEM

Unix is a popular multiuser time-sharing operating system primarily intended for program development and document-preparation environments. It is written in a high-level language, C, with careful isolation and confinement of machine-dependent routines, so that it may be fairly easily ported to different computer systems. As a result, versions of Unix are available for personal computers, microprocessor-based systems, minicomputers and midicomputers, and large mainframes and supercomputers. The source-code-level compatibility of programs developed under Unix makes it possible to transfer applications between personal computers and larger machines, such as the IBM 370, Univac, and even the Cray and Amdahl machines.

The first version of Unix was written by Ken Thompson, later joined by Dennis Ritchie, at Bell Labs in the late sixties. It was a single-user system for the PDP-7 computer written in assembly language. After a major rewriting in C and porting to the PDP-11 family of computers, Unix was made available to users outside of AT&T. Favorable licensing fees for educational institutions were instrumental in the adoption of Unix by many universities. Unix is now commercially available from AT&T, together with numerous variants of the system provided by other vendors. Several specialized versions of Unix, such as the Programmer's Workbench (Unix/PWB), and the Writer's Workbench (Unix/WWB) are also available.

Some of the major features of Unix discussed in this chapter are listed below:

- Portability
- Multiuser operation
- Device independence
- Tools and tool-building utilities
- Hierarchical file system

As already discussed, Unix is portable and available on a wide range of different hardware. It is somewhat of a curiosity that portability was not one of the design objectives of Unix. Rather, it came as a consequence of coding the system in a high-level language. Having realized the importance of portability, designers of Unix have confined hardware-dependent code into a few modules in order to facilitate porting.

Unix supports multiple users on suitable installations with memory-management hardware and the appropriate communication interfaces. In addition to local users, remote users are availed log-in facilities and file transfer between Unix hosts in network configurations.

Virtually all the aspects of device independence described in Chapter 8 are implemented in Unix. In particular, files and I/O devices are treated in a uniform manner by means of the same set of applicable system calls. As a result, I/O redirection and stream-level I/O are fully supported at both the command-language and system-call levels.

The Unix system makes a strong case for the philosophy that a good way to build tools is to provide useful building blocks which are combinable according to the user's needs and preferences. Following this approach, Unix utilities are usually simple and they concentrate on accomplishing a single function as best they can. Numerous Unix utilities, called *filters*, can be combined in an unusually flexible manner by using the facilities provided by I/O redirection and pipes. This is to be contrasted with the alternative approach of providing complex utilities which are often difficult to learn and customize and are frequently incompatible with other utilities.

The sharing and cooperation among users desirable in program-development environments is, among other things, facilitated by the hierarchical file system. The hierarchical file system of Unix spans volume boundaries, thus virtually eliminating the need for volume awareness among its users. This is especially convenient in time-sharing systems and network configurations.

Following the adopted order of presentation in this chapter, we describe Unix from the command-language user's view and system-call user's point of view and then outline some aspects of Unix implementation.

11.2.1 Command-Language User's View of Unix

Unix users invoke commands by interacting with a command-language interpreter called the *shell*. In addition to interpreting users' requests and invoking the corresponding system services, the shell is also a programming language suitable for construction of elaborate command files, called *shell scripts*. The shell is written as a user process, as opposed to being built into the kernel. When a user logs in, the system invokes a copy of the shell to handle interactions with the related user. While the shell is the standard system interface, it is possible to invoke any other user-specified process to serve in place of the shell as a system interface for each particular user. This allows dedicated interfaces developed for users of specialized applications, such as clerical workers using text-processing facilities, to coexist with the default shell and thus provide quite different views and working environments for different users of the same system.

In this section we describe the shell mainly in its role as a command-language interpreter. The shell supports I/O redirection, pipes, and concurrent execution of user programs. We explain each of these features briefly.

Capitalizing on the high degree of device independence provided by the Unix system, the shell supports redirection at the command-language level. Since I/O devices are treated in Unix as files, files and devices may be treated interchangeably in the discussion that follows.

All programs run under the shell start out with three predefined files: *standard input* (which is normally the terminal keyboard), *standard output*, and *error output*. Both standard and error output are normally assigned to the terminal display. The symbols $>$ and $<$ are used to indicate temporary redirection of standard input and output. For example, the command

ls

lists the contents of a directory on the standard output, that is, on the display of the terminal from which it is invoked. By using the redirection operator, this output can be diverted to a file KEEP as follows:

ls $>$ keep

Similarly, input to a program or a command may be taken from the standard input, the keyboard, or from any other file. For example, the command

ed $<$ script

instructs the program ED (editor) to take its input from the file SCRIPT. The purpose of the standard error output is to allow error messages, if any, to be displayed on the user's terminal even when standard output is being redirected to another file or device. Of course, standard error output can also be redirected as desired.

From the command-language user's point of view, pipes allow the standard output of one program to be used as the standard input of another program. Several programs can be connected via pipes to form a pipeline. It is through this facility that Unix tools, called *filters*, can be combined to perform complex compound functions. The shell is instructed to form pipes by means of the vertical bar character (|). The output of the process to the left of the bar is connected (via the pipe) to the input of the process to the right of the bar. For example, the Unix command WHO, which lists logged-on users, can be combined with the filter SORT to provide a sorted listing of users as follows:

who | sort

In this simple example of a pipe, the output of WHO is piped to SORT, which sorts the list of users and outputs it to the standard output, the terminal display in this case. SORT is one of the many Unix filters, programs which take standard input, perform some processing on it, and output the result to the standard output. Depending on the particular command line, the standard input may come from a device, a file, or a pipe. All of these options are also available for standard output. Thus, the sorted list of users can be printed in two-column format on the line printer by means of the following command:

who | sort | pr $-$ 2 | lpr

where PR is print formatter, and LPR causes the output to be spooled to a line printer. The same example could be expressed without pipes by several command lines involving creation and removal of temporary files. However, pipes provide a much more economical and convenient way to combine several programs.

I/O redirection and pipes allow Unix utilities built as filters to be combined in order to accomplish more complex tasks. As mentioned earlier, Unix designers advocate the view that tools should be simple to build, to learn, and to use. As a corollary, flexibility should be provided by allowing basic commands to be combined in arbitrary ways. For example, the WHO command can be combined with the WC filter, which counts characters, lines, and words in a file, to obtain the number of logged-on users in the line count filed:

who | wc

To find out whether Bob is currently on the system without going over the possibly long listing of users generated by WHO, the following command can be used:

who | grep bob

GREP is another Unix filter which outputs only those lines of a file which contain the specified pattern, such as BOB in our example.

Even these simple examples illustrate the flexibility and power of the Unix command system and philosophy. This may be contrasted with the rather common alternative approach of building complex commands with scores of options to learn (and forget). In addition to being difficult to build, such commands are inflexible because their designers cannot possibly anticipate all of the options that users may need or desire. For example, it is unlikely that any system would provide all of the options to do what we have just done with the WHO command. Neither does Unix, but it still allows us to do all those things in a natural and convenient way.

The third capability of shell is concurrent activation of programs. Users indicate their intention to invoke several programs concurrently by putting the & character at the end of a command line. Thus, the command sequence

cc cprog &

causes the shell to return to the user with a prompt immediately upon launching compilation (command CC) of the CPROG and without waiting for the compilation to finish. This mode of operation allows users to do some unrelated work while potentially lengthy operations are being performed on their behalf.

In the remainder of this section we describe some of the Unix commands for program development and execution, file-management, and document preparation. We also briefly discuss two specialized Unix subsystems—the Programmer's Workbench and the Writer's Workbench. Since Unix has over 150 different commands, it is beyond the scope of this chapter to present either an exhaustive or even a systematic representative subset of them. Instead, we discuss the broad range of available operations and only occasionally mention some specific commands.

Since Unix is primarily intended for program development, it offers several editors, compilers, symbolic debuggers, and utilities. Some of the more interesting utilities include TIME, which measures execution time of programs, and PROF, which gathers and displays statistics about where and how a program spends its time. Such tools, commonly called *profilers*, are very useful for identifying potential bottlenecks and time-critical sections of code. This information may guide programmers as to where a redesign of algorithms or extra careful coding are likely to be most beneficial for the overall performance of a program. Other useful program-development facilities of Unix include a general-purpose macroprocessor, M4, which is language-independent and the MAKE program, which controls creation of large programs. MAKE uses a control file specifying source-file dependencies among the constituent modules of a program. When object modules are linked together to form an executable program, MAKE identifies modules that are possibly out of date by means of the related date of the last change and causes them to be recompiled. Unix also provides extensive facilities for the construction and maintenance of user and system libraries of programs and modules.

A much more elaborate system for large programming projects, called the Source Code Control System (SCCS), is also available under Unix. Although SCCS was designed to assist production of complex programs, it can be used to manage any collection of text files. SCCS basically functions as a well-managed library of major and minor revisions of the program modules. Authorized users may check modules out of the SCCS for revision and subsequently return them. The system keeps track of all changes, the identity of those who made them, and other administrative information. SCCS provides utilities for rolling back to any previous version, displaying of complete or partial history of changes made to a module, validation of modules, and the like.

As the development language for Unix, the C programming language enjoys some special treatment. Special utilities for C programs include a beautifier, CB, and a very useful program, called LINT, which checks C programs for potential bugs and wasteful or nonportable statements.

The user can execute Unix programs by typing the names of program image files. Programs can also be scheduled as regular actions at specified times by means of the CRON command or executed as a one-shot action at a specified time by means of the AT command. A user can put a program to SLEEP for a specified time, notify or terminate a named program (KILL), WAIT for termination of asynchronously running processes, or run a program at low priority (NICE). The current status of processes can be obtained by means of the PS command.

Unix provides a hierarchical file system capable of spanning multiple volumes. Files are organized in a tree-structured hierarchy of directories, beginning with the root, which is usually placed at the system boot volume. No cross-links between directories and volumes are allowed, and each directory must be listed in exactly one parent directory. Some of these restrictions were not present in earlier versions of Unix, which allowed arbitrary graphs of directories to exist. Difficulties encountered when processing volume dismounts in such systems have led to the current approach of a tree structure of directories.

In addition to user-created directories, the system maintains several standard directories, where programs implementing Unix commands, system libraries, and standard devices may be found. Files may be specified by full path names beginning with the root or by partial path names beginning with the current working directory. Numerous commands are available to manipulate files. Some of those are listed in Table 11.2. In addition to the usual range of commands to rename, link, and copy files, Unix has explicit commands for the concatenation and splitting of files. A number of standard filters (not shown in Table 11.2) can also be used to manipulate the contents of files. Some examples include comparison, identification of differences, elimination of duplicate lines, and printing of a few first and last lines of a file.

Directories are managed by means of a more or less standard set of commands, some of which are presented in Table 11.2. The MOUNT command is used to add a tree structure of a volume as a leaf of the existing directory tree. The UMOUNT command has the opposite effect. Other commands allow verification of file and volume integrity (ICHECK, NCHECK, DCHECK), as well as backing up and restoring of files and volumes.

File protection in Unix is accomplished by associating an owner's ID with each file when it is created. At that time, the owner of the file specifies the allowed modes of access for himself or herself, his or her group, and for other users of the system. The allowable modes for each individual class of users (owner, group, world) are a combination of three bits, one each for reading, writing, and execution of the file. This information is recorded as a group of 9 bits. The tenth protection bit, when set, informs the system to temporarily change

rm	; remove (delete) files
ln	; link files - used to create aliases
mv	; move files - used to rename files
chmod	; change attributes of files
cp	; copy files
cat	; concatenate one or more files
split	; split a file into more manageable pieces

a. General file manipulation

ls	; list names of one or more files in directories
mkdir	; make a new directory (subdirectory)
rmdir	; remove a directory (subdirectory)
cd	; change working directory

b. Directory manipulation

mount	; attach device, add to the tree of directories
umount	; remove the file system contained on a device
n/i/dcheck	; verify integrity of files
dump	; backup devices or files selectively
restor	; restore dumped file system

c. Volume/media manipulation

Table 11.2 Some Unix file commands

the user identification to that of the file owner in order to execute the file. This feature, called the set_user_ID, provides for privileged programs that may use files inaccessible to other users.

Unix does not automatically enforce protection against concurrent access to the same file. While some interlocks exist to preserve integrity when two users are creating files in the same directory or deleting each other's files, the system does not prevent two users from simultaneously writing the same file. Although arguably not needed in the program-development environment that Unix was originally intended for, the lack of a file-locking mechanism is generally perceived to be a drawback in database applications. For this reason, several Unix variants provide a file-locking mechanism.

Unix designers take the view that document preparation is closely related to program development. As a result, Unix provides a comprehensive set of utilities for document preparation. Among these are the popular NROFF text formatter and the TROFF formatter, which prepares output for typesetting equipment. Other utilities include EQN for mathematical texts and equations, MM for memoranda, MMT for transparency masters, and others.

Preparation of large texts, such as user manuals, may best be handled under Unix by means of the set of programs available as a part of the Writer's Workbench (WWB) software. WWB is a set of programs that helps with two stages of document production: evaluation and editing. Over a dozen programs are available in WWB to analyze prose documents and to suggest improvements. In addition to the usual proofreaders and spelling checkers, WWB software includes a punctuation program, PUNCT, a program for the detection of split infinitives, SPLITINF, and programs such as STYLE and PROSE for comprehensive analyses of the writing style based on linguistic and psychological research. Other inputs to WWB analysis routines consist of actual documents considered to be exceptionally well written and cumulative statistics of the documents analyzed by the system in the past.

The last set of Unix commands discussed in this section is provided for operations between remote Unix hosts. These include CU for remote log-in and UUCP for file transfer. The CU command (call Unix) allows a user connected to a Unix host to log-in to a remote host via a communication link. After invoking the CU command, the user can access facilities of the remote host in the same way as its local users. In addition, the user may temporarily escape to execute a command on its local host, capture on the local host output from operations on the remote host, and send output of local commands to the remote system. The UUCP command (for Unix-to-Unix copy) allows file transfers between two Unix sites. UUCP is actually a collection of utilities for file transfer between Unix sites connected via communication links.

11.2.2 System-Call User's View of Unix

In this section we describe some of the Unix system calls for process-management and communication, as well as for file operations.

Unix system calls are executed in response to the related statements placed in user programs. When invoked, a Unix system call acts as an extension of the calling program. The two are never executed asynchronously. Input/output operations also appear to users as synchronous and unbuffered. As we shall see later, the actual implementation of I/O routines is somewhat different.

A new process can be created by means of the FORK system call:

$$process\_ID = fork ()$$

As a result of execution of FORK, the calling process is split into two related but separate processes. The two processes, parent and child (called father and son in Unix terminology), have independent copies of the original memory image and share all open files. Unlike the processes described in Chapter 3, the creator and the created Unix processes execute from the single shared code segment. Among other things, this results in the somewhat peculiar coding of processes in Unix. The parent and the child processes differ in that the PROCESS_ID returned to the parent is the ID of the child (and is never 0), while the child process always receives an ID of 0 from the FORK. This information may be used by each process to determine its own identity by using the sequence of code given in Program 11.1.

As suggested by Program 11.1, the parent process creates the child process by invoking the FORK system call. In response to this call, the Unix kernel creates the child process. While the parent process naturally continues to execute

```
{Parent process}
  . . .

{Parent creates child}
process_ID := fork ();
if process_ID not = 0       {Parent and child execute test}
    then
        begin
          {Parent's code continues here}

          . . .

          done_ID := wait(status)      {Parent waits for child's termination}
        end
    else
        begin
          {Child's code continues here}

          . . .

          exit(status)      {Child terminates execution}
        end; {if}
{Parent continues here after child's termination}

  . . .
```

Program 11.1 Process creation in Unix

in its own environment, the child obtains a fresh copy of the parent's variables (these remain separate thereafter) and a unique PROCESS_ID. The child also inherits the parent's list of open files, and both processes share the same code segment.

After completion of FORK, the two processes continue to execute on their own. Since they execute from the same code segment, PROCESS_ID returned by the FORK is examined by each process in order to establish its identity. Since it receives its child's ID, the parent finds the PROCESS_ID to be different from 0. This fact is used in Program 11.1 to distinguish the parent from the child. After possibly executing a few statements, the parent may opt to await the child's termination by means of the WAIT system call. This situation is assumed in Program 11.1. Before discussing operation of the WAIT call, let us investigate what happens with the child.

Since parent and child share the same copy of code, both parent and child execute the test of PROCESS_ID returned by the FORK. Having been formed as essentially a distinct process, the child finds PROCESS_ID to be 0. As a result, it executes the sequence of statements following the ELSE part. Thus, although both parent and child share the same code, they still can perform different activities. The example presented in Program 11.1 assumes that the child terminates itself after having executed its sequence of operations. This is accomplished by means of the EXIT system call. As indicated, EXIT takes one parameter, STATUS, which it returns to the parent at the time of completion of the related WAIT. This variable can be used to transmit some information between the terminating child and its parent. The WAIT call is invoked as a function. As such, it returns to its caller the identity of the terminated program, in response to whose EXIT the WAIT issued by the parent is completed. This allows a parent with several children to determine which particular child's termination has caused a WAIT to be completed.

A program can be executed in Unix by means of the EXEC system call. EXEC requires the name of the file that contains the program to be executed. Optionally, additional arguments of the EXEC command can be passed on to the target program when it is activated. Unlike FORK, the EXEC call overlays the caller with the program to be executed. As a result, the caller's image is lost, and EXEC never returns.

Given the nature of process creation, Unix processes form a family tree. The "ultimate ancestor" process is created by the system as a part of the startup procedure. This process and its offspring detect active terminals, start the log-in procedures, and execute shell or whatever other command language is indicated for each individual user by the account file. Thus, there may be as many instances of the shell process as there are active users on the system. In fact, there may be more, because each shell may call itself recursively when processing user requests for execution of commands. Namely, shell normally processes user requests by forking and creating a child, which in turn uses EXEC to execute the user's command. The parent shell process normally awaits its child's termination, at which point the parent outputs a prompt. However, when a user requests concurrent execution of commands, the parent shell process in charge of the related terminal immediately returns the prompt and then creates another child to execute the new command. Since the shell can call itself recursively and all copies of shell share the same code, implementation of the concurrent execution of a succession of user commands is fairly straightforward in Unix.

Different processes can exchange timing signals by means of the matching KILL and SIGNAL calls. The basic format of KILL is

$$\text{kill (process\_ID, signal\_ID)}$$

Individual signals are identified by the integer SIGNAL_ID. About a dozen of those values are predefined to signal exceptional conditions, such as a floating-point overflow and divide by zero. Other values may be used to indicate the occurrence of some user-defined events.

KILL normally terminates the target process, but the victim has the option to survive. Namely, the target process may intercept, or "catch," the signal in Unix terminology and then ignore it or invoke a specific procedure by issuing the SIGNAL call.

The interprocess synchronization mechanism provided by these two calls is rather crude, and it is quite different from contemporary theory and practice. Another problem is that Unix signals, unlike semaphores, have no associated variables and thus can be lost when the recipient does not catch the signals fast enough. Realizing these drawbacks, many variants of Unix and the official licensed version of AT&T, beginning with the release called System V, include semaphores for interprocess synchronization.

Interprocess communication in Unix is primarily carried out by pipes. A *pipe* is a unidirectional channel that may be written at one end and read at the other. A pipe is used for communication between two processes. The producer process writes data into one end of the pipe, and the consumer process retrieves them from the other end. The system provides limited buffering for each open pipe. Control of the flow of data is performed by the system, which halts the producer attempting to write into a full pipe and halts the consumer attempting to read an empty pipe. Pipes are normally created by a common ancestor of the two communicating processes. For example, when executing a pipeline

$$a \mid b$$

the shell first creates the pipe. The PIPE system call returns file descriptors of the two ends of the created pipe. The shell usually redirects these to its standard input and output channels. The shell then forks to create two children which EXEC commands A and B, respectively. Since children inherit the parent's open files, process A simply writes its data to the standard output, which happens to be the input of the pipe in this case. Similarly, process B reads its input data from the standard input file without necessarily even being aware that it is a pipe. Most of the redirection and pipe fitting at the command level is performed by the shell in this way. System commands and filters are rarely even aware of the redirections and piping that they may participate in. This transparency is made possible by device-independent I/O, where files, devices, and stream-level I/O (pipes) are treated uniformly at both command and system-call levels.

A drawback of Unix pipes is that they can be used to communicate data only between processes that have a common ancestor, the creator of the pipe. In general, it is practically impossible for unrelated processes in Unix to exchange data or to synchronize. In Chapter 3 we demonstrated how performance can be improved by splitting a single logical activity into a set of independent but possibly cooperating processes. This concept cannot easily and naturally be expressed with Unix system calls for the creation of and interaction among processes. For this reason and because of the round-robin scheduling discussed later, standard Unix is not very suitable for applications with a real-time flavor.

Unix services for file manipulation include most of the functions provided at the command level. Prior to being read or written, files must be explicitly open. The basic format of the OPEN call is

$$\text{filep} = \text{open (filename, access\_mode)}$$

where FILEP is essentially the connection_ID returned by the system. This identifier is normally used in all future references to the file. ACCESS_MODE specifies the desired type of access to the file, such as read-write.

The contents of open files can be obtained and modified by means of READ and WRITE calls. The relative position of the file marker can be changed via the LSEEK call. The CREATE call functions as an implicit open. Creation of the existing file causes it to be truncated to zero and overwritten by the new contents. Files are normally closed by means of the CLOSE call. The syntax and parameters of these Unix calls are very similar to those of the equivalent generic calls discussed in Chapter 8.

11.2.3 Unix Implementation

In this section we describe some aspects of Unix implementation. Following our usual order of exposition, we begin with process-management and continue with memory-management in Unix. The section closes with a discussion of the file-management system.

The Unix kernel is essentially a medium-size monolithic monitor. System calls are implemented as a set of coroutines. A kernel coroutine is synchronous to the invoking (user) process. In effect, the system coroutine is an extension of the calling process, or its different phase in Unix terminology. Unless preempted by an interrupt, kernel coroutines normally do not give up the processor until completed. Some system processes exist for handling device interrupts.

The Unix kernel keeps track of user processes by means of the data structure, which is a partitioned implementation of the process control-block. In particular, information about a process is divided into two parts; one part is permanently resident in main memory, while the other may be swapped out with the rest of the process image. Some of the information maintained in the permanently resident part of a process control-block includes process name, pointers to its memory image, and scheduling information. The swappable part of a process control-block contains, among other things, saved CPU registers, a list of files open by the process, and accounting information. Permanently resident portions of process control-blocks are kept in the process table.

For scheduling purposes, each process is assigned some priority. The priority level of a system process is usually related to the relative importance of the event handled by the process. For example, disk events have high priority and terminal events have low priority. All system processes have higher priorities than user processes.

The priority of a user process varies depending primarily on the amount of the CPU time recently used by the process. Namely, the system computes the recent ratio of compute time to real time and stores it in the related process-table entry. This value is updated in 1-s intervals. As typical of time-sharing systems, Unix gives higher priority to user processes that have used little CPU time in the recent past. The priority of a process that exhibits CPU-bound behavior is lowered in order to allow interactive processes, generally characterized by low compute-to-real-time ratios, to get their share of the CPU.

When the Unix scheduler is invoked, it simply selects the highest-priority process ready to run. This gives preference to system processes in order to provide acceptable response times to device interrupts. Scheduling is preemptive in the sense that a higher-priority awakened process preempts a lower-priority running one. In effect, preemptive event-driven scheduling is provided to system processes, and an adaptive variant of round robin is used for scheduling user processes.

The memory allocated to each Unix process is divided into two segments: a read-only code segment and a read-write data segment. The code segment, called a *text segment* in Unix, is shared by all processes that execute the same code. Recalling our earlier discussion of process creation in Unix, this means that a parent shares the code segment with its children. However, as suggested by Program 11.1, the parent and its children are distinct processes that normally execute different sections of shared code.

The data segment contains variables and the stack of the process that owns it. While the system automatically increases the size of the stack area as needed, the data portion of a data segment can grow or shrink only as a result of explicit requests made by the related process to the operating system. The data segment is private to each process. Even processes that share common code have distinct data segments. When a (parent) process forks, a new data segment is created for the child. In the course of FORK processing, the contents of the parent's data segment are copied to the newly created child's segment. The parent's list of pointers to open files, stored in the swappable portion of parent's control block, is passed on to the child. In this way a child has access to a copy of its parent's variables, and the two processes share open files.

Pointers to the data segment of each process are kept in the related process-table entry. Since code segments are shared, a separate table—called the *text table*—of pointers to code segments is kept by the system. A pointer to the related entry of the text table is kept in each entry of the process table. The relationship between these tables is illustrated in Figure 11.2, where both the resident and the swappable portions of a parent and a child process are shown. The former are kept in the process table, whose entries also point to the location of the swappable part of the control-block of the related process. In order to reduce swapping latency, versions of Unix keep the swappable portion of each process control-block adjacent to the data segment of the related process.

Memory is allocated to requesting processes using the first-fit algorithm. Growth of data segments is implemented by allocating a new larger area and copying the contents of the old segment to it. When the requirements of active processes exceed the capacity of available memory, one or more processes are swapped out to the disk. Since code segments are never modified, only data segments and swappable parts of process control-blocks are actually copied to secondary memory.

Swapping is delegated to a separate kernel process. When selecting a victim, the swapping process takes into consideration the current status, memory residence time, and size of each resident process. Processes waiting for slow events are most likely to be swapped out, provided that they are of some age. Consideration of age is intended to prevent thrashing by ensuring that processes just brought into memory are not immediately swapped out.

The swapping process selects candidates for swapping in by consulting the process table. Ready-to-run processes are ranked on the basis of their storage

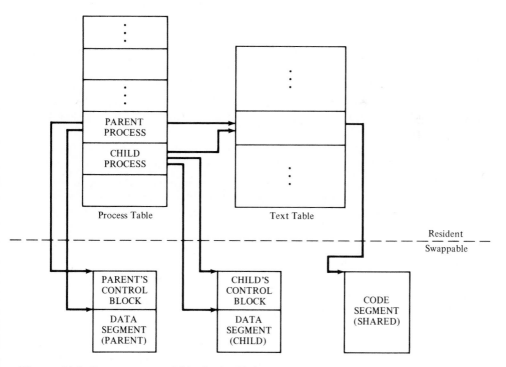

Figure 11.2 Process control-blocks in Unix.

residence time and size. The process which spent the longest time on secondary storage is swapped in first. A slight penalty is given to larger programs.

The Unix kernel consists of some 10,000 lines of C code and approximately 1000 lines of assembler code. This figure represents some 5 to 10% of the total Unix code. When the original assembly-language version was recoded in C, the size and execution time of the kernel increased by some 30%. Unix designers feel that the benefits of coding the system in a high-level language far outweigh the resulting performance penalty. The list of benefits includes portability, higher programmer productivity, ease of maintenance, and the ability to use complex algorithms and to provide sophisticated functions. Some of these complex algorithms could hardly have been contemplated if they were to be coded in assembly language.

The Unix file system features a tree-structured hierarchy of directories which may span volume boundaries. However, each individual file must completely reside on a single volume. Similarly, free blocks on different volumes cannot be pooled together for allocation purposes.

Files in a Unix system can belong to one of the three types: ordinary files, directories, and special files. The latter are used to access and manipulate I/O devices. With minimal exceptions, directories are stored and manipulated like any other file. For processing purposes, all files are regarded as featureless arrays of bytes. While sequential access is supported for all files, random access is possible only to files stored on block-structured devices.

Disks are normally divided into fixed-size blocks. Depending on the version of Unix, block size varies between 512 and 1024 bytes. Some variants have even larger block sizes. Disk drivers provide an abstraction of disks as linear arrays of blocks numbered from 0 up to the device size. The first few blocks of a disk are normally reserved for the boot block, "superblock," and i-list, a list of file definitions. The superblock contains volume-specific parameters, such as size, and the addresses of other areas on the disk. The system volume also contains the root directory of the system.

Each directory contains at least two entries: a link to its parent directory, and a pointer to self. Other entries, when used, contain file names and i-numbers. All other information about a file is contained in its i-node. An i-node allocated to a file contains the following information:

- The user and group ID of the file owner
- File-protection bits
- Physical address of the file contents
- Time of creation, last use, and last modification
- The number of links to the file (usage count)
- File type (ordinary, directory, or special)

A variant of indexing is used to keep track of and to allow access to the contents of a file. In particular, the address field of the i-node contains 13 addresses. The first 10 addresses point directly to the first 10 data blocks of the file. For larger files, the eleventh block points to a first-level index block that contains pointers (128 with 512-B sector size) to data blocks of the file. For still larger files, the twelfth address of the i-node contains a pointer to the first of the two-level index block, and the thirteenth address is a pointer to a three-level indexing structure. Thus, access to the data block of a file may actually require from one to four disk accesses, depending on the file size and on the relative position of the target block within the file.

In practice, fewer accesses are normally required because of the rather extensive disk caching in Unix. As mentioned in Chapter 8, over 100 disk blocks may be buffered in large Unix installations. Read-ahead is performed by the system for sequentially accessed files. Delayed-write policy is employed for disk writes. That is, both reads and writes are satisfied from memory buffers whenever possible. When a new buffer is needed, a victim is selected among recently unused buffers. Only if the victim is marked as "dirty" (written into) are its contents physically written to disk before the buffer is reused.

While significantly improving performance, disk buffering creates several problems. One of them is that the asynchronous disk I/O makes meaningful error reporting virtually impossible. Another problem is that unwritten buffers in a suddenly stopped system may cause files to be corrupted. This is some-what alleviated by a special system call to flush buffers which is executed at regular intervals. The use of buffers may cause the physical sequence of disk writes to differ from the logical sequence of writes performed by user processes. Reversal of the order of writes can adversely affect the integrity of database applications.

Unix keeps track of free space by means of a chained list of indexes to unused blocks. In particular, some 50 pointers to free blocks are collected in one disk block. These blocks are chained together, so that each of them points to the next one in line. The first index block is normally kept in main memory. Thus, the system has immediate access to addresses of up to 50 free blocks and to a pointer where to find 50 more.

The nature of the Unix file system, and its typical applications, normally results in a large number of files per installation. In order to provide fast access to them, without excessive memory overhead, Unix keeps i-nodes of actively used files in main memory. When a file is open, its i-node is copied from the disk into the system table of active i-nodes. The relevant entries are accessible through the list of open files associated with each process. For concurrently open files, only a single copy of the related i-node is kept in main memory. When the last reference to the file goes away, the i-node is copied to the disk and removed from the table.

11.2.4 Unix Summary

Unix is a time-sharing operating system primarily intended for program-development and document-preparation environments. Due to its high degree of portability, Unix is available for a variety of CPUs ranging from microprocessors to supercomputers. The resulting ability to execute applications written under Unix on vastly different hardware makes the system attractive to both users and software designers.

Other major Unix features include device-independent I/O and a hierarchical file system that spans volume boundaries. The Unix command interpreter, shell, makes effective use of these facilities and provides I/O redirection and pipes. These are versatile interconnection components that allow numerous Unix utilities, filters, to be combined in different ways to form complex tools. Specialized versions of Unix with additional tools and utilities are available for program development (Unix/PWB) and document preparation (Unix/WWB).

In addition to file processing and I/O manipulation, Unix provides system calls for process-management. Processes can be created and destroyed, they can synchronize and communicate with each other, and they can execute other processes. Unix processes form a family tree, and strong ties exist between children and their parent processes. Parent and children processes share the same code segment but have separate private data segments. Signals are the primary form of interprocess synchronization, while pipes provide for communication between syblings.

Unix uses event-driven scheduling for system processes and an adaptive version of round robin for user processes. Swapping is used to support multiprogramming (demand paging is available in some versions for larger computer systems). The swapping algorithm partly bases its decisions on the relative age of processes in order to prevent total thrashing.

A variant of indexing is used to keep track of and to access data blocks of files. In order to reduce physical disk I/O and effective disk-access time, Unix provides extensive buffering of disk blocks.

11.3 iRMX 86 OPERATING SYSTEM

iRMX 86 is a real-time operating system provided by Intel for products based on their 86 family of microprocessors. The iRMX 86 is included as a case study in this chapter for three major reasons:

1. It embodies many of the process-related concepts discussed in this book.
2. It provides an illustration and possible guidelines for the functional extension of the KMOS system described in Chapters 9 and 10.
3. Its kernel is implemented in silicon in the form of an operating-system firmware (OSF) component.

For a number of reasons, there is a considerable gap between the findings of the operating-system theory and the actual design practices of implementers of commercial operating systems. In order to preserve the available base of supporting software, many vendor-supplied operating systems tend to follow a slow evolutionary path from one release to another. As a result, even when new concepts are incorporated, they tend to become add-on features that do not always mesh well with the original philosophy of the system.

Having started "from scratch" with no predecessor product to maintain compatibility with, designers of the iRMX 86 have incorporated many sound theoretical concepts into their system. Some examples include multiprocess operation, interprocess synchronization and communication via semaphores, messages, and regions, a hierarchical file system, and device-independent I/O.

The first marketed release of the iRMX 86, designed in the late seventies, was a single-user multiprocess system. When hardware-assisted memory-management became available in the iAPX 86 family of processors, subsequent releases of the iRMX 86 provided support for multiuser operation.

Being primarily intended for real-time applications, the iRMX 86 provides extensive multiprocess facilities and preemptive, priority-based scheduling. The major features of the system include

- Object-based architecture
- Multiprocess operation and multiprogramming
- Error-handling facilities
- Device independence
- A hierarchical file system

Using the object model, the iRMX 86 classifies the resources that it manages into a set of object types, such as processes and mailboxes. Dedicated system calls are provided for the manipulation of each particular type of object. This abstraction results in a more regular definition of the nature and scope of particular system calls and presumably aids comprehension and learning of the system.

Multiprogramming mainly refers to the iRMX 86 facilities for separation of different applications when they coexist in the same system. A special type of system object, called a *job*, is used to define the confines of each particular application. A job consists of a collection of related processes and their common resources, such as semaphores and mailboxes.

Realizing the importance of error handling in real-time systems, the designers of the iRMX 86 have provided a flexible system for exception handling at the process and job levels. At its option, each process can handle its own error conditions, have them processed by system-supplied handlers, or field exceptions to the online system debugger for immediate analysis.

The general advantages of device-independent I/O and of hierarchical file systems were discussed in earlier chapters and in the Unix case study. The specific implementation of these concepts in the iRMX 86 system is discussed later in this chapter.

Following the basic structure of this chapter, the iRMX 86 operating system is described from two different points of view: those of the command-language and the system-call users, respectively. The section closes with a description of an implementation of the iRMX 86 kernel in silicon.

11.3.1 Command-Language User's View of the iRMX 86

The iRMX 86 is primarily intended to provide run-time support for applications running on target machines. This bias may be deduced from a rich set of system calls and a fairly modest collection of services provided to command-language users. Accordingly, we provide a brief section on the command-language user's view and a more extended one on the system-call user's view of the system.

Since programming languages, such as PL/M, Pascal, and C, as well as text editors and language-oriented debugging tools, are available as optional packages, in this section we discuss only the basic offerings of the iRMX 86 operating system. In particular, we omit presentation of program development and execution and just discuss briefly file-related commands of the iRMX 86.

An interesting feature of the iRMX 86 operating system is that it provides three different types of system debuggers. Two of them are more or less standard: a crash-dump analyzer and a static debugger that freezes the system under examination and allows user-controlled debugging actions. The third debugger, however, is unusual in the sense that it is a symbolic operating-system debugger. Namely, this debugger allows the user to examine certain system objects, such as process and semaphore queues, while the balance of the application is running. In other words, the user can dynamically examine interactions of a process both with its cooperating peers and with its execution-time environment. Although quite rare, such debuggers are very useful tools in the integration phases of complex applications, when many more or less independently tested processes are combined to form a working system.

The iRMX 86 operating system supports the notion of *logical device names*. That is, physical devices can be specified by means of logical names. These may be assigned at the system-generation time or at a later time via system calls. Some default logical names, such as CO (for console output), are predefined by the system. The use of logical names facilitates the porting of software between iRMX 86 systems with different hardware configurations.

The iRMX 86 provides a hierarchical file system that can be manipulated by commands or via system calls. Files are accessed in the iRMX 86 by using syntax very similar to that described in Chapter 8 and in the Unix case study in this chapter. Except for default-user and system devices, logical or physical device specifications are required in path names.

Redirection and pipes are not directly supported in the command language. Some redirection is possible by means of prepositional parameters, such as TO and OVER, that are accepted by certain commands.

Several file-related commands of the iRMX 86 are presented in Table 11.3. As indicated, the standard commands for the deletion, renaming, and copying of files are provided under familiar names. The DELETE command acts on both files and directories. The COPY command can also be used to create files when the console is specified as the source file.

In addition to calls for listing and manipulating directories, the standard set of calls is provided for volume maintenance. The FORMAT command allows users

DELETE   ; delete files and empty directories
RENAME   ; rename files
COPY   ; copy and create files

a. General file manipulation

DIR   ; list names and attributes of files in a directory
CREATEDIR   ; create directory

b. Directory manipulation

FORMAT   ; format iRMX 86 volumes
DISKVERIFY   ; verify data structures on iRMX 86 volumes
BACKUP   ; back up files to backup devices
RESTORE   ; restore files from backup devices

c. Volume manipulation

Table 11.3 Some file-related commands of the iRMX 86

to specify the default granularity of a volume. *Granularity* refers to the size of the cluster used by the system as the file-allocation unit for block-structured devices.

Command files can be executed by means of the SUBMIT command. Other iRMX 86 commands include TIME and DATE. File transfer between the iRMX 86 and Intel development systems is possible by means of UPCOPY and DOWNCOPY commands.

Command language of the iRMX 86, called *human interface* in Intel literature, also provides a set of system calls to assist in the definition and processing of additional user-specified system commands.

11.3.2 System-Call User's View of the iRMX 86

In this section we describe some system calls of the iRMX 86. As usual, we begin with the overall system description and then concentrate on calls for process-management and interprocess communication and synchronization. After a brief presentation of memory-management calls, we discuss the basic philosophy of the I/O system. The section concludes with an overview of I/O and file-related system calls of the iRMX 86.

As indicated earlier, the iRMX 86 is an object-based operating system. Objects represent both a concept and a tool. In general, objects are abstract entities in terms of which we think. In our present context, components of the operating system—such as processes and mailboxes—may be regarded as types of OS objects. Each particular process or mailbox is then an instance of the generic operating-system object type, process and mailbox, respectively. All objects of a given type share some common properties. For example, all processes are characterized by having priority and state. In terms of implementation, an object consists of a given type definition and of the related set of system calls for manipulating that specific type of objects.

The following object types exist in the iRMX 86 operating system:

- Job
- Process
- Semaphore
- Mailbox
- Region
- Segment
- Extension and composite objects

The last category of objects, intended for user-defined new types of objects, is not discussed further in this chapter. Other iRMX 86 objects are discussed in the order of their appearance in the list above.

The name *job* may be somewhat unfortunate, because a job in the iRMX 86 has nothing to do with the common notion of batch jobs introduced earlier in this book. In the iRMX 86, a job is an environment in which other iRMX 86 objects reside. More specifically, a job is a collection of related processes and the resources they use. The primary purpose of a job is to provide a boundary between different applications when they coexist in the same system. Although the sharing of objects that reside in different jobs is possible, the sharing of objects belonging to the same job is much less restricted and cumbersome.

Resources held by a job, such as processes and memory segments, are cataloged in the related job directory of objects. Thus, a job consists of a collection of processes and their resources, a directory of objects, and a pool of memory. Jobs are passive objects in the sense that jobs cannot invoke any system calls. It is the active objects, processes, that do the work of the system.

The division of processes into jobs is the responsibility of systems programmers. Related processes that share many resources and have similar life spans are commonly placed in the same job. Jobs in iRMX 86 systems form a family tree. In essence, all jobs in a system are offsprings of the root job which is created by the nucleus (kernel). When a new job is created, it is allocated a pool of memory which is taken from the parent job (the creator). This memory is used for the creation and maintenance of objects, such as processes and segments, that belong to the related job. The basic principles of dynamic memory-management in iRMX 86 systems are discussed later in this section.

Some iRMX 86 system calls for the manipulation of jobs are as follows:

CREATE_JOB
DELETE_JOB
OFFSPRING

As suggested by their names, these calls allow the creation and deletion of jobs. A call to create a job takes a number of parameters which define certain job characteristics, such as the size limits of its memory pool and the maximum allowable priority of processes in the new job. Each job is created with one process in it which can then invoke system calls to create other objects as needed.

The DELETE_JOB call allows a childless job to be deleted with all of its containing objects. The OFFSPRING system call can be used to identify all offspring of the calling job. This call is often used to locate offspring for termination while preparing to delete a job.

Processes are familiar objects to which we have devoted a lot of space in this book. Processes, called *tasks* in iRMX 86 literature, are assigned priorities between 0 and 255—0 is highest—which can be dynamically changed at the run-time by means of the SET_PRIORITY call. Abuses of this call are prevented by the restriction that no process may raise its priority above the maximum limit defined for the enclosing job. Some other process-related system calls in the iRMX 86 are as follows:

CREATE_PROCESS
DELETE_PROCESS
SUSPEND_PROCESS
RESUME_PROCESS
SLEEP

As mentioned in Chapter 3, the iRMX 86 operating system keeps track of the depth of suspension of each process. Thus, a suspended process is actually resumed only after the RESUME_PROCESS (RESUME_TASK in the official iRMX 86 syntax) call, after which the suspend count of the related process becomes 0. The SLEEP call is used for timed delays, and it is functionally equivalent to the DELAY call in KMOS. A few other system calls are provided to handle inquiries regarding dynamic and static attributes of processes.

Interprocess synchronization and communication in the iRMX 86 system are handled by three different mechanisms discussed in earlier chapters of this book. In particular, semaphores, messages, and regions are available to system-call users. In the words of the iRMX 86 literature, semaphores are custodians of abstract units. The maximum number of units per semaphore may be defined at its creation time. Thus, both binary and counting semaphores can be used. System calls for semaphores are

CREATE_SEMAPHORE
DELETE_SEMAPHORE
SEND_UNITS
RECEIVE_UNITS

The SEND_UNITS call generates an exception when attempting to increase the semaphore unit count above its declared maximum. Similarly, the RECEIVE_UNITS call may ask for no more than the maximum number of units defined for a given semaphore. Since queuing semaphores are implemented in the iRMX 86 system, a queue of processes, possibly empty, is associated with each semaphore. A create-time option is to have this queue managed in FIFO order or in the decreasing order of priorities of waiting processes.

Asynchronous, system-buffered messages are provided for interprocess communication and synchronization in iRMX 86 systems. Messages are exchanged by means of mailboxes, so that many-many mapping between senders and receivers is possible. Normally, each message contains a single token for an object. A token is a unique object_ID returned by the system following the successful completion of the call to create the related object. (iRMX 86 also provides object directories and system calls that allow referencing of objects by ASCII names, but we will not discuss those here.) Thus, messages may conveniently be used to pass object tokens between processes. When data communication via messages is desired, the common procedure is to first create the data segment and fill it with the data to be transferred. The message can be used to pass the token for the related data segment to the receiving process. The receiver may then access the data by means of the supplied segment token. Obviously, this approach is safer and more orderly than what we have implemented in KMOS. The price paid for this convenience is the overhead of the several system calls necessary to transfer a single data message.

Some message-related calls of the iRMX 86 are as follows:

CREATE_MAILBOX
DELETE_MAILBOX
SEND_MESSAGE
RECEIVE_MESSAGE

The RECEIVE_MESSAGE call accepts an optional time limit. As with semaphores, process queues can be FIFO or priority ordered.

The third mechanism for interprocess communication provided in the iRMX 86 is called *region*. A region is a data area that may be accessed only in a mutually exclusive manner. While semaphores allow mutually exclusive access to common data, iRMX 86 regions enforce it. That is, the system allows only one process to have control of a given region at any time. Regions also prevent the undesirable behavior of semaphores where a process within a critical section can be preempted by another process wishing to enter the same section, thus hindering the progress of both. Regions alleviate this problem by making it impossible for a process within a region to be preempted by any of its competitors. This is accomplished by temporarily raising the priority of the process within the region to match the highest priority among the processes waiting in the associated priority-based queue. Some system calls for the manipulation of regions are as follows:

CREATE_REGION
DELETE_REGION
SEND_CONTROL
RECEIVE_CONTROL

The SEND_CONTROL call is used by a process to signal its departure from a region to the operating system so that other waiting processes, if any, may be admitted to the region. A call to RECEIVE_CONTROL suspends the caller if necessary until the desired region becomes available.

Device interrupts in iRMX 86-based systems are handled by means of special routines, called *interrupt handlers*. Although they are essentially processes triggered by external events, interrupt handlers are treated differently than ordinary iRMX 86 processes. In particular, interrupt handlers run with all interrupts disabled, and they may invoke only specific, interrupt-related system calls. These calls allow interrupt handlers to connect themselves to interrupt vectors, to enable or disable various interrupt levels, and to communicate with interrupt processes. Since they normally run with interrupts disabled, interrupt handlers should be very short. When more demanding processing of interrupts is required, interrupt processes can be used to perform it. An interrupt process is just an ordinary process which is synchronized to a specific interrupt handler. The two may synchronize via the dedicated SIGNAL_INTERRUPT (invoked by the interrupt handler) and the WAIT_INTERRUPT (issued by interrupt process) system calls. This form of interaction is asynchronous, and the system queues outstanding interrupts signaled by the handler but not yet processed by the interrupt process.

The iRMX 86 operating system provides management of dynamic pools of memory for the needs of its constituent jobs and, ultimately, for the needs of system-call users. A pool contains the memory available to a job and its descendants. Whenever a new job is created, a pool of memory is given to it by the parent (this memory comes from the parent's pool). In order to prevent overallocation of memory, minimum and maximum pool sizes are specified for each job being created. If the parent job does not have enough memory for the purpose, the operating system refuses to create the offspring.

Memory is allocated to requestors in terms of segments, that is, contiguous areas of free memory. The idea is that, statistically speaking, not all jobs may need all of their memory at all times. In other words, the system can provide a useful service by borrowing memory where it exists and lending it where it is scarce. In the iRMX 86 case, memory pools have a treelike hierarchy which directly corresponds to the tree of jobs. When a process requests some memory and none happens to be available, the operating system attempts to borrow memory from the parent—all the way up to the root job. Memory freed by deletion of objects is returned to the pool of the related job. Memory freed by deletions of jobs is automatically returned to their parents.

System calls for the management of memory pools include facilities for the creation and deletion of segments. The segment token, returned by the operating system upon successful creation, is the base address in memory of the related segment. This token is used to identify the segment, say, when being used to transmit messages, and eventually to delete it. Several system calls are also available for inquiries about pool sizes and predefined limits.

This completes our discussion of the iRMX 86 kernel, called *nucleus* in the Intel literature. In addition to the nucleus, the iRMX 86 operating system provides additional layers for input/output and file-management. The iRMX 86 provides device-independent I/O and hierarchical directories of files. All I/O devices are treated as files and manipulated by a uniform set of system calls. Three different types of files may coexist in a system: named files, physical files, and stream files. Named files may be kept on block-structured devices. Hierarchical directories and access control are provided for the manipulation of named files. Physical files allow only one file per volume. They are normally used for character-oriented devices and for the manipulation of volumes with file structures different than that of the iRMX 86. Stream files correspond to Unix pipes, and they may be used for interprocess communication.

Two I/O subsystems, called the *basic I/O* and the *extended I/O system*, are available in the iRMX 86. As a system-generation option, none, basic I/O, or both basic and extended I/O can be configured into any particular system. The basic I/O system provides asynchronous system calls that can execute in parallel with the calling process. The extended I/O system supports logical device and file naming and provides automatic buffering similar to what is described in Chapter 8 and in the Unix case study. System calls of the extended I/O execute synchronously with the caller. That is, control is returned to the caller only upon completion of the related call.

Practically all file-related services available to command-language users may also be obtained through system calls. For example, files can be deleted and renamed, and directories can be listed and modified. In addition, system calls are provided to read, update, and append both data files and directories.

Whenever a file is created, the owner's ID is recorded together with the specified access rights, such as read-only, write-only, or read-write. The access rights of other users are specified by means of Access lists associated with related files. Each entry of the Access list contains the identity of the specific user together with the indication of his or her access rights. In order to prevent excessive growth of Access lists, two special categories of users are defined: system manager and world user. The latter class essentially encodes access rights of all users not explicitly mentioned in a given Access list. Access masks have a somewhat different meaning for directories and for ordinary files, respectively.

Authorized users can read and write files by means of the READ and WRITE system calls. SEEK is also available for random access to files on block-structured devices. Since the iRMX 86 allows the run-time addition of devices, special calls exist for the attaching and detaching of physical devices. New files may be created only on attached devices. The creation of a file does not imply its opening, so the OPEN call must be explicitly invoked prior to manipulation of new or existing files. The OPEN call accepts two parameters in addition to the identity of the target file. These are the open-mode indicator and the share-mode indicator, respectively. The open-mode indicator specifies the intended type of access, while the share-mode indicator specifies the type of sharing that concurrent users are willing to tolerate. The TRUNCATE call is also available to write the end of file at the current marker position. A special call, UPDATE, is used to flush file buffers from memory, say, before removing a volume.

Processes which invoke asynchronous I/O calls may synchronize with the I/O system by means of response mailboxes or by using the WAIT_IO call. Following completion of the related operation, the I/O system notifies the caller by sending a response to the mailbox or by returning control to the first statement following the WAIT_IO call.

With the exception of random access and hierarchical directories, most of these calls are usable for all types of files: named, physical, and stream files. Stream files are somewhat special in that they use no devices and provide no access control. They are primarily used for transferring large amounts of data between processes. In effect, stream files extend the notion of device independence to include processes.

11.3.3 iRMX 86 Implementation

No specific information regarding implementation of the iRMX 86 system is in the public domain. However, it is reasonable to assume that the basic kernel (nucleus) implementation concepts are similar to what we have described in relation to the KMOS. Since the iRMX 86 provides device independence and a hierarchical file system, the material in Chapter 8 and in the Unix case study provides an indication as to how such systems can be designed. Instead of a description of possible iRMX 86 implementations, in this section we briefly discuss the silicon version of the iRMX 86 nucleus.

Several microcomputer operating systems, mostly real-time, are available from software vendors in the form of a collection of read-only memory chips. Such devices, often called *software on silicon,* may be designed into microprocessor-based products to provide the added functionality of a set of operating-system primitives. In order to be usable with a wide range of configurations and designs, such software products are usually written using position-independent code. Since their use alleviates the problem of linking user code with the operating system, software interrupts are a popular method for invoking the services of software on silicon.

The Intel 80130 Operating System Firmware (OSF) component goes a step beyond ROM designs by providing a collection of hardware components necessary to support execution of the operating system, in addition to the kernel code. More specifically, the 80130 OSF component consists of an interrupt controller, three hardware timers, and an ROM that contains about two-thirds of the iRMX 86 nucleus described in this chapter. All of these are housed in a single 40-pin chip.

The interrupt controller, among other things, provides hardware vectoring, arbitration of priority, and selective enabling and disabling of interrupt levels. Three programmable interval timers are intended for the system timebase, timed delays, and for baud-rate generation, respectively.

The 80130 kernel is described as providing 35 additional instructions and 5 new data types to the basic architecture of the related microprocessor. Given that most kernel functions run with interrupts turned off, it is quite justified to regard the operating-system instructions provided by the chip as an extension of the basic instruction set of the microprocessor connected to the 80130. The 5 new data types provided by 80130 are job, process, mailbox, region, and segment. All of them are described under System-Call User's View of the iRMX 86 in Section 11.3 of this chapter.

One interesting implication of operating-system software in silicon is that the kernel contained therein is considered to be stable enough to warrant its "freezing" into the ROM. For example, the 80130 nucleus is compatible with several major releases of the iRMX 86 operating system. Moreover, the selection of system primitives provided in operating-system components provides a good indication as to what designers of such systems consider to be the essential functions of a kernel.

The system calls provided by the 80130 OSF component are presented in Table 11.4. Similar to our reasoning related to the creation and deletion of objects in the KMOS, the 80130 kernel supports only the creation of jobs. While a rather exhaustive subset of iRMX 86 calls is provided for process-management and interprocess communication, semaphores are not supported in the 80130 kernel. Probably pressed with limitations imposed by chip area and production considerations, the designers of the 80130 have opted to exclude semaphores on the ground that similar functionality may be accomplished by means of messages and regions. The OSF component also provides a rather extensive set of services for interrupt-management. This is to be expected, since one of the common uses of the 80130 is to serve as the complete operating system on embedded single-board computers serving as intelligent preprocessors for communications, process-control, and other I/O-intensive applications. Two dedicated calls are provided for the management of segments.

The remaining eight calls implemented in the 80130 OSF component are a subset of the iRMX 86 that was not discussed in detail in this chapter. They are included in Table 11.4 in order to provide a complete set of OSF system calls. A brief description of the basic function of each of these calls is also given in Table 11.4. The first two calls allow selective enabling and disabling of object deletions. For example, these calls can be used to temporarily prevent deletion of a segment participating in a DMA transfer. Two subsequent calls satisfy queries about object types and allow a process to get its token or the tokens of some related jobs. Vectoring to exception handlers, as well as canceling of such assignments, is made possible by the two exception-related calls. Finally, the last two calls in this group allow the definition of user-specified object types, called OS extensions in the iRMX 86, and permit those to activate their own exception handlers.

11.3.4 iRMX 86 Summary

The iRMX 86 is a multiuser, real-time operating system for iAPX 86-based computers. The iRMX 86 provides a rich set of system calls for the run-time support of applications such as process control and transaction processing. The system also includes an object-oriented debugger for the interactive debugging of processes while the remainder of the system continues to run.

The iRMX 86 is object-oriented. Multiprogramming is facilitated by the object type job, which collects related processes and their resources and

CREATE_JOB	; create a job with one task in it

a. Job-related calls

CREATE_TASK	; create a task with specified attributes
DELETE_TASK	; terminate the specified task
SUSPEND_TASK	; suspend, increase suspension depth if suspended
RESUME_TASK	; decrease suspension depth, resume if 0
SLEEP	; delay task for the specified period of time
SET_PRIORITY	; alter priority of a task

b. Task-related calls

CREATE_MAILBOX	; create mailbox, specify type of queueing
DELETE_MAILBOX	; delete mailbox, notify waiting tasks
SEND_MESSAGE	; send object token to the mailbox
RECEIVE_MESSAGE	; receive object token from the mailbox
CREATE_REGION	; create region, specify type of queueing
DELETE_REGION	; remove region, return memory to pool
SEND_CONTROL	; relinquish control of the specified region
RECEIVE_CONTROL	; wait for permit to enter a region
ACCEPT_CONTROL	; enter region if free, do not wait if busy

c. Intertask synchronization and communcation

ENABLE	; enable interrupt line
DISABLE	; disable interrupt line
ENTER_INTERRUPT	; enter interrupt handler
EXIT_INTERRUPT	; exit call for interrupt handlers
GET_LEVEL	; of the highest priority active interrupt
SET_INTERRUPT	; connect to interrupt vector
RESET_INTERRUPT	; disconnect from an interrupt vector
SIGNAL_INTERRUPT	; interrupt handler to interrupt task
WAIT_INTERRUPT	; interrupt task to await interrupt signal

d. Interrupt-management

CREATE_SEGMENT	; create memory segment of specified size
DELETE_SEGMENT	; remove segment, return memory to pool

e. Memory-management

ENABLE_DELETION	; enable deletion of specified object
DISABLE_DELETION	; disable deletion of specified object
GET_TYPE	; determine type of a given object
GET_TASK_TOKENS	; get tokens of certain objects (task, job)
GET_EXCEPTION_HANDLER	; obtain address of an exception handler
SET_EXCEPTION_HANDLER	; connect to an exception handler
SET_OS_EXTENSION	; connect to a new object type definition
SIGNAL_EXCEPTION	; from OS extension to exception handler

f. Other calls

Table 11.4 System calls provided by OSF component

provides isolation between different applications coexisting on the same system. Semaphores, messages, and regions are provided for interprocess synchronization and communication. The system dynamically allocates memory from a hierarchy of job-related memory pools.

The iRMX 86 provides device independence and a hierarchical file system. Named, physical, and stream files are provided for data storage, device manipulation, and interprocess communication. Logical device and file names are supported to aid program development and portability. Two configurable input/output systems offer both asynchronous and synchronous forms of system calls for device and file manipulation.

New user-defined object types may be integrated into the system by means of appropriate system calls. Extensive facilities for exception processing by either user or system code are available at the process and job levels. Most of iRMX 86 services can be included in the target system or excluded during system generation.

11.4 DESIGN OF A REMOTE-TELEMETRY UNIT (RTU)

This case study is an analysis of an actual design and implementation of a remote-telemetry unit (RTU), the basic component of distributed data-acquisition and control systems. Our primary purpose is to discuss and to illustrate certain aspects of real-time applications on the example of a system with a wide range of applications, from automated hamburger production to the remote control of vehicles in space. This particular application is used as a vehicle for describing common considerations present in multiprocess and high-performance systems, such as the use of a multiprocess kernel, the organization of processes, and interactions between them. To that end, we do not delve much into the peculiarities of RTUs. Instead, we stress design for high performance and investigate those parts of the system which are also of interest in a variety of other environments, such as distributed systems and computer networks, for example.

We begin with a brief description of distributed data-acquisition and control systems in order to identify the role and functions of a remote-telemetry unit. We then discuss the software organization of an RTU from the perspective of division of labor into processes, their relationships, and their relative priorities. Special emphasis is placed on the elements of the communications software and on some provisions necessary for support of multipoint configurations.

11.4.1 Computer Data-Acquisition and Control Systems

The primary function of a computer-based data-acquisition system is to monitor the state of the process to which it is connected. There are a great variety of processes that may and have been monitored by computerized data-acquisition systems. Some examples include industrial plants, such as an oil refinery, office buildings (monitoring of heating and cooling systems), and power generation and distribution systems. The data-acquisition system is usually connected to the monitored process by means of various sensors and transducers that acquire the process variables (such as temperatures, flows, and pressures), condition them, and relay them to the computer system. The described signals are usually analog voltages or currents. The process interface of the computer system filters and converts such signals into digital values by means of analog/digital (A/D) converters. The process variables, which are digital by their nature, such as on/off statuses of switches and open/closed states of valves, are brought into the computer by means of digital inputs. In order to prevent damage, such inputs are usually isolated by placing relays or optocouplers between the process inputs and the computer I/O ports.

The data-acquisition system basically monitors the states of the related process, performs some processing, such as filtering and statistical correlation, and presents measured or derived information to the system operator on display terminals and log printers. In geographically dispersed systems, such as power distribution systems and oil pipelines, the acquisition of process data is usually most effectively accomplished by means of a distributed data-acquisition system, such as the one depicted in Figure 11.3.

As indicated, a cluster of process variables whose sensors are located within a geographic locality is connected to the closest *remote-telemetry unit* (RTU). An RTU is usually microprocessor-based. In addition to the CPU, it contains the process interface necessary for attachment of local sensors and status inputs. An RTU monitors its local subset of process variables and communicates the gathered information to the control center. Depending on the distances involved and on the performance requirements, remote-telemetry units can be connected to the center by means of local-area networks, by long-distance cables, or by radio links. A distributed data-acquisition system consists of one central site and remote RTUs, whose number may vary from several to several hundreds. The actual number and locations of remote-telemetry units are determined in accordance with the number of process variables to be monitored, their geographic clustering properties, and cabling costs.

The central site consists of a supervisory computer installation which is connected to RTUs at one end and to human-interface devices at the other end. Operator interface can include numerous types of devices. The most common ones are depicted in Figure 11.3. They include graphic display terminals, mimic boards with process schematics and dynamic indication of the process state by means of lights and indicators, log printers, chart recorders, and the like.

The control-site computers maintain a database of process variables that represent the operator's view of the monitored system. Functions of the central site include presentation of process variables on demand and in regular intervals, such as shift logs. Based on the limits defined by process engineers, dangerous values of process variables are detected and displayed as various alarm conditions. In addition, the central computer can also calculate certain derived process indicators that are difficult or impossible to measure directly. For example, dangerous trends arising from a specific combination of values of process variables, none of which may be in an alarming condition by itself, are often monitored by supervisory

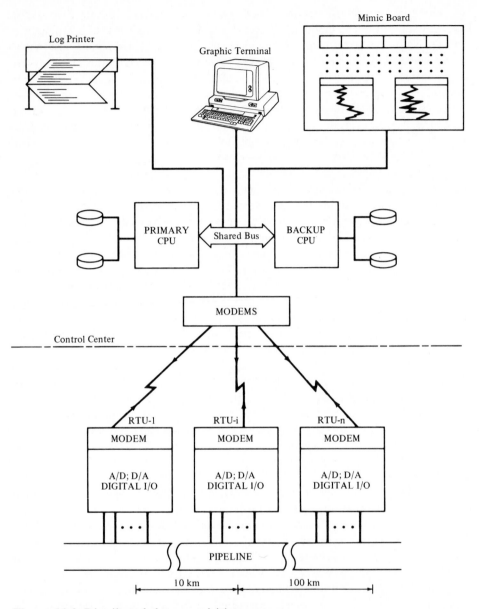

Figure 11.3 Distributed data-acquisition system.

data-acquisition systems. Since most processes require continuous monitoring, it is a common practice to improve the reliability and availability of the central-site computer equipment by means of redundancy. The system depicted in Figure 11.3 includes a primary and a backup computer system operating as a standby that goes online when the primary fails or malfunctions.

By incorporating control algorithms and the actuator-output interface, a data-acquisition system may provide the added dimension of controlling the monitored process. The result is called *supervisory control and data-acquisition* (SCADA). It uses the acquired process data to determine the control actions necessary to maintain satisfactory performance and stable behavior of the process. These control actions are then carried out by activating the related actuators. As a result of control actions and of some disturbances, the controlled process can change its state. Given the dynamic nature of controlled processes, SCADA systems permanently monitor process variables and apply control actions whenever necessary. In distributed implementations, local control algorithms and actions may be delegated to remote-telemetry units. This frees the central site to perform global process optimizations and to disseminate the resulting control settings and parameters to the RTUs.

Sophisticated SCADA systems are the backbone of computer-aided manufacturing (CAM) and computer-integrated manufacturing (CIM) systems. When coupled with an expert system, the basic functions of SCADA may be augmented with advising the operator as to the probable cause and remedy for some emergency process situations. Advanced commercial SCADA systems include elements of computer-aided design (CAD) techniques in the form of verifying the system topology and RTU layout and configuration design rules.

The inevitable merging of CAD and CAM technologies will facilitate much faster transitions between product development and manufacturing. The integration of expert systems is likely to aid both processes, for example, by identifying design problems in manufacturing and field tests and by feeding this information back into development to assist engineering changes. These and other aspects of integrated CAD/CAM systems will help the evolution of contemporary control systems toward meeting the requirements of factories of the future.

11.4.2 The Role of a Remote-Telemetry Unit

In order to avoid the details and peculiarities of control systems, we focus our attention on the remote-telemetry unit functioning in an ordinary SCADA system.

As suggested by Figure 11.3, a remote-telemetry unit collects process data from local sensors and communicates them to the central computer. In terms of hardware, a typical RTU consists of the processor with RAM and ROM, the communications interface (such as an asynchronous interface and a modem), and the process interface. The latter may include an A/D converter and the associated multiplexer, isolated digital inputs, and isolated digital outputs for activation of the local on/off actuators. Special hardware provisions are usually made to enable RTUs to function unattended and to cope with harsh environments. Some of these are described in later sections.

Remote-telemetry units usually permanently scan their local inputs and store the obtained values in the related tables. In other words, an RTU maintains a database describing the local subset of the state of the monitored process. On the other hand, the center maintains a database which reflects the global state of the monitored process, as described by its measured and derived variables. This database represents the operator's view of the process, and it provides input to the control algorithms executed by the central site.

As illustrated by Figure 11.4, the global database is a superset of individual RTU databases. In effect, the process state is represented by means of a distributed redundant database whose primary fragments are maintained in the RTUs and whose integral copy is maintained at the central site. Changes of the states of process variables are detected by the RTUs and recorded in their local databases. The central database is updated by means of center-RTU communications. Due to variable communication delays which are typically several orders of magnitude larger than CPU-memory communication, redundant copies of the process database are not identical at all times. This is inevitable in distributed

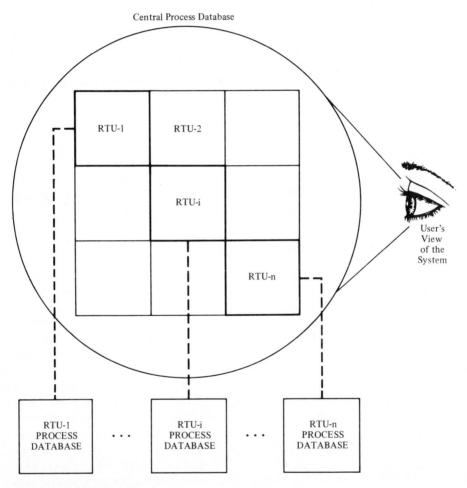

Figure 11.4 Global database.

systems, and it is not generally a problem when redundant copies of data are *converging* to the same state. This means that if the update activity were to cease, all redundant copies of data would attain identical values in finite time. Convergence is ensured in distributed control systems since practically all updates are originated in the RTUs, which pass them on to the center. It is the speed of database convergence, however, that sets telemetry systems apart. In order to be acceptable, a system must be able to acquire data, send them to the center for processing, and receive and apply the resulting control action in real time, that is, fast enough to make the control action relevant.

Thus, one of the primary considerations when designing a distributed control system is the speed with which process changes are reflected in the database. In the remainder of this section we discuss some related tradeoffs in RTU design. We begin by outlining the common form of center-RTU communication and proceed with RTU software organization.

Since most control systems have a hierarchical structure, communication between the center and remote-telemetry units is often of the master/slave type. In particular, the center (master) polls the RTUs (slaves) whenever it wishes to obtain some data from them. In this arrangement, an RTU responds only when polled, and it cannot send unsolicited messages. Polling is popular because it is simple to implement, and it enjoys several advantages, including

1. Flow control
2. Variable polling rate
3. Multipoint operation

The center regulates the flow of data on communication channels by polling the remote units only when it is ready to accept and to process information from them. Thus, the central computer can vary the frequency of polling in accordance with its load variations. Moreover, some RTUs can be polled more frequently than others. The resulting variable polling rate can be employed to monitor critical or fast-changing process variables more closely than the less important or slow-changing ones. Collisions in multipoint configurations, where the center and several RTUs share a common communication channel, may be avoided by fairly simple protocols based on one node (the center) dictating who talks and when.

When polling is adopted as the basis of internode communication, the next decision to be made regards the extent of RTU status reporting and its related mode of operation. The common options include

1. Full-status reporting: The RTU reports the status of all local process variables when polled.
2. On-demand reporting: The RTU reports only the status of a specific subset of the local process variables when polled.
3. Exception reporting: When polled, the RTU reports only the status of local process variables that have changed since the last time the RTU in question was polled.

Full-status reporting tends to overload communication channels and the central computer by indiscriminately sending entire copies of local RTU databases whenever one is polled. On-demand reporting reduces the load by reporting only the values of the specific subset of process variables designated in the polling message. In effect, on-demand reporting is center-driven as opposed to event-driven. As such, it may miss certain dangerous trends or fail to detect and process certain alarm conditions in time. Exception reporting is based on the observation that only changes of state of process variables need to be communicated to the center. Since it maintains a copy of the system database, only the actual updates, as opposed to indiscriminate reporting, need to be sent to and recorded by the center. Implementations of exception reporting require more complex and sophisticated RTUs which are capable of detecting significant changes of states of their local process variables. This potential disadvantage is largely offset by the resulting offloading of communication lines and of the central site. Since only the actual updates are communicated, the center can apply them directly to its database instead of sifting through piles of received RTU data with little or no information content.

11.4.3 Functional Organization and Activities of an RTU

Given its many advantages, our remote-telemetry unit uses exception reporting in a polled communication system with the center as a primary control node. Consequently, the RTU maintains a private database consisting of the values of local process variables. By continuously scanning its process inputs and comparing the obtained values against those stored in its database, the RTU is in the position to detect significant changes of process variables when they occur. The changed values can then be used to update all copies of the database that they are part of. In particular, significant changes are recorded in the local RTU database and communicated to the central copy. In this section we briefly discuss a possible organization of RTU software that meets these requirements. More specifically, we describe the processing of digital and analog inputs and sketch the principles of handling digital telecommands in response to orders issued by the central site. For the sake of simplicity, we ignore other types of process inputs and outputs, such as pulse and counter I/O and digital/analog outputs.

Although they are conceptually simple, there is a fairly large variety of digital inputs. For example, 1 or 2 bits can be assigned to each process input, resulting in single or double signalizations, respectively. The latter variety is useful for detecting when a switch is actually in transition from an ON to an OFF position, or vice versa, in addition to the usual detection of ON and OFF states which are also provided by single-bit digital inputs. Digital inputs can be permanent or transient. Transient inputs have one stable state (normally ON or normally OFF) and can occasionally trip into the signaling state (OFF or ON, respectively), from which they automatically return after a period of time. For such inputs, only the onsets of the transient state are normally reported to the central database.

These variations are usually handled by the introduction of a logical representation of inputs, often called *logical* or *virtual points*. Low-level software drivers then perform the necessary physical-logical mapping, and vice versa, thus allowing the higher-level RTU and SCADA system software to operate with uniform logical representations of inputs. This approach results in simplified software development and maintenance, as well as in more efficient code due to the removal of specific hardware considerations and peculiarities from a majority of software layers. In our description of digital-input processing, we mostly discuss handling of the logical inputs and ignore the actual physical details whenever possible.

Digital inputs are periodically scanned in order to detect status changes. Given the possibility of electromagnetic noise in industrial environments, digital inputs are normally filtered in hardware or in software prior to any other processing. The remote-telemetry unit under consideration scans digital inputs every 10 ms and uses software filtering. In particular, a status change is considered to be valid, as opposed to noise-induced, if it persists for at least two consecutive scan cycles, that is, if it lasts for more than 20 ms. The double-bit inputs are additionally filtered in order to detect indeterminate states (2 bits not complementary) that last for more than 100 ms. Changes of state are detected by maintaining a table of the validated input values obtained during earlier scans. For filtering purposes, a table of the last readings is also kept in the RTU. A valid change of state is detected when a new reading is identical to the previous one but different from the validated state stored in the RTU database. Such changes are recorded in the RTU database and sent to the control center for updating of the central database.

Analog inputs are interfaced and converted to digital representation by means of a bipolar analog/digital (A/D) converter and the associated relay multiplexer. As suggested by Figure 11.5, the multiplexer is used both for isolation purposes and to enable sharing of an expensive resource, the A/D converter, by several analog inputs. Thus, a typical processing of an analog input begins with a command to the multiplexer to select a given channel and thus bring the related input to the A/D converter. After verifying that the desired channel has indeed been selected, the A/D conversion is initiated. Upon its completion, another channel can be selected and converted in the same way.

The particular type of relay used in the RTU under consideration has a maximum operational frequency of 75 Hz, thus requiring some 13.3 ms to settle after changing its state. For security, a break-before-make philosophy is used for relay manipulation. This means that an active channel is first deselected, that is, safely disconnected from the A/D converter, before a new channel selection commences. In this way, the two process signals should never be able to interact with each other through a temporary multiplexer connection. In terms of the scanning rate, opening of one and closing of the other relay must elapse between two consecutive A/D conversions. With the type of relays used, the maximum scanning rate is some 37 channels per second. The A/D conversion time is approximately 45 μs.

In principle, analog inputs may also be scanned continuously in order to detect changes of process variables when they occur. In practice, many industrial processes have fairly long time constants, which can conveniently be handled by

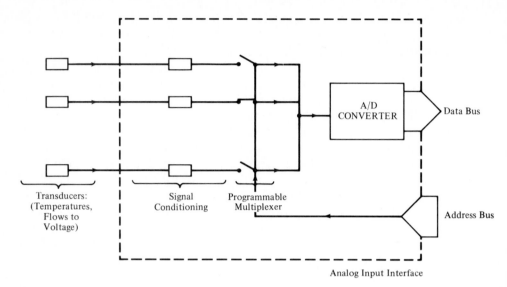

Figure 11.5 Analog inputs.

periodic scanning. This relieves the RTU to do some other tasks in the interim and prolongs the life expectancy of systems with the relay multiplexers. In the RTU under consideration, the analog scan rate is programmable from the center. By default, analog inputs are scanned every 5 s.

Telecommands are implemented by means of output relays. For reasons of security, the telecommands are activated from the center using the two-phase protocol. Namely, the desired relay is first selected and its setting is verified. When both the center and the RTU are satisfied with the outcome of this operation, an order to actually activate the selected command is given and executed by the RTU after a battery of second-phase tests.

Due to its inherent two-level hierarchical structure, star configurations are the most common topology of the communication network of distributed data-acquisition and control systems. Individual RTUs can be connected to the center by dedicated lines, or they can share a common communication channel. These two arrangements are often called *point-to-point* and *multipoint configurations*, respectively. Both of them can be mixed in the same system, as illustrated in Figure 11.6. In either case, communication channels may allow the simultaneous transmission of data in both directions (full duplex) or in a single direction at a time only (half duplex). A simplified view of a full-duplex and a half-duplex multipoint communication line is depicted in Figures 11.7a and b, respectively.

As indicated in Figure 11.7a, a full-duplex channel provides separate lines for transmission and for reception of data. This implies that each RTU connected to the channel receives all polling messages sent by the center. With the exception of broadcast messages, the explicit address of the target RTU must somehow be encoded in each polling message in order to ensure that only one RTU responds

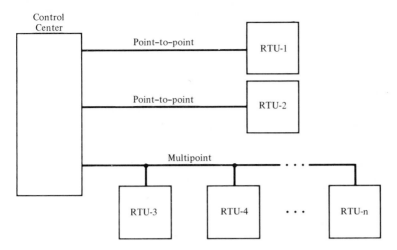

Figure 11.6 Communication links.

to it. Since such responses are sent on the center's receive line, other RTUs generally do not "hear" them.

The half-duplex channel, as shown in Figure 11.7b, can use a single line for both transmission and reception of data, since it is used in only one direction at any given time. This mode of communication introduces the added complexity of RTUs receiving not only the poll messages, but all communications between other RTUs and the center. This tends to complicate the communication protocol for synchronization among nodes on half-duplex channels. For this reason, many computer networks quoted as supporting point-to-point and multipoint configurations on full- and half-duplex channels exclude the multipoint half-duplex variety in small print.

11.4.4 RTU Software Organization (Processes)

Having described the basic organization of a remote-telemetry unit, we now turn our attention to the RTU software organization. Our primary concerns in this section are the process-related aspects of RTU software. These include the division of labor into processes and the design of basic interactions between them.

As discussed earlier, the remote-telemetry unit periodically scans and processes its digital and analog inputs. Whenever a significant change of state of a monitored process variable is detected, the new value is stored in the local database and prepared for sending to the center. The RTU must also receive, decode, and carry out all orders sent to it from the center. The most frequently used operational commands that the central site may issue to the RTUs are as follows:

SEND_CHANGES: The RTU is requested to send only the values of its process variables that have changed significantly from the time of the last poll.

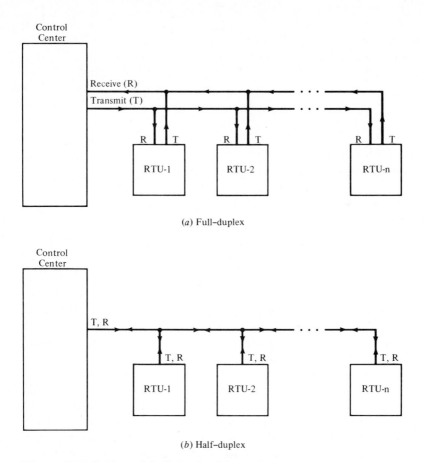

Figure 11.7 Full- and half-duplex channels.

SELECT_COMMAND: The RTU is requested to select a specified telecommand. After attempting to do so, the RTU informs the center about the outcome of the operation.

EXECUTE_COMMAND: The RTU is requested to activate a previously selected telecommand. After readying to execute the command the RTU informs the center about the outcome of the operation.

SEND_ALL: The center requests the values of all RTU process variables. The RTU responds by sending a copy of its entire local database.

Although based on exception reporting, the RTU under consideration is also capable of full-status reporting in response to the SEND_ALL request from the control site. This mode of operation, sometimes called the *general check*, is used for initialization of the central database during the system startup and after disruptions of service caused by communication line or RTU malfunctions. System startup with the actual measured values of the process variables, as opposed to defaults, ensures smooth operation and avoids an avalanche of exceptions necessary to update the central database initially.

The design process begins by investigating and specifying the RTU functions at approximately the presented level of detail. The next design step is to coarsely divide the labor into processes and then proceed with their more detailed specification. In order to do so, let us first summarize the basic RTU activities:

- Scanning and processing of digital inputs
- Scanning and processing of analog inputs
- Detection of significant changes
- Acceptance of messages from the center
- Decoding of the center's orders
- Processing of individual orders:
    - (a) Status reporting
    - (b) Selection and execution of telecommands
- Sending of messages to the center

The two rather obvious RTU functions that can be structured as separate processes are the handling of digital inputs and the handling of analog inputs. Both functions are periodically rescheduled, which suggests their implementation as cyclic processes that never terminate. At this point, it is quite natural to charge each process with detection of significant changes of the subset of the monitored-process variables that it operates on. As a result, each of the two processes needs to interact only with the communication module in order to have significant changes transmitted to the center.

The communication-related functions of the RTU include the acceptance and decoding of messages from the central site and the sending of responses to it. In order to support the full-duplex mode of operation, it is customary to implement the reception and transmission of data as separate processes. These processes can also be charged with implementing the low-level communication protocol. In this way they can remove hardware considerations, such as carrier control and error checking, from other layers of RTU software.

Decoding of and carrying out of orders can be implemented as separate processes or as a part of the reception process which receives messages from the center. Other than improving modularity, creation of a separate command-interpreter process allows decoupling of reception from the handling of messages. As a result, the reception process can permanently monitor the communication line for incoming messages. By assigning a high priority to it, the probability of losing messages due to internal command processing can be significantly reduced. Alternatively, if the same process both accepts and carries out each order after receiving it from the center, it may not be able to intercept all messages from the center in due time.

Let us summarize and name the different processes in order to facilitate further references to them. Scanning and preliminary processing of digital and analog inputs is handled by DIGITAL and ANALOG processes, respectively. Communication messages from the center are received by the LINE_IN process. The orders contained therein are decoded and carried out by the CLI process (command-line interpreter). Finally, messages are sent to the center by means of the LINE_OUT process. Given their acyclic nature (on-demand) and short execution times, telecommands may be implemented as routines callable from the CLI process.

11.4.5 RTU Data Structures and Interprocess Communication

This particular division of labor into processes allows both the reception and the transmission of data to proceed in parallel with other RTU functions, such as scanning and processing of digital and analog inputs. In terms of interactions between processes, DIGITAL and ANALOG must somehow communicate detected significant changes of process variables to the LINE_OUT process. The LINE_IN process forwards messages received from the center to the CLI process. The CLI process also interacts with the LINE_OUT process in order to forward response messages to the central site.

The main data structures in RTU software are the database of local process variables, lists of events, and communication buffers. As suggested earlier, validated values of local digital and analog inputs can be maintained in dedicated tables. In this way, each process—DIGITAL and ANALOG—operates with a separate set of tables, and no synchronization between them is necessary. The only other user of these tables is the CLI process when handling a SEND_ALL request from the center. Since CLI is a reader in this case, no serious conflicts in accessing the database should arise.

We now briefly investigate some tradeoffs involved in designing communication buffers and event-recording lists. Communication buffers are needed for assembling incoming messages and for storage of messages that need to be transmitted to the center. Messages received from the central site generally contain the RTU address, the code of the specific command, and a collection of error-checking bits. All of this fits into several bytes, thus making it reasonable to dedicate a small RAM area to serve as an input buffer. Outgoing messages, on the other hand, can be quite long. For example, response to a SEND_ALL request can be on the order of 1000 bytes. Responses to SEND_CHANGES requests consist of 3 bytes per changed variable, and they can also become quite lengthy when an RTU is polled infrequently or when some sort of increased activity is happening in the related portion of the monitored process. For these and other reasons, the allocation of fixed-size output buffers is quite inefficient and restrictive. For example, it requires that the maximum length of an RTU message be specified in advance in order to dimension the buffer accordingly. The dynamic nature and variability of message sizes attributable to exception reporting do not favor such a decision. A more pressing problem is that certain types of RTU responses, such as the ones to SEND_CHANGES requests, must be buffered until their successful receipt is acknowledged by the center. Thus, two large communication buffers may be needed—one to hold RTU messages awaiting acknowledgment and another to assemble new messages.

Before committing ourselves to a solution, let us investigate the requirements of event lists for a possible relationship to communication buffers. This may be important because those two structures are major consumers of RAM capacity. An event list is a list of significant changes accumulated by the DIGITAL and ANALOG processes between two successive polls of an RTU. Given the variable arrival rate of monitored-process changes, as well as the potential variability of the polling rate, the number of entries in an event list can vary considerably. Thus, both output communication buffers and event lists may best be handled by some sort of variable-length data structures, such as linked lists.

Power consumption, slow peripheral buses, and reliability considerations often prompt designing of the remote-telemetry unit's processor in the form of a single-board computer. In other words, the CPU, ROM, RAM, USARTs, and other supporting chips are placed on a single printed-circuit board. This approach, among other things, tends to limit the amount of RAM that may be available to a remote-telemetry unit.

One of the major challenges facing designers of such RTUs is to devise suitable data structures that can handle variable-length event lists and communication buffers effectively while taking as little memory as possible. An interesting possibility, which is implemented in the design of the RTU under consideration, is to combine event lists and communication buffers into a single dynamic data structure.

In particular, two linked lists—called the EVENT and FROZEN_EVENT lists, respectively—are used as both communication buffers and event lists. They are, together with other major RTU data structures, depicted in Figure 11.8. Initially, all memory remaining after autosizing of the RTU tables for storing of the validated values of digital and analog inputs is linked up into the Free list. The DIGITAL or ANALOG process, upon detecting a significant change, obtains a node from the Free list (not shown in Figure 11.8), fills it up with the related data, and places it at the end of the EVENT list. Thus, the EVENT list

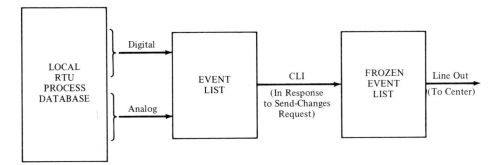

Figure 11.8 RTU data structures.

contains all significant changes of process variables accumulated since the last poll. When a SEND-CHANGES request is received from the center, the RTU is supposed to respond by transmitting the contents of the EVENT list. To that end, the contents of the event list at the time the SEND-CHANGES message is received, is "frozen" for shipment. This is accomplished by transferring the EVENT list into the FROZEN-EVENT list. Since both lists are linked, this operation involves a simple manipulation of the related head and tail pointers. Note that this effectively empties the EVENT list by setting its head and tail pointers to NIL. The contents of the FROZEN-EVENT list is then sent to the center by the LINE-OUT process. The list is kept for possible retransmissions in case of communication errors until a positive acknowledgment is received from the center. At that point, the FROZEN-EVENT list is discarded by having all of its nodes returned to the Free list.

Being of lower priority than the list-swapping operation, a negligible amount of synchronization is needed to make the DIGITAL and ANALOG processes continue their uninterrupted operation when the EVENT list is emptied for transmission purposes. As a result, no events are missed due to list processing.

Due to dynamically managed memory, the presented approach to buffering and event-recording conserves the scarce resource (RAM) and adapts to the actual needs of the system. The BUFFER-OVERFLOW condition, which is essentially a failure to allocate memory, can occur only when all available memory space is consumed by EVENT and FROZEN-EVENT lists. This should be contrasted with the static memory allocation, where a buffer overflow can occur in either a communication-buffer space or in an event list, while other related data structures may be underutilized at the same time.

11.4.6 Operation of RTU Processes

In this section we briefly outline the structure of DIGITAL and ANALOG processes and describe in some detail the communication processes LINE-IN, CLI, and LINE-OUT and the protocols of the distributed data-acquisition and control system under consideration.

The process DIGITAL reads all digital inputs present in an RTU, performs their software filtering, and detects status changes when they occur. The data structures used and modified by the process DIGITAL consist of the table of validated input states, VALTAB, and of the table of last input readings, PREVTAB, which is used for filtering purposes. To speed up processing, VALTAB and PREVTAB are parallel tables.

The basic processing is fairly simple. After reading a group of 8 input bits, process DIGITAL compares their values to the ones read in the previous cycle (stored in PREVTAB). The same input value is also compared against the validated states of the related inputs stored in the VALTAB. Changes that persist for at least two consecutive readings (values read identical to those in PREVTAB but different from the corresponding values in VALTAB) are recorded as validated and linked to the EVENT list. When all inputs are processed, the process delays itself for approximately 7.5 ms by calling the DELAY service of the operating system.

The ANALOG process scans analog inputs every 5 s, or with whatever scanning period is programmed from the center. As discussed earlier, input channels are successively connected via the multiplexer to the A/D convertor for conversion. After a conversion, the selected channel is first deselected and the next one in line is selected for the subsequent conversion. Since a relay multiplexer is used, deselection and selection of a channel take some 13.3 ms each. In order to improve throughput by increasing CPU utilization, the ANALOG process suspends itself for some 15 ms after commanding relay opening or closure for deselection and selection purposes, respectively.

When a new channel is safely selected, the analog/digital conversion is initiated to obtain the digital equivalent of the related analog input. The obtained value is then converted into two's complement representation for subsequent processing and eventual communication to the center. After optional digital filtering, the ANALOG process determines whether the related value has undergone a significant change relative to the one recorded in the table of reference analog readings, TANALOG. This process is somewhat more involved than a simple comparison, because analog values tend to oscillate slightly even when maintaining a constant average value. As a result, successive readings of the same analog channel are likely to be different even in the absence of any significant changes. These variations can be caused by a number of reasons, such as drift, quantization errors, and superimposed noise.

In order to avoid constant reporting of analog inputs and to make sure that all significant changes are detected, the ANALOG process uses the concept of a hysteresis, or the *deadband*. The deadband is used to distinguish between significant and nonsignificant changes in the following way. *Deadband* is defined as a percentage of the full range of the A/D converter. It is programmable from the center, and its default in this design is some 4%. A converted and filtered analog reading which is within the deadband of its reference reading stored in the TANALOG table is considered not to have changed considerably, and no further processing of it is performed by the ANALOG process. Conversely, if the obtained measurement differs from the reference reading for more than the value of the deadband, it is considered as having undergone a significant change. Such values are recorded as new reference values in the TANALOG table and linked in the EVENT list for sending to the center. Obtaining of a free node from the Free list and linking of events to the EVENT list are implemented as common functions callable by ANALOG and DIGITAL processes.

Communication between RTUs and the central site is handled by three processes, LINE_IN, CLI, and LINE_OUT. The LINE_IN process receives messages from the center and passes them on to the CLI process for further processing. The CLI process decodes and executes orders from the center and sends responses via the LINE_OUT process. The CLI and LINE_OUT processes perform fairly standard functions, and we do not describe them in great detail.

Certain communication-related features of the LINE_IN process warrant some elaboration.

The LINE_IN process is charged with receiving error-free messages addressed to the RTU that it executes on. Such messages are then relayed to the CLI process. LINE_IN hides all details of the line-communication protocol from other layers of RTU software. This protocol is designed to handle point-to-point and multipoint communication lines in both full- and half-duplex modes of operation. It is also supposed to be reasonably reliable in the presence of temporary and permanent communication-line failures. At the same time, the protocol is fairly simple in order to conserve computational resources of remote-telemetry units.

For brevity, we omit many interesting hardware details, such as carrier-controlled communication, operation with or without modems, and line-turnaround considerations imposed by half-duplex lines. All of these are performed when necessary without any reprogramming or reconfiguring of RTU software. From the system programmer's point of view, the communication protocol operates as follows. The central site polls a given RTU whenever it wishes to issue some order or to obtain changes of local RTU process variables. A simplified format of the poll message is depicted in Figure 11.9. As indicated, the poll message contains two synchronization characters (ASCII, NUL), the address of the target RTU, the code of the command for that RTU, and a longitudinal redundancy check (LRC) byte calculated on the basis of the contents of the message.

As discussed earlier, in some versions of half-duplex configurations, the RTUs receive all messages that traverse the communication channel in either direction. In particular, the RTUs receive messages sent by other RTUs or from the center. The danger here is that some of those may accidentally appear as legitimate polling messages to other RTUs and may cause some of them to respond. Such unsolicited responses may collide with other regular messages and thus cause considerable harm manifested as loss of synchrony and possible inability to communicate over the related channel for prolonged periods of time. In order to cope with this problem, a dedicated direction bit is included in each communication character. By convention, the center clears this bit in each character of its messages, and the RTUs set this bit in all characters of their responses. By testing the setting of this bit, the RTUs can distinguish messages sent by the central site from those sent by other RTUs. As illustrated later

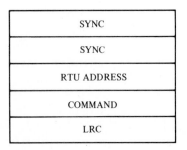

Figure 11.9 Simplified format of a poll message.

by means of the LINE_IN process, this approach considerably simplifies the communication protocol and places little burden on RTU resources. Its drawback, however, is that one data bit in each character must be sacrificed to indicate the direction of the related transfer.

The LINE_IN process in each RTU listens to the communication line and assembles polling messages from the center. The logic of this activity is depicted in the form of a state diagram in Figure 11.10. When an RTU becomes operational, the LINE_IN process is activated and it enters the LISTEN state. Whenever an error-free character (no parity, overrun, or framing error) is received from the line, its direction bit is tested. All characters sent by other RTUs ($D = R$) are ignored. Successive error-free characters received from the center ($D = C$) are considered to be a polling message if they conform to the format depicted in Figure 11.9. Two NULs at the beginning of each message are intended to allow

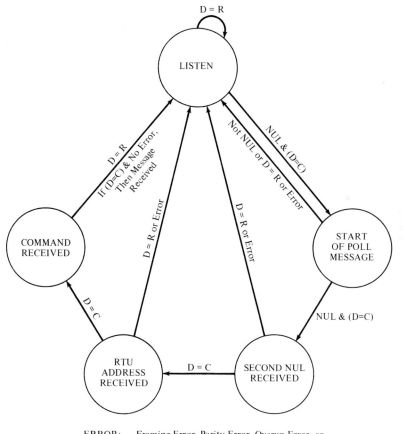

ERROR: Framing Error, Parity Error, Overun Error, or
Time-out, or Carrier Lost

Figure 11.10 Detection of a poll message.

synchronization of the RTUs that are brought online when the communication channel is already operational. This facilitates online addition of new RTUs and recovery after transient failures. Since the protocol is constructed in such a way that no other messages ever contain NUL characters, the RTU can be fairly confident that reception of two consecutive NULs from the center within a specified time limit constitutes the beginning of a polling message.

Provided that all subsequent characters are also received without errors, the LINE_IN process calculates the LRC on received characters and compares it against the one received from the line. If all is well, the received message is considered to be a valid poll message. The LINE_IN process compares the ADDRESS field of such messages against the address of its local RTU, which is encoded by the related configuration switches. If the two match, the poll message is addressed to this RTU and it is forwarded to the CLI process by means of the SEND directive. The LINE_IN process then returns to the LISTEN mode in order to be ready to accept other poll messages. In case any mishap is detected at any point of the described procedure, the LINE_IN process immediately returns to the LISTEN mode to resynchronize for other receptions. This mode of operation implies that no RTU will respond to polling messages that become garbled during transmission. Attempts to reconstruct messages in error are dangerous because two or more RTUs may "recognize" their address and respond, thus causing collisions and other problems discussed earlier. Instead, garbled messages are simply discarded and the central site can detect the fact by receiving no response within a prescribed time limit. When this happens, the center repeats the related message. If no response is received after a few retries, the target RTU is declared as temporarily unreachable and the remedial testing and repairing sequence is undertaken.

This concludes our exposition of the operation of RTU processes. In the next section we briefly outline some of the services of the operating system used by RTU processes and describe their priority assignments.

11.4.7 RTU Processes and KMOS

The presented remote-telemetry unit uses a version of KMOS with services identical to those described in Chapter 9.

The DIGITAL and ANALOG processes use the DELAY service to periodically reschedule themselves. The ANALOG process also uses the DELAY service to deactivate itself after commanding relay closures and openings on the analog multiplexer. The only other communication of these processes with the rest of the system is the linking of events to the EVENT list for subsequent forwarding to the center by CLI and LINE_OUT processes. No system services are used for this purpose, because dedicated shared routines with their own internal synchronization are charged with this activity.

As described, the LINE_IN process forwards relevant poll messages to the CLI process by means of the SEND directive of KMOS. The LINE_IN process also uses the RECEIVE directives to accept input interrupts from the communication line (via the related USART). The CLI process, naturally, receives messages from LINE_IN by means of the RECEIVE directive on the same mailbox used by LINE_IN's SEND and forwards messages to the center by invoking SEND on the mailbox dedicated for data exchanges between the CLI and LINE_OUT processes. The LINE_OUT process accepts these messages by means of the RECEIVE service and uses RECEIVE on another mailbox to accept transmit interrupts from the USART.

The assignment of priorities to RTU processes follows the usual logic of real-time systems that most important and time-critical processes should get high priorities and, with them, preferential service. Another common technique is to make the high-priority and interrupt-related processes as short as possible and to do whatever lengthy processing may be required at lower priority. In this spirit, some logically related activities, such as the reception and decoding of external messages in the described RTU, can be split into separate processes. One of them usually collects the data; it is short and runs at high priority. The other, usually longer process handles the acquired data at a much lower priority. This approach provides good response time to most events while keeping the CPU busy in the interim. Moreover, separation of the data-collection from the data-processing activities facilitates use of multiple data buffers when very high performance is desired. The use of multiple buffers is discussed in Chapters 2 and 3.

Following these basic rules and the RTU hardware-interrupt assignments, the two interrupt-driven processes, LINE_IN and LINE_OUT, are assigned high relative priorities corresponding to USART interrupt priorities, 8 and 9 in this particular design. In order to prevent loss of input characters, as discussed in Chapter 2, LINE_IN is assigned higher priority than LINE_OUT. The remaining processes are not directly connected to interrupts, and they are assigned priorities greater than 129. In order to keep communication with the central site as fast as possible, the CLI process has the highest relative priority in this group, 130. It is followed by the DIGITAL process, whose timing and frequency of execution are more critical than those of the ANALOG process. Consequently, DIGITAL and ANALOG are assigned priorities 135 and 140, respectively. The last user-assigned priority in the RTU is given to the WATCHDOG process, which is in charge of restarting the RTU upon unrecoverable software failures. The two standard system-related processes, KMOSCLOCK and KMOSNUL, are assigned priorities 0 and 255, respectively.

11.4.8 Concluding Remarks

As described, the remote-telemetry unit is a prototypical example of an embedded static system. As such, the RTU is well equipped for unattended operation in harsh industrial environments. Although it provides a great deal of flexibility in the sense of supporting a wide range of different hardware configurations with no reprogramming or reconfiguring of the software whatsoever, the presented design of a remote-telemetry unit is essentially a closed static system. This apparent paradox is common in more sophisticated embedded systems, such as those found in weapons, medical instruments, traffic controllers, and many other applications where the computer is a programmed black box buried within and servicing a larger enclosing system. Namely, all existing flexibility is preprogrammed within its operating system and application programs, and no additional functions can be incorporated without disruption of service.

Like most embedded system, the presented RTU's operating system (KMOS, described in Chapters 9 and 10) and application programs (described in this chapter) are placed in nonvolatile read-only memory (ROM). This provides a rudimentary form of protection and allows the RTU to be self-starting without the need for secondary storage devices. Random-access memory (RAM) is reserved for storage of variables, such as the local database and communication buffers. All application processes are present in all configurations of the RTU, but they are activated only when needed. This is accomplished by a self-configuring routine executed during the RTU startup which tests the hardware and identifies all modules present in the RTU. If modules necessary for a particular function, such as the A/D converter and the multiplexer, are not present in a given configuration, the related process—ANALOG in this example—is simply not created. This approach provides for ease of manufacturing and servicing because all ROMs delivered to all customers are identical, regardless of the particular RTU's hardware configuration. The net result is elimination of the need for configuration of RTU software (cheaper and faster manufacturing of the product), simplified bookkeeping in sales and service departments, and reduced inventory—all accomplished at the expense of possibly a few hundred extra bytes of ROM per station.

Perhaps an interesting datum for potential designers of embedded systems is that the actual product partly described in this chapter contains over 30% of error-detection code which consumes a similar percentage of the execution time. Error-detection considerations were included in the design from its very inception in order to facilitate servicing of geographically dispersed installations where RTUs may be located in difficult-to-access areas (pipelines are not always built on highways). Error detection begins with a thorough power-on self-test procedure and continues with execution of all processes. The selection and deselection of virtually each relay are verified, the A/D converter is tested for accuracy at the beginning of each scan, the protective fuses are read and tested in parallel with each related group of digital inputs, and the execution of telecommands can detect some 15 distinct errors in each of its two phases. In addition, the hardware watchdog timer is combined with the WATCHDOG process to ensure the automatic restarting of the RTU whenever any of its processes attempts to monopolize the processor.

While the design and debugging of error-detection features were simply hard work and little fun for most of the time, the results were well worth the effort. Coupled with the proprietary SCADA software for the central site, the combined system is capable not only of detecting, but also of isolating the probable causes of errors up to the individual RTU, board, and even component level. Depending on the severity of each particular error, the related board, function, or the entire RTU is disabled pending removal of the problem. Extensive error checking and reporting to remote sites are of extreme importance in computer networks and in distributed systems with many potential sources of problems that may be difficult to pinpoint by classical diagnostic techniques, which frequently require the system to be brought down for testing.

OTHER READING

Paterson (1983) describes the design philosophy and details of the file structure of early versions of the MS-DOS. Among the numerous books dedicated to PC-DOS and MS-DOS operating systems, the one by Norton (1985) provides a wealth of information on the hardware, BIOS, and the operating system of the IBM PC and computers compatible with it. Other useful sources are the PC-DOS User's Reference (IBM Corporation 1985), the PC-DOS Technical Reference (IBM Corporation 1985), and the MS-DOS Programmer's Reference (Microsoft 1984) manuals.

An overview of the Unix operating system is provided by Ritchie and Thompson (1974). In another article, Ritchie (1978) examines the goals of Unix and discusses the system's strong and weak points. Implementation of Unix is described by Thompson (1978). Unix porting is discussed by Johnson and Ritchie (1978), by Jalics and Heines (1983), and by Bodenstab et al. (1984). Some real-time extensions to, and derivatives of, Unix are described by Lycklama and Bayer (1978) and Cohen and Kaufeld (1978). Bourne (1978 and 1982) describes the shell. Unix tools and tool-building philosophy are presented by Kernighan and Mashey (1984). The Unix Programmer's Workbench is described by Ivie (1977) and Dolotta, Haight, and Mashey (1978). The Unix Writer's Workbench is presented by Frase (1983) and Macdonald (1983). A detailed treatment of Unix system programming is provided by Kernighan and Pike (1984). The details of Unix commands and system calls may be found in the Unix Programmer's Manual (AT&T 1985).

Industrial process-control systems are the subject of a special issue of the IEEE Computer magazine (IEEE 1984). A concise but thorough overview of the area can be found in an article by Schoeffler (1984). A four-part tutorial by Jaeger (1982) explains the principles and practice of data acquisition.

ASSEMBLY-LANGUAGE PORTION OF KMOS CODE

```
        PAGE    35,132
        TITLE   KMOSA: Assembly Language Portion of KMOS Kernel
        SUBTTL  Procedure INIHDW - Initialize Hardware

        **************
        *** INIHDW ***
        **************

; FUNCTION:    Initializes hardware. In the IBM PC case, just relocates
;              BIOS timer interrupt vector (IBM PC lev 8 = hardware
;              level 0) and vectors timer interrupts to KMOS. Also
;              disables all interrupts (except kbd and disk on PC)
;              to ensure uninterrupted system initialization. Interrupts
;              are enabled later by DISPATCH.

; ATTRIBUTES:  Far, KMOS internal, callable from Pascal when declared as
;              PROCEDURE INIHDW; EXTERNAL;

; PARAMETERS:  No parameters

; RETURN:      No values

; MODIFIES:    Nothing (saves and restores all regs used)

; CALLS:       None
```

```
                        PAGE
                ;       Data segment to access interrupt vector table

0000            VECTAB  SEGMENT AT 0H                  ;Data segment mapped to page 0
0020                    ORG     8*4                    ;Set it to timer vector
0020 ????       TIMVEC  DW      ?                      ;Timer int_serv IP is here (BIOS)
0022 ????               DW      ?                      ;Timer int_serv CS is here (BIOS)
01A0                    ORG     68H*4                  ;Will relocate it to vector 68H
01A0 ????       TIMREL  DW      ?                      ;Will relocate timer int_serv IP here
01A2 ????               DW      ?                      ; and its CS here.
01A4            VECTAB  ENDS
```

```
                                PAGE
                                PUBLIC  INIHDW
0000                    KMOSA   SEGMENT PUBLIC 'CODE'
0000                    INIHDW  PROC    FAR
                                ASSUME  CS:KMOSA,DS:VECTAB

0000  FA                        CLI                         ;Disable interrupts
0001  50                        PUSH    AX                  ;Save registers used by INIHDW
0002  1E                        PUSH    DS
0003  B0 BD                     MOV     AL,10111101B        ;*PC* Set 8259's mask so that only
0005  E6 21                     OUT     021H,AL             ; kbd and disk interrupts are ON.
0007  2B C0                     SUB     AX,AX
0009  8E D8                     MOV     DS,AX               ;DS=0 to access vectors on page 0
000B  A1 0020 R                 MOV     AX,TIMVEC           ;Relocate BIOS timer vector to
000E  A3 01A0 R                 MOV     TIMREL,AX           ; the level 68H.
0011  A1 0022 R                 MOV     AX,TIMVEC+2
0014  A3 01A2 R                 MOV     TIMREL+2,AX
0017  B8 0072 R                 MOV     AX,OFFSET HDWLVO    ;Vector timer interrupts to KMOS,
001A  A3 0020 R                 MOV     TIMVEC,AX           ; ITSERV: hardware level 0.
001D  8C C8                     MOV     AX,CS
001F  A3 0022 R                 MOV     TIMVEC+2,AX
0022  1F                        POP     DS                  ;Restore caller's DS and
0023  58                        POP     AX                  ; AX registers.
0024  CB                        RET
0025                    INIHDW  ENDP
0025                    KMOSA   ENDS

                                SUBTTL  Procedure DISPATCH - Dispatch the Top Priority Process
```

509

PAGE

```
          ****************
          *** DISPATCH ***
          ****************

; FUNCTION:      Activates the highest priority ready process.
;                Re-creates that process's environment (stack,
;                registers,flags) and surrenders control to it,
;                thus effectively exiting the kernel.
;
; ATTRIBUTES:    Far, KMOS internal, callable from Pascal when declared as
;                PROCEDURE DISPATCH (PROCESS:PTRPCB);EXTERNAL;
;
; PARAMETERS:    PROCESS (word) - address of the PCB of the process
;                to be dispatched, on stack as per IBM PC Pascal
;                calling sequence.
;
; RETURN:        ** NOTE ** Transfers control to the dispatched process,
;                does not return to caller.
;
; MODIFIES:      All (but sets the new process's environment)
;
; CALLS:         None


;       Equates

INTOO   EQU     20H                    ;8259A interrupt controller, address A0
INTO1   EQU     INTOO + 1              ;8259A address A1 (bit A0=1)
PREEMP  EQU     4                      ;Status = PREEMPTED
```

= 0020
= 0021
= 0004

Procedure DISPATCH - Dispatch the Top Priority Process

```
                        ;     Data segment (in DGROUP)

                              PUBLIC   SYSMSK
                        DGROUP  GROUP    DATSEG
                        DATSEG  SEGMENT
0000                    SYSMSK  DW       0FFH              ;System interrupt mask: global var.
0000  00FF             DATSEG  ENDS
0002

                              PUBLIC DISPATCH
0025                    KMOSA    SEGMENT PUBLIC 'CODE'
0025                    DISPATCH PROC    FAR
                              ASSUME  CS:KMOSA,DS:DGROUP

0025  8B EC                    MOV     BP,SP               ;BP points to top of stack
0027  8B 5E 04                 MOV     BX,[BP+4]           ;BX gets addr of the desired PCB
002A  8B 67 0A                 MOV     SP,[BX+10]          ;Restore process stack as of last run
002D  8B 47 16                 MOV     AX,[BX+22]          ;AX gets process interrupt mask
0030  0B 06 0000 R             OR      AX,DGROUP:SYSMSK    ;Enable higher priority interrupts,
0034  25 00BD                  AND     AX,0BDH             ;  *PC* [except kbd and disk]
0037  E6 21                    OUT     INT01,AL            ;  and disable all lower priority ints.

                        ;     Check if the process was preempted (interrupted)

0039  83 7F 10 04              CMP     WORD PTR [BX+16],PREEMP    ;See if status = PREEMPTED
003D  75 10                    JNE     CHKMSG                     ;If not, process non-preempted

003F  C7 47 10 0000            MOV     WORD PTR [BX+16],0   ;Was preempted, set status = READY
0044  17                       POP     SS                  ;Restore process's context
0045  07                       POP     ES
```

511

KMOSA: Assembly Language Portion of KMOS Kernel
Procedure DISPATCH - Dispatch the Top Priority Process

```
0046  1F              POP     DS
0047  5D              POP     BP
0048  5F              POP     DI
0049  5A              POP     DX
004A  59              POP     CX
004B  5B              POP     BX
004C  58              POP     AX
004D  5E              POP     SI
004E  CF              IRET                        ; and do an interrupt return (restores
                                                  ; flags and returns control to the
                                                  ; point of interruption).

                              ; When here, process was not preempted.
                              ; Check if it is to receive a message.

004F  8B 6F 08        CHKMSG: MOV  BP,[BX+8]      ;Restore process's frame pointer (saved
                                                  ; by SSTACK in PCB.FRAME field.
0052  83 7F 06 00          CMP   WORD PTR [BX+6],0    ;A message ? (PCB.DELAY <> 0)
0056  74 18                JE    NOMSG                ;To 'NO Message' if none.

                              ; When here, the process should receive a message.
                              ; Its address is contained in the PCB.DELAY field,
                              ; since it was put there by SEND.

0058  8B 77 06             MOV   SI,[BX+6]            ;SI gets the address of the message.
005B  C7 47 06 0000        MOV   WORD PTR [BX+6],0    ;PCB.DELAY := 0
0060  83 7C 04 01          CMP   WORD PTR [SI+4],1    ;See if an interrupt message, TYPE 1
0064  74 06                JE    INTMSG
0066  83 7C 04 02          CMP   WORD PTR[SI+4],2     ; or TYPE 2 ?
006A  75 02                JNE   NOTINT               ;If neither, to 'Not an Interrupt Msg.'
```

```
006C  89 34        INTMSG: MOV    [SI],SI      ;An interrupt message, indicate that it
                                               ; is not enqueued at a mailbox, by
                                               ; setting its link to point to itself.

006E  8B C6        NOTINT: MOV    AX,SI        ;In any case, AX gets msgadr for
                                               ; function return on behalf of RECEIVE
0070  FB           NOMSG:  STI                 ;Message or no message, enable eligible
                                               ; interrupts and surrender control
0071  CB                   RET                 ; to user's process (exit KMOS).
0072          DISPATCH ENDP
0072          KMOSA    ENDS

              SUBTTL  Procedure ITSERV - Interrupt Sevicing
```

513

PAGE

```
;       **************
;       *** ITSERV ***
;       **************
; FUNCTION:      Interrupt service routine. Recognizes the
;                vector thru which the interrupt came in, saves
;                context of the preempted process, and sends the
;                interrupt message to the mailbox associated
;                with the hardware level that generated the
;                interrupt. If no takers, dispatches the preempted
;                process itself.
;
; ATTRIBUTES:    Far, KMOS internal, accessible thru hardware
;                ONLY - should never be called by user or KMOS.
;
; PARAMETERS:    None
;
; RETURN:        None (interrupt message sent, or set to type 2
;                if was sent already but not consumed.
;
```

```
DATSEG   SEGMENT
         EXTRN    IMBLVO:WORD,IMBLV4:WORD,RUNNING:WORD
DATSEG   ENDS

         EXTRN    SEND:FAR
```

0002

0002

```
0072                           PAGE
                     KMOSA   SEGMENT PUBLIC 'CODE'
                             ASSUME  CS:KMOSA,DS:DGROUP
0072                 ITSERV  PROC    FAR

0072  56             HDWLV0: PUSH    SI                       ;Save SI of the preempted process
0073  BE 0000 E              MOV     SI,OFFSET DGROUP:IMBLV0  ;SI gets address of int. mailbox
0076  EB 08 90               JMP     ALLINT                   ;To 'Common Interrupt Processing'

0079  56             HDWLV4: PUSH    SI
007A  BE 0000 E              MOV     SI,OFFSET DGROUP:IMBLV4
007D  EB 01 90               JMP     ALLINT

0080  50             ALLINT: PUSH    AX                       ;Save all registers of the preempted
0081  53                     PUSH    BX                       ; process. IP,CS, flags are saved
0082  51                     PUSH    CX                       ; by hardware and SI saved earlier.
0083  52                     PUSH    DX
0084  57                     PUSH    DI
0085  55                     PUSH    BP
0086  1E                     PUSH    DS
0087  06                     PUSH    ES
0088  16                     PUSH    SS

                     ;       Save stack pointer and set status to PREEMPTED

0089  8B 1E 0000 E           MOV     BX,DGROUP:RUNNING        ;BX gets address of process's PCB
008D  89 67 0A               MOV     [BX+10],SP               ;Save stack ptr in PCB.STACK
0090  81 4F 10 0004          OR      WORD PTR [BX+16],PREEMP  ;PCB.STATUS := preempted
0095  81 FE 0000 E           CMP     SI,OFFSET DGROUP:IMBLV0  ;See if timer interrupt ?
0099  75 06                  JNE     NORMAL                   ;If not, to 'Normal Processing'
```

The IBM Personal Computer MACRO Assembler   PAGE   1-10
KMOSA: Assembly Language Portion of KMOS Kernel
        Procedure ITSERV - Interrupt Sevicing

```
009B  CD 68           INT     68H            ;Timer, fake hardware interrupt to DOS,
009D  FA              CLI                    ; disable interrupts that BIOS
009E  EB 05 90        JMP     GOMSG          ; enabled, and send an interrupt msg.

                              ; Normal (other than timer) interrupt processing:
                              ; acknowledge interrupt to 8259 interrupt controller.

00A1  B0 20   NORMAL:  MOV    AL,020H        ;8259 EOI message
00A3  E6 20            OUT    INTOO,AL

                      ; Send an interrupt message after setting its type as appropriate.

00A5  8B DE   GOMSG:   MOV    BX,SI          ;BX gets address of the interrupt mbx.
00A7  83 C6 0A         ADD    SI,10          ;AX points to INTMSG.LINK
00AA  39 77 0A         CMP    [BX+10],SI     ;Is link pointing to itself?
00AD  74 08            JE     SNDMSG         ;If yes, to 'Send Interrupt Message'
00AF  C7 47 0E 0002    MOV    WORD PTR [BX+14],2  ;No, so message was sent but not
00B4  EB 0D 90         JMP    DISPAT         ; consumed, set its type 'MISSED INT.'

00B7  C7 47 0E 0001 SNDMSG: MOV WORD PTR [BX+14],1 ;Msg not sent, set type to 'AOK'
00BC  53               PUSH   BX             ; and send it to the appropriate
00BD  56               PUSH   SI             ;mailbox - SEND(MBXADR,MSGADR)
00BE  9A 0000 ---- E   CALL   SEND           ;*NOTE* if a process is waiting on
                                             ; int. mailbox, it will be dispatched
                                             ; by SEND's call to DISPATCH, and
                                             ; control will not return to ITSERV
```

```
                    PAGE
              ;     When here, the interrupt message was sent, but no processes
              ;     were waiting for it (hence SEND would return control here),
              ;     so DISPATCH a process. This will effectively resume the
              ;     preempted process itself, but the posted interrupt message
              ;     will remind the system of the pending interrupt processing.

00C3 A1 0000 E        DISPAT: MOV   AX,DGROUP:RUNNING
00C6 50                       PUSH  AX                ;DISPATCH expects a parameter (RUNNING)
00C7 9A 0025 ---- R           CALL  DISPATCH          ;Dispatch a process.
00CC                  ITSERV  ENDP
00CC                  KMOSA   ENDS
                              SUBTTL  Procedure ENABLEV - Enable an Interrupt Level
```

```
              PAGE
              ***************
              *** ENABLEV ***
              ***************
       .
       .
       .
      ; FUNCTION:     Makes the specified hardware interrupt level
       .              eligible for activation, subject to priority
       .              of the running process (remember 8259 int. controller
       .              itself masks off all interrupts of lower priority
       .              than the level being serviced). Enabling an enabled
       .              level has no effect. No action for invalid levels.
       .
      ; ATTRIBUTES:   Far, public = user service, callable from Pascal
       .              PROCEDURE ENABLEV (LEVEL:INTEGER); EXTERNAL;
       .
      ; PARAMETERS:   LEVEL, an integer between 0 and 7 designating
       .              a hardware interrupt level, passed on stack
       .              as per IBM PC Pascal calling conventions.
       .
      ; RETURN:       None (if valid, level enabled)
       .
      ; MODIFIES:     AX,BX,CX,SI,flags
       .
      ; CALLS:        None
       .
0002          DATSEG  SEGMENT
0002          MSKTAB  DW      1,2,4,8,16,32,64,128     ;Masks table, powers of 2
0001 0002 0004 0008
0010 0020 0040 0080
0012          DATSEG  ENDS
                      PUBLIC  ENABLEV
```

518

                    Procedure ENABLEV - Enable an Interrupt Level

```
00CC                KMOSA    SEGMENT PUBLIC 'CODE'
                             ASSUME  CS:KMOSA

00CC                ENABLEV  PROC    FAR
00CC  55                     PUSH    BP                      ;Save caller's frame pointer
00CD  8B EC                  MOV     BP,SP                   ;Establish own frame & pointer
00CF  8B 76 06               MOV     SI,[BP+6]               ;SI gets param (LEVEL)
00D2  83 FE 07               CMP     SI,7                    ;See if valid (in 0 thru 7 range)
00D5  7F 12                  JG      ERRLEV                  ;If invalid, to 'Do Nothing' return
00D7  83 FE 00               CMP     SI,0
00DA  7C 0D                  JL      ERRLEV
00DC  D1 E6                  SHL     SI,1                    ;OK level, multiply SI by 2
                                                             ; to get word offset into mask table
00DE  BB 0002 R              MOV     BX,OFFSET DGROUP:MSKTAB ;Set BX to base of mask table and
00E1  8B 18                  MOV     BX,[BX+SI]              ; index with LEVEL to get the mask.
00E3  F7 D3                  NOT     BX                      ;Set desired bit in mask to 0 and
00E5  21 1E 0000 R           AND     DGROUP:SYSMSK,BX        ; make the corresponding interrupt
                                                             ; level eligible for servicing.
00E9                ERRLEV:
00E9  5D            OKRET:   POP     BP                      ;Restore caller's frame and
00EA  CA 0002                RET     2                       ; clean-up the stack.
00ED                ENABLEV  ENDP
00ED                KMOSA    ENDS

                             SUBTTL  Procedure SSTACK - Save Stack
```

519

PAGE

```
**************
*** SSTACK ***
**************
```

FUNCTION: Saves the stack pointer and the frame pointer
             of the procedure that called the caller of SSTACK.
             This is necessary when a user process calls a KMOS
             service that causes it to be suspended, so its
             stack and frame pointers must be saved for proper
             subsequent resumption. In KMOS this may happen when
             user's process executes RECEIVE and no message is
             available. When the process is to be resumed, it
             should continue from the last call to KMOS, hence
             DISPATCH should return control to it and not to KMOS
             routine that had called SSTACK before preempting user's
             process. In effect, SSTACK sets the stage for a direct
             return two levels up in the calling hierarchy.

ATTRIBUTES: Far, KMOS internal, callable from Pascal when declared as
             PROCEDURE SSTACK (PROCESS:PTRPCB); EXTERNAL;
             NOTE This implementation is highly IBM PC and IBM/MS
             Pascal release-specific (this works with IBM
             Pascal version 1.0 and Microsoft Pascal versions
             lower than 3.11). SSTACK is also
             very restrictive in the sense that it will
             function properly only when called from a
             procedure with two parameters and when invoked
             AFTER the last reference to any of them in the
```
```

```
;                    calling procedure is made (SSTACK destroys both of
;                    the caller's parameters).
;
; PARAMETERS:   PROCESS (word) on stack, as per IBM Pascal calling conv.,
;               BP = caller's frame pointer.
;
; RETURN:       PROCESS^.STACK := SP; (caller's stack pointer)
;               PROCESS^.FRAME := BP; (caller's frame pointer)
;
; MODIFIES:     Flags, BX, CX
;
; CALLS:        None
```

KMOSA: Assembly Language Portion of KMOS Kernel

Procedure SSTACK - Save Stack

```
                             PAGE
                             PUBLIC  SSTACK
00ED              KMOSA      SEGMENT PUBLIC 'CODE'      ;Code segment linked with other 'CODE'
                             ASSUME  CS:KMOSA

00ED              SSTACK     PROC    FAR                ;Far to secure long return
00ED  55                     PUSH    BP                 ;Save caller's frame pointer
00EE  8B C5                  MOV     AX,BP              ;AX points to stack: return address
00F0  2D 0002                SUB     AX,2               ;Two words of return address (far)
00F3  8B 5E FC               MOV     BX,[BP-4]          ; are moved 'up' on stack, thus
00F6  89 5E 00               MOV     [BP],BX            ; overwriting the params of the caller
00F9  8B 5E FA               MOV     BX,[BP-6]          ; of SSTACK. This avoids stack buildup
00FC  89 5E FE               MOV     [BP-2],BX          ; and allows for two-up-level return.
00FF  8B EC                  MOV     BP,SP              ;BP to top of stack as of SSTACK call
0101  8B 5E 06               MOV     BX,[BP+6]          ;BX gets parameter PROCESS from stack
0104  89 47 0A               MOV     [BX + 10],AX       ;PROCESS^.SP := moved return address
0107  5D                     POP     BP                 ;Restore caller's frame pointer and
0108  8B 46 F8               MOV     AX,[BP-8]          ; save it in PROCESS.FRAME field.
010B  89 47 08               MOV     [BX + 8],AX
010E  CA 0002                RET     2                  ;Return to SSTACK's caller.
0111              SSTACK     ENDP
0111              KMOSA      ENDS

                             SUBTTL  Procedures KMOSNUL
```

```
                    PAGE

                    PUBLIC   KMOSNUL, INTON, INTOFF

            ;       **************
            ;       *** KMOSNUL ***
            ;       **************

            ; FUNCTION:     KMOSNUL is a nul or 'Do Nothing' process that runs
            ;                   at the lowest level of priority (255). Its STD
            ;                   is automatically generated by STD.MAC, thus
            ;                   making KMOSNUL an integral part of every KMOS
            ;                   configuration.

0111        KMOSA   SEGMENT PUBLIC 'CODE'
                    ASSUME  CS:KMOSA

0111        KMOSNUL PROC    FAR
0111 EB FE  IDLE:   JMP     IDLE
0113 EB FC          JMP     IDLE
0115        KMOSNUL ENDP

                    SUBTTL  Procedures INTON, INTOFF
```

523

```
                    PAGE
                  ; ******************
                  ; *** INTON/OFF ***
                  ; ******************
                  ;
                  ; FUNCTION:    INTON and INTOFF are two parameterless internal KMOS
                  ;              procedures that are used to turn interrupts on and
                  ;              off, respectively.

0115               INTON   PROC    FAR
0115  FB                   STI
0116  CB                   RET
0117               INTON   ENDP
0117               INTOFF  PROC    FAR
0117  FA                   CLI
0118  CB                   RET
0119               INTOFF  ENDP
0119               KMOSA   ENDS
                           END
```

Segments and groups:

N a m e	Size	align	combine	class
DGROUP	GROUP			
DATSEG	0012	PARA	NONE	
KMOSA.	0119	PARA	PUBLIC	'CODE'
VECTAB	01A4	AT	0000	

Symbols:

N a m e	Type	Value	Attr			
ALLINT	L NEAR	0080	KMOSA			
CHKMSG	L NEAR	004F	KMOSA			
DISPAT	L NEAR	00C3	KMOSA			
DISPATCH	F PROC	0025	KMOSA	Global	Length	=004D
ENABLEV.	F PROC	00CC	KMOSA	Global	Length	=0021
ERRLEV	L NEAR	00E9	KMOSA			
GOMSG.	L NEAR	00A5	KMOSA			
HDWLVO	L NEAR	0072	KMOSA			
HDWLV4	L NEAR	0079	KMOSA			
IDLE	L NEAR	0111	KMOSA			
IMBLVO	V WORD	0000	DATSEG	External		
IMBLV4	V WORD	0000	DATSEG	External		
INIHDW	F PROC	0000	KMOSA	Global	Length	=0025
INTOO.	Number	0020				
INTO1.	Number	0021				
INTMSG	L NEAR	006C	KMOSA			
INTOFF	F PROC	0117	KMOSA	Global	Length	=0002

Symbol	Type		Value	Segment	Attribute		
INTON	F PROC	0115	KMOSA	Global	Length =0002
ITSERV	F PROC	0072	KMOSA	Length =005A
KMOSNUL	F PROC	0111	KMOSA	Global	Length =0004
MSKTAB	L WORD	0002	DATSEG
NOMSG	L NEAR	0070	KMOSA
NORMAL	L NEAR	00A1	KMOSA
NOTINT	L NEAR	006E	KMOSA
OKRET	L NEAR	00E9	KMOSA
PREEMP	Number	0004
RUNNING	V WORD	0000	DATSEG	External
SEND	L FAR	0000		External
SNDMSG	L NEAR	00B7	KMOSA
SSTACK	F PROC	00ED	KMOSA	Global	Length =0024
SYSMSK	L WORD	0000	DATSEG	Global
TIMREL	L WORD	01A0	VECTAB
TIMVEC	L WORD	0020	VECTAB

Warning Severe

Errors Errors

  0   0

CONFIGURATION MACROS

PAGE   35,131

```
;     Configuration module, contained in file CONFIG.ASM, is used
;     to define initial system configuration, i.e. the names and attributes
;     of all processes and mailboxes that should be known to KMOS for proper
;     system startup. The data structures and declarations necessary for this
;     purpose are provided by invoking system macros: SPD, GENPD, MBXADR, and
;     CRTAB. All those are supplied in the file MACS.INC. For this reason,
;     the file MACS.INC must be included in the file CONFIG, via system
;     directive
;         INCLUDE d:MACS.INC
;     where d: is the directory (drive+path) that contains the file MACS.INC.
;
;     CONFIG is also used to include two system processes, KMOSNUL and
;     KMOSCLOCK in the initial system configuration. These two processes are
;     an integral part of every KMOS configuration and their code is supplied
;     in KMOS object modules. However, these are actually the processes that
;     RUN under KMOS, so they must be created by invoking SPD macro once for
;     each of these processes. Finally, KMOSNUL must be the first process
;     created into a configuration, i.e. SPD KMOSNUL ... must be the first
;     invocation of the SPD macro in CONFIG. A minimal sample CONFIG file
;     required for proper system initialization is given below. Note that
;     lower case letters are used throughout. It is strongly recommended
;     that users copy and edit this file as a template for CONFIG, rather
;     than creating their own. Note the compulsory setting on nprocess to 0,
;     the two system required SPDs, and the order of invocation of GENPD
;     and CRTAB macros.
;

C         include macs.inc              ;assumes MACS. INC in the same directory
C         TITLE   *** INITIAL CONFIGURATION: MACROS & INVOCATIONS ***
```

```
C                  SUBTTL  * SPD - CREATE STATIC PROCESS DESCRIPTOR *
C
C          ;; *** macro SPD ***
C          ;;
C          ;; FUNCTION:   Builds a Static Process Descriptor (SPD) as a
C          ;;             component of the Initial Process Table (IPT) that
C          ;;             is used by KMOS for creation of the initial
C          ;;             environment.
C          ;;
C          ;; PARAMETERS: Accepts 3 parameters as described below
C          ;;             (1) The name of the user's process (entry point),
C          ;;                 10 chars maximum.
C          ;;             (2) The size, in bytes, of the stack required by
C          ;;                 this process.
C          ;;             (3) The priority of this process (0 <= pri <= 255).
C
C          SPD       MACRO   NAME,STKLEN,PRI            ;;Paramlist
C                    LOCAL   PSTK,L1,L2,TOPS            ;;Local labels
C
C                    IF      NPROCESS EQ 0              ;When called the first time:
C          NMAILBOX = 0                                ;; .set initial # mailboxes to 0,
C          DGROUP    GROUP   DATA,SSEG                 ;; .data and stack segs in DGROUP,
C          DATA      SEGMENT                           ;; .open data segment, and
C                    ASSUME  DS:DATA                   ;; .establish reference for data.
C                    ENDIF
C          DATA      ENDS                              ;Close current segment and reference
C                    EXTRN   NAME:FAR                  ;; proc name defined in an unknown seg.
C          SSEG      SEGMENT                           ;Open data segment (in DGROUP)
C          PSTK      DB STKLEN DUP ('S')               ;Reserve stack space in SSEG.
C          SSEG      ENDS                              ;(stack is filled with 'S')
```

529

```
                    * SPD - CREATE STATIC PROCESS DESCRIPTOR *

C    DATA     SEGMENT    DS:DATA                          ;;Resume data segment
C             ASSUME
C             IF         NPROCESS EQ 0                     ;;IPT table begins with the
C    IPT      EQU        THIS BYTE                         ;; first process's SPD.
C             ENDIF
C    L1       EQU        THIS BYTE                         ;;Labels L1 and L2 used for padding
C             IRPC       CHAR,<NAME>                       ;;ASCIIs for process name go here
C             DB         '&CHAR'
C             ENDM
C    L2       EQU        THIS BYTE
C             REPT       10 - (L2-L1)
C             DB         ' '                               ;;Pad with blanks if name < 10 chars
C             ENDM
C             DD         NAME                              ;;Pointer to process's entry point
C             DW         DGROUP:PSTK                       ;;Pointer to bottom of process's stack
C             DW         STKLEN                            ;;Stack length
C             DW         PRI                               ;;Process's priority
C             DW         DGROUP:(TDBASE + (NPROCESS*24))   ;;Point to this proc PCB
C             DW         0                                 ;;no special hardware, flags: 0
C    NPROCESS =         NPROCESS + 1                       ;;Keep track of the number of processes
C             ENDM

C             SUBTTL   * INITMBD AND SYSINI MACROS *

C             *** macro INTMBD ***

C    ;; FUNCTION:   Creates an interrupt mailbox descriptor =
C    ;;             standard mailbox descriptor + interrupt message.
C    ;;             This macro is invoked from SYSINI macro, which is
C    ;;             itself invoked from GENPD. Users should never
```

530

```
*** INITIAL CONFIGURATION: MACROS & INVOCATIONS ***
        * INITMBD AND SYSINI MACROS *

C   ;;                      invoke INTMBD directly.
C   ;;
C   ;; PARAMETERS:  Name of the interrupt mailbox
C
C   INTMBD MACRO   INTMBD
C          LOCAL   MSGADR
C          PUBLIC  INTMBD
C   INTMBD DW      5 DUP(?)                  ;;Standard mailbox descriptor
C   MSGADR EQU     THIS    WORD
C          DW      DGROUP:MSGADR             ;;Interrupt message: link = self
C          DW      6                         ;; length is fixed, 6 bytes
C          DW      1                         ;; type = interrupt message.
C          ENDM
C
C   ;;              *** macro SYSINI ***
C   ;;
C   ;; FUNCTION:    Creates an interrupt mailbox descriptor for each of
C   ;;              the eight hardware interrupt levels in IBM PC.
C   ;;              This macro should be invoked ONLY from GENPD macro.
C   ;;
C   ;; PARAMETERS:  None
C
C   SYSINI MACRO
C          INTMBD  IMBLV0                    ;;IMBLV0 is for hardware level 0 (lev 8
C          INTMBD  IMBLV1                    ;; on *IBM PC*), etc. for other levels.
C          INTMBD  IMBLV2
C          INTMBD  IMBLV3
C          INTMBD  IMBLV4
C          INTMBD  IMBLV5
C          INTMBD  IMBLV6
```

531

```
C               INTMBD    IMBLV7
C               ENDM
C
C               SUBTTL  * GENPD MACRO *
C
C      ;;       *** macro GENPD ***
C      ;;
C      ;; FUNCTION:     Creates space in RAM for Process Control Blocks (PCB)
C      ;;               of all processes defined in CONFIG via SPD macros.
C      ;;               Also creates interrupt mailboxes for all 8 interrupt
C      ;;               levels of the IBM PC in the Initial Mailbox Table.
C      ;; PARAMETERS:   None
C      ;;
C
C      GENPD   MACRO
C      TDBASE  DB (NPROCESS*24) DUP ('D')      ;;Reserve 24 bytes for each PCB
C               SYSINI                         ;;When invoked, create
C      IMT     DW      DGROUP:IMBLV0           ;; all hardware interrupt mailboxes,
C               DW     DGROUP:IMBLV1           ;; and enter them in IMT.
C               DW     DGROUP:IMBLV2
C               DW     DGROUP:IMBLV3
C               DW     DGROUP:IMBLV4
C               DW     DGROUP:IMBLV5
C               DW     DGROUP:IMBLV6
C               DW     DGROUP:IMBLV7
C      NMAILBOX =      NMAILBOX + 8
C               ENDM
C
C               SUBTTL  * MBXADR, CRTAB MACROS *
C
```

```
*** INITIAL CONFIGURATION: MACROS & INVOCATIONS ***
          * MBXADR, CRTAB MACROS *

C  ;;            *** macro MBXADR ***
C  ;;
C  ;; FUNCTION:    Builds one component of the Initial Mailbox
C  ;;             Table (IMT) each time it is invoked.
C  ;;
C  ;; PARAMETRS:   Name of the mailbox
C  ;;
C  MBXADR  MACRO   NAME
C          EXTRN   NAME:NEAR            ;;Name of the mbx. defined elsewhere
C          DW      DGROUP:NAME          ;;Create user's mailbox, enlist in IMT
C  NMAILBOX =      NMAILBOX + 1         ;;Keep track of the # processed so far.
C          ENDM
C
C  ;;            *** macro CRTAB ***
C  ;;
C  ;; FUNCTION:    Builds the Create Table (CRTAB). It must be invoked
C  ;;             after all SPD and and MBXADR macros to work properly.
C  ;;
C  ;; PARAMETERS:  none
C  ;;
C  CRTAB   MACRO
C          PUBLIC  INITAB               ;;INITAB public, for use
C                                       ;;by other KMOS modules.
C  INITAB  DW      DGROUP:IPT           ;;Pointer to IPT goes here.
C          DW      NPROCESS             ;;Number of processes in IPT.
C          DW      DGROUP:IMT           ;;Pointer to IMT.
C          DW      NMAILBOX             ;;Number of mailboxes in IMT.
C  DATA    ENDS                         ;;Close data segment.
C          ENDM
C          SUBTTL  Processing od a Configuration File
```

533

```
                              C
                              C          PAGE

= 0000                                   nprocess  =   0
                                         spd     kmosnul,80,255
0000                                   + DATA   SEGMENT
0000                                   + DATA   ENDS
0000                                   + SSEG   SEGMENT
0000  50 [                            + ??0000  DB 80 DUP ('S')
           ]
0050                                   + SSEG   ENDS
0000                                   + DATA   SEGMENT
0000  6B                               +        DB    'k'
0001  6D                               +        DB    'm'
0002  6F                               +        DB    'o'
0003  73                               +        DB    's'
0004  6E                               +        DB    'n'
0005  75                               +        DB    'u'
0006  6C                               +        DB    'l'
0007  20                               +        DB    ' '
0008  20                               +        DB    ' '
0009  20                               +        DB    ' '
000A  0000 ---- E                      +        DD    kmosnul
000E  0000 R                           +        DW    DGROUP:??0000
0010  0050                             +        DW    80
0012  00FF                             +        DW    255
0014  0030 R                           +        DW    DGROUP:(TDBASE + (NPROCESS*24))
0016  0000                             +        DW    0
                                         spd   kmosclock,80,0
0018                                   + DATA   ENDS
0050                                   + SSEG   SEGMENT
0050  50 [                            + ??0004  DB 80 DUP ('S')
```

534

Processing of a Configuration File

```
00A0
0018                    + SSEG    ENDS
0018                    + DATA    SEGMENT
0018 6B                 +         DB      'k'
0019 6D                 +         DB      'm'
001A 6F                 +         DB      'o'
001B 73                 +         DB      's'
001C 63                 +         DB      'c'
001D 6C                 +         DB      'l'
001E 6F                 +         DB      'o'
001F 63                 +         DB      'c'
0020 6B                 +         DB      'k'
0021 20                 +         DB      ' '
0022 0000 ---- E        +         DD      kmosclock
0026 0050 R             +         DW      DGROUP:??0004
0028 0050               +         DW      80
002A 0000               +         DW      0
002C 0048 R             +         DW      DGROUP:(TDBASE + (NPROCESS*24))
002E 0000               +         DW      0
                        ;           spd     pname,stklen,pri      ;initial user process here

                                    genpd
0030   30 [             + TDBASE  DB      (NPROCESS*24) DUP ('D')
0060   05 [             + IMBLV0  DW      5 DUP(?)
006A 006A R             +         DW      DGROUP:??0008
006C 0006               +         DW      6
006E 0001               +         DW      1
0070   05 [             + IMBLV1  DW      5 DUP(?)
007A 007A R             +         DW      DGROUP:??0009
007C 0006               +         DW      6
```

*** INITIAL CONFIGURATION: MACROS & INVOCATIONS ***
Processing of a Configuration File

```
007E  0001        +         DW   1
0080     05 [     +  IMBLV2 DW   5 DUP(?)
008A  008A R      +         DW   DGROUP:??000A
008C  0006        +         DW   6
008E  0001        +         DW   1
0090     05 [     +  IMBLV3 DW   5 DUP(?)
009A  009A R      +         DW   DGROUP:??000B
009C  0006        +         DW   6
009E  0001        +         DW   1
00A0     05 [     +  IMBLV4 DW   5 DUP(?)
00AA  00AA R      +         DW   DGROUP:??000C
00AC  0006        +         DW   6
00AE  0001        +         DW   1
00B0     05 [     +  IMBLV5 DW   5 DUP(?)
00BA  00BA R      +         DW   DGROUP:??000D
00BC  0006        +         DW   6
00BE  0001        +         DW   1
00C0     05 [     +  IMBLV6 DW   5 DUP(?)
00CA  00CA R      +         DW   DGROUP:??000E
00CC  0006        +         DW   6
00CE  0001        +         DW   1
00D0     05 [     +  IMBLV7 DW   5 DUP(?)
00DA  00DA R      +         DW   DGROUP:??000F
00DC  0006        +         DW   6
00DE  0001        +         DW   1
00E0  0060 R      +  IMT    DW   DGROUP:IMBLV0
00E2  0070 R      +         DW   DGROUP:IMBLV1
00E4  0080 R      +         DW   DGROUP:IMBLV2
00E6  0090 R      +         DW   DGROUP:IMBLV3
00E8  00A0 R      +         DW   DGROUP:IMBLV4
```

Processing of a Configuration File

```
00EA  00B0 R              +          DW       DGROUP:IMBLV5
00EC  00C0 R              +          DW       DGROUP:IMBLV6
00EE  00D0 R              +          DW       DGROUP:IMBLV7

                          ;        mbxadr   mbxname                  ;initial user mailboxes here
                                   crtab
00F0  0000 R              + INITAB   DW       DGROUP:IPT
00F2  0002               +          DW       NPROCESS
00F4  00E0 R              +          DW       DGROUP:IMT
00F6  0008               +          DW       NMAILBOX
00F8                      + DATA     ENDS
                          +          end
```

*** INITIAL CONFIGURATION: MACROS & INVOCATIONS ***

Macros:

N a m e	Length
CRTAB.	0005
GENPD.	0007
INTMBD	0004
MBXADR	0002
SPD.	000F
SYSINI	0005

Segments and groups:

N a m e	Size	align	combine class
DGROUP	GROUP		
DATA	00F8	PARA	NONE
SSEG	00A0	PARA	NONE

Symbols:

N a m e	Type	Value	Attr		
IMBLV0	L WORD	0060	DATA	Global	Length =0005
IMBLV1	L WORD	0070	DATA	Global	Length =0005
IMBLV2	L WORD	0080	DATA	Global	Length =0005
IMBLV3	L WORD	0090	DATA	Global	Length =0005
IMBLV4	L WORD	00A0	DATA	Global	Length =0005
IMBLV5	L WORD	00B0	DATA	Global	Length =0005
IMBLV6	L WORD	00C0	DATA	Global	Length =0005

*** INITIAL CONFIGURATION: MACROS & INVOCATIONS ***

Symbol	Type		Value	Seg	Attributes
IMBLV7	L	WORD	00D0	DATA	Global Length =0005
IMT.	L	WORD	00E0	DATA	
INITAB	L	WORD	00F0	DATA	Global
IPT.	E	BYTE	0000	DATA	
KMOSCLOCK.	L	FAR	0000		External
KMOSNUL.	L	FAR	0000		External
NMAILBOX	Number		0008		
NPROCESS	Number		0002		
TDBASE	L	BYTE	0030	DATA	Length =0030
??0000	L	BYTE	0000	SSEG	Length =0050
??0001	E	BYTE	0000	DATA	
??0002	E	BYTE	0007	DATA	
??0004	L	BYTE	0050	SSEG	Length =0050
??0005	E	BYTE	0018	DATA	
??0006	E	BYTE	0021	DATA	
??0008	E	WORD	006A	DATA	
??0009	E	WORD	007A	DATA	
??000A	E	WORD	008A	DATA	
??000B	E	WORD	009A	DATA	
??000C	E	WORD	00AA	DATA	
??000D	E	WORD	00BA	DATA	
??000E	E	WORD	00CA	DATA	
??000F	E	WORD	00DA	DATA	

Warning Severe
Errors Errors
0   0

BIBLIOGRAPHY

Aho, A. V.; J. E. Hopcroft; and J. D. Ullman. 1974. *The Design and Analysis of Computer Algorithms*. Reading, MA: Addison-Wesley.

Akkoyunlu, E. A.; Bernstein; and R. Schantz. 1974. Interprocess Communication Facilities for Network Operating Systems. *Computer*, vol. 7, no. 6 (June): 46–54.

Allworth, S. T. 1981. *Introduction to Real-Time Software Design*. New York: Springer-Verlag.

Andrews, G. R.; and F. B. Schneider. 1983. Concepts and Notations for Concurrent Programming. *Computing Surveys*, vol. 15, no. 1 (Mar.): 3–43.

Atwood, W. J. 1976. Concurrency in Operating Systems. *Computer*, vol. 9, no. 10 (Oct.): 18–26.

AT&T Corporation. 1985. *Unix System V Programmer Reference Manual*. 307–627. Winston-Salem, NC: AT&T Corporation.

Baer, J. L. 1980. *Computer Systems Architecture*. Rockville, MD: Computer Science Press.

Barstow, D. R.; H. E. Shrobe; and E. Sandewall. 1984. *Interactive Programming Environments*. New York: McGraw-Hill.

Bartlett, J. 1978. A "Nonstop" Operating System. *Proceedings of the Eleventh Hawaii International Conference on System Science*.

Bayer, R.; R. M. Graham; and G. Seegmuller, eds. 1978. *Operating Systems: An Advanced Course*. Berlin: Springer-Verlag.

Bays, C. 1977. A Comparison of Next-Fit, First-Fit, and Best-Fit. *Communications of the ACM*, vol. 20, no. 3 (Mar.): 191–192.

Beck, L. L. 1982. A Dynamic Storage Allocation Technique Based on Memory Residence Time. *Communications of the ACM*, vol. 25, no. 10 (Oct.): 714–724.

Belady, L. A. 1966. A Study of Replacement Algorithms for a Virtual-Storage Computer. *IBM Systems Journal*, vol. 5, no. 2: 78–101.

Ben-Ari, M. 1982. *Principles of Concurrent Programming*. Englewood Cliffs, NJ: Prentice-Hall.

Bensoussan, A.; and C. T. Clingen. 1972. The Multics Virtual Memory: Concepts and Design. *Communications of the ACM*, vol. 15, no. 5 (May): 308–318.

Bernstein, P. A.; and N. Goodman. 1981. Concurrency Control in Distributed Database Systems. *Computing Surveys*, vol. 13, no. 2 (June): 185–221.

Bodenstab, D. E.; T. F. Houghton; et al. 1984. UNIX System Porting Experiences. *The Bell System Technical Journal*, vol. 63, no. 8 (Oct.): 1769–1789.

Bourne, S. R. 1978. The Unix Shell. *The Bell System Technical Journal*, vol. 57, no. 6 (July-Aug.): 1971–1990.

Bourne, S. R. 1982. *The UNIX System*. Reading, MA: Addison-Wesley.

Bowen, B. A.; and R. J. A. Buhr. 1980. *The Logical Design of Multiple-Microprocessor Systems*. Englewood Cliffs, NJ: Prentice-Hall.

Brinch Hansen, P. 1970. The Nucleus of a Multiprogramming System. *Communications of the ACM*, vol. 13, no. 4 (Apr.): 238–250.

Brinch Hansen, P. 1972. Structured Multiprogramming. *Communications of the ACM*, vol. 15, no. 7 (July): 574–578.

Brinch Hansen, P. 1973. *Operating System Principles*. Englewood Cliffs, NJ: Prentice-Hall.

Brinch Hansen, P. 1977. *The Architecture of Concurrent Programs*. Englewood Cliffs, NJ: Prentice-Hall.

Brinch Hansen, P. 1978. Distributed Processes: A Concurrent Programming Concept. *Communications of the ACM*, vol. 21, no. 11 (Nov.): 934–941.

Brinch Hansen, P. 1982. *Programming a Personal Computer*. Englewood Cliffs, NJ: Prentice-Hall.

Brown, R. L.; P. J. Denning; and W. F. Tichy. 1984. Advanced Operating Systems. *Computer*, vol. 17, no. 10 (Oct.): 173–190.

Bryant, R. E.; and J. B. Dennis. 1980. "Concurrent Programming." In *Operating Systems Engineering*, edited by M. Maekawa and L. A. Belady, pp. 426–451. Berlin: Springer-Verlag.

Bunt, R. B. 1976. Scheduling Techniques for Operating Systems. *Computer*, vol. 9, no. 10 (Oct.): 10–17.

Calingaert, P. 1982. *Operating System Elements: A User Perspective*. Englewood Cliffs, NJ: Prentice-Hall.

Cheriton, D. R.; M. A. Malcolm; et al. 1979. Thoth, a Portable Real-Time Operating System. *Communications of the ACM*, vol. 22, no. 2 (Feb.): 105–115.

Chu, W. W.; and H. Opderbeck. 1974. Performance of Replacement Algorithms with Different Page Sizes. *Computer*, vol. 7, no. 11 (Nov.): 14–21.

Coffman, E. G.; and P. J. Denning. 1973. *Operating Systems Theory*. Englewood Cliffs, NJ: Prentice-Hall.

Coffman, E. G.; M. J. Elphick; and A. Shoshani. 1971. System Deadlocks. *Computing Surveys*, vol. 3, no. 2 (June): 67–78.

Coffman, E. G.; and T. A. Ryan. 1972. A Study of Storage Partitioning Using a Mathematical Model of Locality. *Communications of the ACM*, vol. 15, no. 3 (Mar.): 185–190.

Cohen, H.; and J. C. Kaufeld. 1978. The Network Operations Center System. *The Bell System Technical Journal*, vol. 57, no. 6 (July-Aug.): 2289–2304.

Comer, D. 1984. *Operating System Design: The Xinu Approach*. Englewood Cliffs, NJ: Prentice-Hall.

Conway, R. W.; W. L. Maxwell; and L. W. Miller. 1967. *Theory of Scheduling*. Reading, MA: Addison-Wesley.

Courtois, P. J.; F. Heymans; and D. L. Parnas. 1971. Concurrent Control with "Readers" and "Writers". *Communications of the ACM*, vol. 14, no. 10 (Oct.): 667–668.

Daley, R. C.; and Dennis, J. B. 1968. Virtual Memory, Processes, and Sharing in Multics. *Communications of the ACM*, vol. 11, no. 5 (May): 306–312.

Deitel, H. M. 1984. *An Introduction to Operating Systems*. Revised 1st ed. Reading, MA: Addison-Wesley.

Denning, P. J. 1968. The Working Set Model for Program Behavior. *Communications of the ACM*, vol. 11, no. 5 (May): 323–333.

Denning, P. J. 1970. Virtual Memory. *Computing Surveys*, vol. 2, no. 3 (Sept.): 154–189.

Denning, P. J. 1971. Third Generation Computer Systems. *Computing Surveys*, vol. 3, no. 4 (Dec.): 175–216.

Denning, P. J. 1976. Fault-Tolerant Operating Systems. *Computing Surveys*, vol. 8, no. 4 (Dec.): 355–389.

Denning, P. J. 1980. Working Sets Past and Present. *IEEE Transactions on Software Engineering*, vol. SE-6, no. 1 (Jan.): 64–84.

Denning, P. J. 1983. "Operating Systems: Principles and Theory." In *Encyclopedia of Computer Science and Engineering*, 2d ed., edited by A. Ralston and E. D. Reilly, Jr., pp. 1060–75. New York: Van Nostrand Reinhold.

Denning, P. J.; D. T. Dennis; and J. A. Brumfield. 1981. Low Contention Semaphores and Ready Lists. *Communications of the ACM*, vol. 24, no. 10 (Oct.): 687–699.

Denning, P. J.; and S. C. Schwartz. 1972. Properties of the Working-Set Model. *Communications of the ACM*, vol. 15, no. 3 (Mar.): 191–198.

Dennis, J. B.; and E. C. Van Horn. 1966. Programming Semantics for Multiprogrammed Computations. *Communications of the ACM*, vol. 9, no. 3 (Mar.): 143–155.

Dependahl, R. J. Jr.; and L. Presser. 1976. File Input/Output Logic. *Computer*, vol. 9, no. 10 (Oct.): 38–42.

Devillers, R. 1977. Game Interpretation of the Deadlock Avoidance Problem. *Communications of the ACM*, vol. 20, no. 10 (Oct.): 741–745.

Dijkstra, E. W. 1965. Solution of a Problem in Concurrent Programming Control. *Communications of the ACM*, vol. 8, no. 9 (Sept.): 569.

Dijkstra, E. W. 1968a. "Co-operating Sequential Processes." In *Programming Languages*, edited by F. Genuys, pp. 43–112. London: Academic Press.

Dijkstra, E. W. 1968b. The Structure of the "THE" Multiprogramming System. *Communications of the ACM*, vol. 11, no. 5 (May): 341–46.

Dijkstra, E. W. 1971. Hierarchical Ordering of Sequential Processes. *Acta Informatica*, vol. 1, no. 2: 115–138.

Dijkstra, E. W. 1975. Guarded Commands, Non-Determinacy and Formal Derivation of Programs. *Communications of the ACM*, vol. 18, no. 8 (Aug.): 453–457.

Dodd, G. G. 1969. Elements of Data Management Systems. *Computing Surveys*, vol. 1, no. 2 (June): 117–133.

Dolotta, T. A.; R. C. Haight; and J. R. Mashey. 1978. The Programmer's Workbench. *The Bell System Technical Journal*, vol. 57, no. 6 (July-Aug.): 2177–2200.

Donovan, J. J. 1972. *Systems Programming*. New York: McGraw-Hill.

Doran, R. W. 1976. Virtual Memory. *Computer*, vol. 9, no. 10 (Oct.): 27–37.

Eswaran, K. P.; J. N. Gray; et al. 1976. The Notions of Consistency and Predicate Locks in a Database System. *Communications of the ACM*, vol. 19, no. 11 (Nov.): 624–633.

Feldman, J. A. 1979. High Level Programming for Distributed Computing. *Communications of the ACM*, vol. 22, no. 6 (June): 353–368.

Filman, R. E.; and Friedman, D. P. 1984. *Coordinated Computing: Tools and Techniques for Distributed Software*. New York: McGraw-Hill.

Folts, H. C.; and H. R. Karp, eds. 1978. *McGraw-Hill's Compilation of Data Communication Standards*. New York: McGraw-Hill.

Foster, C. C. 1981. *Real Time Programming: Neglected Topics*. Reading, MA: Addison-Wesley.

Frase, L. T. 1983. The Unix Writer's Workbench Software: Philosophy. *The Bell System Technical Journal*, vol. 62, no. 6 (July-Aug.): 1883–1890.

Freeman, P. 1975. *Software System Principles: A Survey*. Palo Alto, CA: Science Research Associates.

Geschke, C. M.; J. H. Morris, Jr.; and E. H. Satterthwaite. 1977. Early Experience with Mesa. *Communications of the ACM*, vol. 20, no. 8 (Aug.): 540–553.

Glass, R. H., ed. 1983. *Real-Time Software*. Englewood Cliffs, NJ: Prentice-Hall.

Gonzales, M. J., Jr. 1977. Deterministic Processor Scheduling. *Computing Surveys*, vol. 9, no. 3 (Sept.): 173–204.

Goodenough, J. B. 1975. Exception Handling: Issues and a Proposed Notation. *Communications of the ACM*, vol. 18, no 12 (Dec.): 683–696.

Gray, J. 1979. "Notes on Data Base Operating System." In *Operating Systems: An Advanced Course*, edited by R. Bayer, R. M. Graham, and G. Seegmuller. Berlin: Springer-Verlag.

Grogono, P. 1979. On Layout, Identifiers and Semicolons in Pascal Programs. *ACM Sigplan Notices*, vol. 14, no. 4 (Apr.): 35–40.

Habermann, A. N. 1969. Prevention of System Deadlocks. *Communications of the ACM*, vol. 12, no. 7 (July): 373–377, 385.

Habermann, A. N. 1976. *Introduction to Operating System Design*. Palo Alto, CA: Science Research Associates.

Habermann, A. N.; and D. E. Perry. 1983. *Ada for Experienced Programmers*. Reading, MA: Addison-Wesley.

Hardy, N. 1985. KeyKOS Architecture. *ACM Operating Systems Review*, vol. 19, no. 4 (Oct.): 8–25.

Henry, G. J. 1984. The Fair Share Scheduler. *The Bell System Technical Journal*, vol. 63, no. 8 (Oct.): 1846–1857.

Hoare, C. A. R. 1974. Monitors: An Operating System Structuring Concept. *Communications of the ACM*, vol. 17, no. 10 (Oct.): 549–557.

Hoare, C. A. R. 1978. Communicating Sequential Processes. *Communications of the ACM*, vol. 21, no. 8 (Aug.): 666–677.

Holt, R. C. 1972. Some Deadlock Properties of Computer Systems. *Computing Surveys*, vol. 4, no. 3 (Sept.): 179–196.

Holt, R. C.; E. D. Lazowska; et al. 1978. *Structured Concurrent Programming with Operating System Applications*. Reading, MA: Addison-Wesley.

Holt, R. C. 1983. *Concurrent Euclid, the Unix System, and Tunis*. Reading, MA: Addison-Wesley.

Hoppe, J. 1980. A Simple Nucleus Written in Modula-2: A Case Study. *Software—Practice and Experience*, vol. 10, no. 9 (Sept.): 697–706.

Horowitz, E.; and S. Sahni. 1982. *Fundamentals of Data Structures*. Rockville, MD: Computer Science Press.

Howard, J. H. 1973. Mixed Solutions for the Deadlock Problem. *Communications of the ACM*, vol. 16, no. 7 (July): 427–430.

Howard, J. H. 1976. Proving Monitors. *Communications of the ACM*, vol. 19, no. 5 (May): 273–279.

Hsiao, D. K. 1975. *Systems Programming: Concepts of Operating Systems and Data Base Systems*. Reading, MA: Addison-Wesley.

Hunt, J. G. 1980. Interrupts. *Software—Practice and Experience*, vol. 10, no. 7 (July): 523–530.

Hunter and Ready Corporation. 1982. *VRTX/68000 User's Guide*. 591312001. Palo Alto, CA: Hunter and Ready Corporation.

Hwang, K.; and F. A. Briggs. 1984. *Computer Architecture and Parallel Processing*. New York: McGraw-Hill.

IBM Corporation. 1981. *Macro Assembler*. 6172234. Boca Raton, FL: IBM Corporation.

IBM Corporation. 1983. *Technical Reference for the IBM Personal Computer*. 1502234. Boca Raton, FL: IBM Corporation.

IBM Corporation. 1984. *Pascal Compiler Version 2.00* for the IBM Personal Computer. 6361111. Boca Raton, FL: IBM Corporation.

IBM Corporation. 1985. *Disk Operating System for the IBM Personal Computer*. 6138519. Boca Raton, FL: IBM Corporation.

IBM Corporation. 1985. *Disk Operating System Technical Reference*. 6138536. Boca Raton, FL: IBM Corporation.

IEEE. 1985. Special Issue on Software for Industrial Process Control. *Computer*, vol. 17, no. 2 (Feb.).

Ichbiah J. D.; J. G. P. Barnes; et al. 1979. Rationale for the Design of the Ada Programming Language. *ACM Sigplan Notices*, vol. 14, no. 6 (June).

Intel Corporation. 1981. *iRMX 88* Reference Manual 143232-002. Santa Clara, CA: Intel Corporation.

Intel Corporation. 1983*a*. *iAPX 86, 88, 186 and 188 User's Manual*. 1210912-001. Santa Clara, CA: Intel Corporation.

Intel Corporation. 1983*b*. *iAPX 286 Operating Systems Writer's Guide*. 121960-001. Santa Clara, CA: Intel Corporation.

Intel Corporation. 1984*a*. *Microsystem Components Handbook*. 230843-001. Santa Clara, CA: Intel Corporation.

Intel Corporation. 1984*b*. *iRMX-86 Operating System Manual Set*. 146194-001. Santa Clara, CA: Intel Corporation.

Isloor, S. S.; and T. A. Marsland. 1980. The Deadlock Problem: An Overview. *Computer*, vol. 13, no. 9 (Sept.): 58–78.

Ivie, E. L. 1977. The Programmer's Workbench—A Machine for Software Development. *Communications of the ACM*, vol. 20, no. 10 (Oct.): 746–753.

Jaeger, R. C. 1982. Analog Data Acquisition Technology. *IEEE Micro*, vol. 2, no. 2 (May): 20–37.

Jalics, P. J.; and T. S. Heines. 1983. Transporting a Portable Operating System: Unix to an IBM Minicomputer. *Communications of the ACM*, vol. 26, no. 12 (Dec.): 1066–1072.

Jensen, K.; and N. Wirth. 1974. *Pascal User Manual and Report*, 2d ed. Berlin: Springer-Verlag.

Johnson, S. C.; and D. M. Ritchie. 1978. Portability of C Programs and the Unix System. *The Bell System Technical Journal*, vol. 57, no. 6 (July-Aug.): 2021–2048.

Jones, A. K.; and A. Ardo. 1982. Comparative Efficiency of Different Implementations of the Ada Rendezvous. *Proceedings of the AdaTEC Conference on Ada*, pp. 212–223.

Joseph, M.; V. R. Prasad; and N. Natarajan. 1984. *A Multiprocessor Operating System*. Englewood Cliffs, NJ: Prentice-Hall.

Keedy, J. L. 1978. On Structuring Operating Systems with Monitors. *The Australian Computer Journal*, vol. 10, no. 1 (Feb.): 23–27.

Kenah, L. J.; and S. F. Bate. 1984. *VAX/VMS Internals and Data Structures*. Burlington, MA: Digital Press.

Kepecs, J.; and M. Solomon. 1984. SODA: A Simplified Operating System for Distributed Applications. *Third Conference on Principles of Distributed Computing*, reprinted in *ACM Operating Systems Review*, vol. 19 (1985), no. 4 (Oct.): 45–56.

Kernighan, B. W.; and J. R. Mashey. 1984. "The Unix Programming Environment." In *Interactive Programming Environments*, edited by D. R. Barstow, H. E. Shrobe, and E. Sandewall, pp. 175–197. New York: McGraw-Hill.

Kernighan, B. W.; and R. Pike. 1984. *The UNIX Programming Environment*. Englewood Cliffs, NJ: Prentice-Hall.

Kernighan, B. W.; and P. J. Plauger. 1978. *The Elements of Programming Style*, 2d ed. New York: McGraw-Hill.

Kernighan, B. W.; and D. M. Ritchie. 1978. *The C Programming Language*. Englewood Cliffs, NJ: Prentice-Hall.

Kleinrock, L. 1975. *Computer Applications*, vol. 2 of *Queueing Systems*. New York: Wiley-Interscience.

Knight, D. C. 1968. An Algorithm for Scheduling Storage on a Non-Paged Computer. *Computer Journal*, vol. 11, no. 1 (Feb.): 17–21.

Knuth, D. E. 1973a. *Fundamental Algorithms*, 2d ed., vol. 1 of *The Art of Computer Programming*. Reading, MA: Addison-Wesley.

Knuth, D. E. 1973b. *Sorting and Searching*, vol. 3 of *The Art of Computer Programming*. Reading, MA: Addison-Wesley.

Kohler, W. H. 1981. A Survey of Techniques for Synchronization and Recovery in Decentralized Computer Systems. *Computing Surveys*, vol. 13, no. 2 (June): 149–183.

Lamport, L. 1974. A New Solution to Dijkstra's Concurrent Programming Problem. *Communications of the ACM*, vol. 17, no. 8 (Aug.): 453–455.

Lamport, L. 1977. Concurrent Reading and Writing. *Communications of the ACM*, vol. 20, no. 11 (Nov.): 806–811.

Lamport, L. 1978. Time, Clocks, and the Ordering of Events in a Distributed System. *Communications of the ACM*, vol. 21, no. 7 (July): 558–565.

Lampson, B. W.; and D. R. Redell. 1980. Experience with Processes and Monitors in Mesa. *Communications of the ACM*, vol. 23, no. 2 (Feb.): 105–117.

Lampson, B. W.; M. Paul; and H. J. Siegert, eds. 1983. *Distributed Systems: Architecture and Implementation*. Berlin: Springer-Verlag.

Lauer, H. C.; and R. Needham. 1978. On the Duality of Operating System Structures. *Second International Symposium on Operating Systems, INRIA*, reprinted in *ACM Operating Systems Review*, vol. 13 (1979), no. 2 (Apr.): 3–19.

Leventhal, L. A. 1978. *Introduction to Microprocessors: Software, Hardware, and Programming*. Englewood Cliffs, NJ: Prentice-Hall.

Levy, H. M. 1984. *Capability-Based Computer Systems*. Bedford, MA: Digital Press.

Levy, H. M.; and R. H. Eckhouse. 1980. *Computer Programming and Architecture: The VAX-11*. Bedford, MA: Digital Press.

Linden, T. A. 1976. Operating System Structures to Support Security and Reliable Software. *Computing Surveys*, vol. 8, no. 4 (Dec.): 409–445.

Lipsky, L.; and J. D. Church. 1977. Application of a Queueing Network Model for a Computer System. *Computing Surveys*, vol. 9, no. 3 (Sept.): 205–221.

Lister, A. M. 1979. *Fundamentals of Operating Systems*, 2d ed. London: Macmillan.

Lister, A. M.; and K. J. Maynard. 1976. An Implementation of Monitors. *Software—Practice and Experience*, vol. 6, no. 3 (July): 377–385.

Lorin, H.; and H. M. Deitel. 1981. *Operating Systems*. Reading, MA: Addison-Wesley.

Lycklama, H.; and D. L. Bayer. 1978. The MERT Operating System. *The Bell System Technical Journal*, vol. 57, no. 6 (July-Aug.): 2049–2085.

Macdonald, N. H. 1983. The Unix Writer's Workbench Software: Rationale and Design. *The Bell System Technical Journal*, vol. 62, no. 6 (July-Aug.): 1891–1908.

MacGregor, D.; and D. S. Mothersole. 1983. Virtual Memory and the MC68010. *IEEE Micro*, vol. 3, no. 3 (June): 24–39.

Madnick, S. E.; and J. J. Donovan. 1974. *Operating Systems*. New York: McGraw-Hill.

McKuscik, M. K.; W. N. Joy; et al. 1984. A Fast File System for UNIX. *ACM Transactions on Computer Systems*, vol. 2, no. 3 (Aug.): 181–197.

McNamara, J. E. 1982. *Technical Aspects of Data Communication*, 2d ed. Bedford, MA: Digital Press.

Metcalfe, R. M.; and D. R. Boggs. 1976. Ethernet: Distributed Packet Switching for Local Computer Networks. *Communications of the ACM*, vol. 19, no. 7 (July): 395–404.

Microsoft Corporation. 1984. *MS-DOS Operating System: Programmer's Reference Manual*. 8411-310-02. Bellevue, WA: Microsoft Corporation.

Microsoft Corporation. 1985. *Microsoft Macroassembler for the MS-DOS Operating System* 410610002-400-R00-0985. Bellevue, WA: Microsoft Corporation.

Milenkovic, M. 1981. *Update Synchronization in Multiaccess Systems*. Ann Arbor, MI: UMI Research Press.

Morris, J. B. 1972. Demand Paging Through Utilization of Working Sets on the Maniac II. *Communications of the ACM*, vol. 15, no. 10 (Oct.): 867–872.

Motorola Corporation. 1980. *M68000 Real-Time Multitasking Software Users Guide*. M68KRMS68K(D2). Phoenix, AZ: Motorola Corporation.

Motorola Corporation. 1984*a*. *8-Bit Microprocessor and Peripheral Data*. Phoenix, AZ: Motorola Corporation.

Motorola Corporation. 1984*b*. *MC68020 32-Bit Microprocessor User's Manual*. MC68020UM(ADI). Englewood Cliffs, NJ: Prentice-Hall.

Muntz, R. R. 1975. "Scheduling and Resource Allocation in Computer Systems." In *Software Systems Principles: A Survey*, by P. Freeman, pp. 269–307. Palo Alto, CA: Science Research Associates.

Norton, P. 1985. *Programmer's Guide to the IBM PC*. Bellevue, WA: Microsoft Press.

Ogilvie, J. W. L. 1985. *Modula-2 Programming*. New York: McGraw-Hill.

O'Grady, E. P.; and R. Lozano. 1985. A Performance Study of Mutual Exclusion/Synchronization Mechanisms in an IEEE 796 Bus Multiprocessor. *IEEE Micro*, vol. 5, no. 4 (Aug.): 32–47.

Organick, E. I. 1972. *The Multics System: An Examination of Its Structure*. Cambridge, MA: MIT Press.

Organick, E. I. 1973. *Computer System Organization: The B5700/B6700 Series*. New York: Academic Press.

Organick, E. I. 1983. *A Programmer's View of the Intel 432 System*. New York: McGraw-Hill.

Parnas, D. L. 1972. A Technique for Software Module Specification with Examples. *Communications of the ACM*, vol. 15, no. 5 (May): 330–336.

Paterson, T. 1983. An Inside Look at MS-DOS. *Byte*, vol. 8, no. 6 (June): 230–252.

Peterson, J. L. 1977. Petri Nets. *Computing Surveys*, vol. 9, no. 3 (Sept.): 223–252.

Peterson, J. L.; and T. A. Norman. 1977. Buddy Systems. *Communications of the ACM*, vol. 20, no. 6 (June): 421–431.

Peterson, J. L.; and A. Silberschatz. 1983. *Operating System Concepts*. Reading, MA: Addison-Wesley.

Pohjanpalo, H. 1981. MROS-68K, A Memory Resident Operating System for MC68000. *Software—Practice and Experience*, vol. 11, no. 8 (Aug.): 845–852.

Popek, G. J.; and C. S. Kline. 1979. "Issues in Kernel Design." In *Operating Systems: An Advanced Course*, edited by R. Bayer, R. M. Graham, and G. Seegmuller, pp. 209–227. Berlin: Springer-Verlag.

Ravn, A. P. 1980. Device Monitors. *IEEE Transactions on Software Engineering*, vol. SE-6, no. 1 (Jan.): 49–53.

Reed, D. P.; and R. K. Kanodia. 1979. Synchronization with Eventcounts and Sequencers. *Communications of the ACM*, vol. 22, no. 2 (Feb.): 115–123.

Ricart, G.; and A. K. Agrawala. 1981. An Optimal Algorithm for Mutual Exclusion in Computer Networks. *Communications of the ACM*, vol. 24, no. 1 (Jan.): 9–17.

Ritchie, D. M. 1978. Unix Time-Sharing System: A Retrospective. *The Bell System Technical Journal*, vol. 57, no. 6 (July-Aug.): 1947–1969.

Ritchie, D. M., 1984. A Stream Input-Output System. *The Bell System Technical Journal*, vol. 63, no. 8 (Oct.): 1897–1910.

Ritchie, D. M.; and K. Thompson. 1974. The UNIX Time-Sharing System. *Communications of the ACM*, vol. 17, no. 7 (July): 365–375; revised and reprinted in *The Bell System Technical Journal*, vol. 57 (1978), no. 6 (July-Aug.): 1905–1929.

Rosin, R. F. 1969. Supervisory and Monitor Systems. *Computing Surveys*, vol. 1, no. 1: 37–54.

Schoeffler, J. D. 1984. Distributed Computer Systems for Process Control. *Computer*, vol. 17, no. 2 (Feb.): 11–18.

Seitz, C. L. 1985. The Cosmic Cube. *Communications of the ACM*, vol. 28, no. 1 (Jan.): 22–33.

Shatz, S. M. 1984. Communication Mechanisms for Programming Distributed Systems. *Computer*, vol. 17, no. 6 (June): 21–28.

Shaw, A. C. 1974. *The Logical Design of Operating Systems*. Englewood Cliffs, NJ: Prentice-Hall.

Shore, J. E. 1975. On the External Storage Fragmentation Produced by First-Fit and Best-Fit Allocation Strategies. *Communications of the ACM*, vol. 18, no. 8 (Aug.): 433–440.

Shore, J. E. 1977. Anomalous Behavior of the Fifty-Percent Rule. *Communications of the ACM*, vol. 20, no. 11 (Nov.): 812–820.

Siewiorek, D. P.; C. G. Bell; and A. Newell. 1982. *Computer Structures: Principles and Examples*. New York: McGraw-Hill.

Siewiorek, D. P.; and R. S. Swarz. 1982. *The Theory and Practice of Reliable System Design*. Bedford, MA: Digital Press.

Sites, R. L. 1980. "Operating Systems and Computer Architecture." In *Introduction to Computer Architecture*, 2d ed., edited by H. S. Stone, pp. 591–643. Palo Alto, CA: Science Research Associates.

Smith, A. J. 1978. Sequential Program Prefetching in Memory Hierarchies. *Computer*, vol. 11, no. 12 (Dec.): 7–21.

Smith, A. J. 1980. Multiprogramming and Memory Contention. *Software—Practice and Experience*, vol. 10., no. 7 (July): 531–552.

Smith, L. 1976. Using the 8251 Universal Synchronous/Asynchronous Receiver/Transmitter. Application Note AP-16. Santa Clara, CA: Intel Corporation.

Spier, M. J.; and E. I. Organick. 1969. The Multics Interprocess Communication Facility. *Second ACM Symposium on Operating Systems Principles*. New York: ACM.

Stallings, W. 1984. Local Networks. *Computing Surveys*, vol. 16, no. 1 (Mar.): 1–41.

Stankovic, J. A. 1982. Software Communication Mechanisms: Procedure Calls versus Messages. *Computer*, vol. 15, no. 4 (Apr.).

Staunstrup, J. 1982. Message Passing Communication versus Procedure Call Communication. *Software—Practice and Experience*, vol. 12, no 3. (Mar.): 223–234.

Stone, H. S., ed. 1980. *Introduction to Computer Architecture*, 2d ed. Palo Alto, CA: Science Research Associates.

Stone, H. S. 1982. *Microcomputer Interfacing*. Reading, MA: Addison-Wesley.

Stonebreaker, M. 1981. Operating System Support for Database Management. *Communications of the ACM*, vol. 24, no. 7 (July): 412–418.

Tanenbaum, A. S. 1981. *Computer Networks*. Englewood Cliffs, NJ: Prentice-Hall.

Taylor, R. N. 1983. A General Purpose Algorithm for Analyzing Concurrent Programs. *Communications of the ACM*, vol. 26, no. 5 (May): 362–376.

Thompson, K. 1978. UNIX Implementation. *The Bell System Technical Journal*, vol. 57, no. 6 (July-Aug.): 1931–1946.

U.S. Department of Defense. 1983. *Reference Manual for the Ada Programming Language* (ANSI/MIL-STD-1815A-1983). Washington, DC: USDOD.

Verhofstad, J. S. M. 1978. Recovery Techniques in Database Systems. *Computing Surveys*, vol. 10, no. 2 (June): 167–195.

Waite, M.; and R. Lafore. 1983. *Soul of CP/M*. Indianapolis, IN: Howard W. Sams.

Wakerly, J. F. 1981. *Microcomputer Architecture and Programming*. New York: Wiley.

Watson, R. W. 1970. *Timesharing Systems Design Concepts*. New York: McGraw-Hill.

Weitzman, C. 1980. *Distributed Micro/Minicomputer Systems: Structure, Implementation, and Application*. Englewood Cliffs, NJ: Prentice-Hall.

Wicklund, T. L. 1982. MINI-EXEC: A Portable Executive for 8-Bit Microcomputers. *Communications of the ACM*, vol. 25, no. 11 (Nov.): 772–780.

Wiederhold, G. 1983. *Database Design*, 2d ed. New York: McGraw-Hill.

Wirth, N. 1971. Program Development by Stepwise Refinement. *Communications of the ACM*, vol. 14, no. 4 (Apr.): 221–227.

Wirth, N. 1977. Towards a Discipline of Real-Time Programming. *Communications of the ACM*, vol. 20, no. 8 (Aug.): 577–583.

Wirth, N. 1983. *Programming in Modula-2*. Berlin: Springer-Verlag.

Wulf, W. A.; R. Levin; and S. P. Harbison. 1981. *HYDRA/C.mmp: An Experimental Computer System*. New York: McGraw-Hill.

INDEX

INDEX